Literature
and Western Man

BOOKS BY J. B. PRIESTLEY

FICTION

Bright Day
Angel Pavement
The Good Companions
Daylight on Saturday
They Walk in the City
Faraway
Let the People Sing
Wonder Hero
Blackout in Gretley
Three Men in New Suits
The Doomsday Men
Adam in Moonshine
Benighted
Jenny Villiers
Festival at Farbridge
The Other Place: short stories
Low Notes on a High Level

PLAYS

Volume I
Dangerous Corner
Johnson over Jordan
Eden End
Music at Night
Time and the Conways
The Linden Tree
I Have Been Here Before

Volume II
Laburnum Grove
The Golden Fleece
Bees on the Boat Deck
How are they at Home?
When we are Married
Ever Since Paradise

ESSAYS AND AUTOBIOGRAPHY

Delight
Rain upon Godshill
Midnight in the Desert
All About Ourselves and other essays
(chosen by Eric Gillett)
Thoughts in the Wilderness

Volume III
Cornelius
An Inspector Calls
People at Sea
Home is Tomorrow
They came to a City
Summer Day's Dream

CRITICISM AND MISCELLANEOUS

Meredith (E.M.L.)
Peacock (E.M.L.)
Brief Diversions
Journey down a Rainbow
(with Jacquetta Hawkes)
The English Comic Characters
English Humour (Heritage Series)
Postscripts
The Art of the Dramatist
Topside
Literature and Western Man

LITERATURE
AND
WESTERN MAN

BY

J. B. PRIESTLEY

1817

HARPER & ROW, PUBLISHERS

NEW YORK, EVANSTON, AND LONDON

LITERATURE AND WESTERN MAN

FOR JACQUETTA

Contents

Introduction ix

Part One: *The Golden Globe*

1 Movable Types   3
2 The Italian Scene and Machiavelli   10
3 France: Rabelais and Montaigne   18
4 England and Shakespeare   26
5 Spain and Cervantes   42

Part Two: *"The Order'd Garden"*

6 "And All was Light"   53
7 The Drama   62
8 The Novel   82
9 The Enlightenment   98

Part Three: *Shadows of the Moon*

10 Rousseau and the Romantic Age   113

vii

11 Germany and Goethe   122

12 The English Romantics   139

13 The Romantic Movement in France   159

14 Russians and Others   173

PART FOUR: *The Broken Web*

15 The Age and its Prophets   187

16 The Poets   206

17 The Novelists   222

18 The Dramatists   274

PART FIVE: *The Moderns*

19 Background to the Books   301

20 Mostly before 1914   336

21 Brief Interlude   370

22 Between the Wars   376

    CONCLUSION   441

    APPENDIX Brief Biographies   447

    INDEX   489

Introduction

THE TERM 'Western' in my title has nothing to do with our being out-side iron curtains; it is used in the old geographical and cultural senses, to show that Russia is included as well as America, and that all Asia is excluded. Had it not made the title too unwieldy, I would have qualified 'Western Man' with 'Modern', for our story here begins in the second half of the fifteenth century, after the invention, or at least the first use in Europe, of movable types for printing, a device that has given us the book as we know it. Medieval literature, therefore, is outside this record; nevertheless, it includes nearly five centuries of literature in every form, more than enough, however broad the scanning method, for one author and his reader to look at together.

We should remember, however, that these centuries represent less than a fifth of the time for which we possess some historical and literary records; and not a fiftieth part of the time when our remote ancestors, with one brief unrecorded generation following another, gradually shaped and coloured the human psyche that they bequeathed to us as surely as they did our muscular and nervous systems. The men who figure in this chronicle of five centuries are not merely the product of those centuries; they have behind them thousands of generations of human beings who acquired, and handed on, certain patterns of behaviour, feeling, thought, that find their way into literature, either emerging from the unconscious or coming from various conscious modifications of culture itself. Though a great deal has happened during these centuries—and the increasing tempo of change in our own age seems terrifying—we must still remember that the procession we lead in time is very long indeed, winding back into the remote dusk of pre-history, or, to change the image, that the men who did those wonderful cave paintings, say, at Lascaux, so highly charged with vitality and magical feeling, might be said to be still alive in us today. These centuries we know best are so crammed with history and artifacts that we are apt to forget that they represent a very short section of the life of Man. And in writing this book at least I have tried, somewhere at the back of it all, to keep something like a long view.

This is not a work of scholarship. If it had been, my name would not have been attached to it, for among my dwindling pretensions there is no pretence of scholarship. I have said of this book: "A young man couldn't write it, because he wouldn't have the necessary reading; and an elderly man, who might have the reading, would have more sense than to attempt such a book." And if I have not had more sense, undertaking, at a time when most men begin to slacken off, to sit in the sun, a most formidable task, often both laborious and irritating (I possess about 10,000 books and can hardly find any of them without a search), this was not because I was tempted to make some use of nearly half a century of wide if desultory reading, together with much experience, not to be despised for this task, of the writing and publishing and criticism of books and the writing of plays and the managing of theatrical enterprises, experience that has taken me, so to speak, out of the dining-room, where many critics and most literary historians may be found, into the kitchen where the dinners are cooked. What really tempted me, so that I fell, was my conviction that ours is an age of supreme crisis, when the most desperate decisions have to be made, and that some account of Western Man, in terms of the literature he has created and enjoyed, might help us to understand ourselves (and doing the work has certainly helped *me*), and to realise where we are and how we have arrived here.

So, strictly speaking, this is not a literary history, although at a pinch it could be used as one, and because they might be useful to some readers, I have added the forty pages of brief biographies as an appendix. The final emphasis here, as the title suggests, is not on Literature but on Western Man. I have never had in mind a purely literary study; but if a twenty-volume history of Western Man were being issued, then this might be the volume devoted to his literature; and indeed, throughout, I think I have had a vague notion of a sort of composite Western Man, to whom everything has been related. The appalling business of deciding which writers should not be merely mentioned but given some critical consideration, decisions that could not be made on any national basis, has had to be settled from the standpoint of this Western Man. (If it is objected that it is really I, in the last resort, who must make the choice, my reply is that I am the Western Man I know best.) I have also tried to keep in mind the sort of people who might be best served by a study of this kind: neither critics and literary scholars at one extreme (though I hope some of them will read it), nor at the other the very large public that asks only for digests, rough outlines, bottled and packaged culture (though I hope some of them will read it too); but chiefly the considerable numbers of people, in many different countries, who are sufficiently intelligent and sensitive to enjoy most good literature but are, for various good reasons, rather wary of it, especially the literature of our own age to which I have devoted the largest section of this book. Much contemporary literary criticism is intended for a small minority of persons intensely concerned with literature or for students who are required to read such criticism; and this leaves outside, wondering what it is all about, all these other people, who may well be more valuable and influential members of our modern world community, helping to make the decisions on which the fate of Western Man now depends. Except where I felt it to be absolutely essential, however, I have avoided any discussion of criticism and critics: dog should not eat dog.

Finally, I ask the reader to accept the limitations that have made this task possible at all. Too often our progress together will be uncertain, here too fast, there too slow, over roads that are too rough. The comment along the way will sometimes be too scanty, sometimes too wordy, often arbitrary, insensitive, unjust. Nevertheless, with the reader's goodwill and co-operation, together we may learn something about what Western Man—haunted, bedevilled, inspired, by ideas and feelings that often seem new just because they are very old—has made out of his literature.

Literature
and Western Man

PART ONE

The Golden Globe

1   Movable Types   3

2   The Italian Scene and Machiavelli   10

3   France: Rabelais and Montaigne   18

4   England and Shakespeare   26

5   Spain and Cervantes   42

Author's note on the Elizabethan stage (see pages 30–31):

*It was not until the first edition of this book was on press that I had the oppor-
tunity to read Dr. Leslie Hotson's recently published* Shakespeare's Wooden O.
*In this work, the result of a brilliant piece of research, Dr. Hotson dismisses the
familiar idea of the Elizabethan stage, with its forestage jutting into the auditorium and its back wall with a curtained recess for "the inner stage" and a
balcony above it. He argues that the Elizabethan stage, which had the audience
all round it, was a direct development of the waggon stages used by the medieval
"pageant" productions and by the later touring companies, making use of inn-
yards. It was a long raised platform with a "house", a framework curtained
except when it was used as an interior, at each end, where there were steps for
the actors to "mount the stage" from the dressing room or "tiring-house" running
underneath the platform. This economical arrangement explains not only many
hitherto puzzling allusions (for which see Dr. Hotson's book) but also the fact
that a theatre like the Globe could hold so many people, at least three thousand,
and yet still have a comparatively intimate relation with its audience. Dr. Hotson's
arguments and examples, to which I must refer any interested reader, have convinced me that his theory is right, but I must add that it only gives more force
to what I have written here in praise of the Elizabethan stage. The fact that it
was "in the round", as we discover in* Shakespeare's Wooden O, *is to my
mind an additional mark in its favour.*

—J. B. PRIESTLEY

CHAPTER ONE

Movable Types

THE EARLIEST PRINTED BOOKS are Chinese. One of them, printed from blocks, dates back to the ninth century. Only two hundred years later the Chinese were experimenting with movable types, but their written language demands so many characters that this method of printing was thought to be too laborious. Pictorial wood-blocks had been used in Europe before the middle of the fifteenth century, but 'block books', in which each page had first been engraved or cut out of a solid wood-block, were contemporary with books first printed from movable types. Both the date and the original place of origin of movable types have been sharply disputed between the Germans, Dutch, French and Italians. General opinion has favoured the German claim, represented by the Vulgate Bible (known as 'the Mazarin Bible' because a copy of it was found in Cardinal Mazarin's library in the seventeenth century), printed by Johann Gutenberg at Mainz. And what is certain is that most of the first printers in other countries arrived there from Germany. Before the century was out, books were being printed in the Low Countries, Italy, France, Spain and England. They were mostly of fine quality, far better than the books produced during the sixteenth and seventeenth centuries.

The first English printer, William Caxton, learnt the art in Cologne and practised it in the Low Countries, where he had been living for many years as head of a company of English merchants. He founded his press in Westminster in 1476, and before his death in 1491 he had published about a hundred volumes. These were not in Latin, like those printed abroad, but in his own native language, and many of them he wrote and translated himself. He also printed from type faces that were neither

Gothic nor Roman in design, and altogether was an industrious innovator, to whom English letters owe much.

It is wrong to imagine, however, that this invention of printing from movable types arrived, like rain on a desert, in an age when the copying of books was the work of a few devoted monks. That age had passed. Professional copyists and students had long been furnishing whole libraries, especially in Italy, where wealthy scholars, often writing a beautiful hand themselves, were in the habit of commissioning the most exquisitely written and decorated books. Indeed, for some years these patrons of literature laughed at the barbarous German invention and refused to own a printed book. But students and the poorer scholars, who had only been able to acquire the most modest little library at the cost of much travel, aching hands and smarting eyes, turned eagerly to these printed pages, which soon offered them Greek and even Hebrew. And as more and more books were published, towards the end of the century, there was one consequence that should not surprise us: in Rome, under Alexander VI, the censor got to work. Power, which has its intuitions, soon recognised its enemy. The book had arrived.

That other age, when learning and literature were transcribed by the monk in his cell, was further away both in time and in spirit than is generally realised. The two to three centuries of the true Middle or Gothic Age were gone for ever. With them vanished a truly religious basis and framework for the life of Western Man. As Carlyle wrote, placing himself and his readers squarely in the twelfth century:

. . . Our Religion is not yet a horrible restless doubt, still less a far horribler composed Cant; but a great heaven-high Unquestionability, encompassing, inter-penetrating the whole of Life. Imperfect as we may be, we are here, with our litanies, shaven crowns, vows of poverty, to testify incessantly and indisputably to every heart, That this Earthly Life and *its* riches and possessions, and good and evil hap, are not intrinsically a reality at all, but are a shadow of realities eternal, infinite; that this Time-world, as an air-image, fearfully emblematic, plays and flickers in the grand still mirror of Eternity; and man's little Life has Duties that are great, that are alone great, and go up to Heaven and down to Hell. . . .

To all of which the great Gothic cathedrals, vast, communal, and anonymous, deeply symbolic structures, still grandly testify. It was an age that from one point of view seems narrow, ignorant, brutal—and we could no more return to it than we could divide ourselves between cells, castles and hovels—but the Western mind, in both its conscious and unconscious aspects, found a home in it and was for a little time at peace with itself, related and integrated as it has never been since. If this age produced little literature, perhaps it needed none; certainly it would never have understood so much that has been written since out of men's divided minds, their feeling of loneliness and despair, their homeless spirit. The world of these nameless designers, carvers and builders of cathedrals, was not one more spinning globe lost among the stars; it was a green platform fixed between paradise and hell; and most of it was Christendom, where the wars were feudal and dynastic and the armed nations had not yet arrived, where a man might be given authority because he was a saint, where scholars speaking a common language wandered from one seat of learning to another, where goodness was goodness and evil was evil and there was no tormenting confusion of values. It was this age, not considered as a political-economic system nor a social hierarchy, but as a period when the mind achieved a harmony and a feeling of relatedness, that began to haunt men of other ages like some half-remembered dream. Western Man never left it entirely behind—and in his moments of easy escape could never resist playing with its more picturesque trappings—so that much of his literature faintly echoes its solemn chanting, and one man of genius after another, long afterwards, asked himself how and when this unity with God and His universe could be achieved again, cried out his hope, thundered his rage and despair. For man has come down the eons a religious being, who must needs worship something, and the Gothic, its consciousness soaring with its towers and steeples, was for the West the last truly religious age.

The world into which the movable types found their way, to multiply books and scholars, had long emerged from that age. Except in Italy, which as we shall see was staring already at the brilliant sunlight and murderous shadows of the Renaissance, Western Europe in the fifteenth century was living in the twilight and ruin of the Middle Ages. It was a strange time. Shakespeare catches the tone of it in his historical plays, brutal and turbulent, stiff and heavy with death. (Charles Reade caught much of it too in his historical novel, *The Cloister and the Hearth*.) The Dukes of Burgundy, with their ostentation, violence and half-mad pride, are perhaps its representative rulers. It was at their Court that the *Dance of Death* was performed. The true and living symbolism of the Gothic Age had declined and hardened into pedantic allegory. Universal religious belief and feeling, like a shattered glass, had broken into fanatically held creeds, superstition and a despairing atheism. People of a sort that had once steadily worshipped now wept with the wandering preacher one week and the next week planned murder. There is something over-heated and theatrical in both the pageantry and violence of these years, which smelt, as someone said, "of blood and roses". (In England the long ferocious duel between the Houses of York and Lancaster, which wasted the country and brought it close to ruin, came to be called The Wars of the Roses.) The man of this age was neither the religious hierarchic man of the true Middle Ages nor the sharply individualised man of the Renaissance. He was between two worlds, in a time without apparent foundations, probably heading for doomsday. He was divided between a new and often cynical realism, acquiring or sharing the wealth of the rapidly growing cities, and mad pride and violence, wild superstition and fantasy, an unending *danse macabre*.

In the literature of the time there was a similar division, a widening gap, between what was rooted in observation and actuality and what was essentially fanciful and fantastical. As the cities grew and the castles fell before the cannon, as war itself lost its knightly character and became grimly professional, an affair of money and strategy, heavier weapons and gunpowder, more and more people were fascinated by the romances of chivalry, by invincible swords and enchanted forests and castles in the air. So on one side, as in France for example, there were the new satirical tales that mocked the ideals of chivalry, there were the strictly realistic political memoirs of a Commynes; and on the other side, created as much for the wives and daughters of the new merchant class as they were for the gallants and ladies of the nobility, there were the elaborate romances of Charlemagne and his paladins, Arthur and his knights, adventuring in some dream of chivalry. The stories on which these romances were based, especially those of ancient Celtic origin, were deeply symbolic and often profound interpretations of life, belonging in essence to myth and folk-lore. (Of these *Gawaine and the Green Knight* is an excellent example. And indeed not all the old symbolism and the mythical element have vanished from Malory's version of the Arthurian legends, which was finished in 1469 but not published until 1485.) But what had been once an imagina-tive penetration into the deeper levels of man's being was now, in its guise of romance, floated far above earth and the roots of our existence into the airy kingdoms of fancy and allegory. So there was now already that division we have come to know only too well, a split only closed by great art, a division between a sardonic 'realism', cynically taking the worst for granted, and 'romance' that deliberately loses all contact with actuality, a dream life that tries to reject even the psychological responsi-bilities of our actual dreams. Such a division, a sort of schizophrenic condition of art, is characteristic of an age of transition, a bewildered passage between two worlds. The fifteenth century knew it; and today, with all our fiction, movies and television programmes, we know it again.

The age, however, was changing fast. The movable types were finding their way to one expanding city after another, to keep the great wooden presses hard at work. Books of many kinds were now being printed and distributed. The Greek scholars who had fled before the Turks had long been teaching in the Italian academies; but it is easy to exaggerate the contribution made by classical learning to the new age, the Renaissance, already existing in Italy. After all, Italy, where the ruins of the Roman Empire could be seen everywhere, had never really been outside classical influences. And north and west of the Mediterranean a great deal that was new was happening, and much of it was at least as important as the revival of classical scholarship. The interminable wars had to be financed, and most of the money had to be found in the cities, among merchants and burghers who could not be fitted into any feudal pattern and equally could not be ignored. (It was not only for the sake of their pretty wives that Edward IV flattered and knighted his London merchants.) This new powerful class, which rapidly developed its own ideas, became the patron of arts and letters. In its world of wharves and warehouses and counting-

7

houses and news from agents abroad, what was left of the Middle Ages, apart from the great buildings, began to crumble and dissolve. The merchant did as much as the scholar to bring in the new age.

Perhaps the sea-captains did even more. For years the Portuguese had sailed along the African coast, going further and further in search of slaves, gold and ivory, until finally, in 1486, Bartolomeo Dias, driven by gales far out of his course, rounded the Cape of Good Hope. Beyond the Azores, now colonised by Portugal, there were believed to lie various islands notably 'Antilha' and 'Brazil', that would serve as midway stations (for legend declared them to be wonderfully fertile) on the westward passage to the Indies. Moreover, there lingered a tradition, which unlike most medieval geographical stories happened to be true, that the Norsemen had once discovered a land far to the West that they called 'Vineland'. For years the seamen of various nations persisted in searching for these fabled islands somewhere beyond the Azores, and when they failed to find them they tacked and turned, in the belief that they must have passed them. But a Genoese captain, a man of much experience and of great determination, sailing in the service of Spain, dismissed any notion of discovering the legendary islands, and set a direct course across the Atlantic, where at last he came to the islands he called 'the West Indies'. Thus, in 1492, Christopher Columbus opened the way to a vast new continent, and enlarged the globe. Within the next few years, Cabot had sighted Labrador, Columbus had found the mainland beyond the West Indies, and Vespucci and Pincon had sailed along the coast of Brazil. Not much later, in 1507, the professor of geography in Lorraine, after publishing Vespucci's account of his travels, suggested that the new continent might be given Vespucci's first name—Amerigo. Before the end of the sixteenth century, the movable types and the presses had found their way to Mexico City, Goa, Lima, Manila and Macao; there were printers at work around the great globe.

This discovery of the New World, of great consequence politically and economically, had some direct effect upon writers. It showed them that the earth was much larger than had been imagined, much richer in promise. Here was a whole enormous continent outside all European traditions. What kind of people lived there? Were they cannibals, savages sacrificing to monstrous idols, or innocent and charming beings, living in some Arcadia far removed from the vanities, vices and diseases of civilisation? As authors began to ask these questions—and Montaigne, after seeing some Indians brought from Brazil and having their mode of life described to him, was half-ready to believe they would lose more than they would gain—the romantic notion of the Noble Savage came to men's minds, though it had to wait two hundred years to achieve its greatest effect. Poets and philosophers might not want to set out to discover mountains of gold, but the very thought that beyond the sea there was so much that was strange, illimitable forests in which anything might be found, vast, vacant but habitable spaces where life might begin afresh, all the mystery and wonder and vague promise of a still unknown continent, fired the imagination of the poets, widened and deepened the speculation of the philosophers. This world, so suddenly enlarged, was bright with the promise of new knowledge, new freedom, new opportunities. Men knew they lived on a globe; and now, in the sunlight of this new age, it began to look like a golden globe.

CHAPTER TWO

The Italian Scene
and Machiavelli

THE NEW AGE flowered first in Italy. All that was necessary was there: classical and other learning; the prosperous cities, with their new kinds of men, that were now independent republics or principalities; the changing Papacy itself, still unchallenged except as a political power, still far from the Reformation and Counter-Reformation; the arts that could flourish under ruling patrons who understood them and could reflect the sumptuous new style of life; and the idea of Man the inheritor of the golden globe, no longer a humble creature of God on trial here for a brief season, no longer fixed in the medieval hierarchy, but free to reach the heights or plunge into the depths and by his own abilities, choices, actions, to triumph or to ruin himself. Before the fifteenth century had gone, Pico della Mirandola, the brilliant young Platonist who died when he was thirty-one, had said it, in his oration on the Dignity of Man: . . . "Constrained by no limits (Thou, Man) shalt ordain for thyself the limits of thy nature. . . . As maker and molder of thyself, thou mayest fashion thyself in whatever shape thou shalt prefer. Thou shalt have the power to degenerate into lower forms of life, which are brutish. Thou shalt have the power, out of thy soul and judgment, to be re-born into the higher forms, which are divine. . . ." Fine brave words! But the time and the place seemed to call for such a salute. Was not Florence itself ruled by Lorenzo de Medici (Lorenzo the Magnificent), not only the patron of humanists like Pico, artists like Michelangelo, poets of the stature of Poliziano and Pulci, but himself an accomplished and versatile author?

An astounding versatility was the mark of these Italians of the new age. No other time or place can show us individuals equally many-sided and accomplished. Their energy, capacity, powers of application, must have been phenomenal. For example, Leon Battista Alberti was a painter, a poet, a philosopher, a musician, and an architect; his physical strength and dexterity (it was said he could jump, with his feet together, over a man's head) were as remarkable as the force and range of his mind; he appeared to know everything and to be able to do anything; even the gift of prophecy was not denied him. When Alberti died, in 1472, there was among the pupils of Verrocchio, himself a sculptor, painter, goldsmith, and teacher of the arts, a prodigious youth of twenty, the incredible Leonardo da Vinci, who was to prove himself an original genius in both the arts and the sciences, whose gifts and achievements set him towering above his time. Such men were exceptional but the level from which they rose was itself uncommonly high. The Florentine merchant-bankers were also statesmen, scholars, patrons and connoisseurs of the arts; the artists turned confidently from one medium to another; the humanist scholars attempted to master all accessible knowledge and, while doing so, might be called upon to act as secretaries, officials, diplomats. During this brief time—and this is one reason why it was so brilliant and created so much—society and the individual had one outlook, one aim, looked and moved in the same direction; no energy was lost in misunderstanding, cross-purposes, and conflict; genius drew strength from the community in which it was rooted, and the spirit of the community was leavened and raised by the genius it helped to nourish. But that is not all. Such wide application, such versatility and wealth of accomplishment, imply a prodigal zest, which in turn suggests a sharpening and heightening of consciousness and, supplying the zestful energy, a tremendous release of forces hitherto held in check in the unconscious. This was man, as Pico cried, exulting in his new-found freedom.

Not only man in the narrower sexual sense. The daughters of those rich Florentines were being educated too. Woman shared the glittering spoils of the new age, as indeed she had every right to do, according to its equally new precepts. Man might be now 'the maker and molder' of himself, but it could hardly be denied, after such a pronouncement, that woman was herself very much a 'maker and molder', so this was no time to order her to return to her stillroom and needlework. Moreover, beneath men's creative urges—and this was, above all, an age that saw them flame and flower—there are hidden feminine depths. Eros, not Logos, ruled these years, for all their show of virile and triumphant masculinity. So, first in Italy, then in the next century in France, England, and elsewhere in Western Europe, the Renaissance shows us its highly educated princesses. Erasmus, who numbered many women among his regular correspondents, introduces a sharp-witted learned lady into his *Colloquia*. The first Margaret of Navarre, sister of Francis the First, wrote allegorical and Platonic verse, and kept a circle of poets and philosophers round her. Being as much concerned with the antics of this world as with the secrets of the next, she helped to write, probably edited, and posthumously gave her name to the *Heptameron*, naughty anecdotes in the manner of Boccaccio's *Decameron*. Mary Queen of Scots and her cousin Elizabeth, Queen of England, were as unlike as any two women of rank in that age, but some things they had in common and one of them was a sound early education under the best available scholars. All these educated noble dames, found in one Court after another, made a welcome addition to the patronage and public of philosophers, poets, scholars and romancers, enlarging opportunity but not as yet—setting aside the whims of individual patronesses—deciding the matter and manner of authorship. This was to come much later, largely in response to a masculine notion of what was fit for a virtuous woman to read. Some of the learned ladies of the Renaissance, as for example Ronsard's obdurate last love, Hélène de Surgères, might pretend a chilly Platonic idealism; but what men of genius could write, these ladies were only too willing to read; and they made no pretence of shrinking from any mention in print of those facts of life which it is far easier for men than women to ignore. And if they tolerated, and even enjoyed, some bawdy passages, this does not mean, as some masculine critics appear to imply, that either they were pretending or were sexually corrupt. They were women under the sign of Eros, free for a time to be themselves. That very Margaret of Navarre who could collect the stories of the *Heptameron* was yet deeply religious, morally and socially anything but irresponsible, a reformer herself and the protectress of reformers, at once a loving woman and a learned great lady; she was the type at its best. The astonishing development of versatility, accomplishment, character, in the individual of the Renaissance, included both sexes. The fact should not surprise us.

The Italy of Pico's oration on the Dignity of Man had long been the scene of intrigues, shifting alliances, skirmishes and sieges, minor wars between the various principalities and republics and the soldiers of fortune that they employed. But there was nothing here to prevent the cities and their arts from flourishing, nothing to silence Pico's fine brave words. However, after his death, which came so soon and was attributed to poisoning, the scene changed. War arrived in earnest: what had been military chess-boards were turned into real battlefields. The invasions began: down came the French cavalry and their famous artillery, the hired Swiss pikemen and German *Landsknechte*, and, last to arrive and most formidable of all, the dreaded Spanish infantry, armed with the arquebus. But though, year after year, the invaders marched and countermarched, joined forces with or fought against the Papacy or Venice, Florence or Milan, the brilliant Italy of the Renaissance still survived. Indeed, in the Rome of Julius II and Leo X (except in his final and almost bankrupt years, when he lost men of genius to keep his buffoons), the arts, especially the visual arts, blazed in a last dazzling display. But neither in Rome nor elsewhere could the writers, though numerous enough, well-rewarded, and enjoying international reputations, successfully challenge the painters and sculptors or the three past giants, Dante, Petrarch, Boccaccio, whose Florentine language Pietro Bembo was urging his fellow-poets to imitate. True, there was Ariosto, all grace and charm and subtle mockery in his ultra-romantic epic, *Orlando Furioso*; there was the diplomat, Castiglione, polishing his social and philosophical dialogues of the court of Urbino; there was also—a sinister figure this, presaging our own world of unscrupulous journalism and publicity—the incredibly popular Pietro Aretino, impudent and obscene, who made an opulent living out of his pen by blackmailing important persons.

The political ruin of Italy dates from the summer of 1527, when an army ostensibly serving the Emperor Charles the Fifth, but by this time half-starved and on the edge of mutiny, swarmed down to Rome and sacked the city. The troops, tough Spanish veterans, German mercenaries largely Lutheran in sympathy, were out of hand; the great rich city was at their mercy and they had none; not for days but for weeks at a time they murdered and raped, burnt and plundered. Later the plague spread among the ruins. The population was halved. In the autumn of 1528 Erasmus could write that contemporary Rome had suffered more cruelly than the ancient capital sacked by the Goths, that not the city but the world had perished. The Italian Renaissance of the Medici and Leonardo and the younger Michelangelo, the era when an essentially Italian pagan spirit was still contained within the easy bounds of the Church, when a sense of beauty and a natural piety still worked in harmony and the new humanism modified without defying tradition, may be said to have died in these smoking ruins of Rome. Certainly, the other cities, independent capitals, still stood: Florence, Milan, Genoa, and the rest; and now, above all, though the republic was already past its prime, Venice, where Aretino and his friends brought life, sometimes smelling a little rank, to the new comedy. But the literature of the second half of the sixteenth century, of the Italy not of the Renaissance but of the embittered Counter-Reformation, found its greatest voice in the poet Tasso, who moved from the pastoral idyll of his *Aminta* to his fantastic but deeply impassioned epic of the First Crusade, *Gerusalemme Liberata*. Tasso had genius, of the kind that brought innumerable readers to exult and suffer with him down the years; but genius not only enables a man to express his time but also leaves him wide open to all its pressures, strains, deep divisions and hidden conflicts; and Tasso spent his later years in the shadow of madness.

So remembering what Pico had cried, long before, in the proud high noon of the age, telling his countrymen they could ordain for themselves the limits of their natures, fashion themselves in whatever shapes they might prefer, and considering what came afterwards, we will dismiss the poets, epic or lyrical, the letter writers, the playwrights and satirists, in fact all the general literature of the time, to examine, as the spokesman of the age, a far less brilliant but far more renowned contemporary of Pico's —the Florentine political theorist and historian, Niccoló Machiavelli. (He also wrote one of the best Italian comedies of the sixteenth century, *La Mandragola*.) This official and diplomat in the service of the Florentine

Republic, who took to writing only when the Medici family dissolved the Republic and had him placed under house-arrest, may appear a rather humdrum literary figure when compared with an Ariosto or a Tasso; but, after all, he is one of that very small group of authors whose names have contributed an adjective to all the languages of Western Man. Millions of people who have never read a word he wrote know what 'machiavellian' means, though, ironically enough, it does not mean what Machiavelli meant. He was not a conspicuously successful diplomat, but his various missions to Rome, France, Germany, enabled him to take a close view of ruling princes in action, notably Cesare Borgia, whom he knew at the height of Cesare's swift and dazzling triumphs. He was also a thoughtful student of ancient Roman history. The combined result of these studies and his immediate experiences is to be discovered, though he wrote other historical and political works, in his most famous book, *The Prince*.

No doubt the term 'machiavellian' originally carried a darker shade of meaning than it has had more recently. There was about it almost a suggestion of black magic. During the sixteenth century the rest of Europe regarded Italy not only with admiration and awe, because of its magnificent cultural achievements, but also with mistrust, as a land of sinister magicians, sorcerers, witches, astrologers, fortune-tellers, mysterious poisoners and assassins. Wild superstition was all too often the dark side of Humanism. The broad religious framework of life had vanished and the sciences had still to make their major discoveries, so the mind, which has to believe something, was invaded by notions of magic, sometimes white, too often black. And the morality of the Italian Renaissance was notoriously dubious. If the Italians called all foreigners 'barbarians', the other Europeans held Italians to be over-subtle, treacherous, sinister, possessing dark secrets. So in Elizabethan and Jacobean England the 'Italianate Englishman', the man who had lived long enough in Italy to discover these secrets, was thought to be very wicked indeed, a satanic fellow; and the most lurid and ghastly English plays of the period, such as those of Webster, are all set in Italy. (And this tradition of the wicked Italian, trafficking in black magic, lasted a long time.) Machiavelli himself, a diligent and conscientious Florentine civil servant, might be wildly unlike this Mephistopheles of the South, but undoubtedly 'machiavellian' at first carried a hint of intrigue so unscrupulous and powerful that there was sorcery in it.

Later, down to our own time, 'machiavellian' came to mean power-mongering and plotting without that generous altruism, that sound ethical basis, claimed by all politicians who know their business. But in fact it is precisely this claim that Machiavelli himself strongly advocates. He also tells us, among other things, that while everyone admits how praise-worthy it is in a prince to keep faith, and to live with integrity and not with craft, his experience has been that those princes who have done great things have held good faith of little account, and have known how to circumvent the intellect of men by craft, and in the end have over-come those who have relied on their word. He does not recommend deceit and treachery for their own sake. He is not, as so many people seem to imagine, pleading for villainy. He does not demand that a ruler or ambitious statesman should be a scoundrel. He merely points out that, men being what they are, there are many occasions when lying, treachery, cruelty, will succeed, and truth, good faith, benevolence, will be disastrous. The fact is, of course, that he is examining his various problems of power politics outside ethics altogether, in what may reason-ably be called a scientific spirit. That men in power, and the historians who admire such men, should pretend to be so deeply shocked by him is part of the hypocrisy he advises on occasion, though not on as many occasions as we discover in modern political life. No doubt Machiavelli would have approved of the earlier tactics and stratagems of Hitler and Goebbels but would soon have been astonished that such crude bare-faced impudence could have succeeded so easily. But he wrote chiefly in terms of small city-states and lived long before the time of vast urban masses and all our techniques of mass persuasion.

Nevertheless, as Bertrand Russell has pointed out, "the world has become more like that of Machiavelli than it was" (that is, between his time and ours), if only because the Renaissance and our own era are alike in having much that is new in them, have both seen the rapid breakdown of what belonged to slow evolutionary growth, of a society held together by traditional codes of conduct, of power modified by common ethical values and judgments. Our revolutions followed by dictatorships, our almost omnipotent states and ubiquitous politics, return us to Machiavelli's world, except that we are aware of dangers that would have appalled him. So let us listen carefully when he tells us that if a prince (to us a dictator, party or statesman in power) has the credit of conquering and holding his state, the means will always be considered honest, and he will be praised by everybody, because the vulgar (that is, people in general) are always taken by what a thing seems to be and by what comes of it; and when he concludes by indicating a prince of his time (it was Ferdinand of Aragon, but Machiavelli dared not say so) who "never preaches anything else but peace and good faith, and to both he is most hostile, and either, if he had kept it, would have deprived him of reputation and kingdom many a time". He does not dismiss religion and all the virtues it teaches; he says they are good for a kingdom within their limits; but he deliberately puts the prince (political power) outside those limits, to adopt or discard those virtues as it suits him, while still seeming to have them—and this he stresses—and appearing to be religious. So power is not contained within the religious framework, which is now largely illusory, a popular superstition. Though not intended as such, Machiavelli's examination and analysis of real situations, in terms of power, is like an ironical commentary on Pico's enthusiastic oration on the new Dignity of Man. And though it is true, as history was to show, that there are many decisive factors Machiavelli left out of account, that his whole study of the matter is over-simplified, this careful Florentine official must be considered one of the great originals among writers, revealing to Western Man (who largely out of self-deception coined 'machiavellian') a new insight into experience, and sending, even if unintentionally, across the centuries to us a prophetic warning voice. And this too came from the Italian Renaissance, from its shadow-side, just as the glorious works of art, which we still marvel at today, came from its sunlight.

CHAPTER THREE

France: Rabelais and Montaigne

CERTAIN PLACES at certain times seem to men, perhaps in very different places and long afterwards, to possess a magical quality, capturing and holding the imagination. This is true of the Italy of the early Renaissance; it is equally true of France during most of the sixteenth century. We cannot have travelled south-west from Paris without returning in thought, almost as if we shared a dream with men long dead, to the French Renaissance. Above the rich meadows and the mirrors of the water we see the entrancing châteaux built when Francis the First was King, or the castle at Blois where the Valois so often held court; we pass through Vendôme, which was Ronsard's town, Chinon, where Rabelais was born, and when we have done with the Loire country we probably reach the Dordogne, where Montaigne retired to write his essays. It is a corner of Western Europe nobly provisioned to this day with fine regional food and wine, so that the very dinner-table seems rich with historical and literary associations; we eat and drink and wander through the neighbouring streets or across the fields in this dream of the Renaissance, remembering a line by Ronsard or Du Bellay, a phrase by Rabelais or Montaigne. Perhaps most of our affectionate allegiance to France, our readiness to forgive her so many faults, comes from our feeling for these places and this time, when her smiling image seems to be finally and exquisitely formed.

It was during these years that French, as a written language, began to be perfected, like an instrument to which more and clearer notes were added, both for verse, especially the lyric (though for this form, which asks to be free from too much over-rational public criticism, the recipe was found, only to be lost for over two hundred years), and for that prose, infinitely persuasive, a marvellous instrument, which soon came to be recognised as one of the nation's greatest possessions. From Marot at the beginning of the period, through the Pléiade, more especially the two leaders of the movement, Ronsard and Du Bellay, whose haunting lyrics of love and death were to return much later with the Romantics, to d'Aubigne and Du Bartas, both grave but impassioned Huguenots, at the end òf the period, this was a century of French poets and poetry, the richest, except in drama, until the nineteenth. Yet it was two prose writers who had the widest influence outside France and seem to have contributed most to Western literature in general. And though no two writers could seem more strikingly different than Rabelais and Montaigne, both emerge from the Renaissance in France, one expressing the earlier and wilder phase of it, the other the later and graver phase.

During this century both the Reformation, with Calvin as its chief French spokesman, and the inevitable Counter-Reformation, which sent the Jesuits swarming into Paris, pressed hard upon France, whose history now is a confused tale of religious-cum-political intrigue, of key personages changing sects and sides, of persecutions, executions and assassinations, of massacres and civil wars. But the fundamental difference was not between the fanatics at each embittered extreme but between fanaticism itself and any remaining spirit of tolerance, any idea of moderation in religion and politics, what was left of the Renaissance as Italy had known it. There was still a broad middle road along which the sensuous life of the time went jangling and glittering, and there most of the men of letters are to be found. In the first half of the century Rabelais, roistering and roaring, is somewhere along that road, and during the second half Montaigne is at the end of it, exploring the inner world of his own personality. Both authors were notable originals, and their influence, direct and indirect, can hardly be over-estimated.

It could be said of Rabelais that he is more often referred to than read, that a great many people are aware of him who have in fact never made his acquaintance as an author. This is partly because he is not easy to read in his own language and has been notoriously difficult to translate adequately. But it is also a measure of his true stature. Even though it may have sometimes been reduced, in squalid corners, to a pornographic whisper, his is one of the great voices of Western culture. Indeed, it is a voice that, if we chose to listen to it carefully, might bid us hope among our present fanaticisms and despairing negations. For this monk-turned-wandering-scholar-turned-physician was above all 'a life-enhancer'. So far as he was a man of ideas, he was as much a Renaissance humanist as Erasmus, and in certain important respects there can be said to be more of the Renaissance in his work than in that of any other writer of the age. For example, there is more of its astonishingly exuberant energy, there is more of its almost frenzied demand for knowledge of any sort, there is more of its sheer love of words, there is more of its mixture of nobility and grossness, there is more of its delight in elaborate fantastifiactions. We are probably closer to the essential character of the age with Rabelais than with anybody else. But we have to bear in mind what was his own essential character. He was monk-scholar-physician, a humanist, at heart a sensible moderate who could tolerate anything except black fanaticism, life-despisers, power-worship, a bogus spirituality based on narrowness and pride; but he was also a humorist, in fact one of the greatest humorists of all time. And unless we understand this, we cannot begin to understand him. It is here that he is easily misunderstood, if only because literary historians and critics all too often are by temperament and outlook incapable of appreciating humour, as distinct from wit and satire, or the character, outlook and method of the essential humorist.

We cannot begin to understand and enjoy Rabelais, for example, if we accept the view that he was a serious satirist, an anti-clerical reformer, a Protestant, or even an agnostic or rationalist, who to escape charges of heresy disguised himself as a buffoon, hid himself and his purpose behind a carnival display of giants, dwarfs, freaks, wild clowning and obscenity. This is to turn Rabelais into somebody quite different and much smaller, to turn exuberant genius into careful talent, to take away his greatness. The real Rabelais is not lurking behind what he fantasticates for us, the mad arguments, the impossible journeys and battles; he is not using his drollery as a bait; but being a humorist he is extending himself into everything he creates, and its expansiveness and extravagance, breaking into sheer nonsense, bawdy, or lists of names that are like heraldic processions, are what properly belong to humour. Much of it is like the talk and comic invention of men sitting late over wine, except that it has, to sustain it, the energy and creative richness of genius. Almost every laughable device used by later comic writers may be found somewhere in Rabelais. But their scale is smaller than his. He presses into service everything that comes to mind, scraps of learning from anywhere and everywhere, real characters and monstrous creations, places that range from the smallest villages in Touraine to whole kingdoms of nonsense and crazy wonderlands, talk that runs from philosophical disputes to the grossest tales. But nearly all his grossness, which has worried so many of his more refined critics, is part of his acceptance of everything, of his grand scale, of his challenge to the types of mind that prefer to forget we have bodies and are therefore rooted in Nature. Here both the challenger and the challenged belong to a masculine world, and although Rabelais, like a true son of the Renaissance, admitted women on equal terms into his Abbey of Thélème, he has (unlike Shakespeare) little of value to say about woman herself and apparently very little to say about anything that women want to hear. His acceptance of our bodily functions is nothing new to them and they find his exuberance and extravagance, his colossal pagoda-building of absurdity, both childish and tedious. He is a man's author.

Yet, ironically enough, this robust masculine genius, this mad wag whose cheap cynicism about woman is his weakest feature, makes war everywhere on what is patriarchal, whatever is dominated by the masculine principle, whatever is one-sided, intolerant, harsh, bigoted, fanatical, pedantic, legalistic, tyrannical, life-denying, to defend and to celebrate what is in effect matriarchal in its values, owing allegiance to the feminine principle, whatever makes for a free and joyful acceptance of life in all its genuine manifestations, of nature as well as culture, of man as body, mind and soul. His is the genial anarchism of Eros, rebelling against all repressions and restrictions, laws and regulations, all attempts to turn natural impulses into the galley slaves of an idea; and yet, as we discover in the conduct and talk of Gargantua and Pantagruel and in his description of his Abbey of Thélème, he understands what civilisation should mean, the wisdom of tolerance and magnanimity, the lofty delights of mind and soul as well as the appetites and pleasures of flesh and blood. Though he expands to grotesque limits his accounts of a mad world, he himself is not mad but in essence sane and healthy; no matter how crazily he invents, how monstrously he exaggerates, he is never lost in fantasy but always returns, as all the greatest writers do, to a reasonable and balanced acceptance of continuing life; his enormous roars of laughter have only cleared the air and made it sweeter. "I class Rabelais," wrote Coleridge, no lover of uproarious bawdy, "with the creative minds of the world, Shakespeare, Dante, Cervantes . . ." He is, Hugo tells us, "the soul of Gaul". True, for just as he expresses the Renaissance itself, so too he expresses the France that was discovering and revealing herself in this age. But it is a thicker, richer, more full-blooded France than we find in her later literature, as if this wandering monk and doctor, for all his journeys with cardinals and the like, as their personal physician, to Rome and other cities, kept the country-bred boy, the peasant stock, alive in him and stayed close to the common people, whose humorous and deeply realistic outlook, in spite of his learning and philosophical clowning, he shared; he probably does to this day, when we need him badly. He remains their author, perhaps their greatest.

Montaigne, the scholarly country gentleman meditating in his tower among his books, is a very different figure from Rabelais, born fifty years before him and representing an earlier and wilder phase of the Renaissance in France. Their literary manners are even more widely different than their backgrounds and modes of life. It is the difference between a town fair in full swing and a lecture delivered to the local Philosophical Society, between its largest tavern at closing time and mid-afternoon in the quiet room of the municipal library. Nevertheless, both men move along the same broad middle road; they share a common dislike of pedants, intellectual bullies, bigots and fanatics; they are not irreligious but deeply sceptical about the claims of the theologians; they are humanists under God. Their popularity was equally great, but it is Montaigne who has had the wider influence. Out of what began, in the rather tedious fashion of the time, as a mixture of classical quotations and brief comments on them, there emerged the famous essays, gaining both in length and depth with each volume. And with these Montaigne performed a triple act of original creation: he fashioned a prose style that appears to be as easy and flexible and racy as good talk, a style that could serve as a model for many generations of French prose writers; he created a literary form, the personal essay, that has been since used, more or less as he originally used it, by innumerable good authors not only in French but in other literatures, notably English; and finally, and most important of all, as he developed this essay form he came more and more to take his own character, his own habits, idiosyncrasies, preferences, prejudices, hopes and fears, as his chief subject-matter, turning his attention inward, into consciousness itself and towards the mysterious depths of the unconscious, first setting sail on what has become since a vast expedition of discovery. This Périgord gentleman in his tower, smilingly referring to some fad or whimsy, is the ancestor in literature of Proust, desperately disengaging the last shred of motive, three-and-a-half centuries later, in his cork-lined room.

Men had written about themselves before Montaigne. But they had presented themselves for a purpose outside self-discovery, to make a confession, to prove something; and what they had revealed had not been a true self but a faked image, a mask, a *persona*. Amused, tolerant, neither well-pleased nor angry with himself, Montaigne the observer regards and considers Montaigne the observed as he might look at a pear ripening on the wall or the summer's crop of hay. This had not been done by anybody before him, and, although long after his time elaborate self-analysis would be widely attempted, it has rarely been done as he did it, perhaps never in his prevailing spirit, by all the introspective writers since his time. For Montaigne, for all his scepticism and his dubious queries about death, felt himself to be more securely placed than these later writers did. He did not stare at himself until he saw nothing but a skeleton at the edge of the abyss. This man he had to live with, whose foibles and likings and doubts he describes with such frankness and charm, was nourished and refreshed by Nature, and consoled, for all that was relative and impermanent in this life, by his constant thought of God's eternity. He did not know, nor want to know, too much about either; what he knew was the man lodged between them, above the green grass and beneath the blue dome. His scepticism, lightly ironical, was broadly based, as we may see in his longest essay, *An Apologie of Raymond Sebond* (the spelling here is Florio's in his English translation, which, incidentally, Shakespeare must have read); but if it slyly mocked the bigots and the warring sects, turned sharply away from the torture chambers and the reek of burning flesh, it kept its hold upon this earth and refused to darken the sky. Montaigne's own acceptance of orthodoxy is that of a man who falls in with the custom of the country; his conservatism has in it nothing cynical, nothing aggressive; his distrust of the abstract, the high-flown, the intellect on stilts, iron dogmatism, everything that tries to break the human scale, has warmth and heart behind it, a feeling for what is real and alive, for what can be seen and touched. Heroes and saints, martyrs and mystics, may be made of other stuff, but so too are all the life-haters, the black oppressors of the human race. And in this moment of our history, we are in no position to despise that smaller, but smiling and sun-lit, world of Montaigne.

The chronicles of his time, the age seen as history, repel us; the very air seems stifling, murky with dark fanaticism, intrigue, murder and civil war. It is only in literature, around these little essays in self-knowledge, that the sun seems to shine and the air to have some sweetness. But then the essayist does not claim to know too much outside himself; God is a mystery and not a fellow-conspirator in the power-plot; the universe still escapes the limits of the human mind, and does not obligingly dwindle to suit a sect; there is so much that cannot be known, that exactitude, logic, consistency, must be sacrificed, with some loss of force and pride, to humility and good sense, which can at least enjoy what God appears to have provided. All this there is in Montaigne, and in all those who have travelled, then and since, that broad road with him. But there is something that can begin to be known, as he proved to his and our profit, something much closer and more comprehensible than the doctrine of the Trinity or the world plan of the Absolute, and that is—the mind, the inner world, that shapes and colours both character and action. No wonder that Montaigne was free from the raging and murderous fanaticism of his time. He had taken a peep into the kitchen where that hell-broth was being stirred. Not for him, with his self-knowledge, the consciousness that claims too much, the rising tide of doubt in the unconscious, the

24

barriers hastily raised against this tide, the savage repression of all feeling of uncertainty, the over-compensation bursting into the world as intolerant dogmatism, violence and cruelty. This, the shadow-side of the brilliant Renaissance, darkened the sixteenth century; and if now, four hundred years later, we imagine we are in clear daylight at last, we had better look at the nearest newspaper or switch on the television set. We may feel, not unreasonably if we are thinking in terms of literary form, manner, style, that we have outgrown, left far behind, the gigantic and uproarious buffooneries of Rabelais, the quaint, modest self-revelations of Montaigne; but what lies and lives at the very centre of their thought and feeling, the truly religious good sense to which Rabelais returns after his wildest sallies, the double recognition of the human scale and the surrounding mystery that accompanies Montaigne's self-knowledge, all of this is even more salutary and precious to us now than it was to Renaissance France. Perhaps we are dimly aware of it, are quickened by the spirit of these great Frenchmen, as we stare across the meadows and the water at the châteaux of the Loire, order an *Omelette Gargamelle* at the old inn at Chinon, or descend the thirsty limestone hills of the Dordogne in search of the local wine.

CHAPTER FOUR

England and Shakespeare

THE WINDS that scattered the Spanish Armada blew English Literature, which had been merely smouldering for generations, into a blaze of genius. Elizabeth, who was to give her name to this glorious outburst, had in fact reigned for thirty years before it arrived, and most of its supreme achievements in poetic drama and in prose argument came in the reign of her successor, James the First. Nevertheless, we are right to call this great age of literature 'Elizabethan', for its greatness belongs in spirit to that strange indomitable Queen, just as its decadence later seems to share the stifling atmosphere of James's Court. And clearly there are two questions about this Elizabethan age we must ask and try to answer. Why did it arrive so late, after the Queen herself had been reigning for thirty years, long after the Renaissance in Italy and France had come to an end? And why, when it did arrive, when the sixteenth century had only twelve more years to run, should it suddenly break into that firework display of poetic genius?

The first question is easily answered. Great literature demands a language that is at once a powerful and very flexible instrument, an organ with more than one keyboard and many stops. This instrument was not ready; the organ was only being assembled. English literary forms were either borrowed from Italy and France, as in much of the verse of Surrey and Wyatt, or, as with the prose-men, also often busy with translation, were still crudely experimenting with syntax, with the first creaky wooden machinery of prose style. Nor is this surprising. The England of the Tudors was a new country, even though in some respects it was more medieval and traditional than most of Southern Europe; and it was a new country out on the edge of things, as yet away from the main stream of civilisation. Its famous long-bows had been made obsolete by gun-powder, it had a militia but no real army; it had plenty of ships, boldly exploring, trading and privateering, but as yet they hardly constituted a navy. True, its wealth was rapidly increasing, London was growing fast; its new social order, created by Henry the Eighth and confirmed and stabilised by the adroit Elizabeth, was proving effective and a source of new energy; and the nationalism of the age, nothing strange to these islanders, was triumphant and irresistible here. But too much was happen-ing all at once; enormous effort was required, as nobody knew better than Elizabeth herself, to cope with every immediate situation. So those first thirty years of her reign were years of effort, of solemn endeavour, of will and purpose, all reflected in the writing of the time, in the didactic prose work of Ascham and Elyot, even in the little that was done by the splendid Sidney and in the earlier poetry of the great Spenser. Then came the threat of the Spanish Armada, crammed with the dreaded infantrymen of Spain: the ultimate challenge. The challenge was met, the Armada defeated and, the very elements being on England's side (as they ought to be, in English opinion), finally destroyed; the great black shadow of Spain suddenly vanished; Elizabethan England had come through, where the sun was out and the bells were ringing.

This explains the sudden release of energy, the nation in flower. But it does not provide a complete answer to our second question—why this flowering should reach, in a few years, such a dazzling height of poetic genius. Perhaps a complete answer cannot be found, the *Zeitgeist*, then as now, having too many secret operations. But some contributions towards it are possible. First, the energy was there, ready to be released into art. Next, this was a nation highly conscious of itself as a nation; a late Elizabethan, a subject of the magnificent old Queen, was very much an Elizabethan. Now to this release of energy and this national self-conscious-ness we must add a third factor. Within the national unity of this com-paratively small society there was astonishing variety; it contained, for example, not only Anglicans but also Catholics, Puritans, sceptics and atheists. It was grimly ascetic and wildly licentious; it reached extremes of brutality and refinement, and a building that offered bear-baiting on Wednesday would be playing *Romeo and Juliet* on Thursday. A merchant

27

might invest his money in wool or in a search for El Dorado; good advice might be sought from Francis Bacon, the father of scientific method, or Dr. Dee, the necromancer; capitalism in a black suit rubbed elbows with the velvet or rags of dying feudalism; the great Queen's Court seemed equidistant between the Tower, with its thumbscrews and scaffolds, and fairyland. The life of this London was an incredible medley of lutes and lice, silks and ordure, madrigals and the plague, industrious apprentices and pimps and harlots, white-faced Puritan preachers and red-faced drunken poets. During this brief period, each class had something almost theatrical about it, appeared to be over-playing its part: the great nobles moved in an unending pageant, and the lesser sold estates to buy a suit and three sets of livery for a possible appearance at Court; the new middle class counted its money, donned clean linen to listen to sermons, ate beef and pudding, locked up its daughters, all suddenly and tremendously bourgeois; the common folk, the crowd, the mob, shook its fists or threw up its caps, rioted or rollicked, like the chorus in an opera. To this age, we feel, everything was titanic. Was there a glimpse of some new moral order in the universe, then it came looming through the mists of ignorance and superstition, colossally intimidating; but the mounting individualism, prepared to defy it, went marching on stilts. Love raged like a fever or was all honey, fragrance and a May morning; the very thought of Death brought an arctic winter, darkness and despair. There was then this variety; there were all these contradictions; there were these poles of opposites where the newly released energy went flashing. Words, magnificent words, wonderful words, words of power like those in some magician's incantation, were needed now to express all that must be expressed; and fortunately the language, suddenly arriving at maturity and an extraordinary richness of vocabulary (Shakespeare's is phenomenal), had such words; a man could get drunk on them, a society turn to poetry as it turned to food and drink. And this it did. Finally, perhaps because the rapid transformations of the time and the flood of energy stirred the depths of the unconscious, where all is magical, there seemed to be a strange magic pervading and illuminating the whole scene, miseries and cruelties and all, a magic that lingers to this day in an Elizabethan song, a speech by Hamlet or Cleopatra.

It was a poetry largely meant to be heard rather than silently read. But the exceptions are important. Spenser undoubtedly asks for the co-operation of a devoted and leisurely reader in his immense unfinished epic, *The Faerie Queene*, with its metrical ingenuities, its unwinding richly-dyed panorama, and the complicated political, moral and religious allegories of its adventures in chivalry. So too the younger and less-esteemed poet (who was to have a great influence upon twentieth-century English poets), John Donne, who must have had a private reader in mind when he wrote his impassioned but introspective and quasi-metaphysical verses, to be followed later, when he had hearers in plenty, by sermons of much the same quality. But even outside the drama, to which we will come soon, much of the verse of the age has a challenging rhetorical air, as if bidding the listener mark its inner meaning and moral structure, or is purely and enchantingly lyrical, as if written—as indeed so much of it was—to be set to music and sung. For these Elizabethans were always singing; it was part of the gentry's education to learn to sing in company the intricate polyphonic music of the time. And some of the most ravishing Elizabethan lyrics were simply the contributions of the poets to this pastime.

Before the great age properly declared itself, prior to the very last years of the century, there were signs that prose fiction, beginning with translations of Italian tales and continuing with imitations of such models by men like Lyly and Greene, might leave the drama behind, to keep the crowd entertained by its crude sword-and-dagger tragedies and rough farce. But this prose fiction, as yet remote from the life of its readers and monstrously affected in manner (often parodied by Shakespeare in his early comedies), was too enervated, too bloodless, too narrow in its appeal, to attract the genius of the age. So it was passed over in favour of that form which fascinated the crowd, which might still be crude but had blood and magic in it—the drama. It was in the theatre that the genius of the age suddenly began working its miracles.

Shakespeare and his fellow-dramatists, many of them the younger sons of impoverished landed families who found they could make a living only by writing for the theatre, could never resist jeering at 'the ground-lings', the crowds who paid their pennies to see the play. Most of this was excusable because it did not come from any snobbish desire to flatter their richer patrons but from their exasperation, no doubt after many an argument with the managers, at having to please the crowd by finding room in their plays for fencing matches, jigs and buffoonery. Nevertheless, taking a broad view we may say these dramatists were ungrateful. It was by attracting the crowd and not disdaining it, by accepting popular taste and not rejecting it in favour of what was scholarly, cultured, and fashionable abroad, that Elizabethan drama raised itself to such a height. By adapting itself to temporal and local conditions, it created a unique form, one that offered a Shakespeare an opportunity that almost matched his genius, and a form that had special virtues of its own not sufficiently appreciated even today.

For years the wealthier nobles, for reasons of prestige, had kept troupes of players among their retainers, and these troupes frequently toured the country. (The records of one small town, Abingdon, show that in one year seven such troupes played there.) In addition to these professionals, there were a great many amateur performers, like those caricatured in *A Midsummer Night's Dream*, acting traditional morality plays and folk entertainments that included plenty of singing and dancing and clowning. There was in the country a wealth of crude but useful dramatic stuff. The men who built the new theatres in London had to look to the Court and the more influential nobles for their licences, but they knew that to keep these buildings filled and their companies in employment they had to depend upon the crowd and what the crowd had learnt to enjoy. Not for them, therefore, the neo-classical drama, something in the manner of Seneca. This might have pleased 'the university wits' but would have left the pit and galleries empty. So the new dramatists, soon called upon between them to supply dozens of plays a year, disregarded such knowledge as they had of the classics, and drew upon this rich store of popular dramatic entertainment, with its singing and clowning and sword-play, while hastily devising a kind of drama specially adapted for both the audiences and the playhouses.

The touring companies had set up their stages, when playing for townsfolk and not for the nobility, in the large inn yards, where the crowd could sit or stand around the platform and the superior patrons could seat themselves in the galleries outside the bedrooms of the inn. The London theatres more or less reproduced this setting, though they were usually round or oval in shape and the stage was more than a mere platform, having entrances at each side, a curtained inner stage, and an upper stage or balcony, as the illustrations make plain. For imaginative poetic drama this type of stage had many advantages over the 'picture frame' stage that superseded it. There was no scenery to be changed; the dramatist could move freely and swiftly from place to place, often building up his story by a succession of short scenes. Having only words at his command for any description of places, any suggestion of atmosphere, he had to use his imagination and compel his audience to use theirs. The play could move at great speed. Finally, the actor on the outer stage, surrounded by his audience as he delivered with great effect one of the famous speeches, had an intimate and compelling relation with them very difficult to recapture on the later 'picture frame' stage. Even with such limited evidence as we possess, it is not hard to believe that an Elizabethan audience, attending a poetic tragedy or comedy, found in the theatre an imaginative experience of a richness and intensity that we cannot discover in our own drama.

Though some of them might want clowns, bawdy, bloodshed, there can be no doubt that most of these patrons of the Elizabethan theatre took with them to the playhouse a taste for fine language and a quick comprehension. We know roughly the time required then to perform plays we still produce, and the pace of their performance is astonishing. But we also know that the actors, after severe training, were highly accomplished both in voice and gesture. They created—and probably excelled in—a tradition that lingered among Shakespearean actors into this century; it is not the naturalistic acting demanded by the prose drama of our age; it probably consisted of a tremendous heightening of the actor's personality, aided by every trick of voice and gesture. It did not so much deceive as impose itself upon the audience, probably as much delighted by sheer virtuosity as people are now at the opera. The boys who played the women's parts, in which naturalistic performances would be impossible, were probably trained to act in a highly stylised fashion. All the evidence proves that English acting during this period enjoyed a great reputation;

travellers abroad were disappointed by the acting there; and English companies were in great demand on the Continent. They were also much admired for the splendour of their costumes. Leading players like Alleyn and Burbage had substantial shares in their playhouses (Shakespeare was 'a sharer' too, probably both as dramatist and actor), and made a great deal of money out of them. But with so many new plays to find, put into rehearsal, and then perform, the work, worry and strain must have been wearing; we should not be surprised that Shakespeare retired, probably worn out, before he was fifty.

Those splendid costumes, renowned at home and abroad, were all contemporary in design; no attempt was made to suggest the particular period of the play. This was not because the Elizabethans knew no better; they were not interested in creating that particular realistic type of effect. They assumed, quite rightly, that an audience knows that it is in a theatre looking at actors, that it is quite ready to imagine that a bare stage is a street or a garden, to accept Caesar or Macbeth in doublet and hose, and that the production of a play, no matter how it is staged, must be artificial, based on certain accepted conventions. It is possible that they knew instinctively—what later theorists of the drama failed to understand—that the theatre exists to provide a unique type of experience, to which we respond on two different levels of the mind at the same time, one level concerned with the imaginary life of the play, the other with the play's performance, with all that belongs to the actors and the theatre. And this is true, no matter what convention happens to be established. The most elaborate scene-painting and effects will not persuade an audience that it is actually looking at a street or a forest, that it is not in a theatre. And though there may be some pleasure in admiring a painted scene, imaginative people will take more delight in sharing the imagination of the dramatic poet as he transforms a bare stage into a dozen different scenes. Moreover, the actor almost surrounded by his audience, on a stage where he is not dwarfed and dimmed by the scene painter, is a solid compelling figure; and he and the dramatist, creating everything between them, can reach a far more imaginative and intimate relationship with the audience. Shakespeare could have worked wonders on any stage, using any theatrical convention; nevertheless, he was fortunate in finding, and then helping to develop, a theatre so flexible, adaptable, swift-paced, passionate and poetic.

Before turning to Shakespeare we must consider, even if briefly and inadequately, his colleagues and rivals in the theatre. There are two familiar attitudes towards these other Elizabethan and Jacobean dramatists. Some critics suggest that they have been over-estimated simply because of their relation to Shakespeare, because some of the light on him spills on them. Other critics have held that we undervalue their talents, which were considerable, because they are so outshone by Shakespeare's genius. And this is the sounder opinion. They form a remarkable group of dramatists, with a very wide range of talent, and if there had been no Shakespeare, to represent the age at its best both in tragedy and comedy, their finest work might have been far more often staged. The first of them, an innovator to whom Shakespeare owed much, is Marlowe, who, if he had not died young, murdered in a tavern brawl, might have rivalled Shakespeare in tragedy, where he has sweep and passion, great magic lines, and bold if rather careless designs. Then there is Ben Jonson, scholar and poet as well as dramatist, whose best comedies, notably *The Alchemist* and *Volpone*, have in recent years returned triumphantly to the English stage. They have a sharply satirical sense of character, careful construction, and some wonderful bravura speeches; they are as massive and formidable as their author himself, but, possibly like him, lack easy gaiety and charm. An older man, George Chapman, the translator of Homer, has been less fortunate, both in his series of French historical tragedies and his rather rough comedies, which are often as clumsy as those of his occasional collaborator, John Marston, a coarsely powerful and unequal writer, capable however of passages of unexpected beauty. His fault in tragedy, a common fault among these dramatists, was a wilful extravagance in the action, piling up the horrors. They were much in the habit of collaborating, especially in comedy, and one of them, Dekker, worked so often with other men that it is hard to tell where his work begins or ends. He wrote a great deal of lively prose, both in and out of the theatre, but is chiefly remembered for his exquisite lyrics and a romantic-pathetic touch in his handling of female characters found in none of the others except Shakespeare.

Of the later dramatists, writing under James the First and beginning to show signs of a descent from the high Elizabethan level, perhaps the best are Middleton, Heywood, Webster, Beaumont and Fletcher, Massinger and Ford. Middleton wrote many bustling comedies of contemporary life, but it is in the tragic scenes of *The Changeling* that he shows a flash of genius. They are better than anything in Heywood, a most prolific playwright and something of a hack, who deserves mention, however, because his plays of domestic life seem almost to anticipate the realistic prose-drama of the nineteenth century. Webster was the finest poet of this group—he is indeed a great poet in flashes—but limited and faulty as a dramatist: his two best-known tragedies, *The White Devil* (easily the better of the two) and *The Duchess of Malfi*, contain wonderful lines but strain so much towards horror that they come close to absurdity. Beaumont and Fletcher, who wrote a great many plays together, were ingenious, versatile and very successful, especially with the upper class to which they both belonged; the tone of their plays and their blank verse itself are easier and looser, and with the arrival of their most characteristic work we feel that the true Elizabethan theatre, with its packed pits, its comic breadth its poetic grandeur, has vanished for ever. Massinger was equally industrious and versatile; an adroit master of effective acting scenes rather than of consistently good whole plays, though his tragi-comedy *A New Way to Pay Old Debts* was played regularly for two centuries after his death. John Ford wrote much occasional verse and prose pamphlets before turning dramatist; he constructs with more skill, is more compact, than Webster but has not Webster's intensity and verbal magnificence; he aims at sustained pathos, created by the unending frustration of his lovers, rather than at true tragedy; the ill-starred giants of the earlier tragedies have gone. This is now a theatre almost waiting, we feel, to be closed by the victorious Puritans.

Whole libraries have been written about Shakespeare. There are shelves and shelves of books all attempting to prove that the plays attributed to him were really the work of other people—Bacon, the Earls of Oxford, Rutland and Derby, the Countess of Pembroke (probably as a member of a syndicate), his fellow-poets Marlowe and Raleigh, and even Queen Elizabeth herself. The authors of these strange claims make the same mistake as many Shakespearean scholars who tell us that he must have been at one time a soldier, sailor, lawyer, traveller in Italy, and so forth: they cannot grasp the simple fact that a highly imaginative and sharp-witted young man like Shakespeare, familiar with theatres and their various patrons, dodging in and out of London taverns, could soon pick up all the scraps of expert knowledge and professional jargon he needed for his plays. The astonishingly wide acquaintance and sympathy with all manner of folk, including yokels, watchmen, tapsters, peddlers, harlots, bawds, broken-down soldiers, that we find in these plays do not suggest they were written by a great aristocrat or a committee of earls and countesses. We happen to know that *Pickwick Papers* and *Nicholas Nickleby* were the work of young Charles Dickens, but if we were uncertain about their authorship we would hardly consider the contemporary Lord Chancellor or Duke of Norfolk to be likely claimants. Dickens's background, circumstances, youthful experiences, made it possible for him to write those novels. And Shakespeare's background, circumstances, youthful experiences, instead of barring him from the authorship of the plays (as we are so often told by these Baconians and others), are about what we should expect, given that the man was a genius. He was born and brought up in a small country town, and the plays are filled with evidence of this upbringing; he belonged to the middle class, like so many great writers, and it is from the middle, neither too high nor too low, that most can be seen; and he went to London, where his early years of struggle probably brought him such a wide acquaintance, to work in the theatre, as actor, dramatist, part-manager, frequently returning to Stratford during the summers the theatres were closed, and finally retiring there; and all this too seems more likely than unlikely from what we find in the plays themselves. What the objectors do not make any allowance for, because they do not understand it, is dramatic genius.

Let us deal briefly with other mistaken ideas about Shakespeare. Though he was able, and probably preferred, to work at tremendous speed, hurrying the words on to paper as the images swarmed into his mind, he was not a kind of idiot-medium, taking dictation from someone in the next world, but a fully conscious great artist. On the other hand, he was not—as some of the Romantic critics seem to suppose—incapable

35

of going wrong or of doing botched, careless work. Thousands of hours have been wasted by commentators searching for mysterious hidden meanings, for depths of profundity, in passages that were just hasty bad writing. He was not a member of any secret cult, merely making a pretence of writing for the theatre. His characters (with the exception of the historical personages, of course) belong entirely to the plays in which we find them, cannot have any life outside the plays, so that it is a waste of time and effort—and how much have been wasted!—trying to take these characters outside the theatre, as if they were real people, and wondering what Hamlet did in England or how the Macbeths first met. A better acquaintance with the theatre itself would have saved many Shakespearean critics and commentators from writing a great deal of nonsense about him. As a dramatist he was essentially *of* the theatre, inspired by it but also conditioned and limited by it. There may be some of his plays, especially the great tragedies, that we would rather read than see performed in theatres very different from his, using methods of production and acting too far removed from the methods which he knew and for which he wrote; but even so, we must read them as plays, seeing and hearing them performed, as it were, in a theatre of our imagination. And perhaps this is what Shakespeare himself, who in the end grew weary of the playhouse, would prefer us to do.

All down the centuries Shakespeare has been compared with Nature. It is a tribute to his fertility, his vast range, the breadth and depth of his sympathy, in which he excels all other writers. But this must not lead us to believe that Shakespeare himself cannot be discovered behind this multitude of characters, that his own face is lost for ever among these living masks. No matter how protean, how 'myriad-minded' he may be, a man cannot create so much as a dramatist, and, what is more important, express so much in great poetry, without revealing himself. He may take his stories from Italian novels, old plays and chronicles, Plutarch's *Lives*, but his handling of these stories, what he left out, what he added, tell us something about him. So do the parts played in the action by the major characters he created, the way in which these characters are developed, the interest and sympathy allotted to them. More subtly and profoundly revealing still is his choice of imagery, that astonishing wealth of imagery which, after his two narrative poems and the early plays, ceases to be mere decoration and becomes a pictorial mode of thought and communication. It is characteristic of him that all his best plays, both tragedies and comedies, have each a special tone, atmosphere, almost a climate, as if a distinctive little world had been created for each drama; and this effect is largely produced by the widely different streams of images, gushing from the unconscious. Sometimes, when he was writing to order or felt jaded, what he gives us is slackly conventional stuff that a dozen other men might have written; but as soon as a scene, characters, speech, come to life, then Shakespeare himself is there, telling all he knows and has dreamt, trying to escape, through the fullest possible communication within the limits of the art he has chosen, the sheer pressure that life puts upon so rich and sensitive a nature. It is nonsense to declare, as some anti-Romantic professors have done during recent years, that he was cheerfully and perhaps cynically supplying a demand, ready to follow any change of fashion in the theatre, coolly performing. Great dramatic poetry cannot be created in this tradesman's style—these professors should take a month off and try to give us a companion piece to *Hamlet* and *Macbeth*—it demands all that the total personality can contribute, all that the mind, conscious and unconscious, functioning at its highest pitch, can give it. And this, if we knew enough to interpret all the signs we are offered, suggests the fullest and deepest revelation of personality. The time may come when Shakespeare is better known than any other man who ever lived.

Here, however, with neither adequate space nor knowledge, we can only show enough of the man, briefly exploring the mind and personality of this incomparable genius, to relate him to our story of Western Man in his literature. Such evidence as we have concerning the outward Shakespeare, the man in his time, has surprised and disappointed many of his admirers, who long for some great glittering noble in place of this pleasant, well-liked but essentially bourgeois Shakespeare of contemporary report, cautiously ambitious, saving, temperate, always with one eye on a comfortable retirement at Stratford. True, there are the sonnets, with their shadowy drama of the fair adored youth seduced by the poet's wanton mistress, whose velvety white skin and black hair, brows and roving eyes find their way (when they are uncalled-for, proving that he cannot resist her image) into so many plays. It must have been this woman, or another like her, who indirectly, by constantly disturbing his memory, compelled him against the balance of his art to daub the tragedies and the bitter comedies of the same period with images of sexual disgust and disease. This does not suggest the comfortable bourgeois figure, but reports of the outward man can be deceptive. The world at any time has in it plenty of quiet busy men whose inner life would startle and shock us, whose dreams may be terrible, who as they go about their business know something of Hamlet's disillusion, Macbeth's despair, and Lear's madness. Shakespeare was one of these men on a giant scale. He went down into the depths of his being, hung over abysses there until he too was close to madness, and reached heights of joy and tenderness and love, for the wonder and delight of generations of ordinary people.

Shakespeare can be said to be further along that middle road where we found Rabelais and Montaigne. More wonderfully gifted than they are, with his incomparable imagination and range of sympathy for ever tugging at him like a colossal captive balloon, nevertheless he is, like them, a balanced man. But once he had passed his golden Maytime, of which *A Midsummer Night's Dream* is perhaps the finest flower, and life began to challenge him, this balance became more and more difficult to achieve. He found himself caught between the mounting and challenging opposites, between what he found in consciousness and what came unbidden, giving vitality to his work, from the unconscious. For example, consciously he believed in order, like any good bourgeois then and now, except that his idea of order was on a universal scale. Music, to which he was devoted, was itself a symbol of this order, the harmonious working of things. Disorder was the sign of a profound disharmony, threatening chaos, which he frequently used, as he did metaphors involving thunder, lightning, tempest, as an image of evil. Consciously he supported everything that in turn upheld this order: mighty Julius Caesar; the strong successful English Kings; any social system in which degree and duty were clearly acknowledged; tradition and conformity and a sense of obligation. But as he worked, under the pressure of his dramatic imagination, the released unconscious swung him over to the opposite, giving vitality to his rebels and rogues and misfits and failures, the Kings who did not succeed, the great Falstaff whose every action and word mock and defy order and conformity, whose stature and quality are so dominating that he has to die offstage in order that the play of *Henry V* can be written at all. The whole period of the historical plays can be seen as a mighty tug-of-war between these opposites.

Hamlet, a character into which Shakespeare poured himself without stint or regard for the play's needs, is a man desperately trying to find a balance. He is far more intensely aware of both goodness and evil than anybody near him; he catches sight of receding sun-lit heights and widening black gulfs invisible to the rest of the Court; and he cannot act because he is no longer in a world where decisive action is possible, except on blind impulse, moved by the "Divinity that shapes our ends". Evil in these tragedies can be loosed by man but is not man-made; it rises, a black fog and stench, from unknown depths; it descends, with the lashing rain and lightning, from skies suddenly given over to iniquity; the world is out of the hands of God. Sexual love is transformed, in this murky atmosphere, into lust, treachery, disease, filth, abomination; the chaste, the pure in heart, the Ophelias and Cordelias, are struck dead. The tragic victims of their large imaginative natures (for Hamlet, Othello, Macbeth, Lear, different as they are, have this in common) go to their doom. There is of course no balance here; this is life terribly divided between the opposites, with chaos conquering, disharmony triumphant. But Lear, at the last moment, recovers from his madness: he is out on the other side, beyond the storm. The wonderful *Antony and Cleopatra* begins, entirely within conscious planning, as if it would be a moral tale, showing how world-wide order (the images suggest this enormous scale) is disrupted by middle-aged passion, lust and folly; then suddenly, when all is lost and the tale almost told, the moral is swept aside, the great verse, whose very intensity proves the presence there of the poet's whole personality, rises triumphantly, finding immortal words for immortal longings, now transforming passion, lust, folly, into love: the dying wanton queen cries "Husband, I come", and is woman herself. And then the poet himself is out on the other side, beyond the power of the opposites, where there is harmony, balance; now almost more the indulgent narrator than the quick impassioned dramatist; less interested now, like all ageing men, in variety of character, and more concerned with humanity itself and its values and fortunes; the poet of the last romantic story-telling plays; until he invents, thus breaking his habit, the closely-knit dramatic parable of *The Tempest*, bidding farewell to the magic of the island, to his theatrical genius, to the world and to us, in the most famous speech in all literature.

"Be cheerful, sir," cried Prospero, "our revels now are ended. . . ." That "Be cheerful" coming before a speech that dissolves the very globe itself is wonderfully characteristic of Shakespeare. With him, though he takes us as far as human imagination can reach, we always come home: the balance is restored; life—ordinary sensible life, in which it is best to be cheerful—goes on. He has been accused of being "the first supreme artist in literature who seems to be absorbed in character for its own sake", failing to leave us, as the Greek dramatists did, with a sense that the characters reveal something greater than themselves, a divine idea beyond humanity. It is true that, unlike the Greek dramatists or Dante and a few other great poets, Shakespeare has no universal system to act both as a frame and a reference. Such philosophy as he has, held lightly in his consciousness, for ever liable to be swept away by the unconscious under the pressure of creation, belongs to his time and place. Anything more profound comes in intuitive flashes. But if we consider his whole personality, which is displayed in the best of his work, he steps outside his age, even while expressing so much of it. Thus, it is his conscious villains, led by Iago, who are Renaissance men, believing themselves to possess boundless free will, to be the sole architects of their fate. And it is his heroes who are deeply conscious of the mysterious interventions of what they generally choose to call Fortune. In the narrower sense of the term, Shakespeare was not a religious man—the story that he died a Catholic is hard to believe— but in the broader sense—and this man needs breadth—we can justly call him religious. This is not simply because he has this illimitable charity of the imagination, a tenderness for so much in man and Nature, an instant appreciation of whatever makes for love, affection, understanding, good-fellowship, sympathy and harmony, but because he recognises that life is a mystery, that man and Nature are symbolic representations, that we can feel if not think our way, through our sense of beauty and goodness, to a reality behind appearances, as the lives of the dramatist and players are in a deeper reality behind the shows of the playhouse. Making no use of sect or dogma, only by pursuing his art and bringing to it his whole personality, daring the conflict between consciousness and the unconscious, he might be said to have begun to restore, not intellectually but entirely through feeling and intuition, that religious basis and framework which had been broken and then lost. This takes him outside his time, for here, as in his mistrust of one-sidedness, he was moving against the tide.

In his desire to keep a balance, his wrestling with the opposites, even the very kinds of opposites they were, despite his immensely rich nature (and *rich* is surely his favourite word) and many-sided genius, he comes close to generations of ordinary Western men of intelligence and good-will. It is perhaps the secret of his hold upon our world, century after century. This magnificent king of all our poets and dramatists might be not unjustly described as a gigantic ordinary man of goodwill, who desires, no matter how many adventures of the depths and heights his spirit undertakes, what sensible Western men, all down the years, have themselves desired. He is not, like so many later and lesser geniuses, trying to take us by storm, through the sheer intensity of the unbalanced, the one-sided. He does not want to huddle us into some nightmare otherworld, or leave this one in ruins round us, perhaps out of vengeance on our stupid common humanity. Though he conjures up everything from lyrical young love and gossamer fairylands to darkest witchcraft and bloody murder, always he leads us home: "Be cheerful, sir, our revels now are ended." It is no wonder that millions of men and women, through all the changing fashions of literature, have kept for this man not only their greatest admiration but also their deepest affection. If the day ever comes when Shakespeare is no longer acted, read and studied, quoted and loved, Western Man will be near his end.

CHAPTER FIVE

Spain and Cervantes

In 1580, when Philip II brought Portugal into the vast dominions he ruled, there died the one epic poet who truly celebrated in verse the astonishing explorations and conquests of the past hundred years, that enlargement of the globe which contributed so much to the Renaissance. This was Camoens (*Camões*), the great Portuguese poet, who after some misadventures at home served in Africa and then in India, suffered severe hardships, but was able to compose his epic, *The Lusiad* (*Os Lusíadas*). Written around Vasco da Gama, this poem is really a heart-warming tribute to the Portuguese nation itself, that small impoverished nation which had taken its ships and swords to the ends of the earth. In spite of its classical structure and its eloquent prophecies about Portugal, and over and above its poetic mastery, which Camoens had shown earlier in various lyrical forms, this national epic is important because it is based on actual historical events, is realistic in feeling, humanistic in outlook. It arrived very late in the Renaissance; belonged to a small country about to vanish for the time being from the stage of history; but it expressed one important side of the whole movement better than any other poetical work. Western Man should honour Camoens.

The Spain that swallowed Portugal was now at the summit of its power; with all its territories in Western Europe and its huge empire in America, it was easily the wealthiest and most formidable of the new nations. But its power could be successfully challenged, as the fate of the Armada was soon to prove; its wealth, depending too much upon the gold of the Aztecs and Incas to be economically sound, was badly distributed, as its new realistic novels ('epics of hunger' they have been called) clearly proved. It was a country that ran to extremes, from the most stately magnificence to the grimmest poverty, from the mysticism of saints to cynically realistic scenes of low life. Its people were mixed, for not only did they belong to what had recently been separate kingdoms, but there were among them many converted Jews and Moors. (Jewish ancestry has been claimed for several major writers of the 'Golden Age'.) Yet the mixture, as we discover it in the literature of the sixteenth century, seems already as Spanish in its flavour as a dry sherry. There had been considerable French influence earlier, and after the invasion and occupation of Southern Italy, Italian influence, especially on the poets, was stronger still. Nevertheless, whatever was written in Castilian, now the official and literary Spanish language, had about it something—a tone, air, atmosphere, character—that belonged to Spain and to nowhere else.

This 'Golden Age' chiefly belongs to poetic drama, but it is a writer of prose fiction, Cervantes, who captured the world and so must claim most of our attention. However, we cannot completely ignore the drama. It had three patrons: the Church, which ignored the theatre but commissioned and staged religious dramas, *Autos Sacramentales*; the Court, which must have favoured the tragedies as stately as itself; and the general public, which had a voracious appetite for tragedies, comedies, tragi-comedies, anything that kept a stage occupied. We can estimate the demand from the supply. Lope de Vega, in addition to an astonishing amount and variety of non-dramatic work, wrote over 1500 plays, usually in fairly elaborate verse forms, at times, it is said, completing a three-act (and this division was one of his innovations) verse play in a day, with the managers waiting to carry off the sheets. He was only one of many dramatists, and great though his reputation might be, this work at high pressure, with managers round the door, suggests a tremendous public demand. Many hundreds of these plays must have been made out of stereotyped plots, with love and religion, honour and loyalty, set in familiar opposition, with high-souled, eloquent, but not very individual characters, and with lines that must have done service before; but the best of his surviving plays, probably the fittest to survive, including some in which he came down from the upper air of high chivalry to the sensible earth and the peasants who lived on it, show little trace of these weaknesses. The other master of this Spanish drama, Calderón, came later, outside our period in time but not in spirit, so that he must be mentioned in this place. Because he came late, the days of mere lively improvisation were over, and some of his best-known plays (e.g., *The Mayor of Zalamea*) are careful reconstructions, based on a sound stagecraft, of earlier plays by other men, Lope de Vega or Tirso de Molina. He was successful with many kinds of drama, from the religious allegories of the *autos* to powerful tragedies in a realistic setting, but he makes his most characteristic and most valuable contribution to world drama, joining the great poetic dramatists of Western Man, with such symbolic pieces as *El Mágico Prodigioso* (which Shelley preferred to call *The Wonder-working Magician* in his translation) and, probably his masterpiece, *La Vida es Sueño*, of which various adaptations, rather than direct translations, have been produced in most European countries. It is probably the difficulty of translating Calderón's sumptuous verse—and his *Life is a Dream* demands something better than a prose paraphrase—that has kept these symbolic poetic dramas of his from so many stages, and not his lack in them of the richly human quality of a Shakespeare, though that deficiency is plainly there. Finally, between Lope de Vega and Calderón were many lesser but sufficiently accomplished dramatists who did good service not only to the Spanish theatre but to theatres elsewhere, notably the French, whose classical comedy owed much to these Spaniards. Corneille found his *Cid* in Spain, and the world, thanks to Tirso de Molina, found there the immortal Don Juan.

Among Lope de Vega's unsuccessful rivals in the theatre was an old soldier, who had been badly wounded at the battle of Lepanto and afterwards captured and kept in slavery by the Moors, who had many adventures and had known (and was to go on knowing) poverty and hardships, who had written satirical verse as well as plays and a pastoral novel, *Galatea*: his name was Miguel de Cervantes. The abundant fiction of the Spanish had been chiefly divided between fantastic romances of chivalry and, rather later, the idyllic novels of pastoral life; but from the first publication of *Celestina*, in 1499, the sixteenth century had seen the gradual development of another kind of writing, based not on idealised knights and shepherds but on the observation of real life, found in *Lazarillo de Tormes*, the first *picaresque* novel, and Alemán's *Guzmán de*

Alfarache. And now Cervantes took hold of these three different but equally popular forms of fiction, mixed them and added what belonged to his own genius, and in *Don Quixote*, published in two parts with some years between, gave us one of the unquestioned masterpieces of Western literature. (His *Exemplary Novels* must be mentioned, for some of them are very good indeed.) *Don Quixote* is the first modern novel—and out of it whole libraries of fiction have come—and in many respects it still remains the best. Its fame in Western fiction is unequalled. It has given us the term 'quixotic', and two immortal characters in the Don and his squire, Sancho Panza. Its universal popularity has given it the quality of a myth. It is known without being really read as a novel—though many of our wisest men have read it over and over again—perhaps because some simplified version of it, as a comic romantic tale of adventure, has delighted generation after generation of children. Critics in every succeeding age have given us different accounts of it. As a comic tale, a huge glowing panorama of a period and a place, a novel dominated by two gigantic characters, or a profound parable of human life, it has fascinated all manner of readers, throughout the whole Western world, for more than three centuries. Probably only Shakespeare has captured and delighted more minds than Cervantes. And by the strangest chance, they died on the same day, the 23rd of April 1616.

This great masterpiece is not faultless. In Part One, Cervantes (who had many literary enemies) occasionally lacks confidence in his superb story of the knight and his squire; he introduces subsidiary stories and other matter, to bolster up the main narrative, that merely make us long to return to Don Quixote and Sancho. In Part Two, completed rather hurriedly because a spurious second part had already been published, he no longer suffers from any want of confidence, having basked for several years in the success of Part One (which had been published in Madrid, Brussels, London and Paris before 1615, when Part Two came out), and this second part is more carefully constructed and less episodic and rough in its humour. But now Cervantes's weakness is his self-consciousness, with which he infects to some extent both Don Quixote and Sancho, who, in this part, share their creator's success and are recognised everywhere. This is in fact a very odd development—really making the knight and

squire of Part Two conscious of themselves as characters in Part One—
and we could truthfully say that *Don Quixote* is not a single novel in two
parts but two different novels about the same people. And it is significant
that the Don Quixote who lingers in the popular memory, probably
from the simplified tale for children, is the hero of the early adventures;
the mythological element is in the first part. The second part offers us
the more carefully controlled and also more elaborate fiction.

The secret of *Don Quixote's* wide and timeless appeal is that it can be
appreciated on many different levels. But first, before enlarging on this,
we must dispose of the monstrous notion, which is death to all but the
most superficial criticism, that we must not discover in a work of art anything outside the limits of the artist's conscious intention. So if Cervantes
says that *Don Quixote* is a satire on the romances of chivalry, then that is
all it is. This is nonsense. First, Cervantes may have been merely playing
safe, as many old writers did, by limiting himself publicly to some such
social-didactic purpose. He may have knowingly intended much else, but
preferred not to say anything about it. Secondly, he may have begun
with some such simple plan and then consciously enlarged and enriched
it. Thirdly, in the act of creation, what he consciously intended may have
been swept along by the flood of scenes, incidents, talk, rising from the
unconscious. He is creating something that begins to have a life of its
own, and this life, like any other, may be regarded, appreciated, interpreted, in many different ways, on many different levels. And we may
take it that first, second, and third are all true of Cervantes, great novelist
and battered old soldier, who by the time he came to write his masterpiece was wonderfully rich in experience (but not in money), had looked
and listened and meditated throughout years of journeyings, and—
certainly when he had a pen in his hand—was a wily, ripe, deep old
character. So we had better take what we can from him, this unfathomable humorist, asking such wisdom as we have to discover *his* wisdom,
in greater measure at greater depth, and not be in a hurry to imagine that
our minds can contain his mind. If *Don Quixote* had been nothing but a
satire and knock-about burlesque of the fading romances of chivalry, it
would have been dying by 1650, dead by 1700, and forgotten by the time
it actually set so many good eighteenth-century novelists writing. No, a

man does not write a world masterpiece to be popped into the nearest academic pigeonhole.

This comic tale, romance, fable, parable—take your choice!—revolves round these wonderful characters, the long, lean, fantastic gentleman, the fat little earthy peasant, whose talk alone, if nothing else ever happened, would keep the book alive. The knight, it will be said, is mad; he decides to be a knight errant, after reading and losing himself in so many wonderful stories about them; out in the real world, which cares nothing about knight errants, he has one misadventure after another, because he mistakes windmills for giants, sheep for men-at-arms, and so forth, until he has to be taken back home in a cage. But he is courteous, gentle, brave, long-suffering, and indeed has all the virtues most highly praised in a Christian society. Unless there should be some wicked enchantment, all the women he meets are beautiful and worthy of the highest respect, the men are assumed to be as lofty and selfless in their principles and aims as he is. The world replies by laughing at him, kicking and cudgelling him, humiliating and beating him. His squire, Sancho Panza, cares nothing for knight errantry; his mind runs on food and drink and a good sleep; he is earthy common-sense and talks in peasant proverbs. He ought to be sane enough. But is he? What is he doing so far from his family and village, pretending to be squire to a mad knight? Common-sense cannot hold out against imagination, nor flesh entirely resist spirit. Sancho, doubting and grumbling, has to follow Don Quixote, entering the realm of high fantasy. Soon, as the barber tells him, he is as much enchanted as his master. He has been promised an island to govern, and he is sure that Don Quixote, to whom he cannot help being deeply devoted, will keep his knightly word. This much he understands, but very little else, for in spite of their unending and glorious talk, real communication is almost impossible between these two. But Sancho shares enough of the con-tinuous day-dream to look forward more and more eagerly to his island, where at last he finds himself, prepared to rule with great sagacity. True, many of his expectations are unfulfilled, the life of a governor not being what he imagined it to be; but then that is what has happened to in-numerable men who have sought and found power. As the story becomes more involved in the second part, if only because the knight and the squire are conscious of themselves as characters and public figures, Sancho is at least as mad as his master, some of whose illusions are beginning sadly to fade; he is at times the dominating figure, arguing confidently about wicked enchanters, especially their cunning transformation of Dulcinea from a princess into a village drab breathing garlic. Common-sense has vanished.

The grave Spanish irony descends beneath the surface of boisterous humour and obvious satire like a mine-shaft, taking us to level after level, each more profound and universal than the last. We are involved in the regressive tragi-comedy of illusion and truth, appearance and reality. On one level it is merely laughable that Don Quixote should mistake a miserable inn for a castle, the landlord for a generous custodian, the village whores for ladies of quality, a mean supper for a noble feast. On the level below, all this seems tragic; it is the butt of the company, the man out of his wits, who sees what everybody ought to be seeing, if our values were really what we claim them to be, if Christendom existed outside our sermons and dreams. On the next level, it is comic again, though now carrying a bitter flavour, for how does the world behave when it is challenged by Don Quixote and his illusions? It laughs but, its complacency shattered, there is anger in its laughter, and so it daubs his long mild face with mud, thumps and cudgels his bony frame, and tries to beat the nonsense about knighthood, high chivalry, spells and enchantment, out of him. But this angry brutal world itself is under a wicked spell, has become its own spiteful enchanter, has disinherited itself, by means of the miserable 'collective representations' it calls reality. And below this could be tragic irony again, that what is better is derided and defeated by the worse, that a mean madness overcomes a glorious madness.

Taking a closer view, we cannot even talk of madness. For Don Quixote is by no means stark staring mad, with a consciousness entirely dominated by the unconscious, fixed in a permanent dream. There would be no real humour in the misadventures of a wretched lunatic. Cervantes shows us, with grave irony and with one subtle touch after another, that Alonso Quijano, the solitary elderly gentleman of La Mancha, after years of day-dreaming over his romances, turns himself into Don Quixote the knight errant, building up his illusions until he can begin to live in them, and then taking care, in the submerged consciousness of Quijano which is now the unconscious of Don Quixote, that these illusions, now a superior reality, do not fail him. So when he makes a beaver, as part of his face armour, out of pasteboard, only to find his sword cuts through it at one blow, he repairs it and even strengthens it but does not test it again with his sword, preferring his illusion that it is now the strong beaver he needs. And from now on, as Madariaga points out and proves from further examples: "Don Quixote will never again trust reality and will avoid putting his beliefs to the test whenever he scents the slightest danger of being belied by facts." Which is what we all do, what indeed the whole world does, when cherished illusions are challenged by facts. (A further irony—and the reader must not assume that Cervantes is not aware of it and not enjoying it—is that throughout the novel the author himself cannot resist his own illusion, that there exists somewhere the idyllic pastoral life of poetic imagination.) And, as we have seen, Sancho, the one who knows all about the brute facts, not only begins to share the knight's illusions but plunges further into them just when his master is emerging from them. So Sancho talks eagerly, in the end, of enchanters, to explain why illusion and fact cannot be reconciled; he is like the electorate who have been won over by a half-crazy politician; and as for the enchanters, whose spells wreck our illusions, we all believe them to be at work on us but give them different names—Church, State, Finance, Party, Press. Lastly, why, as the story draws to a close, do Don Quixote's illusions begin to fade, his mind begin to clear? On one interpretation, offered to us by the text, he sees at last that the romances, which in his long fit of madness he tried to live, are false, and so returns to reality. But a deeper interpretation, caught in the sad undertones of the narrative, tells us that he begins to say good-bye to his illusions because he is aware of the approach of Death, the great reality, the triumphant enemy of all illusion.

We are told that Cervantes first conceived the plan of this great book (and surely it is the best idea an author ever had!) when he was in prison. Though no criminal, indeed a man of a proud, chivalrous, generous nature, he saw the inside of several prisons. He came out of them to what was only another kind of prison, a life of poverty, disappointment, un-successful appeals to the rich and powerful, ignominious tasks that ended badly. He was a member of that class of proud but hungry hidalgos which, ironically enough, had been ruined by Spain's fabulous importation of gold and silver and the inflation that followed it. And now the Armada was destroyed, that Armada for which Cervantes went round the country collecting taxes; the national glory was fading; and in the gathering shadows of the age and his own time (in contemporary terms he was an old man), with no patron, no salaried place, few prospects, rich only in experience, memory, knowledge of men, the one-handed old soldier began to write his book. Then out of that experience, memory, knowledge, and an eruption of genius, he wrote the best novel in the world. Through its bustle of roads and inns, its sense of movement, colour and life, he reached far forward to inspire all the novelists who set their characters wandering, and gave godspeed to Gil Blas and Tom Jones and Wilhelm Meister and Mr. Pickwick and Sam Weller. And as the magical ironist of the relativeness of reality, of truth at war with illusion, he might be said to have pointed further forward still, beyond where his faith and hope could reach, towards Ibsen, Unamuno, Proust, Pirandello, Mann and Joyce. Of all our great novelists he is the youngest, because he is the first, and the oldest, because his tale of the mad knight is an old man's tale. He is also the wisest.

Here then, with another age about to begin, is the last gleam of the golden globe, which had once shone like the sun above Florence and Pico and Machiavelli, or down on the middle highway that Rabelais and Montaigne knew, or between the galleries on to the fore-stage of Shakespeare's playhouse. And before this last gleam fades, we see it illuminate, most fittingly, the long melancholy nose and dream-dazed eyes of Don Quixote, Knight of the Rueful Countenance.

PART TWO

"The Order'd Garden"

6   "And All was Light"   53

7   The Drama   62

8   The Novel   82

9   The Enlightenment   98

CHAPTER SIX

"And All was Light"

THE TITLE OF THIS PART TWO, *The Order'd Garden*, was borrowed from the poet Alexander Pope. It was Pope who wrote a well-known epigram on Newton:

> *Nature and Nature's laws lay hid in night.*
> *God said "Let Newton be", and all was light.*

It would be difficult to find two other lines of verse that told us more about the age than those do. They are worth examining. First, there is about them an air of cheerful pride. Everything, we feel, has gone well; God, Nature, Newton, have all behaved properly; what was dark is now in the light. Next, we are made to feel that Nature and its laws (not 'her' laws for a reason that follows) are now completely known, not as a person is known but as a machine is known. The machinery was working, but all in the dark, with nobody understanding anything about it, probably not even guessing it was there. Newton revealed it entirely. There is no suggestion that this age knows rather more than previous ages, that Man is now groping towards a better knowledge of the universe; it is darkness to light, ignorance to full knowledge, in one move. Again, it is typical of the age that it does not leave God out of the picture, does not, as we would, give science all the credit. (But in view of what we have now done with our discoveries in nuclear physics, we should have some difficulty in bringing God into the picture.) The poet asks us to believe that God is inspiring and directing scientific enquiry, like the all-powerful head of some institute of research. This is a very different deity from the one we find, for example, in the Book of Job. He is not the God, the unknowable presence somewhere in the mystery of our life, of the great writers of the previous age, of Rabelais and Montaigne, Cervantes and Shakespeare. He is no longer associated with the night, with what is mysterious, superhuman, magical, fateful, with the unconscious. He has changed sides. He is now associated with light, with all that belongs to reason and the enquiring mind, with consciousness.

Clearly it is impossible to give exact dates to these ages. They overlap considerably and have different limits in time in different countries. But roughly we can say that this age began in the last quarter of the seventeenth century and lasted for about a hundred years. Some of the scientists who contributed so much to it, of whom Galileo and Kepler are notable examples, preceded it by many years; and so did the inventors of scientific instruments, the telescopes, microscopes, thermometers, barometers, the more exact clockwork mechanisms, that made accurate observation possible. Bacon had pleaded for such observation, and the inductive method based on it, as early as 1620. Two of the thinkers who had much influence on the age, Descartes in metaphysics, Hobbes in political theory, belonged to a generation outside this period. On the other hand, the most influential of all, Newton, Locke and Leibniz, were first published in the 1680s just in time to complete the foundations of the age. (Spinoza, who combined a massive and lofty intellect with a simple character, died young, in 1677, and for a long time was either condemned or ignored.) All the general philosophies, the political theories, and the sciences, with mathematics and physics at their head, tended to move in one direction and to present more or less the same picture of Man and the universe. God still existed, but now only as a remote First Cause somewhere behind the machine, which once it had been set in motion could be left to be discovered, sooner or later, by the illumination of Man's reason, God's supreme gift. This rational deism might be condemned by all the various Churches and sects—and during these hundred years many evangelical sects made their first appearance—and it might leave the mass of people untouched and have little appeal to the new middle class; but it captured the spirit of the age.

It was a time when the society that controlled both politics and the arts was small and very closely knit. It might be grouped around a single magnificent despot, as in the France of Louis XIV, or a governing aristocracy, as in England after the Revolution of 1688. And in spite of the wars, especially the conflict between Louis XIV and the Allies that cuts through the middle of the period, these ruling groups throughout Western Europe might be said to be interwoven, in a closer fashion than they were earlier or later, to form one society. One pleasant feature of the age was the extra-national patronage of authors and artists; a writer in trouble with his own government would be invited by another to accept its hospitality. And though a general reading public came into existence and rapidly increased during this period, and was of great importance towards the end of it, most successful authors depended upon royal or aristocratic patronage, were members of this ruling society if only on humble and insecure terms, or if still outside it were determined to please it. So with Reason, the triumph of consciousness, came Taste, not private but public, concerned with what reasonable cultivated persons could enjoy together. One of the most admired essayists and critics of the age, Joseph Addison, made this clear: "The Taste is not to conform to the Art," he announced, "but the Art to the Taste."

Because it was the fashion throughout this age to refer to it as being 'Classical', because ancient Greek and Roman models were held up for admiration and imitation, we must not make the mistake of thinking that we have anything here that is more than negative and superficial. It is negative because what it really does is to express a contemptuous rejection of the barbarous dark waste of the immediate past, across which the classical civilisation gleams faintly. The attitude is more truly anti-medieval than pro-classical. It is superficial because, as we have already seen, this age is living in the new world discovered by the sciences and already enlarged and enriched by them, a world unlike anything either known to or imagined by the ancients. It all amounts to little more than this thought: the great ages of Greece and Rome were successful, civilised, highly culti-vated, and so is this great age of ours, after a thousand years of barbarism, and therefore we are the successors and heirs of the classical ages at their best. But even the direct literary influence is far less than is generally assumed. A Racine might use classical themes for his tragedies—and, after all, so did Shakespeare—but his drama is entirely his own, belonging essentially to this age and no other.

On the other hand, if by 'classical' we merely mean the opposite of 'romantic', then the term can justly be attached to this age, even though it tells us so little. 'Romantick', as it was generally spelt, was indeed a term of abuse or at best easy contempt, certainly during the earlier and more confident years of the period. It indicated the kind of fantastic stuff no longer acceptable to men of Taste, to this age of Reason. It was tainted by the unconscious—to use our terms and not theirs—and this was, above all, the age of consciousness, when God could be found only in the light, not in the darkness. And therefore Art must conform to Taste, which in turn has been carefully cultivated (and this we must allow, adding that it never happened again) by the members of the ruling groups, the society that controls, among other things, the appreciation and patronage of the arts. In this period then, authorship is public and social, as if anything worth serious attention could be read aloud at a large party, where nothing could be less suitable than the kind of poetry that is not only private but is like a secret whispered by the poet to his reader. Authors are now addressing society and not individuals. Most of them therefore are more anxious not to make fools of themselves than they are to give expression to deep personal feelings. The result is an age of satirical and didactic verse and essays, of criticism determined to establish rules so that literature, like society, learns to conduct itself properly, of formal tragedy and cynical comedy, and of prose narrative of various kinds.

Out of all the unceasing production of verse during this age—and it used verse on all occasions—not one great poet, recognised as such by Western Man, comes to us. (Milton? Undoubtedly a great poet, and undoubtedly recognised as such throughout Western Europe. But he pre-dates this age, and is really a latecomer to the previous age; in his earlier poems, before he had fully developed his 'organ voice', he is linked to Spenser, Ben Jonson, the Jacobean dramatists; the equally fascinating verse and prose of Milton and his contemporaries belongs to a period falling between our two ages, but it is closer in outlook, manner, style to that of 'The Golden Globe' than to that of 'The Order'd Garden'.) The truth is, the obstacles were too difficult. This age did not want what we now consider great poetry, and it dictated its terms to men of talent very clearly and sharply. Consciousness must appeal directly to consciousness; the unconscious, where the magic words lie hidden, must be excluded. The general must be preferred to the particular, the abstract to the concrete, the allegorical to the symbolical. Everything must be written and then read in the clear light of reason. And though verse of wit and charm and moral force can be—and was—created within these limitations, they are death to great poetry. But then again, this was an obviously one-sided age, with all its emphasis upon what was fully conscious and rational, and therefore it could not be expressed in great poetry, which is never one-sided. Yet men are only superficially the creatures of their age; a talented young man of 1700 had a mental inheritance, an unconscious, hardly different from that of a young man of 1600 or 1800; there were more or less the same naked men inside the wigs, laces and embroidered coats, silk stockings and high-red-heeled shoes; and therefore, no matter how much the authors acclaim the spirit of the age, we must not be surprised if its one-sided development, leaving so much unexpressed, rotting in the dark of the mind, induced in many of them an hysterical and morbid strain. This in turn often gives their work, which otherwise might be altogether too bluffly rational and optimistic and confident, an added interest and value, bringing shadows and sombre tones to the high-lighted picture.

One example of this morbid strain, only one out of many but the most impressive, is that mutilated giant, Jonathan Swift. He had one of the most formidable intellects of the age; he had perhaps the best plain prose style in all English literature; he had in a large measure both wit and imagination. Among Queen Anne's Tory politicians and men of letters he seems a colossus. But much of his best work, his pamphlets and topical satires, recedes and dwindles with the political conflicts and intrigues of the time, from which he retired, bitterly disappointed, because his party service did not even bring him the bishopric he expected. If he had devoted himself entirely to literature, especially during the years when his genius was at its height, he would undoubtedly have become one of the greatest figures of the century in European literature. (And it is useless for his admirers to say that he is, because in terms of general recognition and esteem clearly he is not.) As it is, the world remembers him for his *Gulliver's Travels* but rarely reads this masterpiece as he intended it to be read. Swift is a master of irony; but Fate is a greater master of it, so decided that Gulliver should be kept alive and in favour by children, who read with delight Gulliver's adventures among the tiny Lilliputians and then among the giants of Brobdingnag. Is there any other instance of a savage satire, one of the most ferocious indictments of the human race in all literature, being transformed into a nursery favourite? But that it should give so much pleasure to children, with their sharp eye for detail, is a tribute to the quality of Swift's imagination. It was a stroke of satirical genius to realise that you have only to alter the scale to make humanity seem contemptible: make people small enough, and all their affairs of state, their armies and navies, are ridiculous; turn them into giants and observe them closely, and they seem disgusting. The Third Part, the voyage to Laputa and the other islands, a satire on contemporary philosophers and scientists, is less successful, though it has moments of triumph that impress us today (imagine what Swift would have made out of our nuclear physicists!) more than they would our grandfathers. The last voyage, to the Houyhnhnms and Yahoos, is almost a nightmare of misanthropy; the return home, when Gulliver cannot endure the sight and smell of his wife and family, is even worse, as if the author were glaring like a madman at us. And indeed he was, for already the shadows were creeping up, the darkness that came long before death to cover that great dazzling intellect, turning him, as Dr. Johnson wrote, into "a driv'ler and a show". Swift has often been called another, if drier, Rabelais; even Voltaire makes the comparison in his *Lettres sur les Anglais*; but this is to misunderstand both men, who may each have had satirical genius but stand at the extremes of it. Swift is not a humorist, not expansive and exuberant but controlled and intense; he did not live in a comic world and laugh at himself in it; he had too much pride and too much disgust, born of pride, to love life; he was all masculine intellect, and some reconciling feminine element, found in most artists, seemed to be absent in him; so his stupendous gifts were largely wasted. Perhaps in any age he could not have avoided madness; but the fact remains that this massive figure of the Age of Reason lost his reason, the light vanished in the darkness.

One of Swift's earlier sardonic inventions had been his *Battle of the Books*, which mocked the dispute as to whether the modern French authors were superior to the ancients. It had been argued for years in Paris, with much loss of temper, far more than the subject deserved, between Fontenelle and Perrault (yes, the one who gave us the charming fairy-tales) and Boileau and others. This ridiculous dispute was taken seriously outside France, for if it was good enough for French poets, critics, scholars, it was good enough for all cultivated persons (except Swift) outside France. That Taste to which we have already referred was a French export. Though later in the period it was modified to some extent by English influence on German and Scandinavian literature, this Taste throughout the age proved the supremacy of French classicism. Malherbe earlier in the seventeenth century and Boileau later decided what was correct and what was incorrect in poetry; the creation by Richelieu of the Académie Française gave literature an official standing, at a time when France was the most powerful single state in Europe; the French theorists of the drama triumphantly established the 'unities', while the theatre of Racine showed what might be made of them, as we shall see in the next chapter; and writers and readers abroad were asked, not in vain, to admire the way in which Paris and Versailles had turned literature, which in the previous age had been like a great wild landscape, into an ordered garden where ladies and gentlemen could take their ease.

Only small tame poets can accept so many rules and such an atmosphere, and the world does not want small tame poets, preferring to leave their verse for honest prose. We can make an exception of La Fontaine, whose Fables in verse, if not his more ambitious Contes, are remembered, often with affection, even though we may associate them with French classes at school. But, outside the drama, this age of Louis XIV returns to us through its prose, though not by way of the funeral orations of Bossuet, the speculations of Bayle and Saint-Évremond, Fénelon (though there is Télémaque) and Malebranche. No, it is not these heavy-weights who are still read outside France. It is the writers who can hardly be said to have had a literary career at all. It is the astonishing Saint-Simon, who from the age of nineteen kept a journal, became an unusually exact observer and chronicler, and so finally in his Memoirs, not published in full until the nineteenth century, gave us a panorama of the French Court unequalled in that or any other age. It is Madame de Sévigné, whose devotion to her daughter has provided us with a bountiful series of letters, which, whether one likes the writer or not (and opinion is sharply divided), cannot be challenged as an intimate record of a whole period. It is La Bruyère and his Characters, an original who was soon to have many imitators; and, even more, the earlier and justly more celebrated (especially outside France) La Rochefoucauld, whose *Maxims* are quoted to this day throughout the Western world. But too often they are quoted without complete understanding either of them or their author. He was not creating an epigrammatic testament of cynicism. He was in his own fashion following Montaigne, helping us to explore ourselves without the coloured glasses of self-love, illusion and hypocrisy. He was not attempting a total account of humanity, only wittily presenting some odd tricks and shifts of the ego. So for example, when he points out, quite truthfully, that there is something not altogether displeasing to us in the misfortunes of our friends, he is not asking us to believe there is no such thing as friendship and that really we dislike the people we call our friends, he is not denying that we will sympathise with and try to help our friends. He is laying bare for us that element of self-esteem, of selfish egoism, which cannot resist a flicker of gratification when we hear our friends' bad news. To make us confess such feelings, momentary though they may be, as La Rochefoucauld does time after time, is to deepen our honesty about ourselves. It is significant that the various maxims about women and love are in general far less penetrating and sometimes even doubtful; La Rochefoucauld discovered his best maxims by self-analysis, of which he must be considered one of the earliest masters.

Philosophy and mathematics are not our subjects here, but we cannot entirely ignore Descartes, who not only contributed to both of them but also, with the aid of a prose style that served as a model for generations, somehow succeeded in pleasing the orthodox while encouraging the sceptics. Blaise Pascal, following him, displayed an astonishing genius for both mathematics and prose, though his writing was too sharply individual to serve equally well as a model. His *Provincial Letters*, an attack upon the Jesuits, smooth and ironical and murderously effective, and his posthumous *Pensées*, never arranged by him for publication, are much easier to admire as writing than to imitate. Delicate and constantly in pain, a condition that his extreme ascetic practices did nothing to discourage, Pascal died before reaching his forties, having sacrificed to his idea of God most of the extraordinary genius God gave him. He is perhaps the supreme example of a self-torturing temperament that appears more than once in our Western literature, where it cannot fail to make some mark because of the very intensity of its expression. Men of this temperament are utterly lost outside religion and half-mad with anxiety inside it; all that matters is salvation and God has devised for it an appalling obstacle race, with traps for the intellect and baited hooks for the senses. Pascal's powerful intellect compelled him to reject every approach to the God of his Church through reason, so belief, which he passionately desired, had to be a matter of faith, a faith unceasingly at war with his intellect, ferociously suppressing the doubts that tormented him more than the pains of his racked body. So everything had to be sacrificed, even the humblest pleasures, the minimum decencies of ordinary life, the smallest sign of family affection, to keep alive this faith in a deity that he was transforming into a monster. Montaigne was one of the few authors he had read for pleasure in his youth, before pleasure was a sin, but though his intellect towers above Montaigne's, he had nothing of Montaigne's intuitive wisdom, which rejected any notion of taking over, with emotional compound interest, the whole debt of sin from Adam down, which was content to be thankful for what God had created without seeing in it a perpetual challenge, which recognised with true humility, needing no hair shirt, that men can see only a little way into the vast mystery that surrounds them. It is these others, like Pascal, so bent on torturing themselves and yet so often, again like him, greatly gifted, courageous, noble at heart, who will continue to appear and to suffer, sometimes to the point of self-destruction, until our Western civilisation discovers a religion that can ultimately contain it, giving it both a basis of thought and emotion and an ample framework of living.

CHAPTER SEVEN

The Drama

I

IN THE THEATRE we look to this age for comedy, not tragedy. (Unless we are French; and French Tragedy shall have its place in this chapter.) The whole spirit of the time favours comedy. Its classicism, rationality, brisk optimism, social view of art, preference for what is general and abstract, suspicion and fear of the unconscious and complete trust in consciousness, all create an atmosphere in which comedy can flourish and tragedy, as most of us see it, can only offer a parody of itself. If this should be doubted, it can easily be proved. How many tragic plays written during this period still have a place in World Theatre? How many comedies? These questions are no sooner asked than it is clear at once that this was an age of comedy. It is the smiles and not the tears of these be-wigged authors that we welcome now.

Unluckily for the Theatre, the flexible and swift-moving Elizabethan Stage vanished for ever. The only trace of it left in the English Theatre was 'the apron' or fore-stage that remained well into the eighteenth century. The European Theatre now was committed to the 'picture frame' method of staging, with painted scenes behind some sort of proscenium arch. Throughout the seventeenth century and for some time later, it was the Italian theatre architects and scene-designers who were in greatest demand and had most influence. But it was opera and not the spoken drama that encouraged more and more elaborate stage effects and the use of 'machines'. Regular tragedy and comedy asked for little in the way of scenery. In a tragedy that obeyed the rules, as we shall see, all the action took place in one rather featureless 'ante-chamber'. Comedy allowed itself more latitude, but was frequently content with one room in a house, or a public square where the chief characters could be seen coming out of or going into their respective houses. Towards the end of the period, dramatists asked for more scene changes, most of the new playhouses were larger, and depended more and more upon public patronage, especially that of the middle class, who had no great love of either poetic tragedy or highly artificial comedy but had a marked taste for sentimental domestic pieces. Careful reproductions of typical eighteenth-century performances—for example, those in the theatre attached to the summer palace at Drottningholm outside Stockholm—show that the chief difference between that stage and ours today is in the lighting, which seems to our eyes hopelessly inadequate. Not only was there not enough light in the eighteenth-century theatre, but there was hardly any distinction between the lighting of the auditorium and the stage.

Perhaps when the eye was not pampered, the ear did more work. Such evidence as we have suggests that there was great auricular style in the acting. (Racine, we are told, took his plays away from Molière's company to their rivals of the Hôtel de Bourgogne, risking a charge of ingratitude, because the latter seemed to him to have a superior style of declamation, more majestic and resonant.) All female parts, except grotesque old women, were now played by actresses, and it is clear that it was neither the beauty nor the powerful protectors of the leading actresses that made them famous but their sheer histrionic ability, of which we have many records. One of the best of them, Adrienne Lecouvreur, dying in 1730, was refused Christian burial, though in the same year the English actress, Anne Oldfield, had been buried in Westminster Abbey; a contrast that gave Voltaire a subject for a sharp attack on the Church. Eighteen years later, Voltaire, who in his *Sémiramis* had introduced some crowd scenes and spectacular effects, was insisting upon the stage being cleared of the fashionable gentlemen who up to that time had taken their seats on the stage. There can be no doubt that this practice must have had some influence on French drama. An author who knew only too well that his actors would be surrounded by tittering and sneering men of fashion would be very careful to obey all the rules, would ask himself if any situation or speech could make him look foolish, would not be anxious to reveal his mind too intimately. In short, this practice of seating the more fashionable members of the audience on the stage, which lasted longer in France than elsewhere, would not discourage satirical comedy but would tend to keep tragedy regular and formal, impersonal and unadventurous. It would sharply reinforce the whole spirit of the age.

The rules mentioned above were supposedly based on Aristotle's *Poetics*, in which there is an analysis of Sophoclean tragedy. In the second quarter of the seventeenth century, French dramatists, led by Mairet, generally agreed to follow these rules, of which the most important were the Unities—of time, place, and action. (Only the last is definitely laid down in the *Poetics*.) A play written with strict regard to the Unities would develop a single action, and would therefore have no sub-plot, would use only one scene, and ideally would represent no greater passage of time than that taken by the play's actual performance. Now it is a mistake to assume, as some critics have done, that these three make impossible demands upon the dramatist. Some of us have written plays for the modern theatre that perfectly fulfil these conditions. And indeed, when a dramatist wishes to achieve great intensity in the development of a single action, of which the supreme example is the *Œdipus Rex* of Sophocles, the other two unities of time and place are immensely helpful to him, preventing any slackening and lowering of tension. Where the French theorists went wrong was in trying to impose these Unities, helpful to one kind of play and merely a nuisance to other kinds, as an absolute condition of good drama. When to these was added a further rule for tragedy, that violent action should not be shown to the audience but merely described to it, the theorists were not uplifting and purifying tragedy, as they imagined, but making it almost impossible to write tragedy with any force and grandeur.

As Schlegel pointed out, the spectator of many French tragedies might well believe that great actions were actually happening but that he had chosen a bad place to be a witness of them. Moreover, as only one scene could be used, no matter how many great personages were involved, the unity of place was preserved only at the sacrifice of sense and credibility. Either the scene would be a mysterious vague ante-chamber belonging to nobody or characters would meet and exchange the most intimate confidences in the most unlikely places. Again, as so much could not be shown but had to be described, the chief characters had to be supplied with confidants, usually featureless persons who merely wondered and exclaimed; and messengers, of no interest themselves as characters, had to bring the terrible news; so that all too often half the cast were mere dummies. Nor was the unity of time any more helpful, for unless the dramatist was wonderfully ingenious, he had both to stretch the time and to bring one crisis so close to another that his action became incredible and absurd. A Sophocles, creating a scene heavy with doom, can succeed in rapidly piling up disaster and horror so that we are held and spellbound; but an attempt at the same unity and rapid development on a level of gentlemanly neatness can easily appear more comic than tragic. The truth is, tragedy of any size and depth demands precisely what these French neo-classical rules tried to deny it: a thick rich atmosphere, belonging to the tragic world that Shakespeare could always create; distinct individuals instead of types, who belong to comedy; concrete significant details, a button, a handkerchief, a mouse, and not a scene carefully emptied of them; men and women, actions and motives, that have something elemental and timeless about them and do not suggest the attitudes and manners of a section of society at a certain time.

It is true that the rules were always being broken. Pierre Corneille was attacked for breaking them in *Le Cid*, the play that in 1636 ushered in the great period of French drama. Based on a Spanish original, this famous piece was classed as a tragi-comedy, because it had a happy ending, but Corneille followed it with some true tragedies, turning to Roman themes, and becoming the foremost member of a group of tragic dramatists that included Du Ryer and Rotrou. A few facts about Corneille help us to understand him. He was a Norman, belonging to a legal family, and was himself a magistrate in Rouen. A stiff awkward man, he was never at home in Paris or Versailles. There is something genuinely classical, in the old "high Roman fashion", about *le grand Corneille;* the lofty ideas of duty and patriotism we find in his plays are more than a dramatist's device to create tragic dilemmas, they belong to the man. He was a romantic lawyer coming from a stock that always drove itself hard. But because he was romantic, he was never at ease with the rules, which he could not put to his own uses as Racine could, and there can be no doubt that simply as a dramatist Corneille would have been more rewardingly creative in a freer theatre. As it is, we feel that the poet in him is waiting for the dramatist—and sometimes waiting far too long—to hoist a character on to a platform from which that character and the poet can launch some magnificent clashing sonorous lines, remembered ever since by French men of action like the sound of drums and trumpets. When the poet cannot take fire, too often we feel that nothing is happening. Yet Corneille had a genuine feeling for the theatre itself; he wrote at least one excellent comedy, *Le Menteur;* and his later pieces, tragi-comedies or romantic melodramas, which for a long time were dismissed as the failures of an ageing disappointed man, are now attracting the attention of scholars of the drama. But he has always meant a great deal more to French readers and playgoers than he has to any public outside France.

This is equally true—and indeed the contrast is even sharper—of Corneille's much younger and more successful rival, Jean Racine. In other respects the two dramatists have nothing in common. A more pliable and subtle (and not altogether admirable) character, Racine was soon a Court favourite, and at the age of thirty-eight left the theatre to become the royal historiographer, writing no more plays except two religious pieces for Mme. de Maintenon's young ladies at St. Cyr—the second of which, *Athalie,* is now considered one of his masterpieces. Racine had studied Greek as well as Latin authors in his youth, and later made full use of his knowledge of Greek mythology. Encouraged by Boileau, he not only did not rebel against the rules but carefully refined them for his own particular purpose. What were limitations to Corneille were to Racine the means of achieving a peculiar intensity of his own. So he became, and has remained, the supreme tragic dramatist of French literature and its theatre. And it is here, while recognising that Racine was a man of genius, that we part company from French critics. It is not simply that they find everywhere in him a haunting poetic beauty to which our foreign ears are deaf, our eyes are blind; that is understandable, and similarly applies to many poets in many languages. The real difference is that his fellow-countrymen discover in his drama a uniquely profound tragic feeling that the rest of us, in all goodwill and without wanting to do battle for Shakespeare and our own tragic poets, cannot discover. As there is probably no other author of importance whose reputation abroad is so different from the one he enjoys at home, and as time has done little to bridge this gulf, it may be of some interest and value to summarise the arguments for and against Racine as a supreme tragic poet.

Our French friends ask us to admire his superb and perhaps matchless economy of means, the way in which he does not lift the curtain until the hour of crisis; his capacity for creating the maximum amount of profound tragic feeling with the minimum of violent action—if necessary with none at all, as in *Bérénice*, which, though inferior to *Phèdre* as an acting play, is often considered the most astonishing triumph of his method. In *Bérénice* nobody dies, not a sword or dagger is out, not a voice roars in anger or screams in fear. King Antiochus, friend, subject and guest of the Roman Emperor, Titus, was once the lover of Bérénice, Queen of Palestine, and loves her still. But she is in love with Titus, who loves her but decides he cannot marry her because his duty to Rome forbids such a marriage. He asks her to leave him, accompanied by Antiochus. She sadly accepts his decision but begs leave to go without Antiochus, declaring that the three of them offer the world the most mournful instance of blighted love. It is a triumph of ultra-refined neo-classical tragedy, providing innumerable opportunities for melancholy declarations of devotion; but does it seem to those of us who are not French, who are not haunted by Racine's cadences and undertones that he contrives with such art out of plain language, a tragedy on the grand scale? It does not. Too much has been refined away. Where is the 'great action' of which this classical drama boasts? Is this Titus a Roman Emperor, this Bérénice a queen? Where is Rome—the huge, clamorous, demanding city—in this quiet, dim ante-chamber? Where is the sensual, cruel, monstrous world ruled by Imperial Rome? Not here, where we feel we are in some corridor in Versailles, listening to three sensitive and melancholy subjects of Louis XIV. It will be objected, by the defenders of Racine, that we are asking for another kind of drama, that we must try to understand and appreciate him within the limits he has set himself, that the scene he presents is deliberately austere and idealised in order that he can express, sometimes in a flashing epigram, sometimes with a mysterious music suggesting wonder and awe, every inward twist and turn of the spirit, the last glimmers of hope and the darkest depths of the soul. If we grant all this, they will tell us, then we are wrong to complain that he does not allow us to see the fatal net closing round its victims, that the curtain rises long after the supreme tragic moment, as for example when Phèdre first discovers she loves Hippolytus, and that the characters seem fixed in their tragic attitudes too early, for it is by this device, robbing the scene of movement and our curiosity, that he compels us to listen and to explore the depths of the characters. So, as they say of parliaments all too often, "the debate continues". What is certain is that Racine has provided a succession of great French actresses with parts that called for every possible resource of the tragédienne, and generations of French critics with characters, situations, lines, that have demanded their most subtle powers of analysis.

After Racine's early retirement from the theatre, tragedy was in the hands of minor writers like La Chapelle, La Fosse, the boy prodigy La Grange-Chancel, and Crébillon, who left the bare classic heights and descended to melodrama and cheap horrors. Voltaire was a great deal better than Crébillon, but his enormous success with what were still considered poetic tragedies does not entitle him to be ranked with Corneille and Racine. He was immensely industrious and enterprising in the theatre to the very end of his long life, but he brought to it a showman's flair—he was particularly adroit in finding original and arresting settings for his plays and contriving new theatrical effects—rather than a genuinely poetic and dramatic imagination. He might be said to have had a complete understanding of the theatre on a rather low level, and none whatever of it on any higher level. Nobody can be stupider than a very clever man out of his depth, and Voltaire's criticisms of Sophocles and Shakespeare are very stupid. In plays he made some sensible innovations; he brought 'local colour' into the theatre; he transformed decaying formal tragedy into lively romantic melodrama with some semi-philosophical trimmings; but no amount of sympathy with his aims or admiration for his wit and courage can transform this jester of genius into one of the world's tragic poets.

2

It is a relief to turn to comedy, so much closer to the spirit of the age. Here we are no longer at cross-purposes with French criticism. The pre-eminence of Molière cannot be disputed. He is one of the world's great comic writers, and in classical artificial comedy he is supreme. The basis of this comedy is not humour (though Molière had humour) but satirical wit; it makes no attempt to create immense comic characters in the round, as Shakespeare did with Falstaff; it is not suggesting to us that life itself is absurd, only that certain types of people behaving in a certain fashion are ridiculous and should be laughed at; it belongs to an age that essentially takes itself seriously. We should not be surprised that Molière, after touring with his troupe in the provinces for twelve years, should then on his return to Paris so soon win the favour and patronage of Louis XIV. So long as the dramatist avoided certain dangerous subjects, he was doing what the King wanted somebody to do, not only amusing him but correcting the follies of the society he ruled. The affectations Molière satirised in his *Précieuses Ridicules*, his first outstanding success, had probably seemed equally absurd to Louis for some time. As a satirist Molière made many enemies, and as manager and actor he had many rivals, and against all these the King's patronage was a sure shield. For so much we must be grateful to Louis. On the other hand, if Molière's theatre had existed in a freer society, if he had not had to write, so to speak, with a despot looking over one shoulder and the Church over the other, it is more than likely he would have given us tragi-comedies of even greater insight and depth than the best of what he has given us. He was a responsible, anxious man, no jovial comedian; desperately overworked as author-manager-actor and never in good health, with a troublesome young wife in the company; and it is typical of him that when, a dying man, he insisted upon going to the theatre to perform, he pointed out that he had fifty people dependent upon his going. He died later that night. The play was *Le Malade Imaginaire*.

He was only fifty-one when he died, and for years he had had to keep his theatre going, to defend himself against innumerable attacks, and to provide entertainment of various kinds, not only straight plays but also what we should now call 'musicals' with songs and ballet in them; sometimes simply for the Court and sometimes for the general public. The wonder is that he achieved so much. He was great in two different ways, one strictly as a dramatist, the other as an author expressing himself. As a creator of artificial comedy, he was astonishingly fertile, inventive and ingenious. For the next hundred years, comic dramatists may be said to have lived off his bounty. There was a queer lack of dramatic invention in this age, especially when compared with the age that preceded it or with the last hundred and fifty years. Men who could write brilliant dialogue seemed unable to invent an original plot or even a good new situation or two. Plots, situations, scenes, were always being borrowed without acknowledgment. Now Molière, like Shakespeare, might pick up any story or idea he found useful, but what he finally created was his own. And he could make an actable comedy, often a glorious one, out of almost anything—a fashion, a fad, even the criticism of a previous play. He was both broadly inventive and wonderfully ingenious and effective in all the details of a scene. Not for nothing had he managed a company and tried for years to amuse all manner of people. He is a superb theatrical contriver. Every stroke has its effect; every scene or speech makes its point. When Congreve shocked Voltaire by telling him that he considered himself a gentleman not a dramatist, he spoke the truth about himself in terms of technique, for in spite of their brilliant wit his comedies, in their confused action, are indeed amateurish. Molière would have regarded them with horror. He is the great professional.

This is something, but if it were all, then Molière, working in a tradition of comedy narrow and outmoded, would be only the most expert member of a group of half-forgotten dramatists. What lifted him above his age and brought him triumphantly out of it is his personal quality as a writer. He is a satirist with a difference. What distinguishes him is that rare quality in authorship which might be called a warm common-sense. It belongs to wisdom, not cleverness. It is compounded of the right mixture of heart and head. Just as there is no sentimentality in Molière, so too there is no unfeeling intellectual arrogance. His criticism of life— and except for the farcical trifles, all his plays are that—proceeds from a

70

centre that is itself a delicate but sure balance. This enables him to see at once what is ridiculous, pretentious, inflated, one-sided; and he can say with Cléante in *Tartuffe* that he is "no dupe of all your formalists". Some of his critics ought to be included among the formalists. They can understand him when he is laughing at affected society women, blue-stockings, mean old men, rich bourgeois trying to be fashionable, and all his obvious victims; but as soon as he comes closer to us and is stealthier in his pursuit of folly, they begin to misunderstand him. So Schlegel could find the *Misanthrope* dull, and calls it improbable because, he tells us, Alceste would never have fallen in love with Célimène or had Philinte as a friend. But this is to miss the point of the play. Alceste is not an ideal hero but another one-sided character, as over-fond of savage criticism and blunt honesty as Célimène is of intrigue and malicious gossip. They are both egoists. And his infatuation is not surprising; it could happen anywhere except in the mind of a German critic. Nor is the play, on its own level, 'ambiguous', for what Molière is telling us is that a man may be right in general but put himself in the wrong by becoming one-sided in his rightness. His Don Juan play, though on the same level for the most part, can really be accused of ambiguity, as if Molière were uncertain how far he might go; but it seems to some of us more fascinating than the theatrically more effective *Tartuffe*. Schlegel, who is important because he best represents the romantic reaction against Molière and classical comedy, also condemned his "didactical and satirical vein which is peculiarly alien to Comedy; for example, in his constant attacks upon physicians and lawyers. . ." But this is to blame him for doing what the age and its dramatic style expected him to do; and as for the physicians and lawyers, who ask to be satirised at any time and must have been irresistible in the seventeenth century, it is their extreme pedantry, pretentiousness and conceit that make them such tempting targets.

That Molière sometimes hit hard, not always sparing individuals, is true enough. After all, he himself had to take plenty of knocks, from life as well as from rival poets and actors. But to suggest, as Schlegel did, that behind his satire is something ill-bred and ill-natured, tainted with a cold conceit, seems to us to contradict everything we feel about this man and his work. For with that balance, that illimitable common-sense of the born satirist and comic writer, is an unusual warmth; not sentiment, not tenderness, but a feeling for and appreciation of the central dignity and worth of human beings. It is this, time after time, that seems at least momentarily to transform the comic types, demanded by this form of drama, into real characters. The situation, the spoken line, may be absurd, but it throws on them a warmer light, as when Henriette excuses herself from being embraced by Vadius because she does not understand Greek, or Jourdain, in that famous moment, delightedly discovers he has been speaking prose for forty years. Too many satirists leave us with nothing in the end but an uneasy conviction of their cleverness; the foolish human race has vanished. But with Molière, though there may be no romantic glow, no memory of characters larger than life, though the scene may be severely classical, may seem to hold little but didactic wit, may almost appear an operation theatre of social surgery, something not only sensible but warmly sensible, belonging to the real relations between husbands and wives, parents and children, the life of the sturdy affections, seems to linger like fire-light on the page or in the playhouse. The heart as well as the intellect and gaiety of old France is here. She does well, through all the changing fashions in dramatic literature, to honour Molière as her great comic writer.

Sixteen years after Molière's death, his company was joined by another, moved into a new theatre, and became the Comédie Française. The only other company licensed to perform in Paris was the Comédie Italienne. Originally the Italian players had largely restricted themselves to the *Commedia dell' Arte*, in which there was a mere outline of a plot and the actors, often brilliant comedians, improvised the dialogue, usually as the kind of characters who have come down to us in the Harlequinade. It was probably the success of these characters, as played by the Italians, that helped to stereotype the casts in so many French classical comedies— the cunning valet and the sprightly artful maid, the Harlequin and Columbine types of young lovers, the foolish Pantaloon old characters. Before the end of the seventeenth century the Italian company had begun to produce French plays. Then it was suppressed for nearly twenty years, but finally returned as the King's Italian Players. Young writers who disliked the Molière tradition at the Comédie Française took their plays to the Italian company.

Regnard began with the Italians and then went over to the Comédie Française, where some of his comedies, notably *Le Légataire universel*, remained in the repertoire down to our own times. Superficially he continued the Molière tradition, with increasing emphasis on the scheming valet, but he turned comedy into farce, relying upon a bustling high spirits to persuade the audience to overlook his wild improbabilities. A far more solid comic writer is Lesage, author of the novel *Gil Blas*. His *Turcaret*, a satire on the financial rogues of the early eighteenth century, is the best French comedy of its time, though never very popular because it is too hard and its characters, who form a sort of grand chain of dupers and duped, probably too unpleasant. Its action is more elaborate than that of most classical French comedies, and is consistently and grimly worked out, without a glimmer of sentiment. With Marivaux, a little later, who preferred to work with the less traditional and perhaps more subtle Italians, sentiment takes the place of hard satire, but it is not the lachrymose sentimentality now beginning to invade the theatre, through the comedies of La Chaussée and others. With an almost feminine sensibility, Marivaux rejected the strongly masculine satirical humour of classical comedy, brought the parts played by young actresses into prominence, and perfected an odd personal style (the critics called it *marivaudage*) in which to express the delicate advances and retreats of his young lovers, often improbably disguised. The total effect, which impressed the nineteenth century more than it did the eighteenth, was rather like that of some polite psychological Harlequinade.

By the end of this period in France the new writers for the theatre, including even Diderot, had abandoned classical comedy and, inspired by the sentimental novels of Richardson and others, had turned to didactic and tearful domestic plays that were called 'comedies' only because they were certainly not tragedies. And then the old comedy, newly and freshly contrived, suddenly sparkled and blazed for the last time. Pierre Augustin Caron, who called himself Beaumarchais, was the author. He was a great many other things as well: watchmaker, musician, speculator, political agent and adventurer, very much an impudent cool card, to whom dramatic authors owe something, for he was one of the first to fight with some success for their rights. His own famous comedies, now equally famous as operas too, are *The Barber of Seville* and *The Marriage of Figaro*. They are not original in conception, being basically comedies of familiar intrigue, but they are devised and written with enormous zest and brilliance, the characters are types lifted into individuals, every situation is fully exploited, and they contain a good deal of cheerfully impudent social criticism. It was this criticism that kept them off the stage for some time and, when they finally arrived there, perhaps gave them a special significance over-flattering to Beaumarchais, strictly considered as a dramatist.

In point of fact, Goldoni was at least as severe on the aristocracy, whom he clearly disliked, and was the more original and of course incomparably the more fertile dramatist. (In Venice he promised to write sixteen comedies in one year, and did it too, several of them being among his best.) After being appointed manager of the Italian Theatre in Paris, in 1761, he frequently wrote in French. He is unequal naturally, but his more solid work has frequently been revived, in more than one language, and the great Eleonora Duse kept his *La Locandiera* in her repertoire. His young women have far more life and individuality than those in French classical comedy. He is very deft in keeping up a bustle of lively intrigue, often very ingeniously contrived, as for example in that comedy of his in which a fan keeps changing hands, to create one misunderstanding after another. But though he remained in France, dying in poverty after the Revolution, he belongs to Italian dramatic literature.

3

The English Theatre, closed during the Commonwealth, began again under Charles II, who granted patents to two companies of players. But these companies, which now for the first time included actresses, performed chiefly for the Court and the small fashionable world and its hangers-on. There was no return to the Elizabethan Theatre, rooted in the national life, and it is doubtful, in spite of the widespread theatrical activity in contemporary England, if the drama has ever really regained the place it once had, when in its first glory. Among the Restoration dramatists were Shadwell, much influenced by Ben Jonson, and Otway, who had a vein of genuine pathos and whose *Venice Preserved* has had many revivals right up to the present day; and the great John Dryden, who attempted both tragedy and comedy, was better when he was serious than when he was not, and was better still well outside the playhouse, either as a poet or critic. It is worth remarking that the best prose of this time, like Dryden's, has a peculiar charm, for though it is beginning to assume a classical correctness there still lingers in it, like the scent of flowers, some trace of the previous age; and even a generation later this charm has not entirely vanished from Congreve's comedies, for all their bite and brilliance. Congreve wrote one tragedy, *The Mourning Bride*, now only remembered in one line—"Music has charms to sooth a savage breast". Addison, the essayist, who had a knack of succeeding beyond his merits, produced in *Cato* a stately and tedious Roman tragedy in the French style. Nicholas Rowe wrote pathetic 'fat' parts for actresses in *The Fair Penitent* and *Jane Shore*. Later, and more important because of his vogue and influence abroad, came George Lillo, who in his *The London Merchant* and *The Fatal Curiosity* created a new form, bourgeois pathetic melodrama, by dramatising old ballads. It was a type of play highly popular in France and Germany as well as in England, with the new playgoing public, unfashionable family audiences, of the later eighteenth century. But nothing here makes any contribution to literature.

The comedy is a different matter. The best of it falls into two groups, divided by an interval of about seventy years, during which there was a marked change in theatrical taste. The earlier group consists of Etherege, Wycherley, Congreve, Vanbrugh and Farquhar. Of these the best from a literary point of view is unquestionably Congreve, who wrote all his plays in his twenties and then, as Voltaire discovered, preferred to be thought an English gentleman. For style and wit, especially in his final play, *The Way of the World*, (though it was far less successful in the theatre than his earlier *Love for Love*), he is magnificent, perhaps incomparable; but he is better to read than to see in the playhouse, where his faulty construction and confused action tease and irritate the spectator. Wycherley is a much coarser writer and has nothing of Congreve's sheer

75

brilliance, but in his own rather brutal fashion he is more effective in the theatre. And so is Farquhar, who if he had lived—he died before he was thirty—might have become the best English writer of comedy of the century, for already he had successfully broken away from the narrow and highly artificial comedy of manners, tending to monotony both in character and action, and both in *The Recruiting Officer* and *The Beaux' Stratagem* (which is still frequently revived) had taken the scene from London into the country, had begun to create some characters in the round instead of the usual flat types, and had brought a breezy fresh humour into comedy that was in danger of turning stale.

After this long interval, filled with sentimental pieces or routine comedies imitated from the French, two Irishmen, Oliver Goldsmith and Richard Brinsley Sheridan, saved the situation for comedy, giving us plays that have held the stage up to the present time. Of Goldsmith's two comedies, the first, *The Good-Natur'd Man*, never successful at any time, is perhaps as much under-estimated as its triumphant successor, *She Stoops to Conquer*, has been over-estimated. Both have highly improbable main plots, not entirely original, and in both the author's natural humour, unborrowed, coming out of his own observation and invention, lights up the scene. While agreeing with the majority that *She Stoops to Conquer* is the better comedy, some of us who have seen many productions of it would be ready to forgo the next one in favour of a revival of *The Good-Natur'd Man*. Sheridan is wittier, though less naturally humorous, than Goldsmith, and both *The Rivals* and *The School for Scandal* (his other dramatic work is negligible) are closer to the tradition of artificial comedy. Indeed, *The School for Scandal* might be described as a Restoration comedy, following Wycherley and Congreve, without the impudent indecencies, and so entirely suitable for family entertainment. This is its strength, and in spite of its genuine wit, here too is its weakness, for its theme, the contrast between the rather raffish but frank and generous Charles Surface and his brother, the slyly sensual, hypocritical Joseph, really demands bolder treatment than Sheridan can afford to give it. So, for all its elaborate and triumphant construction, it is in many respects a less original and satisfying comedy than the earlier and less ambitious piece, *The Rivals*, which has a freshness and unforced gaiety that made a recent revival of it in London an outstanding success. But we are merely comparing these two comic dramatists with themselves. Compared with any other writers of English comedy, for more than fifty years before or after their time, they stand by themselves, high above the rest. Their triumphant Irish invasion of the English comic theatre was to be resumed, again triumphantly, in the 1890s by Shaw and Wilde. There is some witty theatrical element in the Anglo-Irish (which is what all these men were) that enables them, when they settle in England (which is what all these men did), to become masters of comedy. One final note before we leave the London Theatre of the eighteenth century. It was devoted to ballad opera, and, taking a hint from Swift about the possibility of "a Newgate pastoral" (Newgate was a famous prison), the poet Gay wrote the dialogue and lyrics of a ballad opera, all in a sardonic mock-operatic style, about highwaymen and women of the town; and he succeeded so well that it can still be enjoyed, in different musical arrangements and settings, to this day: he called it *The Beggar's Opera*.

4

Managers of theatres, together with their leading actors and actresses, are more inclined to follow fashion, to avoid taking risks, to aim at pleasing their more influential patrons, than publishers and booksellers are. Vogue is more important in the theatre than it is in the bookshop. Plays that have behind them the prestige of great capital cities, from which travellers return to boast of what they have seen in the theatres, seem to anxious managers in other countries both more exciting and far less of a risk than the work of local dramatists. Indeed, often the fashion for importing plays can for some time prevent a native school of drama from coming into existence at all. And although a solitary dramatist of genius from a small country, like Ibsen, can have enormous influence, it will generally be found that if a country occupies a dominating position, through its wealth, political and military power, and also has an active Theatre, the plays of that Theatre will be eagerly sought by other countries.

This was as true of the France of Louis XIV as it is today of the United States, with the difference that our new communications have speeded up the process. It was after Louis XIV had gone, and had taken some of the glory of France with him, that the French drama of his reign was most widely translated and imitated.

In Russia, for example, it was not until 1743 than an actual French company took the places of the previous German and Italian companies, to play Molière and Regnard. These companies had to be brought in because as yet there were no professional Russian actors. But at the Cadet College, where literature, dancing and recitation were taught among other things, amateur productions were made possible. Out of these came the first Russian dramatist of note, Sumarokov, who adopted the French classical style of tragedy in all its severity but took his themes from Russian history. After the cadets had played several times before the Court, a professional company was formed, subsidised by the Court and very firmly controlled by it. In 1782, Fonvizin's *The Minor*, which is still played in Russia, was first produced. In Sweden, which had its Royal Theatre in Stockholm by 1737, French influence was paramount, though both Olof von Dalin and Carl Gyllenborg, in comedy, were also indebted to Ludvig Holberg, a Norwegian by birth who settled in Copenhagen. Denmark and Norway were united then, and the language of the educated classes was more or less the same. Holberg, a well-travelled scholar, not only contrived to be at one and the same time the Professor of Metaphysics at the University and the director of the Danish Theatre (how much we miss in these days of specialisation!), but also created a genuine Danish-Norwegian comedy, which in its lively use of native types and manners came, as we have seen, to have some influence in Sweden. Later, after 'The Age of Holberg' had passed, Johannes Ewald, the Danish lyric poet who died in his thirties, created a native poetical drama, at first in the German manner but later finding his own dramatic style; but though he died as early as 1781, he belongs to the Romantics and so has no proper place here.

It has been pointed out that whereas in most countries we find that creation comes before criticism, in Germany this is reversed and criticism precedes creation. The critic has to clear the ground before the artist can flourish. This is certainly true of German dramatic literature during this age. When the eighteenth century opened there was plenty of dramatic activity of a sort in Germany, with its many towns and Courts. Much of it was crude stuff, with plenty of clowning for the crowd, though visiting French companies played their classics at the larger Courts. The French influence was much strengthened by the enthusiastic support of a dictatorial critic, Gottsched, and his wife, who did much translation from the French, and they in turn, for some years, found a valuable ally in the actress-manager, Caroline Neuber. With its belief in authority and rules, this whole age was favourable to literary dictatorships—witness Boileau earlier and Voltaire later in France, or Dryden and, much later, Dr. Johnson in England—and Gottsched, with Leipzig as his base of operations, for some time ruled German taste both in and out of the theatre. The first challenge to his authority came from the Swiss poet and critic, Bodmer, and his friends in Zürich, who found both in medieval German literature and in Milton and other English poets some potent and magical elements denied them by Boileau and the rules, thus preparing the way for the German Romantic Movement of the following age. The second and more important challenge came from one man, Gotthold Ephraim Lessing, one of the most attractive and influential figures in German literature. With him the characteristically German process of criticism preceding creation takes place in one mind. Apart from some very early work, obviously imitated from French comedy, his major contributions to the theatre represent the triumphant conclusion of some equally creative (in their influence) critical research and speculation. His most famous piece of criticism, *Laokoön*, though important as an early and widely successful example of that type of critical aesthetics to which the Germans are still devoted, is in fact inferior to the best of his dramatic criticism, which appeared originally in a weekly journal associated with the Hamburg National Theatre. Earlier, as a youth in Berlin, Lessing had met and admired Voltaire, but this did not prevent him from revealing the absurdities and aridities of Voltaire's tragedies or even those of Corneille, the gulf there was between French and Greek tragedy, and the immense superiority of Shakespeare. He did not altogether understand Shakespeare and he still depended too much upon Aristotle, but this age cannot show us any better dramatic criticism than Lessing's. It cleared the way, as the way had to be cleared, for Schiller and Goethe and the other dramatists of the next age. But Lessing did more than this, as we have seen: he provided his criticism with its own examples. His 'bourgeois tragedy' *Miss Sara Sampson*, which had an English setting, is not a good play; too much reading and not enough life went into it; but it took tragedy off its classical stilts. In *Minna von Barnhelm* he created genuine comedy out of the German life he knew—an immense step forward. His Italian tragedy, *Emilia Galotti*, rises to an improbable climax—unless one believes that girls ask their fathers to kill them when they feel they cannot resist seductive but unscrupulous princes—but its tight and effective construction made it a good model for future German dramatists. Finally, in his last years, he wrote *Nathan the Wise*, a play in blank verse and—though Lessing was not really a poetic dramatist—his masterpiece. He was at this time librarian to the Duke of Brunswick, and he had published some extracts from the posthumous work of a liberal theologian called Reimarus. He was attacked by an orthodox pastor, Goeze, as an enemy of religion, and replied in a series of pamphlets, *Anti-Goeze*, defending the new biblical criticism and taking a more or less pragmatic view of religion. An official decree forbade any further publication of these pamphlets, so Lessing decided to write a play on a religious theme, hoping that, as he said, "they will at least let me preach on undisturbed in my old pulpit, the theatre." Adapting the story of the three rings in Boccaccio, using a romantic medieval background and making the action simple theatrically but deeply symbolic, Lessing was able to give dramatic expression to all that during these last years he had thought and felt about religion. The wise Jew, Nathan, can bring together, as members of one family, Mohammedans and Christians. What is expressed here is neither the vaguely deistic rationalism of the age nor the inflexible dogmatism of the Lutherans or any other Church. Of the three rings the genuine one has the magic power to bring its wearer the love of God and man, so long as it is worn with faith in this magic power. All religions that ennoble men's relations with one another are partially true, none is exclusively and finally true, and man has still a long way to go. All this reveals an attitude of mind, pragmatic and evolutionary, that is familiar enough now, though by no means common, especially during recent years when we have seen more and more fanatics of atheistic materialism glaring at more and more fanatics of dogma and fundamentalism. It was certainly not familiar in 1779, when as much wisdom as men had heard for a long time now arrived in blank verse for the German Theatre. Two years later, after publishing *The Education of the Human Race*, in which he elaborates his evolutionary view of religion, Lessing died. He had always been poor; he had had to sell the fine library he had collected; he lost both wife and child after less than two years of marriage; his last years were darkened by ill-health, over-work, quarrels with the orthodox; but the essential spirit of the man, nobly serving a mind both critical and creative, vigorous and wide-ranging, liberal and deeply humane, appears to ride so high above poverty, misunderstanding and loneliness, that he seems one of the most triumphant, as well as one of the most appealing, figures of the age. He gave Germany a Theatre of her own, a sound body of criticism, an example of liberal thought without extravagance. He showed the eighteenth century the German mind and temperament at their best.

CHAPTER EIGHT

The Novel

NOW OUR DIFFICULTIES BEGIN. First, in response to an increasing demand, sheer production grows and the names multiply. This means that, while we must sketch the development of the form, we must not imitate the literary historian, crowding these pages with names only remembered in literary histories, but must ruthlessly apply the test hinted at in the Introduction, asking ourselves which writers of prose fiction made a definite contribution, both directly and through their influence, to the literature not of this country or that but of Western Man. Secondly, we must avoid the mistake, common among literary historians, of taking too narrow and too personal a view of the novel. Indeed, the very breadth of the form, offering a wide welcome to all comers, often encourages an intolerant narrowness in its historians and critics. If they are extroverted themselves, then they demand that fiction should be panoramic, offering us as many characters and backgrounds as possible. If they are introverts, they tell us that this breadth of scene is of no significance and that all that matters is that the novelist should reveal with increasing subtlety human motives and states of mind. But if possible it is better here, as in life, to keep a balance and not be one-sided. But does this answer the question, *What is a novel?* No, it does not. In detail the question need not be answered. In place of exact definition, a few observations might be helpful. Coming into existence to please an increasingly varied number of readers, novels, good novels too, can be of various kinds—a statement that only the narrowest and most intolerant critic of fiction would deny.

The novel, whatever its kind, occupies the centre and most of the outlying parts of prose fiction, but the novel and prose fiction do not completely overlap one another. Just within the edges of prose fiction are works that cannot be called novels. Coming to the seventeenth century and the first half of this age, we may say that the interminable romances of Mademoiselle de Scudéry and her friends are not novels. On the other hand, Scarron (whose widow was afterwards Louis's Madame de Maintenon), though busy imitating the Spanish, was beginning to write novels, especially in his unfinished *Roman Comique*, a story of strolling players—a subject that was to fascinate many later authors, including Goethe. Madame de La Fayette's little masterpiece, *La Princesse de Clèves*, though cast in the form of an historical romance, can be accepted as a novel, because as she wrote it she was thinking about herself and her husband and her friend, La Rochefoucauld, and not dreaming about the Court of Henry II. But, looking across at England, what are we to say about John Bunyan's famous *Pilgrim's Progress* and *The Life and Death of Mr. Badman*? The answer must be No, these allegorical sermons, though a kind of prose fiction, cannot reasonably be classed as novels. For the novel must not only have acceptable individuals as characters, but it must make these characters move in a recognisable society. Characters in a society make the novel. (And as we shall see, society itself becomes more and more important to the serious novelist, and indeed turns into a character itself, perhaps the chief character.) And because Don Quixote and Sancho Panza are characters, among the greatest ever created, and, no matter what dreamland may be taking shape in their heads, we see them moving about and related to a completely realistic society, that of sixteenth-century Spain, it is absurd to ignore Cervantes, as so many literary historians do, and go poking around the late seventeenth or early eighteenth centuries for the origins of the novel, for the novel is there, complete and glorious, in *Don Quixote*.

It is particularly absurd when, as often happens, parentage of the novel is claimed for Lesage, largely on the strength of *Gil Blas*. We have already met Lesage as a dramatist but he was even more successful as a story-teller. A friendly abbé, who gave him a small annuity, told him to study Spanish literature, and Lesage translated and adapted several Spanish novels and plays, and these gave him the background for *Gil Blas*. (He never actually visited Spain.) The earlier and more sharply satirical tale, *Le Diable*

Boiteux, was immediately popular, but it was the leisurely and massive *Gil Blas* that gave him a European reputation. (But, oddly enough, it had more influence on the English novel than on the French.) Comparison with *Don Quixote* is fatal to *Gil Blas*, for it exists entirely on one level and lacks any great theme: it is an intelligent entertainment, not a vision and searching examination of life. But as a robust *picaresque* novel and a piece of story-telling on the grand scale, it is superb. No doubt it is too long and cannot help a certain monotony creeping into it, chiefly because no character grows or ever surprises us. But though it may lack great characters it has an immense range of convincing and diverting minor characters, a huge cast of princes, dignitaries, officials, soldiers, lawyers, doctors, merchants, innkeepers, brigands, peasants, countesses, actresses, courtesans, chambermaids. This is not Spain in particular, which Cervantes gives us to the last proverb and wine-skin, but it is a great panorama of the Western European world of the late seventeenth and early eighteenth centuries. And within the limitations Lesage imposed upon himself, or unconsciously his temperament imposed upon him, he tells his long wandering tale with fine skill, keeping the same even texture throughout its length, explaining exactly what happened with an economy that is itself a kind of irony, and preserving a detachment unique in a writer of that period and rare enough at any time. A whole world of poetry, of rich humour, of strange depths of character, is closed to him; but what is open to him he surveys, with smiling sagacity, like a master. As a pioneer of story-telling on the grand scale, his influence and value have been immense; and in spite of some creaking and groaning in its old joints, some repetitions and tedious passages, his *Gil Blas* can still be enjoyed.

Another novelist we have already met in the theatre is Marivaux, Lesage's junior by twenty years. In his *Marianne*, though it contains scenes and characters of ordinary life that Lesage could have used, the novel takes another turn, inward instead of outward. Sensibility has arrived with the heroine. Marianne, the poor and rather calculatingly virtuous girl, has her mind *marivaudaged* on a tremendous scale; and, as Crébillon *fils*, a frivolous but far from stupid writer himself, points out, in this fiction we are told not only everything the characters did and thought, but also everything they would have liked to think. Though

Marivaux's notorious manner was very much his own and he had not the power of invention to sustain his sentimental saga, much that happens in his life of Marianne, especially his pursuit of finer and finer shades of thought and feeling, is happening in fiction for the first time. Marianne herself is the first in a long line of slightly dubious heroines, suffering from but somehow enjoying their extreme sensibility, immoderately self-questioning behind their tentative smiles and all too frequent tears, very much their own psycho-analysts. But we will not stay with Marivaux to relate this introverted hot-house fiction to the age, because he stands close to Richardson, whom he may or may not have influenced, and as Richardson carried this kind of novel as far as it would go and had the greater European reputation, we will wait for him.

The French translator of Richardson was the Abbé Prévost, an odd character who as a young man had been both monk and soldier, was twice exiled from France, spending some years in England, and was an indefatigable writer, compelled to keep going by sheer necessity. His translations, which commanded a wide public in France, did good service to English authors. His own novels are immensely long and verbose, eccentric and discursive, their chapters packed with anything he might be thinking about at the time of writing, from geography to parliamentary institutions. Yet among all this stuff, a jewel in a heap of litter, is a little masterpiece, one of the archetypal love-stories of our civilisation, *Manon Lescaut*. It was originally an episode in his first long novel, and only later was published separately. It has a directness and economy, an objectiveness and force, unmatched in the novel for many years. Apart from the unhappy Des Grieux's conversion at the end, which looks like a gesture of submission to the Church, we believe and are held by everything we are told about these lovers. With Manon herself, at once so tender, weak, pitifully treacherous, very far removed from the vague ideal images of romance, a real woman enters fiction, to make the inevitable tragedy of Des Grieux's infatuation only too believable and deeply moving. The final flight to the desert may belong to romance, but all that Des Grieux narrates before belongs essentially to the novel, as a reasonably realistic account of people and a society.

It was in England, however, that fiction had already arrived at the most astonishing realism, by way of the singular efforts of one man, Daniel Defoe. After mixing, not always very scrupulously, in all manner of public affairs and being for some time what we call now a political journalist, Defoe retired to the outskirts of London to write books. These were in fact works of fiction—though frequently based on accounts of real experience, as *Robinson Crusoe* was based on Captain Cook's account of the castaway, Alexander Selkirk—but in most instances Defoe was not offering them to the public as novels but as fake memoirs—adventurous, as with *Robinson Crusoe*; historical, as with the *Journal of the Plague Year*; scandalous, as with *Moll Flanders*. His first object therefore was to make his readers believe that what they were reading was true. So a complete realism was essential. Fiction with Defoe becomes entirely convincing just because it is not supposed to be fiction. And for this matter-of-fact magic Defoe had a genius. His very limitations as a man and a writer— his narrow outlook, lack of poetry and humour, prosy moralising—help to create this genius. What he does looks easy, just plodding away adding one apparent fact, one commonplace reflection, to another, but it is a method very difficult to sustain with any success, making everything completely credible and convincing, and here Defoe is a master. The first part of his *Robinson Crusoe*, which contains the story that conquered all our world and its children, is a triumphant example of his method. It is hard to believe that what we read is not the truth but an invention; and his convincing detailed realism is not peculiar to *Robinson Crusoe* (though this is easily his most fascinating story, if only because of its central situation, a shipwrecked man on an island) but may be found in the other two books mentioned above and his *Memoirs of a Cavalier, Captain Singleton, Colonel Jack*, and *Roxana*. In describing the adventures of Gulliver, Swift undoubtedly owed something to Defoe and his method, and claims have been made that most English novelists of this century, from Richardson onwards, were directly in his debt. This is probably claiming too much for him, just as it is to declare, as some enthusiastic fellow-novelists and critics have done, that the success of his method makes him a great novelist. Any novel that begins to approach greatness must be something more than a close imitation of a chronicle or memoirs, no matter how deceptively truthful it appears to be. But clearly to some temperaments Defoe's method has a particularly strong appeal, and it is an appeal that has outlasted many changes of fashion in fiction.

From the middle of the century onwards it is English and not French novels that dominate the European scene, the novels of Richardson, Fielding and Sterne. Of these three, Samuel Richardson, the eldest, has had the most curious history. Today, apart from scholars of literature and students of it acting under compulsion, few people read either *Pamela; or Virtue Rewarded*, or *Clarissa; or the History of a Young Lady*, or *The History of Sir Charles Grandison*. It is true that by this time the circulating libraries, eagerly patronised by young ladies (there is an amusing scene in Sheridan's *The Rivals* showing this), were crammed with novels now forgotten; the trade in fiction was booming. But Richardson was no popular ephemeral novelist, ignored by serious critics. He had not only the greatest immediate success, but also the widest reputation and influence, of any novelist of the century. His *Clarissa* drew tears and cries of admiration from all Western Europe. Among its most fervent admirers were French authors, from Diderot, who was ready to put Richardson alongside Homer and Euripides on his bookshelves, to Balzac and George Sand and Alfred de Musset, who called *Clarissa* "*le premier roman du monde*". This absurd; pompous little printer, surrounded by his admiring middle-aged ladies in a suburban villa, created whole schools of literature. Indeed, among more cultivated male readers, he enjoyed a bigger and more lasting triumph abroad than he did at home, where from the first there were some robust masculine intellects, well represented by his fellow-novelist, Fielding, that refused to honour him. But how did this rather effeminate, dubiously pious, narrow-minded tradesman, past fifty when he turned author, come to be regarded, in one country after another, as the greatest novelist of the age? The answer is that he had some powerful allies: his peculiar skill in story-telling; the kind of story he chose to tell; and the spirit of the age itself, the *Zeitgeist*.

Richardson became a novelist almost by accident. The circumstances are important. Being a printer he was well acquainted with bookseller-publishers, and two of them commissioned him to write a series of "Familiar letters on the useful concerns of common life". Remembering a story he had heard of a virtuous young domestic servant who had resisted her master's attempts to seduce her, he decided to tell this story in letters, in the hope of creating "a new species of writing" that would turn young people away from the reading of improbable romances and so "promote the cause of religion and virtue". He began to read what he had written during the day to a growing and increasingly-admiring circle of ladies who met in the evening to exclaim and wonder and weep at what happened between Pamela and her Mr. B. It is this feminine audience, so immediately responsive to every tiny twist in the narrative, that taught Richardson his business as a novelist and brought him fame. It encouraged him to create what Coleridge later, comparing him un-favourably even as a moralist with Fielding, called his "close, hot, day-dreamy continuity". After *Pamela* came the far more ambitious *Clarissa*, in which seduction moves from the backstairs to the front and is now on a grander scale and tragic. The hapless, beautiful Clarissa, pursued relentlessly by the villain of all villains, Lovelace, spurned by her family, finally goes into a vast slow-motion decline and dies, inch by inch, of a broken heart. As one volume followed another, and one fine strand after another of the fatal web was woven around the doomed beauty (who, as spellbound as the reader, made little or no attempt to avoid her fate), strong men and tough women, who every day witnessed unmoved and without protests the kind of scenes we discover in Hogarth's drawings, dissolved into tears, hurriedly broke off to calm their agitation, begged the author, that inexorable magician, to save his heroine. Not only in England, where indeed some mighty eaters of beef and drinkers of claret and port, coarse fellows like Fielding, were left unmoved, but, through translation after translation, in one country after another, hearts were rent. But his last novel, the interminable *Sir Charles Grandison*, had different aims, being the story—and Richardson had it once as a possible title—of 'A Good Man'. There is no doubt about Sir Charles's goodness. It is described and admired without stint, as it might be in the endless chatter and gush of housekeepers, governesses, nurses, discussing over their tea the handsome young head of the family they serve. Which adoring girl is good enough for him? When and where will the marriage take place? What will everybody wear? It is not a novel about a man—there never was or could be such a man—but a novel about a foolish feminine middle-class dream of an aristocrat, the longest girl's novelette in the world.

From his early youth, as one of his admirers tells us, Richardson "was fond of two things, which boys have generally an aversion to: letter-writing, and the company of the other sex". Out of these two things, with the powerful aid of the *Zeitgeist*, he built his astonishing reputation as a novelist. By telling his story in letters he was able to do what women like to do, namely, to look at everything that happens from everybody's point of view. We learn, as we often do in some kinds of feminine company, what Kate thought about what Dick had said to Alice. Of this elaborate method Richardson is the supreme master. Not for nothing did he begin his career as a novelist by reading every evening to his ladies: he had a captive audience on which to test the method. This everybody-writing-to-everybody way of telling a story is of course the most wildly improbable of all; Clarissa writes long letters when she ought to be screaming for help; and at the crisis in her affairs everybody concerned must be writing and reading letters for twelve hours a day. But all this is beside the point. Richardson is not worried about probability. He is taking the reader out of the world, not into it. His main task is to create and then keep going that "close, hot, day-dreamy continuity" in which any reader, not deliberately unsympathetic, will soon suspend all disbelief, almost become hypnotised. For creating so successfully his own little hot-house world and its own semi-hypnotic slow-motion, he must be praised. But the extravagant praise lavished on him by Diderot and others, who ask us to admire his unique knowledge of the human heart, the truth of his characters, the nobility of his pathos, is mostly nonsensical. What is mistaken for real insight is simply a masterly understanding of the weaknesses of a feminine audience. His characters have some truth to themselves, as creatures moving in the hot-house, but open a window and they wither. The whole fantastically elaborate business of Clarissa and Lovelace, over which so many eighteenth-century readers wept, could only exist in an over-heated evangelical-erotic dreamland. A noble pathos is brief, involuntary, a sudden twisting of the hands, wringing of the heart: Hamlet's "Absent thee from felicity awhile" or Lear's "Pray you, undo this button". A pathos artfully spread over hundreds of pages, using every possible device to jerk a tear, is ignoble. It is sensibility for sensibility's sake; it is tears with tea and cake; it is the clever canting little printer at work on his foolish admiring ladies.

Yet the encyclopædic Diderot and the rest were no foolish admiring ladies. No, but they were products of an age that had been too one-sided, too masculine, too rational, too calm and unfeeling, and so was now ready to indulge its feminine side, inferior and negative, in an orgy of sensibility. One tainted unconscious, that which expresses itself in Richardson, calls to others, struggling to balance too much calm enlightenment. The calculatingly virtuous and sly Pamela, the strangely passive and passion-less Clarissa, do not represent woman herself, but only this inferior and negative femininity, far removed from a truly feminine realism, accep-tance of life, deep capacity for love, and contempt for a canting morality. This is the rejected feminine side of man at work and taking its revenge. The faint and pallid but persistent eroticism in these novels, so much unhealthier than Fielding's occasional coarseness, and suggesting that it has emerged from a cellar, belongs essentially to this inferior feminine side. So does any vitality possessed by the magnificently villainous Lovelace, who is a day-dreaming governess's idea of a thrillingly bad man. And on this view of him, it is not surprising that Richardson should soon have enjoyed a greater reputation abroad, especially in France, than he had at home, for by this time the age was more itself, in its one-sided emphasis upon consciousness and the intellect, among the clever French and the earnest Germans than it was among the more instinctive English. The tears that came gushing at his command were more refreshing nearer the desert of reason.

One of these more instinctive English, though he had a sound intellect, was Henry Fielding, a character who had nothing in common with Richardson except a desire to write novels. He belonged to a different class, the landed aristocracy, and largely wrote for a different class, having no hope of catering for Richardson's pious middle-class customers or of promoting virtue among their anxious sons and daughters. Having a living to earn, he turned to fiction after censorship had closed the theatres to him. His first novel, *Joseph Andrews*, began as a burlesque of Richard-son's *Pamela*, but once he had set his characters in motion (especially the glorious Parson Adams) Fielding was too good a novelist to continue a mere burlesque. Now he claimed to be producing something new in literature—a comic epic in prose. His next novel, the massive *Tom Jones*, is his largest and best example of the form. Fielding's last years were a struggle against ill-health—he died at forty-seven—and by this time he was a London magistrate (and a very good one too), and after *Tom Jones* he published only one more novel, the much slighter *Amelia*. But there is also his *History of the Life of the late Mr. Jonathan Wild the Great*, which is a mock appreciation of villainy and the finest piece of sustained irony in English outside the works of Swift. There is a great deal of irony elsewhere in Fielding, who, in spite of the bustle and knock-about comedy and caricaturing of minor characters in his fiction, is a novelist who demands to be read carefully. Behind the coarse and hearty realism of his usual scene, his immense panorama of roads and inn parlours and country houses and dingy town lodgings, is a solid masculine intellect, generally expressing itself in a grave irony, sometimes easily missed by hasty or stupid readers. His warmest admirers include a notable company of fellow-authors: Gibbon said his work would outlive the Escurial and the Hapsburgs (with whom Fielding could claim kinship); Coleridge declared that *Tom Jones* was one "of the three most perfect plots ever planned"; Byron called him "the prose Homer of human nature"; and Scott wrote that "Of all the works of the imagination to which English genius has given origin, the writings of Henry Fielding are perhaps most decidedly and exclusively her own". These are powerful testimonials.

There are two reasons why such tributes are worth recording here. First, because his reputation among English critics and readers is not what it was. Secondly, because his reputation and influence abroad were at no time equal to those of Richardson and Sterne. Unlike them, he made no contribution to the cult of sensibility, never asked for its tears. The women who flocked to more and more circulating libraries rarely went to ask for *Joseph Andrews* and *Tom Jones*. The new reading public, at home or abroad, was not Fielding's. Yet he had both a warmer heart and sounder morality than either Richardson or Sterne. He had a great dislike of the evangelical cant and formal piety of the class to which Richardson and his friends belonged, believing them to be responsible for much hypocrisy, in his opinion the worst of all vices. He was fond of contrasting generous if faulty natures, like his Tom Jones, with cold-hearted sanctimonious scoundrels. He had had a far wider experience of life than either Richardson or Sterne, had been familiar with people of all kinds, was equally at home either in London or the country, had a wonderfully sharp eye for all forms of rascality, cant and self-deception; but there was no cynicism or despair in him, though he believed the world to be crammed with knavery of all sorts ("It is easier," he said, "to make good men wise than to make bad men good"), and he was immediately responsive to any flash of genuine feeling, any indication of deep-lying goodwill. There is indeed behind his immense parade of grim ironic judgment, his classical worldliness, more than a suggestion of romantic morality, the test of the generous heart, the unperverted sympathetic imagination.

Fielding may be said to have been unlucky. Though nineteenth-century English critics generally hailed him as the first great novelist, who successfully attempted something quite new in literature, most critics and readers, especially those outside England, during the years following his death in 1754 probably held a contrary opinion, already considering him old-fashioned, not in line with the forward movement of the age. They had some excuse for believing this. His 'comic epic' definition of his novels; the essays, good as they are, interpolated as introductions; the rather stiff and self-conscious presentation of the fiction, as if it were not good enough to stand by itself: all this must have given him very soon an old-fashioned look, dating him back to an earlier period. And though there are not twenty years between most of his work and Sterne's, for example, his language too seems to belong to a much earlier period. Add to all this his lack of appeal to the new sensibility, to the inferior feminine side of the age, and it is easy to understand why outside England he has not had the prestige of Richardson and Sterne. Yet simply as a novelist representing his own age to ours, not as an influence on movements in fiction between his age and ours, Fielding is unquestionably the greatest of these three; and Tom Jones, to any masculine taste, the finest single achievement in fiction of the whole epoch. And he and his masterpiece are big enough and strong enough to endure neglect, to await the time when fashion will swing from introverted to extroverted novels and novelists, when comic characters and a general liveliness and bustle (together with occasional horseplay) no longer alienate critics, when readers with pretensions to intellect will not object to a certain masculine weight and thrust of intellect in their fiction.

In the library of the vicar of Coxwold, the Rev. Laurence Sterne, there was only one contemporary novelist, Fielding, but there were three editions of Cervantes, four of Montaigne, and no fewer than five of Rabelais. Clearly these were his masters. Yet in *Tristram Shandy* and *A Sentimental Journey* (which can be included here because it has as much fiction in it as travel), apart from a few minor devices, Sterne appears as a complete original. No matter what material he borrowed, he transmuted it into his own Shandean stuff. Some of it has worn badly. The empty pages and rows of asterisks and other cheap tricks in *Tristram Shandy* are more embarrassing than amusing. As he brought the book out in two small volumes at a time, writing as if for serial publication, he was inclined to give it a twist here, a turn there, purely for personal and topical reasons. His sniggering and rather adolescent little indecencies have lost any shock value they ever had, and now mostly seem merely unworthy of the writer, making us feel rather ashamed for his sake. More important still, his pathos, which seemed to his contemporaries as wonderful as his humour, no longer brings a tear to the eye. This is because, as it were, we can see him watching that eye, waiting for the tear. His pathos does not fail because it is so enormously and yet carefully expanded, as Richardson's was; it is sufficiently brief, but it is forced and has about it an air of calculation and showmanship, like so much in Sterne's own not very admirable character. He played on the new sensibility of the dying age. He is nothing if not sentimental, as the title of his travel-cum-fiction volume suggests. He talks too much about his heart to be ever really endangered by it. (Byron said of him: "He preferred whining over a dead ass to relieving a living mother". But so, in effect, did this whole age of sensibility, being, as it was, also an age of appalling and unchecked brutalities.) Finally, to link his name with Rabelais and Cervantes, as his contemporaries frequently did, is absurd. No doubt he read them constantly and with profit, but he is far below their size and weight, their range of genius, their depth of insight.

Nevertheless, he is something more than the literary jester and tumbler of Thackeray's description. Though no Rabelais, he is a humorist of genius, and, what is perhaps more important in this record, a literary innovator of the very highest order. Method, manner, style, all are completely original, completely different from those of any other author of his time, and seem astonishingly modern. So instead of the usual eighteenth-century lumbering or roundabout approach, he jumps straight into his narrative, such as it is. In place of the usual eighteenth-century *written* style, he gives us the very rhythm of intimate speech, in an inimitable style that combines a nervous force with an exquisite delicacy. Richardson and Fielding seem to be writing for people with far more leisure and patience than we have nowadays, but Sterne contrives and writes as if anticipating our modern impatience, cutting away all inessentials. This may seem queer praise of *Tristram Shandy*, in which it takes scores of chapters for the hero to get himself born, and the narrator wanders as the whim takes him, and there are more irrelevancies than anything else. But this of course is Sterne's humour, and if we take away most of his touches of affection and add a dash of bitterness or despair, it is largely the humour of our own time, certainly far closer to us moderns than it is to any of Sterne's contemporaries. He will omit weeks, months, then split a minute into its seconds, to concentrate on the tiniest significant details. Everything the Shandys have is in the way of everything else. The house is a nest of booby traps. The people cannot understand one another; there is no real communication; they are all at odds and ridiculous cross-purposes. Any attempt at conversation is a series of maddening misunderstandings: Mrs. Shandy neither knows nor cares what Mr. Shandy is talking about; Uncle Toby imagines Mr. Shandy is discussing artillery when in fact he is talking philosophy; and if Corporal Trim is called in, he will misunderstand everybody and march the talk in a new direction. Every one of them pursues his own ideas, mounted on his hobby-horse. No conclusion can ever be reached. Even their possessions seem to go their own way, as if they had a malicious elfin life of their own. In this queer household, the master of it, Mr. Shandy, exists in a permanent state of exasperation. Priding himself on his debating powers, having "one of the finest chains of reasoning in the world", he has a wife who does not know what he is talking about, is either stubbornly deaf to all argument or complacently agrees with him so that no argument is possible; and has a brother, Uncle Toby, who is no better, perhaps worse, because he has a habit of showing some gleam of interest, so that Mr. Shandy delightedly brings out his proofs, only to discover that Uncle Toby has suddenly lost all interest and is whistling 'Lillabullero'. Such a character only needs a slight twist to become tragic. This whole lack of communication could plunge us into despair. In our fiction, usually it does. But Sterne, with exquisite art, keeps it comic; and without over-playing sentiment, as he does in his *Sentimental Journey*, he suggests a strong family affection, and makes his chief characters, whom he creates in the round by a series of tiny strokes, as lovable as they are absurd. It is a book that would be improved now by judicious editing, pruning it of cheap tricks and topical nonsense; what remained would be a master-piece of brilliant comic writing, likely to be more fully appreciated today than it was two hundred years ago. So long as Sterne has a sparkle in his eye and not the tear of sensibility and sentiment, he is one of us.

For a long time another novelist, Tobias Smollett, was assumed to be the equal of Richardson, Fielding and Sterne. He is not, though he must be allowed a higher place than any other of their contemporaries. Before writing for a living he had been a surgeon's mate in the Navy and had seen a great deal of rough life, and much of it finds its way into his equally rough but droll *picaresque* novels, inspired by *Gil Blas*. His *Roderick Random* and *Peregrine Pickle* and *Humphry Clinker* (his most amiable and best work) had an admiring following, especially among boys and young men, for some generations, and had some influence upon Dickens in his earliest period. Until his last years, spent abroad, Smollett was compelled to undertake an immense amount of underpaid hack writing, like his friend and fellow ex-medical man, Oliver Goldsmith, who also toiled away in 'Grub Street', turning out volumes of biography, natural history, criticism, and innumerable miscellaneous articles and reviews. Yet Gold-smith, this galley-slave of the booksellers, was able to write not only his two comedies and some later verse that became famous, but also his one and equally famous novel, *The Vicar of Wakefield*. It tells, and carelessly too, an improbable story, largely set against a suspiciously vague idyllic background, but its charm and humour are irresistible, like everything that Goldsmith wrote for his own pleasure. He had a touch of genius; and Smollett, with all his faults, had a rare talent; and one died at the age of forty-six, the other at fifty; and though both were imprudent men, apt to overspend when they had money, and though both may have had constitutional weaknesses, it is probably safe to say that both had their lives cut short, robbing the world of their maturest work, because at one time they had had to write too much while eating too little.

The literary scene had changed completely during the past fifty years. Under Queen Anne, a poet, essayist or pamphleteer looked for a patron; the wits gathered in the coffee-houses were his most important critics; the reading public was comparatively small, but might be influential and directly rewarding. Monthly reviews and magazines did not exist, for the *Spectators* and *Tatlers* of Addison and Steele and their friends hardly come under this heading, though their European reputation and influence were much greater than anything achieved by the periodical writing that came later. But by the time Smollett and Goldsmith had left medicine for letters, the monthly reviews and magazines were everywhere, the publishers—though they were still called 'booksellers'—were commissioning, generally on shockingly bad terms, all manner of books, particularly informative works for the new reading public; every successful novel had its immediate imitators; the circulating libraries were multiplying and expanding; and in 'Grub Street' men and women of every sort, from a Goldsmith and a Smollett down to miserable hacks who only knew how to string a few words together, drudged away to feed themselves and the equally hungry printing presses. The great Dr. Johnson, whom everybody was soon to know intimately through the marvellously faithful reporting of his friend Boswell, had only lately emerged, into dignity and security, from this obscure slavery of the pen. Sterne, who had escaped this grim apprenticeship by jumping from his parsonage into fame, came playing Yorick, bowing and grimacing and philandering all round the town, on his way to Paris, where he would dine at Baron d'Holbach's and there be congratulated by Diderot and the other Encyclopædists. The new English novelist, following the new English novel, had arrived on the Continent; and in the London he had left and the Paris that was welcoming him, the literary scene, with all the elaborate business of supplying reading matter, from the dimmest and most dubious pieces of information up to work of high genius, was assuming a pattern, hardening into a shape, not very different from what we know today.

CHAPTER NINE

The Enlightenment

WE DO NOT KNOW where literature begins and ends. And even when we are certain that something is literature, we cannot be equally certain that we know how far its roots go and from what it draws its nourishment. The movement known as the 'Enlightenment', which had its home in France but reached out to all Europe and indeed further still, was not primarily a literary movement. The literature it created was a by-product. The work of its mathematicians, naturalists, political theorists, cannot be considered here, unless, as with Diderot, it breaks through into literature or may be said to have had strong literary influences. But the general movement itself cannot be ignored. Too much came out of it, and we have not done with it yet. The French Revolution, of course, owed much to the *philosophes* of the Enlightenment. though they were not themselves politicians and did not concern themselves with political action. We are apt to forget, however, that something even more important to us today came out of the eighteenth century of the Enlightenment, namely, the American Revolution. If the vast American continent, the wide rich land itself, able to feed and shelter uncounted millions of immigrants, is the mother of the United States, then the father, the creative *logos*, is the characteristic thought of this movement and its era—the concepts of freedom, equality, tolerance, a refusal to believe that war is inevitable, the idea that men inspired by these concepts can progress by giant strides. The note of brisk rationalistic optimism sounded in the American Constitution might have been heard, almost any night in the mid-eighteenth century, in the *salons* of Madame Geoffrin and Mlle. de Lespinasse or round the dinner tables of Baron d'Holbach and Helvétius.

The three great figures of the movement are undoubtedly Voltaire,

Diderot and Rousseau. Nevertheless, we shall leave one of them, Rousseau, for consideration in Part III, where he belongs because of his tremendous influence upon the Romantics. He is really the figure that bestrides the transition from this age to the next, which explains, apart from his various personal weaknesses, why Voltaire and the *philosophes* viewed him with mistrust: when they looked at him they were looking beyond their own age, into the next. (The contemporary French term, *philosophes*, is worth keeping, not only because this is how these men were known, in and out of France, but also because to call them 'philosophers' would suggest they were metaphysical rivals of a Leibniz or a Kant when in fact they were not metaphysicians at all.) Voltaire and Diderot, then, are our men. They are very different but may be seen against the same fantastic background. It is fantastic because its elements are so wildly mixed. The Paris of Voltaire's plays and tales and Diderot's Encyclopædia is an incredible city. It represents all that is most luxurious in a highly artificial age, and yet is almost bankrupt and is surrounded by starvation and despair. Louis XV's mistress, Madame de Pompadour, encourages him to waste fortunes, often on idle entertainment, and yet is herself a cultivated woman, ready to befriend men of letters. Boucher is painting his dainty marquises, while round the corner, before a crowd of all ranks, a man is having boiling lead poured over him before being torn to pieces by wild horses. Some of the drawing-rooms and supper-tables are loud with scientific discussion and arguments between liberal deists and atheistic materialists, yet at any moment the Jesuits may strike, officers bearing a *lettre de cachet* may arrive, and one of the theorists may be removed to the Bastille. The new age of reason and the fifteenth century seem to jostle each other in this city, where there is at once more progress and more reaction than in any other capital in Western Europe. A Montesquieu can be laying the foundation of modern political science, a Buffon can begin exploring and recording all natural history, a d'Alembert can produce his treatises on dynamics, a d'Holbach enlarge upon his dogma of determinism and atheism, all within a society still officially committed to a despotic monarchy and the most rigid and bigoted ecclesiastical censorship. Books may be burned by the common hangman, authors hurried away to prison, unbelievers threatened with torture; yet Louis XV, idling among his girls, is almost as ready to cancel a *lettre de cachet* as to sign one; Marmontel finds himself with a comfortably furnished room and an excellent dinner in the Bastille; the gayer gentlemen in holy orders arrange elaborate seductions and adulteries; the powdered and beribboned aristocratic ladies argue and quarrel not only about the latest poem or play but also about religion, the rise of civilisation, the origin of life; and a rich kind-hearted Madame de Geoffrin, with no pretensions to culture or science herself, can spend much of her time and most of her money entertaining and helping to support the *philosophes*, the most dangerous men in the country. One or two of them may have to leave the country at any moment, but the age is well supplied with eccentric despots ready to receive them. So Frederick the Great flatters Voltaire into staying with him, and Diderot spends months with the Empress Catherine of Russia, arguing with her at length every evening. In our time Bernard Shaw visited Stalin, but not on these easy terms. He would have done better—or much worse—in this fantastic eighteenth century.

Earlier than d'Holbach, a young man called La Mettrie, in *L'homme-machine*, had advanced the theory that man was simply an automaton, with an enthusiasm rarely found among automata. In advanced intellectual circles—though Voltaire declared himself outside them in this matter—it was generally held not merely that man should be guided by reason, to which Voltaire would have readily agreed, but that, having been produced by an entirely material universe, itself a great machine, man is a kind of little machine, with no claim to immortality and only a mere verbal one to a soul or mind. And if we believe that whatever is built too high, unbalanced or one-sided in consciousness will be compensated for in the unconscious, which will produce the opposite in an inferior form, we might expect to discover in the intimate lives of these people, behind the be-wigged masks, a compulsive emotionalism, all the ecstasies and miseries of romantic passion, the ravages of mad infatuations. And this is what we do find, beginning with the nervous frenzies and amorous antics of Voltaire, the tearful literary taste of Diderot, and culminating in the tragically impassioned correspondence, the appalling secret life, of that smiling hostess of the *philosophes*, Julie de Lespinasse. Already the next age was being formed in these disturbed hidden depths, which even now were beginning to shape and colour the romantic image of Western Man. No wonder its prophet, Rousseau, was not much liked.

It could be argued that Voltaire was cudgelled into greatness. His talent and facility brought him immediate success as a poet and dramatist; he had a pension from the Court, and was a favourite of its glittering society. But he made one witticism too many at the expense of one of its members, the Chevalier de Rohan-Chabot, who hired some toughs to give him a cudgelling. It was not the beating itself but his reception afterwards by his aristocratic acquaintances that angered Voltaire. They received him coldly; the police refused to take any action. But they took action when the Chevalier and his influential family learnt that Voltaire was taking fencing lessons; they removed Voltaire to the Bastille, after which he left for England. His knowledge of English thought, chiefly represented by Locke and Newton, and of English political institutions was never profound, but it served, if only as ammunition in his campaign against Versailles. After that his long years of retirement with his learned mistress, Madame du Châtelet, gave him the reputation of being not only a great man of letters but also a supreme *philosophe*, a master of all the new, exciting, dangerous knowledge. Her death left him free to accept Frederick's invitation to live in Potsdam; and his fantastic relations with the Prussian King and Court were the talk of Europe. Finally, retiring to Ferney, where he was secure from arrest because he was so close to Switzerland, rich and famous, living into an astonishingly protracted old age, all the more astonishing because his health had never been good and more than once he had felt he was about to die, with all his powers not merely unimpaired but actually strengthened, he conducted a political-social-philosophical campaign unique in its force and magnitude. "*Écrasez l'infâme*," he screamed; and all Europe heard him. If he had been allowed to return to Paris, had been restored to anything that looked like favour at Versailles, and these were temptations he was never quite proof against, he might have lost his immense authority; but Bourbon stupidity, one of the great monuments of the age, held out to the end; so Voltaire remained at Ferney, until his last triumphant entrance into Paris, just before his death, like a sort of independent monarch of the intellect, an emperor of deadly mockery.

Neither before nor since his time has any author dominated his society as Voltaire did during the last twenty-five years of his life. (How many millions of us have been set to draw, in our art classes, the plaster cast of that impish sardonic old face!) Erasmus comes nearest, of earlier authors. Later, though Goethe and Tolstoy had a richer creative genius, they never reached his commanding fame as European figures; and Anatole France and Bernard Shaw look like pale copies of him. His energy and copiousness were as formidable as his reputation. Plays, poems, philosophical tales, histories, essays, letters by the thousand (14,000 are known), came in an unending flashing stream from him. It was not a calm acceptance of reason in all things that gave him this prodigious energy. He owes much of it to the furious contradictions in his nature, for with all his great qualities he was also unscrupulous, vain, jealous, untruthful, and lewd. But the energy released by interior explosions was used to fight for reason, to seek out, challenge and denounce superstition, bigotry and intolerance, all misuse of power, all obstacles to free enquiry and discussion, all claims, sacred or secular, to be above criticism, and all excuses for war. His hatred of war, which he ridiculed and condemned over and over again, seems to us now one of history's ironies, for Voltaire helped to bring about the French Revolution, which in turn helped to create more and bigger wars, far more extensive and murderous than any wars his age had known, and pointed the way, via the armed nation and the idea of total war, to the mass slaughter and global lunacies of our own age, on a scale to drive ten Voltaires out of their minds. But Voltaire in his own time, though he had his frenzied moments, kept his wits, and systematically and gleefully used them to lash the cruelties, irrational privileges and follies of Church, State and society. He was from first to last a writer, asking only for pen and paper, but his performance and its effect were so tremendous that he seems to us now, as a figure in history, less like an author and more like some great man of action.

Indeed, at our distance from him, his purely literary achievements may seem disappointing. We can ignore his seven-volume *Dictionnaire philosophique* and all else in that vein. His plays we have already noticed. His verse at its best has elegance, wit, sense, agreeable fancy, almost every merit except that of being poetry. His criticism of the drama is obviously inferior to Lessing's. And though he could write witty good sense about the literature he understood, he shows no special critical insight and there was too much he did not understand. He was much better as an historian, first in his *History of Charles XII* (of Sweden), 1731, then, twenty years later, in his *Age of Louis XIV*, this being his most considerable history, though neither his last nor most ambitious. It has been said with some truth that the writing of history, as we know it today, begins with these two books, especially with the account of Louis and his age. With Voltaire as historian we take leave of the old laborious and narrow chronicles of kings and their wars, we begin the wide surveys of men in general, their movements and manners, to which we are now accustomed. And his style, easy yet lucid, flowing yet pointed, is as original, as new for this subject, as his outlook.

It is possible that David Hume, who had been in France as early as 1734, owed something as an historian—but not as a philosopher, for in this capacity his intellect far outranged Voltaire's—to Voltaire's broad approach and lucid exposition. It was in Paris, where in 1763 he became secretary to the British Embassy, that Hume enjoyed his greatest social triumphs, being lionised not only by the *philosophes* but also by the exquisite ladies of the *salons*, aiming their sparkling glances, as we are told, at his broad, placid Scots face. All this enthusiasm, even though it involved him in some embarrassing social antics, was in sharp contrast to the neglect he had suffered in England; and perhaps the difference between the English and French treatment of authors and authorship is well suggested by some insolent remarks made by Horace Walpole to Hume in Paris: "You know in England we read their works, but seldom or never take notice of authors. We think them sufficiently paid if their books sell, and of course leave them in their colleges and obscurity, by which means we are not troubled with their vanity and impertinence." This observation, itself a piece of vanity and impertinence, owes something to Walpole's jealousy of Hume's success, but it was not untrue when it was made, on 11th November 1766, and it is not untrue today. There was a feline as well as a foppish streak in Horace Walpole, but he had more sense and judgment, especially of public affairs, than he is generally credited with; his *Letters* are a wonderful introduction to the high society, manners and gossip of this age, and, unlike the glances of Hume's admiring ladies in their lost world, these letters still sparkle at us today.

Voltaire's comparatively brief and brisk historical studies may be closer to the taste of our own time than any other eighteenth-century histories, but the age has a greater and even more truly representative historian than Voltaire. This is Edward Gibbon, a late arrival in the age but one of its immortal voices, just as his *Decline and Fall of the Roman Empire* is one of its imperishable classical monuments. It is like a vast winding procession, unresting, unhurrying. Though the age of reason came to an end while Gibbon was still writing the later (and somewhat inferior) volumes of his great history, he and his work remain fixed in it. This is how a thousand years of human affairs look to a rational scholar, who has assembled most of the facts. Gibbon has definite limitations. It is doubtful if he begins to understand religious feeling, and it is this gap in his understanding that makes his account of the rise of Christianity, though it is diabolically clever, one-sided and untrustworthy. Again, there seems something rather absurd about his style, just as there does about Gibbon himself, a strutting fat little man; but a closer acquaintance with both of them increases our respect. This man triumphantly completed his task, like building a city with one pair of hands; and all in a style that has something of Rome's own ponderous manner and yet is also pointed and slyly ironical to fit and please his own time; a style that looks easy to imitate but can only be poorly parodied and degraded; a style that has a classical air to suit the subject and yet is very personal to the historian. And except to fanatical opponents of Gibbon's religious scepticism, his *Decline and Fall of the Roman Empire* remains one of the greatest historical works produced by Western Man.

No, it is not in his histories, good as they are, that Voltaire fully earns the immense literary reputation he enjoyed. It is in a form now out of fashion but very much the vogue in his own time—the philosophical tale, generally with an Eastern setting. The eighteenth century, as much of its furniture and decoration proves, was fascinated by the East—or by its own rather vague idea of the East—and in France, as early as 1721, Montesquieu in his *Persian Letters* had made satire-in-Eastern-masquerade effective and popular. Voltaire may have learnt the trick from Montesquieu but he improved on it. He also tried to improve on Swift in his *Micromegas*, in which a colossal giant from Sirius visits the earth, but though he is sharper and more personal than Swift, he has not Swift's force and weight, his terrible universal irony. Though they can be read and enjoyed as tales—*Zadig* and *Candide* especially—these things of Voltaire's are far outside the novel; they are not about people in a recognisable society; they are vehicles, in a popular acceptable form, of his satire and irony, the light cavalry of his army invading superstition, bigotry, despotism, intolerance. (If Voltaire were alive now, he would probably be writing detective stories, among other things, and there is a chapter in *Zadig*, showing his hero's power of deductive reasoning, that suggests they would have been very good detective stories.) His masterpiece in this form is, of course, *Candide*, which he is said to have written in a few days. It is probably far more widely read and appreciated at the present time, which has no difficulty in matching its most pessimistic passages, than it was during the nineteenth century. It is a curious work, impossible to explain as just another sally in his endless campaigning. [There is the obvious satire of Leibniz's "best of all possible worlds"; there is his usual and tireless mockery of religious persecution, war, and the rest; there is the extra horror, not man-made this time, contributed by the then recent Lisbon earthquake; but in addition, behind the easy mockery of the narrative, which has a brisk movement from disaster to disaster that is itself a kind of irony, there yawn depths of disgust and disillusion inexplicable in terms of his customary philosophical and satirical writing. Voltaire never favoured an easy optimism—it is indeed in *Candide* and elsewhere one of his chief targets—but he generally held the view that if men made sensible Church and State reforms, put an end to persecution, adopted rational institutions and a liberal outlook, preferred reason to prejudice, then a good life might be possible for them. But in *Candide* this possibility seems to have vanished. Humanity itself is mostly vile, wickeder than many fervent believers in original sin would imagine it to be. And what men have left untouched, to blossom for a while, a malignant Chance will wreck and ruin. So what is the use even of cultivating one's garden in Candide's world, when disaster is inevitable? To show us such a world is not to make a plea for reason and tolerance, for what it demands, to be endured at all, is an iron stoicism or a permanently numbed sensitivity. *Candide* is Voltaire almost at the end of his tether. If we compare the whole tone and spirit of it with what we find, for instance, in his *Treatise on Toleration*, which begins with—and is really based on—a statement of the Calas case (John Calas, a decent elderly Protestant, was falsely accused of murdering his Catholic son, actually a suicide, and then tortured and executed; the whole family were the victims of hysterical intolerance, and Voltaire fought their case for years), we see that *Candide* is not, so to speak, a campaign document, just another attack, but is mockery dissolving into utter despair. It is a bright rationality cracking like thin ice, to give us a glimpse of the black depths. It is this despair and these depths that make it popular again today. But the people who welcome it, unlike Voltaire, have not been fighting endless one-man battles against superstition, bigotry, and intolerance.]

Excluding Rousseau, to be considered later, the next most important figure of the Enlightenment after Voltaire is undoubtedly Denis Diderot. The great instrument of the Enlightenment was the *Encyclopédie*, originally begun as a publishing enterprise borrowed from England. There had been a number of earlier attempts to provide readers with works of universal knowledge, usually in dictionary form, but the *Cyclopaedia, or an Universal Dictionary of Arts and Sciences*, published in two volumes by Ephraim Chambers in 1728, was more ambitious and systematic than any earlier work because of its cross-references. The French *Encyclopédie, ou Dictionnaire raisonné des Sciences, des Arts et des Métiers*, though taking its start from the English compilation, was more ambitious still and ran to 28 volumes, between 1751 and 1765. Its early volumes were quickly suppressed, and then it began to lead an underground existence. All the *philosophes* contributed to it, but the man who had to do most of the work, both as editor and contributor, was Diderot. It is easy to say, strictly speaking, what Diderot was not, for he was not really a scientist, he was not technically a philosopher, he was not a novelist or dramatist of any great talent, he was not actually a man of letters of real distinction, and even his friends admitted that he was always too enthusiastic and in too much of a hurry to correct his faulty gift of expression. He could not have written the preliminary discourse to the *Encyclopédie* as well as the mathematical d'Alembert did; and he has not the easy flow of his contributor, Marmontel, whose *Moral Tales* were widely read throughout Europe for many years, and whose memoirs, written in old age, give a very pleasant, if obviously idealised, picture of a country childhood in the earlier eighteenth century. Yet Diderot emerges as the most considerable figure in his group. He seems to reach forward to our own world. A lot of things, important now, appear to date from him. His editorial labours, his central position in the group, and his tremendous zest for ideas, together seem to produce in him a profound intuitive feeling for what is germinal and of widening and deepening significance. This explains the growth of his reputation. Though he cannot be placed exactly —and is so unlike a monumental author that most of his best things were only properly published long after his death—he has a looming if indistinct importance: he is a figure not steadily illuminated but either half-lost in the blur of two centuries or suddenly and brilliantly lit by some flash of genius.

Here are some examples of the way in which he seems to reach forward to us. Though educated by the Jesuits, he early turned deist, and then became a thorough materialist (a metaphysical one, not a materialist by temperament, for thought was his passion) and atheist. And much of his thought after that seems to anticipate the dialectical materialism afterwards elaborated by Marx and Engels. Indeed, though nobody could be less like the typical Communist intellectual than Diderot, so enthusiastic, impetuous, emotional, his varied criticism has in it a suggestion of the 'socialist realism' of Soviet critics. This is particularly true of his periodical art criticism, a form of journalism he may be said to have invented. It came into existence through his friend Grimm, a German who lived in Paris and long supported himself by sending a monthly letter, giving news of literature and the arts in Paris, to private subscribers, mostly German princes. To these cultural news-letters Diderot contributed criticisms of the picture exhibitions in the Salon. Their æsthetics are dubious and they are not the kind of art criticism much appreciated now, outside 'socialist realist' circles, but such was Diderot's enthusiasm, both in praise and blame, and so apt was he in communicating his pleasure at what he thought a fine picture (he greatly admired Greuze, and very frequently attacked Boucher and Fragonard), that his art criticisms when published became extremely popular, and, years later, even Carlyle refers to them, with a few German exceptions, as "the only Pictorial Criticisms worth reading". In the theatre his own two plays are of no importance; Diderot was no dramatist; but here as elsewhere he did some pioneer work in criticism and theory, and Lessing wrote that he owed his own change of taste, towards realism, to Diderot, whose two plays and Essay on Dramatic Poetry he translated. And the best eighteenth-century discussion of acting can be found in Diderot's *Le Paradoxe sur le Comédien*, in which he argues that an actor can best move his audience not, as was thought then, when he allows himself to be gripped by an emotion but when he keeps his head and simulates the emotion. He is excellent, too, on the danger of over-emphasis, the dramatic value of silence, the necessity of establishing through constant rehearsal a balance between players. His direct experiments in fiction were not successful; he tried to follow Richardson in his novel *The Nun*, and Sterne in *Jacques the Fatalist*, which Goethe admired and which contains at least one story, that of Madame de Pommeraye's revenge on her lover, that has offered a powerful plot to later authors. But his admiration for these two novelists, his understanding of new techniques and interests in fiction, combined as they were with his interest in and knowledge of many crafts and trades, acquired through writing articles about them for the *Encyclopédie*, make us feel that he is already pointing the way to the sharply realistic fiction a hundred years ahead. And indeed, in one of his innumerable occasional pieces, his most extraordinary production, he pointed much further still, to our own century.

This piece, a long dialogue but sometimes referred to as a novel, is *Rameau's Nephew*. It had an odd history. Twenty years after Diderot's death, Schiller gave Goethe a manuscript copy of it that had probably been given to him by Grimm. Goethe translated it into German, then returned the manuscript to Schiller. But Schiller died shortly afterwards, and then the manuscript disappeared. For years it seemed that *Rameau's Nephew* only existed in Goethe's German translation. Then in 1823 Diderot's daughter produced a copy, but there was some doubt about its being genuine. It was in fact not until 1891 that the original manuscript was found and all doubts settled. There had never been any doubt among good judges that in its own way *Rameau's Nephew* is Diderot's master-piece. Its form suggests his limitations as an artist; if Voltaire had been visited by these thoughts he would have found some better form in which to display them, probably that of his philosophical stories. But the dialogue, in which he dramatises himself talking to this impudent scoundrel, the nephew of Rameau, was probably more than a convenient literary form to Diderot. It helped him to discover, to face, to express, the shadow-side of his own mind. Not all the dialogue is on this profound level. Some of it merely attacks enemies of the *Encyclopédie* like Fréron and Palissot; and the first version of the dialogue was probably written just after the production in 1760 of Palissot's comedy satirising Diderot and his friends. Some of it is concerned with the intense rivalry between the French and Italian schools of music. There is indeed much of the dialogue devoted to topical subjects, and very amusing it is. But its originality, force and phosphorescent brilliance belong elsewhere. Rameau's nephew was a real person, and Diderot was later accused of making him appear a great deal worse than he actually was. This could never have been said by anybody with the slightest appreciation of the work. Rameau's nephew here, though no doubt sharing some traits and a style of life with the real person, is essentially Diderot's creation. The dialogue wherever it is most brilliant and original is between the Diderot known to his friends and the public, the man who risked a return to the Bastille and toiled for years at the *Encyclopédie*, who devoted his life to the Enlightenment, and the other Diderot nobody knew, the *alter ego*, the Shadow, whispering and chuckling like Mephistopheles in the dark. We are seeing the shining medal reversed. Something had happened to Diderot. It may have been the impact of his love for Sophie Voland, an exceptional woman with whom he could be completely frank—a significant fact that appals his most prudish biographer, John Morley—and whose combination of masculine and feminine qualities delighted him. Whatever crisis it was, out of it came this tremendous dialogue, in which all the brilliant wit, daring and originality are given to the con-fessions and brazen arguments of the parasite, the shameless preyer on a society that is in its turn both predatory and without shame; in which we seem to catch a glimpse of a sinister regress spiralling down to some eternal darkness of the spirit, infinitely removed from the bright surface of Diderot's rational optimism, altruism, alert social conscience, reasonable benevolence. It is a work that does not seem to belong to this age of reason, nor to the following age of romance already beginning to take shape, nor to the one following that. It appears to leap forward two centuries, to this very time of ours, when what was lying in the dark then has come blinking and grinning into the glare of our lights, when you may take up half a dozen novels, in the movement and much admired, and find as their central character, hardly different except for a change of costume and style of dialogue and a decline in wit, no other than Rameau's nephew.

Diderot, in whom all the minds of the Enlightenment seem to meet, to share something of his enthusiasm and natural warmth of heart, lived until the high summer of 1784. In the last conversation his daughter remembered, he said: "The first step towards philosophy is incredulity." A little later, at the dining-table, his wife asked him a question, and then, when she received no reply, she looked at him and saw that he was dead. It was probably the only question Diderot had left unanswered for the last fifty years. He had tried to answer all the questions, in his attractive, impetuous fashion; and yet, when he was getting old and putting an end to a series of notes on anatomy that he had been collecting for years, he could write: "What do I perceive? Forms. And what besides? Forms. Of the substance I know nothing. We walk among shadows, ourselves shadows to ourselves and to others." By this time, the age at an end, Pope's "order'd garden" where all was light could no longer be recognised; strange weeds covered it and among them flowers, scarlet or deathly white, began to bloom mysteriously; and above it the moon was rising, to create fantastic shadows, in which reason was lost to romance.

PART THREE

Shadows of the Moon

10 Rousseau and the Romantic Age   113

11 Germany and Goethe   122

12 The English Romantics   139

13 The Romantic Movement in France   159

14 Russians and Others   173

CHAPTER TEN

Rousseau and the Romantic Age

IT WAS INEVITABLE that Jean-Jacques Rousseau should have quarrelled bitterly with Voltaire and the Encyclopædists. As Lytton Strachey has pointed out: ". . . he possessed one quality which cut him off from his contemporaries, which set an immense gulf betwixt him and them: he was modern . . . he belonged to another world." We are still living in the world that owes much, for good or evil, to Rousseau; but the age that flourished just after his death in 1778, the Romantic Age, owed a great deal more to him: its most characteristic attitudes of mind either were imitated from him or were exaggerations of various attitudes of his. It is not a matter of vague influences but of direct inspiration: the Romantics, first in Germany, then in England, later in France and elsewhere, discovered in him their prophet. No doubt the Age of Reason, decaying to make room for its opposite, would sooner or later have been succeeded by an Age of Romance, even if there had been no Rousseau, but he hurried on the process of transformation; he was the catalyst. So large was Rousseau's legacy to romantic literature that, before estimating it, we had first better dispose of those elements in later eighteenth-century life that contributed to the Romantic Age without the intervention of Rousseau.

These elements belong to the natural reaction against the Age of Reason, against the over-valuation of consciousness, against what was rational, general, abstract, public, existing only in daylight, not in the dark. A one-sided attitude, if persisted in, inevitably produces its opposite, equally one-sided. Too much dependence upon reason sooner or later inspires the glorification of unreason. So the later eighteenth century ushers in a new and widespread interest in the occult; it was a time when pseudo-mystical secret societies flourished all over Europe, when charlatans like Cagliostro found their way into the highest society, when alchemy and astrology, love-philtres and elixirs of youth, became fashionable and profitable again, as in the Renaissance. These new or revived tastes owed nothing directly to Rousseau but ultimately contributed something to romantic literature.

Again, when in 1765 Thomas Percy published his *Reliques of Ancient English Poetry*, revealing long-forgotten treasures of medieval romance and ballad poetry, he opened a door for many later romantic poets, especially in England and Germany; and this new interest in medieval life and literature had nothing to do with Rousseau. It is easy, however, to over-estimate the importance of this discovery of the Middle Ages to the Romantic Movement, as Heine and many others have done. The Movement was not set going, as they have suggested, by this discovery. The Romantic Age did not depend upon its use of medieval scenery and costumes. It could—and often did in its more important manifestations—exist without them. It needed a dream-world, and found one in the Middle Ages, or at least in what it chose to take from medieval life; but what is fundamental here is not its particular choice of a dream-world but the fact that some kind of dream-world was necessary at all. The romantic poets were not medieval scholars; they were men who wanted to present the drama and mystery, ecstasy or agony, of their inner life in the outward terms, the symbolical trappings, of a world very different from the one in which they and their readers found themselves. It might be a simplified and idealised Middle Ages, an Ancient Greece conjured out of its statuary and ceramics, Arcadia or fairyland, or an Arabian Nights version of the East; and no matter which, so long as it was remote, strange, at least half-magical, to suggest the secret life of the soul. And it is significant that the grand prophet of romanticism, Rousseau himself, did not find it necessary to turn medievalist. He did not need any dream of the Middle Ages; his own romanticism was such that, whenever he felt like it, he could turn the France of Louis XV and Choiseul, even though they may have given orders for his arrest, into Arcadia. He carried his own Arcadia about with him. And while smiling marquises in fancy dress played at being there, such was the force of his unconscious drives, over-whelming consciousness with dream-images, that what was play to them could become to him reality, enabling him to leave his stamp for several generations not only upon literature but also upon political theory.

The poets who followed Rousseau, creating in literature this Romantic Age, found the world about them increasingly difficult to present directly and to interpret in Rousseau's own romantic terms. For now modern life began. This was the age of the Industrial Revolution, of new economic and political forces, of rapidly growing and darkening cities, of widening divisions between different classes and types of readers. A poet is now no longer a member of society who happens to write poetry. Literature no longer represents society's expression of itself in well-chosen words, which any intelligent member of that society can enjoy. The poet is now sharply conscious of himself as a different kind of man. He has no well-defined and widely recognised place in the community, is no longer, whatever his fame may be, a public man, like a statesman, a general, a rich banker or manufacturer. In the increasing complexity of communal life, some-how he has been squeezed out; and this in turn, whether he regards him-self as an exile, a rebel, a prophet—and most romantic poets assumed all three roles at some time or other—compels him to be more and more private and personal, less and less a public spokesman, broadly expressing in literature the society of his time, and to declare that nothing has value to him except what he discovers in the depths of his own personality. It would not be true to say that Rousseau was outside all this, for the root of it is in him; but the world changed far more rapidly and dramatically after his death than it did during his lifetime, and if, as we must believe, there would have been a Romantic Age, reacting against the previous Age of Reason, even if Rousseau had never existed, it is certain that these changes would have had the same effect upon the romantic poets. And indeed these effects are still with us, having long outlasted the force of Rousseau's direct influence. We are now far removed from his spell, may never give him a thought, whereas we take it for granted that the poet, whether he is above, below, or eccentrically away from it, is not planted solidly in the centre of our society.

All those critics who have tried to explain the difference between the Classical and the Romantic would have saved much time, temper and paper if they had been acquainted with the discoveries of depth psychology. For the Classical depends upon conscious mind, the Romantic upon the unconscious. So each misjudges the other: the Classical considers the Romantic unbalanced, childish, mad; the Romantic sees the Classical as drearily formal, tedious, lifeless. When either is hopelessly one-sided, it moves towards death; the Classical, deprived of zestful energy, dying of anaemia and boredom; the Romantic, losing all contact with reality, destroying itself in madness. When Rousseau was dying, after suffering for years from persecution mania, he thought himself "alone on the earth" and condemned to be alone for eternity. The fantasies of the unconscious had invaded his consciousness; he was living in a dream, or indeed a nightmare, out of which he could not wake himself. Not only his outlook and opinions but the major events of his life, the very shape of it, had been dominated by his unconscious. He lived the romanticism he was to bequeath to the age that followed him. His life and work, as Romain Rolland observes, "offer in literary history the case, perhaps unique, of a man of genius, upon whom genius descended not only unsolicited, but against his will". Will belongs to the conscious mind; the genius of Rousseau exploded from the unconscious. He describes the very moment of this explosion, on a hot summer day on the road to Vincennes, where he was going to visit Diderot, who was imprisoned there. He was thirty-seven, and had spent years wandering and idling and brooding, making little use of his quite able conscious mind, but storing energy, stoking up the boilers, so to speak, in his unconscious. Then in an instant, as he tells us, he lived in another world, he became another man. 'Great truths' descended upon him in a torrent; he saw in a flash his life's work. A prophet was born. The shy Swiss idler became an impassioned orator, an author of great force and originality, whose influence was so strong and far-reaching that a massive genius like Tolstoy, a century later, could declare himself to be inspired by Rousseau's teaching and example. The immediate effect of his political and social discourses, and his didactic fiction and confessions, was electrical. It was as if, by-passing the wary and dubious conscious mind, unconscious called to unconscious. But then of course the time was ready: the solution had been prepared, and here was the catalyst.

There are elements in Rousseau, reaching from Kant to Marx, that must be ignored here, but sufficient is left to show how much the Romantic Age owed to Rousseau's unconscious bursting like a dam. It is not that all the romantic poets and story-tellers wished to imitate him; we are not considering here an ordinary literary influence; but what was released in him soon came, with of course many individual differences and developments, to be released in them. So the age represents first the reaction and then the triumph of the unconscious, challenging and then defeating the rational conscious mind. The medal was not re-fashioned but merely reversed. What had been formerly admired was now despised; what had been distrusted and feared was now exalted. Created in this way, Romantic Western Man is as unbalanced and one-sided as Rational Western Man had been. There is, however, one important difference. In the previous age, the authors were expressing the society of their time; Molière and Louis XIV, as we have seen, had more or less the same outlook; Pope the poet and John Churchill, Duke of Marlborough, knew they were living in the same world. But when we come to the Romantic Age, we are no longer concerned with the character of a whole society but only with one small, though deeply significant, part of it; so that, for example, Chateaubriand the Romantic and Napoleon have not at all the same outlook; and Byron the poet and Arthur Wellesley, Duke of Wellington, seem to be living in two very different worlds. Literature has begun to move away from the general society of its time; and this oblique movement, as we shall see, now continues down to our own day.

Everything released by the explosion of Rousseau's unconscious, creating romanticism, must necessarily be intensely private, never general and public. So the romantic writer, like Rousseau, is not at home in society. He must discover himself in solitude, far from salons and cities, musing in the forest, lost in reverie among the mountains or on the sea-shore. He is not trying to express what men in general are thinking and feeling, not seeking any common denominator. It is what arises from the depths of his own being—really whatever comes from the unconscious—that deserves expression, which means that, when all is well with his genius, he will in fact discover for us original and profound truths, states of mind never described before, hidden treasures of the soul, but that, when he is below his best, he will tend to be merely affected, egoistic, even touched with megalomania. Exploring himself, he will give us what is either far richer and more valuable than common-sense or considerably worse, just nonsense. This is the risk the romantic writer and his readers run. But it is worth running because the romantic writer in his moments of genius illuminates, with an effect that is magical, the reader's own depths. For that balance of thought and feeling understood by the conscious mind and the classical writer, the Romantic, who sees nothing in this balance but tedium and lifelessness, substitutes the sense of infinity, the sudden ecstasy justifying all the mere mechanics of living, the supreme magical moment.

So the Romantic, following both Rousseau's practice and precept, seeks solitude and reverie. He is a wanderer, like the remote ancestors stirring in his unconscious; to become a settled member of a society is to frustrate his genius. Though longing for the most intensely sympathetic relationship with another soul, in undying love, eternal friendship, he is for ever being misunderstood, the world of men being the wretched thing it is, and almost welcomes the persecution that for poor Rousseau became a nightmare mania. Now the young child is only struggling into full consciousness and still enjoys a profoundly satisfying relation, through the unconscious, with Nature, like the *participation mystique* of primitive men; so to the Romantics, again following Rousseau, the child is no longer a half-grown man or woman, the young of our species, but the archetypal holy innocent, whose joy and unthinking wisdom we should try to recapture if only for a moment, whose happiness irradiates a lost world. So the cult of childhood begins. A companion figure to the holy child is the unspoilt savage, the dusky Arcadian, flower-crowned in some Eden of the South Seas or the Amazonian jungle, whose very existence proves how hollow and false our boasted civilisation is. It is true that the literary members of this cult did not take leave of civilisation to share the lives of these glorious creatures—for they could hardly expect to find them on walking tours or visits to Italy—but they lived with them in imagination and various editions of their works. And again, Rousseau, whose political theory is haunted by this dream, began it.

The magical images of the unconscious are projected by the Romantic on Nature and Woman. What seemed 'a horrid wilderness' to the Age of Reason, which hurried through it in search of roast chicken and clean linen, is now welcomed as a reflection, beautiful or terrible, of the beauty or storm in the Romantic's soul. Nature, especially when remote from traffic and agriculture, responds like a devoted mistress to his every mood. Oceans and mountains, forest and heath, provide the enchanted scenery for his unending drama of the defiant lonely spirit. But somewhere across the ocean or beyond the mountains is the Woman for whom the Romantic is searching, the Woman who will lead him out of his dream of love, those erotic reveries that Rousseau describes, into a real but endlessly ecstatic relationship. The love is there, as it is in the mind of a dreamy adolescent, before the Woman. And as there arise from the unconscious certain strange symbolical images of the other sex, images that may be vague but are still illuminated by the green and gold of the depths, the Romantic turns away from ordinary sensible women who cannot help thinking about children, houses and a steady income. So there flit through the literature of this age feminine creatures who are anything but ordinary sensible women, a host of faerie beings, nymphs, water sprites, savage queens, Oriental princesses, mysterious gipsy girls, anybody in fact who is sufficiently strange and cannot be domesticated. For love here is a pursuit, a torment, an unquenchable thirst, a fleeting ecstasy, a bitter aftermath, disillusion, unending regret, anything but the foundation of an enduring and fruitful relationship between a man and a woman. The Romantic, following Rousseau, is not turning outward, to look at and enjoy women as they are, but continues to turn inward, lost in erotic dreams and reveries, entangled in the uncriticised, unchecked fantasies of the unconscious.

Unless the end, however, is to be madness—as it so often was—a sense of reality must break in, the conscious mind must make its comparisons, and then unless some sort of balance can be arrived at, the result is the famous romantic melancholy, the canker and the worm, the inexplicable sadness, the gnawing homesickness that never knew a home. It was said of one romantic poet: "He wanted better bread than could be made of wheat", and that is true of them all. So they go in search of the blue flower, the lost kingdom of childhood, the happy valley of Arcadia, the forests of fairyland, the tower where they will find at last the strange woman who will enchant them for ever, forgetting if they are foolish, remembering if they grow wiser, that these things do not exist in the outward world, as revealed to consciousness, but belong, with much else, to the hidden realm of the unconscious, to the dreamer in his dream, to the solitary drama of the soul. To ignore the romantic as an aspect of life is to be blind to the rainbow; to accept the romantic as a way of life is to try and pack a rainbow in a crate. Rousseau cannot be considered among the poets, but he was a creator of poets, just because his example helped to release the dark energy, the zest that consciousness can control but cannot produce, the magical symbols that transform verse into unforgettable poetry, all from the depths of the unconscious. The conscious mind can accept and refine, but cannot create those phrases and lines that seem pregnant with many meanings and haunt us like music. The best of the authors of the Romantic Age opened themselves to the fire and sorcery of the unconscious without abandoning themselves to it, without leaving the conscious mind helpless, its will and judgment shattered, its sense of reality lost for ever. The less fortunate of them drifted rudderless into the dark, beyond communication, into madness. Rousseau, the prophet of Romance, the prototype of the romantic writer, ran the whole course. He ended by seeing the world as a conspiracy against him. Drifting into madness, he cried: "Here I am, alone on the earth, no brother, neighbour, friend, society, save myself . . ." He had turned his gaze inward too long, stared too hard into the dark depths of the unconscious. He should have looked the other way, for it is our consciousness that shows us brothers, neighbours, friends, society.

"Man is born free; and everywhere he is in chains." It is the most famous of all Rousseau's pronouncements, and it still reverberates. So far as it merely means that men in our civilisation have allowed a reasonable personal liberty to be dangerously reduced by power organisations, it was true when he wrote it, and it is true today, when we cannot even move about the world without state permission. But in its larger sense, it is untrue and perilously misleading. However man may be regarded, he is not born free. A baby is not free but severely conditioned by its helplessness. Primitive men, moving fearfully and warily in their own elaborate world of menacing spirits, taboos and tribal customs, have less freedom than we have. With the famous *Social Contract* and the arguments that Rousseau based upon it, we have nothing to do here. But what does concern us, because it is something he bequeathed to the Romantic Age and we have not done with it even yet, is his idea that freedom has nothing to do with any appreciation of necessity, any accommodation to the real world, the right balance between the conscious mind, looking outward, and the unconscious; but that, in practice if not in theory, man comes nearest to freedom by breaking that balance, by interpreting the objective world entirely in terms of the subjective inner world of dream and desire, by running away from any challenge to that inner world, escaping from, instead of facing and mastering, reality. A man who prefers erotic reveries to living in love with a real woman will certainly have more liberty, but all that it offers him is an unrewarding erotic relationship with himself. He will be freer if, like Rousseau, he deposits the children he has by his mistress in foundling hospitals, but only at the price of forfeiting parenthood and self-respect. He has more freedom as something; but not as a father, good lover or husband, decent citizen. The complete Romantic, for ever looking inward, swelling his ego into vast proportions, may tell us that he demands freedom to be completely himself—and undoubtedly there are times in an artist's life when he must have such freedom at all costs—but if he keeps running away, refusing to be bound by any obligation, then he cuts down this self by not allowing it new functions, responsibilities, relationships, diminishing instead of enriching his real life, until at last, when the final and narrowing path of escape turns into a *cul-de-sac*, he cries out in terrible despair that he is alone. Thus there is all of romanticism, exploding from the unconscious, in Rousseau: its sudden release of creative energy, its triumph as an aspect of life to be celebrated in literature, its ultimate danger, hurrying to despair and madness, when it is taken unchecked as a way of life.

CHAPTER ELEVEN

Germany and Goethe

THE ROMANTIC MOVEMENT in Germany began about 1770 and lasted until about 1830. This is not the view of most literary historians, who are in the habit of separating the brief 'Storm and Stress' of the 1770s from the main Romantic Movement, which began towards the end of the century. But if storm and stress are not romantic, what is? Therefore it is simpler and more sensible to accept the earlier date for the whole Movement, which may be said to have started when, in 1770, Herder, an excitable young pastor from East Prussia, went to Strassburg and met an even younger law student called Goethe. In Königsberg, Herder had known Hamann, an eccentric scholar who had taught him English, using *Hamlet* as a text-book. Herder had a passion for poetry, which he regarded as the mother-tongue of mankind; but he also believed that the early and truer poetry of a people reflected its history and spiritual outlook, so that although such poetry ought to be translated it should not be imitated. This was an attack on the whole classical tradition. Germans should express their own native genius, the German soul, and not try to write like Ancient Greeks. The greater poetry, full of the "action, passion, feeling" he desired above all else, came from people not tamed and deadened by civilisation—and here he joined Rousseau—and so he wrote with enthusiasm about the old ballads and folksongs that had lately been collected in England and elsewhere, about Shakespeare, who was still regarded as a kind of gigantic inspired savage, and *Ossian*. This last source of romantic inspiration is worth examining. James Macpherson, a young Highland schoolmaster, claimed that he had merely put together and translated into a rhapsodical English prose these ancient Gaelic poems attributed to the warrior bard, Ossian. He said he had transcribed them from the recitals of old people in the remoter parts of the Highlands. Dr. Johnson unhesitatingly denounced Macpherson as a fraud, and he was followed by Hume and many others. Oddly enough, their chief argument is really the weakest, for they protested that thousands of verses could not possibly exist simply in an oral tradition, the human memory not being able to retain so much, all down the centuries; and this is certainly not true, for we know now that people not dependent on the written word are capable of vast feats of memorising. A far stronger argument against *Ossian* is that in its entirety it carries far less suggestion of an ancient Celtic bard than of a young schoolmaster in 1760, who on the basis of a few genuine fragments of the old poetry turned prose-poet himself in a dashing new-romantic style. And the irony of *Ossian* is that, while it was received with suspicion and contempt in the country of its origin, it was welcomed with the greatest enthusiasm abroad and helped to inspire the Romantic Movement.

Herder's doctrine of the supreme importance of energy in great literature, of the intensity produced by wild untutored genius, was one calculated to appeal to young men anywhere, especially to German students in 1770. Wild geniuses responded at once to the call. The result was the earlier phase of the general Romantic Movement, called, after one of its characteristic works, an absurd play by Klinger (*Sturm und Drang*), Storm and Stress. Apart from the two authentic young men of genius, Goethe, an early and dazzlingly successful member, and Schiller, whose first produced play, *The Robbers*, may be said to have concluded the Movement, the other young men, Klinger, Lenz, Müller, Wagner, to name only the more prolific, do not merit any individual examination of their work here. They represent a violent explosion of undisciplined creative energy —and violence is the key-word—unlike anything elsewhere in the eighteenth century. Nothing came out of it, nothing grew; apart from Goethe and Schiller, reputations blazed and then fizzled out, leaving a few delightful lyrics and a pile of unplayable plays. It was followed by a strangely dead time, like the sinister calm that often succeeds a violent explosion, a time of uncertainty and infertility that dominated even Schiller, young and enthusiastic as he was, and more surprisingly even Goethe, the one tremendous figure in the group, whose drama of old

Germany, *Götz von Berlichingen*, had made him known throughout the country, and whose novel, *Werther*, had brought him a European reputation. There is something very German about such an explosion, bursting with work that is itself shapeless, violent, explosive, something that suggests an unusual and not healthy relation between consciousness and the unconscious, compelling the latter to erupt in this fashion, threatening the insanity that finally overcame some of these "wild young geniuses". The romanticism that was achieved gradually elsewhere, freeing itself by degrees from classicism and the rational, came roaring immediately out of these German student 'geniuses', accepting intensity of feeling as the supreme test of both character and art, inflating the ego into megalomania, abandoning all sensible restraint, welcoming the most destructive passions, and heightening the real and generous sympathies of youth—with, for example, the victims of oppression or a merciless legality—beyond any level where something useful might come of them. It was Rousseau seen at the end of a wild *Bierabend*; a students' performance of romantic literary genius. It was not something that could be lived with and matured: a real writer had either deliberately to grow out of it, as Goethe and Schiller did, or, in his disappointment as the storm subsided, to drink or dream his time away. But though a lull followed this Storm and Stress, here in Germany, the first country to welcome it, the Romantic Movement had arrived.

The Germany these Romantics knew was somewhere half-way between the land that had barely survived the Thirty Years War and the heavily industrialised and formidable empire of the late nineteenth century, with an unusual number of splendid cities. Then it had no great capital like London or Paris. Even Vienna, easily the largest German-speaking city, was not half their size. Berlin, in the process of being re-built, had not yet reached a population of 100,000. There was no metropolis beckoning to German authors. This explains why the universities and university towns, Strassburg and Göttingen, Jena and Heidelberg, played such an important part in the German Romantic Movement, and why so many professors and students are prominent in it. And a literature largely cut off from the main current of national life and produced in or around universities, by old professors and tame students, young professors and wild students, could easily swing to extremes, from a dreary formalism and pedantry to excessive self-assertion and irrational rebellion. In any event the German writer was bound to be cut off from public affairs. Whether he found himself in Prussia or Austria, in one of the other kingdoms, dukedoms, or the rest, he had to submit to a severe censorship, was told sharply to mind his own business, and was somewhere on the far edge of an official society chiefly made up of military men and civil servants. For one intelligent duke, like young Karl August who invited Goethe to Weimar, there were twenty like the Duke of Württemberg, who ordered Schiller, then one of his regimental surgeons, to publish nothing but medical works. It is true that there was a large element of mere escape in the German Romantic Movement, but it is only fair to add that there was much in Germany to be escaped from. Its laws were harsh and oppressive; and outside the innumerable Court circles, in the comparatively small middle class, its society was provincial and narrow, stiff in its manners, frugal and uncomfortable in its style of living (the stuffy comfort, heavy furnishings and meals came much later), and, away from the universities, consisted chiefly of pompous officials and professional men and their timid, conventional wives. Any high-spirited imaginative youth, growing up in such a society and finding it too strongly rooted for him to change, would either want to leave it or take refuge in his own or other men's dreams. The romantic Germany that lingers in our imagination, with its quaint little Courts, its misty castles, forests touched with enchantment, peasants singing over their wine, wandering student-poets falling in love with tender golden-haired maidens, belongs to those dreams, being largely the creation of romantic literature, rebelling against reality. The fact that now it seems real, part of the world's geography and history, while the actual Germany of the period is buried in text-books and forgotten, is a tribute to that literature.

It is, however, a literature that has had a mighty ally: music. Not only can we hear Beethoven thundering behind it, but so many of its beautiful lyrics have been set to music by Schubert and Schumann, Brahms and Wolf, that for every one of us at all familiar now with the work of these poets and story-tellers, ten thousand of us know snatches of them, catching a vague glimpse of their dreamlands, through these immortal songs.

Which is perhaps as it should be. The German Romantic Movement, being very German, walks along a forest track, narrowly between the infinities of music and metaphysics. The latter were chiefly supplied by Kant and Fichte, Schelling and Hegel. Of these the least important from a purely philosophical point of view was the most important as a literary ally, and this was Schelling, who incidentally had a considerable influence upon Coleridge and, through him, on some of the English Romantics. Schelling taught that "the system of Nature is at the same time the system of our mind", that "Nature is mind made visible and mind is Nature made invisible"; that these two are completely united and identified only in the Absolute or God, are gradually self-revealed in history, and that in our time Nature and mind are reconciled, brought together on a higher level, through art. This gave the romantic poets, story-tellers and critics what they wanted: Nature was no longer alien and hostile but a friendly collaborator, contributing to the creative process, and the supreme function in our world and time belonged to art. The romantic temperament and outlook now had their own philosophy. In Jena too, where Schelling lectured, there was published romanticism's own critical review, the *Athenäum*, edited by the brothers August Wilhelm and Friedrich von Schlegel. Indeed, Jena—with Weimar, where Goethe was, not far away—was in the first years of the Romantic Movement its acknowledged centre.

Though his *Wilhelm Meister* was regarded almost as the contemporary bible of the Movement, Goethe must be left out of it; so must Schiller— for reasons we shall see later. There were other writers of merit who cannot be included, as for example, at one extreme of popularity, the eccentric novelist, Jean Paul Richter, a sort of German-Gothic Sterne, much admired by Thomas Carlyle (who caught many of his mannerisms) and most of his contemporaries but now almost forgotten; or, at the other extreme of popularity, hardly recognised at all, the mad but greatly gifted poet, Hölderlin, with his inward vision of Greek classical beauty, whose poetry had to wait almost until our own age, for poets like Stefan George and Rilke, for Hermann Hesse the novelist, to make its full effect. The chief names associated with this Romantic Movement are these: Tieck and Novalis; Brentano and Arnim; the two dramatists Werner and von Kleist; the later story-tellers and poets, Eichendorff, Uhland, Kerner, Chamisso and Fouqué; that master of queer tales, Hoffmann; and, in its last phase, Hauff, who died at twenty-five, and Heine in his more romantic youth, before he became sufficiently detached to become the rather cynical historian of the whole Movement. Clearly it is impossible to examine or even enumerate the individual works of these fourteen writers, many of them very prolific. Indeed, it might be thought unnecessary to waste more valuable space on any but a very few of them, for nine-tenths of their work has meant little or nothing outside Germany. And if, as we propose, they are taken together as members of a movement, and that movement is examined, the same objection might be urged. To that objection there are two replies. First, this Romantic Movement is worth examining because of the place it occupies in the history and development of German literature. Secondly, and more important for our purpose here, any analysis, however brief, of this Movement, no matter how few of its works are now read outside Germany, will show us how wide and far-reaching its direct or indirect influence has been, ever since 1830, on the literature of our Western world. Many tendencies, attitudes, idiosyncrasies, of our world literature since 1830 down to the present time originated in, proliferated from, this German Romantic Movement.

Many of these writers were poets and followed a fashion of including short lyrical poems, ballads and songs, even in their prose tales. And some of these, as we saw earlier, are now famous. The German language lends itself most happily to verse of this kind, especially in a naïve folk style, a style in which the younger Goethe was supreme, offering magnificent examples of it to later poets. And obviously the romantic temperament, whether in its recklessly abandoned or melancholy yearning mood, can express itself perfectly in brief lyrics and ballads, in which nothing need be sustained. A fine harvest of such poetry has been garnered from this Movement, probably representing its best direct contribution to literature. Nevertheless, the Movement as a whole made less use of folksong (though Brentano and Arnim made a wonderful collection in their *Boy's Wonder Horn*) than it did of folklore and the folktale, the *Märchen*, the fairy or dream tale. It took over, re-made and developed the *Märchen*, led by its

127

senior story-teller and playwright, Tieck, who even wrote *Märchen*-comedies, completely unlike anything ever found in a folktale. The term became a kind of passport for new dream countries and kingdoms of romance.

Within a movement of this size were many varieties of talent and temperament, so that one man's *Märchen* style was different from another's, but all were intent upon escaping from ordinary reality, Germany as it was. Most were making no attempt to balance conscious and unconscious elements, were one-sidedly favouring the unconscious, no matter how inferior and negative its promptings might be, just as the writers of the previous age had one-sidedly favoured a bright, clear consciousness. So now, with romance and the *Märchen*, came darkness, mystery, strange magic. Their characters, outside reality and beyond the help of consciousness, were often entirely at the mercy of fate, cruel, senseless, impossible to understand. (Tieck and several of the playwrights were ingeniously devoted to this fate theme.) Or they were condemned to undertake unending quests, to suffer hopeless longing. The all-pervading and usually sinister magic frequently transforms people into something like puppets, and turns puppets, life-size dolls, automata, into something like people. And with these and similar devices we are now brought close to the hallucinations of minds so disordered that they have lost contact with reality, consciousness having been overwhelmed by the unconscious. Indeed, in some of the later writers, notably in von Kleist the dramatist, *Märchen* sorcery is abandoned for the psychic alchemy of the unconscious, producing a dissociation of personality, bringing out a terrible secondary self. (The theme has been familiar ever since.) Among nearly all the story-tellers much use was made of material, fashionable at the time, fetched from the dubious territory between science and mysticism, called by one of its explorers "the night-side of science", resulting in much traffic with 'animal magnetism', mesmerism, hypnotism, of which Hoffmann, with his peculiar genius for transforming real scenes and people into a fantastic and sinister *Märchen*, is the master. And with all this, the love that can never be attained except in a flash of ecstasy, being a withering flower, a mask to be plucked away, a light dying on the hills, not something to be achieved by men and women in an enduring conscious relationship. These lovelorn characters are adolescents 'in love' not with real women but with magical feminine images from their own unconscious.

One of the characteristics of almost the whole Movement is its 'romantic irony', which Friedrich Schlegel quite wrongly confused with the genuine and very profound irony of a Cervantes. This 'romantic irony', which was supposed to express the artist's 'inner detachment' and 'spiritual freedom', demands that the writer should suddenly break the spell of his creation, display his hand on the puppet strings, lure the reader towards terror or tears and then show him a wide grin. It is the tale-within-a-tale technique, the play-within-a-play-within-a-play, which was one of Tieck's formulas in his *Märchen*-comedies. On a few, a very few, occasions this 'romantic irony' can be used legitimately, but as a constant teasing device it is an adolescent trick, not expressing detachment and freedom but suggesting the immature artist's uncertainty about himself and his work, a reluctance to stake his all upon what he is doing, an uneasy desire to anticipate and so be safe from the audience's scepticism or mockery. It represents the reverse of Goethe's maxim: "Art rests upon a kind of religious sense, upon a deep immutable earnestness; this is the reason why Art so readily unites itself with Religion." But such art must be rooted in reality. There is no true religion in this *Märchen* romanticism. A picturesque and sentimental religiosity, very different from the sharp and often grim certainties of real medieval belief, comes flickering in with the scenery and fancy costumes of a vaguely imagined Middle Ages. The mystical secret societies always finding their way into these tales have no genuine religious basis; like the actual secret societies of the later eighteenth century, they are rationalism gone rotten, their superstition the phosphorescence of decay. The supernatural that so often plays with and then destroys these helpless characters, moving in some huge anxiety dream, is either a mere story-telling device or on a deeper level the recognition, really pre-religious and primitive, of unknown forces, menacing and uncontrollable, striking out of the dark. And one of the tasks of true religion is to free us from this nightmare. It asks us to stand and face reality, knowing that if we keep on running away, with fear at our heels, hoping to forget the landlord and the bank manager, the magistrate and the police, we shall exchange daylight for darkness, arrive where fear is our host, and then find ourselves in much worse company.

The last of these Romantics, and never quite one of the brotherhood even in youth, Heinrich Heine, finally left Germany for France and achieved a European reputation probably more impressive than his German reputation. He did this in spite of the fact that the peculiar magic of his songs vanishes in translation: his *alte Märchenwald* has deeper shadows and brighter green, where the sunlight comes through, than our "old, enchanted wood" has. His characteristic irony is not merely the 'romantic irony' of the whole group; it is the expression of a complex personality, whose elements are at war, German romanticism with Jewish realism, the bourgeois with the revolutionary, the sentimental lover with the cynical sensualist; and these conflicts can be heard in his poetry, together with a beautiful lyrical note that is all his own. He is not a great poet; he lacked the size and scope and probably the ambition; but among the world's more introverted lyrical poets, 'sweet and sour' like the Chinese dish, he must rank as one of the masters. The same rapid changes of mood, from romantic feeling to mockery, the same brilliance with even more impudence and wit, can be found in his prose, especially in the *Travel Pictures*, which in their own audacious-young-man style have probably never been bettered. But by the time the last of these had appeared, in 1831, Heine, the best-known representative of the rebellious 'Young Germany', had left behind the little that remained of the old Romantic Movement, to which later he was to look back, while still laughing at it, with a certain wistfulness.

We must now return to Schiller and Goethe, the two who touched the Romantic Movement in its 'Storm and Stress' beginning, but then could not be contained by it, deliberately choosing to keep clear of it. Schiller detested the military school he was compelled to attend, and, as we have seen, was forbidden later to write plays at all. After resigning his commission and quitting the state, not without some fear afterwards of being kidnapped by order of the tyrannical Duke of Württemberg, he continued to write plays and some verse during several unsettled years, overshadowed by an unhappy love affair. This time came to an end in 1789, when he became professor of history at Jena. Now he abandoned the drama for history and philosophy, and it was during these years that he made his contribution to æsthetic theory, basing art on the 'play-impulse' (which did not mean that he thought art mere play), and making his famous distinction between 'naïve' poetry (direct, extroverted, classical) and 'sentimental' poetry (reflective, introverted, romantic). It was his friendship with Goethe—long-delayed because of an imagined antipathy —and their work together at Weimar that returned Schiller to the theatre, and it was during the few remaining years of an all-too-short life that, in spite of his rapidly failing health, he produced the poetic drama that has had an immense and enduring reputation in his own country and is at least known and respected wherever there is a serious Theatre. It might be said of Schiller, especially by a non-German critic, that he always appears to be—or about to be—a greater dramatist than he actually is. His work has a dazzle-and-shade effect on our minds, having the shadow of his early death (at forty-six) over it and also the bright attraction of his personality, so high-minded, courageous, enthusiastic. It is good work for the serious Theatre; it offers us great themes, lit by his own overmastering passion for freedom, a passion that came from his tormented youth; it shows us one long cast after another of carefully considered characters, many of them great historical personages, mostly fine parts for ambitious and intelligent players; it is filled with ringing eloquence and high-minded sentiments; and it is the work of a man who, unlike his friend Goethe, understands and enjoys purely theatrical effects, the entrance of a crowd here, of one sinister masked man there. The Theatre, especially in Germany, owes much to Schiller.

He is a good dramatist, but not a great dramatist. His preoccupation with ideas and the philosophical bent of his mind blunt the edge of his drama. Too often his plays make us feel that some magnificent senate is debating a great theme, rather than that a number of hard-pressed human beings are living it. There is too much general eloquence, not enough that seems to be wrung out of baffled minds and hearts at the breaking-point. We are hardly ever close enough to anybody. Too many scenes suggest the theatrical historian, not a tragic poet. This famous historical dramatist contrives to be historical in the wrong way; all the appropriate personages are there, behaving as they might have behaved; but somehow the light in which we see them seems to belong to Weimar in 1800. Except in its final scenes, *Don Carlos* never suggests the stifling atmosphere of Philip II's Court. The elaborate action of *Mary Stuart* does reproduce the plotting and counter-plotting of the period, but we seem to be a long way from Elizabethan England, with its high colours and fantastic mixture of tragedy and low comedy, beauty and brutality. In spite of its action, carefully worked out to embody a medieval conception, somehow neither the mysticism nor the muck of the Middle Ages find their way into *The Maid of Orleans*. With the possible exception of the simpler and heartier *William Tell*, where a whole people's struggle for freedom arouses Schiller's natural enthusiasm, these dramas need both more poetry and more realism. A more deeply poetical and imaginative method with these characters would bring us far nearer to them, whereas so many scenes of high-minded debate and rhetorical eloquence leave them blurred, half-realised figures, as if they were taking part in a kind of verbal opera. And with so much history spread before him waiting to be dramatised—for after all Schiller accepted a professorship in the subject—he was not dramatically adroit in his choice of subjects, allowing himself to be fascinated by very difficult, ambiguous characters like Wallenstein, who finally contributes very little to the vast ambitious drama Schiller built all round him, or Mary Queen of Scots, who loses too much by being turned into a simple figure of tender suffering womanhood. (Thus, the scene in which Mortimer tries to make love to her is an embarrassment if she is mere injured innocence, instead of a woman who could not help using her sexual charm.) Unfortunately, a dramatist must still solve his problems to our satisfaction, no matter how much 'moral grandeur' his work has and how 'nobly idealistic' his characters may be. The Marquis of Posa, in *Don Carlos*, may be the fine flower of revolutionary idealism, capable of inspiring crusades for freedom, but the play in which he appears, to cut across the original theme of Don Carlos's hopeless love for the Queen, still remains confused and unsatisfactory. That Schiller was a born writer for the theatre (as Goethe was not), we do not doubt; and to this we must add certain great personal qualities of mind and heart unusual in born writers for the theatre; but between this high realm of ideas and ideals and the much lower one of theatrical contrivance, there is a middle kingdom of the completely dramatic imagination, enabling a writer to enter intimately into a wide range of characters and scenes, fusing poetry and drama into one marvellous substance, the realm where the supreme dramatists live at ease, in which Schiller is only an occasional visitor.

The greatest European man of letters of this Romantic Age is, of course, Goethe. But even to call him a man of letters is to do him an injustice, for he was also a minister of state, a theatre director, a natural philosopher, a student of many sciences, and was indeed the most many-sided and complete man of his time. He spent his final years, still in Weimar (not risking any loss of stature by visiting great cities like London and Paris), like some fabulous old emperor of literature. Ever since he had startled and fascinated all Europe, as a very young man, with his *Werther*, his reputation had grown and grown. In his later years he was much concerned with the idea of 'world literature', a term he invented, and he must be considered one of its more commanding figures. After his death in 1832, a year that seems to mark the end of the whole Age, there was the inevitable reaction, for too many German writers had lived too long in his immense shadow, and although his vast fame has persisted, so too has this reaction. Indeed, T. S. Eliot, who is usually cautious, if condescending, in his literary judgments, has written: "Of Goethe perhaps it is truer to say that he dabbled in both philosophy and poetry and made no great success of either; his true role was that of the man of the world and sage, a La Rochefoucauld, a La Bruyère, a Vauvenargues." With this astonishing statement still ringing in our ears, let us put the opposition's case against this world-renowned Olympian Goethe.

As a man, the charge would run, he was too self-satisfied and too self-centred; he lacked patriotic feeling and was out of sympathy with the liberating movements of his time; unusually fortunate in his life and adroit in his management of it, except possibly in his all-too-frequent infatuations, he avoided suffering himself and did not fully understand what it meant to others, hence his indifference to or even dislike of Christianity. He accepted as his due the praise of his fellow German writers but did not use his great prestige to help those with real talent, preferring to bestow his praise on the second-rate. (With the exception of Schiller, to whom he was genuinely devoted.) His scientific researches were both pretentious and amateurish, and, apart from some suggestions about evolution, were soon proved to have little value. As a writer, his versatility is more remarkable than what he actually achieved, time having robbed him of the supreme achievements demanded by his reputation. His lyrics have survived and are still exquisite, but a master of world literature needs more than a few songs to keep his place for him. He cannot be considered a great dramatist—*Götz von Berlichingen* is young rough stuff, *Iphigenia* and *Tasso* are altogether too static, *Egmont* is unhistorical and lacks real conflict, *Faust* is too complicated and demanding —and outside Germany he has never captured the theatre. Nor was he a great novelist—for *Werther* has vanished with its own brand of sentimentalism, the first *Wilhelm Meister* is a heavy *Bildungsroman* rather than a genuine novel, the second never comes to life at all as fiction, *The Elective Affinities* is too German and dates badly—and so what have we for world literature? Certainly not the narrative verse of *Hermann and Dorothea*. The autobiography, no doubt, and the *Conversations with Eckermann*; but a great deal more than this is needed to sustain that colossal reputation claimed for him. A good poet, yes—for even this opposition cannot agree with T. S. Eliot's accusation of mere dabbling here—but where are the supreme achievements, the enduring massive stature, that would give him a place beside Homer, Dante, Shakespeare?

But when all this has been said, his greatness remains, except to those whose fanaticisms, religious or political, he offends. Madame de Staël came close to the secret of this greatness when she said that Goethe, resembling Nature, "should not be criticised as an author good in one kind of composition and bad in another". Unless we deliberately check all imaginative sympathy, as T. S. Eliot obviously did, we cannot help feeling, just as most of his contemporaries felt, that there is a final element in Goethe that represents more than the sum total of his accomplishments and his magnificent physical presence and his tremendous reputation. We catch a hint of it in the innumerable tributes to him, as for example in Matthew Arnold's *Memorial Verses*:

> "Physician of the iron age,
> Goethe has done his pilgrimage."

It is as if Goethe had performed a double act of creation, creating his works within the larger containing act of self-creation. "One must be something in order to do something." When Goethe in his old age told Eckermann, on one occasion, that if he had lived another kind of life, in greater solitude, he would have been happier and would have done much more as a poet, he was allowing a mood to blur and darken his self-knowledge. We do not need to be told that Goethe was not the dramatic poet that Shakespeare was. But Shakespeare had only to create the poetry, he had not to create the Elizabethan Age; he took flight from high ground. But Goethe had no such high ground; he could not trust his time, his world, could not open his wings and let the wind carry him; he had to create, so to speak, an age of his own within the age, had to *be* Goethe before he could write Goethe. And the two works to which he gave most thought, year after year, namely, the two parts of *Faust* and the *Bildungsroman*, the very pattern of all such cultural chronicles, of *Wilhelm Meister*, are deeply concerned with this double creation, leading from himself to the symbolic presentation and interpretation, in the Second Part of *Faust* (where, like Blake before him and others after him, he is handicapped by having to be mythological without an accepted mythology), of the life of our whole species. The typical writers of the Romantic Age all seem like helpless victims of chance and fatality; but not Goethe, who makes us feel that he deliberately raised himself above this tragi-comic level, to exist, we might say, in his own atmosphere. Hölderlin may have had an equal genius for the short poem; but Hölderlin drifted into insanity. Purely as a theatre poet, Grillparzer was more than his equal, but, embittered and despairing, Grillparzer ceased to write for the theatre at a time of life when Goethe had still to produce his mightiest works. It is not simply that Grillparzer was faced with the Vienna of Metternich, while Goethe was at home and at ease in friendly Weimar. Goethe's Olympian good fortune was part of his own creation.

As the youthful leader of the 'Storm and Stress' group, Goethe was never again so wildly productive as he was during these early 1770s. Of this period, sailing with the wind, *Werther*, sentimentalising the whole tendency towards self-destruction, was the high point. After going to Weimar, to exchange dreams for actual affairs of state, Goethe moved sharply away from romantic violence and the inflated ego, as he did from his followers, Lenz (who later went mad), Klinger, Wagner and the rest. If they could not save themselves and still write (and not one of them survived as a writer), he could—and did. But now, even though some of his finest lyrics belong to these years, he was almost as infertile as he had been productive before; not because he was too busy with other things, for creative genius cannot be dominated by administrative routine, but because he did not feel ready . He had to subdue, to harness, that essentially German demonic element; he had to create for himself the balance, the right relation between consciousness and the unconscious, that in other times and places the whole spirit of the community might have discovered for him. The famous visit to Italy that followed was both his *Lehrjahre* and *Wanderjahre*, the travel that completed his apprenticeship. (But too much must not be attributed to mere Hellenism, in spite of the tremendous lasting influence of Winckelmann's classical archæology and art criticism.) Goethe returned to Weimar committed to neither the century that was ending nor the one, complete with its Romantic Movement, that was approaching. From now on he belonged to no school, no movement, and was careful to show no particular sympathy with the very Romantics who claimed to be inspired by him: he was a unique Classical-Romantic going his own way; he was Goethe. In a time of vast upheaval, of destruction and self-destruction, when so many roads led the way to dreamland or madness, he had to create his own world in which to create his own work. And it is this, the twofold endeavour that is the very opposite of dabbling and dilettantism, that really sets him apart, as if he belonged to a different time, to a different order of authorship, making him appear to be the detached Olympian, the calm and smiling sage, the Culture Hero arriving from some remote higher civilisation, in the German scene.

"Man is born," Goethe told Eckermann, "not to solve the problems of the universe, but to find out where the problem applies, and then to restrain himself within the limits of the comprehensible. His faculties are not sufficient to measure the actions of the universe; and an attempt to explain the outer world by reason is, with his narrow view, vain. The reason of man and the reason of the Deity are two very different things."

It is the same central outlook we discovered among the greatest writers of the sixteenth century, whose natural approach to man and his mystery Goethe toiled to obtain. Readers of the Second Part of *Faust*, with its confused riot of symbolism, may well feel that here Goethe had not restrained himself "within the limits of the comprehensible", possibly because he had not only been compelled to invent his own mythology but had also lived with the work too long. But here, in his scene of the Mothers and elsewhere, the old poet reaches forward to the discoveries of the depth psychology of our own age. There is indeed in the older Goethe a strange prophetic element. So, in a time of aggressive and triumphant nationalism, he continually speaks of world literature and a world view. Again and again he shows himself wonderfully sensitive to social dangers then only beginning to manifest themselves, mere streams in that day that are now gigantic roaring torrents: the pressure upon "fine talents" of "the demands of an age so full and intense as the present, and one, too, that moves with such rapidity"; the increasing temptation "to swim with the stream of time"; the tyranny of news and publicity, with nothing being allowed to reach maturity, "each moment spent in consuming the preceding one" and the day wasting the day, so that "no one may rejoice or suffer but as a pastime for others; and so it goes on from house to house, from town to town, from kingdom to kingdom, and at last from continent to continent—all helter-skelter"—a surprising description of the early nineteenth century but a perfect one of our own time. It is as if from the eminence to which he has raised himself he can see far more than any of his contemporaries, this poet and sage who joins her great musicians in representing all that is best in the German character and spirit. Germany has never turned away from him without becoming the victim of the demonic element he tamed and civilised. A wonderful poet, from early youth to old age, as the leading voice in the great German lyrical chorus, he may never have reached the supreme creative achievements of the earlier masters, his Wilhelm Meister and Faust and Mephistopheles falling short of a Hamlet or Don Quixote; but his act of creation, which involved himself as well as his writing, was wide and deep and strong, the greatest of our later time. "I can imagine," said Hölderlin's Hyperion, "no people more dismembered than the Germans. You can see workmen, but no men, thinkers, but no men, lords and servants, boys and middle-aged persons, but no men . . ." But Germany in Goethe—as even Napoleon saw—had found a man.

CHAPTER TWELVE

The English Romantics

I

THE 'English' in the above title really refers to the language in which these romantic authors wrote, not to their nationality. True, most of them were English in both senses of the term, but not all. Indeed, Robert Burns, who cannot be ignored, was not only a Scot but also wrote almost all his best verse in a broad Scots dialect, almost a separate language. He is entirely an eighteenth-century figure, and stands outside the Romantic Movement, though there are romantic elements in his work. He is very much of his country, which even today regards him affectionately as a national representative figure rather than as one of its authors. He passionately proclaims what almost every Scot, from lords at the head of ancient clans to peasant ploughmen, have thought and felt. The Scots are an odd people, more sharply divided than most between an austere piety and a rather grim devotion to knowledge, on the one side, and, on the other, a violent and reckless love of wine, woman and song, that no poet has celebrated more lustily than Burns, though he was equally capable of praising the industriousness, frugality and innocent family life of the opposite party. He was not concerned about having a fixed attitude and being consistent; he was a poet of the people, both the virtuous and the wicked, conscientious peasant proprietors and jolly beggars on the road, understood them all, having shared their lives, their toil and frugality and their debauchery; and it is all there, expressed with frankness and gusto, in his narrative poems and songs, especially in his songs, which have both satirical sharpness and lyrical beauty. Burns has the wide range of sympathy, the balance of classical and romantic elements, of a great poet, all the breadth if not (except to the Scots) all the height and depth; he might be described as one of the humbler and more limited master singers.

Another poet who is outside the Romantic Movement—and one who could never be included in any movement—is William Blake, artist, writer and seer. He lived and died in poverty and obscurity, and his complete originality of outlook and a few personal eccentricities encouraged those who knew him only slightly to believe he was insane. And no doubt those who believe that the society we have created during the last hundred and fifty years is essentially sound and healthy will continue to believe, if they ever think about him, that Blake was insane. But there is more profit for mind and soul in believing our society to be increasingly insane, and Blake (as the few who knew him well always declared) to be sound and healthy. And as doubt about our mechanical progress has grown, so has Blake's stature both as a poet and thinker, and it has not stopped growing yet. He was born in 1757 but decisively rejected everything that the eighteenth century upheld, and even a rebel like Rousseau was among his dislikes. He looks back to Böhme, to the strange and obscure sects of Germany in the sixteenth century and of England in the mid-seventeenth century, and forward to the analytical psychology of Jung and his school in our time, men whose criticism of our society he would have applauded; and the only contemporary to whom he can be linked at all is that odd and strongly original Scandinavian religious philosopher and mystic, Swedenborg. Both men boldly described their visions, but Blake was better equipped for the task, being both poet and painter. His writing consists of his poems, largely lyrical and, in spite of occasional faulty diction and careless phrasing, blazing with genius; his aphorisms and critical notes in prose, frequently very profound and always lively reading; and his 'prophetic books', highly symbolic and very obscure and often rather repellent narrative poems. In his early *Songs of Innocence*—and the contrast between innocence and experience was one of Blake's great themes—he seems to recapture an Elizabethan freshness, zest, careless ecstasy, as no other lyrical poet has done before or since his time. And between these early songs and the mysterious craggy 'prophetic books' he produced a small number of poems, usually lyrical in style, equally remarkable for their force, bold originality, and the haunting beauty of their symbolic imagery.

We have seen how ever since the high Middle Ages, when Western Man achieved a complete religious basis and framework to his life, men had felt the loss of this basis and framework. The secret of William Blake, and the key to both his strength and his weakness as a poet, is that he recreated this basis and framework for himself. He can be called a one-man religious revival. But it is the fundamental religious attitude, not the beliefs and dogma, forms and ceremonies, once associated with it, he is reviving. He makes this very plain:

> *I must Create a System, or be enslav'd by another Man's;*
> *I will not Reason and Compare: my business is to Create.*

At the centre of his system is the creative imagination, which he associates with Christ, as against the Jesus who belongs to mere ecclesiasticism, to the accusers and judges of sin. He was the enemy of eighteenth-century Reason, which he recognised, with profound intuition, as the analytical intellect, losing itself in lifeless abstractions, entangling us more and more in the opposites, destroying the natural balance and the interplay of psychic energy between consciousness and the unconscious. One of his strongest pieces, *The Marriage of Heaven and Hell*, not only anticipates the discoveries of depth psychology but also reveals how close his thought came to the profoundest Oriental philosophy, then unknown. Again, his understanding of sex, his mistrust of the growing demands of collective organisations on the individual, his dislike of the Industrial Revolution (his "dark satanic mills") then in its first phase, his equation of all serious art with the religious attitude, help to explain why a man once regarded as a harmless lunatic, or an eccentric with lyrical genius, is now more and more carefully studied as a man of prophetic insight and deep natural wisdom. And even among English-speaking readers he has not yet arrived at his full stature. Here, in this steady growth and deepening of interest, is the proof of his strength. His weakness, when he is considered as anything except the author of a few enchanting lyrics, is that the religious basis and framework are of his own creation; he had to discover and use his own symbols, so that much of his work seems almost as obscure as if it had been written in a private language. His drawings, which often illustrate his poems, are of some help, but too often they are filled with figures from his own personal mythology. There are some men, of great personality and power, who seem by some mistake of the divinities to have been dropped on the right planet but at the wrong time, or to have arrived at the right time but on the wrong planet; and Blake is one of them. His work, ranging from pure song to obscure epics of unconscious processes, at its best blazes with genius and at its worst still flickers with it, the genius of a seer who looks beyond the immediate ages of Reason and Romance, and cannot be adequately interpreted in terms of either. Probably his own time has still to come.

This period in English literature, giving it some of its finest poetry, is often called the Romantic Revival. But this is misleading, for nothing in fact was revived. The typical eighteenth-century judgments on the value of medieval and Elizabethan literature were sharply reversed, and so was that century's opinion of itself. Much from the more distant past was re-discovered, both by the romantic poets and by the few critics, notably Hazlitt, Lamb and Leigh Hunt, who were in sympathy with them. But they were not returning in spirit to these earlier ages, were not attempting to revive them; they were consciously expressing a new age, a new spirit and outlook. These Romantics were the up-to-date men; it was their hostile critics, the spokesmen of the ponderous official reviews, still drearily trying to maintain eighteenth-century standards, who were old-fashioned, out of date. But these English poets and the few critics and essayists who admired them did not see themselves co-operating in a definite movement, conducting an æsthetic campaign. Unlike the French and Germans and other continentals, the English never have such campaigns. There has always been in English writers a strong individualistic strain that discourages any such concerted action, and the Romantics were individualists to a man. Again, English society is neither fiercely hostile to new literary ideas nor enthusiastic about them; it is blandly indifferent to any æsthetic problems. How the English, who mostly care less about literature than other peoples, have contrived to produce such an astounding array of literary genius is one of the mysteries of this life. What is certain is that what was elsewhere a definite Romantic Movement, as in

Germany complete with periodicals and publishers, philosophers and courses of university lectures, was in England a mere drift towards romantic writing.

This drift, however, produced some of the great literature of the language. Not the greatest, though, and not great at all in some forms of literature. This age failed in the drama, though not from want of trying. Apart from the incomparable Jane Austen, who had no more to do with the Romantics than if they had been on the moon, and whose whole tone and quality are exquisitely classical, it failed in the novel proper. Its history and biography show us nothing to compare with Gibbon's *Decline and Fall* or Boswell's immortal *Life of Johnson*. But it is great and triumphant in its poetry and its miscellaneous prose, the essay and very personal occasional criticism. And being a highly individualistic age, even for this nation of individualists, it is particularly rich in authors who are fascinating personalities, around whose lives scores of volumes have been written. The political differences of the time were sharply challenging, especially during the years immediately following the French Revolution and then later during the reaction that followed the defeat of Napoleon; but it is typical of this English period that the romantic writers cannot be found all in one political camp, that they too were divided in their opinions and sympathies. Thus Hazlitt, as literary critic, stoutly championed the work of Wordsworth and Coleridge, but, in his polemics, fiercely attacked them for what he considered their apostasy to the principles of the French Revolution. Byron and Scott, though the two greatest romantic influences in Europe, were poles apart in politics. Shelley was too extreme for anybody's agreement. The aristocrats among them became the revolutionaries; the poor young men gradually transformed themselves into High Tories. The period is as rich in contradictions, ironies, absurdities, as it is in personalities.

One of its ironies, more important to us here than the rest, is that its two most influential figures, Scott and Byron, who for many years dominated the Romantic Movement throughout the Western world, were not themselves the kind of Romantics that Rousseau produced, and at heart did not belong to the Movement at all. Let us take Walter Scott, the older man, first. His narrative verse had its day—he survives as a poet through a few short pieces in the manner of the Border ballads—but of course it was his Waverley novels or historical romances that made him famous both at home and abroad. Their immediate success was stupendous; they were read with enthusiasm by all classes of readers in all civilised countries, and very soon imitated: Scott is the father of nineteenth-century romantic and historical prose fiction. Now that he has long been out of fashion— though sensible and wide-ranging readers return to him—it is hard to suggest the excitement that followed, in country after country, the publication of his novels, the power and the glory of the 'Magician of the North'. The extent of his influence may be judged by the fact that, years after his death, Mark Twain, who disliked him, attributed the elaborately chivalrous airs and graces of the rich planters and their ladies in the Southern states of America to their devotion to Scott's romances. He was described as one of the wonders of the age; even sober critics of the succeeding generation placed him not far below Homer and Shakespeare. That he was over-estimated throughout the nineteenth century is certain; but that he has been under-valued by criticism since then is equally certain. An honourable and punctilious man, he considered it his duty to pay off the debts of a publishing firm in which he was a partner, with the result that he wrote too much, too quickly, and his later work, when his health was failing, obviously suffers from hasty and careless writing. He always wrote quickly and was apt to put too much trust upon his exceptionally capacious memory; his style, except when responding to the challenge of heightened moments, is frequently turgid and unpleasing; his young women and heroic young men are nearly always mere dummies, and their love-affairs are handled in a perfunctory manner; his thought is limited, his general outlook is that of his time; and though his historical sense and imagination are sufficiently broad for him to give us a spirited sketch of any period, he is not able, as some later writers have been, to enter completely and with subtle conviction into the life of any distant age. It is these limitations, emphasised by later critics, that have driven him out of fashion.

Too often, however, his work has not been examined in the right light. He has been accepted, and then criticised, too often simply as a medieval romancer, the author of *Ivanhoe* or *The Talisman*. But his strongest work belongs, as his own upbringing did, to the eighteenth century. And too little has been made, as breadth and sanity and a certain generosity of temperament have themselves gone out of fashion, of his genuinely rare massive virtues, his feeling for character in all but its most subtle and tormented aspects, his command of a wide scene in almost any period, his ability to present a great action in all its greatness, his masculine breadth and sweep and generous force. In spite of his romantic influence, he is in fact one of the supreme extroverted writers, with a boyish passion for historically picturesque and gallant action and for famous characters larger than life, but never losing the cool shrewd judgment of men and affairs that belonged to the Edinburgh advocate that he was trained to be, and that he never quite ceased to be, among all his romancing. And the irony of his position, as one of the great influences of the Romantic Movement, is that at heart he belonged far more to the old eighteenth century than he did to this new age, that in the narrower but truer psychological sense of the term he was not a Romantic at all. He owes nothing whatever to Rousseau, whom he would certainly have detested, and is completely different in temperament and attitude from those writers who obviously stem from Rousseau. Scott is the great romancer who does not belong to romanticism.

Now for Byron, a harder nut to crack. We find him, at the age of twenty, writing to his mother: "I do not know that I resemble Jean Jacques Rousseau. I have no ambition to be like so illustrious a madman . . ." In one of his later journals, he repeats that he cannot see any point of resemblance, gives a score of examples of the ways in which he and Rousseau differed, and concludes: ". . . Rousseau's way of life, his country, his manners, his whole character were so very different, that I am at a loss to conceive how such a comparison could have arisen . . ." But, as he admits, it was frequently being made. If Rousseau was the prophet of the Romantic Age, Byron became its hero. Europe accepted him as the archetypal and symbolic figure of romance. It was as if one of Rousseau's day-dreams came to life. Byron had every qualification the for role of leading man in the drama of the Romantic Age. He was a prolific, impassioned and glorious poet; he was an aristocrat and as beautiful as Apollo; he was misunderstood and abused by his fellow-countrymen; he was wickedly amorous, a satanic philanderer, though capable—or so a million women dreamed—of being reformed by the love of a good woman; when weary of brittle gaiety and debauchery, he retired, a solitary exile, to various picturesque places, and there, wrapped in a cloak, with the clear-cut, pale, sad face of a young Lucifer, he composed immortal stanzas to the ocean, the mountains, thunder-and-lightning; he worshipped the wild beauty of Nature and strange women and man's liberty, for which he fought and died at last in Greece. This was his legend; he wrote it in one poetic tale or drama after another, in sparkling lyrics by the hundred; and he lived it. Only Goethe, forty years older, loomed larger. The advantages Byron possessed over his companion English poets were immense. Not only did he look and behave like every romantic reader's idea of a poet; he had all the prestige of a rich English milord, with the further prestige of having quarrelled with all the other milords; he took the centre of the international stage doubly illuminated by literary glory and scandal; and most of his verse could be easily enjoyed in its original English and lost little or nothing in translation. No wonder that his legend captured Europe, from the great ladies ready to lose their hearts to him down to wistful young clerks, with a taste for romantic verse, who tried to imitate his appearance. The very Age turned Byronic.

Let us admit that Byron's real character was far from simple, containing many conflicting elements, and innumerable close studies have been made of it, producing many different judgments of him. Any account of him within the limits imposed on us here must be inadequate. But it can be said at once that his legend, turning him into the supreme European figure of romance, grossly exaggerates one aspect of his real nature, a side of him deliberately turned toward the public, like that of a man of action —and Byron might be described as a romantic man of action—who knows he has a role to play. (Had he lived another twenty years, it is more than likely that he would have destroyed the whole romantic-poetical legend and created a very different public Byron.) He was quite right when he saw himself in the sharpest contrast to Rousseau, who was at the mercy of his unconscious as Byron never was. There was in fact securely held in Byron much of that eighteenth century against which

Rousseau rebelled. Byron among his close friends, and in his journals and letters, never appears like a man abandoning himself to his dreams; he has much wit, humour, common-sense and shrewd judgment; he is essentially masculine and often appears insensitive to feminine values, and, for all his famous amours, he seems happier in male than in female company. He has far more of the conventional mind of his time than the other romantic poets. As Hazlitt, who did not like him, pointed out, there is in him a strong element of mere dandyism. He never forgets his rank. Much of his misanthropy, world-weariness, dust and ashes of despair, is part of the romantic-poetic performance, for in his longer poems especially he is a highly-skilled and astute entertainer, knowing exactly what mixture of the picturesque, the historical, the dramatic, the amorous, the grandly misanthropical, will hold his readers. Not that everything is false: the melancholy satiety is probably true enough, and the injured pride, and the dislike of obvious tyranny and stifling conventions, and the feeling of guilt left him by his relation with his half-sister, Augusta Leigh. But except in a few splendid lyrics, quite different in poetic quality from his large performances, he is not at heart a romantic poet at all. *Don Juan*, his best work, which shows us his strong masculine intellect, his witty impertinence, his rhetorical gusto, all at their best, is, only in its time and not in its spirit, one of the great romantic poems. There was much of the eighteenth century living on in Byron, together with some occasional flashes that make him suddenly seem startlingly modern. But this magnificent king of the Romantics was never at heart one of their company.

England's nearest approach to a romantic movement was in 1798 when William Wordsworth and Samuel Taylor Coleridge together produced *Lyrical Ballads*. It contains several poems long recognised to be masterpieces, but the critics at that time disliked it. The official critics, who contributed anonymous reviews to the quarterlies, continued to dislike and misunderstand the new poetry for the next thirty years, and as they enjoyed being offensive, to be reviewed by them was something of an ordeal. This probably explains why Wordsworth postponed the publication of his long poem, *The Prelude*, and never completed its philosophical companion, *The Excursion*. Shortly after the publication of *Lyrical Ballads*

Wordsworth returned to his own countryside, the Lake District, and there spent the rest of his long life. He and Coleridge and Robert Southey were frequently called 'The Lake Poets'. (Southey, once thought to be the poetic equal of the other two, his monumental epics greatly impressing his contemporaries, is now chiefly remembered for one or two of his prose works, notably his *Life of Nelson*.) But Wordsworth's poetry is quite unlike that of his friends; he is an original. Once past his rebellious youth, he sternly rejected much of what romanticism offered—nobody could have been more unlike Lord Byron—but he retained and even heightened Rousseau's passion for solitude and communion with Nature. Indeed, Wordsworth is the supreme poet of this passion. Deliberately discarding the usual romantic stage effects, avoiding the use of a tinselled-and-spangled poetic vocabulary and largely expressing himself in plain language, making no attempt to be entertaining in the Byronic manner, he created his own kind of poetry.

A good deal of it, perhaps most of it, is very dull, like a long walk on a grey day. But just as somewhere on that walk there might be a sudden and superb flash of beauty, so in Wordsworth's poetry there are short passages, perhaps only a line or so, that are miraculous. An apparently simple unadorned phrase will suddenly blaze in the reader's imagination. These great moments of his, once experienced, are never forgotten, and we never entirely lose our response to them. Wordsworth is essentially a poet of such moments, and there can be no doubt that on his endless walks among the bleak fells, as he brooded in solitude, the familiar but ever-changing scene spread wide before him, he was in search of these moments, when the mountains and the bare trees and the grass would seem to be lit up from within, when simple words in some magical arrangement of the unconscious would rise to consciousness. There are times known to most of us when, the conscious mind having been quietened and slowed down by hours of solitary walking and brooding, we suddenly relate ourselves to the natural scene through our unconscious, return to the enchanted unity with it which we knew in childhood, seem to lose the ego and our separateness; and of these times Wordsworth is the prophet and high priest. One of his greatest poems is his *Intimations of Immortality*. But in almost all his heightened moments, suddenly soaring out of the dull page, he is revealing such intimations. He is not a pantheist; he does not see Nature as God but as the symbol of God, making a sign, when we are ready to receive it, of our immortality. His essential poetry, as distinct from his uninspired verse-making, can be reduced to a very small volume, containing ecstatic moments of communion expressed in lines unlike those of any other poet, apparently simple in language and structure but curiously haunting, necromantic, as if brought from some depth of ancient incantation. So this long-faced, priggish trudger, meditating his dreary Ecclesiastical Sonnets as he does his twenty miles a day, must be included among the great Romantics.

Of the other two Lake Poets we might say that the industrious Southey had character without genius and Coleridge had genius without character. The promise of Coleridge in youth was boundless; it is agreed by all his contemporaries that the range and the force of his mind were extraordinary—"A hooded eagle among blinking owls", Shelley calls him; but years of opium encouraged him to meditate, dream and talk—he was the greatest talker of the age—and discouraged him from sitting down regularly at a desk to work. When we consider his unequalled reputation in his own time and the extent of his influence, we seem to inherit from him only mere fragments, a few terraces, pillars and broken statues representing a vast empire. But these fragments easily justify that reputation. His finest poetry was written while he was still young and the close friend of the two Wordsworths, William the poet and his remarkable sister, Dorothy. Later, when he had turned to prose, he was able to complete his *Biographia Literaria*, but the astonishing breadth and depth of his mind are best discovered in the various volumes, edited long after his death, that collect for us his scattered essays and notes and passages from his lectures. In his youth he learnt much from German criticism and philosophy, especially that of Schelling, but the criticism of his mature years surpasses the finest German criticism of his time both in its range and its remarkable insight. Though he swung over, like Wordsworth, from youthful rebellion to what looks painfully like High Tory and Church reaction, his perception and understanding of what is important in great literature remained with him, and in his own fragmentary fashion he must be considered the finest critic in this whole European Age of

Romance. All his poetry worth cherishing could be printed in a very small volume, giving us *The Ancient Mariner*, *Kubla Khan* and *Christabel* (both unfinished), and a few shorter poems. But their quality more than redeems the lack of quantity. *The Ancient Mariner* is the most wonderful romantic narrative poem in the English language, one of the supreme triumphs of the romantic imagination, unforgettable in its horrors, marvels and lyrical beauty. Coleridge has described for us how he came to write *Kubla Khan*, that elixir distilled from the very essence of romance, a poetic fragment that is as mysterious, evocative, vague and yet charged with meaning, as a piece of great music. He fell asleep while reading the old traveller's tales in *Purchas's Pilgrimage*, dreamt the poem or at least experienced it as a succession of dream images, and on waking "instantly and eagerly" wrote down what he remembered, immediately composing the poem. He could not finish it, he tells us, because he was interrupted by somebody coming to see him on business. There could be no better example of the contribution of the unconscious to poetry of this order: it is the whole romantic process dramatically demonstrated. Professor Irving Babbitt, who detested Rousseau and romanticism, quotes Coleridge's line "O Lady! we receive but what we give" as an example, following Rousseau, of the false 'Arcadian imagination' turning us away from reality; but in these very chapters of his, Babbitt shows how close to reality Coleridge's observation is, how a profound psychological truth is expressed in it, for being prepared to give little to Rousseau, Coleridge, the whole Romantic Age, Babbitt receives equally little from them. Had Coleridge possessed the will-power, conscious purpose, ethical severity, that Babbitt recommends to literature and its authors, he would undoubtedly have left us a much larger body of work. But it would not have included *The Ancient Mariner* and *Kubla Khan*.

Shelley, who saw Coleridge as "a hooded eagle", was drowned at the age of thirty, and, perpetually young himself, he is one of the supreme poets of and for impetuous and enthusiastic youth. He combines in himself and his work two very different things that are often found together in the young. The foundation of his thought is the ultra-rational atheism and philosophical anarchy not uncommon in the later eighteenth century and expressed at length by William Godwin, the desiccated Prospero to whom Shelley was the Ariel. (Godwin's daughter, Mary, was Shelley's second wife. She ought to be remembered, if not by readers then by filmgoers, as the creator of *Frankenstein*.) Using this foundation merely as its runway, Shelley's poetic imagination took off into the blue. It is an imagination differing in degree but not in kind from that of many enthusiastic romantic young people, to whom this poet always had—and let us hope always will have—a very special attraction. More mature readers are apt to note a lack of ordinary human feeling, a remoteness from common interests, in this poetry; and when it is below its highest level, a certain gaseous quality, a blurring of images, a use of words too reminiscent of the absurd philosophical romances the poet read (and wrote) in his early youth. And Shelley, a rapid and prolific writer, is too often well below his highest level.

But when he is in full high flight—and he is a poet we associate with air and fire, not earth and water—his poetry is marvellous in its innocence and loveliness, its swiftness and grace, its opalescent colouring and shifting lights; as if it already belonged to—and is indeed celebrating—some future Golden Age, when men have rid themselves of their heavy bodies and iron laws, when the imagination can dissolve and recompose any scene, when all are Ariels free of their last tasks and Prometheus is unbound for ever. What any generous youth, preferably in rebellion against tyranny and injustice, imagines for a few minutes, losing himself in excited fancies, goes soaring and glittering and singing through volume after volume of Shelley. But though neither the beautiful melancholy nor the high and sometimes shrill ecstasies, the vague music and perfume and multi-coloured transformations of these lyrics, are quite of this world; there are signs here and there, flashes of psychological insight, notably in his drama, *The Cenci*, that had Shelley lived longer and come to the end of his urge to soar and sing (for even his narrative and dramatic poems are lyrical in feeling), he might have broken the spell condemning so many of the English romantic poets to try, and fail, in the theatre, and so restored the tradition of poetic drama. As it is, he remains a lyrical genius, a romantic figure of eager revolt and poetry that, at certain ages and always for some readers, completely captures the imagination.

John Keats was the youngest of these great romantic poets, but he was the first to die, in 1821 at the age of twenty-six. His first book, containing the long narrative poem, *Endymion*, was denounced with such ferocity by the official reviewers, who did not begin to understand what they were reading, that it was widely believed, by Byron among others, that out of sheer disappointment and mortification his health failed him and so he died young. This is completely untrue. He met this savage criticism in the manliest spirit. "The imagination of a boy is healthy, and the mature imagination of a man is healthy; but there is a space of life between, in which the soul is in a ferment, the character undecided, the way of life uncertain, the ambition thick-sighted: thence proceeds mawkishness . . ." This is well said, but it was said by Keats and not by one of his critics. Indeed, this young surgeon's apprentice had more wisdom and a finer understanding of the arts than could be discovered in a total muster of the *Quarterly Review*'s contributors. His letters, more mature in thought and feeling than most of his poems, make us appreciate what must have been lost to literature by his early death. A handful of the poems he left us, the great odes and the best of the sonnets, gives him a place of equality beside Wordsworth, Coleridge, Byron, Shelley; but before his last fatal illness he developed and matured so quickly, adding to his poetry the high spirits, good sense, flashes of unusual insight, of his letters, that potentially he seems the greatest of these poets, promising to be master of almost any form of literature.

The suggestion, often made, that here cut off in youth was a poet possibly of Shakespearean stature is not at all absurd, even if the poems alone are considered and the wider promise in the letters is ignored. For there is a likeness to the younger Shakespeare of the poems, in this work of Keats. There is the same wide and deep sensuality, the same richness, the same attempt to express fairly common thoughts and moods with the utmost felicity. What is being expressed is neither very original nor profound—Keats is at the opposite extreme from a poet like Blake—but the poetry achieves its own originality, and even profundity, through this richness, this wonderful felicity of image and phrase, its unusual evocative quality, its undertones and overtones. Keats's great lines, like Shakespeare's, haunt the memory, and he soon became one of the most frequently quoted of English poets. Though the themes he chose, the moods he expressed, are extremely romantic, belonging to a day-dreaming youth, the mind behind the strongest poems, the mind deliberately enriching the lines like a composer using the full resources of his orchestra, is a mind already finely balanced between consciousness and the unconscious, that of a major artist, far removed from the pathetic figure of boyish romance that Keats is sometimes assumed to be. He is indeed too often considered in terms of his tragi-comic love-affair, his tuberculosis, his melancholy flight to Italy, his grave in Rome, as if he were a sentimental schoolgirl's idea of a romantic poet. But the poetry itself, his letters, his life in its factual details, show us a very different sort of man, immense if shadowy in his promise, solid and enduring in his performance, brief though it was. And there is not a more attractive figure in all the annals and legends of this Romantic Age than young, for ever young, John Keats.

Though the prose of this Age in England falls well behind the poetry, it shows the same influences and transformations at work on it. The best essayists and critics reflect the intense individualism of the poets, and the impersonal prose of the eighteenth century gives way to a highly mannered prose as personal and intimate as talk, even if infinitely more elaborate. Charles Lamb—and, to a lesser extent, William Hazlitt— deliberately returned to seventeenth-century models, to Sir Thomas Browne and Jeremy Taylor; and the prose of their essays, rich and quaint in Lamb, more sinewy and masculine in Hazlitt, has much of the elaboration, the music and imagery, of the old seventeenth-century prose. Like their essays, the criticism of these two and of Leigh Hunt, criticism that did good service both to contemporary and the older literature (for example, the Elizabethan drama) that had largely been ignored by the previous age, was frankly personal, admitting no standard but the critic's honest likes and dislikes. These romantic prose-men were not behind the poets in expressing themselves first of all, and even their criticism is a chapter of autobiography. One of them, Thomas de Quincey, produced a masterpiece of actual autobiography, day-dream and fantasy, in his *Confessions of an English Opium-Eater*, using a very elaborate and rather too self-conscious prose style. An equally romantic and eccentric figure, Walter Savage Landor, who outlived the whole age and is chiefly remembered now for a few exquisite epigrammatic verses, preferred to avoid the romantic manner in the many volumes of his prose *Imaginary Conversations*, which are written in a massive, classically balanced prose, impressive but a little somnolent, like public oratory. Another original, who sympathised with the romantic rebels but also laughed at them, was Shelley's friend, Thomas Love Peacock, who wrote a number of odd satirical novels, consisting mostly of table-talk, of which one, *Nightmare Abbey*, provides us with the wittiest comment on the whole Romantic Age. It is also a burlesque of the popular 'novels of terror', blood-and-thunder tales of mystery and horror, generally in a 'Gothic' setting, for which writers like Mrs. Radcliffe, Maturin and M. G. Lewis created a large public appetite. Many of their devices—for example, bringing in what appears to be the supernatural and then keeping the reader waiting for a natural explanation—may be found in popular fiction to this day.

Scott soon had imitators in historical romance, but they had most of his faults and little of his merit. It says much for his perception that he was among the first to recognise the supremacy of Jane Austen in her own kind of fiction, the domestic novel, which was also being written by Fanny Burney, Maria Edgeworth, Susan Ferrier, all three women of talent but well below the delicate art, the astonishing perfection, of Jane Austen, who has fascinated every succeeding generation of English readers. Her acute sense of character, her bland irony, her exquisite powers of organisation and presentation, turned the uneventful lives of well-fed people in quiet corners into enchanting novels. Into those same corners William Cobbett might have ridden, to take a look at the crops or the pasture, a kind of rebellious John Bull, whose plain, strong, descriptive and polemical writing may be found in his *Rural Rides*. Of the regular contributors to the official reviews—all of them a long way removed from the romantic—easily the best is the Rev. Sydney Smith, more concerned with liberal and liberating principles than with literature (or religion), a notable wit and humorist, who can still be read with pleasure and makes many a welcome appearance in the diaries, journals, memoirs, of the period. It is very rich in these chronicles, from the journals of political high life kept by men like Greville and Creevy to the diarists of literature and the arts, like Thomas Moore (a poet whose verse, once immensely popular, chiefly survives in a few songs), Haydon the painter, and Henry Crabb Robinson, who in his youth met Goethe and Schiller and whose later acquaintance included most of the English romantic poets and essayists. He outlived this period, which may be said to have ended about 1830 in England, by nearly forty years, but did not live long enough to see the last of the romantic outlook and manner in English poetry, for these persisted, with ever weakening force, until nearly the end of the century.

2

As we have agreed that, in the title of this chapter, 'English' refers to language and not to nationality, we can end it by noticing some American writers, too few during this age to deserve a chapter to themselves. Round about 1800, Charles Brockden Brown was producing his American versions of the 'Gothic' novel, of which the best is *Wieland, or The Transformation*, which had several of the English romantic poets and critics, some years later, among its admirers. But the first American authors to have European reputations were Washington Irving and Fenimore Cooper. Irving spent much of his life in England, which he described with some charm and humour but with little that was original (or American) in matter and manner. He reads more like an eighteenth-century English essayist than an American visitor and man of business. He was indeed much better in his twenties when he was writing about New York, and writing very much in the style of American youth and not at all in the style of a gentlemanly English second-rate man of letters. He is probably best remembered for his tale (borrowed from a German original but cleverly transplanted) of the Dutchman who slept twenty years in the Catskill Mountains and then went back to his village, to become the famous Rip Van Winkle. Fenimore Cooper also spent some years in Europe, then returned to Cooperstown (founded by his father) in New York State, to be that very English and very un-American type— the country gentleman. He wrote a good many novels, mostly bad, and he owed his reputation, which was perhaps more solidly established in

Europe than at home, to his Leatherstocking tales of the wilderness and the Indian fighting, seventy years earlier. Mark Twain, who disliked all Cooper's fiction, revealed all its weaknesses in a savage attack on him, and everything he says is true. But it is not the whole truth, and Twain in his blind prejudice misses the great point in Cooper's favour. In spite of his slack narration, the dubious historical background to his tales, the genteel bad writing, the simpering girls mouthing impossible dialogue, all the schoolboy nonsense about superhuman tracking and sharpshooting that Twain guffaws at, Fenimore Cooper offered the world something essentially and, in its own fashion, deeply and poetically American, just as Twain did when he stopped clowning and remembered the mighty Mississippi. For there came with these Leatherstocking tales, especially to readers on the other side of the Atlantic, a sense of the vastness and mystery of the American scene, of the presence in it, half poetic, half sinister, of these vanishing tribes of red men, of painted shadowy faces in the forest, of fading clouds of dust on the prairie. And all this is as deeply American, even though it is presented with less truth and skill, as Twain's Mississippi. In his own uncertain fashion, Cooper struck a note, heard for the first time, that was to go clanging and echoing through all authentic American writing.

Edgar Allan Poe was twenty years younger than Fenimore Cooper and is a little late for our Romantic Age (though we shall have to stretch it for the Russians and some others), but he is best dealt with here. It is possible to admire some things that Poe wrote, and to feel sorry for him in all his variety of miseries, poverty, years of hack-work, alcoholism, sexual frustrations and aberrations, while still holding that, after the first period of neglect, he has received more attention and praise than he deserves. It is true that after Baudelaire discovered and translated him, passing him on to Mallarmé, who in turn persuaded Paul Valéry (who said so) that Poe was a master misunderstood and slighted by the Americans and English, Poe can be said to have inspired, if indirectly, the whole Symbolist Movement. The French poets who wanted to write about their inner world, not the outer one, felt that Poe had shown them the way. Though exquisite poets in their own language, they were not acutely aware of Poe's faults of taste and style in English, but, on the other hand, they knew that much of his verse and fiction was symbolic fantasy, an attempt to express and to release through art a psycho-pathological condition, which Baudelaire, for one, shared to some extent. And from this point of view Poe is undoubtedly important. It is also true that in his short stories he was an innovator of two kinds, the scientific wonder tale and the detective story, that in our time have entranced a vast body of readers everywhere. Let us admit that he was a highly original writer of some importance. It is when we are chided for misunderstanding and slighting him, for not recognising him as one of the masters, that we feel compelled to state the case against Poe.

To begin with, his critical theory is dishonest, an attempt to rationalise his compulsive necrophilia and sexual perversity, and to transform his own limitations—for example, his incapacity for sustained effort—into supreme literary virtues. He declares in effect that what he wants to do, and is capable of doing, is exactly what literature should be trying to achieve. Both in his verse and his prose there is too much that is typical of the pseudo-literary society in which he lived and worked, reproducing its bogus romanticism, Southern eloquence, the horrible clichés of 'Gothic' fiction. No doubt some of his tales of horror, having their roots in his diseased sexuality, have moments that chill the blood, moments when we forget the elaborate machinery of blood-chilling he has assembled and set in motion. It is true that occasional lines with genuinely evocative undertones and overtones come flashing out of the verse; that some good judges of literature have discovered genius in *Ulalume* and do not see its "dank tarn of Auber" and "ghoul-haunted woodland of Weir" as faded theatrical backcloths; and it has even been argued that the frequent sprightly rhythm of these charnel-house verses indicates an underlying sardonic humour. But what is wrong with Poe's inner world, quite apart from its necrophilia, the embalmed corpse always found on its altar, is that it uses too many tawdry sets and properties borrowed from second-rate romanticism; it is too cheaply and tastelessly furnished; and Poe is unable to use for his utter rejection of life a profound and haunting symbolism. So on purely literary grounds he is unsatisfactory, an original but no master. But partly through his influence, then by way of Baudelaire, there will arrive the idea that literature created out of uncommon energy, zest, an eager acceptance of life, is somehow inferior to the literature that is psycho-pathological in origin, compensating some deficiency, expressing some perversity. And it is a bad idea.

CHAPTER THIRTEEN

The Romantic Movement
in France

THE ROMANTIC MOVEMENT began in France about the time it was ending in Germany and England. More than half a century passed before Rousseau's exported influences were re-imported into France, with other names attached to them. Rousseau was translated into action, in the Revolution. Minor upheavals, like the July Revolution of 1830, are generally favourable to literature, but great upheavals, social earthquakes like the original Revolution, are almost death to it. The guillotine, viewed from either the Right or Left positions, is not inspiring. Moreover, the Republic, the Directorate, the Empire, all affected a certain classical taste, like Napoleon himself, though as a conqueror, with his star and his legend, he may be regarded as another of the Romantics, easily the most extravagant and wasteful of them all. Again, whereas in Germany and England the romantic spirit had merely to overcome a classicism largely imitated from France, and never quite at home among the German forests and in the English haze, in France it had to do battle— as it almost literally did on the first night of Hugo's *Hernani*—against the old standing army of classicism in its central citadel, Paris. And just as the elfin German forests and the magical English mists were not to be found in France, there were essential elements of German and English romanticism that never found their way South, vanishing a long way from the vineyards and the Mediterranean. Though the French Romantic Movement owed much to the German, enthusiastically interpreted by Mme de Staël, and even more to English literature, especially to Shakespeare (played triumphantly by an English company at the Odéon in

Paris in 1827), it differed widely from both of them and had a character all its own.

The French are renowned for their excellent manners, yet their political history suggests they can be more explosive than most Western Europeans. When they are not being formally polite, they are apt to be more informal and impolite than most other peoples. Now the classical style they adopted first, and then retained longest, was more than a collection of technical rules, though the rules were there, and deliberately to break them, as Hugo did, was to declare war on the whole tradition. Classicism assumed certain psychological restraints, imposing on its authors the moderation and good sense of a public literature, the manners of the drawing-room. The Romantic Movement in France changed all this. And with the tremendous energy it released there came a freedom from restraint, sweeping away moderation, good sense and manners, that encouraged boundless displays of egoism, a new cult of personality, the literary ego inflated like a monstrous balloon, with the poet, the artist, no longer expressing society but challenging it and defying it. For after the Restoration, and still more after the July Revolution and the arrival of a bourgeois monarchy, the commercial middle class, the patrons of the new press, became increasingly important. As a class it had old-fashioned classical tastes. (Stendhal thought that the difference between classical and romantic was merely the difference between the old and the new.) But its younger and rebellious members, enthusiastic youths and dreamy girls, gave their support to the new romantic authors, who, ironically enough, through their colossal egoism and their deliberate separation from and defiance of society, were often able to turn themselves into successful professional men of letters. In this they received considerable help—for even strong disapproval was good publicity—from the new popular press. And no matter what they wrote about the solitary grandeur of their souls, the more successful romantic writers were well aware of what the newspapers could do for them, and were often adroit in their use of the press.

Indeed, by the time the Romantic Movement was well under way in the early 1830s a pattern was laid down that has been repeated ever since. Paris has been the centre of almost every new movement, not because the

French are revolutionary-minded in the arts, for they are mostly very conservative, but because, at least in Paris, they care just enough to provide a
really hostile and noisy opposition. It is public indifference, the yawning
tolerance of London, that defeats a new movement, which can soon begin
to thrive on the loud hostility of Paris. There was another feature of the
French Romantic Movement that was peculiar to it at the time but is
familiar enough to us now. It was more than a purely literary movement.
It attacked along a broad front in the arts. The romantic painters, headed
by Delacroix, arrived before the writers. The Salon of 1824 was one of
the great romantic challenges. And even on its literary side the Movement was strongly pictorial. (And not only in words, for, as we can see
for ourselves, Lamartine, Hugo, de Musset, Gérard de Nerval, Mérimée,
George Sand, were all accomplished sketchers, and Gautier was a painter
before he became a writer.) Nor were musicians absent. Berlioz and
Chopin, and frequent sympathetic visitors like Liszt and Paganini, were
like characters out of ultra-romantic fiction, all fabulous creatures incapable of avoiding public attention.

In 1830, however, one literary figure towered above all the new
romantic young writers. This was François-René de Chateaubriand, then
already in his sixties, and the acknowledged father or high priest of
French romanticism. Though anything but revolutionary in his outlook
and tastes, with much of the eighteenth century living on in him, Chateaubriand represents the first break-through of that soaring egoism typical
of the French Romantics. His childhood and youth in a remote Breton
castle might have been invented by Rousseau: he grew up a melancholy
and dreamily voluptuous Narcissus, and carried this handsome image of
himself throughout a long crowded career, very far removed from the
distant unpeopled landscapes celebrated in his works. "While he pressed
forward in pursuit of honours," Anatole France observed sardonically,
"he would sigh for solitude and the world's forgetting." The genuine
brooding melancholy of Sénancour's *Obermann* is reflected, as if in a fine
but flawed concave mirror, in the impressive but slightly dubious works
of Chateaubriand, in which the fiction suggests autobiography, and the
autobiography, especially when it comes to his travels in America, more
than suggests fiction. When the Empire, in search of stability, turned to

religion, it was Chateaubriand who offered it a romantically floodlit Catholic Church. He wrote about almost everything and for everything except the Theatre, but there is a theatrical element, a suggestion of a lime-lit star performer seen against beautiful but painted vistas of exotic land-scape, in almost everything he did write. His contemporary prestige and influence were tremendous but his best legacy to us is his posthumously published autobiography, *Mémoires d'Outre-Tombe*, which is both an astonishing panorama of historical events and figures and the self-portrait of a man who is half-genius, half-charlatan, and thoroughly romantic in both halves. Like a choir conductor with a tuning fork, he sounded very early the note that was to return to him in full chorus from the Romantic Movement.

For a long time now Mme de Staël has been far more often read about than read, existing more as a character than as a critic and novelist. Her quarrel with Napoleon kept her away from Paris for many years; she died in 1817; but she had a considerable influence on French romanticism. Her very first book was a study of Rousseau, and one of her last and best works was an account of Germany that introduced many of the German Romantics to French readers. Her companion for many years—and a fellow-cosmopolitan—was Benjamin Constant, who spent far more time with politics than with literature, but he wrote one brief piece of semi-autobiographical fiction that is a masterpiece, *Adolphe*. This record of a love-affair between a young man and a woman ten years older than he is, typical of innumerable affairs in which the man wearies of it as the woman becomes ever more deeply and tragically involved, combines a severe economy of method with great insight. But except in its date it does not belong to romantic literature. No illusions flourish in it. Constant here is both older and newer than this Age. He looks back to the eighteenth century and far forward to the post-romantic fiction of exact and detached psychological analysis.

We could say the same of Henri Beyle, who wrote as Stendhal. There is a great deal of the eighteenth century in him, not Rousseau but Voltaire, and yet he is also one of the moderns, a prominent member of the tiny group of novelists (of all countries) who are consistently praised by the intellectuals of this century. Comparatively unknown in his own time (though Balzac was enthusiastic about *The Chartreuse of Parma*), Stendhal is now the central figure of a cult. The fact that he is still not widely popular helps to maintain the cult. Although his enthusiastic admirers cherish every scrap of autobiography he left, and think more highly of his book on love than it deserves, his reputation rests on the two long novels, *The Red and the Black* and *The Chartreuse of Parma*. That these are two highly original and remarkable novels, very close in both spirit and method to some of our best modern fiction, cannot be denied. But being a darling of the *élite*, Stendhal has undoubtedly been over-praised. An odd and rather ambiguous person, deliberately cultivating eccentricities to cover a persistent feeling of social inferiority, as a writer Stendhal can be described as a rebellious Romantic partly hiding behind a determinedly unromantic or anti-romantic manner. He detested Chateaubriand, and so he is a Chateaubriand in reverse or inside out. For the Chateaubriand type of Romantic is like an *omelette surprise* or baked Alaska, all flames and glow and sugared egg on the outside, too often covering something cold and harsh to the palate in the centre. Stendhal reverses this. With him the outside is cold and dry, the flame is within. He avoids all the tricks and devices of the obvious Romantic—the warm and misty eloquence, the studied picturesque poses, the unlimited rhetoric lavished on the big scenes—and sharply and dryly observes, records, dissects, keeping to the business in hand and not stopping to ask for a round of applause from the audience. Nothing could be more unlike the romanticism of his time, or closer in spirit and manner to the realism of later fiction, fifty years after his death, than the justly renowned Battle of Waterloo scene in *The Chartreuse of Parma*, in which everything is exactly observed from the point of view of his bewildered young hero, and there is not a trace of the panoramic, the grandly heroic, the super-horrific, of the romantic fiction of his time. And some of the crucial scenes between his young men and their mistresses have a wonderful clarity, economy, penetration, like master-etchings when compared with the coloured fuzz and blur of most romantic love-scenes.

Nevertheless, behind this cool stare and these surgical knives and scalpels, the dry manner and the style imitated from the legal Code, there was a Romantic in Stendhal, and an unbalanced and rather sinister

Romantic too, suddenly taking charge of the action, blotting out good sense, transforming the cool surgeon or analyst into an hysterical patient. Critics who are one-sidedly intellectual and too conscious of belonging to an *élite* often persist to the point of uncovering a streak of silliness in themselves, making them blind to or delighted with a not dissimilar streak of silliness in Stendhal. Just as there is something unsatisfactory and ambiguous about the man himself, so too, in spite of their originality and brilliant technical innovations, his novels offer us too many dubious elements to be accepted as great fiction, let alone (as André Gide seriously declared) the greatest fiction France has produced. They were for their time, these two novels, astonishing creations—and may remain so for many generations yet—but they lack the breadth and balance and strong hold on life of great fiction. They blow too hot and cold, like winds in an unhealthy climate. The head and the heart behind them are out of harmony. Sound criticism must give him the praise he well deserves; but to put him high above talents more massive, broadly-based, fertile and generous, is to imitate his capriciousness, wilfulness, deliberate eccentricity.

Stendhal was present at that famous first night of Hugo's *Hernani*, when the Romantic Movement made its all-out attack, but he was not there as one of the shock troops of romanticism, being middle-aged and, though anti-classical, not sympathetic to Hugo and his friends. Alfred de Vigny was there, but not Lamartine. These two poets must be placed somewhere on the edge of the Movement. They are alike in this, and in belonging to old landed families, and in their marriages, for, oddly enough, both married Englishwomen. Their talents and careers are very different. The great popularity of Lamartine's verse is easy to explain. Melodiously and gracefully it expresses certain tender and sentimental moods known to some people at all times and to a great many people during the first half of the nineteenth century. It is the poetry of a sensitive and highly articulate diplomat and politician, who is not giving all his mind to it but only the more tender and melancholy side of himself. This is the perfect poetry for readers who in turn do not want to give too much of themselves but can appreciate fine elegiac verses at twilight on Saturday or late on Sunday evening, after a week of hard French bargaining. De Vigny, who was in the army when he wrote most of his best poems, is less facile and easily accomplished, has more weight and bite in his verse; he is a deeply earnest, restrained Romantic, without the wild energy and cheerful impudence of the *Hernani* young men. But if his output of verse was small, de Vigny had the romantic versatility, for although he was not really a man of the theatre (in spite of the fact that one of the best actresses in Paris was his mistress), he did a careful adaptation of *Othello* for the French stage, and contributed to it several prose plays, of which the most successful was *Chatterton*, and wrote the historical romance, *Cinq-Mars*, and some admirable memoirs of both military and literary life. Handsome, gifted, apparently fortunate in every way, there was in Alfred de Vigny from the first a withdrawn, pessimistic strain, as if somehow he knew that nothing would turn out very well for him—as indeed it did not—and was guarding himself against disappointment. He lacked the great buoyancy of the out-and-out Romantics. This cannot be said of Béranger, the immensely popular song-writer who was outside any literary movement and who twice sang himself into gaol but then was elected a Deputy in 1848. He was one of the last poets to be genuinely idolised by a nineteenth-century working class.

For his unofficial *claque* at the opening of *Hernani*, Hugo, the son of a general and a man of action himself, marshalled four hundred young enthusiasts from the Latin Quarter, the Bohemian types that found their way later into Murger's stories. Among the art students was Théophile Gautier, aged nineteen, with his hair down to his shoulders and wearing a strange bright red garment designed by himself. Also in the audience were Balzac, Alexandre Dumas, Prosper Mérimée, Saint-Beuve, Gérard de Nerval, possibly young Alfred de Musset, and certainly Charles Nodier, the librarian and himself a versatile writer, at his best perhaps in short stories, who offered both his scholarship and regular hospitality to Hugo and his friends. (And among the opposition that night, jeering from his box, was Scribe, enormously successful with conventional plays and operatic libretti, the acknowledged nineteenth-century master of mechanical but effective play construction.) After the very first line, which deliberately defied the classic tradition of poetic drama, the storm broke and never subsided during the rest of the evening; and on that storm Hugo and the French Romantics rode like Valkyries to fame and glory. Moreover, while commanding his battalion of applauders and riding the storm to glory, Hugo, in the interval between Acts Four and Five, accepted an offer of six thousand francs from a publisher for the play. He was quite cool about it, though down to his last fifty francs. After all, he was Victor Hugo.

When somebody told Hugo, in his fabulous old age, that the soul ended with death, he replied: "For your soul that may be true, but I know that mine is eternal." There is almost all of Hugo in that retort. Like him it is somehow enormous, nearly sublime but also faintly ridiculous. The secret of Hugo is his stupendous energy and self-confidence, enabling him to hurl the whole of himself into whatever he has on hand, short poems, long poems, plays, novels, pamphlets, letters. He does not attempt something but takes it by storm. He is like the young Napoleon's Army of Italy in literature. He is one side of the French national character, largely concealed during the long classical tradition, and belonging to the people and not to the intellectuals, raised to its highest pitch. It is true that he was devoid of humour, but then humour, with its sense of proportion, its doubts and self-mockery, would have cut down his energy and superb confidence. No doubt his egoism was monstrous, but a man who thought less well of himself could not have risen, as Hugo did in his *Légende des siècles* and elsewhere in his poetry, to heights at which he seems to be expressing in true prophetic vein the tragedies and dreams and aspirations of whole peoples. ("Victor Hugo," some wit declared, "was really a madman who thought he was Victor Hugo.") His longest and strongest flights in verse belong in time to the next age, coming well into the second half of the century, but he himself, although he lived until 1885, never really steps out of this earlier Romantic Age, keeping its ardours and extravagances alive through his own sheer vitality, resisting to the end the creeping maladies of the later nineteenth century. It has been said, with truth, that he has far more words than ideas. But then he is a large loose poet, and though there are times when he seems all grandiose pseudo-mysticism and empty declamation, there are other moments when the words catch fire and seem to illuminate some region beyond ideas. All his plays, though only the first of his huge novels, *Notre-Dame de Paris*, come within our time limit here. Both his drama and his fiction suffer from the same fault, a lack of the wide, protean, sympathetic imagination that enables a man completely to identify himself with his characters, giving each one his or her separate life. The creative energy is there, but the egoism gets in the way. A man so tremendously aware of himself as Hugo always is cannot quite persuade us that his creatures have a life of their own. In addition the plays, though two of them, *Hernani* and *Ruy Blas*, can still hold intelligent audiences, suffer from a dated theatricality, many of their highly dramatic devices, once brilliant innovations, having been used over and over again by succeeding generations of melodramatic playwrights. His fiction wears better, especially for younger readers, chiefly because his immense vitality and sense of the picturesque can give colour, movement, life, to wide scenes, encouraging us to ignore any want of subtlety or even truth in the characters, so that we enjoy them rather as we used to enjoy the crowded and dazzling epics of the silent films. Finally, we shall do well to remember that ever since his death the whole current of criticism and literary fashion has been running away from Hugo and all that he represents, from what is positive in him, his creative energy and fertility and optimism, as well as from what is negative or dubious; and that the tide may turn.

Balzac applauded *Hernani* with the rest of Hugo's *claque*, though afterwards he severely criticised both the action and the characters of the play. It may seem strange, except as a mere matter of time and place, to include him in the Romantic Movement. Here, it might be said, is the first and one of the most ambitious of our realistic modern novelists, the planner and architect of the Human Comedy, the novelist of society itself, in Paris or the provinces, town and country, high life, low life, finance, politics, fashionable intrigues, occult researches, everybody and everything; the man who wrote day and night to feed his enormous appetite for money and fame, and to show us every possible effect of similar appetites. But behind this impressive apparatus of realism, of surveying and analysing and reporting, of tracking down and following up, of whole auctioneer's catalogues of salons and boudoirs and libraries and furnishings and *bric-à-brac*, of confidential accounts of dealings on the *bourse*, ministerial changes, scandal in high society, crimes in the underworld, there is a wild-eyed and impassioned Romantic. With his endless writing and re-writing night after night, his robe and black coffee, his mania for speculation and buying jewellery and *bric-à-brac*, his blind devotion to his aristocratic mistress (who said, "He is infatuated with nobility"), he is himself like a character in some fantastic romance of the literary life. His pompous general preface to the *Human Comedy*, with its references to zoology, mysticism, political science, religion, the marvels of electricity, and animal magnetism, should deceive nobody: here is one of the 1830 Romantics enjoying himself pretending not to be one, and there is behind the grand manner and vague wide references of this preface something at once absurd and touching. That he observed and absorbed much during his provincial boyhood and his first years in Paris cannot be questioned; he had a vast appetite for experience as well as for food; but once he set to work to carry out his vast plan all his energy went into creation. (There exists a book containing biographies of two thousand Balzac characters.) He has really very little in common with the naturalistic novelists, the notebook men, who came afterwards. Crowded though it is, often described in detail to the point of tedium, his is a dream world, very different, of course, from the other dream worlds of romanticism but still one of them. That is why we are neither shocked nor surprised to discover in this world of his, next door to some tale of provincial greed or Parisian intrigue, occult elements and fantastic fables that might almost have been adapted from the *Arabian Nights*. And being a dream world, one edge of it vanishes into sheer boredom and the other extreme edge turns into nightmare.

Between these two extremes there is an astonishing crowd of people, moving through a bewildering maze of stories. These people are not perfect creations: they are apt to be either downright good or downright bad, and the good are apt to be too foolish, too easily victimised, and the bad are apt to be too determinedly vicious, smelling a little of sulphur. The virtuous young women generally lack character, and are like early film heroines photographed through gauze. The young men are better, especially if they are ambitious but uncertain, half-clever, half-silly. But best of all are the middle-aged and elderly, of both sexes, who are the victims of some monstrous appetite, some ruling passion, some mania, for the one-sided Romantic in Balzac has an instinctive sympathy with such characters, though he may pretend to disapprove of them, and so creates them rather larger than life and lends them a terrible energy. When these fascinating monsters are entirely absent, his coarse handling, his obsessive love of detail, his insistence upon the obvious, like a guide in a museum, or, in his other mood, his heavy occult hocus-pocus, bring him below the level of any of the reputable realistic novelists who followed him. But when these big characters take charge, when the situation is right for him and the scene blazes into life, as it does in *Le Père Goriot*, *Eugénie Grandet*, *La Cousine Bette* and *Le Cousin Pons*, and in a few of the fantastic tales, he rises high above that level, reaching by sheer creative force and vitality, in spite of his limitations of style, a kind of poetry of fiction not unlike great drama. When Stendhal came into fashion with the *élite*, Balzac went out, along with much other good reading for robust tastes; but those who have such tastes and care nothing for literary fashion will find him the greater novelist.

Two novelists who are now far more often discussed as characters than as writers are George Sand, whose real name was Aurore Dupin, and Alexandre Dumas. George Sand never fails to appear in memoirs of the period because of her love-affairs, especially her spectacular but unfortunate affairs with two men of genius, Alfred de Musset and Chopin. She represents romanticism in its militantly feminist aspect; she writes with enthusiasm and sympathy of the deeply-loving, misunderstood woman, victimised by custom and convention, a character that was to haunt European fiction for some time; and through many of her exuberant improvisations—for her genuine talent and reckless temperament together encouraged slapdash methods—there runs a very real and sensitive feeling for the French countryside and its people. Alexandre Dumas (not to be confused with his son, the dramatist, whose *La Dame aux camélias* is a late product of the Romantic Movement) was a tremendous character, a swaggering giant who can be found in all reminiscences of Parisian life between 1825 and 1850, after which he left the city; and once he was successful he employed so many collaborators that he might be said to have run a factory for turning out 'cloak and dagger' serials and plays. His *Three Musketeers* series has always been deservedly popular among young readers, together with more ambitious tales like *Marguerite de*

Valois and *The Count of Monte-Cristo*, and later English Romantics like Henley and Stevenson delighted in him. His popular plays, *Antony* and *Kean* and the rest, held the stage throughout the century, and indeed have more theatrical vitality and originality than those of Scribe. The weakness of his historical tales is that, having been mostly written for serial publication in newspapers, they are so brisk in their action, so staccato and snappy in their dialogue, that they are apt to seem absurd in book form. This demand for serial stories or *feuilletons* by the Paris newspapers of the period was also responsible for the great popularity of Eugène Sue and his elaborate tales of crime and underworld, the crude romanticism of the new urban masses, and it is chiefly to Sue's influence we owe our later and almost unlimited development in crime fiction.

Prosper Mérimée may at first sight seem to be completely outside the Romantic Movement, for neither as a man nor as a writer does he share any of its more obvious and flamboyant characteristics. He was a reserved man, who contrived to hold a place under several governments, had a rather cynical manner, and wrote comparatively little, and all with an unromantic economy and apparent simplicity, in what is one of the best prose narrative styles of the century. He is at his best in the *nouvelle*, a long short story or brief and more direct form of the novel, in which he relates, with severe restraint and detachment, some tragic or bitterly ironical tale of passion against an exotic background, as in *Matteo Falcone* and *Carmen* and the rest. He realised—as many authors, following his superb example, have done since—that such tales gain in tragic force by not being told with obvious sympathy in the exuberant manner of the other Romantics. But at heart—and we can learn from his revealing correspondence how deceptive his outward manner was—he belongs to them because the overmastering passion, no matter how dryly he describes its effects, is to him its own justification, life as it must be lived however disastrous the consequences, and this is the pure essence of romanticism. In the sharpest contrast, at least outwardly, is Théophile Gautier, in youth the picturesque and rather absurd banner-bearer to the Romantic Movement, and later one of the noisier heralds of the Æsthetic Movement ("art for art's sake") that belongs to the second half of the century. Gautier began as a painter and, when he failed, took to painting in words. A prolific journalist and periodical critic of the arts, he is more impressive as a figure and a contemporary influence than he is in his authorship. His highly coloured prose, which included some impressionistic travel books and some fiction (his youthful *Mademoiselle de Maupin*, with its bravura and impudent sexuality, was one of the minor successes and scandals of the Movement), has been largely outlived by his verse, greatly admired by Baudelaire among others. (Baudelaire himself just misses this Age and so will appear in the next section.) His poetry has not much weight or penetration but is exquisitely turned and splendidly pictorial—a painter singing. With Gautier should be mentioned his unfortunate friend Gérard de Nerval, notorious for his eccentricities even in this circle, being once discovered leading a lobster along the street and saying, "It does not bark and knows the secrets of the deep." There was madness lurking behind this eccentricity, and he hanged himself; but there was also quite remarkable talent, unspoilt and original, within a limited range, in spite of his wandering life and hack-work. His best poetry, to be found in *Les Chimères*, has a classical concentration and density and yet is also mysteriously evocative in the manner of the later Symbolists. And his semi-autobiographical stories, in *Les Filles du feu*, especially *Sylvie*, have an extraordinary nostalgic charm, the green and gold of long-lost summers.

Alfred de Musset was the youngest member of Hugo's circle, a gifted, excitable, wilful boy. Much of his life and work was dominated by his tempestuous affair with George Sand, shadows and echoes of it finding their way into much of his later work. For an undisciplined and hard-drinking man, generally in poor health and dying at forty-seven, Musset was astonishingly productive, probably because he wrote quickly, a poet in the Byronic style but reaching a higher level of beauty and romantic exaltation than Byron did. His prose tales were more immediately successful than his plays, many of which he wrote simply to be read, in his despair of the Theatre. But gradually more and more of these plays were produced until finally, after his death, he was acknowledged to be one of the finest French dramatists of the century. His is not great drama, but his odd mixture of poetry, fantasy and wit, of the Renaissance and the eighteenth century with the romanticism of the 1830s, is both original and delightful. In view of his reputation in Paris, the wide range of his plays from the Shakespearean historical drama, *Lorenzaccio*, to the witty light comedies of his last years, and the many fine parts he can offer actresses, it is surprising he has not a larger place in our World Theatre.

Like Heine in the German Romantic Movement, Musset may be said to represent the final phase of the French Romantic Movement, from which in 1837 he made a great show of breaking away. He offers us romanticism not soaring into the blue but turning in on itself, disillusioned but unable to correct itself and find a balance, as Goethe did, and covering its defeat with wit and mockery. Romance could not sustain this ultra-romantic "child of the age", as he called himself. In this situation, his natural gift for the Theatre, where a man may usefully divide himself and set his dreams and disillusion arguing and fencing, was of great value to him. Even in his very early twenties he could create Fantasio, in the play of that name, who, reversing Hamlet's famous speech, tells us what a wretched thing man is—not to be able to jump through a window without breaking his legs, to be obliged to play the violin ten years to become a decent musician, to learn even before he can make an omelette. (And then we discover that a certain number of eggs have to be broken too.) His very weakness, the spoilt child in him, the absence of that tremendous energy and self-confidence which could keep a Hugo in full flight into his eighties, enable Musset to understand, if not to recover from, the malady of unchecked egoism, the desire for sensation and heightened feeling at all costs, the hope of real omelettes made with dream eggs. He had the perception but he had not the character for a break-away: he was trapped in the shadow of the moon. So with him romanticism dwindles into something poised between wistfulness and mockery, remaining that size and in that posture for the rest of the nineteenth century. The roaring giants, half-mad with egoism, having vanished, a familiar figure, with a dead-white face for the moonlight, capers or droops on the stage. Pierrot has arrived.

CHAPTER FOURTEEN

Russians and Others

I

THE German, English and French Romantics were eagerly read in Russia. But major Russian writers, like the three we can include in this Age, Pushkin, Lermontov, Gogol, though arriving belatedly on the scene and generally conscious themselves of Western influences, really owe little to anything and anybody outside Russia. It is as if another continent had entered literature. The advantages and disadvantages possessed by Russian writers, during this Age and for many years later, are quite unlike those favouring or hampering the writers of Western Europe. The disadvantages are easy to understand. There was first the crushing weight of Tsardom, at its worst during this period, under the iron rule of Nicholas I. A writer defying the censorship or held guilty of subversive tendencies might be ordered to retire to his estates or be sent to Siberia. This made writing a dangerous trade; and not during these years a richly rewarding trade, for in this huge country, with its slow and difficult communications, its few cities, the comparatively large population was made up of thirty to forty million unlettered serfs, a host of military men and officials of every sort, a number of landowners more likely to fall asleep over a book than to read it, and, compared with Western Europe, a disproportionately small educated middle class. This was, as one kind of educated Russian was always complaining, a backward country, a couple of centuries behind the West. But there was no general agreement, even among the educated, that Russia must learn from the West. Strongly opposed to these Westernisers was another Russian type, not always merely less well educated, but still haunted by the vision of a 'Holy Russia' that was the last remaining refuge of the true Christian spirit, a land apart because it had a sacred mission, a miraculous destiny, so that the Russian Soul, the subject of endless speculation and not a little praise, should be kept free of the contamination of the restless, free-thinking West.

A Russian writer, then, was compelled to face some severe challenges if he was at all serious. Was he ready to defy the censorship, to risk being ordered out of St. Petersburg or Moscow, a possible exile to Siberia? If he had a Western outlook, could he afford to provoke the hostility of his 'Holy Slav' critics and readers? Dare he proclaim his mystical faith in Russia if all the clever sneering Westernisers were eager to denounce him as a bigoted reactionary? And if he compromised—not a line of action regarded with favour by the majority of Russians—was he not in danger of being dismissed by both parties as a timid, shallow trifler? And the Russian writer had to face a further disadvantage. He had to compete, on these awkward terms, with foreign writers at home, for educated Russians were generally familiar with at least one foreign language; but he was unable to compete with them abroad, for Russian, a difficult language to read, was hardly known at all in Western Europe, and it was a long time before Russian literature began to be adequately translated. Indeed, even when the great Russian novelists came to be widely read in translation, it was still assumed that there was little or no Russian poetry worth reading. Russian literature, therefore, not only made a very late start but even then began with some heavy handicaps.

For a Russian writer of genius, however, during this period and the next, his unique situation brought him unique advantages. Everything was new and fresh. The very language, a magnificent instrument for both verse and poetic prose, was new and fresh for literature, not running into familiar patterns after centuries of writing, not demanding to be handled in this style or that, but as free, enticing and promising as English must have seemed to Shakespeare and his contemporaries. Then again, this huge country, thick with atmosphere and crammed with character, this giant plain between Europe and Asia, running to every extreme in climate, types of men and women, and modes of living, eagerly invited interpretation. It was for the novelist and dramatist as much a land of promise as the American Prairie was to its settlers. The splendid boldness of the great Russian novelists is usually explained in terms of the Russian character, and this is as it should be, but it must not be forgotten that these writers of the nineteenth century found themselves more or less in the same position that English, French, Spanish writers were in during the sixteenth and early seventeenth centuries. These Russians were not following on, as contemporary Western writers were, behind great national masters of their art. They were explorers and pioneers in literature, doing everything for the first time. And there was a further important difference. A large section of Russian readers, especially among the young, looked to literature for a sign. They did not ask the poet or novelist for entertainment, but cried to him for help. A Russian writer of any importance was assumed, as we say now, to be committed. And, from the first, Russian criticism made this same assumption, taking for granted the social-political, philosophical-religious purpose of literature. Incidentally, it is this tradition, which Soviet Russia inherited among other things, that makes the relation between Soviet leadership (since Lenin) and literature so uneasy and ambiguous. For if the writer is merely one kind of technician who must take orders and follow the Party line like the rest, what becomes of the writer as he existed (and still does to some extent, in theory) in the great Russian literary tradition, as the warning, inspiring, prophetic voice coming from outside the machine? How can he be both inside and outside the machine?

But during our period here, this tradition was of course being created. Everything for literature was young, new and fresh. And it is strange how all the more important of these early writers died young. Pushkin and Lermontov were killed in duels, Pushkin before he was forty, Lermontov before he was thirty. Griboyedov, the dramatist, who created many famous satirical types and whose comedy *Woe from Wit* is a classic, was killed by a Persian mob when he was thirty-four. Belinsky, the most influential critic of the period, died in his late thirties. Gogol wrote all his masterpieces in his twenties, and had done with the world years before he died, at the age of forty-three. It is like a hurried but brilliant procession to the graveyard.

Unquestionably Pushkin's early death—and it may have been planned, for the duel was deliberately provoked and his antagonist was in the

Tsar's service—meant the greatest loss to Russian literature. Though primarily a poet, he had already shown himself to be equally accomplished in prose fiction, achieving a dry, light manner very unusual in Russian. He was a mature artist, able to succeed in many forms, who must have taken with him into the grave several masterpieces now lost for ever. He was influenced early by Voltaire and later by Byron, while he was still experimenting and discovering himself, but he became a greater poet than either of them. Because of the extraordinary ease, naturalness, grace and peculiar concentration (lost in other languages) of his poetic style, he is exceptionally difficult to translate, which explains why his tremendous and enduring reputation in Russia (in spite of attacks upon him at various periods for his lack of revolutionary fervour) has not yet brought him a secure reputation as a world master. But a great deal that is widely admired in Russian fiction and drama really stems from him. And even if we have to take his unique poetic style for granted, catching only an occasional glimpse of it in translation, we can appreciate his originality and creative richness. For example, his characters lead processions of their kinds through subsequent Russian novels and plays: the bored, lazy, pampered Eugene Onegin, and the clear and glowing Tatiana, who first adores him and then, years later, now married, rejects him; Yevgeni, in the dramatic and symbolic poem, *The Bronze Horseman*, the humble clerk, the little wistful man, helpless in the iron grip of the authoritarian state; the half-mad Hermann and the tyrannical old countess in *The Queen of Spades* and the military types in *The Captain's Daughter*. If he had lived, he would probably have turned more and more to prose fiction and drama, in which he had made an excellent beginning. The main achievement of his middle poetic period, *Eugene Onegin*, with all the variety, movement and depth of characterisation of a good novel together with the rich atmosphere and verbal felicity of a poem, must be accepted as one of the major masterpieces of this whole Romantic Age. Though undoubtedly influenced at first by Byron—but Pushkin took many years over the work, we must remember—it soon outgrows Byron, going deeper than false Byronic romance, presenting Onegin himself, in the round, as a victim of this fashionable trumpery romanticism. There is in fact in Pushkin, though he had a weakness for prevailing Western ultra-romantic modes surprising in so great and original a poet, an understanding and balance of values, a refusal to identify himself with fashionable and admired attitudes, a detachment suggesting more strength and depth than the easy 'romantic irony' of the German Romantics, that make him one of the masters and not one of the victims of the Movement. He took what he needed from the West but planted it in rich Russian soil, and what grew and flowered were authentic masterpieces of Russian literature, widely and deeply influencing the whole culture of his people.

Lermontov's all too short life was curiously bound up with the Caucasus, a region of spectacular beauty not without a suggestion of opera and ballet. He was taken there several times as a boy; he was twice sentenced to military service there; the duel that killed him, at the age of twenty-seven, was fought there. And the Caucasus is the setting of his famous novel, *A Hero of Our Time*, and of his narrative poem, immensely popular for the next half-century, *The Demon*. There is indeed a good deal of the Caucasus in Lermontov, both its genuine romantic beauty and its touches of theatricality. He began writing early—his lyric, familiar to all Russians, *The Angel*, was written when he was eighteen—and though he continued to behave in a high Byronic fashion until he Byronised himself into that fatal duel, the general movement of his work, both in verse and prose, was from the ultra-romanticism of his teens towards restraint and realism. Though there probably is for most of us a curious glamour about *A Hero of Our Time*, few of us outside Russia would agree with the verdict there that it is one of the supreme masterpieces of Russian fiction, and is even considered in some quarters (so Mirsky suggests in his History) "the greatest Russian novel". This seems a fantastic judgment. Strictly speaking, *A Hero of Our Time* is not a novel at all but a series of five tales, and no matter how good the characters are that they share, no matter how beautifully they are told, five tales do not add up to a novel, just as five pavilions cannot equal in their architectural importance a splendid palace. A great novel has a scope and a sweep, a broad continuity of narrative, a massive fundamental structure, with which, fortunately for him, the writer of tales, episodes, anecdotes, novelettes, has not to concern himself. A further reason for this difference of opinion is that while we outside Russia accept with pleasure a character like that veteran of the Caucasus,

Captain Maxim Maximych, we are not so fascinated as Russian critics and readers appear to have been with the central character of these tales, the Hero of the title, Pechorin, a larger and looser Onegin in a Caucasian setting and lighting. The success of this character, with his poetic soul and contempt for everybody, his passions shaking and rattling his withered heart, puzzles us. Were there actually a large number of Russians, round about the middle of the nineteenth century, really like Pechorin? Or were there a lot of Russian young gentlemen who felt they were not like anybody in particular and so decided on Pechorin as a promising model? It is only fair to add that there is more psychological subtlety in Lermontov's hero than there is in the general run of Byronic types, but much of the essential falseness remains. The Caucasus was Lermontov's real hero, and heroine too.

Belinsky, the critic, praised Gogol at first as Russia's great realist. But Gogol is without any doubt one of the Romantics. He is an upside-down, inside-out Romantic. Instead of being a beautifier, he is an uglifier. On the Gothic tower of romanticism, Gogol is responsible for the gargoyles. He is never putting down what he sees and hears, steadily reporting a life he knows, although he may be pretending to do so. It is not that characters like Akaky Akakyevitch (*The Greatcoat*), Major Kovalyov (*The Nose*), the Maniloffs and Nozdreff and the rest in *Dead Souls*, the Governor and his fellow-officials in *The Government Inspector*, are wildly unreal. If they had been, nobody would have recognised them, whereas characters not unlike them were to be found almost everywhere. Nevertheless, they are not real people who might be ourselves or our brothers. They are grotesques, comic monsters, the kind of adults that a dreamy but not happy child might see. Like the spiritual and sentimental Romantics, Gogol is moving inward instead of outward, going into a dream world for his characters and scenes. A timid and ugly little fellow, too closely attached to a neurotic mother, unsuccessful at school, failing at everything (including acting) during his first years in St. Petersburg, afraid of women, indeed terrified of life itself, with a poor intellect and more than his share of vanity and egoism: this is Gogol. But to these negative qualities we must add the positive gift of an astoundingly rich creative imagination, enabling him to invent and then describe, in an equally rich exuberant style, crowded with imagery, this compensatory world of his, which will either be much better than the real world is, as it seems in many of his early tales of the old Cossack life and the Ukraine, or much worse, crowded with grotesques, comic monsters, imbeciles, creatures of one idea, a world without dignity, intelligence, or charm, made up of ridiculous misfits and misfortunes. But even when he has apparently lost us and himself in this comic-horrible dream world, he is able to pass at once, at least for a brief spell, into the other and more familiar romantic world, magnified, highly coloured and gay, as for example in his famous tribute to the troika in *Dead Souls*.

Gogol is perhaps the supreme example in all literature of the comic-grotesque romantic imagination, wildly funny (even to the rest of us, and far more so to Russians) in the audacity and abundance of its satirical invention, but not deeply humorous because the mind responsible for it lacks a sense of proportion and balance. It is like a child's brilliant revenge on a world he fears and hates. Superficially his wonderful comedy, *The Government Inspector*, the greatest of Russia's, and one of the world's, archetypal comedies, is a satire on political corruption and provincial stupidity—it was this slant on his work that brought him praise as a realist and a reformer—but fundamentally it shows us a man laughing in a sort of bitter hysteria at a horrible world, to which finally a real inspector will bring doomsday. And Gogol showed an innocent misunderstanding of the nature of his genius when he thought, as he did for years, that the first, comic-grotesque, part of his *Dead Souls* could be followed successfully by two further parts, no longer droll and satirical but filled with positive characters, solemn projects of all kinds, a religious theme of repentance and redemption. He could lose himself, to his final undoing, in a thick atmosphere of religiosity, asceticism, guilt-ridden devotion, but his genius would not follow him. It worked only in its own negative but superlatively rich and brilliant fashion, to create the masterpiece of the first part of *Dead Souls* (based, significantly, on a hint from Pushkin, with whom Gogol, again significantly, was in close touch throughout his best creative period), a work sustained by all the frustrated, dammed-up energy of his youth. There is of course more than a reminder of Dickens in this comic-grotesque imagination of Gogol's, revenging itself, like an angry child making things up, on a detestable world; but this is only one side, though a not inconsiderable side, of Dickens, a far more positive and stronger character. Gogol never reached maturity. He retreated from life, walled himself up, then died. But the lingering immaturity of his twenties, keeping alive in him the child, half resentful, half wistful, had brought him his strange genius. Its major creations are of that rare kind so widely and warmly popular that their characters become national types, quotations from them seem like folklore, so that they merge into the life of a people, become an element of its social atmosphere. The narrower and more direct literary influence of such work is rarely of much importance, and though Dostoyevsky paid Gogol a handsome tribute, neither inside Russia nor outside it has Gogol been important as a direct influence. He has indeed been brushed aside, neglected, by many important Russian groups, distinguished coteries of men of letters. But when will any of them and their works become part of the nation's life, its cultural climate, almost its weather?

2

For a final gleaning of the Age, we may look first to the South, then to the North. In the South, we find two men as different as two Italians of the same era could be, Leopardi and Manzoni. But they are in their widely separated ways both Romantics. It may be objected that nothing more perfectly classical in form and manner than Leopardi's verse, and indeed much of his prose, can be found anywhere else throughout the whole Romantic Age. But it is what lies behind form and manner, what they seek to express, that compels us to include Leopardi among the Romantics. There is every excuse for his pessimism: he must have had the sickliest constitution of any poet that ever lived; he was rarely free from acute physical pain; the precocious scholarship of his boyhood and early youth severely overtaxed him; he could not express himself freely in an Italy under foreign domination, and was too much of an invalid, dependent on his parents, to go into exile; and though he made many admiring friends, his love-affairs were failures. Had we known half his misfortunes, our outlook might have been no brighter than his, and indeed we might not have written anything at all. Nevertheless, there are Rousseau and romanticism at work in him: for example, in his egocentric assumption that his experience is the experience of all mankind; in the belief that at some time or somewhere else, in childhood or before or beyond civilisation, all is different; in his idea of happiness as something complete in itself, arriving and then departing after a brief stay (a suffering sick man's view), instead of being the unsought accompaniment to certain courses of action and ways of living. But there is perhaps prophetic insight in his theory that modern man's increasing desire for more and more exact knowledge, which must of necessity involve him in more and more analysis in a ghostly world abstracted from the real world, would diminish even his capacity for happiness. Behind this theory, as we shall see, there is a good deal more than romantic melancholy and *malaise*.

Manzoni spent the greater part of his literary life, as distinct from his long life as a good and, later, famous citizen, writing and re-writing his one great novel, *The Betrothed* (*I Promessi Sposi*). Other countries have produced greater novels, but not one have they honoured more than Italy honours Manzoni's. There it is thoroughly alive, quoted on public occasions as well as in millions of private conversations, to this day, nearly a hundred and twenty years after its definitive edition (the third version Manzoni wrote) made its appearance. But though it has long been translated into all major languages, in so many editions that it must have been very widely read, somehow it has never given Manzoni a place in the main gallery of Western literature. But he shall have his own special place here. Comparison with Scott is inevitable, and Manzoni himself said that he had learned from Scott many mistakes to avoid. This is hard to believe, for where he is inferior to Scott is in his technique of narrative, which is something one novelist can learn from another, and where he is the equal of Scott at his best, and much superior to Scott on his ordinary level, it is the result of a breadth and depth of sympathy that cannot be acquired by noting another writer's mistakes. Why Manzoni, writing this one novel over and over again, should insist upon telling his tale so badly, is a mystery. Time after time the excellent narrative is held up for scores of pages while its author, out of what seems like sheer perversity, tells us a great deal we do not want or need to know. There is perhaps no other novel of equal merit in Western literature—Eastern fiction is another matter—that begs so hard to be thoroughly edited with a pair of scissors. And its merit is very considerable. The fact that, while it was unpopular in Rome (where it was banned for a time), it was accused elsewhere of being a reactionary work, smelling of the sacristy, is altogether in its favour: good fiction should always be disliked by narrow fanatics. What distinguish it are the curious charm of Manzoni's manner (when he is telling his tale and not merely giving us the result of his years of research), the variety of characters and incidents, the admirable relation between his two young lovers and the historical background, magnificent in the plague scenes, and, above all, the fact that here is a huge historical novel that concerns itself almost entirely with the fortunes of two young peasants. (Renzo is completely convincing, but Lucia is closer to a romantic-period heroine than to a fairly typical Italian peasant girl of the seventeenth or any other century.) Here at last, against an historical background, we live, suffer and hope, with the poor, at the mercy of the whims of the rich and powerful, and for ever menaced by war, famine and plague. The people whom the older historians forgot are here in the centre of the picture. This is Manzoni's great achievement, and we should honour him for it.

The Romantic trail to the North takes us to Copenhagen, where we discover two Danes of world reputation, as wildly different (though still contained within the romantic tradition) as Leopardi and Manzoni. The first of them, of immensely greater repute now than he was in his own time and for many years after his early death, is Kierkegaard. The influence of this eccentric essayist and philosopher upon a few but important writers, first in Scandinavia, then in Germany, was considerable towards the end of the nineteenth century, and now in our own post-war period, since the arrival of French existentialism, which largely descends from him by way of the Germans he influenced, his work is being constantly reprinted and studied. It is a curious and quite original mixture of witty paradox, flashes of sardonic humour, and argument sharpened and hurried on by a neurotic intensity. He might be described as a loose-limbed Nordic Pascal (with the mathematical genius left out), born into the Romantic Age in a small country. We are not philosophers and theologians here, but something must be said, however briefly and inadequately, about his outlook, if only to justify any mention of him among romantic writers. Whatever he may mean to philosophy and theology, considered as a writer he can be understood as yet another Romantic, not too far removed from some of the older German Romantics. It is true that he is bitterly opposed to the Romantic Idealism accepted as the philosophical ally of the German Movement, just as, in his later work, he is bitterly opposed to the official Christianity of the Churches, which to him is not Christianity at all. Man, he believes, becomes a real individual, and at the same time rids himself of anxiety and despair, by a paradoxical act of faith, taking a leap into the dark to believe in the unbelievable. God cannot be found by reason but only by faith. Religion is all or nothing. No compromises are possible. There can be no such thing as an easy-going Christianity, liberal and reformist. Real Christianity involves a life of suffering, complete helplessness before God, absolute dependence upon divine grace. If there were to be real religion in Denmark, Kierkegaard finally announced, a martyr was needed; and shortly afterwards he fainted in the street, was taken to hospital, and never recovered, dying at the age of forty-two. His childhood had been spent in an atmosphere of neurotic gloom and guilt; after a few youthful years of dissipation, magnified by his temperament into an endless Roman orgy of 'lusts and excesses', he had fallen in love with and finally become engaged to a young girl, only to throw her over because renunciation, he felt, was demanded of him; and after that a series of attacks upon him by a comic paper—no joke in a small country where he was a well-known figure, though again he probably magnified the effect—led him to denounce the press and the masses and the whole demoralisation of contemporary society. Behind all this, whatever the final value may be of its contributions to philosophy and theology, may easily be discovered an ultra-romantic temperament, complete with the familiar boundless egoism, never hesitating to project itself on the whole universe; with its ambiguous attitude to sex, its fear of society and social relations masquerading as contempt, its complete acceptance of a God secretly made in its own image, its domination by the unconscious. So now, in our own anti-romantic age, our newest anti-romantic philosophy has to admit its debt, seriously and without irony, to one of the last and most extreme of the original Romantics.

The other and so wildly different Dane, who can be included here by giving the period a final stretch, is no other than our old childhood friend, Hans Andersen. His claim to be an established figure in our Western literature must be allowed, if only because most of us have encountered him before we became acquainted with any of its greater figures. Andersen tried his hand at almost every kind of writing, poetry, plays, novels, autobiographical and travel books, and he never quite reconciled himself to the fact that all his reputation—at least, outside Scandinavia—rested entirely on his little fairy-tales for children. (Incidentally, his use of easy colloquial language in them greatly helped other Scandinavian writers to break with the belated fashion of writing formal literary dialogue.) These famous tales are both varied and unequal, and some of the most mawkish, we might as well admit, are precisely those that appeal most to many children. In the best of them there is a curious suggestion of something much older and stronger than Andersen's imagination, a gleam of mythology and ancient folklore behind his fairy tinsel. This should not surprise us when we remember that as a young child Andersen spent many a day listening to the old peasant women in the workhouse at Odense, and often they told him wonder tales and legends they remembered from their childhood, when in turn they were told stories by old folk; so as grey heads wagged above golden heads, the tales of magic and mysterious fortune slipped down the centuries. And now, thanks to the last of our Romantics, Hans Andersen, these stories have been known to generations of children, are part of the childhood of Western Man. No matter what kind of literature we prefer in our maturity, we begin with Romance, clapping our hands at the shadows of the moon.

PART FOUR

The Broken Web

15 The Age and its Prophets   187

16 The Poets   206

17 The Novelists   222

18 The Dramatists   274

CHAPTER FIFTEEN

The Age and its Prophets

I

WE ARE NOW FACED with the age following that of Romance, the age coinciding roughly with the reign of Queen Victoria. Let us begin with a quotation taken from P. L. Ralph's very sensible survey, *The Story of Our Civilisation*. Arriving at this same point in time, he writes:

The rise of modern industry changed the picture radically. While it stimulated population growth, it provided the means for integrating the population. Urbanisation, ease of communication, and facilities for disseminating reading matter cheaply made possible at last the attainment of likemindedness among the members of a large community. The role of the printing press in bringing about this situation could hardly be exaggerated. The art of printing from movable type had indeed been known in Europe since the fifteenth century; but far more significant for its effects upon society at large was the invention of power-driven and rotary presses in the nineteenth century, together with paper-making machinery. Now a voluminous output of books, periodicals, and newspapers came within reach of manual labourers and permeated the rural areas. The mechanisation of industry, together with the modern mass-production printing press, created the setting in which the democratic thesis could be given unlimited application. . . .

Among the inventors and benefactors of the age was William A. Bullock of Philadelphia, who gave his name to the first machine to print from a continuous web of paper. Unfortunately, only two years after his machine was put into service, he became entangled in one of its intricate driving bands and was killed. This was in 1867, somewhere about the middle of the age we must now consider, and so, without forcing the symbolism of this melancholy incident, we might accept this year as a look-out point and discover briefly what was happening then in literature.

Beginning with poor William A. Bullock's own country, we find that in 1867 Emerson was publishing some verse and had already produced his best essays; Thoreau had been dead for five years, Hawthorne for four; Herman Melville, abandoning in disgust a literary career, had just started work as a customs inspector in New York; Whitman was publishing a new edition of *Leaves of Grass*; Mark Twain was still two years away from his first great success, *The Innocents Abroad*; and William Dean Howells had relinquished his post as consul in Venice to settle in Boston. In England, Dickens, having published his last completed novel, *Our Mutual Friend*, was about to embark on an American reading tour; Thackeray had been dead for four years, the Brontë sisters had died earlier still; Tennyson was writing the last of his Arthurian idylls; Browning was dining out in London and completing *The Ring and the Book*, and Swinburne was writing his *Songs Before Sunrise*; Carlyle, his *Frederick the Great* behind him, was still mourning his wife's death, the year before; Ruskin was within sight of his appointment as first Slade Professor of the Fine Arts at Oxford, where Matthew Arnold was about to vacate the Chair of Poetry.

In France, during this year 1867, Baudelaire was brought back from Brussels, where he had been living for years, to die in Paris; Flaubert is toiling away at his *L'Éducation sentimentale*; Zola is publishing *Thérèse Raquin*; Verlaine is still the author of one youthful volume, Mallarmé is still seven years away from the publication of *L'Après-midi d'un faune*, and Rimbaud is still at school. This same year saw the arrival of Turgenev's *Smoke*, is sandwiched between the publication of Dostoevsky's *Crime and Punishment* and *The Idiot*, and is clean in the middle of Tolstoy's *War and Peace* (1865–69). In Germany the harvest is poor, and Nietzsche will need another five years; but from Norway, in this very year, comes *Peer Gynt*, the Everyman of this later nineteenth century.

This age offers us many famous names, a wealth of literature (unsurpassed in prose fiction), a mountain of books piled up by all these printing machines; and yet, from our point of view here, it is an age without any particular character of its own. The Bullock machine may use a continuous web of paper, but literature shows us no such continuous web. The web is vast—for now there is far more writing that can fairly be called literature than there was in the earlier ages—but it has been stretched so hard in so many directions that it is broken. As Dr. Ralph points out, the new conditions can bring about "at last the attainment of likemindedness among the members of a large community", but above this level, where literature flourishes, we do not find more but a great deal less "likemindedness" than we found in earlier ages. It is as if all the major writers of the age were working at the top of this gigantic tower of industrial production, scientific discovery, urbanisation, and there had fallen upon them, long before it reached the masses below, the curse of Babel, a wild confusion of tongues. There are literary movements of a sort, but they move in opposite directions, cancelling each other out. The Paris of Zola, with his notebooks, newspaper cuttings, files, his attempt at complete objective realism, is also the Paris of Mallarmé, creating literature out of a few mysterious evocative phrases. It cannot be denied that Baudelaire, Whitman and Tennyson are three representative poets of the age, and it is a fact that *Fleurs du mal*, *Leaves of Grass*, and *The Idylls of the King* were first published in the later 1850s; but where is the literary common denominator here, what monstrous tree is simultaneously bearing such fruit? What Anglo-American mid-nineteenth-century movement in fiction gives us, within a year, both *David Copperfield* and *Moby Dick*? What name can we suggest for the *Zeitgeist* responsible for both Nietzsche's *Beyond Good and Evil* and Tolstoy's *What to Do*?

Again, because this age shows us a tremendous increase in reading simply regarded as mass entertainment, it is tempting to announce that we have now arrived at a time when literature of any importance has for ever lost its wide appeal, is limited to a tiny cultured minority. We have been told as much, over and over again. For example: "With a few exceptions," Erich Auerbach writes in his *Mimesis*, "the significant artists of the later nineteenth century encountered hostility, lack of comprehension, or indifference on the part of the public. They achieved general recognition only at the price of violent and prolonged struggles, many of them only posthumously, or, before their deaths, among but a small circle of followers." It should be understood, before we discuss this passage, that Auerbach, whose subject here actually is literature, is including writers among his "significant artists". (If he were not, if he were referring first to painters and then, though less obviously, to composers, we should have to agree with him at once.) And once we restrict them to writers, these statements are not true. That is, they are not true so long as criticism itself has not a minority-snob basis, a secret dislike of enjoying what a lot of other people can also enjoy. Thus, on any sensible level of criticism, the two greatest novelists of this age are Tolstoy and Dickens, both of them enjoying immense popularity throughout our whole Western world. Easily the most popular poet of Victorian England was Tennyson, and Tennyson, with all his faults, is its greatest poet. *Moby Dick* and *The Adventures of Huckleberry Finn* are two major works of American fiction, and for years one was almost unknown while the other was an immediate popular favourite. The most we can say is that during this age the appeal and popularity of its more important writers varied enormously.

It is true, however, that in Western Europe and the United States this age saw the rapid growth, both in numbers and influence, of a class largely hostile or indifferent to literature. This was the new urban middle class, not professional but generally engaged in commerce. Too many members of it were smug, complacent, narrowly prejudiced and intolerant. In France they first came into prominence during the bourgeois monarchy of Louis-Philippe, and it is not surprising that French writers like Baudelaire and Flaubert who grew up during the Thirties and Forties, in a Paris largely dominated by this class, detested it and deliberately set themselves to defy it. Even Dickens, in spite of the enthusiastic welcome it gave him at first, came to dislike it intensely, and his last completed novel, *Our Mutual Friend*, is largely an expression of this dislike. Carlyle too, who called this class 'gigmanity' (because it was so proud of being able to keep a gig, a one-horse light carriage), made it the target of some of his roughest satire. And when, later, Ibsen turned to prose drama, he revealed time after time the hypocrisy and capacity for self-deception of this class. It arrived late in Russia, still a country of landowners and peasants, but not too late to escape the satirical attention of Russian writers, who, unlike most Western authors, rarely came from this class themselves. For after all, most writers of this age came neither from the nobility and the rich nor from the peasantry or the growing mass of industrial workers. They were themselves of bourgeois origin, growing up in this middle class, and even when they rebelled against it, if they were not content with a tiny minority of readers (and here we have the idea of literature appealing only to a few, the *élite*), then they had to contrive somehow to appeal to a fair proportion of this class, just because it made up the bulk of the reading public. So we find writers now resorting to various literary stratagems and deceptions that not only shape their work but deeply affect their whole outlook. We must therefore not be surprised, when we come closer to them, if we notice how many of them feel embittered.

The relation between writers and this middle class inevitably changes the relation between literature and society. For in spite of some setbacks, and a rising challenge from the new mass of industrial workers, this age, with all that it accomplished in material progress, represents the triumph of the manufacturing and commercial middle class. The world of Victorian and Imperial Britain, of the North after the American Civil War, of the French Second Empire and Third Republic, of the new German Empire, even (though to a lesser extent) of Russia after 1861 and the freeing of the serfs, is the world as this particular class, which has more power and thrust than any other, desires and makes it. The great international exhibitions, from 1851 onwards, reflect the whole glittering triumph of these busy acquisitive people. They control the power-house of all Western society. They shape and colour the social scene. The values that society takes for granted are now their values. But literature, as we have seen, whether it tries to please all but the most narrow-minded of this class or defiantly jeers at it, is really in rebellion against it, either openly or in secret. This means that literature is no longer anywhere near the centre. It is running obliquely away. It is no longer going where society is going. It cannot, as it did before, interpret and express the dominant spirit of the age—not, that is, as the age sees itself, for it would not be literature if it did not interpret and express something vital. But now we can understand why we cannot deal with this age as we did with the earlier ages, why it appears to have no unique spirit, literary character and style of its own, why we found the web broken, as the continuous web of paper must have been broken on the day Bullock's machine caught and killed him. As this society sees itself, literature is no longer near the centre. This is not a society expressing itself through literature. So far as the centre of it can be occupied at all by manipulators of words, it has been taken over by editors of newspapers and the more popular periodicals and their contributing journalists, by easy historians and fashionable preachers and imitation philosophers and those creative writers whose only aim is to please the people they meet at dinner parties.

Such literary movements as the age can show may now be seen in their relation to this confident and dominant class. For example, the romanticism that lingered on into the second half of the century, chiefly content to copy in paler tones the imaginary Middle Ages of the original Romantics, enabled the writer or painter to escape from his bourgeois industrial age and then return to it with goods it wanted. For the best patrons of this belated romantic art were the rich industrialists and their families, trying in the evening to forget Manchester and Birmingham. Tennyson's *Idylls of the King*, a picturesque but highly respectable tour of the Arthurian country, are an admirable example of this relation between a fading romanticism and the mid-Victorian reading public. The Romantic, once defiant, a revolutionary, is now pretending in order to please the wives and daughters of manufacturers; he is sitting in a railway train imagining himself riding through the dark forest; so the vitality of the old movement ebbs away, and its literary significance dwindles; soon it is merely catering to the book trade.

A later and very different movement, apparently very much in the spirit of its time, was that towards a sort of scientific naturalism in fiction. The novelist moved away from creation and the companionship of the poets and became a kind of research worker. Novels were to be compiled out of notebooks. Everything—and this in practice meant anything very ugly and unpleasant—was to be carefully observed and described from life. In France, the de Goncourt brothers began it (and invented the term 'human document'), but it was the surviving Edmond de Goncourt's ambitious young friend Zola who carried the method much further and devoted to it his astonishing energy. This had consequences touched with irony, for Zola compelled his bourgeois reading public to face the spectacle of a working class existing in a jungle and an inferno, and made the more intelligent workers, as they began to read him, more aware of the miseries of their class, with further results, reformist or reactionary, that were political-economic and not literary.

Then there was the so-called Æsthetic Movement, probably beginning with Gautier and ending with Oscar Wilde, that has had more serious attention than it deserved, although its real significance has generally been missed. For it should be seen not as a genuine new movement in the arts, for which it has a very poor claim, but as a spirited attempt to challenge, defy and shock the complacent middle class. These people liked such of the arts as they patronised to be "pleasant and wholesome", therefore the members of this movement had to prefer the unpleasant and unwholesome. If business men dressed in grey and black, then artists must wear bright clothes. If bankers and ironfounders, busy and important, had to keep sober, then it was an artist's duty to get drunk. If respectability was the badge of this central and dominant class, then the arts and artists must traffic in strange sins. When Baudelaire, dining among the bourgeois in a restaurant, would ask his companion in a loud, clear voice if he had ever tried eating children's brains, he was behaving as a founder member of this movement, creating its cheerfully impudent but rather tasteless manner. Wilde is in many respects its best representative, for while he claimed that Art alone was important, he himself in fact never led the life of an artist, never gave his work most of his time and energy, and dedicated himself not to literature but to a social career based on a wittily impudent attitude. The movement was not fundamentally æsthetic at all, but social. It was devoted to the game of bull-baiting the dominant class that cared so little about the arts. It was the existence and the power of this class that really created the movement, inspired by a resentment of a society that had forced literature and the arts away from the centre. This partly accounts for the rather childish irresponsibility, the elaborate naughtiness, the flaunting of absurd affectations, displayed by most members of the Æsthetic Movement: they were behaving like children on the edge of a party to which they had not been invited. But it goes deeper than that, for below the resentment is a kind of acceptance. These Æsthetic writers and painters were in fact behaving, not in accordance with their time-old vocations, which care nothing for such antics, but as the new lords of society, indifferent to these vocations, expected them to behave.

Ironically enough, just because literature lasts longest and inevitably does much to shape our opinions and to colour our thoughts and feelings about a past age, we have to make an effort to see this era, especially the mid-section of it between 1850 and 1880, as it saw itself. We must remember that the ideas of the centre were unchallenged, except of course by neurotic and eccentric writers, considered to be no longer capable of understanding and expressing society. England was leading the way during those years, and Macaulay, to whom the Reform Bill of 1832 was the entrance into the Promised Land, spoke for England. Western Man, now busy taking charge of other kinds of men, the "lesser breeds", as Kipling later would call them, saw before him an endless vista of progress. Everything was getting better, and would now almost automatically continue to get better. There might be differences of opinion, often debated with acrimony, about the cosmic arrangements, but the conclusion was the same. The God of the Churches was on the side of Western Man, now taming and baptising the heathen. If Darwin's theory of evolution was preferred to the Book of Genesis, the prospect was equally bright, for Western Man clearly was the fittest to survive. More and more factories were at work, more and more ships sailing, more and more trains running; and the age was so wealthy and so highly skilled that, as the great exhibitions amply proved, it did not need to have any particular style of its own but could borrow and adapt, with the most astonishing ingenuity, styles from all previous ages. Even the occasional wars, unpleasant though they were (and the American Civil War, perhaps because it was so remote from Europe, was painfully long-protracted and bloodthirsty), were nothing like so wasteful and convulsive as the Napoleonic Wars had been, and never really menaced the progress of civilisation. The prosperity of this new industrial society could suffer only temporary checks at the worst, and the material gains it had brought to men were visible everywhere.

Before we return to the makers of literature, questioning and denouncing this society, we will give the age its immediate due. A member of its more comfortable classes, so long as he had not too much imagination nor too tender a social conscience, was probably better off at this time than at any other, before or since. He shared the age's self-confidence and superb energy, unmatched since the Renaissance. A middling man, a dull fellow compared with the brilliant creatures of the Renaissance, he was yet one of the lords of his world. He could make plans for his family, his business, his retirement, his travels and pleasures, without any doubt that they would mature. He never felt the earth was cracking, the sky falling. As he went to his office or factory, hunted and shot, dined out or enjoyed an opera or play, decided to try some foreign spa, he was not haunted by a feeling that at any moment some unimaginable catastrophe, some new revelation of the depths of cruelty in men, would threaten his world. He moved in a wider area of personal liberty than earlier men had known or than we know now. He could manage his own affairs as he thought best, and could spend his own money (and he was only lightly taxed) and go on his travels without having to ask permission of the state. If he did get into trouble in his own country, he could without difficulty take refuge in another, for there was in his day no international conspiracy of bureaucracy against ordinary citizens. Compared with what men had been before his time and what they are in ours, he was wonderfully free; and the confidence and energy born of this freedom, we must confess, had a marked effect on the age. Indeed, even its severest critics, the prophets crying in despair, though far removed from these average sensual unimaginative men, had their share of this confidence and energy. Even their cries of "Woe, woe!" seem to us now to have an enviably rich and confident tone.

2

In considering the thought of this age, the difficulty is to keep our consideration of it within the limits of our subject here, Literature. The temptation to exceed these limits is all the greater because this thought, so many ideas in books by mild philosophers, social theorists and critics, has brought about such terrible consequences in our own age—wars and revolutions, unlimited destruction, torture and mass murder. All the horrors of our time—the most violent known to history—may be said to have originated in the whirl and clash of nineteenth-century ideas. But this is a literary and not an historical survey. And what is difficult is to decide where one ends and the other takes over. A few thinkers are important because they are literary figures in their own right; others because they have had a direct influence upon writers; others because they helped to create a certain climate of thought and feeling in which writers have had to do their work. But there are so many of them, and, obeying the spirit of the age, they take so many widely separated trails, that only the barest justice can be done to the most significant of them.

In this Babel of voices, cheerful or despairing, certain leading questions can be heard. Is an all-round progress inevitable or even possible? Or is the idea of progress a dangerous illusion? Can Man be safely considered a rational being? Or are men, when they do more than air their theories, when they plunge into action, moved by powerful irrational forces? Are they genuinely reasonable or merely in the habit of rationalising their strongest impulses? Can Evolution, which Darwin scrupulously kept within the terms of his biological enquiry (even the famous "survival of the fittest" was coined by Herbert Spencer, not Darwin), be accepted on the widest possible basis? Is the serenely rational liberalism of a John Stuart Mill, who believed that all would be well if men enjoyed liberty, were free from the pressure of orthodoxies and obscurantism, simply the dream of an unusually sensitive and civilised scholar, far removed and temporarily secure from the bloodstained arena and the howling mob?

One man who had answered these questions before they were asked was Schopenhauer. He was really at heart a Romantic, and his one great work, *The World as Will and Idea*, was first published as early as 1818. But the Romantic Age, to his disgust, had ignored him, and it was not until the middle of the century, a few years after his book had been reprinted, that he began to be widely read and appreciated. From then on, his influence was considerable, especially upon literary men. This was due to the fine sweep of his philosophy, the breadth of his culture, and the unusual wit and eloquent force of his writing. He even wrote on literature in a few occasional essays, without much originality and insight but with fine sardonic humour. (Journalism, he remarks, is the second hand in the clock of history and seldom goes right.) Everything in Schopenhauer's philosophy is implacably opposed to the spirit of the age, an age that regarded itself as a monument to the optimism, enterprise, triumphant will-power of Western Man. For to Schopenhauer there is behind all phenomena, keeping all life in motion and for ever renewing it, the Will itself, fundamentally evil because it must create more and more suffering. The only way out (even suicide being useless), through adequate know-ledge, non-attachment, æsthetic contemplation, victory over sensual desire, is complete extinction, the utter nothingness that alone defeats the Will. Here, it will be seen, Schopenhauer goes further than his Oriental masters, making Hinduism and Buddhism seem by comparison almost gaily optimistic. And indeed there has never been a more pessimistic philosophy. Why then should it have attracted so many intelligent readers, repelled, for example, by the pessimism of Leopardi? The answer is that the pain of existence is evident in Leopardi, while there is in Schopenhauer, who lived, a comfortable old bachelor, to a very ripe age, a certain gusto in writing that suggests that his appalling universe is more an intellectual exercise than a real heart-breaking discovery. He had in fact a two-sided nature, equally strong on its sensual and purely intellectual sides, and his general theory represents their cancelling out, to nothing-ness, while his actual practice in writing shows both of them hard at work and fully alive.

It is a long jump from Schopenhauer, cosily ordering his dinner in Frankfurt in the worst of all theoretical universes, to Concord, Massa-chusetts, and Ralph Waldo Emerson and his eccentric young friend, Henry David Thoreau. And yet, without any direct influence, two im-portant features of Schopenhauer's thought may be found distributed between these two distant New Englanders. In Emerson, though as widely removed in temperament from the sardonic German as he was in space, there is the same rewarding discovery of the contemplative and mystical East. There was in addition, of course, the direct influence of the German Romantic Movement on these transcendental New

Englanders, of whom Emerson may be said to have been the intellectual leader. His purely literary stature has dwindled considerably during the last seventy years or so, but even during this later time he has performed the same function for a great many English-speaking youngish readers, bent on improving themselves, that he performed, both in print and on the lecture platform, for his community during his lifetime: he is a sort of guide-interpreter to the world of great literature and philosophy. Perhaps because he thought largely in terms of the spoken word rather than of the written, his essays are curiously formless, a staccato succession of aphoristic phrases, but he carries the virtue of this defect, often achieving a memorable quality in these phrases, a kind of wit touched with poetry. But too often he seems to be content merely to introduce us into this world of great names and enduring thought, and does not seem himself to be going anywhere in it, merely standing at the entrance. In Thoreau, slighter in bulk and weight but in many respects the more considerable writer, we find no Schopenhauer's escape via the East but something of his despairing attitude towards the West. It is an odd discovery, for to us today life in or around the small town of Concord in the Forties and Fifties of the last century would seem almost idyllic, yet Thoreau could write: "The mass of men lead lives of quiet desperation." This is proof, if any should be needed, that the *malaise* of the century, broadening and deepening as it approached our own, was not simply the result of social conditions and outward circumstances, the roar and smoke of factories, the growth of industrial cities, the stress of life in Western Europe. What gives value to Thoreau is not so much his relation to Nature, as we find it in *Walden*, for other writers have been more rewardingly observant, as his stiff-necked attitude towards society. It may be said, with truth, that he 'contracted out' of too much, not merely out of voting and tax-paying but out of much of life itself; but he is an original, and very much an American original, with an imaginative but conversational manner and style of his own, which have had a greater influence on American and English writers (probably because they read him in youth) than has been generally acknowledged.

These transcendental New Englanders had also read their Carlyle, who had a tremendous reputation both at home and abroad throughout this age, only to lose most of it, and be left unread, during this present century. Carlyle was a Calvinist Scots peasant who early became a student (and translator) of the German Romantics. He was himself a kind of Romantic, though he hated Rousseau. Both the French Revolution and the Industrial Revolution seemed to him appalling disasters. Everything the age prided itself upon he regarded with disgust and contempt. But his habit of railing and snarling, rather in the manner of an Old Testament prophet, should not blind us to the value of his profoundly intuitive insights. It was Carlyle we quoted, early in this book, when we referred to the religious foundation and framework of society in the true Middle Ages. He knew that the nineteenth century could not be transformed into the thirteenth century, but he also knew that without some such foundation and framework the society of his time, for all its material triumphs, was heading for disaster. All his loud criticism of the age, his sweeping condemnation of industrialism, colonialism, parliaments and elections, all the manners and morals of Victorian England, must be seen as frantically exasperated gestures by a prophet who, in spite of his Eternities and Hellfires, could proclaim no God. He was essentially a religious man, deeply aware of the danger of a civilisation without a religious culture, who yet had no religion to offer. It is when he is negative that he is strong and sure, and when he is positive, with his Germanic hero-cult that descends, when he leaves religion and art for history, to an adulation of brute power, that he is weakest. But as a kind of prose poet, with an astonishing visual imagination and sense of character and atmosphere, he is in his own way a master. His *French Revolution* is not so much a history as a huge blazing panorama, often grotesque and monstrous but flashing at us the truth of a scene or a man, like a series of Goya etchings turned into words. And time after time in his essays on his own time, with grim humour and in one picturesque phrase after another, he compels us to see the age and all its triumphs dwindling and shrivelling in the white flare of his imagination. We are further in, not out of, the wood that Carlyle described so vividly, and it is time he was read again, even if only in selected passages.

Carlyle's immediate influence was very considerable, certainly among English men of letters, and one of his more notable disciples was John Ruskin. In his own time Ruskin was regarded as an inspired art critic who decided not to mind his own business but to write about things he did not understand, like the general state of society, the relation of men to their work, and other matters best left to the political economists and the politicians. We realise now that Ruskin was often at his worst when writing about æsthetics and at his best when dealing with those things he was supposed not to understand and which, in fact, he understood much better than the experts. Thus, for example, he cut straight to the heart of the matter when he pointed out that the test of a social system is not what wealth it is producing for some members of society but what kind of men, what kind of human experience, it is producing. And though we have had nearly a hundred years to think it out, we have still not answered most of his challenges. Whether he was writing about the works of Turner or the Alps, medieval cathedrals or political economy, Ruskin was a magnificent stylist, returning triumphantly to the immense sentences of the seventeenth-century prose-men, though easier and more secure in his management of relative clauses than most of them ever were, in a style rich to the eye, exquisite to the ear. It was this splendid prose that Proust, after first translating some of it, used as a model for the style he adopted in his great novel, hoping to reproduce in French at least something of Ruskin's unique combination of strength, complexity and grace, like that of a bridge that appears to be all delicate traceries and yet bears in safety the traffic of a city.

Without any direct literary influence but important as a climate creator is Auguste Comte, who represents the logical conclusion of much that had been first thought during the French Enlightenment. He is perhaps the best example of those over-rational immense systematisers who in private seem half-mad and almost entirely at the mercy of the unconscious urges which they deny in public. (Like the first technocrat-socialist, Saint-Simon, who provides the link between the Enlightenment and Comte, he tried to commit suicide.) His famous three stages of development in human thinking, the theological, the metaphysical, the scientific or positive (which at last gives us exact proof), have never at any time been completely accepted by serious thinkers, but ever since his death in 1857 they might be said to have been haunting the suburbs of modern thought, inspiring the more aggressive rationalists and those camp-followers of science whose claims for it are more sweeping than those of scientists themselves. (And it is easy to see why they should be, for scientists of distinction are themselves imaginative and intuitive, far closer to artists than their followers are.) And even Comte's synthetic religion of humanity, based on a complete absence of the religious sense in its founder, though it may no longer be carefully studied—and Comte's actual writing has that aridity which usually follows a ferocious suppression of all unconscious elements—is still, so to speak, hanging about, perhaps waiting for Communism to exchange its hymns of hate for songs of worship. But where Comte is important to literature is that his positivism creates in its turn the kind of scientific or pseudo-scientific sociology that encouraged the extreme naturalism of some later novelists and dramatists, who felt they were working in the best, if somewhat arid, climate of the age. It had some effect too on French literary criticism, notably on Taine, who fortunately, however, possessed a deep and sure feeling for letters, superior perhaps, so far as the greatest writers were concerned, to that of the patient and diligent Sainte-Beuve, the master of the biographical method of criticism. And among the English students of Comte—though she did not allow his shadow to fall between her and ordinary humanity— was the novelist, George Eliot.

It was in England, though not by Englishmen, that a stronger brew than Comte's was concocted, through the joint endeavours of Karl Marx, an exile living in London, and his German friend, Friedrich Engels, in the Manchester trade. With their economic theories we have nothing to do here; and this is no place in which to criticise the whole Hegelian card-castle of dialectical materialism. But some points must be made. The first is that the contemporary English industrial system, which Marx hated with such ferocity, was indeed hateful, and these two Germans were any-thing but alone in denouncing it, for protests as strong as theirs, though less elaborately formulated, can be discovered in Carlyle, Dickens, Dis-raeli, Kingsley, and many other Victorian writers. The difference is that Marx, in his typically German fashion, built his hatred of it into a tremendous philosophical-cum-historical system, now in our time holding in its iron grip about a third of the world. (And nobody would be more surprised than Marx to discover among what peoples he had succeeded.)

This brings us to the second point. Marx and Engels succeeded where other and perhaps sounder theorists failed, chiefly because they created a new myth when a new myth was urgently needed. What they did ultimately, without being aware of it themselves, was to achieve a *substitute* religious basis and framework for society. It is to this, and not to its economics, not even to its idea of the class war, that Communism owes the breadth and depth of its appeal; and it is this hasty substitution, as a basis and framework, of what is irreligious, not belonging to the spirit, for what should be profoundly religious, and not the political and economic structure of its society, that makes Communism so gravely menacing. Even if it should fulfil all its promises—and it is clear now that Marx's idea that the state would 'wither away' under a proletarian dictatorship was an idle dream—it would still keep the mind and spirit of Man in an iron cage, bringing him appallingly close to the plight of the social insects. But—and this is the final point—it is only fair to Marx and Engels, both highly cultivated men, to add that they would have been astounded and shocked by the attitudes and antics of Marxist critics of literature and the arts, which they were hoping to liberate and not imprison. Unfortunately they reached beyond theories and systems and created a myth, a Frankenstein's monster that went stumping away, taking on a life of its own, growing and growing, until it scooped whole populations between its giant hands, crushing that very freedom which Marx and Engels had imagined that at last they could win for men. History, so ingenious at devising ironies, never did better than this, for now we see how Marx and Engels, in their dream of freeing the industrial workers of Western Europe, helped to establish a grim autocracy stretching from Warsaw to the China Sea. The writing, both creative and critical, inspired by Marxism has been almost always of poor quality. Whatever they intended their doctrines to accomplish, Marx and Engels have done literature more harm than good.

The counterblast to the Communist challenge came from a German too. For though Friedrich Nietzsche was proud of his Polish ancestry, he was in spirit essentially German. Commendably German is his overmastering desire to ask questions, no matter how awkward, and find answers to them, at whatever the cost, to arrive finally at his own picture of this world and this life. Lamentably German is what comes bursting through, after conscious control has gone, the windy vanity, the strutting and screaming, the violence and madness. But here we must add that a good deal of racial and nationalist nonsense formerly attributed to Nietzsche, and pressed into service by the Nazis, has recently been proved to be spurious stuff concocted by his sister, who survived him by many years, and her friends. The popular view that Nietzsche demanded a world supremacy of "German blonde beasts" is quite wrong. He was in fact not at all nationalistic in feeling, and never really concerned about politics. Nietzsche, like Carlyle earlier but with even more piercing insight and brilliant intuitiveness, saw that the age was roaring and rolling on towards disaster. God was dead, he proclaimed; such doctrines as that of Evolution, once they reached the masses, would plunge the world into an era of terrible barbarism ("There will be wars such as have never happened on earth"); and the genuinely individual and superior man, capable of philosophy and art, will be overwhelmed by featureless collective life, will be trampled to death by 'the herd'. (This recognition and increasing fear of the mob, the masses, the herd, or whatever name is chosen for the nameless crowd, reaches its height in the half-crazed Nietzsche, but it had been growing throughout the age. It was obviously the result of the rapid rise in population, the industrial towns swarming with the new proletariat, and of some feeling of guilt about this almost outcast class.) Moreover, Nietzsche saw more clearly than anybody, before the depth psychologists arrived hard at his heels, that most men are far from being rational creatures and do not even want to be reasonable; they are moved by unconscious forces and the power of the accepted myth.

A new myth, then, had to be found. It was here, turning from the negative, in which his brilliant insights cannot be questioned, to the positive and what must be done, that Nietzsche goes from strength to weakness. He had rejected so much: Christianity, rational liberalism (he thought John Stuart Mill a vulgar blockhead), the Hegelian state, Marx's Communism, French or English socialism, Russian anarchy; all were useless. So, not unmoved by vague dreams of his Greek and Renaissance heroes, he offered his own myth of the Supermen, towering high above the herd, beyond present good and evil, tyrant-philosopher-artists who by the splendour of their richly individual lives would more than justify the toil and servitude of common men, the masses that would find their own drab lives enriched by the mere existence of these magnificent beings, by a dazzling new myth. The idea is neither ignoble nor completely absurd, though Nietzsche, as he goaded himself on, in the shadow of madness, wrote both ignobly and absurdly all round it, over-compensating his own feeling of inferiority by insisting upon his supermen being ruthless, violent, cruel, and devils with the women. (In fact, respectively like Hitler, Göring, Himmler and Goebbels.) Nevertheless, he was demanding the impossible. He was asking for qualities that cancel each other out: for beings at once more sensitive and less sensitive than ordinary men are, for ruthless tyrants with the tenderness for life of artists, for military bullies who could turn themselves inside out and be philosophers, for lovers of women who, whip in hand, could not know how to love women. The myth is so inadequate, the positive so pitiful after the negative, the destructive force of his criticism, that it is as if a man had blown up a city in order to stage a second-rate pageant. Nietzsche died in 1900, and it was during the last ten years of his life, when he was in fact hopelessly insane, that he and his ideas (all too frequently misrepresented) became famous. Although he loses much, both in poetry and wit, in translation, his best work—and especially *The Birth of Tragedy*, *Thus Spake Zarathustra*, *Beyond Good and Evil*, and *The Genealogy of Morals*—has been published in all major languages; and his influence upon European writers, including some of the most important during the period 1890–1910, has been enormous.

There were other influences extending from this age to the next, our own; there were many other minor prophets but perhaps major philosophical and social critics of this nineteenth century who have not been mentioned yet but may make a brief appearance in later chapters. But enough has been said already to show us the growing confusion of the age in its thought and feeling, in sharp contrast to the direct line of its scientific and industrial progress. All the voices agree that something is wrong, but then, when proposing remedies, turn into a Babel. (If we have said little about the noisy quarrel between churchmen and scientists that followed the publication of Darwin's *Origin of Species*, this is because it was a false and stupid quarrel. Religion and biology cannot fight a duel, because they cannot meet on the same ground.) Two other features of this nineteenth century are plainly distinguishable. First, the existence and central dominating position of a smugly complacent bourgeois class, detested as a class by most writers, even though they had to look to it for their readers. Secondly, the rapid increase of those urban industrial workers, voiceless in their poverty, faceless in their grime, the people whom one major prophet saw as the inevitably triumphant proletariat, and another saw as the vindictive trampling herd, and of whom all but the most trivial writers in Western Europe were aware. (Both the Americans and the Russians had quite a different view of such people, as we shall see.) But though many names have been left unmentioned, we shall do well here to stop at Nietzsche. An old recipe for the preparation of a salad tells us we need, finally, a madman to mix it. This age, considered in terms of its thought, feeling and taste, is not unlike a vast salad, and in Nietzsche it found a madman to mix it.

brother and escapes to France, has a bad breakdown but finally wakens to the call of his country going to war. On this level, making use of such a preposterous narrative, Tennyson is challenging popular romancers and playwrights at their own game, and as an entertainer is reaching out to their large public. On the second level, where throughout the poem he denounces some of the manners and morals of the time and ends by praising the ennobling influence of war, he is writing in his capacity as Poet Laureate and Queen Victoria's official bard. In this capacity he took himself very seriously. He felt it was his duty not only to write poems on important national events but also to make his poetry a kind of 1851 Exhibition of the representative thought of the time. Now Tennyson was not a foolish man; he read widely and was closely acquainted with many of the best contemporary minds; and if much of what he wrote on this level is silly stuff, the obvious explanation is that his heart and his genius were not in it. Only the craftsman—and Tennyson was always a superb craftsman—was there, finding melodious phrases for these newspaper and clubmen's notions. His poetic genius, which cannot be denied, belongs to the third level, discovered in *Maud* in the love-songs, poetry that is entirely romantic.

The poet on this level, the real Tennyson, though no doubt haunted by Virgil, looks back to Keats. And odd though it may seem, when we think of the big, shaggy Tennyson, at every age a magnificent figure of a bard, and the consumptive little Keats, the romanticism that Keats was moving away from, to achieve the balance that would have been necessary for the full expression of his virile genius, was not only accepted by Tennyson but also warmed and softened, turned into something dreamy and passive, strangely feminine. So whenever Tennyson writes about duty and action and the like, he is at the best merely acceptable, because of his sheer craftsmanship; but when he conjures us into some luxuriant, listless and melancholy dreamland, as in *The Lotus Eaters* and so many of his lyrics, his genius is at work, he is magical. The fact that he has a wonderful eye for the English scene, perhaps being over-sharply observant for what poetry needs to record, and that he often compels himself to be stern, curt, grandly masculine, should not blind us to the more essential fact that he is most magical and most Tennysonian when some vague dream landscape and some mood of nostalgia and melancholy are marvellously blended, when he seems less like the great bearded Laureate than like some girl, half-drowned in love, lingering in a hot-house. One part of him, the public figure, the Victorian bard, kept abreast with the age, putting into respectable verse much of its typical thought and feeling; but the poet himself worked in the sunset and enchanted dusk of the lingering romantic tradition, and may reasonably be considered the last of the great English romantic poets. A foreign lady, astonished at his high reputation, indignantly demanded to know what he could do that Byron could not do better. The answer she should have been given is that Tennyson is essentially English, which Byron was not, and that although he is a less impressive figure and far less fascinating simply as a character, he has a greater gift than Byron ever had—and this is important to readers who share the same language—of arranging English words in a magical and memorable order.

All the English poets who were more or less Tennyson's contemporaries spent their youth reading the great Romantics, their work then still fresh and not covered with the dust of biography and criticism. But whereas we feel that Tennyson appointed himself Keats's successor, we see no such direct link with these other poets. They differ from Tennyson, too, in not making a full professional career out of poetry. For example, Browning seems half a great poet and half an eccentric Victorian man of means. During her lifetime his wife, the Elizabeth Barrett with whom he eloped to Italy, was better known and more popular as a poet. (She is best when securely laced into sonnet form.) It was not until late in the age, when Browning returned to London, apparently to dine out every evening, that he became not only famous but also the subject of an odd cult, his more obscure dramatic poems being studied as if they were runes and prophecies. But his obscurity does not come from any great depth and subtlety of thought, but from technical whimsicalities and a rushing eagerness of temperament. His elaborate portraits and study-dramas, mostly with an Italian Renaissance background, are not to everybody's taste, but nobody who cares about English poetry can fail to enjoy his poems with a contemporary setting, in which he seems far more at ease than Tennyson does, such as *Waring* and *The Last Ride Together* or *Bishop*

Blougram's Apology. Matthew Arnold, who did notable service to the age as a literary and social critic, deliberately tried to steel himself against romanticism, and many of his more ambitious poems read like charming exercises in the classical manner, but in his shorter and more revealing poems, of which *Dover Beach* is a fine example, he expresses with romantic urgency the bewilderment, often darkening to despair, of a sensitive mind in a sadly confused time. Dante Gabriel Rossetti is the opposite of Arnold. Because of a few popular poems like *The Blessed Damozel* and the hot-house romanticism of his paintings, he is too often considered a soft poet, lost in some medieval dreamland, whereas in fact he often writes strongly, with a certain Latin hardness, about his own time and place. (His sister, Christina, who mixed piety with charm and humour, wrote the best feminine poetry of Victorian England.) William Morris, an energetic man of many skills and an important figure in the history of British Socialism, was a medievalist, not out of any weak desire to escape the age, which he faced and denounced, but because the born craftsman in him delighted in the solid old crafts. His poetry, which he wrote with astonishing ease, lacks urgency and concentrated power, but in its usual narrative form has a curious half-somnolent charm, like a bright tapestry unfolding as a panorama. Works of reference still tell us that Algernon Charles Swinburne was not a poet who became popular, but a glance at any later edition of his *Poems and Ballads* disproves this statement, for they have been reprinted year after year ever since they first appeared in 1866 and shocked so many people. In his longer poems and dramas, Swinburne simply brings to the romantic tradition a dazzling technical dexterity, only marred by sheer fluency; but in his shorter and more personal poems, which express an ambiguous sexuality, reminiscent of the night life of London and Paris in the 1860s, a vicious decade, he gives us romanticism gone rotten. It is worth comparing the work of all or any of these poets with George Meredith's long poem about a broken marriage, *Modern Love*, published as early as 1862 but appearing to belong, both in manner and content, to another world. But Meredith, still undervalued as a poet, though he understood the Romantics, mocked them and deliberately rejected their tradition.

2

Whitman's weaknesses and absurdities are obvious, but he gives us America in poetry as no other American poet was to do for a long time. It can be said of America during this age that more of its essential poetry went into its prose than into its verse. Herman Melville, who will be considered in the next chapter, is a good example, for he turned to verse after he had written most of his prose works, but he is more of a poet in *Moby Dick*, even phrase by phrase, than he is in his verse. The harvest of genuine poetry, as distinct from versifying, is so thin not because the America of these years is conquering the West or moving toward, fighting, recovering from, the Civil War, but because its literary production is divided between two quite different societies, neither of them really favourable to poetry. These of course were New England and the South. The latter, for all its dashingly romantic airs and graces, its chivalrous hot-blooded males and pure beautiful females like so many magnolia flowers, was even less favourable than the bleaker Yankee atmosphere of Boston and Concord. The imagination could not work on so much that was fanciful and false. Poe's chief weakness as a poet is mostly due to the strain in it of cheap romantic fiction and boozy oratory. Sidney Lanier, his best successor from the South, is a genuine poet, but suffered too much from poverty and ill-health (he was taken prisoner in the Civil War, in his twenties, and died before he was forty) to make the fullest use of his talent. There was in New England a real literary culture, whose high priest was Emerson, but prose, though it might have poetic overtones and undertones, was its natural expression, as it was with both Emerson and Thoreau. Whittier and Longfellow enjoyed enormous local reputations; and in the heat of his anti-slavery feeling Whittier occasionally forges a splendid line or two, and throughout his work is more his own man than Longfellow, who is too often reflecting or transposing into an American key so much European romantic poetry. Oliver Wendell Holmes and James Russell Lowell were prose-men, wittily versifying. The poet who comes nearest to expressing the New England character and spirit is the one who was unknown until late in the age, Emily

Dickinson, half spinster, half peeping troll, sharp, staccato, often awkward, never far from thoughts of death, but when successful a wonderfully bold and concentrated poet, making the men of her time seem timid and long-winded.

Walt Whitman belonged to neither of these two societies but to something between them, looser and lower in the social scale, to Brooklyn and not Boston or Baltimore; to a new and entirely non-European society, growing and not dying as the other two were; to what seems to us now America. It was an odd collection of people, and Whitman is probably the oddest of all great poets. The outward man, the *persona*, is a fake, a long-sustained character performance. Behind the imposing façade of the 'good grey poet', rough old Walt, the big shaggy prophet of New World democracy and its common men, was a vain and womanish literary character, emerging from third-rate *belles lettres*. He was a tasteless poseur. He was a practising and proselytising homosexual. He wrote a good deal of pretentious rubbish, using a vocabulary that might have been borrowed from an illiterate head-waiter. Often he seems like one of those American literary characters that Dickens created in *Martin Chuzzlewit*, and to be capable of echoing humourlessly the worst of their mock profundities. Altogether, a dubious character. Nevertheless, he is a supremely original and genuinely great poet, who gave America not some European colony but America herself, an epic strain, an authentic voice.

How did he come to do it? In order to answer this question, let us consider him in terms of this original 1855 edition of *Leaves of Grass*, for though some of his finest poems came later (as, for example, the lament for Lincoln), his form, manner, attitude of mind, are fully displayed in this first book. First, he was fortunate in not belonging to either of the two dominating social and literary cultures. If he had been a Southerner, he would have inherited the false romanticism and the hostility or indifference to the democratic idea. Writing as a New Englander, conscious of the long war between the flesh and the spirit, haunted by a sense of sin, he could not have identified his poetry with the claims of the body. But he was free from both these pressures. His not very arduous work as a journeyman printer, newspaper man, carpenter, gave him an entrance into an amorphous new society of workmen and artisans, of careless hopeful males; and at a time too before the long and bitter Civil War, before the wholesale immigrations to provide industry with labour, before business America took shape, a time—as he makes us feel in his earlier work—still fresh and bright with promise. And, because of his inverted sexuality, a common-place scene of men at their tasks, unloading a ship or building a house, would for Walt, loafing there, be invested with emotional significance, largely erotic in origin. But what is undoubtedly rooted in his inversion becomes in most of his poetry—we cannot say all of it because the sexual feeling in some poems is obvious—a curiously selfless identification, not unlike the *participation mystique* of primitive man, with a whole vast panorama of Man and Nature presented to us, we feel, almost in a pre-historical condition, as if human society, as Europe had known it for centuries, did not yet exist. And the democracy about which we hear so much in Whitman seems less the familiar political creed, one system out of many, than it does a term for some new world outside politics altogether, as if the happy anarchy of Shelley's golden age of the future were already here. Behind this poet's rather absurd lists of trades and jobs, his bragging about steam printing-presses and electric telegraphs, is a dream as wide as the sky, impossible to a European poet, an American dream.

Such an outlook demanded an unconventional poetic form, large and loose and rolling. And to this form Whitman brought little taste and talent—he had not enough of either to be an acceptable minor poet— but did bring authentic genius. Even when he is bad, and he can be horribly tasteless and silly, he is bad as a great original, a bard singing and celebrating a new world. He is not always wildly optimistic, for the Civil War and all that followed it hit him hard, but this dream of a new and entirely free society, essentially classless, made up of comrades, because it is seen through a haze of diffused eroticism, never leaves him. And over and over again, through much that is mere formless writing, there flashes the great illuminating phrase. It is as if so many different elements—the time, his background and kind of experience, his inverted but strong sexuality, the loose poetic form he chose, even his lounging indolence of body and mind—combined to create in him the very type of genius required (even though reluctantly acknowledged) by his country and his age. Indeed, in spite of the very different culture of Latin America, where at this time the poets were mostly writing under the influence of the French Romantics, we might add that in Whitman the whole vast continent, where all manner of Western men were settling and creating new societies, could have found its voice.

3

The third of these representative major poets, Charles Baudelaire, declared that poetry has no other end but itself, that if a poet has a moral end in view he has diminished his poetic force. Now there can be no doubt about Baudelaire's poetic force. He brings together—a rare combination—a classical strength and weight and an ultra-romantic evocative quality: architecture and music. The power of suggestion is not a monopoly of modern poetry; it belongs to the art itself; but Baudelaire deliberately heightened this power by his use of strongly associative imagery and by making one kind of sense-impression suggest another; and here he is the first—and remains one of the greatest—of the moderns. This frail little man, looking like a ruined priest, walks at the head of a procession of poets that has not ended yet. But his theorising is nonsense. Poetic force has to come from somewhere, just as a genuine poem, though it may be judged by its intensity of experience, has to be about something. A man cannot write with Baudelaire's precision and passion about nothing. Nor can a man ask us to believe that his poems have no concern with morality, anybody's morality, if he boldly labels them 'flowers of evil'. Baudelaire has in fact other ends in view besides the creation of exquisite verse. The first and less important we have already briefly noticed, in glancing at the Æsthetic Movement. It is the desire to startle, shock, disgust, the complacent bourgeois class, people like the general whom his adored mother presented to him as a step-father. Baudelaire spent a good deal of his adult life revenging himself on his step-father, working off his jealousy as a young child, using his great talent as a form of compensation. And in all this he is very much one of the representative moderns, so often, as we shall discover, negative in their initial approach to literature, which does not come from an excess of vitality and a wider and deeper acceptance of life than is common, but from embittered introversion and a sense of deficiency. In any event, an artist does not gain freedom by this desire to shock stupid conventional people, for he is still compelling himself to accept their standards and outlook by deliberately reversing them: he is only a bourgeois type standing on his head.

The second and far more important end that Baudelaire had in view deserves more consideration. It belongs to the 'ruined priest' aspect of him. The sensuality that Baudelaire parades and celebrates is not that of a self-indulgent full-blooded man, a careless giant like Dumas, a sexual athlete like Hugo. It is cold and careful, and might even be described as conscientious. We can call it conscientious for two quite different reasons. First, there is the poet's pursuit of curious sensations, a pursuit in which Baudelaire led the way for all the æsthetes and decadents of the next thirty years. The artist, they believed, is the supreme taster. They also believed—ruinously, unless they happened to be as cautious as Walter Pater—that an individual sensation, justifying itself no matter what its origin might be, could be removed from the stream of living and enjoyed in a kind of vacuum. This idea is as mischievous as it is false, for it calls for stronger and stronger doses, to produce any effect worth regarding as a sensation, so debauchery has to be spiced with perversion, perverted debauchery helped out by drugs, until nothing works any longer, except to produce boredom and misery, and death is welcome. Now Baudelaire, who unlike so many of his later admirers was not a fool, was well aware of all this, so he was conscientious in his cult of destructive sensuality for another and deeper reason. It was on his part a kind of calculated blasphemy. It is for him deliberate sinning. The flesh, having been alienated from the spirit, is transformed into a goad and a whip. The sensation with him loses its false independence, and is returned to the stream of life, but now negatively, becoming significant because it is linked with death, sin, blasphemy. This is Logos, gone mad, posing as Eros. It is extreme romanticism turned devotionally Catholic, but, in its childish egoism, enlisting under Satan. Behind the fastidious poet and critic, the coolly impudent social poseur, half dandy, half priest, who yet wastes his slender stock of money and vitality on a coarse and vindictive mulatto mistress, is little Charles Baudelaire, his mother's boy, defying all the archangels and turning his back on the Kingdom of Heaven.

Genius, Baudelaire declares, is childhood recaptured at will. The childhood he could recapture showed him two extremes of living, brief felicity giving place to long misery. (After the death of his father he was able to monopolise the attention of his mother, to whom he was passionately devoted, but then she married General Aupick, who remained with him a symbolic figure of all that was stupid, conventional, detestable, and the little boy's long misery began.) He grew up, feeling an exile, and hating the ugly and brutal world in which he found himself. If Paradise was denied him, then he would damn himself deeper with curious, increasingly fantastic sins. And even though fixed in this foolish adolescent attitude, he could bring to criticism a fine taste and powerful intelligence, and he could contrive poetry of astonishing force and beauty. But though his personal history explains a great deal, it does not explain everything. There is the age itself to be taken into account. It could not offer him the broad foundation of religion that his essentially religious nature demanded, but only a sickly religiosity that he stood on its head. What it could and did offer him, for Baudelaire was very much a Parisian, was the Paris of the mid-century, a material and corrupt society, turning the poet in his boredom and disgust into a defiant connoisseur of isolated sensations, making him prefer the adolescent's black standard of Satan to no banner at all, breeding out of his poetic genius the twin and equally mischievous traditions of dandyism and decadence.

That was not all, however. It was the ageing Gautier and not Baudelaire who chiefly inspired that group of poets known as the Parnassians, which included in its earlier years Théodore de Banville, Louis Ménard, Leconte de Lisle, Sully Prudhomme and François Coppée; but the direct line of modern poetry by-passes these poets and runs straight from Baudelaire to the Symbolists. And the Symbolist Movement is important not so much because of the work that came directly out of it but because the major poetry of our own century (to be considered in our final section) mainly derives from it. Oddly enough, this also means that the major poets of our time owe a good deal, in an indirect fashion, to a minor American poet we have already noticed: Edgar Allan Poe. Both Baudelaire, the original Symbolist, and Mallarmé, the chief theorist and metaphysician of the movement, were deeply impressed and influenced by Poe's theory and practice of what he called "a suggestive indefiniteness", his belief that poetry should be evocative rather than descriptive. (There is irony here, for much in Poe's verse that is either mechanical or in dubious taste must have been accepted by these two French poets, both so wonderfully sensitive to their own language.) But more went to the making of this movement than the combined influences of Poe and Baudelaire. In the Paris of Mallarmé, already the capital city of art in rebellion everywhere, other influences were at work. Thus there is an obvious link between Impressionist painting and this new poetry. More important still was the music of Wagner (to which Baudelaire had been an early convert) that was for ever suggesting to Mallarmé some possible parallel development in poetry. And several of these poets spent some time in England, with its hazy landscapes, misty-golden water-colours, its earlier romantic poetry quite different from that of the more rhetorical French Romantics. This was the time, too, when the Russian novels, so exotic and mystical, were first appearing in French; and there were also strange voices from Scandinavia. We can say then that the many nations that were soon to find their major poets inspired by the French Symbolists had themselves, a quarter of a century before, made some initial contribution to the movement.

Yet it was never a very positive movement, nor indeed much of a movement at all, in the usual meaning of the term, suggesting a definite group with a common programme. Its poets shared dislikes rather than likes. All were equally contemptuous of what might be called official verse, traditional, descriptive, moralising, school-book stuff. They detested the pseudo-scientific naturalism of popular novelists and playwrights and the kind of criticism that praised it. In their various ways they all wanted to take poetry out of the heavy materialism of the age, now in its final phase. They were all rebels of one sort or another. But they were not rebels in the spirit of 1848. (Though some of them—Rimbaud certainly, Corbière and Laforgue probably—can be seen as rebels in the spirit of

1958.) Their poetry, differing as it did in many respects, was alike in not having been written to be declaimed on the barricades. Rimbaud, who combines in himself two of our familiar contemporary types, the intellectual and the tough, would have manned a barricade "just for the hell of it", but not in his capacity as a poet. Indeed, in that capacity he was beginning to erect his own and very different barricade, against the understanding of the ordinary reader, unable to appreciate his deliberate "disordering of the senses", his idea of poetry as a disturber of consciousness. But before he had really arrived at the 'new literature' he had promised himself, this astounding youth walked out of literature altogether, preferring to find his relation to the universe in gun-running and the Abyssinian slave-trade, and dying at thirty-seven. The quality of his finest work cannot be denied, whether he wrote, as a boy, about the sea he had not then known or about the lice being taken out of his hair, about the provincial lad under the lime trees or about the colours of the vowels; but he is one of those strange and rare creatures who cannot be seen and estimated as a writer among writers, although their genius or talent is unquestioned, because of the terrific impact on us of their personalities, which seem outside their place and time, as if they were visitors from other planets. Behind Rimbaud's sensitiveness to his own world, which his poetry reveals, there is something not belonging to that world, that age, something implacable and coldly violent, suggesting not that age but ours, and not our literature, in which he has to share influences with the ironic and delicately colloquial Laforgue and of course with Mallarmé himself, but rather our history, as if our present world of character and action fulfilled some sinister vision with which Rimbaud entertained and cooled himself during one of his Abyssinian nights.

That Symbolism was the loosest sort of movement, united negatively in its dislikes rather than positively in its likes, is proved by the prominence in it of Verlaine. For though Verlaine's public abjuration of the eloquence and rhetoric of the Romantics brings him alongside the Symbolists, he is at his best and in essence a kind of poet discovered at many different times in many different literatures, namely, the pure singer celebrating anything but pure life, the lyrical sinner who would be a saint, the drunk murmuring magical regrets at three in the morning. He needs no more æsthetic theory to sustain him than Villon did. But it is far more difficult to be so apparently simple, at once so evocative, melodious and fluid, in French, the language of rhetoric, wit and logic, than it is in English, German, Russian; and there Verlaine triumphs, achieving a popularity (helped by the French composers) denied to the other Symbolists, a strong short-term influence in the Nineties, a decade crowded with bohemian singers and half-repentant sinners, but losing his vogue in later and harder years, among poets with more iron in their systems. Given his marvellous ear and flexible technique, Verlaine succeeded simply by dropping out what he felt to be superfluous; but Mallarmé, a very different character, the central authentic Symbolist, worked positively and laboriously to create a new poetry. In this he was as impersonal as the young Symbolists (who mostly died young) were sharply and directly personal. Moreover, there was in Mallarmé none of the dubious dandyism and decadence that came out of Baudelaire and, for thirty years after his death, dropped from level to level, especially in prose, until it reached the pornography of perverted sexuality. (After which the psycho-analysts arrived and with their clinical phraseology removed the glamour.) It is indeed ironical that Mallarmé, who of all these poets probably had the most satisfying relation with real life, should have moved further away from ordinary reality in his work than any of them. But then Mallarmé did not merely believe that poetry should aim at Poe's 'suggestive indefiniteness', at evocation in place of description, he also believed that it could be made to behave like music, that it could almost be based on verbal notation, that words used symbolically could bring the mind into some eternal realm of the Platonic idea. That among much so obscure that it seems unrewarding and repellent he produced some original and powerful effects, a few poems of beauty, is true enough; but after all, Mallarmé was a poet as well as a determined and subtle theorist, and he might have done as well, if not better, without his years of severe concentration on his theory. He might have had more time for poetry.

Mallarmé, in his theory of Symbolism, suffered from the very circumstance that had wrecked Baudelaire's life, namely, that the society of his time was without a religious foundation and framework. An age with that foundation and framework would have provided him with symbols, for the control of the unconscious by religion is through symbols, and these would have meant as much to his audience as they did to him. His poetry, no matter how subtle, how profound, it might be, would then have had a public language, not a private one. And the weakness of Symbolism, not in its negative aspect, a mere avoidance of what it considers unpoetical, but in its positive aspect, as poetry in a new form, is that it compels the poet, in a secular and non-symbolic age like this, to write in what almost amounts to a private language. Too often his work demands long, close study before it can be understood, and then, after such an effort has been made, it may no longer make its true and urgent emotional impact, its æsthetic quality having withered. As we have seen, the influence of the French Symbolists was immediate and wide. They are partly responsible for the sudden rise and sweep of Belgian poetry, for Fontainas, Gilkin, Giraud, Lerberghe, Mockel, and Maeterlinck (who brought Symbolism on to the stage); and even for the greatest of them, Émile Verhaeren, in spite of his later Whitmanesque realism. Symbolism enters German literature through Stefan George and Rilke, English through Yeats, Russian through Blok; and moves on to Latin America. Without this French movement there would have been no modern poetry as we know it today. By deliberately limiting his range while at the same time demanding from him more concentration, an effort more severely sustained, it gave the modern poet, in an unfavourable time, a new hope, a renewed faith in his art. But it also entangled him in its own limitations. Poetry became more intensely private, almost esoteric. If it still spoke in a public voice, through a Kipling or even a Paul Fort (originally a Symbolist), then it was not quite poetry, which now seemed to whisper in a corner to a few initiates. Enjoying modern poetry was no longer like enjoying a glass of wine, spring blossom, the operas of Mozart, but began to suggest some difficult and mysterious hobby, solving cryptograms or learning to write Chinese. The gap between the poet of genius or great talent and society in general was now far wider than it had been when the age began. The point is not (as we have so often been told) simply that the new urban workers were unpoetical in spirit, not only outside poetry as literature but with no memory now of the songs and ballads their grandparents knew, but that educated, intelligent and not insensitive people, capable of appreciating other arts or older literature, were now all too often alienated from contemporary poetry. It seemed to be written by and for specialists; and, after all, this was increasingly an age of specialisation. And here is the tragic irony of the situation. For poetry does not represent the specialisation and separation of men, cannot be another of the barriers between them. Poetry is the break-through, the whole man addressing other whole men. But now modern poetry, in its sincere effort to be more purely poetical, lost most of its audience, and just when that audience was in need of it. So if the poets were unlucky, so was the age.

CHAPTER SEVENTEEN

The Novelists

I

WE HAVE NOTICED ALREADY that the general drift of this age, from about 1840 onwards, was away from literary culture. More and more people, a large proportion of them middle-class women, wanted something to read, but did not see themselves as patrons, connoisseurs, students of literature. Now it might be said that a poem is literature until we are convinced it is not, whereas a novel is not literature until we are convinced that it is. The novelist does not begin by making a contribution to literature but, if he is considered good enough, ends by making one. To this day, a century later than the period we have entered here, it is still the custom on the literary pages of serious newspapers and periodicals —in many countries, and certainly the English-speaking countries—to review at length poetry and essays, history, memoirs, biography, while fencing off and briefly noticing new fiction. And even now, solemn public men, anxious to prove their cultivated taste, let it be known that the limited time they have for reading is rarely wasted on novels. This idea of fiction goes back to the time when Balzac was publishing some of his best novels in smudgy daily instalments in the popular press, and the novels of Dickens were arriving in fortnightly or monthly parts. But although this delayed the recognition of their genius—"We are inclined to predict of works of this style both in England and France," wrote the *Quarterly Review*, which had learnt nothing, "that an ephemeral popularity will be followed by early oblivion . . ."—it brought them and the novel itself a multitude of new readers in country after country. And this immense popular eagerness, like that of the playgoers in the great days of poetic drama, helped in turn, through some mysterious social alchemy, to produce the genius that satisfied it, making prose fiction the dominant form, raising the level of the novel in one country after another, until now we look back on this time as the golden age of the novel.

The novel that achieved this sudden triumph was a loose mixed form, half a work of art and half something else, the despair of neat analytical minds. It came out of a rapidly growing, sprawling, changing, untidy society, in which older social and cultural patterns were fast disappearing, and it reflected the character of that society. At its best it was literature, but not literature existing within the limits of the accepted literary tradition. The great nineteenth-century novelists were not strictly men of letters but both something less and something a great deal more than men of letters. Their position, unlike that of earlier writers of similar stature, was undefined and ambiguous, in spite of their popularity and wide fame, and this partly accounts for a sense of strain in them, for their bewilderment and unhappiness. Meanwhile, not any public dissatisfaction with the novel as a loose mixed form, but rather some constant pressure of criticism, which the more ambitious novelists later in the age could not disregard, compelled these novelists to move in one of three different directions. They could go nearer the scientist, the sociologist, the reporter; could try to be as objective as possible; could observe and record rather than invent and create: like Zola and the novelists of naturalism. Moving in another direction, they could insist upon rejecting the loose mixed form in the hope of turning the novel into a work of literary art, technically as perfect as a good sonnet, the novelist himself becoming as much an artist as a painter or composer: a dream that haunted Flaubert and gradually imposed itself upon Henry James. Finally, seeking significance neither from science nor art, they could fall back upon an old tradition of prose fiction, while making use of every advance in technique, and deliberately transform the novel into an instrument of propaganda (not necessarily either religious or political), the expression in narrative and dramatic form of a definite philosophy of life, which we discover in the later Tolstoy, in George Eliot, Meredith, Hardy, Anatole France. So the latter half of the age shows us both creation and criticism moving in these three directions.

In one supremely important respect, however, the general reader, directly and naïvely responding to what the novelist offered him or her, came closer to understanding what is essential in the novel than many of its cleverest critics, no longer capable of that response. For what is essential is that the novelist, whatever else he does, should be able to show us people who by some means or other, through delighted fascination, repulsion, or mere conviction that in their own world they exist, catch and hold our imagination. If his characters fail to do this, then the novelist has failed. A novel in which the people do not seem to us to come alive (even though they appear to be almost monsters) cannot succeed as a novel, no matter what merits it may have as a piece of writing. The narrative itself may go through all manner of transformations, the narrator himself may be a wise man or almost a fool, but this vital relationship between us and its people, or at least some of them, remains central in fiction, its keystone. A good deal of critical impatience with fiction, encouraging absurd judgments, is due to the fact that this peculiar but essential ability can be easily recognised, as it has been by millions of ordinary readers, but escapes analysis, and cannot be explained in terms of intelligence or sensibility. (Walter Pater, for example, lacked neither, yet his attempts at fiction are lifeless, so many visits to an exquisite morgue.) The most we can say here about this mysterious creative faculty is that it appears to be linked with childhood, demands a certain imaginative vitality, and only works on a grand scale with men who have rich but not integrated personalities, contradictory characters, divided men, of whom Tolstoy and Dickens are obvious examples. Caught between the flashing poles of the opposites, they generate out of their joy, misery, bewilderment, whole multitudes. And it may not be too fanciful to see in the age itself a similar character, divided and contradictory, demanding to be expressed in the novel.

2

Along with those French novelists, notably Balzac and Stendhal, whom we have already discovered among the French Romantics, the English now took the lead again, as they had done in the previous century. The dates prove this. By the end of the Thirties, with *Pickwick Papers* and *Nicholas Nickleby* behind him, Dickens was already dazzlingly successful and was being translated and read all over Europe. The Forties brought Thackeray and the Brontë sisters to join Dickens, whereas it is not until the Sixties and Seventies that Russia produces its masterpieces. Even in France there is a gap between the death of Balzac in 1850 and the arrival seven years later of Flaubert with *Madame Bovary* and a new kind of fiction. It is then the Anglo-Saxons, both at home and overseas (Hawthorne and Melville), who can justly be considered first.

The Brontë sisters, members of a strange doomed family, both died young, Emily at thirty, Charlotte before she was forty. They were Celts but lived in the West Riding of Yorkshire, remotely and bleakly, with the wild moors on one side of them and the black industry of the valleys on the other side. The secret of Charlotte, whose reputation strictly as a novelist has declined during this present century, is that she combines an ultra-romanticism of spirit, a gift from her family, with an essentially feminine realism, making use, as so many later women novelists were to do, of autobiographical elements. So in *Jane Eyre*, her first and greatest success, she begins without any romantic trappings of any sort, showing us her bleak world as she knew it with what at that time was astonishing boldness, and then, delivering us from consciousness and memory and plunging us into the myths of the unconscious, in the true romantic fashion, entangles us in a mysterious and fantastic tale, only raised above mere melodrama by the sheer force of her imagination. There is in this novel and the three that followed it (*Shirley*, *Villette* and *The Professor*, actually her first but not published until after her death) a certain impatient and sometimes fierce feminist element: it is a protest against the beautiful smiling images created by male writers; it declares in effect that a plain little woman, very different from the ladies of romance, moving about almost unnoticed in the outer world, carries around with her an inner world of gigantic hopes, fears, passion, tenderness and joy. But the tremendous challenging male, Jane's Mr. Rochester, is a figure born of this inner world. And in her sister Emily's solitary masterpiece, *Wuthering Heights*, this demonic dream lover, Heathcliff, imagined with far greater intensity, dominates the whole wild strange scene, one half Yorkshire moorland, the other half some dark tempestuous realm of the unconscious. This story of a demonic passion, devouring one generation and then wearing itself out before a second can be destroyed, is not really a novel at all, if the novel is seen as an account of man in society, but belongs to a rare category of fiction—like Melville's *Moby Dick*—consisting of narratives that are like prose poems and cannot be criticised as novels. Like similar works, Emily Brontë's is unequal, confused, turgid, but both in its grand tragic design and in the visionary intensity of its best scenes it is an astounding performance for a girl in her twenties, leaping in one bound from Victorian fiction to Elizabethan tragedy, and it is not surprising that Emily now overshadows Charlotte. But the whole strange family has been the rewarding subject of many studies.

William Makepeace Thackeray, who at home, though never abroad, successfully challenged the supremacy of Dickens, has almost all the qualities demanded of a major novelist. He has a sharp eye and ear for a character; he can rise magnificently to a big scene; socially he is uncommonly perceptive; and he has a narrative style that is easy and flexible and yet has distinction. His purely literary gifts are impressive; he is one of the best English essayists; and his historical novel, *Esmond*, is a remarkable *tour de force*, recreating the age of Queen Anne as few ages have ever been recreated by a novelist anywhere. His first ambitious novel, and his best, *Vanity Fair*, is unquestionably a masterpiece. It made him famous while he was still in his middle thirties. But in spite of this success and these gifts, his work as a whole is unsatisfactory and disappointing, and this cannot be explained by his failing health and death at the age of fifty-three. Although he still receives lavish praise in all reference books of English Literature, he is no longer widely read even in England, and has not maintained, if he ever had it, the stature of a major novelist in world literature.

He was unlucky in his life and his time. The young wife to whom he was devoted went mad (outliving him by thirty years); he could not re-marry and, partly owing to an unrewarding and rather fatuous attachment to a friend's wife, the primly complacent Mrs. Brookfield, he never found a mistress who could have taken his wife's place; and consequently he spent much of his time at his clubs. Now the London club is very different from the Paris café, where an artist meets other artists, to denounce the critics and the stupid public and to start a new movement. The London club is usually dominated by men who care nothing for the arts, who indeed represent the stupid public, and in their company a writer extremely sensitive to criticism, as Thackeray was, is more likely to abandon any plan for a defiantly original piece of work than to adopt it. Again, Thackeray, who had wasted in his youth the money he had inherited, was determined to provide handsomely for his two daughters, and this meant that he could not afford to alienate the middle-class family readers on whose support he depended. To some Victorian novelists— his admiring and industrious friend, Anthony Trollope, for instance—this limitation of both theme and treatment was no great hardship. But to Thackeray it was almost fatal. The creative writer in him understood the relations between men and women (there was in fact a strong feminine streak in Thackeray the creator and social observer, and often he comments on a scene as a woman would), but dared not explore and describe these relations frankly. Therefore, too often frustrated, even though able to give the disreputable characters, especially the women, more life and individuality than the virtuous types (so Becky in *Vanity Fair* and Beatrix in *Esmond* are far superior to his loving, blameless women), after shaping a plot that must have puzzled or teased his family readers, the creator in him retreats and gives place to a moralist and a rather cynical manipulator of puppets. His life defeated the sexually susceptible and deeply affectionate man, and time and circumstance were too much for the sharply and perhaps tragically perceptive artist in him; and so, to cover these defeats and retreats, more and more he adopts an elderly man-of-the-world, old clubman, half moralising, half shoulder-shrugging manner. (It is typical of Thackeray that while only in his forties, still an upright giant, he should have referred to himself as an elderly man, an old fogey content to pat the hands of the women, in a fashion that would have shocked Goethe and Hugo in their eighties.) So he appoints himself an apparently rather indolent chronicler, poised between humorous acceptance and moral disapproval, of the snobberies, pretensions, petty chicaneries, of mid-Victorian society, though still occasionally revealing, in a flash, the depth and fire of his real creative mind. In *Pendennis*, *The Newcomes*, *Denis Duval*, and other work below the level of *Vanity Fair* and *Esmond*, we are left dissatisfied but catch occasional glimpses even here of a great novelist, almost like finding some gigantic ruin, cathedral or castle, in a dingy suburb. He had all the gifts of a master except the fiercely creative will that lifts an artist above bad luck and an unpropitious time.

"It is usual to compare Dickens with Thackeray," wrote Santayana, who cannot be accused of any lack of fastidiousness, "which is like comparing the grape with the gooseberry; there are obvious points of resemblance, and the gooseberry has some superior qualities of its own; but you can't make red wine of it . . ." Dickens possesses in full measure that fiercely creative will in which Thackeray, a big but slack and rather soft man, is deficient. It is the so-called sentimentalist, not the supposed cynic, who is harder and more militant. (Henry James, who in his youth met Dickens, comments on his 'military eye'.) And much of Dickens's humour is not at all the kind of humour that is affectionate, sentimental and close to tears, but is as sharp and hard and merciless as pure comedy. Children often have this ruthlessly comic vision; and here we shall do well to remember Baudelaire's "Genius is childhood recaptured at will", for in Dickens's creative genius there is a direct access to childhood, to the fantastic world that imaginative children know, a world in which streets, houses, doors, chairs, clocks, are all alive, and people are like goblins and elves, are comic or sinister monsters, and all is cosiness, kindness and fun or is mysteriously menacing, dark with horror. To say that all this is mere exaggeration and caricature, as superior but unperceptive people often have done in condemning Dickens, is to miss his unique quality. The world's fiction—and especially minor Victorian fiction, like that of Surtees, Samuel Warren, Charles Lever, Albert Smith—is crammed with exaggeration and caricature, but it is all a long way from Dickens. The secret of Dickens is that he is able to create and vitalise a whole world of his own, and we delight in it in spite of its limitations (for it is a world without religion, culture, genuine history), because it resembles the world we remember from our childhood. We have only to think of some of our parents' or grandparents' friends, seemingly larger than life, unchanging, immortal, to come close to the comic (or even horrible) characters of Dickens. There is in him, not in his all too eloquent and expansive passages but in his whole act of creation, especially as it proliferates into the comic and grotesque, a kind of poetry. Dickens's triumph is not that of a prose novelist, closely observing man in society: it is that of a Maker, a dramatic and epic poet of inns and parlours, fog and street lamps, a mythopoeic genius.

So much needs to be said, to make plain what is fundamental in Dickens, what lies at the root of his extraordinary genius, what makes him Dickens, but it is necessary to know a great deal more about this very great novelist, who was neither the Father Christmas of English Literature nor the vulgar clown he is supposed to be by intellectual English critics who have never really read him. (The point is well made by the distinguished American critic, Edmund Wilson, in his extremely valuable study of Dickens, the best so far, to be found in *The Wound and the Bow*. We have not to agree with everything this critic says, to appreciate and be grateful for the full advantage he has taken of his position, removed as he is, by being an American, from both the English popular idolatry of Dickens and the intellectually fashionable proscription of him.) Let us consider first the man himself. He was a highly neurotic man, and the increasing strain of trying to satisfy himself as a man and an artist, and at the same time doing his best to please his immense expectant public, did nothing to make him less neurotic. At the age of twelve, an intelligent, sensitive, nervous boy, because his father had been arrested for debt, he was taken from school and sent to work in a blacking warehouse. He was only there six months and may have suffered no great hardship, but his whole world had been turned upside down, the emotional security of his family relationship had been destroyed, and he was therefore the victim of a profound shock from which he never really recovered. (This is proved by his statement to his biographer, Forster, to whom he confessed, when middle-aged, rich, famous, that he still had horrible dreams in which he found himself once more the waif in the blacking warehouse.) So this experience was part, not called but not to be denied, of the "childhood recaptured" by genius. And if there was a bright side, all cosy domesticity, beaming glances, jokes, songs, glasses of punch, there was also a dark side, born of a child's resentment and terror, suggesting the evil faces looking through the window, the murderer's footsteps, and all that menaced innocence and happiness, not merely obvious villainy but everything in society that was mechanical, coldly inhuman, heartless. Dickens was consciously rebellious, often for very good reasons, but there was also in him an unconscious deeply anti-social strain (as there was in Dostoyevsky, who admired and was considerably influenced by Dickens), which explains the fascination that murder had for him both in his life and his work. His novels are not all cosy domestic interiors and high spirits, and where they are not bright and sparkling, they are dark with violence, madness, death.

A man suffering from such an open wound of the spirit can often find healing in a profoundly satisfying relationship with a woman. But Dickens was unfortunate in his sexual life; though this too could have been the result of his neurosis, for he appears to have been fixed sexually at an immature stage, and so may have unconsciously rejected any possibility of a relationship with a mature woman. His marriage to Catherine Hogarth was a mistake, for he was really in love with her younger sister, Mary, who died in her middle teens. This is proved not only by his extravagant grief and frequent references to her but also by the fact that she haunts nearly all his earlier novels. Later, he fell in love with another young girl, Ellen Ternan, an actress, who became his mistress and is said to have borne him a child that died. This relationship lasted for twelve years, in fact until his death, but such evidence as we possess, which includes a statement she is supposed to have made, long afterwards, that she detested the mode of life the liaison imposed upon her, strongly suggests that it was not a satisfying relationship, not one of mutual love but the result of a persistent infatuation on his part; and it is significant that his later heroines, based on her, have the petulance and wilfulness of a young woman spoilt by a lover twice her age. This affair, a well-kept secret for more than half a century, is important because it helps us to understand the later Dickens and the novels of those years. This young actress appears to have been a rather commonplace girl, but she was the wearer of the life-renewing magical feminine image for this prematurely aged man, whom years of creative work at a high pitch had robbed of nervous energy and zest. So there must have been times, when she had been kind and he had been gay, when he looked through recovered eyes of youth at the society that, if it had penetrated his secret, would have instantly condemned him. (And largely out of hypocrisy too, for London life in these Fifties and Sixties was particularly vicious.) At other times, we may be certain, compelled to earn money to keep three establishments going, with a difficult mistress and a dangerous secret, no longer capable of the vast brilliant improvisations of earlier years, wondering if all his powers were failing him together, he must have been a tormented and desperate man staring at a darkening world. This is why, against all good advice, he still left his writing desk for the gas-lit theatrical reading desk he took on his tours: it was not the money he wanted but the cheering audiences, the packed town halls, the old bustle and excitement of life on the road. And perhaps in the end, after he had been warned over and over again that it might be fatal if he continued these public readings, it was not even those things he wanted. For though he was back at his desk when the final seizure took him, writing his most elaborately plotted story, all about a murder, he might be said to have been plotting a murder for the last few years—his own. This is not as fanciful and melodramatic as it might at first appear, for it is impossible to consider carefully the last years of Dickens, up to that time a temperate and careful man, not at all reckless in his style of living, without coming to the conclusion that he died before he reached sixty because he could no longer resist the urge towards self-destruction. The man who had brightened and enriched the lives of millions had had enough of this life.

We can come closer to the real Dickens and his achievement if we remove from them, however hastily, certain popular misconceptions. To begin with, it is generally held that, with the gradual waning of energy and youthful high spirits, his work slowly degenerates. But this is only true if he is regarded simply as a comic entertainer of genius. As a novelist, a serious novelist to be taken seriously, he steadily matured. Briefly considered in purely literary terms, his work shows the following development. His early novels, largely improvised, are created under two different influences, that of the eighteenth-century *picaresque* novels he had devoured in boyhood, and that of contemporary melodrama (Dickens was always fascinated by the theatre) with its alternating scenes of violent action or pathos and of broad comedy, to which of course Dickens brought his own peculiar genius, a childlike outlook raised to a mythopoeic level. But he begins to plan and to plot in a less theatrical manner. After *David Copperfield*, a semi-autobiographical novel taking the place of an actual autobiography (and its earlier chapters use a highly subjective technique that anticipates much characteristic modern fiction), his novels are consciously and elaborately planned and, behind the conventional plots, retained with what is now rather forced humour to please his immense audience, are deeply concerned with society itself, making use of a broad symbolism. (The fog in *Bleak House*, the prison in *Little Dorrit*, the dustheap in *Our Mutual Friend*, are obvious examples.) It is fatal to our judgment of him, and to our appreciation of this later work, to regard these novels merely as unsuccessful attempts to recapture the zest and high spirits of the earlier stories. While hoping, rather desperately, to entertain his audience in the old way, and this explains some of the weakest scenes in these later novels, Dickens is trying hard, and not without success, to create a different kind of fiction, which will enable him to express some of his strongest convictions and most disturbing feelings. In fact he is here one of the savagest critics of the age. And it could be argued that in the later work of this tormented man, still regarded as England's most brilliant entertainer, the outstanding figure of Christmas jollity, we can discover, if we make the effort, some of the deepest and most despairing insights into the structure, pattern, tone, of English society, not only as it was a century ago but as it still is today.

He perceived its weaknesses and dangers because, in spite of his fame, wide acquaintance and innumerable activities, he was really always outside this society and free from its self-deception. For example, although we largely associate him with Victorian London, he spent surprisingly little of his time there and in later life he declared with obvious sincerity that he detested the city. Indeed, it is too often forgotten that, as soon as Dickens could live where he pleased, he went out of England altogether for some years. (This enabled him to look at it from outside and be sharply critical, as for example: "The closed warehouses and offices have an air of death about them, and *the national dread of colour has an air of mourning* . . .")

He loved the England of his boyhood, which still belonged to the eighteenth rather than the nineteenth century, but the very different England of the Fifties and Sixties, with its booming industry and new, hard, narrow middle class, he regarded with a mixture of contempt, fear and horror. He saw its affairs conducted in a fog, its expectations originating in a convict hulk, its society a series of prisons as in *Little Dorrit*, its pursuit of wealth the scramble round the dust-heap of *Our Mutual Friend*. On a long and wide view of the nation, he was very English; but, unlike Thackeray and Trollope, at ease in their clubs, he was not at all a Victorian middle-class Englishman, was indeed the very opposite of one. His outlook and sympathies are very close to those of the traditional working classes, whose mistrust and dislike of institutions, bureaucracy, the official machinery of government, legal hocus-pocus, solemn political humbug and jobbery, he shares and expresses with comic genius. It is easy enough to dismiss his account of politics as a game between Coodle, Doodle, Foodle and Cuffy, Duffy, Fuffy, his foggy Chancery, his Circumlocution Office and its Barnacles, as the wild exaggerations of a comedian; but he is often nearer the essential truth about Victorian England than Macaulay and his pooh-poohing critics ever were. His standpoint was the one that politicians, important officials, all persons in power or seeking to be, always claim to have but somehow never act from and contrive to forget, that of ordinary human happiness, the life-enhancing quality, innocence of mind and heart. And it is useless here to accuse him, as some critics have solemnly done, of inconsistencies, as if he were a social and political theorist and not, as he was from first to last no matter how his work changed and developed, a dramatic artist, one of the world's supreme story-tellers. From his first comic and melodramatic improvisations to his last symbolic narratives of what seemed to him a detestable society, an age profoundly corrupt, he was never an immaculate artist, never free from dubious tricks to keep the crowd amused, always vulnerable to the stupidest criticism; but his positive qualities (not excluding subtleties that have largely passed unnoticed) are gigantic and rare, those of a great creator, equally capable of enthralling a child and winning the admiration of a philosopher. We began with Santayana, deliberately choosing a man very different from Dickens in all essentials; so now let us end with him.

He wrote: "I think Dickens is one of the best friends mankind has ever had."

3

Midway between Dickens's two visits to America, in 1841 and 1867, throughout the decade immediately before the Civil War, his popularity there was challenged by new American novelists on various levels of literary merit. One of them, Susan B. Warner, writing as 'Elizabeth Wetherell', discovered a vein of sentimental religiosity, beginning with *The Wide, Wide World*, that kept booksellers busy and children tearful for many years. Another woman novelist had an international success, not without some political and social consequences, with her first story, written as a piece of anti-slavery propaganda. This was, of course, *Uncle Tom's Cabin*, and its author, Harriet Beecher Stowe, followed it with many other novels but never repeated her first sensational triumph. It is melodramatic and unreal, but its dramatic vitality is proved by the fact that the stage version of it long outlived the settlement of the slavery question, and indeed was a popular touring play, in more than one country, well into the present century. But there also arrived, with these high-minded best-selling ladies, a genuine classic of American fiction, Nathaniel Hawthorne's *The Scarlet Letter*, the first and the best of his novels, though he had already published two collections of short tales and sketches. Of his remaining three novels, none as good as his first, there is most life, together with some unexpected humour, in *The Blithedale Romance*, based on his six months' stay at Brook Farm, the transcendental community settlement. He produced other volumes of short stories, including some for children. This form obviously attracted him, but he is unequal in it and has been over-praised purely as a writer of short stories, rarely improving upon what the German Romantics (whose work he knew and must have been influenced by) had already achieved in this medium, and on the whole inferior to his Swiss contemporary, Gottfried Keller, though Keller did not actually publish his own stories until some years after Hawthorne's death. Finally, Hawthorne left some *Notebooks*, which are curious and fascinating reading, filled with odd notions and clues to his equally odd character.

If Emerson represents the bright side of this New England group, Hawthorne offers us the shadow side. Among the many 'hints', as he liked to call them, for stories in one of his earlier notebooks is this: "A man living a wicked life in one place, and simultaneously a virtuous and religious one in another." There is a great deal of Hawthorne in that idea, not only the opposition of wickedness and virtue but, even more important, the emphasis upon a double aspect and the unspoken suggestion, perhaps not consciously acknowledged, of a reality behind both aspects, the man himself not essentially either 'wicked' or 'virtuous'. But too much can be made out of Hawthorne's Puritan family and background. It was not his great-grandfathers who kept this young man, apparently sound and indeed attractive in mind and body, mooning in the dusk at Salem for years, hardly speaking to anybody except his widowed mother. Not Calvinism, though a glimpse in childhood of its nightmare universe may have had some effect, but some deeply personal sense of guilt was behind these lurkings and silences, twilight flittings and reveries, these allegories of sin and guilt and strange transformations. (Another 'hint' for a story was: "A man to swallow a small snake—and it to be a symbol of a cherished sin." The psycho-analysts ought to erect a monument to Hawthorne.) Fascinated in his introversion by the allegorical and symbolic, always hovering in some twilight region between consciousness and the unconscious, he describes life as if he were the Lady of Shalott staring into her mirror. It is this shadowy looking-glass quality, together with the undoubted charm of his writing, composed for the ear and not merely for the eye, that gives even his weaker tales a unique character. But though he called himself 'a romancer'—and complained not unreasonably that New England life was deficient in the rich materials and trappings of romance—when he is strongest, as in *The Scarlet Letter*, he is in fact a novelist. This enduring work is a novel pretending to be an historical romance. Because novelists choose to write about men in society, it will generally be found that their more significant work, on its deepest level of meaning, is actually concerned with society itself. *The Scarlet Letter* has been variously interpreted, as an allegory or fable embodied in a dramatic tale, but we shall come closest to Hawthorne, not in his conscious intention but totally as a creative artist, making use of unconscious elements, if we assume at once that this is not an historical romance of Puritan New England in the seventeenth century but a novel profoundly concerned with New England society in the middle of the nineteenth century.

Hester, ripe and full-blooded, essentially and richly feminine (like the tragi-comic Zenobia in *The Blithedale Romance*), an Eros figure, does not belong to this society but comes to it across the sea, from which Aphrodite emerged, out of the masculine unconscious. The letter 'A' she is compelled to wear may be the badge of sin and shame, but it is scarlet and brilliant, even seems to glow in the dark: it has life in it. She gradually redeems herself, in the opinion of the townsfolk, but only through a transformation that robs her of her essential erotic femininity, the life and fire that blaze in the scarlet letter. In her cowardly lover, the Rev. Arthur Dimmesdale, we have the religious aspect of this society that denies its debt to Eros, to the feminine principle accepted positively as sensuous and life-enhancing, not negatively as a purely maternal influence. But Dimmesdale is ruined and finally destroyed by the patient, powerful and vindictive Chillingworth, a man of intellect and science, a Logos figure, also arriving, like Hester but later, across the sea. We are left in the end, to represent the future, the strange and ambiguous child, Pearl, and a society that rejects, unless it is transformed or drably disguised, what Eros can offer, and sees its narrow and life-denying religion condemned and finally destroyed by the analytical intellect, itself arid and uncreative, the enemy of a full satisfying existence. We are reminded of yet another 'hint' for a story in Hawthorne's *Notebooks*: "Various good and desirable things to be presented to a young man, and offered to his acceptance—as a friend, a wife, a fortune; but he to refuse them all, suspecting that it is merely a delusion. Yet all to be real, and he to be told so, when too late." He never wrote a novel about that young man, but somewhere, somehow, in his romantic tale of the scarlet letter and old Boston, of adultery and vengeance, he might be telling the society he knew, his world and time, what that young man had to be told, knowing too, in his melancholy and loosening hold on life, that it was too late.

Moby Dick, Herman Melville's masterpiece, was dedicated to Hawthorne, the two writers being neighbours and friends. Melville, the younger by fifteen years, was a great admirer of Hawthorne, whom he praised for his fantasy and allegory, his alternating sunlight and "great power of blackness". But the two men, though sharing much and arriving together at their masterpieces, are very different. Melville is at once the wilder and the weaker, the more desperately neurotic, compelled either to break away from society, romantically going to sea, or to bury himself in the crowd, silent and forgotten, as he was in his later years. He is a morbid, ambiguous, unfinished character; one half of him a belated Elizabethan genius, the other half an untalented, cranky, pseudo-philosophic, mock-profound type, familiar enough in or near New York throughout this age. Though we include him here among the novelists, simply because he is generally accepted as one, he is not really a novelist. Not even his sea stories, including the posthumous, powerful but over-praised *Billy Budd*, are those of a novelist; *Typee* and *Omoo* are romanticised travel books; *Mardi*, though some of its writing has a new power, is an unsuccessful attempt to turn the travelogue into philosophical fiction; *The Confidence Man* is a good idea bungled through inadequate technique; and *Pierre*, though it anticipates some of our newest fiction by rebellious inverts, reads as if a Jacobean tragedian, a Ford or a Tourneur, had tried to collaborate with the young editor of a mid-nineteenth-century college magazine. What remains, like a whale among halibut and turbot, is *Moby Dick*. And where *Moby Dick* is weak, it is worse than the average goodish novel. We do not always know who is telling the story; there is too much information, breaking the narrative, about whales and whaling (probably because Melville originally intended it to be a semi-documentary book); the best characters are not kept steadily in our sight; there is too much eloquence for its own sake, too many salutations "to the possibilities of the immense Remote, the Wild, the Watery, the Unshored". But where it is strong, it is better than a good novel. It moves into another dimension. It takes on the quality of dramatic and epic poetry.

To begin with, the basic idea is a magnificent one. It was a stroke of genius to make use of whaling men's yarns about an enormous and dangerously aggressive white whale (generally known as 'Mocha Dick') as the framework of a symbolic epic-drama. Then the early scenes in New Bedford, the *Spouter Inn* and Queequeg and the sermon, and in Nantucket, the ship *Pequod* and its two captain-owners, all these are grandly imagined, larger and stranger than common life, seen in the light and shadow of some vivid dream world. The ship at sea, with its mixture of races, of ordinary men and fantastic characters, with the monomaniacal Ahab brooding on his quarter-deck, or nailing the symbolical gold coin to the mast, is like some new but sinister ark of humanity (without woman, it should be remembered), and at times brings us close to the large and loose, essentially American, poetry that Whitman is preparing to publish in *Leaves of Grass*. And the final pursuit of Moby Dick and the huge catastrophe of the whale's vengeance, a climax raised to an epic height, is magnificently imagined and described. In spite of Hawthorne's influence, to which we probably owe Melville's more ambitious re-drafting of the book, *Moby Dick* is not allegorical, in Hawthorne's familiar manner, but truly symbolical, which means that a single inner meaning cannot be attributed to it. The whale itself is entirely evil only in the mind of Captain Ahab, the figure on humanity's quarter-deck, the will that drives the ship on its tragic quest, the mind in its complete self-dependence, in its ruthless opposition to the whale as a force of Nature, in its appalling *hubris*. The whale is neither good nor evil. It is the mighty Other or Opposite, what we leave when we split totality and claim half as our own before demanding the whole again, Nature as against Man, the unconscious as against consciousness, the feminine as against the masculine principle; and the more we separate ourselves from it, challenge it, hunt it and hope to destroy it, the more powerful, menacing, and finally destructive it becomes. In the rich but unbalanced and neurotic nature of Melville, like the age to which he belongs, there is no reconciling element, no principle of integration; he cannot help seeing life in terms of the opposites, of a Manichean conflict; and his tragic story of Captain Ahab and the *Pequod* and the White Whale (all colours except black are contained in white), with its epic grandeur and flashing poetry of phrase, is his deepest and truest account of himself and his time.

It is ironical that it was after the Civil War, which destroyed the opposed social systems and cultures of the old North (largely New England) and the South, and then opened the way to the West and a single national culture, that the American press—and it was a time when newspapers were read to the exclusion of almost everything else— announced that it was time now America produced her own literature and was no longer dependent upon England and Europe. For, as we have seen, it was immediately before this war, in its approaching shadow, that, with Melville and Hawthorne and Whitman, major American literature made its appearance, and that Melville at his greatest and Whitman entirely (perhaps even Hawthorne in his true significance) either went unrecognised or were condemned, and for some time were better appreciated across the Atlantic than they were at home. But both Melville and Hawthorne, though essentially American, were rooted in a culture that America had shared with Europe, whereas in the era following the Civil War, during the 'gilded age' of cynical politics, predatory capitalism, and rapidly increasing immigration to meet the demands of industry in the East and land settlement in the West, the American nation, now more widely based and more sharply conscious of itself, seemed to begin all over again. It did this at first culturally on a lower level, almost without literature, certainly without the tragic-poetic insights of Melville and Hawthorne at their best, largely turning to newspapers and magazines, popular humour (often with a Western drawl) both in print and on the lecture circuit. It was from this world, belonging neither to New England nor the old South, but with much of the new rough-and-ready West in it, the frontier and the mining camps, that Samuel Langhorne Clemens, known to the world as Mark Twain, finally emerged. Although it means jumping the years, we will consider him here, just because, after a good deal of knock-about humour, which brought him a large audience that shared his native prejudices, he made his own contribution to what is central and significant in American writing, and what is in turn America's contribution to our world literature. Setting aside Whitman and disregarding in this place the expatriate Henry James, we can say that Mark Twain, after thirty years, takes up the tale that had been silenced in the Fifties.

Twain does it by returning to his boyhood and youth, dominated, as if by a nature god, by the vast Mississippi river, which flows through *Huckleberry Finn*, his one major work of fiction, and brings vitality and enchantment to the first half of his *Life on the Mississippi*. Here his memory of the river returns him to his boyhood and releases in him a poetry that owes nothing to any literary tradition (and indeed is opposed to any tradition), a poetry that wells up from depth of feeling, from a buried life touched with the magic of the unconscious, a poetry that seems to express for the first time (though later American writers will imitate the kind of prose Twain created here) a whole inarticulate folk, a changing region, a vanishing way of life. Huck and the river, the natural innocent spirit in its own mysterious and beautiful realm, are central and life-giving to this novel, which loses much and is almost cut down to the size of its predecessor, *The Adventures of Tom Sawyer*, once it leaves the river. What happens along the banks of the river, observed and reported by Huck with a simple but seemingly absolute realism, is in the sharpest contrast to the dark majesty and mystery of the river rolling through the night. If this is the world, then it is a world of chicanery preying on ignorance and stupidity, of cowardly mean people in ugly mean streets, of prejudice and ignoble passion and meaningless murder. And we may be certain that here Mark Twain is not savaging life as it was lived in remote Missouri when he was a boy. This, as he was to prove in *Pudd'nhead Wilson* and *The Man that Corrupted Hadleyburg* and many passages of comment and reminiscence, was to him the world.

But this will not do. To begin with, he has already abstracted from this world all that is symbolised by Huck's journey down the river, and removed from it the Mark Twain capable of describing that journey, who still existed, to feel the water flowing in the desert of his disillusion and pessimism, or else the book could not have been written at all. Then again, though this may have been the world as it existed in the mud of Missouri about 1850, it is a monstrous parody of the world as it existed elsewhere, even though ignorance, prejudice, knavery, violence, may be universal, a world of religion, art, philosophy, historical tradition, that Twain deliberately rejected. Wishing to demonstrate the tremendous pressure of American society upon its writers, Van Wyck Brooks, an American critic at once scholarly and courageous, took Twain as the most melancholy example of this art-hating process, in his book, which should be read, *The Ordeal of Mark Twain*. Here we are shown Twain, world-famous, idolised by his fellow-countrymen, with all outward circumstances in his favour, inwardly miserable, restless in his dissatisfaction with himself, deeply pessimistic, because "there was something gravely amiss with his inner life", because he was alone with his conviction that he had not fulfilled himself as an artist. But while it is true that in another society, demanding that the writers it honoured should explore the whole of life, Twain might have revealed far more of his total self, including life-enhancing elements he took care not to reveal, and while it is also true that the cultural climate of the America of his middle and later life was unfavourable to the writer as artist, as Henry James early realised, many of the limitations in Twain's work and outlook, astonishing in view of his tremendous reputation at home and abroad, really belong to the man himself. From the first, in his *Innocents Abroad*, he struck an attitude— *let's-have-no-more-of-this-European-nonsense*—and though inwardly he must have grown out of it, he did his best to maintain it. He was sufficiently intelligent to despise, given time, the social and intellectual antics he indulged in—the get-rich-quick, get-healthy-quick, get-happy-quick, get-wise-quick nostrums and quackeries that fascinated American society, but was not intelligent and strong-minded enough to rid himself of them once and for all. He was sharp enough to penetrate the obvious hypocrisy and the complacent optimism of his time, but then remained in a state of adolescent disillusion, which accounts for his pessimism, and indeed for the inflated idea he had of the importance of the autobiography he left to be published after his death. But he lacked the curiosity and patient will to look deeper into life. His constant uneasiness, his suspicion of authorship itself, came from the conflict between his exhibitionist vanity (a trait that probably encouraged Bernard Shaw to over-praise him) and his deeper conviction, for he was at heart a modest man and was aware of limitations he had never tried hard to remove, that he was over-estimated at home for the wrong reasons, and welcomed and fêted abroad partly as a curiosity, America's representative man who wore a white suit and drawled Yankee witticisms at public dinners. And indeed he is often very funny, and his sketches still have some life in them, though inferior to his reminiscences of the old mining days in the West, which, in spite of their pioneer humour of mere exaggeration, are the best of his books of travel. But he was a great writer only when he returned to the river, for him the stream of life.

4

We left the Russian Novel, now in this age to reach great heights, with Gogol. His admiring friend, Aksakov, must at least be mentioned, even though he was a writer of reminiscences rather than a novelist, not only because his leisurely chronicles of his family and childhood, as placid as a lake in these Russian steppes and as clear as the air above them, have been widely enjoyed outside Russia, but also because his objective manner, limpid style, and easy sense of passing time, had an effect upon later Russian novelists. Goncharov's *Oblomov* probably had an effect upon every Russian who could read. It created—or revealed—a type everybody recognised, and added something to the nation's knowledge of itself. As a novel it has many faults; it has little narrative interest and most of its characters are dummies; but as a ruthless study, moving inexorably through a multitude of significant details, of one man's slow decay and final ruin—beginning with Oblomov, healthy, cheerful, well-off, the typical absentee landowner in his bachelor flat in St. Petersburg, then taking him steadily down to his death, a bankrupt dupe and hopeless sloven, with everything lost through mere indolence and ineffectuality—it has probably never been equalled in any other nation's fiction. Appearing in 1859, two years before the emancipation of the serfs, this novel, out of which the term *Oblomovism* (to describe the corresponding weakness in the national character) was coined, highlighted and brought deeper shadows to Russia's familiar problem of her 'superfluous men', possessing good qualities but unable or unwilling to make use of them, talking and dreaming their lives away. Russian fiction throughout this age is crowded with these charming, ineffectual, maddening characters, just as it is today with laconic engineers and busy managers of collective farms.

Turgenev, the first of the three great Russian novelists, might have turned into one of these 'superfluous men' if he had not fallen in love with a French singer, Madame Viardot, quarrelled with his mother, who owned the estate, and followed his siren (to whom he devoted himself for many years, in the strangest fashion) out of Russia, back to the West. True, he was a born writer, but there was in this gentle giant a lack of aggressive energy that might easily have kept him dreamily occupied on the family estate, in the manner described so exquisitely in his *Sportsman's Notebook*, if he had not felt himself compelled to leave Russia, and then in exile, moved by nostalgia, to begin recording his memories. (Thanks to literature, that vast Russian countryside, which must have been so often heavy with boredom, dark with suffering and cruelty, now seems to us touched with enchantment, one of the lovely lost kingdoms that live in the imagination.) Turgenev spent much of his time abroad in Paris: in February 1863 the Goncourt brothers write in their Journal: "Charles Edmund brings us Turgenev, that foreign writer who has so delicate a talent. He is a charming colossus, a pleasant giant, with white hair, who looks like the good spirit of a mountain or a forest. . . . He was touched by the reception we gave him, which put him at his ease, and he talked to us most interestingly about Russian literature, which he regards as in full career towards realism . . ." But Turgenev rarely made such an altogether pleasant impression upon his fellow-countrymen, with whom he was apt to be stiff-necked and to seem arrogant. Nor is it difficult to understand why he should appear to be one kind of man in St. Petersburg, where for a few years during the middle Fifties he reigned as head of the literature of progress and reform, and another kind of man in Paris. The publication of his strongest novel, *Fathers and Sons*, dominated by its 'nihilist' (the term was coined by Turgenev) hero, Bazarov, cost him his popularity with the radicals, who accused him of having caricatured them. Deeply offended—for Turgenev regarded Bazarov as anything but a caricature; this character was in fact his reply to the familiar criticism that he could create Russian heroines but no Russian hero—from this year, 1862, onwards Turgenev remained abroad, except for brief visits, and deliberately alienated himself from Russian life and literature; even if not, as we have seen from the Goncourts, to the extent of refusing to discuss them with his friends in Paris.

We may assume, however, that it was not wounded vanity that led Turgenev to prefer Paris to St. Petersburg. He was more at ease in Paris because there he was an artist among artists, not a political and social theorist, a leader of renegades, a prophet or charlatan. The point is important because it helps to explain Turgenev the novelist. As we already discovered in Part Three, the writer's situation in Russia, with its censorship, suppressions, prosecutions, its political and social ferment and semi-underground movements (creating an atmosphere not unlike that of Nazi-occupied countries during the last war), was quite different from what it was in the West. The Russian writer was read not simply for pleasure but for guidance and deliverance. A serious novel was yet another tremendous manifesto. So Rudin, in Turgenev's novel of that name, could not be accepted by contemporary Russian readers as a complicated living character, whose relation to other characters is traced with magnificent skill, but had to be seen as a representative figure with definite political and social implications. But though Turgenev yielded, with no conscious reluctance, to this pressure to produce fiction of social significance, novels that attempted to satisfy the demand for criticism, guidance, leadership, we can see now, from what is strongest and weakest in his fiction, that fundamentally as a creator Turgenev was not in sympathy with this idea of fiction. In his heart of hearts he did not want to write this kind of novel, and when he breaks clean away from it, as in *First Love* or *The Torrents of Spring*, he makes us feel the sense of release that he has. (Or compare in *Smoke* the deeply fascinating love-story and the tedious and unreal discursive talk it has.) So Turgenev cannot be completely identified with his best-known novels as Tolstoy and Dostoyevsky can with theirs. He is negative where they are positive. He yielded to pressure or the temptation of wide popularity because, like many very big men, he was not aggressively wilful, and was inclined to be suggestible and pliant. There was indeed in Turgenev a deep feminine streak. And if he appeared to be arrogant in Russian literary society, it was probably because he felt uncertain of himself and ill at ease. He was an artist, not a leader, a prophet.

It is here we find Turgenev the enduring novelist, now after a century, when the applause and catcalls of long-dead Russian radicals and reformers are silent. We need not care whose side he was on in the middle of the nineteenth century; he is on our side now. Here is the creator of all those wonderful feminine characters, the fascinating and enigmatic mature women, the enchanting young girls, the writer who must be at least partly responsible for the glamour associated with Russian women in Western minds during the later part of the nineteenth century. This is the poet—even though the form is prose fiction—of lyrical and tender young love, of dawn over the fields, and dusk in the woods of the Russian countryside. His novels proper are weakest when they give us the socially significant talk he felt it was his duty to offer his readers; they are strongest not only in the presentation of complex living characters but also—and this is his most individual contribution to the art of fiction —in their delicate but sure handling of a whole group of people, whose shifting relations with one another are wonderfully suggested. His mind, sceptical and ironical but never without compassion, seems to move among these groups of his like a soft but clear light, illuminating their characters and relationships. This is particularly true of the central set of novels, *Rudin*, *A Nobleman's Nest*, *On the Eve*, *Fathers and Sons*, all published between 1856 and 1862, and soon to have a very considerable influence on the fiction of Western Europe, especially in France and England, where the social and critical elements in Turgenev were ignored and he was regarded as a master of the art of fiction. (With something of the approach to it that the Impressionist painters had to figure and landscape: he shared the same admirers.) And if we add to these central novels the best of his shorter and more poetic novels and his tales (such as *A Lear of the Steppes*) and the exquisite *Sportsman's Notebook*, and his play *A Month in the Country*, good in itself and the spring-head of much later drama, we see that his legacy has been as substantial in bulk as it has been delicate in texture. Russian critics, not necessarily Communist, have sometimes complained that Turgenev has been over-valued in the West while other Russian writers, of equal stature at home, have been undervalued or ignored. But we take what we want from each other's literature. Like Chehov, who probably owes as much to Turgenev as Turgenev does to Pushkin, Turgenev represents a side of the rich Russian character, the gently ironic, tender, vaguely poetic side, that we in the

West can most easily understand and enjoy. And if at the present time, when a pleasure in the coldly over-complicated alternates with a taste for the red and raw, Turgenev is out of fashion, he will return, as all the original masters do.

The second of this trio of great Russian novelists, Dostoyevsky, is so wildly different from Turgenev that it is hard to believe that they belonged to the same nation at the same time. As we have seen, Dostoyevsky much admired and at first was much influenced by Dickens, and we might say of him that he is Dickens without comic genius but with the lid off. Everything that contributed to the dark side of Dickens was immensely enlarged in Dostoyevsky's life. If Dickens's father came down in the world, Dostoyevsky's was murdered by his serfs for his drunken cruelty. (Freud says that Dostoyevsky unconsciously desired his father's death and then felt guilty when it happened.) If Dickens had his six months in the blacking warehouse, Dostoyevsky had a mother who died when he was seventeen, a murdered father, ill-treatment at school, epileptic fits, and, to crown all, nine years in Siberia (after being led out for execution and then reprieved at the last moment), four of those years being spent in prison with the lowest criminals. We are told that during those years he was never alone and was allowed nothing to read except a Bible. Perhaps one part of him, whether later he was writing furiously in Russia or gambling furiously in Germany, never really left that prison, with its robbers, rapists, murderers, and its Bible. As we can discover in his wonderful account of his Siberian experience, *The House of the Dead*, he came to find in these convicts, cast out by society, many remarkable qualities; and on his last evening, while mentally taking leave of the prison, he can even cry: "And how much youth lay uselessly buried within these walls, what mighty powers were wasted here in vain! After all, one must tell the whole truth: these men were exceptional men. Perhaps they were the most gifted, the strongest of our people. But their mighty energies were vainly wasted, wasted abnormally, unjustly, hopelessly. And who was to blame, whose fault was it?" And earlier, while discussing corporal punishment and the sadistic corruption of those with the power to inflict it, he observes significantly: "Society, which looks indifferently on such a phenomenon, is already contaminated to its very foundations." And now one last quotation from this *House of the Dead*, as remarkable in its own way as his greatest novels (in which there is nothing better than his description of the innocent happiness of the convicts watching their theatricals), taken again from his account of the final evening: ". . . Our dreams and our long divorce from the reality made us think of freedom as somehow freer than real freedom, that is, than it actually is . . ."

But can Man, weak and sinful and guilt-ridden, find happiness in freedom? And if not (as Ivan Karamazov's Grand Inquisitor argues), which must he give up? And as between society and the man it condemns so mercilessly, which is the criminal? And if there is a God, why do the innocent, the very children, suffer so terribly? And if there is no God, and we may do as we please, in a society obviously corrupt, why do we long to repent our sins? These and similar questions, frequently linked to various problems and movements of the time (atheistic nihilism or Christianity; Holy Russia or the materialistic West), tormenting questions to which Dostoyevsky really found no answers, are not only discussed in his finest novels—and this kind of talk in Dostoyevsky, unlike Turgenev, is astonishingly vital—but are dramatised in them. We may guess that he himself swung wildly between the opposites, between dizzy antitheses, now in blazing light, now in deepest darkness. It is significant that the reconciling figures in his novels, the saintly 'idiot' Prince Myshkin or Alyosha Karamazov, have not the vitality of the other chief characters, just because they are either contrived or identified only vaguely and weakly with their author's personality. It is the divided men, torn between the opposites, that he creates with all his energy, Ivan Karamazov, not Alyosha; and next to them, those terrible and prophetic figures, still in the underworld in his age, but emerging from it to make history in our age, the cold and empty men, victims of a moral and spiritual anæsthesia; and, with these half-mad males, the girls and women equally divided in their sexuality, part debauched, part innocent, now sadistic, now masochistic. His stage is crowded with screaming and cursing psychopaths, vivid projections of his own inner divisions, his bewilderment, angry frustration, so that we can forgive the French writer who called him the "Shakespeare of the lunatic asylum". But the questions that tormented him were real and indeed profound, and what

247

his wild characters in their wildest moods threatened the world with has come to pass and indeed has been excelled by the events of our time. Our concentration camps, torture chambers, mass murder factories, and all the complicated apparatus of violence, cruelty and death that we have piled up, must be haunted by the accusing ghost of Dostoyevsky.

He is here, however, as a novelist, and to understand what he made of the novel we must turn at once to the four massive works of fiction that occupied his last years: *Crime and Punishment*, *The Idiot*, *The Possessed*, and *The Brothers Karamazov*. (Earlier novels, like *The Gambler*, a semi-autobiographical study of his own mania for gambling, and *The Eternal Husband*, which is like a French comedy of adultery re-written by a cruel psychiatrist, all have their own interest, but would not have survived if these last four novels had not been written.) Let it be said at once that, just as most modern poetry regarded as significant literature came out of French Symbolism, so much modern fiction, equally highly regarded, comes out of Dostoyevsky. It is not that he has been widely imitated, for he cannot be successfully imitated at all. But what he did to and for the novel, for good or ill, has been done again, in their various individual ways, by many of our most ambitious novelists ever since his time: they flourish in the same climate—of dramatised ideas and intensity-through-guilt—as the more massive and profound Russian. Now what Dostoyevsky did was to tear the novel wide open. It was like a bag that would not hold all he wanted to stuff into it. He had to deal with semi-metaphysical and social ideas, not because he was merely interested in them but because they tormented him, tossing him on the horns of their dilemmas. At the other extreme, he felt himself compelled to examine and express human character not in its public and social aspects, in the usual style of fiction, but as far into its irrational depths as his intuition, his astonishing intuition that anticipates many of the later discoveries of the psycho-analysts, would take him. And here we must remember that he was essentially a man at war with himself, in the depths of his own being, and that the years in Siberia had given him time and opportunity to be his own war correspondent. He has then these two extremes—the great challenging ideas and the irrational depths of human nature, character taken as far as it will go. And they must be brought together. But there is in him a third strain, purely literary and there from the first, following his excited reading of Dickens and Balzac. This is the desire to write stories not unlike theirs, that is, crowded with incident, often violent, melodramatic, and full of suspense and mystery, none of your tame Turgenev stuff. So after experimenting in one strange and powerful work, his *Notes from Underground*, bringing the great tormenting ideas and the depths of character together without the framework, incident, atmosphere, of the novel of excitement and melodrama that he had always enjoyed writing, Dostoyevsky in his last four novels combines all three elements, in the hope of fusing them together, to achieve the fiction of psychological depth and symbolic dramatic intensity. And in their finest chapters, and notably in *Crime and Punishment* and *The Brothers Karamazov*, he succeeded magnificently.

We cannot, however, have everything within the covers of one novel, no matter how long it is. If much that is new is brought in, then other things that are old must be left out. If the extremes are to be brought together, then what is between them may disappear. And what is between them is the customary life of man in society with which we associate the novel, the life of our familiar relationships and affairs, our business and pleasure, our homes and families and friends, in fact most of our existence as we commonly see it. Not all of this has dropped out of Dostoyevsky's novels, but a great deal of it has, with the result that although they are concerned with issues of the utmost significance, reveal a profound insight into character and motive, are charged with their own intense reality, they seem to many readers, to all of us at times, not like novels about this world but like rapid semi-hysterical accounts of a phantasmagorical dream life, in which there is no flesh-and-blood, no ordinary streets and houses, no people at work and play, but where fallen angels, demons, loud-voiced spectres and galvanised waxworks, lit by hellfire, hurry to and from terrible deeds, meet to curse one another or sob in repentance, pour out their confessions or debate with the lunatic brilliance, force and obstinacy of madmen. So what the novel has gained in depth and intensity by being turned into metaphysical symbolic drama —and the purely dramatic element in Dostoyevsky is tremendous—it loses in breadth, variety, and the kind of realism that makes us feel it is a fair picture of man in society. The point is very important because of Dostoyevsky's influence upon later novelists, belonging to our own age, especially writers of great talent who, without any superficial likeness to him, share some of his neurotic intellectuality, his deep disunity, his fury of frustration, if not his creative genius. For there can be no doubt whatever about Dostoyevsky's genius. No sensitive person who has read these novels, especially in youth when their ideas strike with maximum force, can ever forget their first shattering impact, unlike that of any other fiction. We may not return to him as we do to other major novelists, but this may be as much our fault, in our wish not to be profoundly disturbed, as it is his, wounding as he does without healing, dividing as he does without joining and reconciling. For though we may feel that religion is the final answer, the religion we do not have, few of us are likely to respond to Dostoyevsky's half-hearted gesture towards the Greek Orthodox Church. On the other hand, if he can be the cruellest of novelists, he can also be the most compassionate. And if he is far from being a perfect artist, he is also more than an artist. No intuitions into the maladies of the age, not even those of Nietzsche (who admitted his debt to Dostoyevsky), were more searching than his. There is no question he asked—no dilemma he dramatised with such intensity—that we have successfully answered yet. We may smile when we read that young Dostoyevsky, as a student of engineering at the military school, once produced an admirable design for a fortress, except that he forgot to provide it with any entrances and exits. But after all, how many have we?

The third of this great trio of Russian novelists, Tolstoy, completes the astounding break-through of the Russian Novel into world literature, one of those sudden explosions of national genius that we can only marvel at and never explain. By the end of this age, when, ironically enough, Tolstoy had condemned the very work that had made him famous, this elderly Russian aristocrat, now trying not very successfully to look and behave like a peasant, had the greatest international reputation of any living man of letters. The age of the novel had found a novelist to crown. And no matter what might have been said in Russia about his early or later work, the fact remains that this world fame was based—and still is, though his reputation may not stand quite as high as it did—on two pieces of fiction, the epic *War and Peace*, perhaps the greatest in the prose fiction of any nation, and that magnificent novel, *Anna Karenina*. His earlier work, notably his stories of military life and his semi-autobiographical novels of childhood and youth, though of considerable value in itself, can be regarded as so much preparation for the writing of these two master-pieces. During these years he rid himself of any trace of the fashionable romanticism, which he detested, and of any temptation to indulge in senti-mental pseudo-poetical fine writing; he tested, exercised, strengthened, his extraordinary grasp and command of significant detail; he made increasing use of his unusual power of psychological analysis, a power not poetic like that of Turgenev, nor profoundly intuitive like that of Dostoyevsky, but conscious and rational, even though in the full sweep of creation, with his tremendous energy of mind at its highest pressure, certain unconscious elements were added. (He could not have shown us the younger Natasha, in *War and Peace*, and Anna Karenina, as he does, without the aid of those elements. And if any masculine reader doubts this, let him try to create a Natasha or an Anna consciously and ration-ally.) But by the time he was finishing *Anna Karenina*, he was already entering a period of bewilderment and depression, ended by his so-called 'conversion'. His later work, excluding the purely polemical books, shows us the prophet at war with the artist, still alive in him and still capable of revealing himself in flashes of greatness. But there are no more supreme masterpieces like *War and Peace* and *Anna Karenina*. It is more than likely that the 'conversion' was inevitable, simply because the creative energy that had gone into these two works left him so exhausted that he could no longer sustain the deep conflict in him, and one side, opposed to his art, had to win.

If the born novelist, as we have already seen, is almost always a deeply divided man (and thus able to identify himself with a variety of characters), we shall expect this master novelist to show us unusually wide and deep divisions, and we shall not be disappointed. The contradictions in this prodigy are prodigious. He was an aristocrat who yearned to identify himself with the peasant. He was an individualist who wanted to lose himself (and us) in the mass. He was an epicurean artist who converted himself to the narrowest puritanism. He had the sexual virility of three ordinary men and feared and finally condemned sexual relations. He had the life-urge of ten ordinary men and went for ever in dread of death. ("Death, death, death awaits you every second," he tells us in *What I Believe*. "Your life passes in the presence of death." And this is no sermonising trick; the cry comes from the shrinking heart; yet it was a strong and brave heart, and went on beating into its eighty-third year.) Both positives and negatives in him seem at maximum strength, until his 'conversion' brings its negative victory; and this probably accounts for the astonishing creative energy of his middle life, which gave us, as triumphs of that energy, his two masterpieces. His essential dualism, which remained with him in spite of the apparent victory of one side, is perfectly illustrated by a story Gorky tells of him. Walking with a friend, Tolstoy saw two splendid-looking young guardsmen marching towards them, and immediately began denouncing their pompous stupidity, like that of animals trained by the whip. But when they actually passed him, he stopped, to cry with enthusiasm: "How handsome! Old Romans, eh? Their strength and beauty!" It is as if two different men had spoken, but it was only two different sides of the same man, the author of *War and Peace*, which, except in a few weaker passages, does not show us this conflicting division but a unified creative personality, all the more energetic and broadly-based because, for the time being, it has triumphed over these contradictions.

That breadth, both in observation and feeling, and that energy, necessary to sustain the impression of reality its great scene gives us, contribute much to *War and Peace*. For this, above all other novels of Western Man, is like a broad river of life. It chooses to show us the Russia that Napoleon invaded, but, though much is made of the history in a deliberate anti-historical way, we feel any other epoch might have served as well. It is one of the great novels, perhaps the very greatest, of passing time, and Tolstoy is a master of its continuous movement. Where other novelists plot and plan, work to a pattern, shape a story, contrive a drama, Tolstoy here merely seems to reveal, now a multitude of significant details, now a wide scene, now a character in its depth. It is an epic with an extra dimension. So not only do the characters, characters as widely different as Natasha, growing up, and Kutuzov, commanding his army, Pierre and the aged Prince Bolkonsky, seem to have a stereoscopic solidity, but behind the Rostov and Bolkonsky families and their circles of acquaintance, all the personages in the foreground, we are made to feel the presence of the nation, and behind the nation Man himself. We also feel that in this vast flow of largely instinctive life there is an essential goodness. It is what interferes with it, from Napoleon's mad egoism downwards, that is bad. Many readers may feel that Tolstoy's own interference is bad, especially when he stops the moving panorama, refusing to let time pass, while he explains his ideas on history and war. (They are extreme, but he is probably nearer the truth than the average military historian.) The trouble is, not that a novel on this vast scale cannot accept some downright expositions of its author's ideas, but that the Tolstoy we meet in these passages, like the Tolstoy responsible for the novel's one important failure in character, Karatayev the super-peasant (and perhaps some of the talk of Pierre and Andrey), is not the fully creative personality responsible for the rest of the novel, and we are conscious of the temporary breakdown. But for the rest, and that means most of the huge chronicle, though terrible things may happen, though no aspect of reality is hidden from us, though we seem to lose ourselves in these people and events and may never give a thought to their author, somehow we come to share something at least of his creative energy, zest, wholeness, and deep happiness in the work; and so we read it and remember it with delight, the flame and smoke of war fading away, even time's passing robbed of most of its melancholy.

To suggest, as many critics do, that *Anna Karenina* is a kind of continuation of *War and Peace*, is misleading. Tolstoy's literary method is almost the same, especially in the earlier part of the story; he brings to it the same handling of significant detail, the same power (perhaps rather heightened) of rapid and sure analysis of character, the same piercing sense of reality. But everything else is different. *Anna Karenina* is no epic, no river of life, and time in it is not simply passing but conniving, shaping, and striking. It is not another panorama of instinctive life, in which the scene, however dark and tragic in the foreground, seems to vanish in the distance into a misty brightness. This may be a drama on an epic scale, but a drama it is, not an epic. How it came to be written is important. After *War and Peace*, Tolstoy began work on an historical novel about the Russia of Peter the Great, but then abandoned it in disgust. A woman called Anna, the mistress of a neighbouring landowner, had committed suicide by throwing herself in front of a train; and Tolstoy had attended the inquest. Here was matter for a novel of contemporary life. The mastery and brilliance of the early chapters of *Anna Karenina* probably owe something to his feelings of relief after discarding the historical novel. But the Tolstoy behind the huge darkening tale of Anna and her lover, Vronsky, and her husband, Karenin, is not quite the same man who wrote *War and Peace*. The total creative personality is just beginning to crack, though still not ready for the 'conversion'. Levin, the only major character in this marvellous gallery of portraits that is not entirely successful, wears a thin mask and his voice is too often not his own. But on the whole the conflict in the depths of Tolstoy's personality, though it begins to darken the story, only seems to heighten the marvellous force and precision of his handling of Anna and her growing tragedy. So real are these people, especially Anna and Vronsky, that we can argue about them and what they did and what happened to them, just as we do about people we know and their affairs. The fatal flaw in the relationship between Anna and Vronsky, so sharply contrasted with that between Kitty and Levin, seems to have unfathomable depth, beyond the measure of any conscious purpose Tolstoy may have had; and her tragedy (which we sense, at our first reading, from the very beginning) certainly cannot be explained in ordinary social and moral terms, as a punishment for leaving her husband, a failure in courage, and so forth; and it may be—to hazard one guess— that the relationship is doomed because Anna herself is too feminine while Vronsky like Karenin, though otherwise so entirely different, is too masculine. What is certain is that Anna is so wonderfully alive and real and moving because to Tolstoy's unconscious, the source of his creative energy, she is symbolic archetypal Woman, whom consciously, with all the values she symbolises, now that he is nearing the break-up, he has to destroy. And we might risk adding that it is the defiant unconscious, working at full pressure before the lid comes down on it, that gives a curious feverish brightness to so many of the scenes in this very great novel.

There was to be nothing like it again, though the artist in Tolstoy, denounced and imprisoned by the prophet, was to break out several times, to add colour and depth to some of the later moral tales. To discuss in detail the odd Christianity-cum-Buddhism to which Tolstoy so elaborately converted himself would be wrong here. But why he should have found it necessary to make this complete change—a literary event of some importance when we remember what effect it had on the work of a man of genius—does concern us here. For being himself a deeply divided and bewildered man, and facing an age that was now a long way from the time when the society of Western Man had possessed a religious basis and framework (and so, as all intuitive men perceived, might be drifting towards appalling catastrophe), in his own need and impatience, born of his personal conflicts, Tolstoy decided that he himself must demonstrate what such a religious basis and framework could be. But a man cannot do this by himself—a religion that gives a whole great society a foundation and a frame cannot be reached in this fashion; it must rise from the living depths of the society itself—and most certainly he cannot do it by cutting himself in half, by ignoring the necessity for any reconciliating principle to rescue him from the clash of the opposites, as Tolstoy did. So everything went wrong, and the man who had written *War and Peace* and *Anna Karenina* offered the astonished world some books conceived in the spirit of street-corner tracts. And in his *What Is Art?* this man of genius, this giant of literature, could solemnly set Hugo's *Les Misérables*, Dickens on the level of *A Christmas Carol* and *The Chimes*, and *Uncle Tom's Cabin* above Cervantes, Molière, and Pushkin, and dismiss Homer and Shakespeare as poets to be avoided. Yet behind this nonsense was something profoundly true and in danger of being forgotten, namely, the idea that art should be religious in origin and feeling and ought to be widely understood and appreciated, not the possession of a few, but enjoyed by the mass of people. Not simply in an ideal society but even in a reasonably healthy one this ought to be largely true. But in his impatience and despair, Tolstoy took an absurd measuring rod of his own to art, making it fit the half of him now in command of his personality (though not in complete command, as his later stories and plays prove), and then applying what is left of art to a society as deeply divided as he was, and suffering from maladies not to be cured by one man's improvised and narrow attempt at a religion. His diagnosis was mainly right, but he was wrong in thinking he could supply the remedy; and in the attempt to supply it he denied the world, which had need of him, the fully creative personality responsible for his two masterpieces. For though in some of the fine peasant tales, and in *The Death of Ivan Ilyich* (powerful but false), *The Kreutzer Sonata* (sex leads to crime), and *Resurrection* (choked with attacks on the legal system), he returns in part to his old technical mastery, the prodigious creator of *War and Peace* and *Anna Karenina* has vanished. But these two great novels remain with us, and at the thought of them we can echo Tolstoy's cry as he stared after the two guardsmen: "Their strength and beauty!"

5

In his Journal entry for 21st April 1883 Edmond de Goncourt makes the following note: "Our old Turgenev is a true man of letters. A growth has just been removed from his stomach, and he said to Daudet, who went to see him one of these days: 'During the operation I thought of our dinners, and I struggled to find the words with which I could give you the exact impression of the steel cutting up my skin and entering my flesh . . . like a knife cutting up a banana' . . ." Turgenev, always so polite to his French friends, may have been flattering them, for this remark reflects the spirit and the literary methods of the group of novelists who held these dinners. The oldest member of it, who did not attend the Paris dinners but occasionally entertained his fellow-novelists at his house near Rouen, was Gustave Flaubert; and the youngest (with Daudet, both born in 1840) was Émile Zola; and, oddly enough, it is these two, so very different, who are the dominating figures in the French fiction of this age, beginning with the publication of Flaubert's *Madame Bovary* in 1857. Edmond and Jules de Goncourt, brothers and collaborators whose Journal (mostly the work of Edmond, his brother dying in 1870) brings us so close to this group, make a link, in more senses than one, between Flaubert and Zola. They pursued the documentary method with much ardour, even if it took them to hospitals and morgues; and in *Renée Mauperin* and *Germinie Lacerteux* especially they succeed with it; but too often they seem like painters and psychologists working alternately and lack the movement, narrative sweep, vitality, of the born novelist. Their friend Daudet is probably best-known to all of us outside France because his *Lettres de mon moulin* (early work but as good as anything he wrote later) and his *Tartarin* burlesques (which have little lasting appeal) were represented so often in our French school-books. He has charm, a sense of the picturesque and the dramatic, and a nice blend—more English than French—of humour and sentiment, all found at their best in sketches and short tales; he has not the necessary weight and drive and intellectual force to bring off the more ambitious novels of society that he attempted, which too often have a suggestion of the stage about them. (*L'Arlésienne*, the play for which Bizet wrote the famous incidental music, is his.) That he never fulfilled the promise of his bright beginning was probably due to his increasingly bad health.

Guy de Maupassant comes into this group, belatedly, through Flaubert, a friend of his family and his adviser, almost a tutor, when he was first learning how to write. It is probably to Flaubert that he owes his superb naturalistic technique, more severe in its economy, if coarser in grain, than Flaubert's. It is Maupassant more than anybody else who made the intelligent short story, bitterly ironic more often than not, so popular for many years, bridging the gap between readers in search of literature and the wide public looking for entertainment. Some of his stories, especially those of Norman peasant life, are little more than anecdotes; his humorous tales do not succeed in being very funny and sometimes are not even passably pleasant; but he is a master of the grimly ironic story that appears to compress a whole life into twenty pages or so, often denying a man or woman all happiness or hope of it by one twist in the action of the tale. But it is mostly appearance, based on ingenuity and clever story-telling. For stories of this kind, which have so often been imitated from Maupassant, pretend to tell us far more about life than they know. In spite of their objective naturalistic manner, which so easily deceives the young and the innocent when that manner is in fashion, they are no closer to the facts of our common existence than the tales of the earlier romancers. They monstrously over-simplify life, rob it of most of its potentialities of change and growth, deny it any power of compensation, just to make their one cruel point, as if they were matadors and life a dying bull. There is as much falsification in the cool, neat, cynical Maupassant type of short story as there is in the sentimental and rosy fiction of the popular magazine. There are as many tricks in this business of leaving characters desolate for ever after three incidents and thirty pages as there are in leaving them in a permanent glow of happiness. Not that Maupassant could not do better than this, in at least a few of his stories, from *Boule de suif* onwards; and then there are his novels, of which *Bel-Ami* and the ingeniously plotted *Pierre et Jean* are the best; but though his talent cannot be denied, there is something, coldly coarse and gritty, in his personality that, if it does not actually repel us, makes us reluctant to return to his work. Nevertheless for some years after his early death, in 1893, his influence was wide if not deep.

Apart from the steady procession of popular novelists, from Octave Feuillet to Paul Bourget, there were some others outside this naturalist group, notably Barbey d'Aurévilly, perhaps the last of the true Romantics, and Huysmans, who, after describing ordinary life with great bitterness, in *À rebours* describes with considerable resources of invention and fine language, but not without silliness, an existence of complete artificiality. There was also Villiers de L'Isle-Adam, who began as a Symbolist poet, then wrote some stories that combine satire of this life with grandiose visions of some other life, and at the end of his vagabond existence, consistent with his rejection of reality, he left behind him a wild symbolical tale, *Axel*. Having found in his castle both a beautiful girl and a fabulous treasure, and falling at once in love with the girl, who is as ardent as he is, Axel implores her to commit suicide with him immediately, before reality can break in, and it is here, arriving at the line that has so often been quoted, he cries in scorn: "Live?—Our servants will do that for us." This is extreme introversion deriding extroversion; it is dream banishing reality; it is the life of the imagination, withdrawn from actuality, preferred to anything life in the world may offer; it is the reverse face of the medal on which naturalism has shown literature being guided by science. It is also a dislike of contemporary society, the later nineteenth-century world, carried to the point of pretending it is not there. (But Axel, before his Sara arrived, and Huysmans's extravagant hero, Des Esseintes, presumably took money from the world they so despised. However, to give him his due, Axel's creator, Villiers, did not do his dreaming on a large private income, did not demand from the world he rejected a daily supply of clean linen and five-course meals, but lived like a sparrow among the cafés and night-houses.) The weakness of this attitude, which belonged to the Symbolist Movement in its widest and most influential form, is that it divides a totality, created out of the mutual reaction between our outer and inner worlds, consciousness and the unconscious, objective and subjective experience, that should not be divided. It makes the poet and story-teller as hopelessly one-sided as the grimmest doctor, lawyer or banker. The great masters of literature are equally open to what outward experience will bring them and what will arise from the depths of their soul. The fact that intelligent and sensitive men could be so one-sided proves how much they detested and feared the society of their age, the world of this later nineteenth century.

Flaubert, though no Symbolist, shared this dislike, this horror of the all-conquering, stupid, bourgeois existence, loathing the class to which economically and socially he belonged. And indeed his work, alternating between the present and the distant past, may be seen as an oscillation between a direct criticism of this society, in *Madame Bovary, L'Éducation sentimentale, Bouvard et Pécuchet*, and an escape from it, at least superficially, in *Salammbô, La Légende de Saint Julien l'Hospitalier* and *La Tentation de Saint Antoine*. One reason why he hated the world about him—and there does seem to have been something exceptionally complacent and gross about French bourgeois life before and during the Second Empire—was that he was at heart a Romantic, and indeed a wildly rebellious Romantic. His devotion to his art, his self-immolation, and perhaps the character of his greatest admirers, between them tend to make us imagine him as one of those small, bony, thin-lipped French intellectuals, coldly logical and orderly, a mixture of the ecclesiastic and the cashier; whereas in fact Flaubert was a very large tempestuous man, given to emotional outbursts; and Anatole France, in his sly fashion, gives us an amusing picture of him looking like a huge Scandinavian chieftain, picturesquely dressed, loud in his rages and enthusiasms, with an innocence behind his absurdity, toiling away for fourteen hours a day, all in a vast muddle of documents and missing information. Here then is yet another sharply divided man turning to the novel. He is a wild Romantic compelling himself to be an exact realist. He is above life, having scornfully rejected it for art, but is also still below it, secretly afraid of it. His coldness and apparent hardness to the women who loved him have this fear behind them, a fear of being involved, of being challenged and then failing; for he was an affectionate son, uncle, friend, feeling himself able to cope with these less demanding relationships. His hatred of the world, loud in his talk and filling his letters, for its stupidity (though even in his own art, to say nothing of science and invention, it had arrived at a great epoch), and for its ugliness (though, not far from him, Manet, Degas, Monet, Renoir, Pissaro, were about to paint it), was not entirely false but neither was it altogether sincere. And he retired into his study, certainly devoted to his art but ready to wrestle with difficulties he had partly invented for himself, as other men have retreated into monasteries. Perhaps some of his later admirers, who set him above Tolstoy, Dickens, Balzac, are secretly more impressed by this retreat than by the work that came out of it.

Although his method, in the novels of contemporary life, is so painstakingly realistic, he is no Zola, writing from outside his chosen subject. His novels have weight and depth just because each of them represented a battle with himself and a partial victory of one side of his nature. In the tragic story of Emma Bovary, with whom he unblushingly identified himself (in the famous admission: "Madame Bovary, c'est moi"), he tried to rid himself of the more foolish aspects of his early romanticism, the dissatisfaction with one's own style of life, the longing for whatever is not easily attainable. Behind the arid social and political futilities of *L'Éducation sentimentale*, Flaubert is trying to justify his frequent statement (perhaps all the more frequent because he still had to convince himself) that the artist must be totally uncommitted, without any social convictions. For here, while redoubling his attack on the bourgeois, who are more cynical and emptier than ever in this Parisian scene, he rejects the socialist solution for the workers and peasants (for whom, both here and elsewhere, he has a natural generous sympathy), perhaps perceiving intuitively, as Dostoyevsky did, a future iron tyranny in the success of a doctrinaire movement of the extreme Left. Following his *Trois contes*, in which he is not wrestling with himself but is genuinely concerned with other people's lives, he began, after a vast preparation that is not unlike the laborious futility he is about to satirise, *Bouvard et Pécuchet*, his novel about the two retired copying-clerks, determined to acquire knowledge, that he never lived to finish. His synopsis of the unwritten chapters suggests that they would have added both breadth and depth of meaning, and it contains, among other things, some curiously successful guesses at the future we are living now. But even as it stands, this story of two absurd little men toiling away in their search for knowledge (and it probably owes something to *Don Quixote*, which Flaubert loved) can be taken on more than one level. For if they are ridiculous, heaping up this mass of information, mostly nonsense, and running into knock-about mis-adventures, so in our own various ways are we all, the author—as he knows very well—included. The final irony is that if Flaubert, ageing fast as he actually wrote the book, had not condemned himself to these immense preparations, had for once written the book straight out of his head, refusing to be the Flaubert of the literary legend, he might have achieved a masterpiece, comparable in its breadth of humanity and depth of meaning with his beloved *Don Quixote*. But though his mind was reaching towards a new freedom, he remained the slave of his method.

This leaves us, as most criticism and a world of readers have testified, with *Madame Bovary* as his most representative piece of work, his master-piece. This tragedy of a foolish romantic woman and her absurd doting husband, her two worthless lovers, her neighbours in the small country town, may well justify the four years of heartbreaking toil that went into its composition, at a time too when its author was in his prime. But if so, then the claim of great genius, made on behalf of Flaubert by critics usually not deeply concerned with fiction, must be modified. It is a remarkable novel, solidly and beautifully planned and written, but as it has been used so often as an argument in favour of the novel as a pure art form, as a rod chastising those novelists (especially the Russians and the English) whose work is looser in form and texture but livelier and seemingly more vital, we might ask ourselves here if *Madame Bovary* really is as close to perfection as we are told it is. Passing minor faults of construction, of which the clumsy first chapter is an example, let us consider two major weaknesses that, if admitted, bring this novel some way from perfection. The whole setting, Tostes and Rouen and the Normandy countryside, is presented to us, throughout the novel, as a series of exquisite little scenes, of which we are delightfully and gratefully aware: it is almost like sauntering through a gallery of Vermeers. But who in the novel is seeing and enjoying these scenes? The answer must be that, except on a few occasions, nobody there is seeing them, that they are being precisely but lovingly described to us by Flaubert. It may be objected that he is entitled, like other novelists, to describe the world in which his drama is unfolding itself; but if he is offering us complete realism, an objective narrative into which he does not intrude, yet all the time we are aware of him, presenting the scene not as his characters see it but as he would see it, then something is wrong. And surely there is also something wrong with Madame Bovary herself. She is very carefully put together and set in motion, but do we feel throughout the novel that she is the same living character? Has she a unique personality of her own, or does she appear to feel, think, behave, merely as Flaubert wants her to feel, think, behave, to go the way he has decided she shall go? Is she truly herself from first to last, or is she one person in one scene, and quite a different person in another scene? Does she ever really move us as the old peasant woman at the Show and Charles Bovary and the child, at the end, move us? Compare her with Anna Karenina, and there is revealed at once the difference between talent-plus-industry-and-patience and sheer creative genius. Flaubert's industry and patience, like his pride in and devotion to his art, are to be admired and if necessary to be imitated; but perhaps if he had given his solid talent an airing, let the sun shine on it, we might have seen it flame into genius.

Zola and Flaubert have nothing in common except a few friends. Zola's naturalism arose out of a belief that the novelist could work, in a spirit of scientific determinism, alongside the biologist and doctor. His plan of the huge *Rougon-Macquart* series was conceived in that spirit; its twenty volumes would show what heredity and environment had made of the various branches of a family during the period of the Second

Empire. And each novel would explore a certain territory or be concerned with a particular style of life, after Zola had made himself thoroughly acquainted with the facts. So, in order to write *Germinal*, one of the most ambitious and (if not widely popular) successful novels of the series, Zola spent six months taking notes in the coal-mining districts of North-Eastern France and Belgium. This preliminary documentation was an essential part of the naturalistic method. The novelist might imagine characters and situations, but the world in which they existed had to be an accurate copy of the real world. This 'documentary' fiction, something between literature and journalism, is not only still written but is on the increase, and there is a great deal of it both in Russia, where it is praised as 'socialist realism', and in America, where it is accepted as 'the low-down'; but Zola was its first and greatest practitioner, and made—or had made for him—the largest literary claims for it. But these claims, though never without serious advocates in Zola's lifetime and since, have not been approved by critics of weight inside or outside France; though the general tendency has been to ignore Zola rather than attempt any final judgment on him.

But he cannot be ignored here. Whatever his literary status may be, he exists as a world figure in modern fiction; he has been read, is still read, by multitudes everywhere; he is the representative novelist of French naturalism of the Seventies and Eighties; he has been called a great novelist by some very intelligent and responsible writers. (Thus, André Gide in his Journal for October 1934 protests against the lack of appreciation of Zola, whom he regularly re-reads. In England, where Zola's first translator and publisher, Vizetelly, was sentenced to imprisonment, Havelock Ellis translated *Germinal*, "a great prose epic" he called it, and now one of the best of the post-war novelists, Angus Wilson, out of his admiration for Zola has written a book about him.) What, then, is the case for Zola? First, he wrote a great deal that is immensely readable; most of his work has breadth and vigour, and the best of it has impressive power; he has an astonishing visual sense, combining an eye for detail with a panoramic style, like that of some painter of vast frescoes; he explores and describes his various selected territories and modes of life, many of them new to fiction, thoroughly and frankly and fearlessly. Next, he is much more than a narrow novelist with a thesis or purpose: his *L'Assommoir* (*The Drunkard*) is not simply a moral tale about the evil effects of drink in the Paris slums but is a genuine novel about a group of poor people. Though he has shot at everybody, from cabinet ministers, millionaires, leaders of society to the poorest wretches gibbering in the gutter, and undoubtedly fails badly with some types, from poets to peasants, he is most convincing among the very people who had up to his time been ignored, or mentioned either with disgust or vague dread, namely, the new people of the nineteenth century, the industrial workers, the masses swarming in city slums, the proletariat. Their lives were ugly and often filthy, as he took pains to show, and much of the outcry against his work was not based on any literary standards but came from a fear of the plain truth. His originality does not lie in his pseudo-scientific method, which need not be taken seriously, but in his genuine feeling for people in the mass and his sense of social justice, a natural sense that has nothing to do with political propaganda. Zola is far from being a Communist, but at his strongest— say, in *L'Assommoir*, *Germinal* especially, and *La Débâcle*, his picture of France's downfall in the war of 1870—he represents better than anybody the kind of novelist the Communists are always hoping to manufacture, chiefly through Party directives and resolutions of the Union of Writers. And his most impressive and memorable scenes, like tremendous moving pictures, are those in which he shows us not individuals but whole masses of people in motion, in a fashion that seems to belong to our age, mass-communicating through mass-media, rather than his. It is nonsense to say he is out-of-date—this comes from the criticism that has taken its tone from his arch-enemies, the Symbolists—because in what is central and original in him, his reportage, his concentration upon a particular way of life, an industry, a national crisis, his sense of people in the mass, he is more modern than most of the moderns, a novelist of our time.

Perhaps *Germinal*, unquestionably his masterpiece and still the best of its kind, allows us to call him a great novelist. But we cannot go very far with his admirers. The trouble with Zola is that, beginning as he did with the idea that the new naturalistic fiction, if written on a grand scale, could be almost a scientific experiment, he forgot what literature is, and so it took its revenge on him. For literature does not put life under a microscope, remaining outside it to observe and to record what it is doing. Literature thinks and feels and imagines its way into life, express-ing it from the inside. But with Zola we are always on the outside, and he is like one of those museum guides who tell us about everything and give us no opportunity of using our imagination. What he does is very difficult to do, and usually he does it very well, but it is not artistic creation. He is our special correspondent or guide to the markets and their workers, the financiers and cocottes, the dram shops and the slums, the big store and its assistants, the peasants sowing and reaping, and so on through the programme; but though he may instruct, entertain, horrify us, he weaves no spell about us, still leaves us outside the peculiar enchant-ment of literature. In his own day he was accused of deliberate sensa-tionalism and pornography (he is still sold in many a dark little shop as a spicy author), but this was unfair to a conscientious and public-spirited man, who finally risked everything by his courageous intervention in the Dreyfus affair. It is true that he often seems vulgarly sensational, over-doing everything in a tasteless fashion, but this is a fault of his method. Instead of identifying himself with his scene and its people, he stares from outside, busy with his notes, and then as his narrative develops and he warms to the work, he releases in himself some rather cheap romanticism. (It is not supposed to be there, but, after all, Zola was from the South and was not brought up with scientific naturalism.) Then he begins to overdo everything, making ugliness too ugly, brutality too brutal, loveli-ness too lovely, goodness too good. And in spite of the indignant denials of his admirers, he does in fact achieve some pornographic effects, as for example in the hot-house relations between Renée and her step-son in *La Curée* and in many passages in *Nana*. He does not do it intentionally; it happens because a certain conscious puritanism in him, when at the full heat of narration, brings into play its unconscious opposite, all lush and leering. And this too comes from a failure to use the imagination on the level where it is both integrating and fully creative. He was never quite an artist, except perhaps, in his own panoramic and mass-conscious fashion, among the coalminers and masters in *Germinal*, that hard but not hopeless epic, ending on a strangely prophetic note, a vision of the germinating mass of workers "growing towards the harvests of the next century".

6

So far we have considered the fiction of this age in terms of those novelists writing respectively in English, Russian, French. But were there no others? Clearly there were many others, writing in their own various languages; fiction, except in translation, had not vanished from Central Europe, Spain and Italy, Scandinavia; there was valuable talent, even if it fell short of genius, displayed throughout the age in all these regions and countries. But there are several good reasons why their writers of fiction did not break through into world literature and become figures of international significance, why major novels in English, Russian, French, focused so much attention on themselves. They are good literary reasons, quite separate from the fact, an important fact, that these major novelists represented communities of greater size, wealth and power. (Germany may seem an exception here, but not until the end of this age was there a genuinely unified German community.) First, these novelists of Paris and London and Moscow led the way; for example, arriving at realism while novelists elsewhere were still working in a belated spirit of romanticism. Secondly, there is a natural tendency for writers developing the prose fiction of their country to turn to the historical novel (or romance, if romanticism is still in vogue), to display to the nation, perhaps just becoming conscious of itself, its wonderful past; or to become exclusively and narrowly regional, writing stories to show how quaint, comical, pathetic, appealing, the peasants and merchants and local officials are in some remote province. Thirdly, many of the best writers in these countries, writers who often felt compelled or were driven by circumstance to do all manner of work from journalism to poetry, preferred the subsidiary form of the short story to the novel proper.

We can find all these limiting factors in the German fiction of this age. So, very early in the period, we have the German-Swiss Gotthelf, an earnest pastor free of all literary influences but a writer of solid merit, believing that didactic fiction would help the simple folk he knew, writing realistic tales of local peasant life, creating what came to be called 'the village novel'. And as Germany itself still consisted of widely different regions, speaking and writing Low German as well as High, Gotthelf's example was more or less followed there, and we have the localised fiction of Reuter and Auerbach and Raabe, and, in Austria, the peasant tales of Anzengruber and Rosegger. And if Gustav Freytag left the village for the town, the peasant for the middle class, both commercial and learned, he is little more than a German Dickens without the magical humour; while Spielhagen has plenty of ideas and is an ingenious plotter but lacks the essential ability to create people and to keep them alive and kicking. Another German-Swiss, Gottfried Keller, has more talent, temperament and breadth of mind than any of them, and is really in the world literature class, but after his very long and very leisurely autobiographical novel *Der Grüne Heinrich*, instead of concentrating on other novels, shorter and more objective, he scattered his gifts among short stories, like the other Swiss, C. F. Meyer, and the Germans, Storm and Heyse. (They were very fond of setting stories within stories, framing a set of tales with another tale, known in Germany as *Rahmenerzählung*. This device seems to have had a fascination for the German mind, so that it survived the Romantics, who had made frequent use of it.) Keller's stories, mostly written in Zürich and not fully and widely appreciated in Germany until the very end of this age, are very good indeed, not for their technique but because they reveal a rich and pleasing personality; but had he chosen and mastered the big novel form, the novel as it was being written in Russia, England, France, German readers would not have had to wait until the next age, our own time, for a major novelist belonging to world literature.

One or other of these limitations, and sometimes more than one, can equally be found in the literatures north and south of Germany, from the peasant tales of Bjørnstjerne Bjørnson in Norway to those of Verga in Southern Italy, from the national historical fiction of Rydberg in Sweden to that of Pérez Galdos in Spain, which also has Alarcón (*The Three-cornered Hat*) and Pereda and other regional novelists, while Holland had Dekker, an official in Java, with his solitary, powerful novel of protest, *Max Havelaar*, and Denmark the short-lived, imaginative realist, Jens Peter Jacobsen. And as far away as the Argentine and Uruguay there was the fiction, half romantic, half realistic, of which the *gaucho* was the central figure, like the cowboy in the American 'Westerns' of today. There was a great deal of fiction being written, throughout this age, in many different places; but the supremacy of England, Russia, France, in the novel (unlike the drama, as we shall see in the chapter that follows) could not be challenged. And we have not entirely finished with these three, for though Tolstoy and Zola brought us to the end of this age in Russia and France respectively, we left the English Novel, which has some developments of its own, only as far into the age as Dickens could take it. And Dickens had some younger contemporaries with their own ideas about the novel, and his comparatively early death in 1870, only seven years after the death of Thackeray, left a wide and inviting place open to these younger novelists.

Dickens's friend, Wilkie Collins, deserves a mention, simply because he brought the fiction of mystery and intrigue, now so popular, not only into public favour but also, as we know from *The Woman in White* and *The Moonstone*, as near to perfection, both in its ingenuity of plot and its thick atmosphere of menace, as it is ever likely to be. Again, it is only fair to point out that before Zola had adopted his notebook-and-news-paper-cutting method, Charles Reade had used it in preparing the earlier of his novels that attacked various public abuses; though, oddly enough, Reade's own masterpiece is his historical novel of the fifteenth century, *The Cloister and the Hearth*, one of the best in this kind in any language. With Collins and Reade may be placed Anthony Trollope, whose reputation has had a curious history. Even before he died he was regarded as an industrious hack (his *Autobiography*, a frank and sensible account of himself as an author, tended to confirm this view of him in minds neither frank nor sensible); for a long time after his death in 1882 he was almost forgotten; but during the last twenty-five years he has been increasingly reprinted and read, and, if anything, is now over-praised. Whether he is writing about clerical life or high politics (and he had little direct experience of either; he was in fact a Post Office official), Trollope is able to achieve a rather flat but utterly convincing realism, chiefly by a consistency of character and tone and by refusing to attempt too much, keeping to a common denominator of general interest. He and Dostoyevsky might be said to divide fiction between them. But he created a genuine little world of his own, and the desire to escape into it, out of our own menacing world, explains most of his recent popularity.

A new kind of English fiction arrives with Mary Ann Evans, who chose to write under the name of George Eliot. (It would be difficult to find two women less alike than the two novelists who both hid themselves behind the same first name—George Sand and George Eliot.) She was a deeply earnest, intellectual woman, who abandoned the narrow religion of her provincial youth, and as assistant editor of the advanced *Westminster Review* she became the colleague and friend of the leading utilitarian and positivist thinkers. (Herbert Spencer, the philosopher, was one of her devoted friends during this period.) Though rightly accepted as an intellectual equal by these males, and looking decidedly unlike the admired female type, all curls and dimples, of this era, she was essentially feminine in temperament; and defied convention by living with G. H. Lewes, the dramatic critic and student of German philosophy and literature, who was already married and could not obtain a divorce. The release she found in this successful relationship with Lewes encouraged her to turn to fiction. She brought to it her knowledge of and concern for ideas, religious, ethical, political, ideas that had been missing from the novels of Dickens and Thackeray; and also a clear picture of the rural and small town life of the Midlands where she had passed her childhood and youth. She was never quite sure of herself, being naturally over-conscientious and anxious and having the burden of talent without the propelling force of sheer genius; but she had an excellent general equipment for the writing of fiction: a fine sense of character, both male and female, sophisticated or naïve; sufficient humour, and a very sharp feminine eye for tiny but significant motives and all the shifts of self-deception. And she was able to plan and organise her novels so that they clearly reflected her own intense moral earnestness, her world of immutable cause and effect, her deep sense of ethical and social responsibility. Whereas Dickens in his huge slap-dash way wrote for anybody and everybody, to the last still hoping to please all tastes, George Eliot—as her publishers might say now—wrote thoughtful novels for thoughtful people, although she was not afraid of strong situations and even melodrama. Her masterpiece is undoubtedly *Middlemarch*, in which she reveals in a cool but searching light the society of a whole town, in which several distinct but interlocking groups of persons are seen in motion, growing, changing in their varied relationships, and we are made deeply aware of the whole broad but flickering tissue of opinion and judgment and illusion and disillusion, aware too of her own capable hands weaving the web. This has brought us a long way from the hit-or-miss story-telling of earlier Victorian fiction. There is an obvious gain, but because so much depends on consciousness in this fiction and so little is left for the creative unconscious to contribute, there is a loss too, of irrational poetic elements, of sudden ecstasy or sudden tragic insights, of life's heights and depths and fury and horror and beauty and wonder. George Eliot, rejecting divine revelations and miracles, was proud of being able, as she said, "to live without opium". But literature likes a little opium.

Meanwhile, even before George Eliot's death in 1880, two novelists who were also poets—and indeed finally came to think of themselves as poets who had written novels—were hard at work to prove, in their very different ways, that English fiction had great flexibility and almost kept open house for all manner of temperaments and outlooks on life. (And this is perhaps the best place to mention that odd figure, half crank, half genius, Samuel Butler, whose fable of an imaginary country, *Erewhon*—anagram of 'nowhere'—is a brilliantly original piece of social criticism, and whose posthumous novel, *The Way of All Flesh*, strips all pretence from Victorian family life.) These two poet-novelists were George Meredith and Thomas Hardy. Both of them, Meredith with showy defiance and Hardy simply and rather naïvely, write their own kind of novel, and bring to their fiction an all-pervading philosophy of life, like a decided climate. Meredith's novels are at their best when they come closest to high intellectual comedy in narrative form, as in *The Egoist*. An impatient, brilliant man, he was bored by the mere mechanics and journeyman-work of novel-writing, the sort of thing a man like Trollope did so well, with the result that his novels never seem solidly based and have an air of unreality about them; but in his big scenes—and he is nearly always hurrying towards a big scene—he is often magnificent, perhaps matchless, in the penetration, speed, fire and wit of his mind, his intellectual high spirits lit by flashes of poetry. His highly subjective treatment of such scenes, making far greater demands on the reader's imagination than any other novelist of his time was making, give him an importance, as one of the early innovators in the technique of modern fiction, that has not been sufficiently recognised. Both his reading of life and his theory of comedy insist upon equality between the sexes, the feminine spirit checking and balancing the masculine, and, holding this view (unpopular in Victorian England and not widely held even today), Meredith was fortunate in being able to body it forth in a series of boldly conceived but attractive heroines. The inevitable reaction set in after his death, as late as 1909, but sooner or later, his many faults forgiven him, he will be read and enjoyed again.

Meredith's last novels were his worst, Hardy's last were his best. The two poet-novelists were as unalike in this as in almost everything else. Meredith is mocking, hard, exacting, but fundamentally optimistic, whereas Hardy (who had nothing of Meredith's touchy vanity) is easier and more broadly sympathetic but deeply pessimistic, going to great and often inartistic lengths to prove how cruelly the universe (born of the Greek tragedians and Schopenhauer) plays with us and then, when tired of its sport, destroys us. (There is much to be said for this view of things, for Hardy, like Schopenhauer, lived to a ripe and contented old age.) The scene to which Hardy brought this idea of cosmic irony and cruelty was the remote rural Dorset ('Wessex' in his novels) that he knew so well in his youth; and indeed in some of the novels, not placed in any historical past, we almost feel we are in some undated era of antiquity, when Stonehenge was still new, and are shocked to hear rumours of railways and factories. But this is a tribute to Hardy's brooding vision, essentially poetic although often clumsily expressed, in which the protagonists, the chorus of rustics (often humorous), and the landscape, itself a majestic and ancient character, are assembled, blended, held together, as if on some vast stage, tremblingly lit against darkness and doom. It is when he succeeds in imposing this vision upon us that Hardy is strongest. He is weakest when he is trying to write an acceptable Victorian novel, especially if it contains what he innocently imagines to be highly sophisticated characters and typical scenes of urban life, where he is no more at home than Meredith is among farm labourers. It has been the fashion, which began before his death, perhaps because he encouraged it, to prefer his poetry to his fiction (though in fact they show exactly the same strength and weakness), but the best of his novels, notably *Far From the Madding Crowd*, *The Return of the Native*, *The Woodlanders*, and *Tess of the D'Urbervilles*, have the endurance of rugged old trees.

A slighter figure is Robert Louis Stevenson, yet another poet-novelist, the Scot who went to the South Seas and died there, at forty-four, just when, as his unfinished *Weir of Hermiston* proves, he was maturing as a novelist, as distinct from a romantic story-teller. Stevenson's enormous popularity, partly the result of his narrative gift but also the reward of his style, which has an unusual and very personal grace and charm (and some of his sourer critics might try to learn something from it before dismissing it as a mere trick), has now lasted a long time, so long that only prejudice would deny this continuing popularity a hard core of genuine literary acceptance. It cannot be explained by the fact that we begin reading him early—his *Treasure Island* being a masterpiece of romancing for boys— for there are many other authors of our boyhood we hurry to forget. Stevenson brought out of his Scots Calvinism a lively sense of evil and its conflict with the good in men, and indeed his symbolic tale of this dualism, *Dr. Jekyll and Mr. Hyde*, though not one of his best stories, is for ever being recalled, throughout the English-speaking world, to signify man's divided nature. His exile in the South Seas, which he described with more charm than Melville had been able to command, gave a welcome exotic flavour to his later work. Life in Western Europe had begun to seem rather drab in the Eighties, and this is one reason why French readers turned eagerly to Pierre Loti, the romantic naval officer, and English and American readers were delighted with Stevenson and the confident, sharp-eyed young man from India, Rudyard Kipling.

The Americans enjoyed Stevenson and Kipling all the more because these were very lean years for American fiction. There was Mark Twain, as we have already seen, and there was his friend William Dean Howells, an honest (though timid) and sensitive novelist of manners, whose *Rise of Silas Lapham* gives a fair parlour picture of Boston in the Eighties, and who made use of his very considerable influence, during the following decade, to help young newspapermen converted to naturalism and a super-reporter's laconic prose-for-the-eye, like Stephen Crane (*The Red Badge of Courage*), who unfortunately died young, as did the American Zola of wheat-and-railways, Frank Norris. The West had been disappointing; Brett Harte was not another Mark Twain, and Ambrose Bierce, with more depth and bite than Harte, wrote too little. There was a kind of lull before the clumsy howitzers of Theodore Dreiser opened the main battle for realism in American fiction. But surely one impressive figure is missing? Yes, Henry James. But although James lived far longer and wrote far more in this century than in ours, the character of his work and the curious history of his reputation take him out of this age and into the next, among the moderns of Part Five. His first successful novel, *Roderick Hudson*, appeared in 1875, that is, during the central and greatest period of nineteenth-century fiction, 1840–80, perhaps the golden age of the novel; but his later work, which mainly accounts for the astonishing resurrection of his reputation after his death in 1916, places him securely, if anything belonging to these years can be considered secure, among the novelists of the twentieth century and in the final section of this chronicle.

CHAPTER EIGHTEEN

The Dramatists

I

WHILE FICTION was enjoying its greatest triumphs, the Drama was suffering an eclipse. Some critics have found cause-and-effect here, as if novel-reading became popular at the expense of play-going. But the facts do not support this argument. Between 1840 and 1880 there was no lack of theatrical activity; new playhouses, mostly smaller but more luxurious than the older theatres, were being built everywhere; and it was during these years, especially in the 1860s, that the elaborately realistic staging of plays, so familiar to us now, was first introduced. It was also a period, beginning in Paris with a Rachel and ending with a Bernhardt, or in London with Irving, in New York with Edwin Booth, of great players, actresses who could behave like mad queens both on and off the stage, actor-managers who looked as if they were permanently fixed in a Shakespearean tragic role but contrived to be shrewd showmen. The theatres, the actors, the playgoers, were much in evidence; all that was missing was any drama worthy of the name. Unfortunately, while the art of Drama cannot exist without the Theatre—for all genuine dramatists write not merely to be read but to be performed on the stage—the Theatre can exist, and even flourish after a fashion, when it is indifferent to the true imaginative art of Drama. And this is what happened during these middle decades of the nineteenth century.

It is true that the great classics were still being produced. Indeed, the actor-managers who dominated the Theatre during this period prided themselves on their Shakespearean productions, spending much time and money on them, calling upon the services of well-known artists to design magnificent stage sets, insisting that antiquarian experts should supervise the costumes, armour, weapons, and so forth. Where a scene asked for a few soldiers or cheering citizens, scores and scores of supers were engaged, drilled, and carefully costumed. Any mention of snow brought tons of salt to glisten on the stage. But all this pageantry and pedantry, often accompanied by a ruthless cutting of scenes, to save time, merely took the imagination out of imaginative drama. Wonderful dramatic poems, referring to no particular time or place, depending entirely on the magical evocation of their words, were turned into scripts for historical and spectacular shows. Shakespeare, the supreme dramatic poet, was not good enough; the audience wanted something more for their money. (The costly imbecilities of our films at their worst are merely an exaggeration of this nineteenth-century Theatre.) No matter how nobly ravaged they might look, for ever haunted by the ghost of Hamlet's father, these actor-manager tragedians were experienced showmen who knew what was needed to fill the large theatres they occupied. If they did not appeal, first and foremost, to the imagination of their audiences, it was because they knew that these audiences either had no imagination, or preferred not to exercise it in the playhouse. These people in fact—and especially the comfortable class whose money paid for the extravagant stage production—no longer went to the play in the same spirit as their ancestors had done, innocently and widely receptive in mind and heart. They paid their money to be amused, to be 'taken out of themselves', not into themselves. And so what is now called 'show business' was born. It may be objected that the Theatre has always been 'show business', that Shakespeare and Molière, both dramatist-managers, were as much aware of it as any nineteenth-century actor-managers. But to them 'show business' represented only one aspect of the Theatre on which they imposed their vision of this life. Certainly they had to please their audiences—the Theatre cannot exist on its patrons' displeasure—but the audiences they had to please were very different from those that filled these nineteenth-century playhouses, who brought so little with them, not wanting the life they knew to be illuminated and interpreted for them, only desiring to forget it, to be tickled out of any consideration of it, for a few hours. Another web, we might say, was broken here.

The very large theatres, where working people could find plenty of cheap seats, mostly staged melodramas, mixing sentiment and farcical humour with strong crude action, and offering spectacular effects—all "horrors and blue fire", to quote one English hack who wrote scores of such pieces. It is easy to condemn or ridicule drama on this level, and harder to realise and appreciate that something essential to the enduring Theatre, a vitality, a swaggering and larger-than-life quality, a very broad and direct appeal to the emotions and moral sense of people in general, was being maintained, kept alive, in these noisy playhouses. They preserved a foundation on which truly imaginative and subtle drama could be raised; and Shakespeare would have preferred their occasional productions of *Hamlet* or *Othello*, which at least had pace and sweep, to the 'conscientious and artistic' productions of the more ambitious actor-managers. And melodramas originally written and produced about the middle of the nineteenth century, robbed of their more spectacular effects, were still touring the provinces in most Western countries up to the outbreak of the First World War, after which the films, equally melodramatic and far more spectacular, captured their audiences.

It was in the new and smaller theatres, built without enormous galleries but with plenty of velvet stalls or *fauteuils* for patrons in full evening dress, that the old conventions, dating back to the seventeenth century, were replaced by an elaborate realism in staging. A room was no longer suggested by a backcloth and wings (with the actors making their entrances and exits between them) and by no more furniture and properties than were absolutely necessary to the action. Now it was by a 'box-set', with walls and a ceiling and doors and windows, and unless it represented a hovel or a garret it was more often than not crowded with pieces of furniture, ornaments and knick-knacks, just like the rooms the audiences had recently quitted. True, there was more here than managers' showmanship. There were now, in the Sixties, capable and popular playwrights who wrote with this new kind of staging in mind, and, from Ostrovsky in Moscow to T. W. Robertson in London, insisted upon realistic detail in the production of their plays, demanding doors with knobs that turned, tea on the tea-trays, snow effects outside the window. (They also insisted, to their credit, on their companies no longer playing on almost empty stages but having to work with so much furniture and properties, being very carefully rehearsed for weeks instead of running through the play in a day or two.) Nevertheless, mere showmanship played its part here. One of the most successful of these innovators, the London actor-manager, Squire Bancroft, recalls in his memoirs the surprise and gratification of his patrons when they first saw his various new effects—autumn leaves falling throughout a wood scene, the snow driving-in each time the door of a hut was opened. But a price was paid for all this material elaboration and these stage-manager's devices, themselves of little or no imaginative value. And, in all the cities where most theatres were operated for private profit, it was a heavy price.

The older theatres, with their scenery of painted cloths, easily raised or lowered from the 'flies', their vague ante-rooms or apartments that could serve several plays with their interior scenes, their minimum of furniture, properties and effects, had no difficulty in staging a whole repertoire of old plays and were able, without much trouble and expense, to introduce new plays into that repertoire. But this new realistic method, involving the building of solid sets and the assembling of all the necessary furnishings, properties, effects, was cumbersome and expensive, and only worth while if a production ran for at least several months at a profit. This meant that the manager felt he could not afford to risk any new play that might displease or bewilder the people who bought his better seats; the stage-manager might be adventurous with his falling leaves or driving snow effects, but the author must not be adventurous; what was needed was something safe, and preferably a plot and some characters that had already been successful elsewhere; with the result that theatre after theatre, in country after country, presented something "adapted from the French". This importation of plays from Paris, and the kind of plays they were, must be considered elsewhere, for here we are still examining the price demanded of the Theatre by this new realistic method of staging the drama. And not only was there a loss of economy and flexibility in theatrical production, with long runs taking the place of the old repertory system in the smaller, newer, more fashionable theatres, but something was lost in the all-important relation between the audience and the play. True, there was some gain for the dramatist, who could now place his characters, not in some vague featureless apartment, but in a room so carefully designed, built, decorated, furnished, that it became itself a kind of large character in the play. And the later major dramatists, Ibsen, Strindberg, Chehov, took full advantage of all that elaborate *décor* could offer them. They transformed mere realism—doors with turning knobs and weather outside the window—into character and atmosphere. But where, then, was the loss? We cannot answer this question unless we understand the relation between an audience and a play, the essential nature of the drama.

True dramatic experience, which is what we go to the theatre to achieve, demands a simultaneous double response from the audience, on two different levels of the mind. On one level our imagination is captured and held by the characters and what happens to them. On the other level we are still conscious of the fact that we are sitting in a playhouse, looking at and listening to actors. It is this double response that gives dramatic experience its unique character and value.* The so-called reality of a play depends upon its hold upon our imagination, and no matter how powerful and moving this may be, we are still aware of the fact that we are attending a theatrical performance, we do not for a moment mistake what we see for real life. It follows therefore that we accept whatever theatrical convention the production represents. We may prefer one style to another but we recognise the conventions for what they are. The curtain may rise on a bare stage or an office scene, cluttered up with desks and ledgers and noisy with typewriters and telephone bells, but we are still in the theatre, waiting for our imagination to be held and enchanted. And extreme fussy realism in production may prevent the imagination from experiencing its own sense of reality. So when Bancroft's audiences were surprised and gratified by the falling autumn leaves in his wood scene, they were probably denying their imagination full entry into what was happening in that wood scene, apart from falling leaves. Again, Shakespeare's words, set down for this purpose, take us further into the Forest of Arden than all the painted canvas and artificial foliage that a producer can assemble. (And a real wood, taking us out of the theatre

* This theory of the drama is fully explained in my lecture and notes in *The Art of the Dramatist.*

altogether, makes true dramatic experience impossible.) Now the old characterless interior scenes, consisting of a rather dim backcloth and wings (which some of us may remember from our youth, when companies touring a repertoire of eighteenth-century comedies still used them), did not look like real rooms, but they were accepted as such, as part of the theatrical convention, and they had the important advantage of not offering themselves for our surprise and gratification but of concentrating our attention on the actors and their words and gestures. These actors performed all the better because they had this attention, had not to compete with walls, doors, decoration, furniture, properties, and had more scope for their acting on almost bare stages. This is particularly true of high comedy, in the old classical style, now in our time generally flattened by and almost buried under elaborate *décor*. The loss therefore was very considerable, and the price the drama as an art had to pay for this new realistic method of production, as its subsequent history proves, was altogether too heavy. Indeed, in spite of many rebellious experiments, our Theatre is still labouring under a weight of debt.

2

The spirit of Paris, during the Second Empire, was probably best expressed in the Theatre by those cheerfully impudent collaborators, Meilhac and Halévy, who supplied Offenbach with the *libretti* for his comic operettas. And to these two we might add the prolific Eugène Labiche, whose best farces, notably *Un Chapeau de paille d'Italie* and *Le Voyage de Monsieur Perrichon* (with its central sardonic idea—that we like those who owe us gratitude, and detest those to whom we ought to feel grateful), can still be enjoyed in performance. This is more than could be said of his more serious but equally successful contemporaries, Émile Augier and Alexandre Dumas *fils*. It is true that the latter's *La Dame aux camélias*, his very first play and a dramatisation of his own popular novel, has never ceased to be played, not only because it offers a star actress the kind of acting part few star actresses can resist (and many plays are constantly revived just because leading performers want to challenge the fame of their predecessors in such parts) but also because its theme, the courtesan purified by love, might be said to be archetypal in its own world of romantic sentimentality. And it is ironical that the younger Dumas should now be represented in the Theatre by this early tearful piece, because his later work displays him as a severe moralist, too often humourless, stiff, priggish. Both he and Augier, who began as a poet but was then swept into the reaction against the Romantics, wrote highly didactic pieces, which later would have been called 'plays with a purpose' or even 'problem plays', attacking the false 'sense of honour' and moral laxity of the aristocracy, the greed, snobbery, materialism of the bourgeois, the threat to family life in the drift towards the *demi-monde*, all that was dangerous or dubious in the morals and manners of the time. Thus it is a mistake to suppose, as many people appear to do, that the nineteenth-century Theatre had to await the arrival of Ibsen before it freed itself from comedies of sexual intrigue or sentimental melodramas and discovered serious social criticism. But these French playwrights are too topical and local. They lack breadth, weight and density. Their stagecraft, though still making use of occasional 'asides' and soliloquies, is neat and often quite adroit, but it is all too thinly contrived (with far too much dependence upon the duel, threatened or taking place offstage, as the climax of the action) and we feel that the characters, who changed their opinions and outlook so rapidly, are merely so many pieces of the play's chessboard.

If this is true of these superior and serious-minded French playwrights, it is the whole and devastating truth about the manufacturers of the 'well-made' play, whose leader, after the long reign of Scribe, was Victorien Sardou, chief of the export business in French drama during the latter half of the nineteenth century. What was wrong with these plays, which finally came under the lash of Bernard Shaw's wit, was not that they were well-made, for plays ought to be well-made and there is no virtue in faulty construction. But the true dramatist has not only to bring life to the Theatre, working, as we have seen, in some theatrical convention or other, he must also bring the Theatre to life, so that we can respond to him fully on the imaginative level; and this these French theatrical experts, with their box of professional tricks, failed to do. Their characters have no life of their own; they exist to be clamped into effectively theatrical situations. Thus Sardou's tremendously successful play about diplomacy—and its English adaptation has had many revivals, as no doubt similar adaptations have had elsewhere—is not about diplomacy, has not a single diplomat who comes to life in it, tells us nothing about anybody, throws no light on anything, and is nothing but a succession of trick situations and the kind of bosh that lazy and timid leading actors, afraid of their art, so often prefer to good writing. But these plays would never have been so successful, as they were in many capital cities for a long time, if the audiences had been looking for something better than a box of tricks. "Drama," Denis Saurat observes, while condemning the whole nineteenth-century Theatre, "demands a great writer, a great public, a great moment." This is asking too much, if the Theatre is to be kept going at all, but we could drastically reduce these demands and still be a long way from Sardou and his colleagues and adaptors and their fashionable audiences, killing time between dinner and supper, clapping their white-gloved hands at every knowing but nonsensical 'Curtain'.

The irrepressible Zola adapted his naturalism to the stage, and was followed by the grimly sardonic Henry Becque, not quite the master he is often supposed to be, even in *Les Corbeaux* and *La Parisienne*, but a dramatist of integrity as well as skill. A home had to be found, well away from the velvet *fauteuils* and white gloves, for this new naturalistic drama, and it was provided by André Antoine, first in his Théâtre Libre, made out of a garret, and later on a larger scale in his Théâtre Antoine. He was revolutionary not only in his choice of plays, which included much new important work from outside France, but also in his style of acting and staging; and his fine example was soon followed in other capitals, so that out of his transformed garret in the Eighties came the whole Experimental Theatre movement, dedicated to something more than pleasing fashionable audiences and raking in a fat profit. Such drama as we have had during the past seventy years owes much, in some instances everything, to these theatres and the enthusiasts who have kept them going, often at considerable financial sacrifice; but the split between what is fashionable, popular, broadly entertaining, profitable, on the one side, and, on the other, what is determinedly experimental, serious, solemnly dedicated, has robbed the drama of our time of the vitality the Theatre possessed, during the great ages, when there was no such division, when everybody in his or her own fashion could enjoy the same play, when there were not theatres for clever people and theatres for silly people—but the Theatre. The drama, a communal art, cannot flourish if the public mind is suffering from schizophrenia.

Among Antoine's dramatists were Ibsen, Strindberg, Tolstoy and Gerhart Hauptmann. (Hauptmann was first produced by the *Freie Bühne* in Berlin, a theatre modelled on Antoine's, like Grein's Independent Theatre in London.) The most important of the newer French playwrights with whom he was associated were Brieux, whose modern morality plays were performed throughout Europe, the satirical Octave Mirbeau, the analytical François de Curel, and Hervieu, who brought a suggestion of classical tragedy into the prevailing naturalism. All these writers, whatever their nationality, were regarded as members of the naturalistic movement in the Theatre, but they were in fact widely different—especially the dramatists of real genius—and the movement itself was more negative than positive, a combined reaction against something rather than a united progress in a new direction. What these dramatists had in common was a determination to break with the artificial manner of the older Theatre, with its 'asides' and soliloquies, its neat formal scenes and unlikely coincidences, bringing their texts into line with the realistic method of production. There was in their work less obvious Theatre, together with the kind of action and dialogue that seemed closer to real life. If they remained with society at the level favoured by the older Theatre, they were either sharply satirical or openly challenging and rebellious. Otherwise, following Zola, they explored very different social regions, bringing on the stage, as realistically as they knew how, the poorest workers and peasants. The most thorough-going and successful of this group was undoubtedly Gerhart Hauptmann, who in his earliest work for the Theatre, grimly silencing the romantic poet in him, brought into his *Before Dawn* and *The Weavers* Silesian workers and peasants, whose style of life and dialect he reproduced with a fidelity and depth of sympathy probably unique in this kind of drama. Here he towered above his fellow-countryman and contemporary, Hermann Sudermann, whose apparent realism, much influenced by Ibsen, was mixed with an element of theatricality, which accounts for the popularity of his best-known play *Die Heimat*, known in England and America as *Magda*, long regarded with much favour by leading actresses.

At the end of this age, however, in the Nineties, Hauptmann was producing *Hannele* and *The Sunken Bell*, verse plays, philosophical and symbolical in a semi-Wagnerian and very German style, a world away from his severe naturalism. The grey tide had turned. This sudden change of fashion, swinging away from the drabbest naturalism to romance in a new symbolical dress, the return to the Theatre of colour, fine language, mystery, wonder, explain the rapid rise to fame of two dramatists who now seem to most of us to have been vastly over-estimated. One was from Belgium and the other from the South of France: Maeterlinck and Rostand. Maeterlinck's early plays, *The Death of Tintagiles* and the rest, are rarely revived and are largely forgotten, but they are preferable to his later and more elaborate pieces, such as *The Blue Bird* and *The Betrothal*; and we have only to read them sympathetically to understand the profound effect they had on playgoers in the Nineties. In sharpest contrast to the drama of exact times and places, ordinary explicit speech and recognisable character types, these little plays of Maeterlinck's seem to take us out of time and any place we know. The personages are as mysterious as the setting; their silences are as pregnant as their strange speech; they appear to move like somnambulists in an atmosphere heavy with doom. The value of this highly original drama has nothing to do with the poet's profundity, which did not in fact exist, as his subsequent attempts to explain it amply proved, but comes from the originality of his technique, from the admirable economy and the tremendous power of suggestion, with its apparent revelation of our unconscious life, attained by his particular method. (Its influences may be discovered in some of the more poetic Irish plays and similar things elsewhere, though the more direct influence of Maeterlinck has been responsible for a good deal of mere theatrical whimsy. What was good and genuinely original in his early method has not had the influence that perhaps it ought to have had.) Rostand, though equally removed from naturalism, is very different, and his work can be seen as a continuation, with much added wit and humour, of the theatre of Hugo and the elder Dumas, an unblushingly romantic and sentimental type of drama, carrying off highly theatrical situations and contrivances with a swaggering gusto. All these qualities are found at their best in his *Cyrano de Bergerac*, which, in spite of the fact that its exuberant poetic wit loses much in even the most careful translation, is still played in many different countries. Years of bad health, resulting in his death at the age of forty-nine, not only robbed Rostand of his youthful gusto but prevented his reaching a maturity, of which there are signs in his last work, that would probably have given him the stature of a major European dramatist. But although Paris had so long dominated the whole theatrical scene, the major dramatists, the acknowledged masters of this age, arrived from other and very distant places.

3

The first of these masters, invading the European Theatre from the far North, was Henrik Ibsen. That a Norwegian should do what the playwrights of Paris and London, Vienna and Berlin, had as yet failed to do in this nineteenth-century drama, namely, create a series of prose masterpieces, is one of the ironies of the time. If we ask why he succeeded, we are likely to be told, except by his more recent critics, either that he brought to the Theatre some important ideas and a serious intellectual challenge (see Bernard Shaw, among many others) or, as Mencken for one tells us, that Ibsen's ideas are of little importance and that he owes everything to his superb technical mastery. Both of these accounts of him are inadequate. They are also, at one and the same time, unjust both to Ibsen himself and to the Theatre he came to conquer, which at its best was neither so lacking in ideas nor so poor in its stagecraft as they suggest. Ideas and social criticism were already coming into the Theatre, and the old artificial and clumsy theatrical devices already going out, by the time Ibsen began in earnest to create his prose drama. What Ibsen did was not only to speed up this coming and going but to raise the whole movement of prose drama to a higher power. He was like an engineer who by simplifying and strengthening the boiler was able to increase the steam pressure. What Ibsen created was a drama of far greater density and depth than any the age had so far known. (Compare his drama with that of his spectacularly successful contemporary, Bjørnstjerne Bjørnson, playwright, poet, novelist, theatre manager, political leader, called "the uncrowned king of Norway". Bjørnson was a splendid personality and a true national poet, but his plays, even the once-famous *Beyond Human Power*, when compared with Ibsen's, now seem thin period pieces.) Ibsen was able to do this, giving the effect of an unusual breadth and thickness of life, not because he made a few technical innovations, following the trend towards realism, doing without 'asides', soliloquies, letters read aloud, and so forth, but because he made a technical discovery of the highest importance, a method of construction that has been followed over and over again by dramatists since his time. Without this method he would never have been able to offer his audiences the apparent breadth and thickness of life, the density and depth, that his best plays appear to possess.

What Ibsen did, after long brooding over his characters and their histories, was to see their combined story mounting to a climax, and then to begin his play just before this climax arrives, all that has happened in the past to contribute to it being told or suggested to the audience in various adroit speeches. This is very different from *showing* all that happened in the past, which is what most earlier or contemporary playwrights did, thereby condemning themselves to be lengthy and cumbersome or restricted to a very slight action. Ibsen realised that all that matters, at least in the kind of drama he was trying to create, is the climax, the final flare-up, the end result of these entangled life-stories. So he devised for himself what has been called his 'retrospective method', which so many modern dramatists have borrowed from him. By the time he arrived at his middle period, to which we owe most of his major work, he brought to this method all the skill and ingenuity it demands if it is to be successful. (He was at this time a slow and unusually painstaking writer, constantly revising and pruning his drafts.) But he also achieved both economy and greater force by his grim determination—and he is perhaps the most grimly determined character in the whole history of dramatic literature—to move steadily forward along one line of development, refusing, unlike most playwrights, to offer his audiences a little variety or relief, by way of comic or picturesque episodes. Writing as he did, for the most part, completely out of touch with managements, players, audiences, at the opposite extreme from the familiar type of playwright who is writing to meet a demand, Ibsen with an astonishing strength of will imposed himself ruthlessly on the Theatre, which had to take him as he was or leave him alone. (This is a course far more difficult for the dramatist to adopt than it is for any other kind of writer.) But though he was a great innovator and often a supreme master of concealed exposition, economy of dramatic means, construction, he was not the perfect theatrical technician he was sometimes thought to be. Thus, to take two examples from the period of his maturity, in *The Wild Duck*, one of his masterpieces, the elaborate staging demanded by Act One, the party at old Werle's house, hardly justifies itself, and the play would have been much easier to stage and could have been equally effective without it; and in *Hedda Gabler*, so often revived because it offers a wonderful opportunity to a leading actress, there are several clumsy improbabilities. We must look to neater, smaller, less ambitious playwrights for a negative perfection in theatrical technique.

"From end to end of his life," Mencken tells us, "there is no record that Ibsen ever wrote a single word or formulated a single idea that might not have been exposed in a newspaper editorial." This is not true, and anyhow is beside the point, for Ibsen was not trying to compete with newspaper editorials but was offering us dramatic experience. And if Mencken really believed that he could adequately summarise *The Master Builder* by the statement "that a man of fifty-five or sixty is an ass to fall in love with a flapper of seventeen", it is hard to imagine why he consented to write an Introduction to a volume of such empty plays. What in fact distinguishes them is their unusual density and depth. This cannot be completely explained by a change of method, a new technique. The boiler may be simpler and stronger, but something has to raise the pressure of its steam. And critics like Mencken are at least quite right when they tell us that Ibsen's ideas, when abstracted from his drama, are not boldly original and revolutionary; he was not another Marx or Nietzsche, and did not pretend to be: he was a dramatist. And the force and depth of his drama, the richness of the experience he offers us in the Theatre, come from the man himself, not from the social critic nor the theatrical master craftsman but from the personality behind them, whose conflicts, tensions, stresses, at various levels, were reflected and re-created in this drama. Ibsen was far from being the cosmopolitan iconoclast he was once thought to be. First and last, as his more recent critics have emphasised, he was a Norwegian poet. Though he remained in self-imposed exile for twenty-seven years, bitterly critical of the only society he knew intimately, that of the superficially formal and dour folk of the fiords, unable altogether to repress berserk explosions and still haunted by trolls and ghosts, he never made a genuine new life for himself in Rome and Germany but kept himself aloof, ruthlessly devoted to his work, proud of the sacrifices he was making, his asceticism, the exercise of his formidable will. Yet he was still the Norwegian poet who struggled against opposition, neglect, poverty, finally to write the defiant *Brand* and the even more revealing and essentially Norse folk-epic drama of *Peer Gynt*, which contains certain elements, capricious, lively, droll, never found again in his work. But once Ibsen was in exile, determined now to create prose drama, compact, hard, searching, as unlike *Peer Gynt* both in form and spirit as it was possible for him to achieve by sheer will-power, he tried to keep the poet in him battened-down below. (He even declared that poetry was bad for drama.) But the poet, dismissed from consciousness, flourished rebelliously in the unconscious. There were now three divisions in his total personality, three enduring conflicts, inevitably producing their own tensions and stresses, that he expressed and tried to resolve (ridding himself of poison, he called it) in progressive stages of his work.

There was first the man exiled from and bitterly at odds with the only society, the only people, he ever cared about, his fellow-Norwegians. Next there was the anti-poet for ever wrestling with the poet. Finally, the conflict that takes possession of his last plays, ending in terrible despair, that between the artist prepared to sacrifice everything for his art and the accusing spectre of manhood, rising from the depths to shake a gaunt fist, who announced that this so-called proud sacrifice had been nothing but slow murder. From this fearfully divided self, these conflicts and tensions, come the unusual density and depth of his finest plays, especially *The Wild Duck*, *Rosmersholm* (in many respects his masterpiece), *The*

Master Builder. It is this terrific pressure from within, finding some relief in his art, that compelled him to reveal more than other nineteenth-century dramatists had done, to suggest to his audiences the misty and often sinister borderland between consciousness and the unconscious, turning himself into a prophet in the Theatre of the depth psychology that was soon to invade the clinics, a Freudian before Freud, a Jungian before Jung. This helps to explain, in part, what seems to us now the astonishing antagonism his work first aroused, the wild abuse hurled at him. It was not so much his social criticism, his attacks on hypocritical bourgeois, his defence of rebellious wives, and the rest, that made critics and playgoers exclaim how repulsive and disgusting his dramas were. Often such people must have been made to feel uncomfortable, disturbed in some fashion they could not name, by these revelations of the hidden sides and depths of personality, just as later the same kind of people, feeling equally un-comfortable, angrily denied the discoveries of the psycho-analysts. There is, however, another reason why so many critics and playgoers disliked Ibsen. They were accustomed to finding in the Theatre playwrights who dealt largely in humour and charm. Now it cannot be denied that Ibsen, both as a dramatist and a man, was lacking in humour and charm. Genius though he was—and of that there can be no question—he was a curiously unlovable man, who for the most part shows us curiously unlovable people. (Though some allowance here must be made for inadequate translation.) It is not simply that they are unhappy, for, after all, Ibsen was not writing cheerful comedies, but that it seems impossible that most of them could ever have been happy, in spite of what they may say. They may reveal depth of personality, but for the creations of a master dramatist they are too often wanting in breadth of personality (not how-ever in *The Wild Duck*, which at moments seems to be anticipating Chehov), without the sudden glow and unexpected glints, the light together with the shade, of fully-rounded characters. Though the later plays especially are filled with imagery, largely symbolic, drawn from the fiords and the mountains, the changing sea and the rushing white streams, they still often seem to us to be taking place in an atmosphere of stuffy gloom. Finally, it must be accepted that Ibsen's earlier and more polemical plays, *Pillars of Society*, *A Doll's House*, *Ghosts*, storm-centres of enthusiasm and violent protest in the last century, have now largely faded into period pieces.

But his great dramas, to which the years only bring more significance, will keep their place in the World Theatre, and indeed may soon reach gigantic new audiences through television, a medium that does less harm to Ibsen than it does to most major dramatists. He gave to the Theatre an *appearance* of strict realism—for that is what his method amounted to— while doing something far more important, namely, giving prose drama the density and depth, the penetration into the recesses of personality, that we associate with poetry, and so transforming, enriching, ennobling, the modern playhouse.

4

The odds were heavily against its happening, yet no sooner had Ibsen established himself as the master dramatist of the age than another genius arrived, also from the North, this time from Sweden. He was August Strindberg. It has been said—and it is a surprising story when we remember Ibsen's opinion of himself—that one day the ageing Norwegian pointed at a portrait of Strindberg, twenty-one years his junior, and called him "One greater than I". It is too early, even now, to decide if Ibsen was right or not. What is certain is that in spite of their difference in years, temperament, outlook, each owed something to the other, for Strindberg could hardly have written *The Father* or *Miss Julie* without the example of Ibsen before him, and the last plays of Ibsen show definite traces of Strindberg's influence. Unlike Ibsen, Strindberg, who was astonishingly copious, did not confine himself to the Theatre but poured out novels, volumes of autobiography, essays and treatises; and in Sweden he is regarded as a great all-round man of letters, as important outside the drama as he is inside it. But though some of his books—especially such frank memoirs as *The Confessions of a Fool* and *The Inferno*—are widely known outside Sweden, he owes his international reputation almost entirely to his plays. Europe has plenty of novelists and autobiographers as good as Strindberg was, whatever the Swedish verdict may be, but in the Theatre he is recognised to be one of the rare masters. Nevertheless, even now, with the possible exception of *The Father*, his plays are neglected rather than over-performed, at least outside Scandinavia; and as yet our Western Theatre has not experienced the full impact of his tremendous two-part tragedy, *The Dance of Death*, or seen, outside a few little experimental theatres, his expressionist *Dream Play* and *Spook Sonata*. While we have gone on producing Ibsen's earlier and weaker plays past the point where they began to 'date' and to fade, we have not yet caught up with Strindberg, even though no sound critic of the drama doubts his genius.

He may not have been the solid master builder that Ibsen was, but it could be argued that he possessed, or was possessed by, a more natural genius for the drama. In his various confessions and semi-autobiographical fiction, he often seems half-mad or cranky and absurd. But he responds at once to the discipline of the Theatre, and is able to appear successfully and severely realistic or creatively experimental in his method, just as he pleases. The strange elements are still there, often casting sinister shadows, but the dramatist himself is masterly, fully in control of whatever the stage demands. No doubt the sheer objectivity of the Theatre—and he came in the end to create a small Intimate Theatre of his own—balanced his own extreme subjectivity, compelled this dangerously introverted man to reach towards extroversion, affording him some relief from his menacing one-sidedness, so close to insanity. It is significant that after his worst breakdown, in the Nineties, while still not entirely free from persecution mania and hallucinations, he moved instinctively towards the Theatre, beginning the vast trilogy, *The Road to Damascus*, that carries him out of naturalism into his more subjective, mystical-symbolical drama, and experiments, of which we cannot appreciate even yet the full effect. What seems a limitation to many writers in the Theatre, the fact that the dramatist cannot speak directly for himself but must devise an action and characters to represent him, steadied and strengthened this writer, who may have been saved from the madhouse by the playhouse.

If he had been born in another age, even after the same unhappy childhood and youth, Strindberg might have found, within the religious framework of the age, the security, peace of mind and heart, enduring sanctions, that he required so desperately, and for which he sought in the huge muddle of scientific materialism, alchemy, Nietzschean prophecy, Swedenborgianism, Old Testament morality, pseudo-mystical chemistry, fortune-telling and superstition that his own age offered him. He seems to go roaring his approval, then screaming his disappointment, through all the movements of the time. And that mysterious borderland between consciousness and the unconscious which Ibsen discovered in his later plays was where Strindberg mainly lived, never entirely leaving it throughout all his angry journeyings. He was an Ibsen with the door off the unconscious, and out of its darkness came the muttering rumours of vast conspiracies against him, the figures of strange persecutors, the sweet-smiling, infinitely seductive, yet terrible image of Woman. In the Japanese Puppet Theatre there is a mask of a girl, her face as smooth and innocent as an egg, that can be instantly transformed into a grinning and ghastly horned demon. This was Strindberg's idea of women, not persons belonging to the opposite sex but angels turning into devils. So he was one of those unhappy men who cannot live with women and cannot live without them. It was inevitable that his three marriages should be unhappy; a man cannot settle down cosily with a creature who is turning into a persecuting demon. Those of us who have received long letters from strangers suffering from persecution mania have often been astonished by the extraordinarily elaborate ingenuity with which these deluded persons explain the ramifications of the plots to kidnap or poison them. And in those plays in which he shows us a wife destroying a husband, Strindberg, using a naturalistic method, displays the same almost diabolical ingenuity. Technically *The Father* is a marvel; we are compelled to believe in the trap that is slowly closing round the doomed Captain; so that when we arrive at the appalling scene in which the old Nurse tricks him into wearing the strait-jacket—a scene difficult to play but when properly played perhaps the most harrowing in all modern drama—we still suspend our disbelief. Both in this play and in the later, more elaborate and subtle *Dance of Death*, the victim is a military man, representing masculinity at its extreme of simple decency, sense of duty and honour, on the positive side, and, on the negative, all its obtuseness and wooden rigidity. And though consciously he makes Woman the villain of the piece, the unconscious feminine element in the dramatist, feeding his desire to create at all, is always triumphant.

To us outside Sweden, Strindberg seems strongest in the Theatre when he is not in the middle region of his historical and national plays but at one end or the other of his dramatic territory, in the naturalistic technique and apparent realism—a wonderful conjuring trick, this—of *The Father* and *Miss Julie* (that powerful and most subtle little play, in which the class war is superimposed upon the sex war, as it was later at times by D. H. Lawrence), or, at the other extreme, in his final experiments, designed for his own theatre, *The Dream Play* and *The Spook Sonata*. Here—and on the whole more successfully in the more original second play—we have completely realistic scenes blended with highly subjective drama, taking place in the inner world of vague associations, premonitions, hopes out of time and fears beyond space, archetypal joys and griefs, and those fateful coincidences that Jung has called 'synchronicity'. The severely, perhaps coarsely, objective character of the drama, which, however it is written, has to be performed by solid, flesh-and-blood actors on a stage to several hundred people who know their names and may be taking supper with them, challenges the creative imagination and technical skill of all the more ambitious modern dramatists, who long to turn this stubbornly objective medium into the magic slave-of-the-ring of the highly subjective life they wish to report and display. Strindberg's replies to this challenge are not only among the first and boldest but must be regarded as perhaps the most successful, and certainly the most widely influential, of what may be (our Theatre being what it is) attempts at the impossible. In his frantic search for God, down all manner of crazy by-ways, in his angel-demon attitude towards Woman, in his bewildering and unattractive oscillations between monstrous arrogance and self-pity (though it is worth remembering that during his final years in Sweden his children visited him daily, obviously out of affection, not duty), Strindberg may seem merely a grotesque figure; but in the Theatre, where so many conscientious and respected writers display nothing but minor talent and industry, he has genius: he was—and still is, for we must not imagine we are ahead of him yet—a master.

5

The third master came from Russia: Anton Chehov. Now it is true that Chehov was born in 1860, four years after Bernard Shaw, who is reserved for our next section; and that his *Three Sisters* and *The Cherry Orchard* even take us out of the nineteenth century. (*The Cherry Orchard*, his masterpiece, was produced in the year of his death, 1904.) Nevertheless, his place is here, as Shaw's is not. He belongs to this age, not the next, and, in the drama even more than in its fiction, he is one of its most original and gifted sons, and perhaps the most lovable of all. His early death, arriving just after he had at last reached complete maturity as a dramatist, was a stroke of the bitterest ill-luck for the modern Theatre. During the last forty years he must have had more performances outside Russia than all the other Russian dramatists put together. In Moscow he is of course the possession of the famous Art Theatre, which, chiefly through the efforts of the actor-director Stanislavsky, arrived at a method of staging and playing Chehov that brought his drama to life. A similar relation with the Maly Theatre had been previously established by Ostrovsky, who demanded a new and more realistic style of production and performance for his lively satirical comedies about the merchant class or a serious play like *The Storm*, which should have had more productions in Western Europe than it has had. Tolstoy, with his *Power of Darkness* and *The Fruits of Enlightenment*, preceded Chehov in the Theatre, but though Chehov regarded him with admiration and the warmest affection, he made no attempt to imitate him. We know from Chehov's letters what he felt about Turgenev's novels—delighting in many of their episodes, but finding the women in them false and tiresome—but how far he was directly influenced by Turgenev's play, *A Month in the Country*, we do not know. But a likeness is there, more than a hint of the dramatic method Chehov was to perfect nearly half a century later. Yet we can safely say that Chehov, not making all manner of experiments like Strindberg but bringing one method to perfection in his maturity, is perhaps the most startlingly original dramatist of the whole age. So when, in London in 1911, a first and single performance of *The Cherry Orchard* was given, many of the critics drifted away long before it was over, convinced that there was no play here worth their consideration. Highly original masterpieces have a sly trick of pretending to look like failures.

Asking for a ticket to see a Norwegian company visiting Moscow, Chehov, as late as 1903, could add: "You know, Ibsen is my favourite writer." Some allowance must be made for Chehov's cheerful exaggeration, but, even so, this is a surprising statement. For as a dramatist, Chehov might be said to be Ibsen turned upside down and inside out. Indeed, he offers us a reversal of all established dramatic procedure, defying all the theories and text-books of play-construction. Drama, we are told, is created out of the conflict between two or more leading characters, usually rather larger (if simpler) than life, exceptionally single-minded and strong-willed. This central conflict and these familiar stage characters were not to be found in Chehov, which is why conventional critics and their readers imagined for years that he was not troubling to write a play at all. Chehov's characters are not more single-minded and strong-willed than we are; they have, if anything, rather less determination and direct purpose. They are never moving towards some great thundering clash and climax. And not, as Western audiences liked to think, because they are Russians, for Russians are perhaps more given to clashes and climaxes than the rest of us are. This does not mean that there is no characteristically Russian element in Chehov's drama. There is, but it is to be found not in the unconventional and untheatrical construction, but in the swift changes of mood, the tears following the laughter, the laughter the tears, so difficult to reproduce on the stages of Western Europe, where for a long time Chehov's plays were performed slowly and gloomily, as if somebody were dying in the next room. (The absence in Russia of a strong classical tradition, with its formal division into tragedy and comedy, enabled Russian novelists and dramatists to feel at ease in this swiftly changing, laughter-and-tears atmosphere, in which, anyhow, the Slav temperament is at home.) But the lack of single-mindedness, purpose, will, strong action, in Chehov is personal to him, is deliberately contrived by his dramatic method, which offers us a new kind of theatrical experience.

It is not a question of realism. Chehov does not come any closer to imitating real life than Ibsen and Strindberg do. Indeed, while he is still feeling his way, until he arrives at the triumph of his method in *The Cherry Orchard*, he takes more risks of appearing artificial or descending into bathos than they do in their naturalistic plays. In *The Seagull* and *Uncle Vanya* he is sometimes nearly off the tightrope he is walking; and even in *The Three Sisters* there are a few moments of danger. But by refusing to heighten his characters and fix them into a decisive action he is able to do several things that make his drama original and, in spite of his wide influence and many imitators, still unique. Thus, by avoiding tight construction, by keeping his action fluid, he is able to allow his characters, not a few of them but almost all of them, to reveal themselves in a score of different ways and at many levels. He is able to suggest the complexity and richness of life, all its overtones and undertones. He is the opposite of those adroit but unsatisfactory playwrights whose characters appear to be at odds with one another in an empty world. Though written in prose, Chehov's drama is essentially poetic. But its poetry, far removed from the heroic and epic style, is not in his people and what they do and say but in the depth and richness of the atmosphere and life in which they seem to move like fish in glimmering, green, purple-shadowed water. Each play and indeed, as he improved and enriched his method, each act of a play—as in the four beautifully contrasted scenes of *The Cherry Orchard*—has its own rich atmosphere. And there in place of the usual sharply contrived action, provoking curiosity and excitement, we have a continual unforced revelation of character, an organised rhythm of mood, a growing intimacy of feeling with the people and an understanding, deepened by emotion, of their world, as if we had shared their experience. So once we have seen *The Cherry Orchard* several times, produced with the care it demands, we almost begin to feel we were actually there when Mme. Ranevsky, Anya, Charlotta and Yasha arrived so late from Paris or when they all left the darkening house except the forgotten old Fiers.

A doctor—and the doctor in Chehov was never completely driven out by the writer—catches a great many people when their pretences and defences are down. No man is a hero to his doctor. Now Dr. Chehov had a sharp eye, an unflinching sense of the truth, much humour, and a tender heart. And what is finally communicated to us by his drama, which represents a much greater and more highly original achievement than his short stories, good though they are, because the medium is so much more obstinate and difficult, is an immense brooding tenderness, unequalled by any other modern dramatist, and all the more remarkable because it never lapses into sentimentality. (He can be played sentimentally, as he often is outside Russia, but this is wrong and is often due to the influence of Western drama that cannot arrive at this tenderness without sentimentality.) The tears in Chehov are not weak tears. The conception of him as a lachrymose, semi-decadent, sentimentally nostalgic writer, mooning over failures, misfits, useless persons, is utterly mistaken. He does not shrink from terrible ironies, pitiless truth. His humour has a cutting edge. (Young authors, avid for popularity and success, should turn to Trigorin's revealing speech on this subject in his scene with Nina in Act Two of *The Seagull*.) And though his drama, with its scenes composed like so many scherzos and nocturnes, should not be regarded as so much realism—and Bunin, who came from a landowning family, declared in his memoirs that *The Cherry Orchard* was wildly unreal, ridiculous—his plays sink deep roots into the Russia of his time. They make us feel with our hearts, and not merely understand with our heads, the emptiness and boredom of existence in Serebrakoff's remote country place or in the little garrison town of the three sisters; the bewilderment and helplessness of Mme. Ranevsky and her brother, Gaev, who are aware deep-down that their class and whole manner of life are coming to an end, as the axe falls on the cherry trees and the harpstring breaks in the sky; and finally, somewhere behind the autumnal sad quiet, the rumbling of discontent, the straining and cracking that will make revolution inevitable, the sudden cries of rebellious hopeful youth, a Trofimov, half fool, half prophet, proclaiming: "All Russia is our orchard." But even when all this is old history, when the plays may be performed in theatres overshadowed by tenements and factories two thousand feet high, within walls insulated against the thunder and glare of moon-rockets, so long as all minds are not deadened and hearts not armoured in plastic and high-duty alloys, this drama of Chehov's, so rich in atmosphere, so revealing and subtle in its changing moods, so funny and sad, so wise and tender, will bring its smiles, its tears.

And now, with Chehov dying in 1904, just ten years before the world clapped on its now-familiar mask of murder, the age is well over, though not, as we shall see, done with; and if we have been careless about strict chronology, we have at least brought this section of the tale to a close, not with one of its greatest figures, the novelists casting longer shadows than the dramatists, but certainly with one of the most lovable writers of his time and ours.

PART FIVE

The Moderns

19 Background to the Books   301

20 Mostly before 1914   336

21 Brief Interlude   370

22 Between the Wars   376

CHAPTER NINETEEN

Background to the Books

I

IN 1892, a French civil engineer resigned his post under the *Ministre des Ponts et Chaussées*, having decided to retire at the early age of forty-five. He had read widely and now, having already produced one book, he needed more time for writing. Here, it would seem, in M. Georges Sorel, the engineer, the retired government official with his pension, decoration, little villa, was the perfect representative of the stuffy petty-bourgeois class. Moreover, unlike many of his type, he was devoted to his wife, who died a few years after his retirement; he was extremely respectable, and indeed something of a Puritan. But what is it that distinguishes and serves to unite, in their variety and inconsistency, the books he wrote? First, a contemptuous rejection of all the accepted values, creeds, institutions of the age. Secondly, raging behind all his arguments and pronouncements, a lust to destroy, to bring the whole age to a violent end. Thirdly, after the state and all traditional culture had vanished in smoke and dust, the desire to create—on one level by an act of will, on another level by offering the mass of men a new myth—an era of vast productiveness, of triumphant technicians and busy workers, untroubled and no longer deceived by any idea, religious, philosophical, cultural, social, that had clouded men's minds in the past. This suggests Communism, but in fact Sorel, whose influence was stronger in Italy than it was in France, came nearer to arguing Fascism into existence.

What is important here, however, is not what Sorel accepted or rejected in Marx or Nietzsche, Proudhon or Bergson; not his belief in the Syndicalist class war and the General Strike and whatever violence might follow it; not his more profoundly intuitive understanding of what can be achieved by a combination of brute power and a sustaining myth. What is important here, especially when we remember how much ruin and misery he helped indirectly to produce for our own age, is the state of mind, the whole psychological condition, of this respectable, retired civil servant and engineer. For this was no outcast, wanting to destroy society because it would not accept him, not one of the proletarians whom he told to seize power and then wreck everything. He was an outwardly successful member of the class whose whole way of life, institutions, education, culture, he wished to destroy once and for all. And if he showed, as he did, a reckless disregard for the consequences of violent revolution and of war between powerful modern states, if he seemed indifferent to the suffering they would produce, that was because there was behind all his polemics and conscious thinking, roaring up from the unconscious, this urge towards violence, this rage to destroy. All the time he had been measuring and taking notes and reporting to his superiors at the Ministry, had been quietly moving towards his pension, red ribbon, early retirement, had appeared to be a typical bourgeois official of the Third Republic, the corrosive acid had been boiling in the dark of his mind. Behind the mask of smiling or anxious conformity, he believed nothing he heard, nothing he read. The liberal democracy, the easy bourgeois way of life, which he appeared to represent, he saw as so much doomed imbecility, to be violently destroyed by the workers as a man might wring the neck of a diseased chicken. If his outward life was one-sided, so, at the opposite extreme, was his inner life, in its furious lust of destruction, its refusal to measure and weigh and consider the consequences. There was nothing in him, nor in the universe as he understood it, to balance these opposites; no integrating principle. God was dead, as Nietzsche had declared; and Man, alone and responsible, was busy cheating himself. So bring the whole edifice of religion, philosophy, culture, education, crashing down; make way for the new myth; let the Life-Force, whose creatures we are, shape the masses, rebellious and triumphant, as it wills and pleases. And already we can hear the dictators screaming at their hypnotised mobs, see the bonfires of books, and catch the stench of concentration camps. Our own age has arrived.

It is true that Sorel was an exceptional man. But he was only exceptional in his wide reading, his ability to express himself, fluently if not happily, his bitter insights. What was behind all this, in varying degrees of disgust and anger, was not uncommon then, throughout Europe if not in America (still under the spell of its dream of unchallenged democracy and rapid material progress); and soon, as our century advanced, it was to be commoner still. Men felt themselves to be living without purpose, in a society without meaning. What might be accepted consciously was violently rejected unconsciously, in the depths no longer controlled by any symbols of a larger containing life, a life in which the individual felt himself to be unique, a complete and responsible person. The great collectives, whether political or industrial empires, began to grow at the expense of common men's feeling of individuality, personal responsibility, spirit. And as this conscious feeling was lost, frustration and anger and a desire for violence for its own sake piled up and smouldered in the unconscious. All of which at least goes some way to explain why this century of ours, which has talked more about peace than any other, has fought the most terrible wars known to history; why at the apparent highest levels of its civilisation it has brought back torture, committed itself to mass murder, and used its concentration of power and its technical skill not to broaden men's freedom but to cancel liberties already won. It is the great age of saying one thing and doing another, of grim realities ironically commenting upon smooth and pious platitudes. "Here's richness!" cried Mr. Squeers (of Dickens's Dotheboys Hall), smacking his lips as he handed his wretched pupils their watered milk. It is the twentieth century congratulating its citizens on their freedom, opportunity, richly satisfying way of life.

For the most part the ideas, born of a growing *malaise*, belonged to the previous age, the nineteenth century; and what our own age did was to translate these ideas into history, to turn these dramatic sketches into dramas of actuality on a vast scale. There were, of course, some gains: the improved conditions of employment, public health, housing, general education; but as industrial populations rapidly increased, together with the urban areas they occupied, there were more and more frustrating exchanges of primary time-old satisfactions, which strengthen a man's sense of himself as a person, for secondary satisfactions, so much convenience and comfort and amusement: it is like a man bartering an affectionate wife and family, a company of friends, a place in society, for a motor car, a washing machine and a cine-camera. It is these industrial and urban people, as we saw in Part Four, who became 'the masses', the dark mob without names and faces, lurking round the edge of the lighted drama, a vast unrehearsed chorus without a part written for it. They are still on the scene, though healthier and better-dressed, when this new age takes over; writers are even more aware of their presence; and Gustave Le Bon has already published his study of the popular mind, *The Crowd*, to be reprinted everywhere in edition after edition; and, after thirty years, the Spanish philosopher, Ortega y Gasset, brings out his *Revolt of the Masses*. But if 'masses' is more than an idle term, does there already exist, as a product of the growth of population and the spread of the industrial-urban environment, a 'mass-man', who might have been imagined by Sorel? And if he does exist, how will he behave, what will he do, this new sort of man? For if he has been so ruthlessly conditioned, is such a finished product of whatever 'mass' may mean, that he is no longer a whole person, entirely human, then, when he finally asserts himself, what will happen to everything necessary to sustain complete humanity, whole persons? On the other hand, if 'masses' and 'mass' merely refer to fellow-men and women living in unfavourable conditions, almost compelled to be faceless and nameless, then it is likely that deep feelings of frustration and resentment must soon rise in such people to an explosive point, to produce even more violence and destruction than Sorel dreamed of or that we in this century have already known. If, then, 'masses' and 'mass' have any meaning at all, is the end human product of the age to be a docile sub-man, perhaps sooner or later too stupid to attend the machines that satisfy his desires, or a man feeling so furiously and deeply frustrated that he is ready to welcome, unconsciously if not consciously, an apocalypse of destruction, whole continents turned to radio-active dust? And this is no mere rhetorical question. It comes home to us and demands an answer. For while it is understandable that political and military leaders, neurotic or too busy and weary to think, should have accepted nuclear weapons and various other monstrous devices, the unprotesting acceptance of such things by the bulk of their people, the so-called 'masses', with nothing to gain and so much to lose, is a fact of great significance. Is it docility and stupidity or frustration and angry despair? Has the sub-man arrived—or the avenger?

These questions, however, take us past the limit set for this final age, which must be separated from us by some years, otherwise writers in their teens, books still warm from the binders, will be demanding consideration. The end term must be clearly marked, so we will put it at 1939, going no further than the outbreak of the Second World War. This will leave us with forty years or so, years packed with authors, piled high with books. And we must come closer, to examine in more detail the background to these books.

2

The nineteenth century produced the ideas that, after some modifying and vulgarising, our own century has transformed into action and history. And indeed there is one curious feature of our age that sets it apart from other ages. In spite of its prodigious and ever-increasing activity in the teaching of philosophy and in general philosophical writing, owing much to the spread of university education (especially in America), it is an age that has failed to produce one of those philosophers, a Hegel for the student of philosophy, a Schopenhauer for men of letters and their readers, whose thought and world-view, *Weltanschauung*, have fascinated and dominated it. The place of any such philosophy and world-view, many people will tell us, has been taken by Science, which throughout our age has made such astonishing progress. (It has also changed so many of its hypotheses that Whitehead, in his last years, could declare that everything he had been taught in his youth was now held to be wrong.) But Science, which works by abstracting what it needs from total reality, is a method, not a philosophy broadening into a world-review. And though professional philosophers had multiplied, grappling with all manner of problems most zealously, not one of them was accepted by the age as its chief guide, its supreme wise man. Just when men needed a contemporary world-view, apparently there was not one to be had. And what was to be had, so far as it could be understood, was not what most men felt they needed.

There were, however, some important influences, especially in the earlier years of this age. One of them was provided by Henri Bergson, a brilliant stylist and personality—his lectures in Paris became fashionable events—but a difficult thinker, who has not had many disciples inside philosophy but a great many, of a much vaguer sort, outside it. Sorel, as we have seen, took something from him, chiefly the idea of a driving creative will, now the hero and not, as in Schopenhauer, the villain of the piece; and Shaw's conception of the ever-experimenting Life-Force was partly borrowed from Bergson, who also supplied Marcel Proust, a relative as well as an admirer, with the idea, essential to his great novel, of two kinds of time. And there were many others, particularly in the years between 1900 and the First World War, who used Bergson to reinforce Nietzsche, the great irrationalist. True reality, in Bergson's view, is an endless becoming, an unceasing flow and flux, that can be perceived and understood only by intuition, and not by the inferior function of intellect, compelled to halt the flow, to abstract something static from it, in order to analyse it. With the immense development of Science, its method triumphant everywhere, it was inevitable that there should be a reaction, on behalf of a richer appreciation of reality, against the abstracting and analysing intellect, taking the butterfly out of the air and presenting it lifeless and dismembered. But intellect and reason should not have been thought to be synonymous. To challenge the supremacy of intellect is not to abandon reason, which may be called upon to justify the challenge. In our ordinary life, especially if we need advice, we have no difficulty in distinguishing between a highly intellectual man and a soundly rational man. What is unintellectual or even anti-intellectual—a poem, for example—is not necessarily irrational. But perhaps because Bergson's intoxicating military metaphors, his galloping armies, his shells bursting into more shells, were more easily appreciated than his ideas about space-time and real time or duration, his influence encouraged a kind of reckless irrationality, favouring irresponsible action, a 'damn the consequences' attitude of mind, both in public and private life, with some results we already know. Some of the sharpest criticism of these irrational tendencies also came from France, in Julien Benda's *La Trahison des clercs* (known in its English translation as *The Great Betrayal*) and some earlier works. But we cannot leave Bergson without mentioning his attempt to explain the Comic in *Laughter* (*Le Rire*); an admirable entertainment in itself, this little work, but an inadequate explanation of the Comic, which Bergson discovers, too narrowly, in whatever is mechanical, automatic, rigid, inflexible, in human life. But this can be terrible as well as comical; and Humour, as distinct from the unfeeling or satirical Comic, certainly demands a wider definition.

Another outbreak of what most contemporary philosophers see and condemn as anti-rationalism came from the other side of the Atlantic. It was associated with C. S. Peirce, John Dewey, and William James, the psychologist and brother of Henry James, the novelist. (Was it Jowett, Master of Balliol, who said: "The psychology of William James is all fiction; the fiction of Henry James is all psychology"?) As William James's contribution, which he called pragmatism, is the best-known, we can confine ourselves to him. An unusually energetic, enthusiastic, attractive figure, he did magnificent pioneer work in several different territories of the mind. (His study, *The Varieties of Religious Experience*, is a masterpiece.) Sharing any active man's suspicion of, and distaste for, "a block universe", the creation once and for all of an immovable, unwinking Absolute, believing in his heart, as most of us do, that Man must do as well as he can in a vast mysterious universe of which only a tiny part has been revealed to him, that he has to act, however incomplete his knowledge of fundamental truth may be, James declared in effect that any idea may be held to be true if it works, that is, if it helps men to live wisely and happily. Naturally other philosophers have severely condemned this doctrine because its general acceptance would put philosophy, as a truth-discovering activity, out of business. Moreover, although this pragmatic view may do no harm when it is held by a man with the integrity and generous altruism of a William James, it is capable of doing much mischief among men who care nothing for truth and the facts, but merely want to justify any line of action they would like to take. If an idea can be assumed to be true just because it enables us to do what we want to do, we have soon left philosophy behind and are in a world of lying propaganda. Which is where the age, once pragmatism was debased to this level, soon found itself, as we know now only too well. But the eager and noble-hearted William James, dying in 1910, did not live to see what happened when the decent coinage of his radical empiricism, his philosophy of action, came to be minted by forgers and cheats; nobody would have been more shocked.

He was shocked earlier, we are told, by the attitude of mind of his Harvard colleague, the Spanish-American George Santayana, who made his own and very elaborate criticism of and reply to the irrational movement in the five volumes of his *Life of Reason*, in which, however, he makes plain what he considers to be the limits of human reason. A Catholic by his upbringing and a sceptic by temperament, Santayana recognises the elements of myth and symbol in religion, but somehow fails to appreciate their depth and emotional force, and removes himself so far from them that he seems like a man who would go to church merely to smell the incense. At his best an exquisite stylist, he is happiest not in the cut-and-thrust of metaphysical debate, to which his style does not lend itself, but in his own kind of philosophical reverie, a prolonged meditation. His *Soliloquies in England* is an enchanting book; but there is nothing in his careful verse or in his one novel, *The Last Puritan*, in spite of the praise it received and its large sale, to make us believe that in him a creative writer was lost to philosophy.

Benedetto Croce, whose long and useful career as an Italian Liberal and educationalist deserves our warmest praise, whatever we may think of his philosophy, must be mentioned here because his theory of æsthetics was much discussed just before and for some years after the First War. (The article on 'Æsthetics' in the fourteenth edition of the *Encyclopaedia Britannica* is his work.) His theory is based on the identity of what he calls 'intuition' and 'expression', but the latter, with him, does not involve communication. Because we fail to distinguish between these two, he tells us, there "arise the confusions between *art* and *technique*. Technique is not an intrinsic element of art but has to do precisely with the concept of communication". And now, he adds, we are out of æsthetics and into 'practical action'. Clearly he is entitled to set what limits he pleases to his æsthetics, and to tell us that what he calls 'art' does not recognise technique as an intrinsic element; but most of us will continue to believe that a work of art is what the artist has actually made, using some technique or other, and that an intuition-expression, really (as he admits when he describes a painter at work) a pre-existing image of what might be made, is not a work of art. An artist is the man who has the intuition-expression plus the necessary technique of communication. Moreover, this technique of communication, though it need not be strictly governed by rules, as Croce rightly saw, at least must come within some accepted convention, on which art, no matter what grand proclamations we make about it, must depend. So a Chinese composer might be inspired by a magnificent intuition-expression, a Ninth Symphony of gongs and drums, but it would never reach us. Nor does Croce seem to understand that a lover of pictures is not only fascinated by the personalities of great painters and what happened in their minds, but is also fascinated by the whole odd but miraculous business of putting paint on canvas, itself a source of wonder and joy to him.

Croce's theory of æsthetics, like his general philosophy, was not regarded with much respect by his fellow-philosophers or the tough-minded critics of art and literature. (He is contemptuously dismissed in a footnote by I. A. Richards in his *Principles of Literary Criticism*, first published in 1925, and a work of much authority among younger critics, at least in England and America.) But all the talk about Croce in so many universities was not without result. Simplified versions of his theory had a considerable effect for some years upon literary criticism. They loosened it and made it less pedantic. They discouraged scholarly critics from continuing the weary old task of trying to define the Sublime, the Tragic, the Epic, and so forth. They made nonsense of any surviving notion that it was the business of criticism to apply certain rules. They suggested that the critic, before dismissing a work because it seemed so new and strange, so unlike other admired writing, should ask himself to discover what the writer had had in mind and had attempted to do. This made criticism more flexible, more sympathetic, more immediately appreciative of originality and experiment. The creative writer, whose primary intuition-expression, on this theory, was itself art, was to be thoroughly understood before being judged. The critic was encouraged to see himself, not as the representative of society who would approve or disapprove of the work offered to it by the author, but as the privileged first receiver of the original intuition-expression, who would then explain it to the reader. He became, so to speak, the experimental and difficult writer's impresario. This change of attitude, which both gained something and lost something, as we shall see, helps to explain much of what happened to literature in the 1920s. And Croce and his æsthetics played some part in this change.

At this same time, from the Germany of defeat, wild inflation, and the ruin of the old middle-class, there came the despairing voice of Oswald Spengler, announcing that our civilisation was doomed, like seven others before it, whatever we did. As an historian of culture, he was quickly challenged and discredited, but we must not follow the example of the scholars who, after riddling his *Decline of the West*, dismissed him too easily. The book's wide success, however brief it may have been, was significant. Not only was Spengler's pessimism infectious but he left behind him, like poison in the flour-bin, an uneasy feeling that the whole civilisation of the West was more than merely insecure, that perhaps it had heard already, from behind some veil, a final judgment, a sentence of death. So perhaps only the violent extremists, Left or Right, who had rejected any idea of liberal democracy and gradual progress, could save Western civilisation. Or, if they could not, if it were inevitably doomed, then why still attempt any restraint and balance, why not recklessly indulge every passion and prejudice? This mood helped to shape and colour the Thirties. Ten years after Spengler had published his *Decline of the West*, when his later work attracted little attention outside Germany and his name was hardly ever mentioned, his legacy of despair had not been exhausted, his influence was still in the air, favouring one extreme or the other; and that is why he warrants a mention here.

Another and far deeper influence, narrowly national at first but reaching out over the years, was that of Miguel de Unamuno, poet and scholar, novelist and philosopher, Basque by birth but long accepted as the voice of Spain. The work that is best-known outside Spain and that has contributed most to this influence, *The Tragic Sense of Life* (*Del Sentimiento trágico de la vida*), was first published in 1912, but it was during the Twenties that various translations of it made their way across Europe and to the United States. Contemptuous of mere debate and the familiar polemical devices, Unamuno writes with the passion of a poet, as "a man of flesh and bone". He sees man, the real man, the individual, not the abstract figure of progress reports and statistics, as being for ever aware of death, and hungering, down to the remotest depths of his being, for immortality. This is man as he really is, no matter what the Renaissance, the Reformation, the political and industrial revolutions, may seem to have brought him. Man's analytical intellect, his critical reason, only strengthen the denial of what his essential individuality demands against all argument, the conquest of death, eternal life. It is this terrible division in him, this endless war between reason and faith, that brings a man a tragic sense of life, and on this dark but secure foundation he can begin to build, despair and agony rising to compassion, compassion to a love of all who share the same hunger and suffering, love to a God who must return it. Unamuno's approach to his theme, by way of death, is very Spanish, like his insistence upon the individual "man of flesh and bone", but always he makes use of his knowledge of many literatures to draw upon all the resources of European culture; and although his reputation outside Spain still falls far below the immense prestige of his name among Spanish writers and readers, he is unquestionably a figure of world literature. The extent of his influence is difficult to estimate, even if we allow him some share in the Catholic gains between the Wars, but that it existed in his lifetime, and has if anything increased since his death in 1936, cannot be denied.

The philosophy belonging to and characteristic of this age came first from Cambridge University, before the First War, and then later, after the War, from Vienna. The two Cambridge men who rebelled against subjective idealism and ended the long reign of Hegel were G. E. Moore and Bertrand Russell. Though we have no concern here with their highly technical theories of epistemology—even if we halt for a moment to applaud their return to something like common-sense, their insistence that objects enjoy an independent reality, that, in Moore's phrase, trains do not have wheels only when they are in stations—Moore and Russell are important to us for two quite different reasons. Moore was anything but a system-builder; he was a highly efficient demolisher of systems; and his scepticism, his sharply critical intelligence, his easy and pleasant style of exposition, so rare among philosophers since the eighteenth century, may be discovered, and enjoyed by the general reader, in his *Principia Ethica*. With his "states of mind", his ultimate goods reduced to the appreciation of beauty and personal relationships, his particular combination of realistic scepticism and what might be called æsthetic humanism created a certain attitude towards life among his admiring students; and as these included the influential Maynard Keynes, brilliant economist and patron of the arts, and Lytton Strachey, whose criticism and diabolically clever biographies reveal this attitude; and because, through Keynes and Strachey, he influenced the whole of the so-called 'Bloomsbury Group' and some original and distinguished English writing between the Wars, G. E. Moore cannot be ignored.

Bertrand Russell offers the greatest possible contrast to his friend Moore. Instead of remaining in Cambridge, he has been everywhere, including prison. (He was an aggressive pacifist during the First World War.) He has in his own supremely honourable career reversed the whole trend of twentieth-century philosophy. He has left the study and the lecture theatre, after doing his share of the world's work in mathematics, symbolic logic, critical epistemology, for the forum and the marketplace. He has been a philosopher in the broadest sense as well as being one in the more fashionable, narrowest sense. There seem to be two quite different Bertrand Russells: one, the earlier, a Cambridge superintellectual grinding his idea of truth to a bitter sharp edge, half sardonic, half despairing; the other, mellowing with the years, taking over a family inheritance of public service and liberalism, determined to use his immense knowledge, his searching intelligence and wit, his moral courage that seemed to develop a cavalier gaiety the more it was tested, on behalf of a spirit of free enquiry, to challenge every form of tyranny, to keep Western society liberal and humane. So in addition to his many philosophical works, he has given us various historical and social studies, such as his *Freedom and Organisation, 1814–1914, Power, The Prospects of Industrial Civilisation*, and popular essays, like his *Conquest of Happiness* and *In Praise of Idleness*, a strange subject for a writer so indefatigably productive. We may believe, no matter how wittily persuasive we find him, that Russell is too rational and seriously undervalues the irrational elements in our life and their effect upon us, so that at times we feel we are back in the world of John Stuart Mill; but only bigotry and fanaticism could prevent our admiring both what he has done and the spirit that has sustained the work.

There is, however, something else that forbids any appreciation of writing of this kind, and that is academic snobbery. Philosophers who wish to keep their reputation, it holds, should not attempt to expound philosophy to the general reading public. Nor should they, because they are philosophers, write on social, political and other topics. A philosopher must not be a philosopher in the older and still popular sense of the term; he must not make a public appearance as a wise man, or, if this is more than he would claim, as a rational and disinterested thinker, freer of passion and prejudice than most men. He is straying outside his 'field'. (The less adventurous the professors are, the more we hear about their various 'fields', as if they were grazing there.) He runs the risk, in search of applause, of vulgarising his subject. So it is said, all too often in universities, where men who have taken their knowledge to the public outside have suffered a loss of reputation. And clearly it is a matter of temperament. One learned man would feel helpless outside his study, lecture room, college; another, who cares just as much about his learning, feels it his duty to address the general public. It is absurd for these two to condemn each other. But the condemnation, even if it is only a sneer or a shrug, has been all on one side, where a mask of scholastic purity can hide both timidity and envy; it is against the scholar who accepts the challenge of a wider audience, and with it the task, often a formidable test, of expounding his knowledge in the plainest possible language. We live in an age of easy mass communications, mostly carrying rubbish, and if knowledge and good sense can occasionally make some use of them, then so much the better. And as for tradition, a philosopher like Russell, ready to offer such knowledge, truth, wisdom as he has acquired to all who will read and listen, is closer to the great old tradition of philosophy than the mysterious experts who only communicate with other mysterious experts, offering solutions of problems that only they can understand. This is very much the new style in philosophy.

A group that met in Vienna in the early Twenties, a group mainly composed of scientists and philosophers who had been scientists, broke with all the older philosophies, on behalf of what became known as Logical Positivism. Its chief exponents, notably Schlick, Carnap, Wittgenstein, visited or settled in England and America, where they were able to make many converts among students of philosophy. What the system achieved, in meaning and methodology, as the logic of science that it professed to be, is far removed from anything that concerns literature; but this is not true of its critical and negative side, which is of some importance. For what the logical positivists did in effect was to reject metaphysics and ethics as mere fanciful speculation, because their conclusions were incapable of verification; and to attach what was left of philosophy, after all this old nonsense had been kicked out, to the sciences. As far as they were concerned, any notion of a philosopher as a wise man, offering other men some sort of world-view or anything to live by, was banished for ever. To them a true philosopher, as distinct from some old-fashioned charlatan doing tricks with metaphysics and emotive language, was a kind of engineer of logic, meaning, real linguistics. This may or may not have helped science, but it was not much help to men wondering what to make of a world so busy with scientists and engineers, so noisy too with pronouncements that, in the opinion of this new philosophy, had no meaning. In theory, now that the clear clean truth was out, the world should have been better; but actually, as a place for a bewildered man, hoping for a little guidance, it was worse. The philosopher-as-wise-man, the philosopher-as-guide-and-friend, was a cheat. The dismissal of metaphysics as mere fancy, ethics as a waste of words, left a vacuum, not to be filled by philosophy reduced to a narrow edge and its ally, science. It may be objected that logical positivism is highly technical and difficult, not for the general public. But any doctrine—and especially one that is new, original, and as irreverent and ruthlessly intolerant as any undergraduate would wish it to be—cannot be brilliantly expounded to some of the brightest young men in twenty or thirty universities without having some effect both inside and outside those universities. A certain atmosphere was created, an atmosphere in which much writing and reading came to be done. And many people did not like it, although they may have always felt that the old metaphysical systems were more like works of art than like truthful statements about reality. It was an atmosphere that seemed to narrow and chill the mind.

Before the logical positivists arrived, however, an earlier Vienna, still the capital of the ramshackle old empire, had seen the depth psychologists at work, driving shafts and tunnelling into the mind. Sigmund Freud was the pioneer and leader of the earliest group; Alfred Adler and Gustav Jung broke away from it to form their own groups. By the Twenties, writers who made no pretence of being psycho-analysts were referring to Freud's 'Œdipus complex', Adler's 'Inferiority complex' and 'over-compensation', Jung's 'introversion' and 'extroversion' and his 'collective unconscious' and 'archetypes'. Of these three, it was undoubtedly Freud, with his emphasis on the parent-child relationship and the unconscious sexual drives behind it, who had the widest influence upon writers and readers in this age ending with the Second World War. A certain narrowness and one-sidedness, suggesting a gloomy determinism, did not make it a very inspiring influence; and the Freudian reports of art and literature, which appeared to make no distinction between a creative artist and any dithering neurotic, were far from helpful. Biographers rather than poets, novelists, dramatists, made use of Adler's idea of the ego in its search for power and its trick of over-compensating some early feeling of inferiority. Jung's thought is at once bolder and more subtle; his theory of the collective unconscious and its archetypes; his account of the four functions, thinking, feeling, sensation, intuition, and the Types that result from them; his equation of the integrating principle—transforming the ego, still at the mercy of unconscious drives, into the freed Self—with religious experience: these not only bring him much closer to and in deeper sympathy with art and literature, but also turn him into one of the few great liberating thinkers of the century. But the wide reach and the complexity of his thought, impossible to condense into a few phrases that anybody can repeat, restricted his appeal and influence during most of these years; and it is only from the late Thirties onward that he has begun to be widely studied and admired, especially in Britain, Northern Europe and America. The immediate effect of all this depth psychology, tearing down the façades of self-deception, rationality, purpose and will, revealing the wild circus of the unconscious, was to increase the feelings of bewilderment, helplessness and despair among the educated, who saw in it, outside the clinics, a final assault upon man's dwindling notion of his own dignity. And from this effect the later literature of the age, produced between the Wars, is certainly not free. Much of it was written, we might say, with an imaginary analyst sardonically chuckling behind the writer's back. So, for example, in any work intended for more sophisticated readers, the larger-than-life heroic, in character or theme, was no longer possible. But though the thought takes us beyond our limits, both in time and subject, the final development of this depth psychology took an unexpected and significant turn, as Progoff has made clear in his study of it, *The Death and Rebirth of Psychology*; for each of these chief theorists and practitioners of depth psychology, heavily committed at first to a reductive and analytical method, found himself reaching a dead end, a trap from which he had to escape; and so they were led, in Progoff's words, "to an experience of the spiritual core of man's being, to the seed of personality that unfolds psychologically in each person and yet is more than psychological. They came, in other words, to the metaphysical foundation of life that underlies psychology; and since each one experienced it in a different way, each gave it a different name . . . and each of them referred ultimately to a contact with a larger realm of reality in which man's psychological nature transcends itself. . . ." So the turning wheel seems to bring us within sight and sound again of Unamuno, ignoring all our reports of progress to stare at the great blank face of death, and passionately proclaiming the hunger of "the man of flesh and bone" for immortal life.

3

A French critic has told us that if we can discover what a writer's favourite word is, the word he cannot help using over and over again, it will give us the essential clue to his personality. Now if the first half of this age in literature, the period from the later Nineties until 1914, had consisted of one writer instead of innumerable writers, if we see it as a person, that clue word would have been 'modern'. Had the term been newly coined, its wide use might have been necessary to describe something equally new, like Impressionism in painting earlier or Cubism later. But of course it was anything but new; what was new was this frequent use of it, as if a great many writers had suddenly realised they were existing in their own present time. And these writers were very different. In the England of the Nineties, for example, the minor poets and æsthetes claimed to be 'modern' because they broke with Victorian tradition, imitated the French Symbolists, and defied middle-class bourgeois morality. In the same England of the late Nineties a much stronger claim to be 'modern' was being made by very different writers, notably Shaw, with his Socialism and epigrams about rates and taxes, H. G. Wells, in his science fiction, and Rudyard Kipling, with his empire-building and steam engines. So it was elsewhere, throughout Western Europe: the ambitious writers, not the elderly and academic, and not those who were content to be easy public entertainers, were all 'modern'. They were alike in this claim, if in little else. And this is something we have not met before; it is a distinct and perhaps significant peculiarity of this period.

No doubt there was a feeling in the air that things were moving fast, with even greater changes on the way. (Wells in his prophetic vein was very sensitive to this feeling, and was probably its master interpreter.) And indeed, several years before 1914, being 'modern' would not satisfy some of the liveliest young men, who announced the arrival of Futurism, and assisted Marinetti to give very noisy and silly performances of it. Not to be outdone by the Latins, the British, headed by Wyndham Lewis, with at least one American, Ezra Pound, decided to whirl themselves and their readers out of time altogether by creating Vorticism. But when their periodical *Blast* appeared, to damn everything they disliked at the top of its voice, it was already 1914; and very soon there was sufficient blasting to satisfy the vorticists and enough banging to please even Marinetti. And, as we know from innumerable memoirs, many persons found a strange and startling beauty—in the time immediately prior to the war—in the excitement of new movements and astonishing works of art, in the blaze and clang of Diaghilev's new ballets, in the negro rhythms of the new revues, in the brilliant promise of the new literature about to be created; but they enjoyed it all with the intuitive feeling, heightening and colouring their pleasure like a slight rise in temperature, that this was no ordinary time, that something was ending. The fact, so often stated, that finally the war came as a complete surprise does not deny this prompting of intuition, which these gayer people were not going to interpret in terms of political alliances, ultimatums and mobilisations. The truth is that from the beginning of the age (with a few prophetic voices earlier than that), behind the claims to be 'modern', the sense of hurrying time and change, the final rush from modernism into futurism, there had been this feeling of an impending catastrophe. And if, as we have so often been told, for the fortunate (not necessarily rich) the Edwardian afternoons seemed so full and golden, the nights of ballet and opera had such a blaze and splendour, they may have been experienced, standing out in relief, against this dark feeling; they were like a last dreamy half-hour in bed when the mind knows it is already time to rise and face the day.

There is, however, another reason why more ambitious writers, differing widely in temperament and talent, should have all begun claiming to be 'modern'. The rapid growth of population, together with the spread of education, created an enormous reading public that had to be satisfied on many different levels. Now on these levels many old forms that had once been new and original, the expression of an age, persisted after a fashion. So, for example, the historical romantic fiction of a Scott or a Manzoni, which when it first appeared a Goethe eagerly read, did not cease to be written; the form did not vanish; but as the reading public grew, more and more writers, unambitious but not always mere hacks, entertained a large section of the public with historical romances written in an easy popular style. And this happened to other forms, originally fresh and vital. For as we pile up people, we pile up periods, which do not perish completely but linger on, though without their first freshness and vitality. Thus there are plenty of Victorians alive today, but they are inferior Victorians, representing more of the vices than the virtues of that age. And similar levels were to be found in the production of books, now an important trade, which had its publishers to match its authors and readers, cosily old-fashioned or rebellious, experimental, eager for something new to catch the spirit of the time. It appeared then that real literature, the vital thing, as distinct from mere agreeable writing down through various levels to hack-work, could only be found to exist on the outer and advancing edge, turned away from the past, facing the present and the future. In short, it was 'modern'. It alone could reflect or express a society rapidly cutting itself loose from the past, or at least appearing to do so, busy changing everything that could be changed.

Not that the writer-as-artist had to approve these changes. But he had to show himself aware of them, even if only to scream in dismay. Two quite different attitudes can be discovered in the types of writers already mentioned. What we have called the æsthetic writers, convinced of the complete alienation of the artist from society, in effect contracted out of it, obeyed as few of its rules as possible, and were its vagabonds or hermits. The other type, a Shaw, a Wells, a Kipling, did not dissociate himself from society, might indeed celebrate much of what it was doing, but joined it to denounce it vigorously from the inside, unlike a vagabond or hermit but very much like a prophet. In the period up to 1914 both these types were held to be making new and valuable contributions to literature; and those who held this view of them were of course the younger critics and their readers, themselves equally 'modern', moving with the same advancing edge. But obviously a Shaw might have playgoers, a Wells or Kipling a host of admiring readers, who were not consciously 'modern' at all; and during these years, unlike those that followed the First War, the support of this large audience did not matter one way or the other. A writer was not important because he was popular, and he was not unimportant because he was popular. Because mass values and tastes, though already known to exist, were not yet regarded as menacing, the extent of a writer's popularity could be ignored. He was capable of creating literature if he had the necessary talent and used it as a 'modern'.

The term, however, could be used in a different way, in which 'modern' equals what we might call the uneaten oyster. This idea of literature and the arts—and actually it came to literature from the fine arts, where it was more at home—must be understood, because it was to have a considerable influence upon taste and judgment throughout the whole age, and especially between the wars. The original artist, with his own particular sensibility and his new and perhaps revolutionary technique, arrives like an unopened oyster, presenting us with an unattractive hard shell. But if we have the enterprise and patience to open the shell, then we can refresh and sustain ourselves with the oyster inside—with what the artist offers us, once we have come to appreciate his new technique. And when we have enjoyed and digested this oyster, we are left with an empty shell, and must now find another unopened oyster, probably rockier and more formidable than the last. This idea of our relation to the arts, without such coarse imagery, is the subject of some of the most exquisite passages in Marcel Proust's great novel that overshadowed the literary Twenties. When we first encounter the work of an original artist, Proust declares in effect, we find it unattractive, repulsive or meaningless; then, perhaps quite suddenly, having penetrated the shell, we discover that it is deliciously rewarding, a wonderful addition to our world; and then, having apparently absorbed it all, we lose interest in the work and its creator, shrug them away, and pass on. We seem to behave to our artists as curious and heartless sensualists do to their women. But while the oyster-shell is open and the delicious creature it offers us not yet swallowed and digested, this is the one we have been waiting for, a marvel and a delight—all fresh, just in, the latest and best. Such are the arts and literature as a series of uneaten oysters and a trail of empty shells.

Now this approach can be made on three different levels of intelligence and sensitivity. And Proust can be found, at ease, on all three. On the highest level, as a writer of genius, who saw in his work the meaning of his existence, he brought his superb intelligence and sensitivity to the work of other great artists, took and absorbed what he wanted, then moved on. On the level below, as a Parisian, living in an atmosphere of artistic movements and manifestoes, of attack and counter-attack, of one original artist displacing another, he would be almost conditioned to take this view of the arts. Finally, on the lowest level, he had been a man of fashion, living in a tiny world of long dining-tables and *salons*, where a fresh topic, something new and exciting, the curious exhibition, the scandalous play, the latest and oddest genius, was always urgently demanded. And while it cannot be denied that some exceptional persons approached contemporary arts and letters, with Proust, on the highest level, it is also true that far more people were with him on the other two levels, where there was revolution in Montmartre and counter-revolution in Montparnasse, or exciting new names and sensations for rich fashionable women. For it is an odd thing about this epoch, both before and after the war, that although the artists and writers themselves might have existed for years in an honourable poverty, no sooner had they attracted attention to themselves than the smart rich made most noise about their work. Much of it first made its way, not as in other times, among romantic revolutionary students or the earnest professional middle class, but among the wealthy, the extremely sophisticated, the more intelligent fashionable persons. Long before the poor man's newspaper had noticed the new arts and letters, the up-to-the-minute 'modern' geniuses, the uneaten oysters, appreciations of them had begun to appear, between advertisements of diamond necklaces and of sables and mink, in the thickest and glossiest fashion magazines. It may have been this curious development, peculiar to the age, and not any social-æsthetic principles, that encouraged the Communists to denounce so much of this new art and writing as examples of capitalist decadence. What had been 'modern' became, like a style of interior decoration or an eccentric hat, the ultra-smart, truly *le dernier cri*.

4

In the very middle of this age the First World War rises like a wall of blood-red mountains. Its frenzied butchery, indefensible even on a military basis, killed at least ten million Europeans, mostly young and free from obvious physical defects. After being dressed in uniform, fed and drilled, cheered and cried over before they were packed into their cattle-trucks, these ten million were then filled with hot lead, ripped apart by shell splinters, blown to bits, bayoneted in the belly, choked with poison gas, suffocated in mud, trampled to death or drowned, buried in collapsing dugouts, dropped out of burning aeroplanes, or allowed to die of diseases, after rotting too long in trenches that they shared with syphilitic rats and typhus-infested lice. Death, having come into his empire, demanded the best, and got it. This was no ordinary generation;

it was the flower and fruit of an exceptionally long summer of European peace and prosperity, so much vintage blood; and the men among us who fought with it and saw it being destroyed, and the women still alive who cannot forget its wonderful bright promise, we believe to this day that the best companions of our youth, the liveliest minds and bravest hearts, all the golden lads (and the English among us discovered how strangely prophetic were A. E. Housman's bitter laments in his *Shropshire Lad*, written so many years before) went to that war and never came back from it. This is something that nobody born after about 1904 can ever fully appreciate. Europe's total loss is beyond calculation. 1919 was a ragged shadow of 1913. What possibilities and potentialities in politics, arts, sciences, vanished among the shell holes and barbed wire, we shall never know. But some consequences of this war we do know, and we cannot ignore them.

The war cut Europe to the bone. (Britain is of course included in Europe here, and so, with some reservations because of their distance from the scene, are the dominions of the British Commonwealth: indeed, the Canadians and Australians fought some of the most desperate battles of the war.) No intelligent and sensitive European—and writers can hardly succeed without intelligence and sensitivity—could escape the terrible impact of these four years. They might be neutrals, but the war was there, all round them. The total effect might be different for different sets of people, the neutrals, the non-combatants of the warring nations, the men who actually did the fighting; but it was not to be avoided. Any sensitive man, perhaps a writer hard at work, who temporarily succeeded in repressing any thought of the war probably only let it loose in his unconscious. The younger writers of the embattled nations who for one reason or another remained at home, but saw their brothers and friends fast disappearing, had the desperate choice of admitting the whole nightmare into full consciousness or risking what deliberate suppression of it would do to their unconscious. As for the actual combatants, if they came out of it in one living piece, they returned to the civilian world like strangers from another life. They knew too many dead men too early; they were closer to them than to the living. Besides, the living had changed, everything had changed. How does a man, weary down to his bones and feeling half like a ghost, begin writing a masterpiece in some new mode? Setting aside the Americans, for both Faulkner and Hemingway, young as they were then, went to the war and were wounded in it, how many combatants survived the war to achieve major international reputations in the new post-war literature? For if something had happened to these men who came out of the armies, it is also true that something had happened, and was still happening, to the literary world in which such men found themselves. It was a world as unfamiliar to most of them as the civilian clothes they were wearing.

But before we look at these post-war years, let us consider that war-time Zürich in which, among so many odd exiles, James Joyce sat staring at Dublin tram tickets, handbills, posters. He needed these, and much else about Dublin that his friends there had sent him, because he was writing *Ulysses*. In the same city in the same year, 1916, three other personages could have been found. First, no refugee but one of Zürich's most distinguished citizens, Carl Gustav Jung, who had already broken with Freud and published his massive study of symbolic fantasies and archetypes, *Psychology of the Unconscious*. It was Jung who was soon to warn modern man that he was now perilously one-sided, so certain of his conscious control of himself and events that his mind, no longer fortified by the symbols of religion, was almost entirely at the mercy of his unconscious drives and fantasies; and who was able to foretell, from his analysis of his German patients, that sooner or later Germany, then suffering from defeat and inflation and consciously rejecting any idea of militarism, would explode into a barbaric fury of violence and destruction. The second of these three was another refugee like Joyce, a young Rumanian poet called Tristan Tzara. Though the youngest, he was the leader of a small group of exiles from the countries at war, a group that had started a movement, more 'advanced' even than Futurism, indeed the movement to end all movements: Dada. These Dadaists, as they called themselves, were not merely bent on ridding the world of the art of the past; they wanted to destroy art altogether. They were artists against the arts. Music was to be turned into sheer disagreeable noise; painting into any mess of paint, paper and canvas; literature into gabbling nonsense. They staged Dada demonstrations calculated to bewilder and infuriate any audience. By all manner of elaborate imbecilities they proved how completely they rejected art, tradition, thought, decency, sense, the world now fighting the war from which they had fled. This movement, in spite of its obvious silliness, spread to several countries for a few years after the war—it held many demonstrations in Germany— and later in Paris it led, through the enthusiastic support of the poet André Breton, to the more considerable and lasting movement—surrealism. It is easy to see why it should. For it is impossible for a man to use words and paint, no matter how determinedly senseless he tries to be, entirely without any expressive significance. If conscious control is completely relaxed, then the unconscious takes over. This release of the unconscious is what surrealism wanted to achieve, though, by having so definite an aim, it brought back, thereby defeating itself, some measure of conscious control.

The last of these three in Zürich in 1916 was also an exile, had been one for years, but was shortly to return to his native country. He grew up there as Vladimir Ilyich Ulyanov, but followed the fashion in Russian revolutionary circles and changed his name to Lenin. And nothing that Jung, Joyce or Tzara and his Dadaists could have said to him would have made the slightest shade of difference to what he thought and felt; he knew, it seemed, exactly what was wrong with the world and how it could be put right. He had an odd trick, disconcerting rather than disarming, of going off into sudden fits of laughter. Perhaps, an intuitive man of destiny, he perceived already that, after being returned to Russia by the German Army in a sealed train, like a germ in a test-tube, he would begin a task that would end in re-shaping a third of the world. And these four, Jung between two analyses, Joyce resting his eyes from his huge novel, the wild young Tzara and the grim Lenin, might have passed one another any late afternoon in 1916 along the Bahnhofstrasse in Zürich. It was still the middle of the war, but already here, away from the guns and the slaughter, the world after the war was taking on its shape, colour, character.

Russia, as always, was different, not in the same picture. There the revolution happened, to reconstruct entirely, with steel rods and cemented limbs, the crumbling colossus of 1917. Once the Bolsheviks, led by the formidable Lenin, were securely in power, the background to Russian writing changed with central Soviet policy. It must therefore be considered separately. Immediately after the revolution, while the civil war was still being fought, there was very little printing, and instead of new books there were readings and recitals in public places, chiefly by revolutionary poets like Mayakovsky. Between the end of the civil war and the arrival of the first Five Year Plan, at the time when Lenin's N.E.P. loosened the hold of the state, writers enjoyed a fair amount of freedom so long as they did not attack the Party. Although, like many revolutionaries, conservative in his literary taste, Lenin was far more tolerant than his successors; if he could not appreciate all the new experimental writing and theatre work, he did not dictate to the poets and producers what they should do. It is to one group of younger writers, the so-called 'Serapion Brothers', intellectuals who had no wish to leave the country, as many of the better-known older writers did, but were not Party members, that we owe the best descriptive writing and humorous fiction that has come out of Soviet Russia. But the Five Year Plan and the tightening grip of the Party, which operated in literature largely through the General Union of Soviet Writers, compelled authors to choose between silence and poverty (for their work would not be published) and even worse things, on the one hand, and on the other the 'socialist realism' that would now rule all the arts. And 'socialist realism' banished all experiments in the decadent style of Western Europe, frowned on whatever was romantic and picturesque in fiction, and allowed about as much humour and satire as any writer faced with the task of seriously describing an earnest Party member building a cement works might contrive to find.

There is no glimmer of sympathy here for any system in which political bosses, who have spent their time seeking power and not trying to understand and appreciate the arts, can dictate to authors, composers, painters, what and how to write, compose and paint. And it is still a bad system if the political bosses say nothing but let various General Unions, largely controlled by political sycophants and composed mostly of envious or frightened mediocrities, do their bullying of the arts for them. Nevertheless, in all fairness, and to free ourselves from propaganda disguised as criticism, we must try to regard this background, so far as it concerns literature, both from a Soviet and a traditionally Russian point of view. For example, as we have already noted, the idea that serious literature must have a strong social meaning and purpose was not invented by the Bolsheviks, but may be found, from Belinsky onwards, in nineteenth-century Russian criticism. Again, the meeting of authors for mutual criticism is not simply yet another distasteful Communist device but was customary long before the revolution. Indeed, much of what is thought in the West to be typically Communist—as for instance an all-or-nothing attitude of mind that forbids compromise, a desire to be completely committed, a preference for a heartily gregarious style of living—may actually be traditionally Russian. We must remember too that the Soviet people, partly no doubt because they had not all the highly commercialised distractions we have in Western Europe and America, were possessed by a passion for the printed word, vast editions of new books being gobbled up in a few days. And the decision, mistaken though it was, to bring down literature and the arts to a level at which workers and peasants could appreciate them, was made at a time when new sacrifices were to be demanded of these people. Moreover, in the years before the revolution, during the first and pre-war half of this age, Russian literature had not only fallen a long way below the nineteenth-century heights but could genuinely be said to be largely decadent, being morbidly sensational or confused and gloomy. And the fear that this could happen again, that the old Slav pessimism would come seeping through once more, played some part, if not a major one, in this decision to have nothing but 'socialist realism'—work easily, all too easily, understood, thoroughly extroverted, mechanically optimistic. After all, we have plenty of this kind of writing (capitalist idealism?) in the West, carted by the ton to the bookshops and handsomely rewarded by the popular magazines. The difference—and to literature it is vital—is that while the Western author may have to resist social and economic pressure in favour of such writing, at least he is not officially and professionally fenced in with it, is not condemned to be "an engineer of the soul" where the soul has been abolished and its majesty and magic transferred to the engines.

5

Having dealt with Soviet Russia separately, we must now return to Western Europe and America and the literary world they created after the First World War. If we seem to assume that everything was happening everywhere at the same time, which of course it was not, this is simply to save both space and the reader's patience. Obviously some people in some places found themselves in the post-war literary world much later than other people in other places did. But the atmosphere, values and general character of the world, sooner or later, and with a few local differences, could be discovered everywhere outside the steel fences of the Soviet Union. As we know now, the First World War settled nothing. What it really did was to speed things up, to heighten temperatures already rising before 1914, to widen and deepen splits in the Western mind that had existed throughout most of the nineteenth century, to turn what was thought to be the world after the war into what we call now "the world between the Wars". And our business here is to consider all this in terms of literature. Perhaps we ought to have said "in terms of Literature". For one of the earliest tendencies of this period, a tendency that continued throughout this half of our age, was to turn literature into Literature. In other words, criticism became less relative, less inclined to discover varying degrees of merit in all manner of books and authors, and more absolutist, transforming reviewers and critics into goldminers washing away the dirt to discover a few grains of precious metal, genuine Literature. The arrogant intolerance that was found before 1914 only in a few *avant-garde* types, who might be genuinely fanatical or merely impudent, soon became widespread among the younger reviewers, critics, lecturers on Literature. It was not enough that a writer possessed some talent and was honestly trying to make the best use of it. (And, after all, that is what we may suppose these critics themselves were doing. But they did not impose their hard, high standards on criticism.) No, the question now was: Does this writer make any contribution to Literature? And some of those who asked this question seemed like bad-tempered customs officials on a busy hot day: *Come, come, come—any Literature to declare?*

To understand this new critical absolutism, so seemingly arrogant and intolerant, we must first understand what the war had done, how, if it had settled nothing, it had unsettled a great deal. Four years had been blown away and millions of young men had gone and never returned. This negative effect is very important, all the more so because it has been so often ignored and forgotten. It denied the years after the war the possible genius, the certain talent, that perished with these young men; and we must bear in mind that, during the first two years of the war, many of these men were the strongest, the most courageous and liveliest-minded members of their generation, young men nicely balanced between introversion and extroversion, neither psychopaths nor wooden-headed insensitives; and that during the remaining two years vast numbers of mere boys, of whose promise and potentialities we know nothing, were shovelled into the furnace. And we are not being sentimental if we suggest that some good literature, possibly some great literature, vanished with those ten millions. We may believe, as many of its consequences implore us to believe, that the First World War was perhaps the most gigantic piece of folly in the history of Western Man; but we are not also compelled to believe—even though some such idea has been in the air ever since—that only men unfit or unwilling to fight would be capable of creating literature.

These men then, together with all they might have done, were missing. And a new generation was arriving with the early Twenties. It did not want to think about the war or to take seriously anything that had helped to bring about the war. The old men who had laid the foundations of that slaughter-house were entitled to no respect, and the kind of life they represented was a huge pompous sham. They and it were no longer worth serious criticism, and anything that could be called Literature had something better to do. So not only was anything and anybody academic, soundly established in the pre-war world, out of fashion with the young intellectuals, but so were the old prophets and rebels. A Bernard Shaw might have dissociated himself from the war, might now in these early Twenties be having his greatest box-office success, with *Saint Joan*, but he was out, finished. An Anatole France might still be selling edition after edition, but as a literary man he was dead, done for. And indeed hardly any of the big pre-war reputations survived among these young post-war intellectuals, who, though comparatively few in number, belonged to those small central groups capable of moulding opinion and establishing new reputations. What they wanted was not literature, the stuff handed out at school and enjoyed by the kind of old men responsible for the war, but Literature. This Literature would not take on any particular form—nobody was going to revive those old quarrels—though it was not likely to appear in any familiar guise, to repeat conventional patterns and textures. But, whatever its form, it would express what any young and intelligent and sensitive person must feel about the world, disillusion ranging from a gay and fantastic derision to the blackest depths of disgust. It would of necessity be introverted, going inward, accompanying—or even leading a way for—the new scientific magicians, the psycho-analysts, whose fascinating technical terms were now being adopted, often with more enthusiasm than accuracy, by all the intelligentsia.

There was from the beginning a suggestion of the esoteric about this new Literature. The general reader was not expected to understand and admire it. In other times enthusiastic critics had waved new masterpieces at anybody able to read; it had happened to some extent up to 1914. But now *serious* criticism, which meant not relative but absolutist criticism, dedicated to removing Literature from the mounds of trash, no longer beckoned the crowd forward but waved it away, muttering darkly about small minorities, the intelligent few, the *élite*. (Though nothing, it must be added, is more likely to attract some sections of the young than this method.) It was felt too—and this was new—that a serious writer, an artist and not an entertainer, ought to be difficult, hard to read, not simply because he was putting into words original thought and strange subtle feelings, as all major writers are bound to do, but because he ought to set up a barrier between his work and stupid or frivolous idle-minded readers. This attitude, though bad for literature in the long run, robbing it of the vitality that comes from a wide appeal and response, was not entirely in-excusable. The new writers and their critics, unlike most of the serious writers and critics before 1914, felt themselves to be increasingly challenged and menaced by mass communications, mass writing and reading, mass standards, mass values. They felt they had to keep guard on their integrity. And if they preferred to be absolutist in their criticism, if they were too self-conscious about literature, turning it into Literature, if they were too often arrogant, intolerant, narrow, this feeling that they and their standards and values were being besieged by the mass must be their excuse. Because the idle-minded crowd must be kept out, they felt, they made their work more difficult to read (often impossible to read with pleasure) and to understand easily and quickly, putting into reverse the efforts of older writers to appear as simple and pleasantly readable as their subjects would allow them to be. And because this new generation of creative writers and critics felt it their duty to keep the mob at bay, a duty that might mean sacrificing money, ease, and popularity, they can be forgiven their decision to appear difficult and unattractive, even though it produced some horrible writing, like a diet of broken glass.

Nevertheless, this refusal to be relative, to recognise that there are all kinds of writers and readers; the new impatient dichotomies, dividing writers into a tiny group of genuine artists and a large group of fakes, clowns, hacks, dividing writing itself into Literature and rubbish, readers into 'highbrow' and 'lowbrow': all these did no good service to literature. As we have already discovered, literature reaches its greatest triumphs, its supreme masterpieces, in work that is able to appeal to and satisfy its readers and audiences on several different levels. *Hamlet* is not only one of our greatest tragedies but also the most popular play ever written, the piece that has filled a thousand playhouses when nothing else would. *Don Quixote* can be read with equal delight by children and wise old men. True, a Shakespeare or a Cervantes cannot be found in every age; nevertheless, every age so far has produced some masterpieces, all with a broad and lasting appeal because they are satisfying on more than one level, beginning with one of simple interest, curiosity, excitement, common human feeling. But this is not true of the Twenties, certainly not in Western Europe. (Much of what is said here must be modified for America, not only because the reaction to the war was not quite the same but also because the general tendencies were slower in their development.) Consider some of the most admired and influential work of the Twenties:

Proust's great novel, Joyce's *Ulysses*, Valéry's *Charmes* (which included *Le Cimetière marin*), Eliot's *Waste Land*, Virginia Woolf's *Mrs. Dalloway*, Hesse's *Steppenwolf*, Thomas Mann's *Magic Mountain*, Kafka's *The Castle*. These have their own genius and depth, but it would be absurd to pretend that they have the old broad appeal on many different levels, beginning with anybody who wants a book to read. They only begin where the average reader wants to stop. Unless a reader puts himself alongside their authors, reaching their level from his, he can hardly make a start, and in some instances may feel he is reading nonsense. This is not a criticism of these works—we shall come to that later—but a proof of how literature, by turning into Literature, one of the arts no longer accessible to the crowd (compare Ortega's *Dehumanization of Art*, though he makes the point in a different way), loses its old capacity, at its best, to make a broad appeal on many levels. And with that, it loses much of its former vitality and its hold upon the society of its own age and future ages.

The truth is that, even though mass communications may multiply and become more and more powerful and mass standards may harden, the relative view is still the more sensible, impatient dichotomies are still unjustified and misleading. People cannot be either justly or profitably divided into intellectuals and blockheads, into sensitives and insensitives, into art-takers and art-refusers, into readers of Literature and consumers of trash, into the *élite* and the masses. Even if these last should exist, there is still room between them for innumerable people who may not appreciate to the full every new and difficult work but are not necessarily unintelligent and insensitive. We have seen already that one result of the Symbolist Movement in poetry was that many educated persons, quite capable of appreciating the other arts or older literature, began to lose interest in poetry. The new Literature of the Twenties produced a similar result with the same kind of people. Among these people, between the *avant-garde*, the intellectuals, the bright fashionables flirting with any new art, and the humble crowds, increasingly catered for on their levels, there was a loss of interest in contemporary literature. And unfortunately this happened at a time when the printed word itself was facing a dangerous challenge. For the world between the Wars was busy stimulating and satisfying the visual sense, chiefly through films, though in many other ways too. During these years, many parents who from childhood had had a passion for literature, for the magic of words, discovered that their children did not share this passion, did not respond to this old magic, but, on the other hand, delighted in whatever appealed to their visual sense. A hundred years before, it would have been a book that united old and young, and people belonging to various classes, in their common enjoyment. But now, no new book could do it, perhaps only a Chaplin film. (Chaplin in the Twenties was doing more or less what Dickens had done eighty years before. And nobody, not even Chaplin, appears to have noticed that these two comedians of genius are oddly alike—in physique, background, temperament.) Against this view, that the literary sense, combining an interest in ideas with a deep feeling for words, was losing as the visual sense was gaining, it may be objected that the world between the wars could record an enormous and steadily increasing sale of books, especially in the new cheap editions. But allowance must be made here for the rising income and expenditure of the whole Western world. Were more books sold at the expense of other things? (It was not publishing but film production that was at one time the fourth largest industry in the United States.) Finally—and this is brute proof that the literary world had suffered a great change—whatever works might be in large and eager demand, it was hardly ever the works of the new giants of Literature, the books that the serious younger critics were declaring to be the masterpieces of the age. That the greatest should not be in most demand, that the poets of genius should not be read and quoted everywhere, that the names of the master novelists and of the characters they had created should not be on everybody's lips, all this does not surprise us; now we take it all for granted; and yet it would have astounded our forefathers.

There is another new and odd feature that can be observed in this Literature of the Twenties. On what is considered to be its highest level, it is no longer national, not even regional. The post-war literary world appears to be carrying to an extreme its revulsion from the insane nationalism, the imbecile prejudices, of the earlier war years. Now most of the new high reputations belong to writers who seem to have no nationality, to be completely cosmopolitan. What they represent are certain types and attitudes of mind, found everywhere though not perhaps in large numbers; and what they do not represent, as so many older important writers did, are the people among whom they were born. So Rilke is like a flittering ghost somewhere between Paris and Austria. Proust sets most of his vast panorama in Paris, but we do not go to him to learn anything about Paris or indeed the French. Though moving between Trieste, Zürich, Paris, James Joyce cannot write about anything but Dublin, but nobody thinks of him as an Irish novelist. Kafka's stealthy fantasies do not take us to Prague or to anywhere this side of the moon. T. S. Eliot, running no risk of being thought uneducated, studied at Harvard, the Sorbonne, Oxford, and his early poetry, which brought him fame so quickly, is really as international as his education. And so it goes on. There is however one link between many of these cosmopolitan figures. It is Paris. The influence of Paris, now reaching the Americans as well as the Western Europeans, is stronger than ever in these years after the war.

This Paris was not the French capital. It was not even the literary Paris, to which Stefan Zweig offers such a charming tribute, all the better because it comes from outside, from an Austrian, in his autobiographical *World of Yesterday*, describing his stay there in 1904; the Paris in which so many French writers of great talent, enjoying what Zweig calls "inconspicuous sinecures" as official librarians and so forth, lived very quietly, in a modest bourgeois family style, and wrote exactly as they pleased, for small periodicals and little literary theatres, without any commercial ambitions; the Paris responsible for so much good French writing in the years before 1914. No, this Paris so important in the Twenties was the cosmopolitan city where tourists scattered their cheaply-acquired francs like confetti, and struggling artists and expatriated writers could live on the smallest incomes and meet so many others of their kind. It was the centre of the international arts, the movements, the experiments. The new post-war Berlin might be even wilder, both in its theatre and the night life that came after the latest Expressionist production. But the domination of Paris, as the cosmopolitan capital of arts and ideas, could not be successfully challenged. The essential spirit of the Twenties, in the arts and in literature, was distilled there. It was as potent as the innumerable *fines* consumed at café tables by writers, from everywhere, arguing for hours and hours, excited not only by brandy but even more by this heady atmosphere of art and ideas. The influence of this cosmopolitan centre of the arts was like that of its talkative late hours and drinks, both good and bad. It was good because it discouraged provincialism, a timid conventionality, any dependence upon accepted ideas and familiar old techniques; because it encouraged experiment, new ideas and techniques, a concentration upon metaphysical Man and his problems. It was bad just because it came from a cosmopolitan centre of the arts, where there were too many uprooted artists, away from the communities that had bred them, where there was too much expression and not enough to express, where movements in the arts, in this thin and over-heated atmosphere, took on something of the feverish haste and solemn triviality of the neighbouring world of fashion. In this air and strange soil, sure and solid growth was difficult and rare; much work, done by the over-stimulated, flowered grotesquely or withered on the stem; and although a few of these writers in exile, those with a certain weight of talent, came through triumphantly, to make great reputations, we cannot be sure whether they would have been better or worse without their years in Paris.

Other reputations arrived with the Thirties, a decade no longer gaily post-war but rapidly darkening with social and political issues. There is no need here to unfold the familiar panorama of the Great Slump and the unemployment it brought, the rise of the Nazis, the Spanish Civil War, the false dilemma of Communism-or-else-Fascism, the huge and terrible approach, for which Berlioz might have written his *March to the Gallows*, of World War II. We have read a great deal, perhaps too much, about the new social consciousness of the young writers of the Thirties, and how different the literary world was from that of the Twenties; but looking back we can see that this difference was comparatively small, that the big change, bringing with it new standards and values, occurred just after the First World War. (And to some extent during the war, when many of the younger intellectuals, civilians or, if in uniform, not on active service, began their own campaign.) The more important reputations established then were not destroyed by the Thirties. The attitudes we

have already described, the attitudes that were new in those years, remained more or less fixed. The social consciousness of the young writers,
the swing to the extreme Left so common in the mid-Thirties, neither
shattered the great reputations made in the Twenties nor successfully
demanded room among them for some 'socialist realists' on the Soviet
model. Some new names arrived but only in a literary world created in
the early Twenties, originally in Western Europe, although it soon
stretched across the Atlantic. (It is worth remembering too that in the
Thirties literature was being taught, in a large and growing number of
colleges, often by men and women who had been students, eager for new
movements, values, names, in the earlier Twenties.) Nor is this so surprising, even though the Thirties made so much history. For literature
has its own time and it changes in its own fashion, not responding to the
most frenzied signals from journalists and radio commentators. It has
access to the unconscious; visions, dreams, prophetic whispers from behind
the veil, all find their way into it. Long before 1914, long before the
century began, literature had given many a sign that Western Man was
beginning to feel homeless, charged with angry frustration, in the modern
world, where ancient patterns of living were so quickly destroyed and so
many primary satisfactions hard to find. One deeply intuitive writer
after another had suggested that combustible material was piling up in the
dark, hidden below the triumphant blaze of factories and stores, hotels
and theatres, all the material progress of the later nineteenth and the earlier
twentieth centuries. Then the First War—the war that was to end wars,
even though nobody but a few prophets knew how it had begun—came
blasting through into terrible actuality, four years of fire and blood. And
though still asserting that literature, on its highest creative level, has its
own time and looks before and after history, we must recognise that this
First War did make some important changes in the literary scene. It
splits this age into two main parts, one before 1914, the other after 1918,
with a war interlude between them; and the chapters that follow, chapters
in which the more significant writers, or those most admired, at last make
their appearance, must be arranged with some modification to fit this
pattern. If it should seem an awkward arrangement, let history take the
blame.

CHAPTER TWENTY

Mostly before 1914

I

THE DIFFICULTY now is plain. These years are packed with authors, piled high with books. To ignore all but a few is to abjure sensible relative criticism in favour of an intolerant absolutism. But the list of writers, if literary justice has to be done, stretches to an appalling length, from Jeppe Aakjær, the lyrical poet of Jutland peasant life, to Stefan Zweig, the Austrian man-of-letters and one of the tragic exiles. It might be possible to marshal these hundreds of writers into some kind of procession, but who would want to see it passing by? Moreover, it would hide and not reveal the relations between this age and its literature; and now we have arrived in our own time, it is more important that this broad relationship should be understood than that every writer of any reputation should be briefly brought forward, like a schoolboy at a prize-giving. It is also more important to have at least a little space in which to examine the personalities and works of those writers of international fame and wide influence. The stories and plays in Yiddish of Peretz, the lyrics of the Brazilian poet, Alberto de Oliveira, the Serbian comedies of Branislav Nušić, for example, may still mean more to some readers and audiences than the works of Bernard Shaw and Anatole France, Thomas Mann and Marcel Proust; but these readers and audiences do not represent the world of Western Man. No doubt a writer belonging to a small nation, using a language that cannot command many readers, is at a disadvantage, especially if he is a poet and hard to translate; although what he loses abroad he gains at home, where he suffers from less competition and has a greater chance of arousing national pride. It cannot be denied that the larger nations, with their great capital cities, bring their writers of power and originality earlier international recognition; but only the sharpest prejudice would deny that these capital cities either produce or draw to themselves far more of these writers of power and originality. And though genuine talent and fine work, which may have done much for a small people, may easily go unrecognised throughout most of the Western world, original genius, able to make a strong appeal to some readers of many nations, will not remain long in obscurity. So in 1924 there died, at the age of forty-one, a Czech-Jewish clerk who wrote odd stories that he hardly ever finished and did not even want to be published; yet in the Thirties such was the fame of Franz Kafka that an adjective, familiar to everybody concerned with literature, had been coined from his name.

The first Nobel Prize for literature, in 1901, went to France, perhaps as a well-deserved tribute to her culture; and to a poet, the popular Sully Prudhomme. If French poetry had to furnish a candidate, this was a bad time. Mallarmé, who anyhow would have been too difficult, and Verlaine, too disreputable, had both died a few years earlier. Mallarmé's disciple, Valéry, had not yet made his late start; Jammes was still too young. There was of course old Mistral, if his Provence could be assumed to be part of France, and the Provençal he used for his verse regarded as one kind of French writing; and indeed his turn came, in 1904. These years in France would not have offered a much wider choice even in drama and fiction. It was a rather barren little interval, so far as major figures were concerned. In the drama, Rostand died too soon, Maeterlinck received the 1911 award but as a Belgian, Brieux had an international theatrical reputation but no standing in literature, and François de Curel, Hervieu, Lavedan, Georges de Porto-Riche, younger men like Bataille and Bernstein, or the deliciously comic Georges Courteline, lacked either the breadth or the weight. There is a similar gap, before a new brilliant generation arrives, in the novel. Thus, Maurice Barrès was giving too many of these years to politics and journalism. And even Anatole France, though now in his sixties and the most commanding figure in the French literary scene, did not produce his strongest work, *L'Île des pingouins*, *Les Dieux ont soif*, *La Révolte des anges*, until the years immediately before the

First War. And he had to wait until 1921, when he was seventy-seven, to receive his Nobel Prize. He died three years afterwards.

By 1924 Anatole France, with his immense reputation both at home and abroad, had enjoyed a very long reign. Moreover, as we know, the literary world of the Twenties had its own new values and standards. So it is not surprising that his death should have been followed by attacks on his work, reputation, personality; though we may feel that the savagery of these attacks did not exhibit French criticism—or criticism elsewhere that followed Paris fashion—in a favourable light. After the knives had done their work, he was ignored. And all these hoots and howls, and, even more, the silence that followed them, have largely succeeded in keeping two new generations of readers away from him, have reduced his fame to a shred of what it was, throughout the Western world, during the last thirty years of his life. There is no more dramatic example, in this whole age, of the sudden collapse of a great reputation. But if the noise of it reached him beyond the grave, Anatole France would not have been shocked, for he had no more illusions about enduring fame than he had about most other things. One of Nicolas Segur's published conversations with him is on this very subject; he tells Segur not to delude himself, that one generation will laugh at what the preceding one adored, that the arts have their fashions too, that we cannot believe in the reality of glory when we remember that the enlightened age of Voltaire looked down on Homer and Dante and regarded Shakespeare as a clown and a barbarian—yet we, who revere and love those great figures, are no more intelligent than Voltaire. He himself, he added, had had the good luck to be praised by the right people at the right time, and his work did not deserve the eulogies and the large circulation it enjoyed. No, Anatole France said it first, but said it better than his detractors. And sooner or later, if the pleasures of reading are to continue, Anatole France will reappear, not quite the giant he seemed to be once, but still dwarfing the writers who made haste to attack him.

The case against him is easily made: he lacks the creative energy and depth of a master novelist; his thought is not original; his famous style has not a contemporary tone and ring, and too often suggests an eighteenth-century pastiche; his elaborate scepticism and irony, at a time when, unlike

Voltaire, he ran no risks, can be irritating or wearisome; and his novels of contemporary life, if we except *Crainquebille*, seem thin and unreal. Much of him—his sly sensuality, his mocking rationalism, his antique-shop tastes, his scholarly dilettante airs, his general view of man and society—suggests a nineteenth-century background, fading rapidly in the years before the First War, and gone for ever after it. But all this does not dispose of him, except in the limited terms of literary fashion; it leaves the best of him, in its own unique mixture of qualities, quite un-touched. For there is nobody like him. It is not an accident that this essentially French writer—and no writer of his time or since is more completely French or owes so little to any outside influences—should have had so great a reputation throughout the Western world. He had something of his own to offer it.

Anatole France, however, owed much to two very different persons. The first was Madame de Caillavet, who not only made him the chief attraction of her *salon* but bullied him out of his natural indolence (though there is hard work somewhere behind that style of his) and made him write books instead of table-talk criticism and occasional short stories. And it was she, being Jewish, who urged him to support Dreyfus, the second of these persons to whom he was indebted. For it was the lengthy and revealing Dreyfus case that made him deeply aware of social injustice, broadened his sympathies, turned him into a vaguely liberal type of socialist (he became a close friend of the great socialist leader, Jaurès), and finally gave his work more originality, force and a deeper compassion. His was an odd development: his earliest writing suggests an elderly smiling sceptic; with increasing fame, fortune, and years, his work reverses the usual trend, displays a more youthful inventiveness, adds a suggestion of generous anger and breadth of compassion to its mockery and irony, makes use of its wit as a weapon against injustice in every form. His fundamental pessimism is still there, but, unlike so much of the pessimism that was growing and deepening with the age, it is not savage and wounding, a kind of revenge, but has pity in it. *Crainquebille*, as early as 1902, sounds a note that later writers echo over and over again. Perhaps his sardonic fable about the penguins who acquired souls, and with them a history, is over-long (an unusual fault with him), building

339

too much on its basic idea; but his *Les Dieux ont soif*, superbly narrated, is not only the story of the French Revolution but of all major violent revolutions, in which Death, taking charge, is hungry and refuses to be satisfied; and there is more than Voltairean irony in the final twists and turns, the metaphysical paradoxes, of *La Révolte des anges*. These later works will one day recapture readers in many countries, who will then perhaps go back to *Thaïs*, to a short story like *The Procurator of Judea*, or to some of the old literary *causerie* pieces, glinting with irony and wise mischief, all so pleasant and easy to read, and all—except of course for those critics who have dismissed this author as a mere fake—so hard to write. When the literary world is tired of alternating doses of syrup and vinegar, perhaps it will return with pleasure to the light dry wine of Anatole France.

There was in fact no other Nobel award to a French author, after that to Mistral in 1904, until the First War. Then, in 1915, the prize went to Romain Rolland. It is hard not to believe that Rolland's outspoken pacifism, which compelled him to leave France for Switzerland, did not play some part in this choice. But it could be justified as a literary award, for Rolland was not only the author of some distinguished biographies and musical criticism but also the creator of that enormous ten-volume novel, *Jean Christophe*, very widely read and discussed throughout Europe between 1904 and 1912. Rolland was a noble character, dedicated from youth to the service of the highest culture and the cause of peace, and bringing to that service a selfless enthusiasm, a remarkable intelligence, and a great knowledge of the arts. He believed that Europe could be saved from disaster by a close understanding, especially on the cultural level, between Germany and France; and *Jean Christophe* is the bio-graphical-epic of the German musician of genius, representing in spirit the old Germany of Beethoven and Goethe, not the intoxicated empire of Wagner's trombones and Nietzsche's supermen, who would bring about this close understanding, with the two cultures, to the sound of glorious music, locked in an embrace somewhere in the Rhineland. The early volumes, filled with youth and hope, were as successful as they deserved to be; but the vast novel, as a whole, did not succeed in its own day and its faults will not dwindle with age. The pressure of the idea was too much for the not very robust novelist in Rolland; he lacked the creative energy and sheer human stuff, essential for fiction, to keep his narrative convincing, engaging, vital, to the end. He had many magnificent qualities (they can be discovered in the biography of his friend Péguy that he wrote in his old age, well outside our limit here), making him so finely responsive to the arts, so lofty an idealist, but he failed as a major novelist from a deficiency of another quality, often too coarse to accompany this high idealism but magical in its effects, the very quality that turns a thinker into a richly creative artist, an idea into colour and movement, character and life. The point is worth making, because this deficiency is so often discovered in men of great intelligence and sensitivity who turn to fiction and drama under the pressure of one dominating idea. It is as if the power of full rich creation, feminine in the male unconscious, refuses to respond to this Logos command. The creative literary form has to be loved, not merely used.

It is just what was missing in Rolland that was triumphantly present in Colette, who had no plan for saving Europe or anything else, cared nothing about marrying two national cultures or any mating without flesh and blood, had no grand ideals and very few ideas, but was fully in possession of this life-giving quality. As a girl, married to 'Willy' (who had a genius, anything but literary, for persuading other people to do his writing for him), Colette produced at her husband's request the sketchy and rather raffish series of Claudine stories; and as they were extremely popular it is almost certain that they delayed the recognition, especially outside France, of her later and completely independent work. For there are many Nobel prize-winners who can show us nothing to equal this Frenchwoman's original and deeply feminine genius. Over and above her treatment, so quick and sure, of sexual relationships, she is able to bring us into the physical scene, into an intimate contact with nature like the *participation mystique* of primitive man or our own childhood, in a manner, at once easy and yet frugal in its power of description, that has never been equalled by any other novelist of our time. Her limitations are obvious, and she knew herself too well to try to escape from them, but within her limited range, in her own world of passion and tenderness and an exquisitely feminine response to physical things and the atmosphere of an exact time and place, she is a marvel, to whom some of us, acting as grateful individuals and not as members of some solemn committee, would have awarded all the prizes within our grasp. If Colette is not good enough for Literature, then we ought to stay with her and let Literature go.

2

None of these earlier Nobel awards suggests any appreciation of what was 'modern' in European literature. They are a tribute to work well done in a previous age. So in 1902 the prize went to the German historian of Rome, Mommsen, born in 1817. Björnson was given the award in 1903, not undeservedly, though the mightier Ibsen was still alive. The following year, the old and rather faded Spanish dramatist, José Echegaray, shared the prize with Mistral. In 1905 Poland was honoured, in the choice of her chief story-teller, Sienkiewicz; Italy's turn came in 1906, when Carducci was chosen, a writer of power and weight both in his poetry and critical and polemical prose, but dating back to the *risorgimento*. But then, in 1907, came a surprise, for the first English writer to be given the award, Rudyard Kipling, was a mere baby of forty-two. He was, however, already descending from the summit of his career. Some of his best verse, in *Departmental Ditties*, and tales of British India, in *Plain Tales from the Hills*, *Soldiers Three*, and the rest, actually belonged to the last 1880s, when he found himself famous before he had reached the age of twenty-five. By 1907, the year of the award, though he had, and continued to have, an enormous number of admiring readers both at home and abroad, it was no longer the literary fashion to read him and to praise him, he was not one of the exciting 'moderns'; he was now the favourite author of the kind of English people denounced or mocked by Shaw and Wells and their young disciples; and, knowing all this, Kipling had already grumpily retired from the literary scene, almost pretending to be a Sussex squire who occasionally wrote something. This cheerless masquerade, which brought him the society of politicians, generals, 'empire-builders', and severed his roots as a writer, an imaginative artist, a man of feeling and intuition, was the outward sign of what had gone wrong within. The secret of Kipling's curious development is that the artist in him, not the brilliant technician he remained to the end but the imaginative, intuitive, warmly and deeply sympathetic artist in him, was born in and nourished by and unconsciously closely attached to India. (And in the early chapters of *Kim*, for example, we discover this artist at work, painting the scene like a master, whereas later in the story he disappears.) If he rejected India, as all his imperialist convictions, strengthened by his youthful dazzling success in England, compelled him to do, then he also rejected, with the grimmest determination, this deeper and more creative part of himself, his unconscious. This desperate battle with himself probably began during his stay in America, which offered him a free-and-easy democratic style of life that he also rejected, continued after his return to the England of the Boer War, when again he was offered a choice and made the wrong one, and ended in a melancholy stalemate, after the tension of it flashed into some of his best work, as he alternated between his Sussex squiredom and visits to South Africa. He lived with two murders, that of his early childhood in Bombay, that of the young reporter in Lahore.

This explains certain elements in Kipling that his enthusiastic admirers prefer to ignore. All of them suggest a narrowing and hardening mind, a cutting off of sympathy from the contemporary scene (with the artist finding some outlet in Indian animal tales or glimpses of the past for children), an inhuman or even anti-human strain in him. Machinery and technical devices become more important than people. (And one of his almost forgotten stories, *With the Night Mail*, describing a flight across the Atlantic in the year 2000, offers us a significant sketch of a highly technological and semi-Fascist world.) His supposedly humorous stories, in which he is at his worst, are childishly sadistic. Cruelty in some form or other finds its way into story after story. His final work, written after he had lost his son in the war and was himself a sick man, is so fantastically contrived and morbid in feeling that it seems pathological: we wander in the dark among the twisted ruins of a great talent. His sheer literary ability was astonishing. He was a complete original. As a poet—and he *was* a poet, even though he wrote a good deal of journalism turned into verse, like his once-famous *Recessional*, which is a Tory leading article in rhyme and an Old Testament costume—he reversed for himself the whole trend of the age, appearing as a public poet, writing for anybody, offering some of his best verse in the Cockney style of the regular soldiers serving in the East. The prose of his tales, very much his own, a prose at which he worked like a craftsman in metal (his father taught such crafts), is at once economic and effective, though often too hard and glittering, rather too brash in manner; but in England and abroad, especially in France, it had a considerable influence on the more literary writers of *reportage*. There have been signs during the last twenty years that the rapid decline of his once tremendous reputation has been halted, that what he did best will no longer be left unread in literary circles just because it is by Kipling. But though his great gifts can still be discovered, he remains a melancholy example of a writer who failed to grow in stature, using his gifts to the full, because he deliberately rejected, and tried to kill, the artist in himself. If he could have returned to the fountain-head, India, accepting all that he had accepted as a child, he might have gone forward from the early chapters of *Kim* to write masterpieces. In what is probably the best-known quotation from his verse, he declares that East and West can never meet. They could have met in him.

One reason for Kipling's loss of stature, both in England and elsewhere, was that during the years following the Boer War the aggressive imperialism he represented became very unpopular among younger literary men. In England they were largely swung over to the Left by Shaw and H. G. Wells. Public debating by men of letters was popular at this time, and Shaw, an experienced and adroit platform performer, revelled in it. Two of his familiar opponents, who argued in favour of their Catholic distributism and peasant proprietors and denounced Shaw's state socialism, should be mentioned here: Hilaire Belloc and G. K. Chesterton. Belloc, the older and more formidable figure, began as a young man of great promise, brilliantly versatile, but, after producing some excellent verse and a few satirical novels, books of travel (*The Path to Rome* is the best) and essays in a highly mannered but captivating prose, he scattered rather than concentrated his various abilities, using too much of his time and energy in fierce polemics and in histories from the Catholic point of view.

Chesterton, as essayist, critic, and fantastic story-teller, with an engaging manner all his own, became a popular figure perhaps rather too soon; his early work, however, is his best; he was too heavily committed to journalism and, like Belloc, to books commissioned by publishers, to give his very considerable talent the time and opportunity it required; his later work tends to be tired and slack; but there are imaginative high spirits in his fantastic tales, and behind the humorous paradoxes (and false analogies) and rhetorical fireworks of his essays there is some very shrewd, sometimes wise, social and literary criticism. Both Chesterton and Belloc, though keeping a solid core of Catholic admirers, were far more important and influential figures during these pre-war years of debate than they were after the war, when both the political and literary worlds, now sharply divided, changed completely. But this is more or less true of Shaw and Wells. It was in Edwardian England (which they condemned) and its afterglow until 1914 that they were the dominating figures.

If H. G. Wells, who died in 1946 in his eightieth year, had had a shorter life, his purely literary reputation would stand much higher than it does now. He belongs as a novelist to the period before the First War, and indeed some of his best science fiction, a term that has some meaning here with Wells, dates back to the 1890s. (That little masterpiece, *The Time Machine*, was as early as 1895.) After the First War, with his *Outline of History* and similar work, Wells became a popular educator on a world scale, a one-man UNESCO. Even before the war he had declared that he was not a literary man, an artist, but a journalist. It was at this time that he began writing novels, of which *The New Machiavelli* is the best example, that were indeed a kind of topical, journalistic fiction. This suited him, as a novelist passionately concerned with ideas, but pleased nobody else: the people who wanted the story and characters resented the intrusion of the ideas; the smaller number who welcomed Wells's ideas preferred to do so outside the dubious atmosphere of fiction; and while Wells could do more with this kind of novel than anybody else, he could not make it successful when it was asking for failure. His earlier novels, outside his science fiction, are a very different matter. *Kipps* and *Mr. Polly*, wonderful examples of character, sharp observation, humour and insight, were essentially new and 'modern' because they looked at life and contemporary society from the standpoint of a very large and neglected class, the struggling and confused lower-middle class of clerks and shop assistants. *Tono Bungay*, his most ambitious novel and probably his masterpiece, is sociological fiction, combining insights into both private and public life, that has a wide reach and yet is very much alive. And because it arrived in the Thirties, when he had long been out of fashion and was neglected by the younger critics, his ample two-volume *Experiment in Autobiography* deserves special mention, for it is in fact a remarkably good account of this whole age, particularly the period up to 1914, by one of its most honest and liveliest minds.

Indeed, it was the open honesty of Wells, even more than his irrepressible liveliness, that got him into trouble, made him vulnerable. Where other public men created an image of themselves, a *persona*, to withstand the wear and strain of public life—and there is no better example of this arena figure than that created by his friend, Bernard Shaw—Wells adopted no attitude, wore no mask, no padded and stiffened costume. What the reader was offered for his money was the candid spectacle of H. G. Wells learning how to live, educating himself, grappling with things. (This explains why this affectionate and friendly man was so often impatient and irascible in his public controversies: he felt that while he was being as honest and candid as possible, his opponents were merely maintaining attitudes; and generally he was right.) The secret of Wells is that his temperament and natural genius were always in opposition to his training and conscious outlook. For the latter were scientific, and acquired at the very time, the Eighties and early Nineties, when science was most sure of itself, while his temperament and natural genius were essentially literary. As a young and enthusiastic teacher of science, he only began to write when his health broke down. Really a born writer, soon able to conquer the literary world, he never really regarded himself as a member of that world, a writer among writers, an artist among artists: his background, he felt, was science. This accounts for his bold but sketchy plans for transforming society, his quick changes of mind, his impatience and growing disgust and despair. (But his very last book, *Mind at the End of its Tether*, with its strange tone of utter despair, should not be accepted as his final testament; what it really shows us is an old and dying man projecting his own approaching dissolution upon the whole universe.) He demanded that the world outside science should order itself as rationally as the world inside science does, and became impatient and angry because its irrational forces were so powerful. This was his weakness. But his scientific training and outlook, when they were allied to his literary genius, brought him and his readers much that was new and valuable: not only the science fiction and the uncannily accurate prophecies; not only a bold disregard for lifeless tradition and mandarin conventions, both in the novel and in his sociology; but a fresh eye and an unusual viewpoint, a range of interest denied to most writers, the honesty and candour of the laboratories, a new tone and temper belonging to his own time. Literary criticism, as it narrowed and became itself more introverted, may have come to undervalue him, even to ignore him; nevertheless he left a whole world, wider than that of Western Man, a world he had helped to educate, deep in his debt.

Though they held many ideas in common and, in spite of some sharp public disagreements, must have encouraged each other, Wells and Shaw were very different men, no more alike in temperament than they were in physical make-up. Whereas Wells faced the world with the thinnest possible *persona*, Shaw, following a fashion among Irish writers (no wonder Yeats praises the Mask), very deliberately built up a formidable *persona*, a figure for the platform and the press, the G.B.S. of legend. The real Bernard Shaw was courteous, kind, generous, shy rather than impudent, physically strong and courageous, yet rather timid and prudish in his relations with the world of food and drink, sex or hearty male companionship and conviviality, no dramatist for the Mermaid Tavern; but this *persona*-creation of his for the world's eye, this tremendous G.B.S., combined impudent wit with ruthless destructive criticism, showed no reverence for anybody or anything, spared no feelings, pulled down and kicked aside all idols, and somehow contrived to suggest, at one and the same time, a puritan prophet and a new Mephistopheles. Out of various elements available to serious 'advanced' circles in the Eighties—chiefly contributed by Marx, Nietzsche, Samuel Butler (the author of *Erewhon* and an iconoclast of great originality), Ibsen and Bergson—Bernard Shaw constructed a platform and philosophy for G.B.S.

347

and gradually acquired, chiefly by speaking in public anywhere and at any time, the most formidable debating style of the age. It is a style that is all the more effective because it is never discovered groping for the truth, never suggests any uncertainty. The man who said he wished he were as sure about anything as Macaulay seemed to be about everything should have read or listened to G.B.S. For it was G.B.S. with the beard and the eyebrows, not the Bernard Shaw who hid behind them, who used this style like a two-handed sword. Wells in debate could lose his head and his temper because he was honestly expressing what he thought and felt and was emotionally involved with his opinions. G.B.S. never lost his head and his temper because, being a *persona*-figure or a permanent character-part, he was not emotionally committed to his ideas. In those years before 1914 Chesterton and others often rebuked their newspaper readers, the crowd, for not perceiving that G.B.S. was a serious consistent thinker, for telling one another that this chap Shaw would say anything for effect, would swear that black was white, and so forth. But in its own clumsy but intuitive fashion the crowd was right, sensing justly that there was a lack of deep-down seriousness in this G.B.S. who was always making for the limelight; he might be clowning on behalf of the Life-force, Lamarckian evolution, Marx's theory of value, Fabian Socialism, but he was still clowning.

The private Bernard Shaw was an honourable and meticulously honest man. The public G.B.S. was dishonest. He was dishonest about sex, which he pretended to have outgrown when he had merely dodged it. He was dishonest about the social and political systems he advocated. G.B.S. could admire and loudly praise a Stalin when Bernard Shaw could never have endured three months of the Stalinist atmosphere of sudden arrests, torture, and murder. G.B.S. existed, having been created for it, in a world of ideas and debate and intellectual comedy, not the real world in which men bleed, women scream for mercy, children cry in bewilderment or terror. To him 'the liquidation' of whole classes is merely their painless disappearance, not mass arrests and murder, corpses dumped into quicklime. It may be objected that this is G.B.S. in old age—and there is grim irony in the fact that Shaw, after making G.B.S. tell us that we did not live long enough, sadly outlived his friends and his world, only to endanger his reputation—but this same lack of feeling for and contact with the real world can be found in the plays of his early middle age. So, for example, when we see *Captain Brassbound's Conversion* now, and watch a cool and smiling Lady Cicely settling everything in that corner of Morocco, we wonder why it never occurs to her or anybody else there that charming ladies like her in similar places have been raped and then had their throats cut. It is true, of course, that some things sincerely held and felt by Bernard Shaw himself were built into the G.B.S. platform. There can be no doubt, for instance, that he reacted violently against the life, messy and sloppy, boozy and bohemian, that he knew as a boy in Dublin, and that this reaction accounts not only for a strong puritanical strain in him but also for the G.B.S. insistence upon order and authority, his preference for imperial Great Powers (he would not denounce the Boer War as most of his friends did), his approval of dictators, from Julius Cæsar to that mock-Cæsar Mussolini, designed by the Life-force to rule the untidy, sensual, idle-minded mob. Shaw's personal temper, tone, style of life, were more aristocratic than democratic. The egalitarian society advocated by G.B.S., who argued in favour of equal pay for everybody, would soon have developed a privilege system (first-grade civil servants entitled to book six opera seats a year, second-grade only three), more galling to people low on all lists than differences in income above a reasonable level. And if G.B.S. had allotted the privileges, there would certainly have been some for master dramatists.

That he is one of our master dramatists there can be no doubt. The copiousness, originality and splendid vitality of his drama entitle him to be recognised as the greatest comic dramatist since Molière. The plays are not entirely the work of the G.B.S. of the polemics, prefaces and public appearances. He had the private Bernard Shaw to assist him; it is their collaboration that gives this drama its unique quality. One of them supplied the power of debate, the wit, the impudence, the iconoclasm; the other contributed the characters (which are much better than many of his critics would have us believe), the cheerful nonsense, the occasional and unexpected flashes of beauty, tenderness, wisdom. There is an Irishman at work here as well as the Fabian Society's famous intellectual clown. And the very lack of any deeply personal emotional commitment to many of his ideas was of enormous value to him in the creation of comedy, keeping the best of it clear of sourness, ill-temper, hysterical injustice, lighting the stage with a golden good-nature, which we remember with gratitude after we may have forgotten what we laughed at, recognising it for what it is—a kind of poetry, the sign of a master, wrung out of satirical comedy. It is this, together of course with the unfailing wit and the manner and style tested by, triumphant upon, hundreds of platforms, that gives him his supremacy in modern comedy. But the actual form in which he succeeded is his own creation. He invented a new comedy, a comedy not of situation and character, though of course he cannot dispense with them, but of debate, of intellectual conflict and high spirits. And although he was one of the most brilliant dramatic critics of this or any other age, he might be said to have begun his own playwriting outside the Theatre, that is, without developing any existing theatrical technique, and to have started at a point where two other lines of interest and experience seemed to meet. One of these came from his years of public speaking, his expert knowledge of platform debating devices, eloquence, humour, and of the reactions and behaviour of audiences. (So directors and actors favour his plays because they dominate the audience so easily and surely.) The other, strange as it may seem, came from his love of opera, which he enjoyed more than he did the spoken drama. He approached his plays as if they were a kind of opera without music—a duet here, then a trio, another duet, then perhaps a quartette, and so forth. And if anybody imagines this to be a guess and far-fetched, we can add that we have heard him explain, in some detail, this curious and very personal manner of conceiving a play.

His limitations are obvious to any intelligent playgoer. His dramatic method, apart from this operatic approach, is far from being subtle. Having learnt from his platform experience that earnest people, capable of appreciating his ideas and wit, are always easily amused by broadly comic effects, he never hesitates, when the debate ought to be interrupted, to introduce some rather rough clowning—a solemn character in a ridiculous costume, a woman shouting, a man bursting into tears, and so on. Having once achieved his own comedy of debate, he makes few experiments in form and technique, is not afraid of wildly improbable situations or of handling his cast as if they were playing an operetta. Some of the basic situations in his most successful plays, as for example *The Doctor's Dilemma*, are sheer impudence. His range of characters, though wider than is commonly thought and including some excellent raffish types with whom perhaps he had an unconscious sympathy (as he had with similar types, like Frank Harris, in real life), is limited, if we accept him as a great dramatist. When he is consciously aiming at a deeply poetical effect, either in situation or character, he can be bad, worse than lesser men. He is uneasy with life on irrational, instinctive, intuitive levels; so, for example, his sexual relationships are inadequately presented, dodged and scamped. But, after all, what he mostly offers us is his own kind of intellectual comedy, in which he is inimitable. (And therefore should not be imitated: his enormous success and influence have persuaded too many playwrights, before they knew better, to attempt Shaw plays.) And the sheer vitality of his drama is demonstrated by the fact that his earliest plays (actually some of his best), having survived sixty years and the disappearance of many social ideas that he challenged, do not seem faded and out-moded, empty of laughter. Nobody now believes in the romantic notion of war ridiculed in *Arms and the Man*, but everybody delights in the play. Or *You Never Can Tell* may no longer seem a play of ideas but is enchanting in its grave nonsense, a companion piece to Wilde's *Importance of Being Earnest*, a gift to the world of Irish wit. No doubt that G.B.S. figure, as guide, philosopher and friend, should be dubiously regarded, being without essential wisdom; and the Bernard Shaw who created that figure is dead; but the George Bernard Shaw of the Theatre, with his wonderful intellectual high spirits and his atmosphere of golden good-nature, fills our playhouses with delight and laughter, and is alive.

During these years before the First War, the English literary scene had more than its share of major writers, especially in fiction, and we cannot leave it without noticing some of them. Though Joseph Conrad was a Pole, he served with the British mercantile marine, then lived in England and wrote in English; but his literary influences were largely French, and there are times when his prose reads like a translation from French, while in temperament and outlook he is closer to Eastern Europe than he is to the West. Before 1914 he was greatly admired by intelligent critics but was not widely read until the war came, and unfortunately the novels he wrote during these last years, for he died in 1923, are inferior to his earlier fiction. The new post-war criticism, excited about Joyce, Proust, Kafka, forgot about Conrad; but there are signs now, when Symbolism in fiction is being so much praised and it is being belatedly discovered in Conrad, that he will yet receive the attention and recognition he well deserves. But he is one of those writers whose importance we find hard to estimate, just because at some time in our lives we are completely fascinated by them, and then later, because we have already taken so much from them, we miss this first enchantment. About some of his shorter and stronger tales, of which *Heart of Darkness* is a magnificent example, there can be no doubt: they are masterpieces of their kind. When, however, he is most ambitious and most involved, he is often much less satisfying, especially when we return to him after a long interval: his slow-motion impressionism, his device of a narrator, a Marlowe, within his narrative, his heavy indications of psychological depths that we never really explore, can even be irritating, making us feel we are being offered a common-place tale of action pretentiously over-dressed. But at his best he does take the tale of action and, losing nothing on the way, raise it to a new high level, giving us a sharp and often terrifying vision of Man himself, with nothing to guide or help him but the skill he has mastered and a few simple loyalties, moving in a little lighted space above the dark destructive elements, which may be the China Sea in a typhoon or the black horror of the jungle or the corruption invading some back street. His outlook is understandable: he spent years as mate or master of lonely sailing ships, and then came, a sailor ashore, an alien with few friends, to try to find exact shades of meaning in a foreign language. Nobody could be further removed from a Shaw or a Wells, from a believer in any -*ism* except stoicism. He was a pessimist, but, unlike so many writers, he was a manly and not an ignoble pessimist, believing that a man by self-mastery and loyalty should be ready to face the worst. He cannot be identified with any literary movement. He is a solitary figure in modern literature, the novelist of lonely men who find themselves hard-pressed and try to do their duty, of unfamiliar and unfashionable heroes who, with some tragic exceptions, are genuinely heroic.

French influence is easily discovered in the earlier fiction of George Moore, an Irish contemporary of Shaw and Wilde, who had once been an art student in Paris and knew the great Impressionists. It is seen at its best, as naturalism in English fiction, in his *Esther Waters*, published as early as 1894. Later, during and immediately after the war, he was to return to fiction, with *The Brook Kerith* and *Héloïse and Abélard*, conceived and written in a very different spirit and style, not unimpressive but very self-conscious in a kind of *édition-de-luxe* manner. But during these years before 1914 he was bringing out what many of us regard as his master-piece, his three-part autobiography, based on his relations with the Irish literary movement: *Hail and Farewell*. This is reminiscence coloured by prejudice, shaped without much respect for truth, but transformed into a delightful work of art, unifying the varied expression of Moore's odd personality, in which sensitiveness and insensitiveness, unusual candour and impudent lying, great talent and silliness, are huddled together. Though as English as Moore is Irish, Arnold Bennett was even more deeply indebted to France. A systematic man, who enjoyed making and carrying out plans, Bennett quitted journalism in London to begin his literary career proper in France, the country most sympathetic to literary careers. His most successful and strongest novel, *The Old Wives' Tale*, was written there, and published in 1908. After fifty years, it will seem to any intelligent reader still a good novel, to any reader, that is, who is not demanding what Bennett is not offering, such as Symbolism, metaphysics, depth psychology, wild eroticism, any idea of ordinary people as dummies or monsters. He never quite achieved this Old Dutch Master solidity again, though he comes near it in *Clayhanger* and, after the war, in *Riceyman Steps*. And his very last novel, *Imperial Palace*, revealing at length and in all its complexity the management of a large luxurious hotel (Bennett was always fascinated by both organisation and luxury), because it appeared when literary fashion had turned away from his kind of extroverted and sharply observant fiction, has not had the attention it deserves as a humanist's account of a typically modern example of social machinery, a little collective at work. (It is, after all, a weakness in deeply introverted writers, entangled in subtle states of mind, groping their way

through the inner world, that they cannot offer us recognisable and convincing accounts of life as it is lived among our elaborate organisations,
social machinery, collectives. So we lose to the inner world, on this level
of literature, the significance of our relations with what is typical of our
outer world.) The comparative failure of Arnold Bennett's later fiction,
sufficiently readable and entertaining but without weight and depth, is
explained by the fact that his success had cut the roots that nourished his
work. He was a novelist of provincial life who no longer had any
provincial life; and the smart rich people with whom he dined, now that
he was a success, could not provide him with an adequate substitute for
this life. And many other highly successful modern writers have suffered
in this fashion. They reach the height they have dreamt of, only to discover that the supply of oxygen is dwindling.

We now come to another Nobel Prize winner, for in 1932, the year
before his death, the award went to John Galsworthy. He enjoyed a very
large international reputation after the war, chiefly because his *Forsyte
Saga*—and the idea of putting together several of his novels under this
title was not his inspiration but his publisher's—was regarded abroad as a
representative portrait of England. But he belongs as a creative writer
and not simply as a literary figure to this period before the war. Both his
best novel, *The Man of Property*, and what may come to be regarded as
his best play, *The Silver Box*, first appeared in 1906. He had been writing
for some years but it was a crisis in his personal life, ending with his
marriage to his cousin's former wife in 1905, that gave his work character
and force. Having quarrelled bitterly with the class to which he belonged,
the solid unimaginative upper-middle class, the men who were always
thinking about property and included their wives in that description,
Galsworthy sharply challenged its pretensions and limitations in his fiction,
and showed his sympathy with its victims in his plays. It was highly
conscious rebellion, and, in spite of his genuinely broad sympathies,
Galsworthy makes us feel that unconsciously he still identified himself
with this class. (This accounts for the greater richness and sense of life
in *The Indian Summer of a Forsyte*.) Both as a man and as a writer he had
fine qualities, but we miss in his fiction and his drama the total commitment, conscious and unconscious, of the artist, and the life-giving element

354

this brings with it. His contemptuous dismissal by the younger critics of the Twenties was unjust; they forgot what he had accomplished years before; but if he had been able to broaden and deepen his vendetta against one section of society into a rebellion against every life-denying aspect of it, if he could have exchanged his real but rather aloof pity for its victims for a warm imaginative identification with them, he would have more than justified the position he occupied as a literary figure. His one act of rebellion before 1906 charged the batteries for some years; to commit further acts, keeping the batteries charged, would have made him disreputable in his own sight; and John Galsworthy was, after all, in his essence a conscientious and respectable citizen, in fact a Forsyte.

A very different writer must make his entrance here, even though his most ambitious novel, *A Passage to India*, did not appear until 1924. This is of course E. M. Forster, and although he does not seem to belong to this pre-war age at all, the fact remains that all his novels except the last came out in the middle of this period, beginning with *Where Angels Fear to Tread* in 1905 and concluding, at least for an extraordinarily long interval, with *Howard's End* in 1910. These dates are surprising, not only because Forster, happily, is still alive and must therefore have been very young when he made his reputation as a novelist, but also because he seems to belong in spirit to the time after the war, to the Twenties and Thirties for which he acted as a remote advance guard. So his reputation was still rising when Wells, Bennett, Galsworthy, in fashionable literary opinion, were fading figures of the past. Yet in some respects his early novels 'date' even more than theirs do. The difference is that while their kind of fiction was going out of literary fashion, his was coming into it. He rejected from the first any idea of being a solid chronicler of a society, of filling with realistic detail a broad canvas, of making his narrative acceptable and convincing by accumulating representative characters and events. He works in brilliant flashes, sudden revelations of character, glimpses of heights and depths, action that is not realistic and typical but symbolic. Loading everything in a scene with meaning, this evocative method, closer to poetic creation than to ordinary prose narrative, makes unusual demands upon a novelist, and this probably explains why Forster in his later years has abandoned fiction for the essay, which he writes with captivating skill and charm. His *Aspects of the Novel*, though a brilliant performance, leaves us with the feeling that he has no great regard for this form of literature. Although he may be said to have changed the direction of the English Novel, and brought to his own fiction a poet, a psychologist, a philosopher of a sort, he is never entirely satisfactory, judged strictly as a novelist. There is an uneasy wobble in his narrative, and the world he shows us, though intensely real at certain moments, never seems steadily there for long. It is like looking at life through glass that is beautifully thin and clear in some places and thick and distorting in others. This is not due to any want of ability—Forster is one of the most intelligent novelists in any literature—but to a Puckish wilfulness, defying the realistic approach and probability. But then the novels themselves point the contrast between what is heavily formal, slavishly and stupidly conventional, life-denying, and all that is life-enhancing, sensuous, personal: the conflict between pot and Pan. The more ambitious *Howard's End*, however, complicates this conflict, and *A Passage to India*, which adds racial relationships (though these are not its subject) to the intricate pattern, is even more elaborate: a novel that requires several readings to be appreciated to the full, undoubtedly Forster's masterpiece. But it has taken us eleven years beyond 1914.

3

That excellent American critic, Van Wyck Brooks, writing as a young man just after the European War (as it was then) had broken out, introduced into an essay, to deplore them, those brand-new slang terms 'Highbrow' and 'Lowbrow'. (He was wise enough, even then, to realise that the common use of these terms, dividing people into two opposed classes and somehow disliking both of them, would do far more harm than good. It has in fact done literature a disservice.) It seemed that what was produced, and handsomely rewarded, at home, in America, was 'lowbrow', and what was 'highbrow' was imported from Europe, especially from England. For all its material progress, or perhaps because of it, the America of the early 1900s, ploughing and hammering and trading across the whole continent, appeared less capable of creating literature than the New England of fifty years before. (Nobody guessed that within a few years the American literary scene would have changed entirely.) There had been Stephen Crane and Frank Norris, who died too young; there were amusing fellows like O. Henry and George Ade, a good satirical regionalist like Ellen Glasgow, sound craftsmen like Booth Tarkington, who might escape from easy sentimentality if they could resist the commercial pressure of the magazines. And if the literary scene appeared bleak and arid during these years, it was not improved by the knowledge that many established American writers, the men headed by Henry James, the women by Edith Wharton, had already chosen to turn their backs on America, to live and work in Europe. These 'expatriates', as they were soon to be called, were often denounced by their fellow-countrymen, who have in turn been attacked for their narrowness and prejudice. This is an American quarrel. Nevertheless, we may observe that the out-and-out defenders of the 'expatriates' are being rather obtuse when they point out that English writers, a long list, were not denounced for preferring to live out of England. The difference between an ancient kingdom and a comparatively new republic, a revolutionary experiment based on a kind of contract between the federal government and its citizens, is far too great for any such parallel. Moreover, it was felt in America—and rightly too—that here across the huge continent, where plainsmen who had fought the Indian and hunted the buffalo now saw cities rising, were a new people and a new style of life, demanding the attention of writers who called themselves American. To stay away, it was felt, was to keep on running away.

That very distinguished Bostonian, Henry Adams, was no ordinary 'expatriate', quite apart from the fact that he repeatedly returned to the Washington that he and his family had known so well; but he might be said to have turned, in his final phase, into an 'expatriate' from the whole modern age. What lured him away can be discovered in his *Mont-Saint-Michel and Chartres*. What he thought and felt as a wide-ranging enquirer and as a baffled kind of historian, bent on instructing his many friends rather than the general public, is to be found in his curious but valuable autobiography, *The Education of Henry Adams*. It has some bad faults.

The device of writing it in the third person is irritating. And though he writes well on the whole, he is too often turgid and confused in his exposition of ideas. Even a reader without scientific bias may well feel that Adams should have either learnt more science or left it alone. Nevertheless, unlike his first readers, we are in position now to appreciate some of his remarkable intuitive insights, prophetic flashes that are far more important than such argument as he attempts. It is not what he systematically thought but what he felt, almost in his bones, that fascinates us now. He *felt* the dangerously rapid acceleration of discovery and invention, the menace of giant forces released like genii from bottles, the perilous one-sidedness of an age that was losing the values of the feminine principle. It is this deeply intuitive feeling, not his conscious ideas of world history in phases, that makes us believe that here is one man in 1904 who, if he had been given a glimpse of the hydrogen bombs of 1954, would have been shocked but not altogether astounded. Thus, any notion of Henry Adams, admiring Norman stained-glass and carvings, as merely one of the most eloquent of American sentimental culture-tourists, must be abandoned. And quite apart from its strange insights, *The Education of Henry Adams* is one of the best accounts we possess of a sensitive enquiring mind in the latter half of the nineteenth century.

Delaying the appearance of the most famous of the earlier 'expatriates', Henry James, and returning to the American scene, we must say something about Theodore Dreiser, even though his importance in the development of American fiction is much greater than any international reputation his own fiction has won for him. He can only be judged abroad by what he contributed to literature, and although his contribution cannot be dismissed, it is inferior to what has since been offered to us by some American novelists who followed him. But they followed him, as a smoothly efficient farmer might follow the clumsy pioneer who first broke the soil. Dreiser was clumsy too, a big, lumbering, oafish man, but in his stubborn fashion he did break off thick chunks of real life, much closer to reality than the highly laundered and prettified selections from it then offered as 'wholesome reading'. It is true that between *Sister Carrie* and *An American Tragedy*, his naturalistic beginning and ending, Dreiser is by no means confining himself to characters and modes of life he

knows directly—there must have been a good deal of guessing and invent-
ing behind *The Titan* and *The 'Genius'*, for example—but he is doing his
best to enlarge and truthfully record the world in which his stories
happen. He has, for instance, stopped pretending, in order to satisfy the
Society for the Prevention of Vice, that sexually moral women cannot
behave badly and that sexually immoral women cannot behave well.
What he did required no profundity, no subtlety, only some honesty and
courage, for he was simply taking fiction out of a completely unreal
atmosphere and bringing it closer to what any group in a bar or a news-
room knew about life. He was not a great novelist, though a considerable one; but he cleared a space in which American fiction could breathe
while it worked.

Did Henry James, who certainly worked hard enough, breathe the
finest oxygen or make do with one collapsed lung? In other words, have
we in him one of the supreme masters of the novel, as we are so often told
now that he is in fashion, or a novelist of great skill and originality who
yet leaves us dissatisfied and dubious? The question does not turn on his
earlier fiction, chiefly concerned with the difference between the American
outlook of the time and the European, but on the value of the Jamesian
essence, increasingly distilled at greater strength. Our reply will depend,
first, on our attitude towards fiction, and, secondly, on our purely
personal response to what is very personal in James. But what will not be
in dispute is his long devotion to literature (we can forget his sad flirtation
with the Theatre), or his high degree of sensitivity and intelligence, his
boundless curiosity, the unfailing literary zest that lights up his massive
personality, or, what is too often forgotten, the wide range and variety
of his life's work. Whatever our attitude towards fiction, whatever our
personal response to him may be, we cannot possibly deny him a kind of
greatness. But there remains the question—is he one of the supreme
masters of the novel?

Those critics, a small but powerful group, who claim for James the
highest rank, may generally be found demanding, first, that a work of
fiction should be a work of art, as a sonata or a painted landscape is a work
of art, and, secondly, that the novelist-artist should be a conscious moralist,
directing the reader through his imagination to draw certain conclusions,

359

critical of man's behaviour in society and belonging ultimately to the sphere of moral values. (But these, it is only fair to add, must not be interpreted narrowly but as widely as possible.) And on this view of fiction, James's stature rises at once. It is he, as he tells us over and over again, who is consciously devoted to the art of fiction. It is he who composes a novel as if it were a sonata, organises it as if it were a landscape on canvas. It is he who insists more and more on the strictly defined point of view. Not for him the random chronicling and slap-dash improvisations of the novelist indifferent to his art. And he is a moralist, quite obviously and firmly at first and then later pursuing and contrasting finer and finer shades of conduct. He brings to fiction, so much in need of them, adult and exquisitely civilised standards, European in their depth of culture, American in their candid purity. If in his later work, where the essence is finer but stronger, he makes heavy demands on the reader, so much the better. This will winnow the 'finer awarenesses' from the coarser; those readers who understand the Master's own "sort of plea for Criticism, for Discrimination, for Appreciation on other than infantile lines" from those who, not belonging to the elect, remain childishly uncritical and indiscriminating, inappreciative of the novel as a form of art and as a presentation of the finest shades of feeling, the highest moral values.

A man might be anxious not only to be fair but to be sympathetic to Henry James, who at the worst was a lovable human being of great talent, and yet feel that there is a certain strain in him, when he has donned the Master's robes, that has produced in his disciples too much complacency or supercilious self-righteousness. This encourages a brutal frankness in the case against him. Now clever persons, especially the more feminine, are adept at transforming their defects into apparent virtues, at painting weakness to look like strength. James may or may not have been a master novelist, but he was certainly a master of that process and illusion. Deeply aware of his limitations as a man and a writer, he created the criticism that would disregard those limitations. What *he* could do in a novel made it a work of art. What he could not do was inessential to fiction on this higher level. Undoubtedly he had a passion for literature —it was his only passion—and especially for the art (always impure) of fiction. And he wrote himself: "The only reason for the existence of a novel is that it does attempt to represent life." But to represent life with any breadth, depth, feeling, a man must have had to be up to the neck in it somewhere, and not have merely gone about on tiptoe, peeping at it. James left America, defeated by it, as he was to be defeated by many things. (However, to give him his due, this became one of his main themes.) But he did not *live* in London: he filled his notebooks and worked there and dined out. He was the nice polite American who came to dinner, without knowing how close Father had been to bankruptcy with that Australian business, why Mother had so many headaches, why Daughter was sulking, why Son was a little drunk, why the butler and the younger parlourmaid exchanged such glances, why the cook had given notice, without really knowing what was happening in the house. True, he was intensely curious, but he was on the outside, not inside the life there.

He was kept on the outside by his odd status, by his lack of ordinary commitment and involvement, by his detachment from the struggle in which most people are engaged, the heat and dust and mess, by his timidity and sexual ambiguity. It is all this, and not his concentration upon "the finer awareness", that gives so much of his fiction a bloodless quality, a spectral air. He had to represent life from the narrowest base that any major novelist has ever had, with only one toe on the ground. Certainly, given such disadvantages, he worked wonders, especially during the Eighties, that compelling decade, when he gave us among other things *The Portrait of a Lady*, *The Bostonians*, *The Princess Casamassima*; and it is fascinating to see how, after he returned from his melancholy debauch with that old harlot, the Theatre, contents of the unconscious pushed their way into his work. For what he accomplished not only in spite of his limitations but by making use of them, he deserves our praise and affectionate thanks. But we are entitled to be suspicious of his own critical attitude, and to resent what his more fanatical admirers have since done with him and his attitude. "Because thou art virtuous, shall there be no more cakes and ale?" Because Henry James so easily imposes a form and pattern on his docile material, have earthier or more exuberant novelists to follow his tame example? If a novel must "attempt to represent life", then why should a grey thin novel, however neatly contrived and finely aware, be any better than a thick rich novel, however untidy and less delicately perceptive? And is James, in his later manner, being more and more subtly aware, or is he often writing very clumsily about nothing very much? If we know already that we must live while we can, reaching while the apple is on the bough, why should we regard this tiptoeing along interminable airless corridors, in search of some further confirmation of such truths, as fiction at its highest pitch? Because he did so much so well, sensible relative criticism cannot help but recognise him as a major novelist. But to use his very deficiencies as criteria for fiction as Literature, to hoist him into the commanding position of a supreme master, is not sensible, and seems a little sinister: as if the newest criticism, establishing Modern Literature, had switched the current from the positive to the negative, as if supremacy required a lack of richness and fullness in life and art, as if a ghost might write better than a man.

4

Because the more important poets and dramatists either lived through the war years or appeared after them, it is wiser to reserve any accounts of the poetic and dramatic movements of the whole age for the last chapter. And without the poets and dramatists, the German and Austrian shelves seem rather bare during the years before 1914. Even Thomas Mann, though he had *Buddenbrooks* and *Death in Venice* to his credit, did not achieve his great international reputation, chiefly through his *Magic Mountain*, until after the war. The German Nobel prize-winners, after Mommsen, were Eucken in 1908, old Heyse in 1910, and Hauptmann in 1912, and with none of these are we now concerned. It was a generous allowance for Germany and suggests some prejudice against any Russian choice, for not only was the giant Tolstoy still alive, at least until 1910, but there was also the writer who had been since the beginning of the century more widely discussed throughout the Western world than any other, namely, A. M. Peshkov, who called himself Maxim Gorky. In the Nineties he had flashed up like a rocket from vagrancy into world fame; and after the revolution of 1905, in which he had taken part, it was the pressure of foreign public opinion that had compelled the Tsar's government to release him. He began a triumphant world tour, to collect funds for his fellow-revolutionaries, and it was during this tour that the momentous discovery was made, in New York, that the woman with him was not his wife. (He had separated from his wife but no divorce was possible under Russian law.) The American public, preparing to pay him the highest honours, felt outraged; Mark Twain and Howells refused to attend the banquet for him; he and his mistress were promptly turned out of their hotel. Gorky retaliated by putting New York into a series of stories as *The City of the Yellow Devil*; the seeds of misunderstanding and ill-will were first sown.

Gorky made good use of his immense literary earnings and astonishing energy by establishing and directing a publishing house, 'Znanie' or 'Knowledge'. The most important of his writers were Bunin, Kuprin, Andreyev. Bunin, who hated the Bolsheviks and, as his memoirs prove, any writers who accepted them, was awarded the Nobel Prize in 1933, as the leader of the Russian writers in exile; probably, for much of his work written before the revolution was not widely known outside Russia, as the author of that laconic little masterpiece, *The Gentleman from San Francisco*. Kuprin has been called a Russian Jack London—for Jack London enjoyed enormous prestige, quite out of proportion to the literary merit of his story-telling, among Russian and other revolutionaries in these years before 1914—and, if not famous, was at least notorious chiefly for his anti-military novel, *The Duel*, and his account of a brothel in Odessa, *The Pit*. Andreyev, unstable and entirely pessimistic himself and a very unequal writer, not without good invention and creative ideas but writing too often in an alcoholic haze, was never taken very seriously by Russian critical opinion, but has had a more lasting success outside Russia, where his *Seven that were Hanged* has been widely read and also drama-tised, and his play *He who Gets Slapped*, probably because of its symbolical circus scene, has frequently been produced. Another who had a large international public for many years was Merezhkovsky, the poet and critic, but almost entirely for his trilogy of philosophical-historical novels about Julian the Apostate, Leonardo, Peter the Great, to which he brought much industry and erudition, a pretentious and irritating use of anti-thesis, and very little evidence of any genuine creative imagination. Two other characteristic works of this period, well-known outside Russia, were the gloomy and perverse Sologub's *The Little Demon*, whose sadistic schoolmaster, Peredonov, was a creation of some power; and the more trivial Artsybashev's *Sanin*, shallow writing about free love and sex, but intoxicating reading for Russian schoolgirls in 1907, and much discussed, a year or two later, among 'advanced' undergraduates in the West. There can be no doubt that between the revolution that failed in 1905 and the one that succeeded in 1917 Russian fiction lost almost all trace of the force and depth it had had during the nineteenth century; such social influence, always important in Russia, as it had was not good, often really corrupting; and, as we have already seen, it was the memory of this melancholy period that influenced the Bolshevik leaders who, after Gorky's return to the Soviet Union in 1928, put the crushing weight of their authority behind his socialist realism.

It is hard to decide about Gorky. As a figure he looms tremendously, not only in his final role as the solitary giant writer of the Soviet Union, which gave him every honour it could devise, but also in his earlier phase, now so often forgotten, when he had a far greater international reputation than his friend Chehov. There are two reasons why he was so successful outside Russia. The first is that he was a political revolutionary at a time when liberal opinion throughout the Western world denounced the Tsar's government. The second reason is more important, from our point of view. In his early stories and drama Gorky wrote about the humblest workers, the vagrants, the outcasts, whom he had known in his teens as he tramped from one odd job to the next. This made him at once a modern of the moderns. He arrived just at the right time, when readers and playgoers, or at least those in search of what was 'modern', entertained a belief very fashionable in literary circles from 1895 to 1905, and one that came back with the Thirties. (And it is now, after another twenty-five years, in fashion again.) It is the belief that novels and plays about low life, about prostitutes, pimps, tramps, casual labourers, thieves, outcast drunks and drug addicts, are somehow more 'real', more vital, more deeply significant, than the fiction and drama concerned with the

vast majority who work regular hours, pay their way, change their under-
clothes, and belong at some level to society. Youthful members of the
comfortable classes, feeling rebellious or bored, have always been
attracted to this idea of fiction and drama. Fundamentally it is not a
realistic view, even though a second-rate writer might find more easy
material for sensational writing on this doss-house level than elsewhere;
it is sentimental-romantic, and merely reverses the convention of the
'nice' novel asked for at libraries, the 'nice' play demanded by matinée
audiences.

Gorky, of course, was not following a fashion—and indeed, though the
taste and the idea behind it already existed, he may have largely created
the fashion—for he began writing, like a sensible youth, about the life he
knew best. But he reached world-wide success all the sooner because
there was in him more than a strain of the sentimental-romantic, together
with a fondness for popular philosophising that masses of his readers
shared with him, just as they shared his lack of any formal education.
And indeed he was regarded as being over-emotional by his grim Marxist
comrades, although in fact his practical and optimistic spirit was of great
service both to the revolutionary cause and then afterwards to the Russian
writers bewildered and victimised by the revolution itself. Even when
we have made allowance for the Soviet incense through which he
loomed in his final years, and for some dubious elements in his personality
as he aged, he remains an impressive figure, but as a creative writer without the stature he was once thought to have had. In fiction, for all his
Twenty-six Men and a Girl and some fine short things, and in drama,
despite the firm hold of his *Lower Depths* on the World Theatre, he is no
longer certain, outside Russia, of any place in the first rank. In neither
form does he equal Chehov, though Chehov's last years seemed to be
spent in his shadow. Where Gorky really excels all his Russian contemporaries, and indeed perhaps any writer in this age, is not in his
creative work but in his reminiscent writing, whether he is describing his
childhood and youth or his fellow-authors. He is one of the great portrait-
painters in literature. Remembering his grandmother or Tolstoy, some
old peasant or an eccentric millionaire, he displays the same astonishing
gift, revealing in a clear but warm light every character he summons from

his memory, in which indeed there is a power of creation, an economy of means, a certainty of touch, he could not bring to his novels and plays. It is only here that Gorky will keep something of the vast reputation he once had: he will be remembered as one of the world's great remembrancers.

Many of these earlier Nobel awards take us away from the main stream of literature into one of the side-channels. Frequently they show us one nation's gratitude, not for a contribution to literature in general, but to some writer who has long and faithfully represented one aspect of the national life. Consider the two Polish prize-winners, Sienkiewicz and Reymont. The former's historical novels and excellent short stories were not widely known outside Poland. What indeed *was* widely known, to millions everywhere, but hardly on the Nobel Prize level, was his popular romance of Ancient Rome, *Quo Vadis?*, which anticipated the technicolor super-film but achieves more convincing effects at a fraction of the cost. And Reymont, who was probably given the award for his epic novel of Polish village life, *The Peasants*, never had a large body of readers outside his own country. Two of the earlier Scandinavian prize-winners were women, and both of them had plenty of readers beyond Sweden and Norway. But the Swede, that enthusiastic story-teller and snapper-up of myths and legends, Selma Lagerlöf, though she lived until 1940, hardly belongs to this age. The Norwegian prize-winning authoress, Sigrid Undset, does belong to this age, and began by writing naturalistic novels, *Jenny* and the rest; but her international reputation was based entirely on her long medieval story, *Kristin Lavransdatter*, which is something far more than the panoramic tapestry it might first appear to be, and does in fact bring us closer to essential femininity than most of the novels of livelier and more cosmopolitan ladies. The two Danish awards, sharing one year, went to Gjellerup, an odd and poor choice, and Henrik Pontoppidan, a good choice, although it never brought the fiction of this powerful moralist and anti-Romantic much attention outside Scandinavia. It was the Norwegian, Knut Hamsun, who received most attention and had for some years an international reputation not unlike Gorky's, if on a smaller scale. At home he succeeded partly because of his highly original style, his revolutionary manner even in the use of language; abroad, in translation, his appeal was much like Gorky's (he had had a similar knock-about early life): he showed the world a remote people; he was more 'real', more vital, than ordinary urban and middle-class novelists, because he dealt at length either with vagabonds preferring nature to society or with peasants tilling and building, as in his famous *Growth of the Soil*. There is in Hamsun an energy, zest and sweep that give him some size; he came from peasant stock and his suspicion of and dislike for industrial civilisation were sincere; but there is in him a great deal of the romantic literary temperament, making the best possible use of vagabonds who love all nature and peasants rooted in the soil, together with a suggestion here and there of the sham primitive, a dubious element that in the melancholy end, even though his years might excuse him, encouraged this famous old Norwegian to accept the flattery of the Nazi invaders.

There were some good prose candidates at the other end of Europe, in Spain, for instance. Pérez Galdós, the old novelist of the whole nation, was still alive, not dying until 1920; there was Unamuno; there was that Basque in the old picaresque tradition, that sun-dried and harder Dickens, Pío Baroja. In Italy, Verga was still alive; there was the astonishing D'Annunzio, half genius and half mountebank, ready to imitate whatever was fashionable in literary Europe and yet able to bring a new sensuous life to Italian poetry, a Fascist caricature of a great writer; and there was Pirandello, but he moved from fiction to drama after the war, and his Nobel Prize, like his place here, comes later. But there was also, over in Trieste, a successful German-Jewish business man, Ettore Schmitz, who did some writing at odd times, when he called himself Italo Svevo. The two novels he had written in the Nineties had not received much notice; they were published locally and written in the unliterary Italian of Trieste. But in 1906 he asked the Berlitz School to supply him with a tutor in English, and this is how he came to meet James Joyce. Years later in Paris, Joyce, who had particularly admired the second of these Svevo novels, *Senilità*, talked to Valéry Larbaud, and to other critics, about this old friend in Trieste. Given a little recognition at last, Svevo began writing again, publishing his masterpiece, *La Coscienza di Zeno* (called in the English translation *The Confessions of Zeno*) in 1923, and leaving behind him, to be published posthumously, the delicious novelette of *The Nice*

Old Man and the Pretty Girl, a very fine short story, and an unfinished novel about an old man. But Svevo did not die of old age; he was killed in a motor accident just as he was at last beginning to enjoy his belated success, a tragi-comic stroke of irony that he might have invented himself. (Perhaps he did. Ettore Schmitz, the business man, created Italo Svevo, the writer; and then Svevo, gathering force and boldness from his fame, dispensed with his creator Schmitz, by having him killed.) And what is certain is that in this odd and highly original writer, who to this day has hardly been generally read and discussed, the later part of this age, from the war onwards, has a truly representative figure, and the inner world of Western Man, as he is now, has found one of its explorers.

For Svevo, especially as we find him as Zeno, cannot be dismissed with vague references to the psychological novel and psycho-analysis. He has his own quality, depth, significance. First he is comic as great clowns like Grock are comic, appearing to us like grave but naïvely enthusiastic visitors from another world who for ever come to grief in this world, where the simplest mechanics of living are unmanageable. And here, with Svevo, the other world is the bourgeois business world of Ettore Schmitz, a world of solid and satisfying appearances that vanish at a touch or become mocking mirages—of personal relationships, finance and business, science and art—in the more inward and real world where Svevo or Zeno tries to make his way and do his best. Reason is a cheat here; cause and effect are playing a malicious game; nothing turns out right; nobody really understands anybody else; no conscious purpose can be achieved: "Man cannot do", as that sardonic magician, Gurdjieff, used to tell his pupils. But then, although Svevo-Zeno recounts his ironical misadventures in the first person, there is no real person, single and integrated, in action here, only fragments of personality, an 'I' who wants this, an 'I' who does that, contradicting and cancelling one another out. And now as we stare harder in these depths, we are like the physicists investigating the structure of the atom, in which energy whizzes arbitrarily in a nothingness. If we do not find horror and madness down there, in these ruins of a disintegrated human world and human personality, if we can still laugh, it is because a touch on the elbow from the bewildered, wistful but still smiling Svevo, who can confess so freely because, a man of mixed nationalities in a city of mixed nationalities, he is without pride, recalls us to the sunlit streets of Trieste, to the cheerful and apparently solid appearances. So we laugh, as this gravest of modern humorists intended us to do. Nevertheless, we have been given a prophetic glimpse, a whisper has come from the innermost recesses of the age: we have been warned.

CHAPTER TWENTY-ONE

Brief Interlude

AFTER the First World War, the general public did not want to read about it. After the Second World War, the general public did not want to read about anything else. (Perhaps reading about high-explosive bombing offers a cosy escape if you wonder about hydrogen bombs.) The writing that came out of the First was a mere trickle compared with the flood of verbiage still roaring out of the Second. But more literature of a sort, even though there is not a great deal of it, can be found in the trickle than in the flood. It is not difficult to understand why. The Second War was too restless, banging about all over the place, and hardly distinguished between soldiers and civilians, whereas the First clearly separated combatants from non-combatants, keeping the combatants, if it failed to kill or maim them, in its own nightmare world of trenches and barbed wire and shell holes perhaps for years. It was this lunatic empire of cold mud and hot iron that most of the soldiers who returned home wanted to forget, which helps to explain the rather feverish high spirits of the early Twenties; but the sheer pressure of remembered experience—and one reason why people write at all is that they want some relief from the pressure of experience—was too much for a comparative few of them, so they wrote about the war and at least came closer to literature than the thousand-and-one tales of the Second War we have had so far. The strange world of the front line that these ex-combatant writers tried to describe, chiefly for those who had never experienced it, was the same for both sides; the hatred and monstrous nationalistic prejudices of politicians, editors, professors, and clergymen could not exist in it; all its inhabitants, to whom the other world of women and firelight and clean sheets began to seem like a dream, were deep in conflict not with other men but with the gigantic machinery dealing out wounds and death, with heat and cold, hunger and thirst, and the dark madness of the age that had swept them into holes in the ground.

Some writers, however, were killed long before they could describe this soldiers' world. One of them was Alain Fournier, who vanished (for his body was never found) as early as September 1914, a year after he had brought out his first novel, *Le Grand Meaulnes*. (It is called *The Wanderer* in its English translation.) To some readers it is nothing more than a charming and gentle romance of boyhood; but to others it has a peculiar magic of its own, a suggestion, all too rare in prose fiction, of a reality behind ordinary reality, and to such readers it seems a little masterpiece. Among the dead in the Battle of the Marne was Charles Péguy, one of those odd figures who, no matter how unsatisfactory their writing is, can never be dismissed, or even much reduced in size, by criticism; they do not really belong to literature—though Péguy gave up everything to keep his famous *Cahiers de la Quinzaine* coming out year after year, from 1900 to 1914—but live first as characters and later as legends. The most sensationally successful of the French war books was Henri Barbusse's *Le Feu*, though published as early as 1916 and inspired, throughout its panoramic length, by anything but official patriotic fervour. Georges Duhamel, who served as an army surgeon, wrote with deep feeling about his patients in his *Vie des martyrs*, 1917; and his former colleague in *unanimisme*, which might be described as an earlier and non-political French version of 'socialist realism', Jules Romains, who like Duhamel plunged, after the war, into those vast fiction-chronicles known in France as *romans-fleuves*, produced in two volumes about the battle of Verdun probably the most impressive account there is of the French at war. A late casualty, for although he died after the war he had been badly wounded much earlier, was the exuberant Polish aristocrat who called himself Guillaume Apollinaire, a poet, a character, and in the years just before and during the war the leading impresario and master of ceremonies for all the *avant-garde* movements in Paris.

In English the most satisfying war literature did not come from the novelists. Few established novelists—though we must not forget Ford Madox Ford, whose war novels are his best—were on active service, but

Maugham made good use of his intelligence work in *Ashenden*, Hugh Walpole wrote what is probably his most durable piece of story-telling, *The Dark Forest*, out of his experience at the Russian Front, and Compton Mackenzie risked prosecution by recounting, truthfully yet with great humour, what he did for the war in the Eastern Mediterranean. Among the poets, Rupert Brooke was an early casualty and a notable loss to English writing. His immensely popular war verses, expressing a mood that was soon to change, have not only removed critical favour from his earlier and much better verse but have also obscured the undoubted fact that he was a writer—maturing slowly, and no worse for that—of great promise in several possible forms, prose as well as verse. Of the poets who expressed the later mood, who wrote as inhabitants of that strange front-line world of the First War, the best were Wilfrid Owen, who was killed in action, Robert Nichols, who wrote in various forms after the war, but, partly because of his bad health, never quite steadied himself down to make the most of his talent; and Siegfried Sassoon and Robert Graves, who also wrote truthful and searching prose reminiscences of their war-time life. W. J. Turner, a richly original poet, now under-valued, served in the war but wrote little about it; another soldier poet, though more widely known for his more recent criticism and æsthetics, was Herbert Read; and lastly, a most melancholy instance, one poet who never returned, Edward Thomas, who for years had drudged away at hack-work and then discovered a fine vein of poetry in himself, in his late thirties, but was killed at Arras in 1917.

It was an excellent traditional poet, Edmund Blunden, who wrote one of the best books of front-line reminiscence, *Undertones of War*, though he maintains throughout it a kind of brisk bird-like cheerfulness typical of only a few fortunate spirits. Very different, bitter in its disillusion, is C. E. Montague's *Disenchantment*, which is often too self-conscious and mannered, like the fiction and essays of this *Manchester Guardian* hero and supreme example (for he created a whole school of highly literary journalists), but it contains some passages of exceptional force and some of equal charm; and it does describe, better than any other English record of the war, the long grim descent from the high spirits and innocent patriotic fervour of the early volunteers. A similar mood of disillusion, expressed in even more vivid and sharper prose, can be found in the war-time essays of H. M. Tomlinson, who had been a war correspondent; but Tomlinson, whose style owes something of its tone, though not its colour, to Thoreau, is at his best, and is one of the finest descriptive writers of the age, in his two books of travel, masterpieces of their kind, *Sea and Jungle* and *Tidemarks*. Finally, there was the most successful of the English war plays, *Journey's End* by R. C. Sheriff, who was fortunate in the fact that his play, which is well contrived but rather conventional and genteel, came out at the right time, ten years after the war when the public was at last ready to accept such a play.

Five years earlier than *Journey's End*, the Americans had had their war play in the very different and uproarious *What Price Glory*, by Maxwell Anderson and Laurence Stallings. Most American writing about the war came from those ardent spirits who did not wait for their country to put an end to its strained neutrality: Alan Seeger, the poet, who died in 1916, fighting with the French; E. E. Cummings, the poet, who volunteered to drive an ambulance for the French, only to find himself at last in *The Enormous Room* he described so well; Ernest Hemingway, who served with the Italians whom we discover, in what is probably his finest passage of descriptive writing, in *Farewell to Arms*; and William Faulkner, who joined the Canadian Air Force. Oddly enough, one of the most memorable brief accounts of what trench warfare really meant was written by an American who was in the army but never got into the war itself: it appears, in a description of a visit to the old front line, in *Tender is the Night*, by Scott Fitzgerald.

It was the other side, however, that produced the war novel that had the greatest public of all, and this was E. M. Remarque's *All Quiet on the Western Front (Im Westen nichts Neues)*. Both the German title and its English equivalent, familiar quotations from news bulletins on each side, have the same grimly ironic sense, implying that what was not even worth reporting, what was indicated by a mere shrug in words, could be a narrow segment of hell for men holding the front line. It was not a great novel, but its staccato manner, with the brutal thud of each detail falling into place, did evoke the whole inhuman scene with a skill that its author, no longer kept taut by emotion, has never quite recaptured in his later fiction.

Arnold Zweig was an older and more experienced writer than Remarque, and if his *Case of Sergeant Grischa* never had the success outside Germany that *All Quiet* did, that is partly because its scene was laid on the Eastern and not the more familiar Western Front, but also because it was not a picture, or a series of strong black-and-white flashes like No Man's Land seen under successive flare lights, that any fighting soldier could recall, but showed a number of carefully observed characters involved in an elaborate action. As a study of the innocent and helpless individual caught and destroyed by the machinery of armies at war, Zweig's novel probably has no rival in fiction before or since its time; and its climax, Grischa's execution by a firing party, comes to us with such tremendous force that we are astonished that its author, entangled later in the Zionist question, never reached the status of a major novelist. But it was possible to show the individual in the military machine in a very different fashion, comic and not tragic and therefore closer to the mood that prevailed between the Wars and since; and the first master of this later fashion was undoubtedly the Czech, Jaroslav Hašek, whose *The Good Soldier Schweik*, a kind of literary counterpart to Chaplin's *Shoulder Arms*, is a droll epic of the little man, half ingenuous, half cunning, who successfully dodges the bullets and shells, the mazes of bureaucracy, and the crashing ruins of the old Hapsburg Empire. We need more Schweiks, both in and out of fiction.

So we come to the end of this brief interlude. Just after the end of the war, fought long past the point of a sensible negotiated peace, to a conclusion of bitterness and ruin, Yeats could write, in one of his greatest and most prophetic poems:

> Things fall apart; the centre cannot hold;
> Mere anarchy is loosed upon the world,
> The blood-dimmed tide is loosed, and everywhere
> The ceremony of innocence is drowned;
> The best lack all conviction, while the worst
> Are full of passionate intensity.

It is possible that if there had been no First World War, or if it had been brought to an end before the old political Europe fell apart, before the worst took over from the best, the centre, not only in politics but in literature, might have held. If it had, then it might have restored to literature a balance between introversion and extroversion, between man's inner world and the outer world of the society in which he lived, between what consciousness discovered groping towards the dark and what it faced in the light, between what a few hypersensitive and perhaps unstable minds wished to reveal and what the mass of men enjoyed reading. On the other hand, while taking into account the obvious changes in the literary scene produced by the war and already described in 'Background to the Books', we may still feel that the vital seeds, flowering eventually into their own kind of literature, were sown earlier and at a depth inaccessible to whatever comes from political events; and that because time moves so slowly and mysteriously in man's unconscious—and, after all, it is the unconscious that both creates and responds to what is best in literature—then on this level what happened between 1914 and 1918 was a mere explosive flash, a sudden loss of temper, and that what was thought and felt and written not only in 1900, or 1880, but long before, when the curious *malaise* of modern man was first experienced, might be carried through unchecked, leading inevitably to what was written and admired in 1920 or 1930 or 1940, when another war was exploding. One thing is certain, that whatever the First War might have done or not done, it did literature no good.

CHAPTER TWENTY-TWO

Between the Wars

I

IN THIS AGE we have never been satisfied and happy with our drama. From the point of view of literature, it has been our least successful form. Our more intellectual dramatic critics and playgoers have steadily complained about it. Modern drama should have more of *something*—perhaps more poetry, perhaps more social content, perhaps more psychological depth. Without that something, whatever it is, our drama lags behind poetry and fiction and hardly begins to express the essential spirit of the age. What is wrong? So long as we are not making a steady income out of pretending to find the answer, it is easy to find. The stage is a bad place on which to try to express the spirit of the age. The Theatre is not for but against our representative literature. Instead of being deeply subjective, it is solidly objective. Whatever tricks may be worked with lights and sets and stage machinery—and almost everything has been tried —actors and actresses remain substantial creatures, very different from words on paper. A great actress, a Duse, may appear to whisper a woman's final secret, but she is still Duse, who is staying at the Grand Hotel. And indeed the Theatre, with its appeal on two different levels, would not be the Theatre without this solidly objective element. But that is not all. If for example we are exploring the finer shades of thought and feeling with Proust, we are alone with his printed page, we can take our own time, we can meditate upon, feel our way into, what he is telling us. A Proust in the Theatre—God help him!—would have to make his point to a thousand people all at once and then pass on to the next point; and these people are very different (they were closer in thought and feeling

376

during the great ages of the Theatre), ranging from bright young nephews in the gallery to bewildered rich old uncles in the boxes; and if the point is made too quickly, some of them will not know what is happening on the stage, and if it is lingered over, others will begin to yawn and cough; and if too many are puzzled, or too many bored, they will tell their friends to stay away, and without an audience there is no play, no drama. A book can spend years selecting its readers; a play—and plays are meant to be performed, not read—has to collect whole audiences. If the poet, novelist, essayist, can offer the reader a private string quartette, the dramatist must offer the playgoer a brass band in the park.

The dilemma of the serious modern dramatist is that what our age wants to express through its literature does not lend itself to his chosen medium, and that what admirably fits the stage fails to give the intellectual what he asks from contemporary writing. So a typical poet of our time, admired for his symbolism, involved imagery, packed meaning, his depths of dubiety, is compelled to modify so much of this for the Theatre that soon he is not typical and is not admired. It is no use asking him to write like Shakespeare or Molière; he is another kind of man in a very different age; and his audience is not Shakespeare's or Molière's. It is equally useless to demand that he should do for the drama what Proust or Mann, Joyce or Kafka, has done for the novel, because the Theatre, where the drama lives, would defeat him by imposing its own enduring conditions. It is not a question of public taste and finance, though these are important in the Theatre, but of the character of the medium itself, the form that must be solidly objectified. Moreover, the dramatist in this age has had to face a new challenge. This of course has come from the film. Our age merely inherited the Theatre but created the film, and so has a special feeling for this new medium, itself a triumph of technology. The film soon removed a large section of the popular audience from the Theatre, and especially the young. And in the film the contemporary world has a medium that is not obstinately objective like the Theatre, that is flexible, so many dissolving images, able to move easily in space and time, show a crowd in the street or suggest one person's inner life. And no matter how much trash it has projected, no matter how rarely it is used intelligently and

377

sensitively, the film, though further removed from literature, has at its best come closer to expressing the spirit of the age than the contemporary Theatre. (So a fashionable, in-the-movement artist-cum-intellectual like Jean Cocteau can offer more of his bright, if brittle, talent on the screen than on the stage.) And between the Wars, especially in Western Europe and America, much of the old youthful excitement, making the Theatre seem magical, deserted it for the film, leaving the dramatist in a colder atmosphere.

The serious modern dramatist, then, wishing to interpret the age, had to face the challenge of this new and more flexible medium, while wrestling with his own intractable medium. And, looking over his shoulder, so to speak, were the three masters, Ibsen, Strindberg, Chehov, who in rather easier circumstances, but with the help of their own genius, had already compelled the Theatre to be new and 'modern', had almost brought it into line with the poetry and fiction of their time. What more could be done, with or without genius, when these other forms became even more deeply subjective, when the spirit to be expressed was even less broadly positive and more subtly and profoundly negative, moving away from and not towards the Theatre? Obviously, not very much. Those writers for the Theatre who took their work seriously, who were not merely filling a playhouse for a season, had either to follow on and try to catch up with poetry and the novel, by being experimental one way or another, or to offer some special dramatic bonus of their own, as compensation for not keeping their audiences in the van of the movement. So we shall find them doing one or the other, that is, once we are into the Twenties. Before the war, though Ibsen was closer, what Strindberg and Chehov had achieved already was not yet widely understood; the dramatists felt freer, less hard-pressed, than they did later; and the interpretation of a national or regional spirit in soundly theatrical terms, it was felt, would pass as serious drama. And if this drama turned away from the grubby naturalism of the Eighties and Nineties, from those consumptive peasants and prostitutes in cellars, then so much the better.

In the earliest years of this pre-war period there was the *Jungwien* group, led by Hermann Bahr, who wrote scores of plays, of which one, *The Concert*, the best of his Viennese comedies, is still in the German repertoire. Beer-Hofmann, who later brought into the drama his Jewish feeling for the Old Testament, was one of this group. So was Hugo von Hofmannsthal, a figure of real importance but best seen as one of the poets of the age; and also Arthur Schnitzler, a sympathetic and very skilful playwright, too often regarded now, outside Austria, as simply the author of the *Anatol* playlets, which were very early work. What kind of drama would a very sensitive and rather weary doctor create out of a dying society? Schnitzler's more mature work supplies the answer. Near-by, in Munich, performing in cabaret after trying nearly everything else, was that odd, shady, but original character, Frank Wedekind, whose monotonous and brutal eroticism is not good enough, whose dramatic construction and writing are not good enough, whose cabaret antics are too dubious, but who has to be mentioned, not without a reluctant respect, because by sheer force and originality he did blast a way for the drama that came to be written after his death in 1918. He is not quite an important dramatist, but as a charge of coarse but effective gunpowder under the Theatre, resulting in a grand explosion, he can be praised wholeheartedly.

The Spanish dramatists, with Unamuno in their midst and with Jacinto Benavente (who received the Nobel Prize in 1922) and Martínez Sierra busy for years translating foreign plays, were extremely well aware of what was happening in the European Theatre, and indeed deliberately broke with the nineteenth-century national tradition represented by Echegaray. And certain of their plays—though here the more powerful Benavente has been less fortunate than the lighter Martínez Sierra and that pair of Andalusian charmers, the brothers Álvarez Quintero—have often been produced, usually with success, outside Spain. Nevertheless, they still seem to be somewhere on the edge of the international Theatre; and even Benavente, with his weighty talent and searching eye, is not quite accepted as one of its representative figures. The national scene, with its own Catholicism alternately the villain and hero of the piece, holds us, even fascinates us, as they display it in their drama; but most of us cannot identify ourselves with this drama, cannot feel—as we can with Ibsen's remote Norwegian villages or Chehov's country houses that seem half-way to China—that its characters involve our own hopes and fears in theirs. Held and impressed by these excellent dramatists, ready to be moved by them to laughter or tears, we still do not quite feel ourselves to be members of their audience, to have completely stopped being tourists. It is worth adding that many of the English translations of these dramatists were the work of Harley Granville-Barker, after he had walked out of the English Theatre, where he had done brilliant and valuable work, as a director and actor in close association with Shaw, and as a dramatist himself. He lacked the final degree of concentration in his own drama, and for an ex-director was curiously prodigal of scenes and characters; but he brought to the London stage an intelligence and a sense of society in both its breadth and depth that was keener than Galsworthy's; and though he never had, nor probably wanted to have, J. M. Barrie's goblin cunning in stagecraft, he had a cool masculine charm less forced and tricky than Barrie's more feminine blandishment. Indeed, for a few years, while he was writing his own plays instead of translating his Spanish contemporaries, Granville-Barker appeared to be Shaw's closest rival in London.

Over in Dublin the Irish literary and nationalist movement was establishing its own theatre, the Abbey. That great poet, Yeats, devoted himself to it for years, with much help from his friend and fellow-playwright, Lady Gregory; and his comparative failure in the drama is significant, proving that poetry, even when the poet has been closely associated with a playhouse, does not give a modern dramatist any supremacy in the Theatre. Unlike Yeats, John Millington Synge was a born dramatist, though it was a stroke of genius on the part of Yeats to divine this, to persuade Synge to leave Paris and go to the West of Ireland and listen to the peasants there. Out of his eavesdropping, Synge created an elaborately heightened speech, every bit of it "flavoured like a nut", but belonging to the literature of drama even though based on peasant idioms and cadences. More than this, however, went into his masterpiece, *The Playboy of the Western World*, which escapes definition and categories, is at once realistic and fantastic, bitterly satirical and yet poetic, and a unique specimen of a new kind of drama, which Synge's death, while still in his thirties, abruptly cut short. The secret of Synge, apart from his instinctive feeling for dramatic form, is that he brought together the discipline his French studies had taught him and the rich harvest he gathered from the peasants' wild talk but self-regarding acts in the West of Ireland. And his unfinished *Deirdre*, similar in style but different in structure and tone from *The Playboy*, suggests he was still developing. Years later, after the First War and the Irish civil war, the Abbey Theatre found another born dramatist, though not quite the genius that Synge was, in Sean O'Casey. He first succeeded, especially in *Juno and the Paycock* (though here the wonderfully rich comic element is superior to the tragic), by a heightened tragi-comic naturalistic treatment of Dublin low life, with the civil war all round it. After cutting his Irish roots, O'Casey might be said to have exchanged the 'bonus' of his rich humour and characterisation for restless 'catching up' experiments that have never quite succeeded, though he might well have complained that they have not been given many chances to succeed.

Shortly before the war, Expressionism arrived, in painting, poetry and the drama; and after the war, during the early Twenties, Berlin was the capital city of dramatic Expressionism. (For years afterwards, dramatic critics in many different countries, whenever they were compelled to notice anything experimental on the stage, dismissed it by saying they had seen something just like it in Berlin in 1922.) It is a waste of time trying to find an exact definition of Expressionism in drama. It is easier to see what it rejected than what it accepted: it rejected realism and naturalism, whatever was conventional and established in the Theatre, the picturesque and the sentimental and the romantic, anything that had the approval of the authorities, the officials, the bourgeois, and was enjoyed by the kind of people that indignant young men dislike. It was not a movement, going steadily in one direction. It moved violently in several directions at once, like an explosion, which indeed is what it was. But what the more serious Expressionist playwrights, as distinct from writers of pretentious bosh, were attempting was important. They were trying to escape from the dilemma of the modern dramatist that we have already described. They wanted to bring the drama into line with the whole contemporary movement, to overcome the Theatre's obstinate objectivity, to give the drama both the breadth of the novel and the film and the subjective depth of poetry and the new fiction. (Strindberg had pointed the way, it is true, but it was only a wave of the hand from a wild genius, not a course of instruction from the head of a drama department.) To do this they had to destroy any painstaking illusion of reality, the kind of drama Chehov and Stanislavsky created between them for the Moscow Art Theatre; they had to abolish definite times and places, characters with names and addresses and distinct personalities, a particular action involving some persons somewhere; so that what happened in a typical Expressionist play offered nothing in the middle region of either newspaper reporting or story-telling but might be welcome material to a sociologist on the broad view and a psycho-analyst on the deep one. Furthermore, defiantly facing the Theatre's objective challenge—we might almost say, grasping the nettle—the Expressionists deliberately made their drama more obviously theatrical, something happening on a stage occupied by performers with painted faces, show-people mouthing and gesturing.

On its broadest basis, as a reaction in one form or another against naturalism and realism, Expressionism turns up in many different places, as a method employed by many playwrights of varied talents, during the Twenties and Thirties. But in its first explosive capacity it was entirely German. The outstanding playwright of the original and very mixed Berlin group, which included Sorge, Hasenclever, Unruh, Sternheim, Kornfeld, Toller, Brecht, was Georg Kaiser, whose *From Morn to Midnight* has been accepted as the standard Expressionist play. He was a prolific playwright, capable of writing effectively in more than one manner; he had indeed that acute sense of the theatrical which, unless it is accompanied by certain qualities demanded by literature in general, seems to hinder rather than help a writer to create enduring drama. While remembering that some excellent German playwrights, including that droll satirist Carl Zuckmayer (*The Captain of Köpenick*), did not come out of Expressionism, we must stop to consider one who did, Bertolt Brecht. Probably no other modern dramatist divides critical opinion more sharply than Brecht. (But this is truer of the years following the Second War, when he ran very successfully his own company in East Berlin, than of the time before it, which is our period, when he was in exile.) His Communist background and his highly individual dramatic theory and practice have aroused prejudice both for and against him. Many directors and critics see in him a poet who out of Expressionism has created a drama that meets the challenge of the age, escapes from the modern dramatist's dilemma, because of its broad social basis and significance, its unique mixture of epic and ballad, of the wide scene and the narrow intimate one, its freedom from all naturalistic conventions, its insistence that the actor should detach himself from ordinary theatrical illusion, should offer the audience his performance as if he were playing in vaudeville. Those in opposition do not deny his original lyrical strain (best-known in the famous adaptation of *The Beggar's Opera*, the *Dreigroschenoper*, to which in fact Brecht only contributed the lyrics) but maintain that his form of drama has been designed to cover his lack of invention and his doubtful dramatic technique, that between its epic style, which can be tedious, and its folk-ballad style there is a great gap in the middle, where genuine drama could be created, and that his tricks with the players, notwithstanding his undoubted ability as a director and trainer of actors, may be useful to Communist propaganda performances but bring nothing of value to the Theatre as it is understood in the West. And even now, twenty years beyond our period here, it is still too early to decide which party is right. What is beyond doubt is that Brecht—and it is to his credit —has at least created much excitement and debate that can do the Theatre no harm.

Brecht went to Russia in the Thirties, before he reached California in 1941. He should have gone to Russia ten years earlier, for then he might have shown Russian playwrights how not to displease the Party and yet write something that did not displease themselves. The wild experiments of the Russian Theatre in the Twenties were not made by writers but by directors and designers, and more often than not at the expense of the classics and plays imported from abroad. Most of us may feel that completely naturalistic production may clutter the stage with too many walls and doors, too much furniture and domestic ornament, but we may also feel that to replace all this with platforms, ladders, bits of machinery, as if the action of the play had been transferred to an equally cluttered factory, does not give the Theatre a new subtlety and depth. (It is worth adding here that the complete domination of the Theatre by a super-*regisseur*, who sees in the whole enterprise an opportunity to express his own astonishing mind, rarely helps the drama.) The situation in which the Russian playwrights found themselves was grimly ironical. Here, at last, they were offered every encouragement—resources unrestricted by capitalist profit-seeking, magnificent troupes of players and designers, playhouses packed with eager and enthusiastic audiences—but were denied the elementary and essential freedom to write about human life and character as they saw them. They did what they could with black-and-white themes of revolutionary triumphs, heroic factory managers in conflict with sabotage, scientists finally coming into line with the Party—and a few of their plays, such as Bulgakov's rather Chehovian *Days of the Turbins* and Katayev's farcical and enormously successful *Squaring the Circle*, have been produced and applauded outside the Soviet Union—but official policy denied them even any attempt to solve the central problems of the serious modern dramatist. Russia, in many respects a theatrical Promised Land, was out of the competition.

These twenty years between the Wars were crowded with playwrights of talent and intelligently written, amusing or moving plays, some greatly successful and admired in the country of their origin and others almost equally successful in the international Theatre; but most of these do not concern us here, for this is not theatrical history, and what we must look for in this crowd are those dramatists trying to bring their work closer to the literature of the age, and not to write local and more topical variations of what had been done already by Ibsen, Strindberg, Chehov, but to produce a drama representative of their own time. And to arrive in the same place just after one of these masters was a misfortune, at least on the international level, for some excellent dramatists. Of these, Hjalmar Bergman and Par Lagerkvist are good examples, for they arrived in Sweden too soon after Strindberg to receive from abroad all the attention they deserved. So the Norwegians, from Gunnar Heiberg and Hans Kinck to Helge Krog and Nordahl Grieg (an impassioned experimenter whose final development was blocked by the Second War, in which he was killed on active service), were still seen from outside Norway in the vast shadow of Ibsen. Yet some other of the smaller national Theatres appear to suffer from the absence of a widely recognised master dramatist. Thus Hungary during this period seems to have produced more than its share of accomplished playwrights, headed by Ferenc Molnár, whose smooth but intelligent comedies were popular almost everywhere; but without the stiffening that one outstanding serious dramatist could have given it, the Hungarian Theatre could not stop the constant drift of its writers to the world's film studios.

From the early Twenties onwards the French theatrical scene is crowded with figures that catch the eye—Raynal, Pagnol, Romains, Vildrac, Marcel, Crommelynck, Giraudoux, to name only a few—but perhaps the most determined efforts to give prose drama a new subjective depth were made by Henri René Lenormand and Jean Jacques Bernard. They are quite different in temperament, outlook, method. Probably because the central character in *Le Mangeur de rêves* (*The Dream Doctor* in the English version) calls himself a psychologist—though any professional would condemn him as an amateur meddler—Lenormand was often thought to have based his drama on Freudian psycho-analysis; but he himself has strongly denied this, and his plays, though obviously belonging to a world in which the psycho-analyst has arrived, an age all too conscious of psychopathology, lend him support. He is chiefly the dramatist of inevitable degeneracy, as in *Les Ratés* (produced in English as *Failures*), of a sinister determinism and fatalism, as in his *Time is a Dream*, of evil being released from the unconscious (which he regards, too simply, as merely containing what has been suppressed by consciousness) and then attracting to itself whatever is hostile, malicious, destructive, in other persons or the very forces of Nature. This is not the great world of tragedy, with its clean bright edge; it is a small world of small characters, helpless against a creeping corruption. Because his mind is fixed on the bitter conclusion, because he is moving stealthily towards it from the very first, Lenormand, unlike greater dramatists, cannot make us feel that what is being destroyed is of any high value. His central characters are not unreal, but, destined to be victims, they have no large hold on life. There is no size to this drama, no spring of poetry; it creeps through a black ooze of pessimism; but its rather obvious psychopathic plotting does happen in a strange and sinister atmosphere that is perhaps Lenormand's most creative achievement, making us wonder if Macbeth's witches had once flitted through his Alpine hotels and sitting-rooms in Nice. The world of Jean Jacques Bernard's drama is small too, and not tragic but tenderly wistful and pathetic. He compels the Theatre to be more subjective by keeping it quiet. He is the master of long significant pauses, which allow us to join his characters in their inner life. He brings drama closer to the contemporary novel by allowing very little to happen on the stage, so that in order to fill the gaps his audiences have to turn themselves into psychological novelists. This makes him a bad dramatist for large noisy audiences demanding entertainment, the kind that the great masters of drama can capture and dominate within ten minutes; but one of the best and most satisfying modern dramatists, a perfect tiny master, for a small playhouse filled with intelligent and sympathetic people. And if his exquisite pieces —and there are half a dozen of these fragile transparencies that represent him perfectly—are not played as often as they used to be, that may merely indicate that the prevailing fashion, in favour of coarsely-drawn characters shouting one another down on the least provocation, is against his kind of drama, or that there are fewer small playhouses and fewer intelligent and sympathetic people to fill them.

The Italian Theatre, later compelled to retreat as the film advanced, had in the Twenties, quite apart from full-blooded theatrical romancers like Sem Benelli, a number of ingenious and experimental playwrights, Chiarelli, Antonelli, Bontempelli, de Stephani, Rosso di San Secondo, and the more sober and better-known Ugo Betti, all of whom were trying in various ways to push the stubborn Theatre in the inward direction that literature was taking. But, to the world outside, this Italian Theatre was represented by Luigi Pirandello, awarded the Nobel Prize in 1934. He came to the Theatre rather late, as a distinguished but not popular writer of short stories, after years of hard unrewarding work, writing and teaching, and a tragic private life. In the Theatre, where he is completely at home, the themes that fascinated him in his fiction take on a new and more important life, just because they enable him to do the great difficult thing, to compel the Theatre to reflect the modern attitude. For Pirandello's drama is nothing if not subjective, and its central theme, dramatically embodied in various highly ingenious actions, is the relativity of our subjective life. The problem of identity, to which so many writers now seem to be turning their attention, can easily be discovered in what Pirandello was writing forty years ago. His drama—which is too often represented by the over-played *Six Characters* and too seldom by the under-played *Right You Are*, *As You Desire Me* and, perhaps above all, *Henry IV*—deserves the attention it has had, indeed more attention than it has had, not because it has any unusual breadth or fullness of life, not because it lifts us into a world of great characters and events, not because it is profoundly tragic or richly comic, but simply because it is satisfying in theatrical terms, grapples successfully with all that is solidly objective in stage performance, and yet contrives to reflect, as in a cunning arrangement of distorting mirrors, the inner bewilderment, the subjective dubiety, the broken vision, of our age. It takes a step, even if not a great one, further than the nineteenth-century masters. It belongs to our time and could not have been created or understood earlier than our time.

It was not until the Twenties that serious writing for the Theatre in New York at last caught up with its direction and acting. The new playwrights who arrived then included Elmer Rice, a lively experimenter whose *Street Scene* had an international success, Sidney Howard, an intelligent craftsman, and, rather later, Robert Sherwood, an adroit provider of star roles though not without ideas, and of course the writer now recognised to be America's leading dramatist, Eugene O'Neill. Even briefly and very roughly, it is difficult to offer an estimate of O'Neill's drama. His weaknesses are plain. For example, everything that makes the short-lived Synge a master is flat and dead in O'Neill, a writer utterly without charm. He is gloomy and funereal rather than tragic. Though technically experienced, he makes his experimental plays, as a rule, oddly clumsy, theatrically tactless; and his symbolism always seems theoretical, not vitally and poetically symbolical. His whole natural equipment as a dramatist looks inadequate. But he has a dogged courage, a determination to make the Theatre obey his will, to compel it to do something new for him, a dour integrity, that not only command our respect but raise the level of his drama as a whole, for all its obvious faults, and already seem to give it, once his complete failures are ignored, a quality of massive endurance. This is particularly true of the plays in which he is disciplined by a definite time, place, style of life, as in the New England *Desire under the Elms* and *Mourning Becomes Electra*, and possibly the semi-autobiographical plays that he left to be produced after his death. Years before the Broadway style became fashionable in Europe, O'Neill had audiences everywhere, as the representative American dramatist (and the first to receive the Nobel Prize), and this claim must be allowed him, all the more willingly because he was, and still is, a pioneer.

Neither in New York nor in the European capitals did the troubled Thirties, setting politics in high relief, do much to bring the Theatre and literature, as the age saw it, closer together. In New York, Thornton Wilder made a successful experiment in *Our Town* (but his one-act *The Long Christmas Dinner*, with its foreshortened time, is perhaps an even more valuable experiment); Maxwell Anderson, who suffered from not writing prose and never arriving at poetry, made a brave attempt in *Winterset* to give dignity and depth to a familiar American scene and situation; Lillian Hellman and Clifford Odets made triumphant entrances; while some of the best theatrical writing of its kind could be found in the tough, uproarious farces of the period. Central Europe passed into the shadow of the new barbarism; Karel Čapek, to whose widely-played *R.U.R.* we owe the term 'robot', and who also wrote, with his brother, the ingenious *Insect Play*, died just before he might have heard Hitler's tanks rolling into Czechoslovakia. The poet Lorca, who was bringing his own zest and strong popular feeling to Spanish drama, was killed in the Civil War. In France, André Obey had written in a new-old style for the Compagnie des Quinze, rather like a theatrical version of those imitation broadsheets, with verses and woodcuts, that cultivated persons used to be fond of printing; and later in the Thirties there arrived a new French dramatist, who at once showed his sombre power to create symbolic action in prose drama, Jean Anouilh. In London, the Scots dramatist, James Bridie, wrote individual scenes of great brilliance but tended to be weak in construction and the economy of character and action; the poet Auden and the novelist Isherwood collaborated in three experimental pieces, intelligent and amusing, that never quite achieved the concentrated force the Theatre demands; and in *Family Reunion*, though it was far less popular than his later plays, T. S. Eliot came nearest to creating drama that did not sacrifice too much and allowed the poet in him to breathe and move: it is his best play. But it is not good enough, just as all the dramatic work we have named in this chapter is not good enough, just as the work that has come since 1940 is not good enough, either to make this a great age of drama or to compel the Theatre to reflect perfectly what is central in the literature of our time. Our Theatre has been served by as much talent in writing (though this has often been denied) as in its direction and acting. But whereas directors and actors can build their triumphs on past greatness, the dramatist is fixed, no matter what subject he chooses, in his own present time. It may be that a supreme master could have shown us, even through the laughter, the tears, the horror, the delight that the Theatre appears to demand if it is to be satisfying, the crumbling floor of our consciousness, all the corroding doubts and fears, the depths of disintegrating personality; and the fact that we cannot imagine how he would do it is no proof that it would be impossible, for genius by its very nature sees what is possible in the apparently impossible. But though some way was gained, a little here, a little there, as we have seen, the Theatre could not be moved into the central position it had enjoyed in some past ages. And the complaints against it, as if it deliberately refused to be significant in the contemporary fashion, are neither valid nor even reasonably intelligent. For while the Theatre can successfully offer us Hamlet and company and one ghost, it can do nothing with one rather spectral Hamlet and a whole company of ghosts.

2

We may believe that in this age fewer and fewer people read contemporary poetry, but the anthologies and studies, the lists and libraries, do nothing to suggest that fewer and fewer people were writing it—or at least were writing verse with some pretensions to being poetry. A geographical sweep would take us from Halldór Laxness producing iconoclastic and sharply modern lyrics in Iceland, to the Chilean Nobel prize-winner, Gabriela Mistral, brooding poetically over the melancholy Patagonian landscape. It would show us her fellow-Chilean, Pablo Neruda, in whose strange poetry French Symbolism and surrealism are mixed with some dark earthy feeling from the Araucanian Indian blood in him (and it is this mingling of the Indian strain with the Spanish or Portuguese that seems to give us the more creative and authentic South American artists in all forms); and then it would take us as far north as the 'New Provinces' poets in Canada, or across the widest sea in the world to Australian poets like Frederick Macartney and R. D. Fitzgerald. But in a space that is shrinking fast we must find some link between the major poets of this time, those who influenced all the others, and some relation between what those major poets wrote and the age itself. The starting-point must be where we left the poetry of the nineteenth century, with French Symbolism beginning to enter other literatures and to influence very profoundly the more ambitious of their new poets. We can easily understand, however, that the Symbolism of which Mallarmé was the high priest, Symbolism in its purest but not most palatable essence, could not be exported, could not pass unchanged through equally, if not more, powerful poetic minds, not only belonging to other nations but, as time ran on, writing in another century, a new age. But one of these major poets did not belong to another nation; though he had a Corsican father and an Italian mother, he was entirely French in his upbringing, education, domicile, temperament; as a youth he had attended Mallarmé's evenings and might be said to be his pupil: this was Paul Valéry.

Though all his poetry would not fill a sizeable volume—and not every poem in this tiny collection, great as Valéry is at his highest reach, is entirely satisfactory—Valéry is a key figure in the poetry of our time. This is not so much because he vastly improved upon Mallarmé's practice, though unquestionably he did, but because he largely created certain ideas about poetry, a general attitude towards the art, from which many of our later poets and critics of poetry have been unable to escape. When such critics prowl about a poem, examining its 'structure', like engineers testing a bridge, they are at work under Valéry's influence. It was Valéry, interested in mathematics and fascinated by Leonardo, who brought this scientific-engineering touch to poetry. Violently reacting against romanticism, and in terror of being thought sentimental (the nightmare of all typical moderns), he renounced the idea of poetry as communication and with it the further idea, common to both the neo-classic and the romantic ages, of the poet as a representative man. Poems were what poets made. And what makes a poet is not his 'poetical' feeling or outlook but his capacity to produce poetical effects. And just as the musician or painter has his special apparatus, so it may be necessary for poetry to have its own special language, different from that of ordinary speech. (Nothing more likely to devitalise poetry than this could happen to it, as so many great poets, abandoning poetic diction for something nearer ordinary speech, have recognised.) As for obscurity, in one of his notes under this heading, Valéry says that if his mind is richer, more rapid, freer, more disciplined than ours, neither he nor we can do anything about it. But if he would stop being so arrogant, he would realise that there is something he could do about it, for he could make better use of his altogether superior mind to avoid obscurity, which is, after all, what minds much richer, more rapid, freer, more disciplined than his, have been able to do. Though, as we are always told, an unaffected and attractive member of any company, Valéry in his occasional criticism and notes, and in his general attitude towards his work and his readers, seems pretentious, affected, intellectually snobbish, capable of turning his greatest admirers into indifferent poets and worse critics. Some sterile and tedious cults have come out of Valéry.

The poetry, however, was not created by the later critic, commentator, lecturer. And if there is so little of it, that is not simply because he worked so long and hard giving it a final shape, had other things to do, was indifferent to a literary career (he was not); it is chiefly because the kind of poetry he wanted to write, digging deeper than Mallarmé and then building with harder material, demanded an original powerful impulse, set going by the emotion released by some personal crisis, that he rarely felt. He is in fact anything but a man looking about him and then making a poem, as another man might paint some flowers or design a piece of furniture. Though capable of lines with a wonderfully evocative descriptive power, he goes inward and inward, not outward. He is a man making a poem about a man making a poem, just as his friend Gide could write a novel about a man writing a novel. (And when literature begins to feed on itself like this, as an ulcerated stomach begins to eat itself, then the society that cannot nourish literature is dying, or the literature that cannot take nourishment is sinking fast.) Let us admit that what Valéry was trying to do was appallingly difficult. He had to use symbols in a non-symbolic age and yet avoid a private language—hence his angels, serpent, young Fate, Narcissus, and the rest, all of which are merely literary, no longer religious, going deep into the unconscious. But Valéry, as a born poet (for this he was), was well aware of the value, in depth and magic, of those lines that arrived unbidden and complete, rising from the unconscious. His conscious attitude and *persona* were for a poet unusually high and dry, obviously over-intellectual; he refused to read most literature, and particularly detested novels; he preferred Descartes and mathematics. This one-sided conscious attitude would inevitably produce its opposite from the unconscious, from the deep source of what he knew was essential to his poetry. (We in turn know he knew this because he says so, without mentioning the unconscious but admitting that he would build poems around these 'given' lines.) We have here, then, a very wide division indeed in the personality, between a one-sided over-intellectualised consciousness that yet depends on an unconscious that it does not understand nor even recognise. "We make poetry," Yeats said, "out of the quarrel with ourselves." It is this quarrel, this great gap that must be explored, this dangerous polarity that is so destructive to personality that it can lead to madness, out of which Valéry creates his poetry, using a powerful will, perilously taut, to bend together what has been given by the unconscious and what is understood and stated by consciousness, the poem itself being like the bowstring quivering and singing as the bow is bent. He is, above all, the poet of this dangerous wide division between what is one-sidedly over-conscious and the unknown unconscious, in a situation that typifies the modern intellectual and that always threatens personality, the central self of earlier poetry, with dissolution. It is here that the age finds in him one of its voices. It is at its best pitch a wonderful voice, capable of speaking with great beauty; but with something disturbing and not humanly satisfying in its thin, high, dry quality and occasional obscurity and confusion; as if poetry, now profoundly self-absorbed. had reached great distinction but only in its old age.

Of the three German poets who came out of the Symbolist Movement, only one, Stefan George, belonged to Germany, and he was a German of the Germans. Hugo von Hofmannsthal, very much a Viennese, had in his ancestry almost every Central European element, including the Jewish. (He was far from being alone among the major artists of the age in having some Jewish blood; and it is a terrible irony that an age that owed so much of its culture to this Jewish strain, at once deeply introspective and creative, should then single out the Jews to be the victims of its mass murders.) And the third, Rainer Maria Rilke, born in Prague, was descended from Bohemian and Alsatian families: he came from the edge of everything, rather like the polyglot attendants on the old international *wagon-lits*. These three poets, born within a few years of one another and closely acquainted in their youth, went very different ways in their maturity. Yet they are alike in this, that, possessing great gifts, creating poetry often of great beauty, they yet miss greatness itself, missing it each in his own fashion. They are very remarkable poets but from the standpoint of world literature they are not great poets. They did much for German literature, over and above what they directly contributed to it, but here we cannot include them among our masters.

Oddly enough, the one who was long supposed to have the least claim might now, or in the near future, be thought to have the strongest. (Edwin Muir, himself a fine poet and much concerned with German writing, took this view.) This is Hofmannsthal, whose lyrical poetry belongs to his youth (he could be called a prodigy); who later turned to the Theatre, making a brave attempt to revive poetic drama, and furnishing Richard Strauss with *libretti*, perhaps too successfully, at least for many years, for the good of his own literary reputation; and he did some fine work in prose, notably the magnificent fragment of narrative, *Andreas*, which might have been a masterpiece, and that curious study of dissociation and alienation, *The Letter of Lord Chandos*. He does nothing badly, and some things, in more than one form, superbly well. He is ultra-sensitive, deeply serious; the mystical strain in him may not be strong but it is not false, not a literary device like Maeterlinck's; and his feeling that catastrophe is on its way, that his world is doomed, has about it something genuinely prophetic. On the other hand, it could be argued that he retreated before this intuitive knowledge that the society and culture, of which he himself was the delicate final flower, were already dying, and that he turned in despair to Baroque masquerade and mystical yearning because he could not bring himself to recognise, in all its raw crudity and destructiveness, what had life in it instead of death. So he clings to the tradition he represents like a man tied to the mast of a ship that is breaking up. His search for "the way into life", perhaps his main theme once his prodigious youth had gone, suggests that he knows he has put himself outside it. But he cannot be dismissed as a figure, elegant and autumnal, of Viennese charm and final melancholy; there is in him more steely strength, more depth too, than that; unlike almost all his contemporaries, he is now gaining and not losing stature; and he is far from being merely the poet whose words we cannot hear, above the brass and percussion of the orchestra, in *Elektra* and *Der Rosenkavalier*.

Stefan George, though originally much influenced by the French Symbolists and English poetry, had the good sense, and perhaps some prompting of genius, to continue the tradition of the magical old German *lied*, to which he added a monumental quality of his own; he is a magnificent poet until he turns almost completely didactic and the enchanting song-birds vanish, leaving behind a Teutonic sermon in concrete. But it is difficult, at least for those of us who are not German, to discover much further good sense in this poet's outlook, career, style of life. Compelled, like every serious poet who came out of Symbolism, to face the problem of coming to terms with a non-symbolic society, Stefan George decided to settle the problem by abolishing society. He lived and wrote for a small closed circle of disciples and admirers, creating his own tiny *Gemeinschaft*. Here in this hot-house, secure against the chilling winds and night frosts of criticism, it was possible to believe anything—that the German Empire might be conquered by poetry and high ideals, the Krupp works crumbling at the sound of exquisite lines about runes and roses; or that a handsome boy from Munich, once he was called Maximin, dressed in a purple robe, crowned with violets, could by his semi-divine presence prove the coming rule of mastersingers. What is certain, among all this phantasmagoria, is that the boy's death, at the age of fifteen, had a profound effect upon Stefan George, and that the poet out of his grief, rising above a mere sense of personal loss, did create work of weight and power, even if the thought sustaining it is not securely rooted in reality. There was indeed a masculine force and dignity about this poet when he was actually writing poetry. Nevertheless, this exclusively male circle of his, banishing woman to the kitchen, was largely at the mercy of its own negative, inferior feminine qualities—for we can never move in a straight line, so that if we run away from woman then we arrive, so to speak, at her back door—and in the end the realities of the German situation, far removed from any poetic ideals, came crashing through the heated glass. For a year or two the ageing poet considered the flattering proposals of the Nazis, but then, recovering his integrity, he kept silent, escaped to Switzerland, there to die, while the books were burning in Berlin, burning like the temple in the curiously prophetic play he wrote. He came out of his charmed circle too late.

The third of these poets, Rainer Maria Rilke, as we saw earlier, was on the edge of everything. Much of his ordinary behaviour might have been inspired by the idea of poets held by people who dislike poets. A rather ruthless parasite not only on the beds and board but also on the attention and emotions of his friends, usually aristocratic cultivated ladies, Rilke freed himself from communal claims and obligations to devote himself entirely to his exquisite sensibility and to his deeply poetic expression of that sensibility. He offers us whatever he discovers exploring his inner world to its furthest recesses. Away from the melancholy chaos of our relations with the outward world, poetry with its symbols can create a real enduring world, more or less the equivalent of what Proust found in his remembered, as distinct from passing, time. And to some extent, to a degree beautifully reflected in some of his elegies and final sonnets, with their Orpheus and his Spirit of Song, this is true. Any art worth the name appears to offer us another and timeless world, made out of elements extracted out of man's experience of the world of time and change, then fused with personality, set in order by the spirit. But we are men, not birds or flowers, and our inner life is still man's inner life, the inheritance of a thousand generations. We can heighten and refine our sensibility, set it hovering and quivering so that it appears to experience the alien life of a landscape, a tree, a flower, in Rilke's manner, but it remains our sensibility. We cannot shed our humanity, and if we try to reject it, then we can only distort and misuse it. True, we are more likely to be whole men if we look beyond Man, as religion bids us do; but Rilke, in his neurotic flight from common human relationships and responsibilities, trying to imagine his own religion, did not really look beyond Man but hoped to cancel him out. And if we keep running away from life, as Rilke did, then we hurry towards death; and Rilke asked for death, not only for himself but for everybody and everything else; the whole earth must die because it did not satisfy his idea of completeness. Again, if our sensibility is such that it seems to detach itself from us, so that whatever is observed appears to be living more intensely than we are, then we are in danger, as Rilke was, of a complete breakdown of the personality. Rilke, creditably, neither committed suicide nor went mad, but, sustained by the powerful ego of the artist (and his egoism was stupendous), wrote his *Elegies*. They contain some magnificent poetry, but it is poetry shining through a crack in the mind of the age. It is art finding a narrow passage between suicide and madness. We feel that something anti-human is on its way: the men who will eventually make the horror bombs are already leaving the other children at play so that they can spend another hour with their text-books. (And the leukaemia their bomb tests will spread round the world is the same leukaemia already infecting and thinning out the blood of Rilke, so that the death he longed for came in the end from a scratch: the roses he was offering a girl—symbol to symbol—had thorns.) Rilke's earlier version of the Orpheus myth contains a marvellous hair-raising passage describing an Eurydice no more a woman, not even the shade of one, but already so much spreading rain and root; and some-how we feel this is not the familiar idea of our bodies returning to the dust, nor a cheerless aspect of pantheism, but that here, utterly alien to the myth and the older poets who have made use of it, is something sinister and anti-human, preferring rain and root to woman. If there ever was a man who needed a society contained within a religion, it is this neurotic, quiveringly sensitive yet monstrously egoistic Rilke. He was really a religious poet condemned to write his poetry and invent a religion at the same time, and all that the age could offer him was the wreckage of its æsthetic movement, Mallarmé's Symbolism, Rodin's sculpture, a remote castle or two, and a society chiefly concerned with heavy industries, bank loans, and guns that could send a shell ten miles. Rilke could not do what he hoped to do, but in trying he did transform the German language into an astonishing new poetic instrument, and provided our age with one of its strange disturbing voices.

Symbolism found its way to Russia, and inevitably suffered a change there, with some essentially Russian mystical element coming into it. We are of course still in the period preceding the revolution. There are many names—Balmont, Bryusov, Sologub, Hippius, Annensky, Byely, Ivanov, and the greatest of them all, Alexander Blok, to whom we shall return. The movement could be stretched to include even Boris Pasternak, although he was not considered one of the Symbolists and began writing as one of a group of so-called 'moderate futurists'. After making all allowance for the difference between the Russian and French temperaments, it is not difficult to discover a certain likeness between Pasternak and Valéry. Both write very little, but such is their concentrated force that they produce an immediate and tremendous impact upon their fellow-poets; both seem obscure and almost meaningless to the ordinary reader, even though Pasternak's original, odd, sharp imagery may be different from Valéry's, because in effect, by a similar effort of will, both of them bring together two widely separated levels, one of emotional intensity, driving from the unconscious, and the other purely and rather dryly intellectual. Thus extremes meet in their poetry, and nearly all that belongs to the mental region between, producing familiar romantic and sentimental verse, is missing. The difference between them is that while the French poet, deeply introverted, is really concerned with his own inner world, almost disintegrating his own personality, Pasternak is looking out at the world, describing life there, but with terrific subjectivity, so that if what he describes seems new and strange, whether repellent or suddenly beautiful, that is because he is making poetry out of the encounter between his outer and inner worlds. (There is a painter behind Pasternak as there was a mathematician behind Valéry.) Although his now famous *Dr. Zhivago* is well outside our limit here, it is worth noting that much of the fascination this prose epic has for us—and it is obviously a poet's creation, not a novelist's—comes from this characteristic effect of time-place-mood, the outer world seen through a window of the inner world.

It is obvious, however, that those of us who cannot read Pasternak's lyrics in their original Russian miss both his originality in diction and rhythmical power; so in many of the English translations, up to now, his typical effect loses poetical force and often seems coldly clever. Nevertheless, we catch at least a glimpse of a powerful poet, whereas, in similar translation, the 'street poems' of Mayakovsky merely suggest an excitable man making a great deal of noise.

Blok is generally held, at least by critics free from the Party line, to be the greatest Russian poet of this century. (But living poets, like Pasternak for example, cannot be brought into comparison, because we do not know what they yet may write nor even what they may have already written that has not been published.) He began writing early but died at forty-one, worn out and sunk in melancholy: he had a cardiac disease, an "insomnia of the heart", one of his friends called it; but it is likely that the revolution, which he had welcomed in its first stages, showed him events and a kind of life that he could neither accept, like Mayakovsky, nor grimly endure, like Pasternak: he withered away, which generations of poets may do long before the Marxist state attempts any withering away. A gentle, handsome creature, more Nordic than Slav in appearance, he suggests a partial throw-back to his father's German ancestry; there is in him nothing of the steely will and intellect to be found in contemporary poets like Yeats and Valéry; he is all emotion and intuition and the instinctive power of creation. His literary background was that of the pseudo-mystical and gloomily decadent period centred around the abortive revolution of 1905; and he never succeeded entirely, except perhaps in his famous revolutionary poem, the greatest of its kind in any language, *The Twelve*, in freeing himself from its influence. But he seems to have had from the first a wonderful instinctive feeling for form, even extending to the drama. In his earliest and deeply symbolic poems he was much influenced by a prevailing cult for the eternal feminine element in divinity, Sophia, or Divine Wisdom, whom he addressed almost directly and personally (as a man might who was talking to his own *anima*) as his Beautiful Lady. (And before we dismiss all this as so much typical decadent Russian nonsense, we might remember what has happened since to the Virgin in Roman Catholicism, or ask ourselves if our almost lunatic technological-masculine society would be any the worse for some possible guidance from a divine feminine principle.) But it seemed to him that his Beautiful Lady vanished—perhaps he could no longer project the *anima*, which took possession of his unconscious, playing the devil with his mode of life but compelling him to write more and better poetry—and he derided the Sophia mystical cult, only to find in Russia herself a similar symbolic image.

Like Yeats, though with never the deliberation and controlled power, Blok broke the mould of Symbolism, his poetry rushing in the opposite direction from that, say, of Valéry. He writes whatever his overwhelming emotional drives compel him to write. And in a new and far more powerful and disturbing manner. Though C. M. Bowra, in his admirable study of Blok in his *Heritage of Symbolism*, is clearly anxious to keep the poet within the symbolic tradition, he has to write: "His whole style had changed. Diffuseness and vagueness have given place to a hard outline, an economy of effects and a boldness of imagery unique in Russian verse. . . . All is clear, grand, direct and powerful . . ." This is obvious even in translation. Thus, most of us must have read several different translations of his famous *Dance of Death*, and although they differ widely in verbal dexterity, what Blok intended comes triumphantly through them all. From now on he is very far removed from anything Mallarmé ever had in mind. Blok is much nearer to the old Romantics in spirit but making full use of essentially modern effects. The significant details, of which he is a master, are realistic: we are in St. Petersburg with him, see the street lamps and the chemist's shop, visit the restaurant where the gipsies are singing, hurry through the snowstorms. There is symbolism here, of course, but only as there is in all poetry of any depth. And there are strange depths in this Blok, prophetic glimpses and warnings of terror and misery to come, as in *A Voice from the Chorus*. From here to his final masterpiece, *The Twelve* (his last published poem, *The Scythians*, reads like political rhetoric, possibly written to order), we have left the Symbolist Movement behind. The only truly symbolic figure in *The Twelve* is that of Christ discovered leading the dozen revolutionary soldiers, and it could be argued that the poem would be better without this rather theatrical ending; but all the rest, the twelve typical soldiers, the prostitute, the bourgeois, the writer, are themselves; the snowstorm is a snowstorm, the city a city, and the revolution a revolution that is happening; Blok is not writing about states of mind, finding images to suggest the depths of his own personality, but is concentrating the revolution and what he feels about it into one narrative-dramatic-marching-folksong. It is simply not the kind of poetry the original Symbolists ever dreamt of. So far as they had any rules, it breaks them all. It is a great poem, but no other great poems, either by Blok or by anybody else, came out of it; modern poetry, after 1918, was not moving in this direction; and of his own later style, in which each uprush of emotion, each explosion in the unconscious, somehow finds expression in perfectly chosen and sharply realistic detail, Blok remains the solitary master.

Yeats too was a symbolist poet—and never ceased to be one—who broke clean away from the French movement, with which he was only vaguely associated in his youth, to become not only a great poet but probably the greatest poet of this century. (If there is hesitation here, it is for two reasons: first, to allow for the natural bias that comes from sharing the same language; secondly, that some of Yeats's finest later poems do demand some knowledge of Irish life and history, to be understood at all, and he can never have assumed he was addressing a world-wide audience.) Great or greatest, he had certain important advantages, and the character to make the most of them. Genius and character are not the same thing, and it is only when we are young that we imagine them to be. Blok and Rilke had genius but were deficient in character, while both Valéry and Stefan George had perhaps rather more character than genius. Yeats had both, to a high degree: a strong personality, increasingly massive with age; unusual self-discipline, enabling him to shape his life as well as his art; and behind the grave and elaborate poet-magician *persona* he faced the world with, not without an inner gleam of Irish impudence and humour, considerably more shrewd common-sense than the saints, drunkards, hard-living horsemen he was fond of praising but did not imitate. These were all advantages, when poetic genius is added to them; but he enjoyed others. He was Irish, a tremendous advantage, because it meant that he had his own small country, a tiny stage on which he could play almost any part he pleased, a society still free from industrialisation and the urban mass, where eighteenth-century country gentlemen still rode among almost medieval peasants and the common talk was still imaginative and salty; and yet, because he wrote in English, he could find publishers and readers and admiring critics in England and the United States, and so could draw, however modestly, upon the resources of large, wealthy, industrialised societies without having to live in them and write about them: a perfect arrangement for a modern poet, and perhaps only possible for an Irish one.

But Ireland did more for him than that. First, it compelled him to break away from the Symbolist tradition; and secondly it gave him an opportunity, which he would not have had in England or America, to create his later and stronger poetry in quite a different way. The break with Symbolism came because too many inferior poets were imitating him, borrowing his

> "coat
> Covered with embroideries
> Out of old mythologies"

(see *A Coat* in *Responsibilities*, the volume in which he makes the break); but also because now, in his mid-forties, he could look back on years of experience, much of it bitter and hard to swallow, quite outside literature and belonging to Irish public life. (Nothing is more blazingly public than the Theatre, which sends a writer stark naked into the market-place.) This experience had to find its way into poetry—for Yeats was a poet first, last, and all the time—and even if his earlier manner had not been imitated and cheapened, it was still inadequate to express his attitude towards this experience. But if his poetry were almost to abandon symbols from Celtic mythology, alchemy, Rosicrucianism, magic, if it had now to deal directly at times with real events, then out of what life, capable of nourishing poetry, could it speak? This was Yeats's problem; and because genius sees possibilities in the impossible, it is not safe to assert that, if he had been English or American, then the problem would have defeated him; but we can say definitely that it was because he was Irish that he was able to solve it so triumphantly. The initial semi-dedicatory verse addressed to his 'old fathers', in *Responsibilities*, the key volume, gives us the clue. There is not one of his old symbols in this verse, which directly addresses and describes, in a heightened romantic manner, his father and grandfathers. The life now out of which his poetry will so often speak, with a wonderfully controlled passion, will be life in Ireland as he has known it, heard or read of it, raised by a continuous act of will to a lofty and heroic level. (Even when he is denouncing the merchants and the mob he is still regarding them from this height, far above economics and sociology.) Of course there will be symbols again—all verse that is not pure song or narrative-dramatic rhetoric cannot avoid their use—but in the poetry that Yeats writes from now to his death, poetry into which politicians, revolutionaries, music-hall dancers, philosophers, tinkers, whores and schoolgirls find their way, in which we are in Dublin, at Coole, listening to the Oxford chimes or sitting in a London teashop, we are—as we are with the later Blok—a long way from Mallarmé's idea of poetry.

But Yeats not only had the character, capable of a continuous act of will, that Blok or Rilke lacked, he also lived much longer, well into his seventies; and instead of trying to recapture the themes and moods of his youth, as so many aged poets have done, he wrote directly and profoundly out of what he thought and felt at each stage of his life. Those readers who dislike the poems of his old age will probably find their own last years, if they have sufficient life in them, equally outrageous. If Yeats's dependence upon Irish characters and history gives him a superficial narrowness, a suggestion of provinciality (though behind every reference is something universal), then breadth, stature, greatness, are more than restored by his astounding ability to express, with passionate plain speech (no Valéry and special diction here) wonderfully organised and most powerfully evocative, each succeeding decade. He is indeed the great poet of the second half of life, who by will and intellect, serving imagination, is able to see his own existence and that of his country raised to a kind of Homeric height, where Maud Gonne and burning Troy, Parnell or O'Leary and Conchubar or Cuchulain, are not brought together by fancy but seem to share the same life. Once he is past his youth, beyond the Æsthetic and Symbolist Movements, his poetry comes from a double act of creation: there are the poems, and behind them the heightened and heroic life out of which they come, itself a creation. What cynical onlookers, like George Moore, regarded as luxuriant attitudinising was really part of this primary act of creation, which, for example, raised the actual unpromising relationship with Maud Gonne to an heroic and tragic level, where she was another Deirdre or Helen of Troy, and from that level the love poems, some of the finest in any language, are launched. So, in Dublin years ago, we heard Gogarty say: "Yeats is now so aristocratic, he's evicting imaginary tenants." But behind the rather innocent Anglo-Irish snobbery and personal vanity, the poet was continually at work, with an unsleeping will and a tenacity belonging to some hard core in him, creating the life, the special heroic-tragic-symbolic world to which Ireland herself contributed so much (as England or America would not have done), and out of which, now with an air of direct realism, his poetry could be created. And it is the effort to sustain this life, this world, that gives his prose memoirs, valuable and fascinating though they are, a too-lofty, over-solemn, hierarchical manner, a style in the stiff robes of some mysterious order, as discouraging to ease and intimacy as he often appeared to be himself.

Too much has been written about what Yeats did or did not believe. He believed in poetry and the life of the imagination. For the rest, we might quote what that eccentric novelist of genius, John Cowper Powys, says wisely of a friend in his *Autobiography*: "He combined scepticism of everything with credulity about everything; and I am convinced this is the true Shakespearean way wherewith to take life . . ." And though there may seem more evidence of the credulity than the scepticism, until we remember that Yeats took no wild gambles on his beliefs, it is the Yeatsian way too. Here he can be contrasted with the friend of his youth and his Dublin contemporary, 'AE', George Russell. The two men are at opposite extremes. Russell was a whole-hearted enthusiastic believer, a genuine mystic in his own fashion; and his verse, like his painting, hastily done and far from carrying the full weight of his impressive personality, is an attempt to reveal what he believes: it is poetry in the service of ideas. But with Yeats, from first to last, from theosophy, Rosicrucianism, magic, to automatic writing, spiritualism, the vast wheel in *A Vision*, ideas and beliefs are there to serve his poetry, the ideas to strengthen, the beliefs to light up, that poetic life, that specially created world of his own, out of which his verse comes. When he no longer needs them, as in so many of his last poems when he is playing the mischievous half-mad old man, speaking out about sex, then they are no longer there. He was not a mystic, a seer, another Blake; he was entirely an artist, committed to "the supreme theme of Art and Song", the life of the imagination, and sceptical-credulous about any enduring reality behind appearances, using whatever was supernatural to give depth and illumination to his poetry. Everything that happened to him, everything he saw, heard, read, thought and felt, was compelled to serve his art, first to create a life possible for a poet, in an age hostile to such a life, and then to create the poetry itself. And he brought to this double task, just as he brought to the labour of giving every line a seemingly inevitable order of the right words, all the concentrated power of his formidable personality. Yeats is not a great poet by accident but by design, and the design, like the poetry, is entirely his own. He had some luck: his country was Ireland, where imaginative life still flourished; he lived in robust health to be old, unlike so many poets; but few men have done more with their luck; and the poetry he has left us, incomparable in this age in its combination of quantity, range and power, proves what poetic genius can accomplish with the aid, all too rare, of character, will, and a noble single-mindedness.

There are nearly a hundred poets represented in *The Oxford Book of Modern Verse* that Yeats edited. (The curious manner, half lofty, half casual, of his Introduction should not delude the reader into thinking it does not contain some very shrewd and pointed criticism.) Still, with time and space shrinking, in pursuit of what is essentially 'modern' in poetry and of major international reputations and influences, we can only note, in passing, the twilight of the pure singers, headed by that fine old poet, Bridges; the arrival, through belated publication, in the Twenties of Gerard Manley Hopkins, whose 'sprung verse', together with his curiously dense but sharp imagery, had an immediate strong influence; and the later arrival in the Thirties of poets like George Barker, Auden, Day Lewis, Spender, MacNeice, whom Yeats considered more 'modern' than himself, and whose work, up to 1939, was still in its early stages. In

America, where any representative anthology would be equally crowded, we may also note in passing, first the rough but effective realism of Middle-Westerners like Carl Sandburg and Lee Masters, then the arrival of sophisticated and highly visual (though with aural deficiencies to an English ear) experimenters like William Carlos Williams, Wallace Stevens, Marianne Moore; with a side-glance at the tragic Hart Crane, tragic not only because he committed suicide in his early thirties but also because he had the wide reach but not the tenacious grasp of the major poet, and at the Californian Robinson Jeffers, all magnificent energy and furious misanthropy, as if an unbroken horse were writing verse. We must stop, however, at Robert Frost, if only because he stands outside the whole modern movement and yet is widely recognised as a major poet and is altogether an odd, original, unexpected figure. His poetry is, in his own phrase, "versed in country matters"; it is not even national but local, New England, in scene and manner; it is as frugal with imagery and metaphor as a farmer with his money; much of it appears to have the rhythm and tone of cautious conversation, spoken out of the side of the mouth by a man not looking at you; yet through this stealthy rusticity comes almost everything, short of the depths of personal dissolution and the blazing heights of ecstasy, that the modern poet is trying to express —bewilderment and horror, wonder and compassion, a tragic sense of life, which he, however, suggests without bitterness or whining. This is a poet, using his poker-faced rural *persona*, who likes to pretend he is being simple and obvious when he is not, just as many other poets, going with the movement, like to pretend they are being profound when they are not.

This brings us to the two American poets who early left America for Europe, to become major influences in the poetry of the Twenties and Thirties: Ezra Pound and T. S. Eliot. Pound we have met already, in the Vorticist explosion just before the First War. A picturesque and exuberant personality, he acted as a kind of showman-ringmaster for the whole three-ringed circus of the *avant-garde*. At first he dashed from movement to movement like a Sinclair Lewis character doing a quick European tour. His odd combination of learning and a wide culture, the Middle-Western salesman manner, seriousness and cheerful impudence, impressed his fellow-poets. And indeed it might be argued that those, like Eliot, who were his friends were so deeply impressed that, for ever afterwards, they added something to his printed page, bringing the lines to life, that the rest of us, never having been under the spell, cannot provide. What is certain is the sharp division, between those who believe him to be one of the poetic masters of the age, great in achievement and influence, and those who see him as a minor poet busy with juggling tricks, and a bad influence. Let us admit that his initial approach is that of a major poet, that he goes to the ends of the earth and backward and forward in time, adding economics, history, philosophy, to literature and linguistics, to create his own framework, his own high platform from which his poetry will speak. Let us also admit that his incessant demand that poetry should be more concentrated, should carry the maximum load of meaning, is within certain limits a reasonable and valuable one. But Pound cannot be contained within limits. His talent, though genuine, is not strong enough to defy his theories. He is capable of compressing a poem, until it looks as if *Haiku* are only round the corner, while actually losing and not gaining in intensity. And what he has built for himself, as framework, platform, special world of chosen ideas for his verse, is such a wobbly, crazy Provençal-pagoda that no wonder he fell off it into bad trouble.

For all his long and deep concern for the art, he has been a bad influence on modern poetry. It is he more than anybody else who has encouraged an unnecessary obscurity, not arising from the flashing broken images of passion, but too often from a cold cleverness working away at compression. For a line can be so loaded with meaning that it can only be understood if the reader regards it as part of an exceptionally difficult crossword puzzle; but at what moment, in this puzzle-solving atmosphere, does æsthetic experience arrive, when does poetry begin? It is he who has encouraged too many younger poets to collect savoury and rare ingredients, but then to ruin the dish because the heat of the oven, the poetic feeling, is too low to cook it properly. Following his example, they have offered us too many recondite allusions, too many scraps of other languages (for a poem is a performance on one instrument, not one of those 'musical' acts in vaudeville), and too many of those cold flat statements, filled with polysyllabic abstractions, that read like quotations from legal documents. What may have been originally conceived in passionate intensity too often somehow loses, through too much concentration and cool brainwork, real poetic feeling, and ends by suggesting an over-self-conscious intellectual sneering and showing off. Pound and those who have followed him may feel, not unreasonably, that they have taken poetry past the point at which an older poet like Yeats worked with white-hot iron; and certainly the art must be kept in movement; but where they have taken it, the whole temperature seems much lower, the music harsher or non-existent, the shapes less comely, the heartbeat fainter, the glory and ecstasy of the art infrequent and fading. It is as if poetry, determined to keep up with the age, were running away from itself.

T. S. Eliot, though closely associated with Pound in the beginning, is entirely different. He has created for himself a poetic instrument, which, though low in tone and rather narrow in compass for a major poet, he uses with wonderful skill. (His prose—a kind of *persona* prose, suggesting behind its chilly didacticism an intolerance and arrogance from which Eliot as a man seems quite free—is in its own way equally skilful.) Sharing some of Pound's dubious devices in his earliest work, expressing disgust and despair and the poet's cleverness, Eliot rid himself of them to achieve a highly distinctive verse, low in tone, slow but subtle of movement, at once easy and yet tense, capable of an almost conversational tone and yet far-ranging in its allusiveness, that justifies his claim to be modern and yet not dissociated from poetic tradition. As a technical achievement, this could hardly be over-praised—a strong statement for once, for no poet, indeed no writer of any kind, in the period between the Wars, has had more praise or been quoted oftener than Eliot. His has been one of the major voices of the age, proclaiming its disgust and despair, its guilt and *angst*, its struggle to find a faith. A cynic, regarding Eliot's literary career itself as his chief creation, might suggest that this poet, having captured the *avant-garde* with his early work, then proceeded to strengthen his position, bringing in a new host of admirers, by announcing his conservatism in literature and politics and his acceptance of Anglo-Catholicism. Though this describes what has happened, it would be unfair to Eliot himself, whose sincerity cannot be questioned. And indeed this strengthening of his position, on a social level of orders and prizes, about which he probably cares little, actually meant a weakening of it on the more important level both of poetic creation and social criticism.

A major poet in this age has to do for himself what society will no longer do for him; he has to create a foundation and framework of some sort, a world within the world, for his poetry, just as we saw that Yeats did. Had Eliot remained in America, which gave him more than is commonly thought, he might have been able to do this, even though America is no Ireland and the pressure he would have had to resist (though Auden went to meet it) would have been tremendous. (But sheer space, the mere distance between New York and Santa Fé, and a certain looseness of texture in American life do something to make up for this pressure.) But remaining in England, becoming a British citizen, turning Anglo-Catholic, royalist, and the rest, meant in actual effect that Eliot rejected creation for mere acceptance. He accepted, whatever he may have thought of it privately, the British Establishment—the dole system, the refusal, until the last minute, to challenge the dictatorships, all the humbug and cant, the politically manipulated snobberies, the hard-faced industrialists and financiers turning up in ancient orders of chivalry, the newspaper proprietors cynically debauching their readers, and even a Church that is timid and time-serving. No doubt Eliot disliked many of these things; but he had to accept them: a man cannot ask to join a nation in order to become one of its most distinguished rebels. Yeats, flashing out of his own world, could strike fiercely and realistically, could be openly and proudly scornful. But Eliot was trapped in his acceptance. The exquisite instrument went murmuring through metaphysical quartettes; there was chilly and arid praise of chilly and arid authors, bone saluting bone; there were cautious notes towards definitions of culture; but the poetry did not ring out, the prose speak out. A major poet in a bad time should make powerful enemies. If he despises the mob, he should openly show his contempt for those who mislead it and fatten on it. Eliot left despair, if not disgust, behind, passed through the wasteland, but the trumpets, either of battle or victory, never sounded on the other side; certainly, modesty and politeness were against it, and perhaps a false fixed attitude, and perhaps something dry and negative that remained.

He turned to drama, perhaps to avoid direct and personal speech, and there made some experiments, much to his credit, in creating dialogue that, without any obvious break, could be flatly conversational and then quickly heightened. But he lacks the breadth of sympathy, the variety in himself to distribute among and give life to many characters, the constant dramatic invention within the main structure, that a dramatist needs. He is the central, best-remembered poet of the mood of the early Twenties; his technical mastery deserves all the praise it has received; he will have some stature even when all his influence has gone; but he would have been a greater poet if he had stayed at home, by the great rivers that ran through his boyhood.

One final note, before we leave the poets. Towards the end of the Thirties, nearing the limit of our period, there came, flashing and thundering, the young Welshman, Dylan Thomas. It is worth adding, though the event lies outside our time here, that his death during an American lecture tour, when he had just reached forty, made him a curious and fascinating figure to millions who had hardly ever thought before about poets and poetry: it was as if some reckless and raging bard, lurching wild-eyed but still magnificently intoning, had come among them out of some forgotten Celtic age; an archetypal figure of the elements rejected by the modern way of life. And indeed, at first sight, or, better still, at first hearing in Thomas's own slow, deep, rich tones, his poetry seems to have been composed in some bardic frenzy. Marvellous lines, satisfying and moving at once, came and went among passages of the densest obscurity, although even these, unlike so much of the earlier and determinedly 'difficult' verse approved by Valéry or Pound, were charged with passion. (Obscurity can be wrestled with, if with meaning comes emotion: what is intolerable is verse that seems charged with nothing but a distaste for other people, one long slight sneer.) With Thomas not only was the emotion there, but with it the intense labour of the serious poet; yet undoubtedly his poetry is hard, or even impossible, to comprehend. Eliot and Pound, earlier, had often seemed obscure because they were so widely allusive in their imagery and leapt from image to image, unlike Yeats, without any frame of argument. Then, for example, Auden, a real and often powerful poet even though apt to keep his cleverness showing, was sometimes obscure because his poetry used private references, private jokes, so that at these times the reader seems the only outsider at a party of old friends. Dylan Thomas's obscurity, important to those of us who grew up with poetry still having some frame of argument, arises from his chosen method of composition, a kind of dialectical process in imagery, very strong in effect when it succeeds, creating the wonderful lines we recognise at once, but leaving us bewildered or irritated when his inner world, from which all his poetry issues, is suddenly too personal and private in its imagery. Thomas remains then, at the end of this epoch, a 'difficult' poet just as Valéry was at the beginning of it; nevertheless, he breaks with the general trend of poetry during these twenty years, by not being over-conscious, too coolly intellectual, emotionally debilitated, by writing with passion and the full force of his essentially poetic personality. It began burning itself out, and his final compulsive drinking merely added quick fuel. Perhaps there is something symbolic about his death, so far from the green bardic hills of Wales, in one of the steel and concrete towers of New York, above the traffic that looks like a plague of drilled beetles, and not far from the big bombs and the plans for rockets to the moon; and about the fact that millions of kind wondering Americans, who knew little or nothing of the poetry he had created in his life, somehow understood his death and were moved by it. For a few days a poet was in the news: he had come, he had gone, and for ever; and then the machines went grinding out their familiar tale of collective insanity, the corruption of power, the ruin of the earth, the day's rat-race, and, like trinkets on a death-bed, all the huge, costly, glittering trivialities of our time.

3

When we come to fiction, as we must do now, let us begin with Marcel Proust. He is a great novelist, possibly the greatest so far in this century. There are two outstanding reasons why he can be called great: first, that he successfully achieved in and for his age what previous great novelists had achieved in and for their ages, and in fact continued a great tradition;

secondly, that he added something new, entirely his own, to fiction, thereby, it is argued, creating another kind of fiction, essentially modern, changing the direction of the novel and indeed the very atmosphere in which serious fiction must now be written, and so on and so forth, etc., etc., etc. Now it is our contention that Proust's claim to greatness, which must not be grudgingly allowed but most happily and gratefully affirmed, is far stronger when he is seen continuing a tradition than it is when he is accepted, as so much criticism tends to do, simply as a breaker away from tradition, an altogether new kind of novelist, revealing an essentially modern consciousness and its relations with the unconscious. For it is here where he is wide open to attack. And this can be easily, even if briefly, proved. Thus, the whole of his vast novel is contained within one consciousness, that of the narrator; but though we have access to his most fleeting and subtle impressions, we never have a reasonably clear idea exactly who this narrator is. And though time is all-important—it is indeed Proust's subject—there is no major novel in which the time-scheme is more muddled and bewildering than it is in this one. So here, in this gigantic and profound study of a narrator's consciousness in time, both the narrator and the time are vague and confusing: "Who is he?" we cry: "And what time is it?" Again, Proust, in his capacity as a new modern master, is considered a supreme if withering analyst of human relationships. But no reader who has gone beyond infatuations, to love truly a member of the opposite sex, could be taken in for a moment by Proust's perverted notion of love coming out of desire that has suffered a check: this is a mere mixture of sensuality and curiosity. His account of Swann's infatuation and jealousy is wonderful, but Swann, here the biter bit, merely goes around tasting women, not loving them, and is trapped by Odette's hold on the æsthete in him; she becomes necessary to him as plovers' eggs might be to a gourmet: but this is not love. Again, there are hundreds of pages, some of them magnificently written, about the narrator's relations with Albertine, but they throw no light on our common heterosexual experience, because Albertine is a mere name, behind which so many page-boys and chauffeurs are hiding, and offers us none of the behaviour, thought and feeling of a real girl. For the reader who is not homosexual, Proust on this level of relationships has not outdistanced older major novelists, not even a minor one like Benjamin Constant, but has merely gone obliquely away from them, heading for some salt desert. Finally, though we have no further space for examples, while there are innumerable pages of astonishing subtlety and depth in Proust, there are also many, far too many, long and wearisome passages, begging to be cut (old Proustian hands turn the pages hastily), of mock-profundity and false depth, especially in the later books, never properly revised; and it can be argued that his concluding ideas about Time and human life, coming very close to the Oriental conception of man's 'long body', cannot really be contained, however hard he works with 'involuntary memory' and 'art', within the scientific-rationalist scheme of existence he seems willing to accept. There is some ambiguity here: his references to another plane of existence, a life outside time, may be metaphorical or may indicate a belief he was not prepared to define. But enough has been said to show that it is precisely in this capacity, as an explorer of consciousness, as an analyst of relationships, as the new and very modern magician, that Proust can easily suffer damaging criticism.

It is when we restore him to the tradition of major fiction, acknowledging his originality but not conceding that the writing of novels begins all over again with him, that he moves from weakness to strength. If the central task of the novelist, yesterday, today and tomorrow, is to show us Man in the society he has created—and with a major novelist, society itself will be an all-important character—it is here that Proust is triumphantly successful. And on a great scale. The enormous length of his narrative is not the result of mere prolixity, even though it could be improved by judicious cutting, but is absolutely essential to his purpose. It enables him to show us a host of characters, indeed a whole society, moving with Time, and not moving in a straight line but always curving, spiralling up or down, aiming at one thing and arriving at its opposite, beginning as one kind of person and ending as somebody quite different. Because he has such a span of years at his disposal, Proust is a master of dramatic ironies, from the superficial or comic to the profound and tragic. In his own life Proust may or may not have been something of a snob (much of the evidence overlooks his bland irony and humour), but it is absurd to imagine that his novel is tainted with and weakened by snobbery because it is concerned with a decadent and foolish society and the social stratagems and antics of its members; this was the society he happened to know, and so this is the society he builds up and then takes to pieces for us, far more thoroughly than his hostile critics could even attempt to do. (A stronger criticism would be that apart from his artists, who are superb, he does not show us men at work, probably cutting a very different figure from the one they display at evening parties, or involved in political and economic affairs: mostly we see his men as old-fashioned women must have seen theirs, but with the same acute perception too.) But all his complexity of movement, all his various levels of irony, his ruthless penetration into the society he offers us, valuable though they are, would not keep us reading and re-reading him if the characters he sets in intricate motion did not appear to us to have a complete life of their own. It is here he joins the tradition. He is an authentic creator, of a world into which we can enter again and again, of an astoundingly wide range of people—an index-guide to them makes a fair-sized volume—a portrait gallery, but never still, always in movement and alive, of artists, aristocrats, professional men and their wives, ambitious hostesses and their guests, courtesans, men about town, headwaiters and valets and peasant servants, old people and young children, from the stupendous half-mad Charlus, like a Goya portrait, to the Dutch interior figures of the grandmother and Françoise. Let us give most credit to where it belongs. Proust's analysis of character and motive, his careful exploration of his inner world, these require sensibility, patience, skill; but the sheer creation of all these characters and their world demands a novelist of genius. (And if any man doubts this, let him sit down and begin to try—we can wait.) And when we add to this essential creative power the breadth and depth of Proust's mind, adding to the long vista of memorable personages and scenes equally memorable passages of subtle analysis and exquisite meditation on life and art, volume after volume of them, we have a great novelist, possibly the greatest our century has yet known.

While we are holding the door wide open for Proust, our French friends, who play this game brilliantly, will try to rush in André Gide, assuring us that he too is one of the master novelists. They will even pretend he is greater than Proust, having had more influence on French younger novelists. They can say what they please, but over this threshold of the masters Gide shall not pass. He may have been for many years the revered *maître*, the one, and there is always one, allowed to wear a skull-cap; he may have written supremely well, as indeed he often did, and left behind him a very full and fascinating journal; he may have behaved honourably and with courage about the Congo and about the Soviet Union and possibly, though uncertainty begins here, about the conflicting claims of a Protestant conscience and a taste for pederasty; he may have had the mostly highly cultivated intelligence in France, in Europe, and unquestionably he made some curious and interesting experiments both in fiction and autobiography; but he cannot possibly be considered a major creative writer, a European master of the novel. *Les Faux-Monnayeurs* (in English *The Counterfeiters*) is very subtle in its intention, very ingeniously contrived even if rather clumsily jointed, but never really comes to life as a novel. A born diarist and self-explainer, Gide is no creator. Suspecting this, some of his admirers have put him forward as a great anti-novel novelist: he deliberately "reveals the inadequacy of all fiction when it is confronted with life". Possibly; but the real masters of fiction prefer to write great novels: Gide shall not pass.

Proust died in 1922 and from then until 1939 the French novel flourished, but no master arrived. Admirers of François Mauriac would deny this statement; but though we on our side could not deny him great talent, an unusual power of telling a story with all the economy of a dramatist and yet still creating atmosphere and poetic feeling, we find his ultra-possessive landowning families monotonous or repellent, and his narrowly theological idea of human relationships as crippling to Mauriac himself as it is to his tortured characters. Even further from Paris than Mauriac, geographically and spiritually, Jean Giono, among his Provençal peasants and his folktale landscapes, reminds us that there are still some regions in France not too far removed from the primitive. Bang in the movement, at one time, was Henry de Montherlant, really a throw-back to the decadence and weary dandyism of the nineteenth century but capable of expressing himself, with considerable skill, in the manner of the Twenties. One of the meteors of the Thirties—we can still remember the excitement about him—was Louis-Ferdinand Céline, whose influence has persisted in spite of his political disgrace. (He preferred the Nazis when the war came.) His *Journey to the End of Night* is not without genuine poetic power, born of shuddering disgust; but the weakness of this nightmare-film kind of fiction is easy to discover. Something satisfying and valuable can be created out of a sane man looking at a mad world, or a madman making what he can out of a sane world; but a mad account of a mad world leaves us dissatisfied, unless we also have felt nothing but sick disgust for years and years. Perhaps the most formidable new talent in French fiction, and the one that best interpreted a world into which Proust never penetrated, belonged to André Malraux, essentially, in the earlier phase before 1939, the novelist of men of action in the new world of violence. But he must not be confused with later novelists of action who are half-journalists offering us undigested *reportage*. The power of Malraux, whose influence both inside and outside fiction has been very considerable, comes from his genuine poetic creation, the personal vision he imposes, his ruthless interpretation of reality in terms of his private myth of revolutionary tragic contemporary man. He is also deliberately and intensely pictorial, almost turning certain moments in his hard violent world into glimpses of Old Masters. Something very old and deeply civilised, and something representing the new barbarism of our time, seem to meet in him, disturbingly, for they do not meet to enhance life but rather to create a death-wish: we feel his chief characters, like Garine in *The Conquerors* (one of the key novels of this period), do not know how to live, only how to die. His personal vision, created world, myth, are not unlike Hemingway's, but though his range is narrower, at least in the three novels he published between 1928 and 1937, his depth of penetration into the confused contemporary scene is more impressive.

Proust, the born Parisian, and James Joyce, the exile in Paris, met only once, and found they had nothing to say to each other. Joyce, even more than Proust, has to be rescued from all the nonsense that has been written about him. Every few days, for years and years now, somebody tells us that Joyce is the master of the modern novel, or words to that effect, and that he opened for younger novelists "completely new avenues of expression" and all the rest of it. Responsible writers keep on making these statements like so many parrots, and nobody troubles to ask them why Joyce is the master of the modern novel, or who and where all the novelists are who have now been writing so long directly under his influence. And then there is the legend—to which he can have contributed only by trying some Irish humour on solemn disciples—of Joyce the lonely arrogant giant of modern literature. And the irrelevant statements, generally given a bullying tone, about his work: that *Ulysses* follows the pattern of the *Odyssey* (what if it does?), and that *Finnegans Wake* took him seventeen years to write, a length of time that suggests an elaborate hobby rather than any passionate desire to create something. We are not about to attack Joyce himself, nor even the Joyce cult, which gives some people pleasure and does the rest of us no harm; but the development of fiction between the Wars cannot be honestly dealt with, nor indeed Joyce and his work clearly seen, unless we are prepared to be reasonably realistic about him. It is simply not true that he is the great influence in modern fiction. Not one younger novelist of any importance derives from him. He did not invent, though he certainly enriched, the various subjective-narrative techniques known as stream-of-consciousness, free association, interior monologue, all of which had been used before. Moreover, if the truth must be told, these techniques, unless used sparingly and very selectively or as a sheer *tour de force*, like Mrs. Bloom's famous free-association-interior-monologue at the end of *Ulysses*, tend to be clumsy, fatiguing, and downright boring. And Joyce did not open new avenues for the novel, but created his own magnificent *cul-de-sac*. He was not himself intensely concerned with modern literature and thought, and, apart from his astonishing linguistic researches, preferred to think about and enjoy music. He can be called a great novelist—anybody can be called anything; and greatness cannot be denied him—but there might have been far less confusion if he had been hailed and praised, as he well deserves to be, in some other style.

"Joyce's books," we are told, "which a few years ago had to be smuggled into the U.S.A., are today required reading in college courses there." But this has been the trouble. *Ulysses* existed too long in this over-charged atmosphere of once-past-the-customs-officers-straight-into-the-college-course, of the division between people who said it was the greatest modern masterpiece of fiction and the people who said it was a lot of filth and ought to be suppressed. Each group encouraged the other to overstate its case. True, anybody who finds *Ulysses* pornographic must be in danger of sex mania; it is to most of us a strong anaphrodisiac. Indeed, Joyce, more a straight Jesuit here than one 'in reverse', can be accused of associating sex, and the whole life of the body, too frequently with disgust. This is not straight realism, just reporting the facts, but comes from the author's manipulation of the scene. Actually, it goes against the complete realism often claimed for Joyce in his handling of Bloom; for when we are first with Bloom, at breakfast time, a number of unpleasant details are sharply presented to us not as they would appear to Bloom, an easy-going unfastidious sensualist, but as they would have appeared to Joyce. *Dubliners* and the *Portrait of the Artist* are all very well, and *Finnegans Wake* much better than that, but Joyce, as the great modern master of the novel, stands or falls by *Ulysses*. Now if, remote from the screams of 'masterpiece' and 'filth', we had been called upon to judge this formidable work simply as a novel among other novels, we might have asked some awkward questions. Is it entirely satisfactory as a narrative? Not having, like Joyce, a love-hate relationship with Dublin, do we want, or need for the purposes of the novel, as much of Dublin as he gives us? Is Bloom really as solidly and convincingly created as he is thought to be? Is Stephen Dedalus artistically essential to a novel about a day of Bloom's life, or is he an occasionally tedious piece of self-indulgence on the author's part? Is the author, in fact, creating characters and scenes as a great artist in fiction would create them, keeping his hobby-horses out of the picture? Or is he, novel or no novel, letting himself rip? And if we can ask this question of *Ulysses*, what is to be said, strictly considered as a novel, of *Finnegans Wake*?

We could fill pages with such questions, not because we dislike Joyce, either as a writer or a man, but because we feel he was so hurriedly rushed by his admirers into a false position, now hardly ever challenged. Joyce was not taking the novel anywhere; he has to be enjoyed but then by-passed. (A point that has been acutely made by C.P. Snow, himself an unusual and interesting novelist because he has brought to fiction what he has learnt in science and public service.) In terms of the novel, Joyce is an eccentric with astonishing gifts and of unquestionable genius. He is not so much a novelist as a unique combination of fantasist, humorist, scholar, poet. (Though it has characters and action of a sort, *Finnegans Wake* is a prose-poem, containing passages of great beauty and others filled with Irish wilfulness and devilment, about dream life and the personal and collective unconscious. And why not?) Let us take a quick look at him as a man. As a youth he broke with the religion that had moulded his thought, becoming the Jesuit in reverse, thereby still keeping some of the mould. He had to leave the only place he ever cared anything about, Dublin. (He lived in Trieste, Zürich, Paris, yet never wrote about them, a fact that suggests an eccentric poet-humorist rather than a novelist proper.) Failing sight, encouraging a natural introverted tendency, drove him further and further into his inner world, there to discover the Dublin of his youth. He had a notable gift for languages, together with a passion for words: he is one of the great word-men of all time. Except for immediate, domestic and convivial purposes—he was a friendly man and good company, in spite of the legend—he stubbornly rejected the outer world, deliberately took himself out of "the nightmare of history". (And *Ulysses*, we must remember, came out of the war years, to which he turned eyes that were psychologically blind before physical defects menaced them.) Except in his final years, and even they were clouded with bewilderment, anxiety about his daughter, and grief, he had a hard life. With uncommon power of will allied to genius, he kept his inward vision fixed, and with immense labour, lightened by the poetry, humour, memories aided by exact research, and general devilment about his loved-hated Dublin and the world of his youth, he created the realistic-cum-phantasmagorical, social-psychological-tragi-comic *Ulysses* and the dream prose-poem, mostly in heightened Jabberwocky language, of *Finnegans Wake*. Even the latter is not, as Mary Colum told him it was, outside literature. But they are both outside fiction, in the reasonable traditional sense of the term; and most of what we have been told about Joyce as the great modern master of the novel, changing the course of fiction, opening a way for later novelists, is nonsense. These are the astonishing creations of a comic poet of genius, who did whatever appealed to his idea of prose narrative in depth; and in these works he is unique and inimitable.

Two years after *Ulysses* first appeared in 1922, Franz Kafka died, having already destroyed much of his work in manuscript, but leaving, with instructions that they should be burnt, three unfinished novels, later known as *America*, *The Trial*, and *The Castle*. (His friend and executor, the writer Max Brod, wisely felt that the circumstances did not justify the destruction of these manuscripts.) The fame and influence of these three strange tales, quite unlike any others, have been tremendous. Kafka was not so much a writer as an atmosphere, in which fellow-writers of the later Twenties and the Thirties found themselves. Schools of criticism, ranging from the mystical and theological, through the psycho-analytic, to the opposite extreme of naturalism and the severest rationalism, have fought bitterly over these three unfinished novels. That they should be thought worth the battle is proof enough of their fascination and uncanny power, and of the genius of Kafka, the unknown, sickly minor bureaucrat who created them. Of these three works, *America* is the least important, and though *The Trial* and *The Castle* are often bracketed together, *The Castle* is the masterpiece. Technically Kafka is superb; his manner and style are perfectly suited to his task; he has a steady forward movement, together with a constant stealthy inventiveness, apparently along a narrow line between dream and reality, and exactly the right narrative tone for his tales: within the limits he sets for himself, he is a master. Whatever Kafka's inadequacies were, they were not literary. And on the level he reaches in *The Trial* and *The Castle*, especially the latter, his is the most triumphantly sustained symbolism in prose fiction.

Symbolism, genuine symbolism, which can release meanings at various levels but will always have a meaning that cannot be fully grasped, is the key to Kafka. The critics have quarrelled with one another over him; one believes he describes the quest of the soul for divine grace, another that he is haunted by his relation to his father, another finds the clue in his sexual life, and yet another, Marxist, sees him entangled in the inefficient bureaucracy of the decaying Austrian Empire. They all miss the secret because they are all confusing symbolism with allegory. If Kafka had been merely writing allegories, he would have been forgotten by now; the world is littered with unread allegories. The reason why Kafka has fascinated intellectuals of all kinds is that he is genuinely and profoundly symbolical. His fiction, moving stealthily between this world and the region of nightmare, along the narrow edge between the light of consciousness and the dark of the unconscious, is symbolical of how modern man feels himself to be situated, no matter—and this is the point his critics miss—what meaning each man may attach to it. His chief characters, in their suddenly alien worlds, mysteriously put under arrest or unable to communicate directly with the authorities demanding service, suffering from a deep unease, a guilt without a crime, tormented by a lack of any direct communication, by senseless obstacles, by apparent contradictions that waver between irrationality and a suggestion of a more profound rationality out of reach, are symbolic figures of modern man trying to live his life. So far as we are fairly typical men of this age, and so long as we have the intelligence to appreciate our situation, and the sensibility to experience it fully, we are Kafka characters. But only if we are men. Woman is different, as the helpful relations with her in the fiction suggest; she is less involved in the situation than man is; she might offer him a way out of it; the world that is half a nightmare, unbalanced, one-sided, represents the masculine principle. And it is no wonder that Kafka could not finish his symbolic tales. Where could he look for an ending? It is forty years since he wrote *The Trial* and *The Castle*, and the situation of contemporary man is no better now: it is indeed much worse.

The year Kafka died, Thomas Mann finished *The Magic Mountain*, the great German *Bildungsroman* of the age, the work that set him in front of Hesse and Wassermann and other novelists writing in German, and did most to establish him as one of the major representative novelists of his time. Purely as an example of Mann's mastery in fiction it is less satisfying than his *Death in Venice*, exquisitely contrived symbolism in narrative; but its sheer size and weight make *The Magic Mountain* important. It is vastly superior to *Buddenbrooks*, although that clinical study of decay was a remarkable performance for a writer in his twenties. (Mann's *Joseph* novels and his *Dr. Faustus*, a post-Nazi fable, fall outside our limit here.) A brilliant example of what Mann could do on a small scale is the political, strongly anti-Fascist, *Mario and the Magician*. But for our purpose here *The Magic Mountain* can be taken as his masterpiece. It was soon accepted as one of the key novels of the epoch; and during the thirty-five years since its publication an impressive amount of critical attention and writing have been devoted to it. Apart from his purely political thought —or, better perhaps, his political instincts—Mann is intensely German in his cast of mind; and whether we accept with admiration his meditations on 'the artist' and 'the bourgeois' and 'culture' and 'spirit' and 'death', or find him on these occasions too inclined to be unnecessarily heavy, turgid and ambiguous, will depend on how much sympathy we have for this characteristically German kind of writing. But even if we believe that he might have lightened his intellectual load, which he never shoulders with ease, we cannot deny his power of solid creation, which is very impressive indeed. He builds a novel as the Germans have always built ships. Formidable creative tasks, to which he could apply himself with typical Teutonic thoroughness, were probably psychologically necessary for him, for in spite of his shrewdness and almost ubiquitous sense of irony, there were in him some equally typical dubious Teutonic elements, notably a compulsive feeling for decay and dissolution, as if there was in his unconscious one of those creatures irresistibly attracted by the reek of a rotting corpse. And the artist in him—and he was essentially an artist, not a philosopher trying to use art—pressed the creature into his service.

The Magic Mountain is a great novel, representing in our time a great tradition, because it is satisfying on various levels, even if, as we shall see, it is not entirely satisfying. It tells us, with a wealth of significant and memorable detail, how simple young Hans Castorp went to visit his cousin Joachim, a patient in a Swiss sanatorium for consumptives, and remained there, a patient himself. It tells us, on the next level, as a typical *Bildungsroman*, how various persons tried, and failed, to convert Hans, now not quite so simple, to one *Weltanschauung* or another. On the next level, it offers us a symbolic drama of the artist in the world before 1914. On the level below that, depth psychology looms, the whole mountain and the Flatland below are contained within one psyche, and we are beyond the novelist's conscious intention. The strength of the novel comes from the central conception of the Magic Mountain itself, a stroke of genius. For this is truly symbolic, like Kafka's narratives. It has not one meaning—and any criticism that declares it has is doing Mann an injustice—but meaning within meaning and, like all true symbols, a final one that cannot be grasped. Once this is understood, Castorp's experiences on the mountain become fascinating and richly rewarding. They reveal an endless duel of opposites, starting with the obvious difference between the mountain and the plain below, life in the sanatorium and life outside it; and these conflicts on every level are indicated with the blandest irony. Nevertheless, this great novel has one artistic blemish that exactly coincides with what the casual reader, only wanting a story, finds irritating or tedious in it. Settembrini and Naphta, by directly representing their opposed points of view in their lengthy debates, break the symbolism. They really belong to a different book. They are like black-and-white figures in a colour film. They are unlike Madame Chauchat and Peeperkorn (a wonderful creation), who are truly symbolic figures, who just by being themselves carry their whole weight of meaning with them: the Russian woman being feminine allure, carelessness and reckless disorder, whatever is mysterious, formless, menacing to spirit, in the East, the sexual drive in the unconscious, and so on; the huge Dutchman, the European capitalist who has made his fortune out of the East, with his masterful yet secretly diseased personality, being life on an instinctive level of acquisition and pleasure, at first a reconciling principle in the breadth and force of its humanity and sheer vitality, but unable to face the challenge of spirit or genius, and so on: there is no end to these two, yet we find them satisfying, enjoy them as characters. But the debaters, Settembrini and Naphta, are not satisfying in the same way; and their debates break the spell of the symbolism, making us impatient, not because what they say is boring but because we feel that with them and their talk Mann has lost control of his method, is suddenly writing a novel with less depth in it. But, these two apart, this is a novel of marvellous solidity, richness, complexity, in which, for once, the outer world is not wrecked or turned into a shadow show for the sake of the inner world, but both worlds are held together, to present one epic-drama capable of being enjoyed and interpreted in many different ways, by a powerful but highly disciplined creative urge. The poets of this age, from Valéry onwards, who contemptuously dismissed the novel as a mere ribbon of narrative, immature stuff for immature minds, should have been compelled to read *The Magic Mountain*.

It was during these middle Twenties, when Mann's masterpiece was making its way throughout the Western world, that the N.E.P. period in Russia offered a breathing space for the writer, between the earlier and wild civil war period and the later Five Year Plan and socialist realism periods. This was the time when Isaac Babel, a Jewish writer of great talent, brought out his *Red Cavalry*, in which tales of violence, similar in background to hundreds of others that had been or were being written, are raised to the level of literature by their richness, complexity, depth. The sardonic humorists, Katayev and Zoshchenko, and the lighter pair, Ilf and Petrov, can write freely, before the steel bars of the Five Year Planners come crashing down. After that, even when Gorky has established his socialist realism and the atmosphere is not quite so oppressive, the odds are against literature. A strongly individual writer of exceptional ability, like Leonid Leonov, who in another time or place might have reached the stature of a major novelist, is still able to write real novels instead of propaganda-department fables; and a wily and ambiguous character like Alexei Tolstoy, an old hand by no means without talent, can put together something that looks like a literary career; but the creation of literature does not come easily to Stalin's "engineers of the soul". The Muse, being feminine, refuses to take orders from a Party, and sulks in silence when notified of resolutions by executive committees. But one writer, at once greatly gifted and admirably obstinate, told the story he wanted to tell in his own way, with the result that Mikhail Sholokhov's *And Quiet Flows the Don* burst out of the Soviet Union, where it has sold millions, and captured the world. It has no pretence to depth, subtlety, penetration into character, this panoramic tale of the Cossacks before and during the First War, the revolution, the civil war; but it has the breadth of its own great plain, vigour and movement, colour and sparkle, and a direct and firmly sustained objectivity very rare in the fiction of this age, inside or outside Russia. In spite of the fact that its central and best-drawn character is a White, not a Red, it is now established as a classic of Soviet literature. In the West it was certainly given more and warmer praise than any other Russian novel arriving between the Wars; but its violence was too remote, its people too simple, its manner too objective, for it to be considered of any outstanding importance by the deeply subjective and introverted guardians of modern Literature. The gap between Western Europe and the Soviet Union was widening.

Just as the Thirties arrived, David Herbert Lawrence died. Half poet, half prophet, and unquestionably a man of genius, his extremely original fiction still leaves criticism sharply divided. The poetic half of him is wonderful; he makes most clever and sensitive people seem dense and thick-skinned; both through his senses and an intuitive perception he is in direct contact with life, in all its natural manifestations, as few men are, and only a minority of women. This gives his fiction, at its best, a strange quality that many readers, especially women, find as fascinating as it is original: what passes between its characters is being reported on a deeper and more mysterious level; in place of the usual clash of *persona* with *persona*, and the familiar rationalisations of motive and conduct, we have encounters and conflicts in the dusk of the inner world, in the dark unconscious; and because on this level our sexual life, which compels us either to accept or retreat from the challenge of the Other, can save us or destroy us, Lawrence is always deeply concerned with sex. (The frequent attempts of official Britain, here at its stupidest, to turn Lawrence, who was a kind of pagan puritan, into a pornographer would be comic in their irony if it were not for their tragic effect upon him and his work.) The prophetic side of him is far less satisfactory than the poetic. Like some other writers who matured between 1910 and 1920, Lawrence was fiercely anti-intellectual; but also like the others he could not escape from being an intellectual himself, could not use thought and self-consciousness to rid himself of thought and self-consciousness; and this dilemma, together with a disease that found some relief in explosions of rage, goes far to explain the anger and bitter intolerance of a man who was at heart friendly and considerate and often an enchanting companion. He knew in his blood and bones that our society was hurrying to disaster, but had not the temperament, the time and patience, the steady energy (for his creative work was compulsive, and a life of restless travel, with inadequate means, anything but easy), to discover for himself, coolly and analytically, what exactly was wrong. An unsatisfactory novel like *Kangaroo*, with its wonderful evocation of the Australian scene at the beginning, and the fine promise of its characters in their political situation, and then its descent into long and querulous autobiography, is a good example of these two opposing strains, the creative-poetic and the prophetic-egoistical, at work in him. Moreover, the official persecution of him in England, added to a physical condition that removed him from the damp, smoky Midlands where his roots were, sent him wandering and rootless, remote from the one kind of society, that of industrial England, that both challenged and nourished the real novelist in him, as distinct from the rhapsodical exotic romancer. So his strongest work as a novelist—apart from the short stories in which he is often at his best—was his earliest, notably *Sons and Lovers* and *Women in Love*. Like most intellectuals he had the bad habit of assuming that his experience was universal experience; so although he was capable of exploring the depths of sexual relationships with an insight and sensitivity rare in fiction, he is not an entirely safe guide here; he cannot help over-emphasising the element of conflict, sex triumphant through a tension between opposites, that he discovered in the relation, odd though satisfying, with his own wife, alien in nationality, class, temperament. And inevitably he under-valued the close understanding, affection, deep friendship, possible between the sexes. Some readers and critics see him as one of the greatest novelists of the age; others, while conceding his genius, find him un-satisfying, sometimes repellent, often irritating. And the debate continues.

There is the same division of opinion, though it is not quite so sharp and emotional in tone, about another English novelist, also perhaps with more innate genius than solid talent, Virginia Woolf. Although she was herself a perceptive and delightful critic, she was arrogantly narrow in her rejection of the novel as Wells and Bennett were writing it, and in her assertion that it is the task of the novelist, abandoning what is external and alien to consciousness, to record life itself—"not a series of gig lamps, symmetrically arranged; but a luminous halo, a semi-transparent envelope surrounding us from the beginning of consciousness to the end . . . " But the novel is a very loose, wide form; and the task of the novelist is to write as well as he can the kind of novel he wants to write. If his fiction is concerned with men in a particular society, and with the character of that society, then this highly subjective, interior monologue, halo-and-envelope method will not serve his purpose at all. In the unending dazzle of thoughts and impressions, society disappears and even persons begin to disintegrate. Indeed, it might be argued that a writer who feels that life can only be described and recorded in this fashion should not be writing novels at all but poetry, and not even narrative poetry. The Impressionists were glorious painters, but if, instead of framing a few square feet of separate canvases, they had offered us glittering panoramas of summer a hundred feet long, we might have found their work fatiguing and tedious. Not that Virginia Woolf is fatiguing and tedious, but she is often in danger of becoming so, and indeed of losing contact with what can reasonably be considered prose fiction, with recognisable characters meeting other recognisable characters in the world of ordinary time and space. It is one thing to feel free of that series of gig lamps; it is quite another thing to atomise narrative, construction, scene, character, so that nine-tenths of what is valuable in fiction vanishes, and what is described as a novel becomes a series of prose poems.

This is not a condemnation of her work, for even in her least successful novels there are wonderful passages, but a complete rejection of her absolutist intolerant theory, which she herself modified in practice. In her masterpiece, *To the Lighthouse* (the next best, as pieces of fiction, are *Mrs. Dalloway* and *Between the Acts*), she is experimental, both in her use of time, actually different kinds of time, and in her two-level structure of prose narrative and poetic symbolism; and she is also a beautifully satisfying novelist. But here, in the family and their visitors, solid figures probably owing something to her memories of real people, she creates character and does not dissolve it in order to catch the tiniest flicker of consciousness; and within the limits of her experimental (and fascinating) form, she is far closer, as she is again in *Between the Acts*, to a more or less traditional method than her initial theory would allow. She is not quite a major novelist; she has the depth but nothing like the breadth, her own range being unusually narrow; she is too consciously a member of a limited class, the cultivated section of the English upper-middle class; but she does, at her best, so shape and colour and intensify the novel that it becomes a wonderful image of her mind, reflecting its poetry and wit, its gaiety sparkling above the tragic depths.

Aldous Huxley made some experiments in his fiction, especially in *Point Counter Point*, but the distinction of his mind and the quality of his writing cannot conceal the fact that his novels are made, not really created, and the further fact that he is concerned with ideas and not with persons. Evelyn Waugh, while still in his twenties, made a brilliant appearance, with his *Decline and Fall* and *Vile Bodies*, and strongly influenced a whole generation, in and out of writing, by creating without previous preparation a new kind of humour, entirely his own. It belongs very much to its time, breaking with traditional English humour by being without affection, entirely detached; it is hard and coolly impudent but superbly comic. An eccentric, over-rhapsodical but often richly rewarding novelist, who creates a world entirely his own, is John Cowper Powys, who has yet to obtain the wide recognition he deserves, either at home or abroad. This can hardly be said of Graham Greene, whose cunningly related novels of action, clouded with *angst*, heavy with guilt, taking place somewhere between the worlds of Mauriac and Malraux, increasingly appealed to the taste of the age. Of the many admirable women novelists, the one who achieved the widest recognition during the Thirties was probably Elizabeth Bowen. Finally, it is not surprising, when we remember how fashionably foolish some critics can be and how original artists not in any movement can be neglected, to find that in a recent work on modern British Literature, crowded with unimportant names, L. H. Myers is merely mentioned with others in a footnote devoted to historical novels. The novel in question by Myers, *The Root and the Flower*, is no more an historical novel than are *Wilhelm Meister* and *The Magic Mountain*; it is in fact an ambitious attempt, by a highly original writer of distinction, to create philosophical fiction, an English equivalent of the *Bildungsroman*. Like Virginia Woolf, L. H. Myers committed suicide during the war, probably having had as much public violence and private literary stupidity as he could take.

American fiction between the Wars deserves some special consideration; and for two good reasons. First, because up to now, lagging behind Western Europe, it has been given little space. Secondly, because now, from the early Twenties onward, the American Novel comes blazing out of obscurity, and several of its practitioners are recognised and applauded and imitated throughout the whole Western world. This is not entirely due to their remarkable individual talents, though these are not in question. For it can be said that after the First World War, in which the United States had to break its tradition of isolation, the nation itself comes roaring and glittering out of a previous comparative obscurity; its economic and potential military power is now recognised to be vast; and with power come increasing attention and respect, the ability to initiate, for imitation abroad, various social and cultural fashions. In 1900 an American novel, just because it was American, was under a disadvantage, certainly abroad, and even to some extent, among the cultivated, at home. By 1940 an American novel, just because it was American, and probably being praised or referred to by periodicals now exported or reproduced in translation through the Western world, enjoyed tremendous advantages. This change is dramatically reflected in the award of Nobel Prizes. Up to 1930 no American writer had received an award. From 1930 onwards the Prizes have fallen like gentle golden rain upon the American literary scene. Nevertheless, all this could not have happened if the talent had not been there, if American fiction had not suddenly come to life in the early Twenties; and this sudden and astonishing development in literature, taking place in conditions quite different from those in Western Europe, to a large extent outside the general movement of European 'Modern Literature', creating influences rather than accepting them, deserves special consideration within the limited space left to us in this chapter.

We shall begin with Willa Cather, not only because she is the oldest of these novelists but also because she is beginning to be neglected. (A recent English study of American Literature, after two pages concerned with Sarah Orne Jewett, gives Willa Cather exactly half a line.) Because she wrote an indifferent war novel that became popular, *One of Ours*, and later retreated—and a retreat is exactly what it was—into historical fiction with a strongly Catholic background, the significance of the two novels she wrote before this retreat, *A Lost Lady* and *The Professor's House*, is being missed, often by the very criticism that looks for symbolism everywhere. For both these novels are essentially if not profoundly symbolic. Mrs. Forrester in *A Lost Lady* is the delicate beautiful lady, seen through the eyes of unsophisticated youth, the lady whose life becomes tawdry, cheap, vulgar; and she is also a certain way of life, a state of manners and society; and she is also the West itself, increasingly plundered and vulgarised. What happens inside that professor's house symbolises the kind of society the novelist herself is now regarding with despair, and Tom Outland's story within the story, his account of his discovery of the Cliff Dwellers' mesa and of his feeling of ecstasy there, symbolises, genuinely though again not profoundly, Willa Cather's own religious conversion. She lacks both size and intensity; she seems curiously ambiguous in her feelings, and always inclined towards rejection and retreat; though a conscientious craftsman, she does not always move her characters and control their scenes with the intuitive skill of a born novelist; but her actual writing at its best reaches a distinction and a certain sober charm not often found in modern American fiction; and the neglect of her, by the kind of criticism that can find significant depth in Hemingway's bullfighters and big game hunters, is somewhat surprising.

When Sinclair Lewis received the Nobel award in 1930, he ought to have shared it with H. L. Mencken. The latter, though no novelist, deserves a place here. His roaring success in the early Twenties, when he battered away at all the idols of the crowd, helped to clear the air. When Mencken is serious, he is nearly always bad; but as a kind of clown-critic, full of impudence and a rough sardonic wit and a vitality that keeps his earlier *Prejudices* still readable today, he was, and still is, good lively company. He was entirely destructive, caring at heart for nothing except a dream Germany born in Baltimore of string quartettes and beer. But destruction, especially of this noisy comic kind, breaking no heads or hearts with its bladders and custard pies, was what was needed. Chief of his clown-philosopher visions was one of America in the Twenties as an immense and almost free circus. (Mencken said President Harding cost him less than eighty cents a year: "Try to think of better sport for the money.") And it is really by way of Mencken's America-as-circus, and not by way of realism about the Middle West, that Sinclair Lewis appears. In the satirical-clown department, where social and literary criticism is represented by Mencken, Sinclair Lewis is in charge of the novel. Or it might be more accurate to say that the novel is in charge of him, compelling him to abandon realism for comic-cum-romantic fantasy. (We mean what we say here. Certainly for his earlier novels, Lewis, a good reporter, set to work like another Zola, filling notebooks with facts and observed details, and then shutting himself up with them, to write his novel. And it is when the method broke down, when the novel began writing itself, that he really created something.) He could not be a serious satirist because he did not possess any central fixed set of values and standards; he looks to Europe when he is in America, to America when he is in Europe, to Eastern America when he is in the West, to the West when he is in the East; as a man, and so as a writer, he was uncertain of the world and of himself, bewildered, confused, homeless and restless. (This is why, in *Work of Art*, he can take hotels so seriously.) He could not identify himself with any kind of life, was always the clever visiting journalist or the tourist. But only in his relation to the actual scene. His best work is raised high above journalism; sheer drive, applied to the mass of recorded detail, and a rare exuberance, bringing the unconscious into action, turn him into a genuine creator, not a conscious deliberate artist but a myth-maker. So his masterpiece, high above *Main Street*, is *Babbitt*, which is at once something less and something more than a novel, just as *Moby Dick* and *Huckleberry Finn* are. This is a truly American creative imagination at work, uncontrolled and outrageous by European standards, just as America itself seems uncontrolled and outrageous; rushing, in *Babbitt*, from heights of satirical buffoonery, often clowning for its own sake, to quick shuddering glimpses of depths where terror and despair are lurking. The real Sinclair Lewis, the enduring writer, should not be looked for in *Martin Arrowsmith*, *Dodsworth*, *Ann Vickers*, but, apart from *Babbitt*, in *Elmer Gantry*, *The Man who Knew Coolidge*, and some parts of *It Can't Happen Here*. He faded away, looking in his last years strangely empty, melancholy, spectral, because there was in him no creative and critical centre that could take over, once the necessary drive, energy, exuberance, were waning. But while they lasted, he was, as he remains, one of those creators who do not make works of art for the cultivated minority, but myths for the multitude. Even if criticism, quite mistakenly, should argue him out of literature, he will remain a figure in American history.

When we consider all these gifted American writers of fiction, shooting up like rockets in the Twenties, out of the dusk covering what was to modern literature almost an unknown country, we cannot help feeling that while their professional opportunities, bringing success, money and prestige, soon surpassed those enjoyed by European writers, their personal situations, the opportunities of the inner world, were inferior, making their lives very difficult. Thus, the afternoon of life, as Jung has so often pointed out, if it is to be lived properly and not in despair, demands a transition from the natural phase, belonging to the morning or first half of life, to the cultural phase, to a wide concern for what is not outwardly and immediately personal to a man, for the culture that binds together his whole community. And this transition is difficult enough for a European, now that religion, which once contained culture, no longer offers indirectly "schools for forty-year-olds"; and for an American it is far more difficult still: he is ageing in a land of youth. There was a further difficulty for these writers of the Twenties—though it is probably an aspect of the wider problem—for it seemed impossible for them to live simply as writers, as artists and intellectuals, to accept the literary life that had brought them money and fame. They would go to France, where the literary life is so warmly accepted that it almost seems too close and fusty, but the idea of settling down at home as professional men of letters, which is what they were, either never occurred to them or frightened them. So Sinclair Lewis behaved more like a Hollywood foreign correspondent than an important novelist. Ring Lardner, it is true, had a sports writer's background and was a sick man, but when he was writing some of the best American short stories of this age he was still wasting time and energy on Broadway producers; yet what he really thought of some of them, and of Broadway, may be found in his *Day with Conrad Green*. Sherwood Anderson left his family and business and got to Chicago, where there were writers, went as far as Paris, where there was Gertrude Stein, but returned home to become a newspaperman. When he was desperate, Scott Fitzgerald shut himself up outside Baltimore to do some writing, but only after years of extravagant clowning between Paris and the Riviera, as if he owned factories, oil wells and a bad conscience, and not simply an exquisite talent. William Faulkner stayed at home and worked hard enough, but somehow well outside the literary life, as if he were an eccentric Southern gentleman, a thousand miles from the nearest semi-colon. Last but not least, Ernest Hemingway, who owed everything to literature and not a little to the heavily-charged literary atmosphere of Paris, made haste as soon as his success was assured to contrive a big-game-hunter *persona*, a fellow who might write something when a decent day's sport was not to be had. These writers had great gifts; the Twenties, in American fiction, shine and glitter with their varied talents. But they made it hard for themselves afterwards, when the transition from morning to afternoon had to be made, and a writer, beginning to look down the long slope, would be none the worse if he were securely inside and not outside the life of authorship, sharing a few responsibilities, trials and triumphs with some fellow-writers. It was a way of life, not Death, that was needed in this afternoon.

Both Ring Lardner and Sherwood Anderson, in their very different ways, strongly influenced American writing in the years following the First War. Lardner seems to have been a strangely divided man, a good friend, helpful and humorously tolerant, but carrying within him some coldly destructive element, which sets to work at once in his more ambitious short stories. (The stories were ambitious; he was not, and never even troubled to collect them.) They are often very funny—after all, Lardner was a very successful popular humorist—but as a report on a society they are terrifying, revealing a wilderness of banality, shoddiness, cheapness of mind and spirit, that is like a glimpse of hell. He had an astonishingly exact ear for flat half-witted dialogue—compare the speech in his tales with Sinclair Lewis's warm and grotesque inventions—and he opened the way for later sardonic realists. Sherwood Anderson opened a way too, though in a very different fashion: he is often as soft as Lardner is hard. When Anderson, at forty, broke away, he left behind him a paint-manufacturing business; and it is as if from then on he was determined to celebrate whatever had a natural naked surface, unpainted. He was a confused man, nearly always in a state of mind better expressed in poetry than in prose fiction. He seemed to have been haunted by a rather Whit-manesque dream filled with lovers and friends and jolly craftsmen and farmers out of picture books, the kind of streets we all remember from childhood, and no heavy industry, loans and mortgages, salesmen and advertising, or purse-proud sour puritanism. He wanted everybody to break away, then be happy ever afterwards. He is not really a novelist, though capable of sketching a character, a situation, in pleasant prose, but a kind of folk-poet who has tried a lot of jobs and has looked at Freud. But he was both exciting and liberating in his day, and took not only himself but some of American fiction out of the paint factory.

The four representative novelists of the younger generation are Scott Fitzgerald, Ernest Hemingway, William Faulkner, and Thomas Wolfe. If there were more space, then some of it would have to be given to Dos Passos, a genuine innovator with an appreciation of social forces but rather thin and dull on the purely creative side; to John Steinbeck, chiefly for his *Grapes of Wrath*; to the patient, intelligent and soberly naturalistic J. G. Cozzens, though his two best novels, *The Just and the Unjust* and *Guard of Honour*, fall outside our time-limit; and to John P. Marquand, not so much for his oblique social satire as for his elaborately contrapuntal past-with-the-present method of narration. Of the four we have chosen, Scott Fitzgerald had the strangest career: a brilliant success in his youth, he lost everything, so that when he died in 1940 all his books were out of print and he had almost been forgotten; and then when he was in his grave every dream he had had came true. Far gone in drink, he was capable of saying and doing many foolish things, but when, towards the bitter end, he would declare that he used to have "a beautiful talent" he spoke the exact truth. He had indeed a natural and beautiful talent, and if he had had anything like the character to match it, he would have been a great novelist. But he was a shockingly divided man, and the continual strain created by this division probably accounts for his compulsive drinking. One half of him, cherishing, guarding, using the talent, was mature, conscientious, and had great integrity. The other half, from which the talent had to be protected, was wildly immature, negative, crammed with adolescent nonsense and silly values, still harbouring resentments, suspicions, feelings of inferiority, that belonged to school and college days. In *The Great Gatsby*, his one novel in which everything went right, a wonderful creative effort brings both halves together, making use even of negative and inferior elements, projecting the Fitzgerald inner world on to the Gatsby outer world, with satisfying symbolic depth. *Tender is the*

Night, on which he laboured for years, is far less satisfactory as a whole, not only because in both versions the construction is unsound but also because Dick Diver and his story refuse to carry the load; but it contains some magnificent scenes and passages, some flashes of insight into the richly decaying society it represents: it is indeed more fascinating than many novels far less open to hostile criticism. As for *The Last Tycoon*, in spite of yet another mistake in construction (Cecilia Brady as the narrator), and certain doubts we may have about Stahr himself, so quick and sensitive, as a motion-picture mogul, it remains the best attempt yet to put Hollywood into a serious novel (Nathanael West's wild but powerful *Day of the Locust* takes Los Angeles itself, not the film industry, as its theme); and it offers us a few scenes that seem to belong to a possible masterpiece. Fitzgerald unites a cool, smoothly realistic method of narration with a certain symbolic depth, making us feel that what is happening and will happen to Stahr, in his dream factory, will relate itself to a whole society. It is ironical that this novelist, so long associated in the American public mind with jazz, sex, wild parties, is always fundamentally concerned in his serious work with society itself. Young American novelists, wanting to find a way between plodding realism, fiction like a long day in a dull town, and sheer phantasmagorical symbolism, novels like screaming nightmares, should look closely at this last unfinished work of Fitzgerald's. But they will be very lucky indeed if they can recapture his apparently careless grace of writing, and his true and delicate feeling for a character, a situation, a unique moment in a certain social atmosphere. For this man, so bewildered, divided, self-tormented, really had "a beautiful talent".

The arts can inspire one another, but it is wiser to leave it at that, and not to assume that a successful revolution in one art can lead directly to a similar revolution in another art. This was the assumption that misled Gertrude Stein, the patron and friend of so many brilliant *avant-garde* painters in Paris. A solid personality, no posturing charlatan, though possibly not above a poker-faced prank or two, she was living in a time, place, atmosphere, where anything might happen, so why not a successful revolution in the use of language? But it was a mistake. (And, if we may risk a paraphrase, a mistake is a mistake is a mistake.) She influenced other

434

writers, however, especially an ambitious young American newspaperman in Paris, Ernest Hemingway, who with her blessing finally created a Style. It has been the most richly rewarded style in modern literature. Its virtues are many and remarkable: it makes sense at once to the most casual reader, who enjoys it without knowing that a style is there; the cultivated reader can appreciate its true rhythms, its deliberate economy, its hard masculine accuracy of statement, its immense power of suggestion and evocation, all the more effective because its suggestion of laconic reporting tricks the reader, so to speak, into using his imagination. Most of us nowadays are suspicious readers, anxious not to waste sympathy and emotion, but if a narrator, describing happiness or terror and horror, is colder and curter than we think he ought to be, then we release sympathy and emotion. Though its rhythms and deliberately limited vocabulary are based on American speech (with at least a few helpful hints from *Huckleberry Finn*), this style of Hemingway's, arriving at its perfection in *A Farewell to Arms*, does not come out of action and the reporting of action, as a simple reader might imagine, but out of the art of literature and Hemingway's intense single-minded devotion to it over many years. This long-sustained effort, for which he deserves the highest praise, not only made him as a writer, but probably saved him as a man from the results of some trauma, some open war wound in his inner life. But sometimes, reading his earlier work, aware of the tension, we feel as if the style were like some magical coat of mail, not keeping its wearer active in the battle but preserving him from threatened collapse.

By a great effort, then, he became master of the magic style, soon to be imitated and cheapened far and wide. But, unlike Yeats in a similar situation, he could not draw on fresh life-giving resources of the spirit, nourishment from responsibility itself, from broadening experience; he was incapable of any great further effort. So the style, in the old sinister magical fashion, mastered him. It took him away from a whole continent of life, his own people, his own maturity as a novelist, and sent him to Spain, to Africa, anywhere, in search of more violence, more death. There was no farewell to arms, no separate peace. Where before he had discovered the effects to express the situation, a situation perhaps demanded by some bitter wound in the soul, now themes were chosen just because they enabled him to use the effects again. True, many of the short stories he wrote during these years have been highly praised, and of course they are written with great skill; but not only do they fail to show any signs of a major novelist arriving at his maturity, they suggest that something false, false to life and to art, is creeping in, a touch of cynical swagger, a hint of bogus profundity, as if he is now unconsciously beginning to parody himself. He is genuinely attracted to Spain, a land of hard obstinate men and haunted by death; the test of lonely courage fascinates him; but while he himself is being brave all over the place, he is refusing the one courageous act demanded of him by his life in art—and he created himself out of literature as an art—and that is, to settle down in or near any American city, take it in all over again, sink down some shafts, if necessary find a new manner and forge a new style, and then write the great American novels of his maturity.

William Faulkner has nothing in common with Hemingway except great prestige, the Nobel Prize, and a love for violent situations. Apart from his war service and a spell or two in Hollywood, he has remained in his own native region, and has written about nothing else. Henri Bernstein, the French playwright, once said that Hollywood was full of genius and all that it lacked was talent. This could be seriously and truthfully said of Faulkner. When his admirers tell us that he is a novelist of genius, the one authentic man of genius in contemporary American fiction, they are quite right. But they do not add that he lacks talent, which would also be true. He has genius because he is able, as few writers are, to force the barrier between consciousness and the unconscious, and so release into his work, as if it were a huge narrated dream, the contents of the unconscious. His novels are at once so powerful and so confused because in them his outer and inner worlds are so inextricably mingled. We are impressed but bewildered because we do not know whether we are being offered Mississippi or mythology. Talent, which the very greatest writers possess in addition to genius, would bring order into this confusion. Faulkner's style, which has the pell-mell richness of genius, pouring out in an unchecked flood of language, would gain enormously if there had been talent to work on it, civilising it. When a writer is overmastered and swept along by unconscious elements, he achieves power and intensity, as

Faulkner does, but without great conscious discipline his work will be unequal, tasteless, without proportion, any steady vision, as Faulkner's is. So a novel of his, say, *Light in August*, can begin wonderfully, so that we feel we are reading a masterpiece, and yet later involve us in all manner of turgid and dubious stuff, like a dream half-remembered but grandiloquently related. Within the limits of fifty pages he can be one of the best and one of the worst novelists in the world. And again, with this unchecked rush of unconscious elements, some foul matter is swept into the novels. *Sanctuary*, we know, is not one of his major works—yet even if it were intended to attract the crowd, why decide on this particular form of attraction?—but it remains one of the ugliest stories in an age crowded with them, not because of its obvious violence and sexuality but because there is a sort of hateful relish behind the ruthless degradation of Temple Drake, as if this modern version of Persephone in the underworld had to be deliberately perverted and soiled.

The huge heaving mass of regional life, in almost every possible aspect, discovered in these Faulkner novels, as if one writhing coil after another of a serpent-like saga were being revealed, undoubtedly strengthens his claim to creative genius. The force and fertility are there. But some doubts remain. For this is a very strange region, certainly to those of us born a long way from it, and so far as it belongs to the outer world, so far as it can be disentangled from Faulkner's inner world, it is not one that throws any light on our own experience. (Unless we are prepared to believe that this peculiarly degenerate society, whose members seem to move almost in a trance from one act of violence to another, is itself a symbol of our world society.) But Faulkner himself seems concerned only with this Deep South of his, which has its own myth, the American dream in reverse, of departed glory, defeat and decay, mysterious curses claiming their victims, men and women implacably doomed to suffer lawless passions, incest, rape and murder; all in an atmosphere, in spite of Faulkner's multitudinous and brilliant detail, oddly reminiscent of Poe's tales. (Though these were written, let us remember, when the South was supposed to be enjoying that golden age which haunts it yet. What it really had, and may still have, if its authors may be realistically interpreted, is a bad combination of sultry weather and thinning blood, hard

437

liquor, the contamination of slavery, a confused sex life, too much eloquence and too little thought, and a romanticism not only over-ripe but going rotten.) It can hardly be a coincidence that the immense prestige of Faulkner has been built up during years when so many of the most influential critics are themselves of Southern origin. This does not mean that they are deliberately over-valuing his genius; but it may mean that, accepting or at least understanding the same myth, they find meaning, significance, emotional depth, in much of Faulkner that seems to the rest of us merely violent, confused, eccentric, embittered, cruel, so many blanks or stains on the pages of a writer who, in other places, can be a richly creative and compassionate artist.

The last of these four—and the youngest: he was born in 1900 and died in 1938—is Thomas Wolfe. He was a gigantic young man, who wrote—and indeed did everything—gigantically, and his weaknesses, faults, deficiencies, are to scale. He is all too easy to criticise adversely, and this probably explains why he has had rather more than his share of such criticism. He never learnt how to construct a novel, nor indeed even how to keep a narrative going, for he runs to vast length not so much because he goes on and on and on as because he tends to hold a scene and go in and in and in. He is monstrously rhetorical and oratorical, as if a dozen old-fashioned Southern politicians and a dozen jugs of corn whisky were at work in him. Like a bewildered but raging adolescent, trying to grasp the whole world, he seizes hold of everything and bangs about, crying in effect—like the old *Punch* parody of Marie Corelli—"I'm sure there is a Something Somewhere if we could only find it." There was so much thinly-disguised autobiography in his vast chronicles, and he was himself so demanding, over-sized and demonic, that he seemed for ever in trouble, living in a permanent storm centre. He was never at home anywhere, always discovering something alien and sinister in the environment, whether it was Asheville or Harvard, London or New York, Paris or Brooklyn, always hurrying away from some evil he could not define towards some ultimate good he could never reach. As if he belonged to some giant race that lived two hundred years and did not come of age until sixty-five, he remained to the end hopefully, despairingly, furiously young. Yet not without acquiring a little wisdom on the way, rather more perhaps than his fellow novelists, as we may discover from his last letter to 'Fox' in *You Can't Go Home Again*; this in its denial of pessimistic and fatalistic conservatism says something infinitely worth saying, once and for all: "Man was born to live, to suffer, and to die, and what befalls him is a tragic lot. There is no denying this in the final end. *But we must, dear Fox, deny it all along the way.*"

The truth is that, once his limitations are accepted, Wolfe is one of the most satisfying and rewarding of all these American novelists. It is not only that his scene is big, as indeed it is, but that he explores the scene with a wonderful eye and ear, with astonishing thoroughness, often taking us to a great depth. Because he invented so little, shaped and cut so little, drove himself so hard while he was writing, he was able to give life, down to the last flicker or whisper, to an amazing range of scenes. We may always feel his own presence in them, always be aware of a romantic-fantastic element in their presentation, but this is more than compensated for by the sheer vitality, the abundance and richness of life, the poetic truth he attains. He may seem wilder, more grotesque, when he is among the literary and theatrical groups on the 'Enfabled Rock' of New York than when he is among his own mountain folk; but behind his shout of defiance and derision, his huge slashing caricatures of New York personalities, there is still a kind of poetic truth that compels us to remember his New York when we have long forgotten other men's. He is always surprising us, for he might seem to be the last man to go lumbering among the delicate expatriates, following Fitzgerald, yet is there anybody and anything in Fitzgerald as solidly created, as subtly observed, as Starwick and the scenes that contain him in *Of Time and the River*? And he has episode after episode, like that week-end in the mansion above the Hudson, that carry their vitality so deep into the memory that they seem like our own experiences. American intellectuals, suspicious of his exuberance and underlying romanticism, should never sneer at this writer, for, to us who are not Americans but know the place and the people, Wolfe is one of the small and invaluable company of essentially American creators, one of its huge, wild, shaggy poets whose creations, which have nothing of Europe in them, release in us the wonder, fear and affection we have felt so often as visitors to the American scene. And Wolfe's

439

faults can be forgiven him, if only because they are mostly the result of a frenzied feeling of time hurrying by. A man's unconscious often knows the secrets of his body, is at least dimly aware of its span of life; and if Wolfe wrote too much too fast, cried to us too often out of bewilderment, confusion, despair, perhaps he too, with unconscious awareness arriving as premonition, recognised that he had to do so much in so little time: he died at the age of thirty-eight. He at least did not refuse the chance to mature; he never really had the chance; he remains one of the few major *young* writers of this age, a giant of the morning; and everything about him, faulty and over-youthful, candid and vital and endearing, belongs essentially to an America that is itself still a giant of the morning. And indeed any America that shrugs him away, forgetting what he did and tried to do, will be smaller, older, closer to death, even though it may never have lived—as its major novelists, accepting their maturity, might have taught it to live—in the glowing serenity of the afternoon.

So Tom Wolfe, whom we remember so towering and awkward, so eager and alive, and who vanished so soon, is the last writer in this long procession. He is not a bad final choice. He nearly tore himself to pieces trying, as a good writer must, to get everything down on paper, all the sights and the sounds and the smells and the moods and the people, hundreds of them, in the land that now has most power, most wealth, most influence. And there was his wise last word: *But we must, dear Fox, deny it all along the way.* No matter how piercing and appalling his insights, the desolation creeping over his outer world, the lurid lights and shadows of his inner world, the writer must live with hope, work in faith. What literature, which is still concerned with Man himself, with persons and not with statistical units, must deny, if necessary against all evidence and reason, is the ultimate despair, the central place of darkness from which the last gleam of nobility and wisdom has gone.

Conclusion

REVERTING with heartfelt relief to the first person singular of the Introduction, I will suggest what we may have discovered along the way, and how it applies to us and our society here and now. After the loosening and decay of the medieval religious foundation and framework, Western Man broke out, shook himself free; he began his printing and started to explore the great globe of earth; and like a boy racing out of school he was filled with new energy and delight. His outer and inner worlds were not yet at variance; the religious symbols had not yet lost their force. The greatest writers of this age, men who have much more in common with one another than might first appear, are nicely balanced between their conscious and unconscious life. They are aware of the mystery of our existence without being fanatically devoted to any particular interpretation of it. They seem to us to this day to have a wonderful life-enhancing, vitalising quality all their own. (The enormous popularity of Shakespeare almost everywhere, since the Second World War, is probably a tribute to this quality, now more necessary to us than ever.) These writers seem neither over-extroverted nor obviously introverted. Their age is neither committed to one conscious attitude nor at the mercy of its unconscious drives and urges; it is not neo-classical, it is not romantic, at least not as the later age will be, and its love of fantastic inventiveness and richness comes out of its feeling of freedom and its exuberance. Its literature is both a public literature and a private literature, and perfectly expresses this. But the age is not being interpreted as a society, which is still seen and taken for granted as a natural social hierarchy; it is men and women as individuals, representing the age, to whom this literature turns, finally creating characters—Gargantua and Panurge, Hamlet and Falstaff,

441

Don Quixote and Sancho Panza, and the rest—of such a size, density and enduring vitality that they seem to belong to the mythology of Western Man.

Then, in the next age, the scientists and philosophers apparently penetrated the mystery and, twitching aside the last veil, revealed the vast but smoothly-running machinery of the universe, of which Man, so long as he knew and obeyed the rules, was master. Everything important was outward, and society on its higher levels, living outwardly, also lived magnificently, with a style we still envy. For a man who had position, or some wealth, or talent *and* luck (for many men of exceptional talent led desperate lives at this time), it was a delightful age. Literature, still important to this society as an expression of itself for itself, was entirely public, essentially a social activity, the product of a heightened proud consciousness, so that this is the age of comedy and satire and the beginning of highly objective realistic narrative. But it was not possible to maintain this one-sided attitude very long; the unconscious inevitably asserted itself. It did this at first mostly in an inferior way: novels and plays were filled with a tearful sentimentality; Gothic ruins, then Gothic romance, became fashionable; secret societies, devoted to the occult, were found everywhere in Europe; and in Germany the new romanticism produced the *Sturm und Drang* writers. The true Romantic Movement followed, and in England and Germany, then later in Russia and France, gave us some wonderful poetry. But this romantic literature never quite belonged to the centre of society, as earlier literature had done; and it is significant that the three dominating literary figures of this age, Goethe, Byron and Walter Scott, were not fully committed to romanticism.

In the age that followed, which I have called 'The Broken Web', literature moves still further away from the centre. There can now be discovered—and it is writers of genius who first call attention to it—that curious *malaise* of modern Western Man. Too many things are going wrong at the same time. Any last pretence of society having a religious foundation and framework, being contained at all by religion, has vanished. Industry creates a new urban 'mass' people, outside the old social structure. Patterns of living that had existed for thousands of years are destroyed within a generation. Deep dissatisfactions, really belonging to Man's inner world, are projected on to the outer world, except by a few profoundly intuitive men of genius, who now begin to prophesy disaster. Other writers, seeing quite truthfully that social conditions are bad, urgently demand reforms or an entirely different kind of political and economic society; and there now comes into existence the belief, which most of the world still holds today, that a full, satisfying, happy life is possible, is waiting for us just round the corner, if we only produce more and more, make some changes in the control and distribution of things, and so forth. Meanwhile, the inner world is largely ignored, the unconscious drives and fantasies remain unchecked. Some literature tries to be completely extrovert, taking in more and more of the outward world. Other literature seeks the inner world, tries to explore it. Some men of genius show themselves to be deeply divided. Compared with earlier ages, this age, lasting roughly from 1835 to 1895, though remarkably rich in great talent, especially in the novel, seems strangely confused, committed as an age to no particular attitude. But somewhere in it can be found almost all the ideas that have shaped men's lives during this present century. The catastrophic outer world of our age is the confused and angry inner world of the nineteenth century dramatised on the largest scale.

The modern age shows us how helpless the individual is when he is at the mercy of his unconscious drives and, at the same time, is beginning to lose individuality because he is in the power of huge political and social collectives. It is an age of deepening inner despair and of appalling catastrophes, an age when society says one thing and then does something entirely different, when everybody talks about peace and prepares for more and worse wars. Western Man is now schizophrenic. Literature, which is further removed from the centre than ever before, does what it can. The writer of genius cannot help responding to the innermost needs of his age; he sees and reports what in its depths it asks him to see and report. He cannot help becoming, through his own relation to his unconscious (and without this relation no creative work of value is possible), an instrument of whatever there is in the general deep unconscious, the inner world of the whole age, that is trying to compensate for some failure in consciousness, to restore a balance destroyed by one-sidedness, to reconcile the glaring opposites, to bring to our outer and inner worlds a life-enhancing unity. But literature itself now becomes one-sided, inevitably because it is over-introverted, often so deeply concerned with the inner world, with the most mysterious recesses of the personality, and so little concerned with the outer world, that it cannot really fulfil the task it set itself. It now becomes a literature largely for specialists, themselves nearly always equally introverted; and people in general, for whom it is really intended, find it either too 'difficult' or too 'neurotic' and 'unhealthy'. (It is a mistake, all too common, to imagine that the new depth psychology created this literature. They are in fact parallel developments, and on the whole we can say that depth psychology owes more to modern literature than that literature does to depth psychology.) And in a sense these people who do not want modern literature, because they feel it is too entirely attentive to the inner world, that it lacks a life-enhancing quality, are quite right. The men who have created this literature have obeyed their daemon, have fulfilled their genius, and we should be grateful to them. But we should also realise that this modern literature means little or nothing to the mass of people, the very people in danger of losing true individuality, personality, to the collectives of our time; and that even for the minority of persons capable of understanding and enjoying this literature, it cannot carry the load. Nothing we have can carry it. Since the Second War, in this atomic age, sure of nothing but sex—and, to take two successful English examples, what is there left at the end of *Lucky Jim* or *Look Back in Anger* but sex?—we are now piling on to sex the whole gigantic load of our increasing dissatisfactions, our despair, a burden far greater than it can safely take.

Religion alone can carry the load, defend us against the de-humanising collectives, restore true personality. And it is doubtful if our society can last much longer without religion, for either it will destroy itself by some final idiot war or, at peace but hurrying in the wrong direction, it will soon largely cease to be composed of persons. All this, of course, has often been said, but generally it has been said by men who imagine that the particular religion they profess, their Church greatly magnified, could save the situation. I think they are wrong, though I would not for a moment attempt to argue them out of their private faith. If such a faith,

444

a Church, a religion, works for them, well and good. But I have no religion, most of my friends have no religion, very few of the major modern writers we have been considering have had any religion; and what is certain is that our society has none. No matter what it professes, it is now not merely irreligious but powerfully anti-religious. And if we all joined a Christian Church tomorrow, the fundamental situation would be unchanged, because no Church existing today has the power—and we could not give it this power by joining it—to undo what has been done. We should be acting on a conscious and not an unconscious level, and the forces from the unknown depths that religion, if its symbols have the right magical potency, can guide and control would still be without guidance and beyond control. For the symbols no longer work, and they cannot be made to work by effort on a conscious level. (The stammering helplessness of the Churches during this age of war and more war and now, the final horror, a nuclear arms race is proof that, whatever they may do for this man or that woman, they are now among the institutions contained by our society, compelled to follow every lunatic course it takes.) No matter what is willed by consciousness, that which belongs to the depths can only be restored in the depths: the *numinous* lies outside the power of the collectives, cannot be subject to state decree, created by a final resolution at an international conference, offered to all shareholders and employees by the board of Standard Oil or General Motors. So we have no religion and, inside or outside literature, man feels homeless, helpless, and in despair.

We must wait. Even if we believe that the time of our civilisation is running out fast, like sugar spilled from a torn bag, we must wait. But while we are waiting we can try to feel and think and behave, to some extent, *as if* our society were already beginning to be contained by religion, as if we were certain that Man cannot even remain Man unless he looks beyond himself, as if we were finding our way home again in the universe. We can stop disinheriting ourselves. We can avoid both the *hubris* and the secret desperation of our scientific "wizards that peep and mutter". We can challenge the whole de-humanising, de-personalising process, under whatever name it may operate, that is taking the symbolic richness, the dimension in depth, out of men's lives, gradually

445

inducing the anæsthesia that demands violence, crudely horrible effects, to feel anything at all. Instead of wanting to look at the back of the moon, remote from our lives, we can try to look at the back of our own minds. Even this *As If* will do something to bring our outer and inner worlds, now tearing us in two, closer together, more in harmony. We may need much more to establish order, justice, real community, in the outer world, and may not ourselves find the right healing symbols for the inner world, but, just as a first step, we can at least believe that Man lives, under God, in a great mystery, which is what we found the original masters of our literature, Shakespeare and Rabelais, Cervantes and Montaigne, proclaiming at the very start of this journey of Western Man. And if we openly declare what is wrong with us, what is our deepest need, then perhaps the despair and death will by degrees disappear from our modern arts. Literature, where the whole man should find himself totally and touchingly reflected, might then look both outward and inward, as it should; and so bring with it a rich new life, a life sometimes tragic, at other times careless and gay: as different and as satisfying as Shakespeare's midnight heaths, where good and evil battle in thunder-and-lightning, and his Forest of Arden, where, the West meeting the Ancient East for a moment, the young voices pipe up in an eternal spring:

> *This carol they began that hour,*
> *With a hey, and a ho, and a hey nonino,*
> *How that life was but a flower . . .*

THE END

Brief Biographies

As MY TEXT contains very few biographical details, it seemed to me that it could do no harm, and might help some readers, if these brief biographies appeared as an Appendix. I have deliberately excluded, for various good reasons, all living authors. Anybody sufficiently knowledgeable to point out the various omissions here—and I am aware of several, though most of them could be defended—is too knowledgeable to be reading this Appendix at all, and is guilty of trespassing.

J.B.P.

ADAMS, HENRY BROOKS: American historian and autobiographer, born at Boston in 1838, died in Washington in 1918. He studied at Harvard, where he later taught history. After continuing his education in Germany, he became secretary to his father at the American Embassy in London. He edited the *North American Review*. His most famous works appeared in the latter part of his life and were the result of many years of thought: *Mont-Saint-Michel and Chartres: a Study in Thirteenth-Century Unity* (1904) and *The Education of Henry Adams: a Study of Twentieth-Century Multiplicity* (1907). Although his ideas were not always clear, and his exposition of them can be confused and rather turgid, he often shows remarkable insight into the weaknesses of modern society.

ANDERSEN, HANS CHRISTIAN: Danish fairy-tale writer, born at Odense in 1805, died in Copenhagen 1875. His early life was a struggle against the poverty of a simple cobbler's home. At fourteen he went to Copenhagen but failed to make a career in the royal theatre though a benefactor enabled him to attend the grammar school at Slagelse from 1822–28. He met many distinguished people on his wide travels in Europe; and it was after a long stay in

Italy that he published in 1835 his first successful novel *Improvisatoren* and the first four fairy-tales. Apart from his famous stories and fairy-tales—he wrote 168 in all—his writings include novels, plays, travel books, autobiography, and poetry. His world-wide popularity as a writer of children's stories is probably not as great as it was, but his best stories, which owe something to the folktales he heard as a boy, are little masterpieces of their kind.

ARIOSTO, LUDOVICO: Italian poet, born at Reggio Emilia in 1474, died at Mirasole 1533. He entered the service of the Estes at Ferrara and became secretary to Cardinal Ippolito, visiting Isabelle d'Este at Mantua in 1507 and being exiled with his patrons in 1512. In 1517 he became director of theatrical entertainments at the Court of Alfonso I and was made Governor of the Garfagnana in 1522. He retired to the country in 1527 and spent his last years revising his famous epic *Orlando Furioso* (which first appeared in 1516) and other works including comedies, love poetry and satires. In Ariosto, the old legends of chivalry, with which he is ostensibly dealing, have arrived in an age very different from the one that first conceived them, so that, although he re-tells them with great skill, his narrative glitters with irony and mockery. Early in the sixteenth century he struck a note that is repeated and echoed through much of the literature that followed.

BALZAC, HONORÉ DE: French novelist, born at Tours in 1799, died in Paris 1850. Educated at Vendôme and intended for the law, he worked in a legal office from 1816–19. An unfortunate venture as printer-publisher ended in bankruptcy two years later. He began writing adventure stories anonymously, then in 1833, after the publication of *Le Médecin de Campagne*, he had the idea for the *Comédie Humaine*. The greater part of the novels and other studies that went to make up this tremendous panorama of French life were written between this time and 1845. Nevertheless, in 1848 and 1849 he failed to achieve election to the French Academy. Later, when Stendhal and Flaubert came to be regarded as the representative French novelists, Balzac was consistently depreciated and under-valued. But though his work, often written in such a hurry, is unequal and he has obvious faults of manner and style, Balzac by reason of his sheer creative force and his large grasp on life cannot be denied his original reputation as a great novelist, a genuine master, though fundamentally a Romantic and not a realist, as he was once thought to be.

BAUDELAIRE, CHARLES PIERRE: French poet and critic, born in Paris in 1821, died there 1867. When he was six his father died and his relations with his step-father were unhappy. In 1841 he went on a ten months' voyage to the east. Despite a small inheritance he was constantly in financial difficulties. The publication of his famous poems *Les Fleurs du mal* in 1857 was followed by his prosecution for immoral writings. The next seven years were devoted to artistic and literary criticism and to translating Poe. In 1864 he went to Belgium but became a victim of aphasia and returned to Paris an invalid two years later. Himself a poet of great originality, power and depth, as an influence it is almost impossible to over-estimate him. He is one of the key figures of the whole modern movement in literature.

BEAUMARCHAIS, PIERRE-AUGUSTIN CARON DE: French playwright, born in Paris 1732, died there in 1799. Although trained in his father's trade as a watchmaker, he devoted most of his life to intrigue and financial speculation. He visited Spain in 1764 and travelled in England, Germany and Austria as a political agent in 1774. He was imprisoned in 1773 and gained a reputation for attacking corruption. In 1776 he supplied arms to American colonists and founded an authors' society in 1780. He became a revolutionary agent, emigrated in 1792 but returned in 1796. Of his five plays and one opera, the most famous are *Le Barbier de Seville* (1775) and *Le Mariage de Figaro*, both being made into operas later. A strange ambiguous figure, Beaumarchais is immensely lively and inventive in his comedy, and its aggressively satirical attitude towards aristocratic privilege had some influence on revolutionary feeling.

BLAKE, WILLIAM: Born, the son of a hosier, in London in 1757, died there in 1827. He was trained in art at St. Paul's with an engraver, and at the Royal Academy, but soon broke away from the convention of the time. He made many illustrations for his own poems and those of past and present writers. Most of his poetry was written during the last twenty years of the eighteenth century, *Songs of Innocence* appearing in 1789 and *Songs of Experience* in 1794. Thought by some to be insane, he died in poverty. He is now regarded as one of England's major poets, and one who, in spite of his difficult private mythology, repays study, if only for the sake of his profound intuitive wisdom.

BLOK, ALEXANDER ALEXANDROVICH: Russian poet, born in St. Petersburg in 1880, died there in 1921. He became the leader of the Symbolists in Russia, but the 1905 revolution shattered his romantic idealism, and his poetry became aggressively realistic. He welcomed the 1917 revolution and wrote the famous poem *The Twelve*. Later he called on the West to join Russia in creating a new and brotherly humanity. But the suffering and cruelties of the civil war caused him to lose faith and gradually cease writing, his death coinciding with the disintegration of the Symbolist Movement. Although Soviet criticism of him has often been unfavourable, foreign critics of Russian literature acknowledge him to be Russia's greatest poet during the period 1900-20.

BURNS, ROBERT: Scottish poet, born at Alloway in 1759, died at Dumfries in 1796. Although his family were small farmers, he had a good literary education and started writing poetry. As a farmer he did not prosper, but when his first volume, *Poems chiefly in the Scottish Dialect* was published in 1786, he at once became famous and was received in literary society. A second edition made it possible for him to marry and return to farming. He was given an appointment with the excise board in 1789. He wrote many songs for the *Scots Musical Museum* (1787–1803) and for George Thompson's *Select Collection of Original Scottish Airs* (1793–1805). Burns was capable of versifying in a conventional eighteenth-century style, but the best of his lyrics and narrative poems in the Scots dialect are magnificent, and here he is a great folk poet.

BYRON, GEORGE GORDON NOEL BYRON, 6th Baron: English poet, born in London 1788, died at Missolonghi, Greece, in 1824. He had a badly deformed foot from birth. Living with his widowed mother in Aberdeen, he went to grammar school there, but on succeeding unexpectedly to the family title he went to Harrow and later to Cambridge. After foreign travel with his friend Hobhouse, he published the first two Cantos of *Childe Harold's Pilgrimage* in 1812 and won instant fame. Having been for years the romantic hero of London society, and having published several more of his fashionable narrative poems, he married disastrously, was involved in scandals over this and over his supposed relationship with his half-sister, Augusta Leigh. He left England in 1816, never to return. He lived in Venice and other places in Italy, where he wrote some of his finest work. The great satire *Don Juan* was unfinished when he left in 1822 to support the struggle for the liberation of Greece. After two years among the rebel leaders he died of fever; when his body was returned to England burial in Westminster Abbey was refused on moral grounds. Byron was one of the great dominating figures of the whole Romantic Age, and had an immense European reputation and influence. Purely as a poet, and not generally as a figure, his reputation among English critics is less impressive; but his complex character and dramatic life have been the subjects of innumerable studies.

CALDERÓN DE LA BARCA, PEDRO: Spanish dramatist and poet. Born in Madrid in 1600 and died there in 1681. After studying at Alcalá and Salamanca he became a dramatist and most of his best-known plays were written between 1628 and 1640. He served as soldier in 1640–41 and then in 1651 became a priest and ceased to write for the popular Theatre. But he continued to produce the religious dramas called *autos* and special plays for the Court. During the eighteenth century he was hardly remembered outside Spain, but the Romantic Movement rediscovered him and now he is generally held to be Spain's greatest dramatist.

CARLYLE, THOMAS: Scottish man of letters, born at Ecclefechan in 1795, died in Chelsea 1881. Educated at Edinburgh University, he taught mathematics at Kirkcaldy, then lived in Edinburgh between 1818 and 1822, studying German literature, writing and tutoring, his *Life of Schiller* appearing in 1825. From 1828–34 he lived in Dumfriesshire, then moving to London, where he remained until his death. In 1836 he published *Sartor Resartus*, first in Fraser's Magazine, where it had little success, then as a book in New York and later in London. His lectures *On Heroes and Hero-Worship* were published in 1841, and his numerous works include history, biography, literary criticism, politics and sociology. Both as a philosopher and a historian, Carlyle no longer enjoys his Victorian reputation. But he is a wonderful grotesque prose-poet, not without some prophetic insights.

CAXTON, WILLIAM: English printer and translator, born c. 1422 in Kent and died in 1491. He was apprenticed to a silk mercer, then went into business in Bruges on his own account and in 1453 was formally admitted to the livery of the Mercers' Company. He was governor of the 'English Nation' company until about 1469, when he entered the service of the Duchess Margaret of Burgundy. He learned the art of printing in Cologne in 1471–72, and on his return to Bruges set up a press and began by printing his own translations from the French, the first of which appeared in 1474. He then established himself in England and the first book to be printed in that country is dated 1477. From then until his death he was fully occupied with printing and writing, a large number of works being produced. He is perhaps best described, and appreciated, not so much as a printer or a translator as what we should now call a publisher: he is the first, and if not the best, by no means the worst, of English publishers.

CERVANTES SAAVEDRA, MIGUEL DE: Spanish novelist, dramatist, poet, born at Alcalá de Henares in 1547, died at Madrid in 1616. He was educated at Madrid, served as a soldier in Italy, and was wounded at Lepanto, and in 1575, on his way home, was captured by the Moors. After five years' captivity, he returned to Spain. He travelled widely in Spain, buying stores for the Armada, and got into trouble with both the ecclesiastical and civil authorities, knowing what it was to be imprisoned. His life, indeed, was hard. His pastoral novel, *La Galatea*, appeared in 1585, and it was followed by some plays and verse and the admirable *Exemplary Novels*, later to be both imitated and plundered by many writers outside Spain. The first part of *Don Quixote* appeared in 1605, and was so successful that false sequels to it compelled Cervantes to bring out his second part in 1615. Enjoying some distinguished patronage, he found his last years easier. *Don Quixote* is Cervantes's great masterpiece, and in many respects it is a work of fiction that has never been excelled, for it can be read and enjoyed with equal satisfaction on many different levels. It is at once romance and satire, realism and mythology, one of the most amusing, the most pathetic, the wisest, tales ever written. Cervantes and his Don Quixote and Sancho Panza are Spain's greatest gifts to the world of Western Man.

CHATEAUBRIAND, FRANÇOIS RENÉ, VICOMTE DE: Born in the ancestral Château de Combourg at St. Malo in 1768, died in Paris 1848. He served in the Régiment de Navarre, visited America in 1791 and lived as an emigré in London and Brussels, returning to France in 1800. After making his literary reputation with *Essai sur les Révolutions* (1797) he became converted to Catholicism and attained fame with his *Génie du Christianisme* in 1804, breaking in the same year with Napoleon. After several years spent mainly at his home or abroad, he was made a peer on the Restoration and became leader of the ultra-royalist opposition. Between 1821 and 1828 he was Ambassador in Berlin, London and Rome and Foreign Minister in 1823, retiring from public life in 1830; his *Mémoires d'Outre-Tombe* were published in *La Presse* in 1848–50. These rich reminiscences are now generally regarded as his masterpiece, his earlier work having lost much of its first highly romantic appeal. But the fact that it appeared a generation before the French Romantic Movement began made him an extremely influential figure.

CHEHOV, ANTON PAVLOVICH: Russian author, born at Taganrog in 1860, died at Badenweiler 1904. Of humble birth, he studied medicine in Moscow, where he wrote for humorous papers. Although qualifying as a doctor, the success of his first book (*Motley Stories*) in 1886 caused him gradually to adopt a literary career. His first play *Ivanov* (1887) reflects the melancholy and sense of futility that, in spite of his humour, was to pervade all his work after that date. As well as a great many stories he wrote four more famous plays, *The Seagull* (1896), *Uncle Vanya* (1900), *Three Sisters* (1901) and *The Cherry Orchard* (1904). A master of the type of short story now found throughout modern literature, Chehov is even greater in the drama, where he developed an entirely original and very flexible method, which allows him to be deeply subjective without losing the hold a dramatist must have on his audience. It is a method that has since been often imitated, but it seems to demand Chehov's pervasive charm, humour, unforced pathos.

COLERIDGE, SAMUEL TAYLOR: English poet, critic, philosopher and talker, born at Ottery St. Mary, Devon, in 1772 and died at Highgate, London, in 1834. Educated at Christ's Hospital and Cambridge, with a short and ludicrous term with the Light Dragoons, he settled at Nether Stowey, where he had his close friend William Wordsworth as a neighbour. Here he wrote his greatest poems, *The Ancient Mariner*, *Christabel* and *Kubla Khan*, and made his famous collaboration with Wordsworth in the *Lyrical Ballads*. Later he embarked on a restless career as journalist, lecturer, and at one time secretary to the Governor of Malta. His marriage was an unhappy one, and poor health led him to become addicted to drugs. In his poetry Coleridge is one of the great Romantics. In his criticism, never systematic and much of it collected from lectures and notes, he has extraordinary insight, and in his inspired flashes he is the finest critic of the whole Romantic Age. His influence in many different directions was very considerable.

COLETTE, SIDONIE-GABRIELLE: Born at Saint-Sauveur-en-Puysaye in 1873, died in Paris in 1954. Her childhood was spent in Burgundy, and inspired her first *Claudine* books (1900–03), which appeared as the work of her husband, 'Willy'. From 1906, when she obtained her divorce, she earned a living on the music-hall stage as a dancer and mime, while continuing to write. In 1913 she married Henri de Jouvenel. She then, as an established member of Paris society, achieved great success with a number of books, including the *Chéri* novels, becoming a member of the Académie Royale de Belgique in 1935 and of the Académie Goncourt ten years later. Her intensely feminine genius created a kind of fiction unlike any other, and delicious.

CONGREVE, WILLIAM: English dramatist, born at Bardsey, Yorkshire, in 1670 and died in London 1729. He was educated at Trinity College, Dublin, intended for the Law but began writing for the stage. He wrote a tragedy, *The Mourning Bride*, as well as the better-known comedies, of which the most successful was *Love For Love*, 1695. His masterpiece (1700), *The Way of the World*, was badly received, and he wrote very little afterwards. All his comedies were written while he was still in his twenties, and this may explain their frequently faulty, confused construction, but it does not explain Congreve's superb dramatic style, the finest in all English Restoration and eighteenth-century comedy.

CONRAD, JOSEPH (originally Teodor Jozef Konrad Korzeniowski): Born in Mohilow, Poland, in 1857, died at Bishopsbourne, Kent, in 1924. He realised an early ambition to go to sea, finally becoming a Master Mariner and British subject. He mastered the English language and began writing in it in 1889; his first novel, however, *Almayer's Folly*, did not appear until 1895. He became a novelist of great distinction, original in outlook, manner, style, especially in the work he did before 1914.

CORNEILLE, PIERRE: French dramatist, born at Rouen in 1606, died at Paris in 1684. He came of a well-to-do line of Norman lawyers, and after being schooled at Rouen by the Jesuits, he qualified for the Bar, and became a magistrate. He produced his first play in 1630 and the most famous comedies and tragedies were written during the next fifteen years, including the much-criticised *Le Cid*. He left the Theatre in 1652, owing to declining success, but returned in 1659 with experimental work including *pièces à machines*. The unsuccessful competition with Racine, relative poverty and the death of his son cast a shadow over his last years. Though his drama can be dull and rather mechanical in its action, it is filled with great moments and great lines; and Corneille is essentially a poet in the drama. If he has never been widely played outside France, he has been securely held in the affection and admiration of his fellow-countrymen.

CROCE, BENEDETTO: Italian philosopher, born at Pescasseroli in 1866, died in Naples in 1952. He was educated at Naples but after the tragic loss of his parents in an earthquake he spent three years in Rome, attending Labriola's philosophy lectures, and going back to Naples in 1886. In 1903 he founded and edited a bi-monthly review of literature, history and philosophy, *La Critica*. His main philosophical works, including the four volumes of *La Filosofia del Spirito* were produced during the next ten years. He was appointed a senator in 1910 and became Minister of Education in 1920–21. He was a confirmed liberal and retired from public life on Mussolini's rise to power, returning after the war to help in the formation of a new government. Although his actual theory of æsthetics has never been widely accepted, he greatly influenced criticism, and on the whole in a liberating fashion, during the Twenties.

DEFOE, DANIEL: English novelist, journalist and pamphleteer, born at Cripplegate about 1660, died at Moorgate in 1731. His parents were Dissenters and, unable to enter university or a learned profession, he endeavoured early in life to earn a living by writing, becoming a journalist and political pamphleteer and continuing in this occupation till he was nearly sixty. His main works of fiction were written in the latter part of his life, beginning with *Robinson Crusoe* (1719). As Defoe was pretending to write other people's memoirs and confessions, he was compelled to be entirely realistic in manner, thus helping to create realism in fiction. Apart from the world-famous *Robinson Crusoe*, his work is either greatly valued, by novelists and critics to whom he makes a special personal appeal, or is dismissed as being too limited in outlook, too coarse in grain, to be enjoyed today.

DIDEROT, DENIS: French philosophical writer, publicist and critic. Born at Langres in 1713, died at Paris in 1784. Despite his education by the Jesuits at both these places, he would not pursue a settled profession but preferred to spend ten impecunious years as a hack-writer and teacher. His friendship with J.-J. Rousseau and others improved his literary prospects. After publishing his *Lettre sur les aveugles* in 1749, followed by a brief imprisonment at Vincennes, he began the task of editing the *Encyclopédie*. This vast compendium of knowledge and progressive thought was banned in 1759, but he continued alone and completed the main edition in 1765. He visited St. Petersburg in 1773 under the patronage of Catherine II. Diderot's creative writing, if we except the extraordinary dialogue *Le Neveu de Rameau*, is not impressive, but he is one of the most important figures, certainly the most attractive figure, in that whole French movement known as the 'Enlightenment', to which he adds a certain warmth, eager curiosity, breadth of sympathy in art and letters, all his own.

DOSTOYEVSKY, FËDOR MIKHAILOVICH: Russian novelist, born in Moscow in 1821, died in St. Petersburg 1881. Son of a surgeon, he qualified as an engineer in St. Petersburg and entered government service. His literary career began with the publication of two short novels in 1846. He was arrested as a member of a revolutionary group in 1849, sentenced to death but instead exiled to Siberia, where he spent four years in a penal settlement and four more in a line-battalion. On returning to St. Petersburg he published the periodical *Vremya*, which was banned in 1863. His great novel, *Crime and Punishment* appeared in 1866, followed by *The Idiot* in 1868. He fled to Western Europe to escape creditors but returned in 1871. Between 1873 and 1880 he published 'An Author's Diary', first in *Grazhdanin*, then as independent issues. His literary fame, which had been increasing steadily, reached its climax with the appearance of *The Brothers Karamazov* in 1879–80. He is a great novelist, whose influence upon the new subjective and symbolic fiction of Western Europe after the First War was tremendous.

DREISER, THEODORE HERMAN ALBERT: American novelist, born at Terre Haute, Ind., in 1871, died in California in 1945. Born into a large, poor and highly religious family, he went from job to job while in his teens, becoming editor of pulp and fashion magazines. His first novel *Sister Carrie* was published in 1900 but subsequently banned for alleged immorality. With the publication of *Jennie Gerhardt* in 1911 he was able to give up hack-work and several novels were produced between then and his death. He is a clumsy though often powerful novelist, and as a courageous pioneer of realism he had a great influence on American fiction.

DUMAS, ALEXANDRE DAVY DE LA PAILLETERIE: French novelist and playwright, born at Villers-Cotterets in 1802, died at Puys near Dieppe in 1870. His father was a Revolutionary general, and he had creole and negro blood in him. He went to Paris in 1823 and was employed by the Duc d'Orléans. He turned to writing to earn his living, and from 1829, when he achieved success in the Theatre, he wrote many plays up to 1860. Ardently devoted to republicanism, he supported the 1848 revolution; went into voluntary exile in 1851, fought for Italian independence with Garibaldi in 1860 and after living for four years in Naples returned to France and died deeply in debt. Of his novels the famous *Les Trois Mousquetaires* appeared in 1844 and *Le Comte de Monte-Cristo* in eighteen volumes between 1844 and 1845, while twenty-two volumes of *Memoires* appeared in 1852–54. If Dumas is not quite a great writer, he is certainly a great character, whose dashing historical romances have entertained millions and have pleased some good judges of fiction.

ELIOT, GEORGE (pen-name of Mary Ann Evans): English novelist, born at Arbury Farm (Warwicks.) in 1819, died in London 1880. Her early life was spent in Warwickshire, managing her father's house until his death in 1849, reading widely and studying classical and European languages. From 1851–53 she was assistant editor of the *Westminster Review*. After translation and critical work her career as a novelist began with three stories in *Blackwood's* in 1857, followed soon after by *Adam Bede* (1859), *The Mill on the Floss* and *Silas Marner* (1861) and others, including the famous *Middlemarch* (4 vols.) in 1871–72. This last, her masterpiece, is now generally held to be a major contribution to English fiction. During the last twenty-five years a good deal of critical attention has been focused upon George Eliot.

EMERSON, RALPH WALDO: American poet, essayist and philosopher, born in Boston 1803, died at Concord (Mass.) in 1882. Educated at Harvard, he followed, after a period of teaching, the family's tradition by entering the Church. A change in his religious outlook made him resign in 1832. He visited Europe, where Carlyle became his friend, but finally settled in Concord, where he helped to found the Transcendental Club and edited *The Dial*. His beliefs were expounded in his first book *Nature* (1836), which, with his revolutionary Harvard address in the following year, made him famous and the eventual leader of the New England writers. Two series of essays followed in 1841 and 1844; he then lectured extensively; and published *Representative Men* in 1850, *English Traits* in 1856, and *The Conduct of Life* in 1860. Though he is at once deeply reflective and eloquent, Emerson's manner and style, discursive and staccato, seem better suited to the lecture than the essay, and he is no longer the great educative influence he was, both in America and England, during the nineteenth century. But he remains an essentially American figure of size and weight.

ERASMUS, DESIDERIUS: Dutch humanist, born at Rotterdam in 1469 and died in 1536 at Basle. Educated at Deventer and 's-Hertogenbosch, he entered the monastery of Steyn in 1487 and was ordained in 1492. After studying in Paris he first visited England in 1499, when he met Thomas More, who became a life-long friend, and John Colet. He spent time in Italy, becoming a doctor of theology in Turin, then in Cambridge and later at Louvain, where he became involved in the Reformation and removed to Basle for safety in 1521. His adherence to the Catholic cause led to his exile at Freiburg in 1529. Apart from his humanistic writings and the famous *Moriae Encomium*, he brought out an important edition of the New Testament. His freedom from the fanaticisms of his age, his broad humanism, his correspondence with so many important personages, his personal influence, make him one of the key figures of the time.

FIELDING, HENRY: English playwright, pamphleteer and novelist, born near Glastonbury in 1707, died in Lisbon in 1754. Educated at Eton, he began to study law but turned to the Theatre and produced a burlesque, several farces and comedies between 1730 and 1735. The Licensing Act in 1735, precipitated by his satire, *Pasquin*, put an end to theatrical success and he returned to the Law, becoming a magistrate in 1748. His first novel, *Joseph Andrews*, appeared in 1742, followed later by *History of Tom Jones* (1749) and *Amelia* (1752). When poor health caused him to travel to Lisbon, he wrote the *Journal of a Voyage to Lisbon*, published posthumously in 1755. Fielding has his limitations, but when younger English critics ignore him, it is usually because they have not read him. He is in fact, as an impressive list of fellow-writers have testified, a great novelist, who brings to his fiction a strong masculine intellect.

FITZGERALD, FRANCIS SCOTT KEY: American novelist and short-story writer, born at St. Paul (Minn.) in 1896, died at Hollywood (Calif.) in 1940. Educated at Princeton, he joined the armed forces as a young man without ever serving overseas as he had hoped. His first novel, *This Side of Paradise*, appeared in 1920 and was followed by others describing the 'Jazz Age', the most famous being *The Great Gatsby* (1925). Later novels were *Tender is the Night* and *The Last Tycoon*, which he left unfinished. His reputation is far greater now than it was during his lifetime. He was a novelist of great natural talent.

FLAUBERT, GUSTAVE: French novelist, born at Rouen in 1821, died at Croisset 1880. A surgeon's son, he studied law in Paris from 1840–43, but as poor health barred him from leading an active professional life he settled with his mother at Croisset. *Madame Bovary* was published in 1856–57, but his first novel *L'Éducation sentimentale* had been written some ten years previously though not finally published until 1869. After much research and a visit to Tunisia in 1858 *Salammbô* appeared in 1862 and *La Tentation de Saint Antoine*, begun in 1845, was published in 1874, and his two plays appeared in the same year. *Trois contes* appeared in 1877 but his last novel, *Bouvard et Pécuchet*, remained unfinished at his death. His importance and wide influence as a novelist cannot be questioned, but whether he is a great or minor master of fiction is still being argued.

FRANCE, ANATOLE (pseudonym of Jacques-Anatole Thibault): French writer, born in Paris in 1844, died at Saint-sur-Loire in 1924. Son of a Paris bookseller, he embarked on a long literary career with a collection of verse *Les Poèmes dorés* (1873), some impressionistic criticism, novels and short stories including *Jocaste et le Chat Maigre* (1879) and *Le Crime de Sylvestre Bonnard* (1881). In the four volumes of ironical novels, *Histoire contemporaine* (1896–1901), inspired by various political factors such as the Dreyfus case, he attempted an analysis of modern society. But his strongest work is the deeply satirical fiction he wrote in the years before 1914. After his death his reputation was savagely attacked in France and his work was neglected, but within his limitations he is one of the masters.

GALSWORTHY, JOHN: English novelist and playwright, born at Kingston Hill, Surrey, in 1867, died at Hampstead in 1933. Educated at Harrow and Oxford, he began writing, largely influenced by Turgenev, rebelled against the propertied upper-middle class, to which he belonged, in the novels afterwards reprinted as *The Forsyte Saga*, and also wrote a number of severely naturalistic plays on topical themes. He was a sound and sympathetic craftsman in both fiction and drama, but was on the whole inferior to several English contemporary writers, who did not, as he did in 1932, receive the Nobel Prize.

GEORGE, STEFAN: German poet, born at Büdesheim in 1868, died at Locarno in 1933. His great gift for languages and extensive travel enabled him to develop a mind capable of embracing the entire cultural tradition of Europe and his numerous translations and adaptations are proof of this ability. In addition to his poetry and prose writings he worked to reform the German language through the journal *Blätter für die Kunst* (1892–1919), while as metaphysician, prophet and founder of a school of thought, he was an important influence in German intellectual life between 1914 and 1933. His finest poetry is in the tradition of the old German *lied* but he adds to it a certain monumental quality of his own.

GIDE, ANDRÉ PAUL GUILLAUME: French author, born in Paris 1869, died there in 1951. Son of Protestant parents, his father from the Midi, his mother from Normandy, he was brought up in a strict puritan atmosphere. He visited Tunisia in 1893–94 and met Oscar Wilde in Algeria in 1895; the contact with the Arab world is expressed in *Les Nourritures terrestres* (1897). In 1925–26 he visited the French Congo and attacked the colonial administration there in two travel books, *Voyage au Congo* (1927) and *Retour du Tchad* (1928). His sympathy with Communism in the 1930s was dispelled after a visit to the Soviet Union in 1936. A versatile and prolific writer, his works include numerous novels—among the most famous being *La Symphonie pastorale* (1919) and *Les Faux-monnayeurs* (1926)—plays, criticism, and autobiographical writings. His reminiscences and his Journal are fascinating, but, whatever French criticism may say, he is not a major creative writer.

GOETHE, JOHANN WOLFGANG VON: German poet and man of letters, born at Frankfurt-am-Main in 1749, died at Weimar 1832. Son of an imperial counsellor, he was educated privately, then at Leipzig and Strasbourg, and practised law in Frankfurt from 1771 to 1775. His early work owes much to the influence of Herder, whom he first met in 1770. *Götz von Berlichingen* appeared in 1773 and the famous *Werther* in 1774. He settled in Weimar in 1775 and from then until his visit to Italy (1786–88) administrative duties and scientific interests left little time for writing. On returning to Weimar he produced the great classically inspired poems and from 1791 to 1817 directed the Weimar theatre. By 1800 he had become the leader of German letters and among the numerous works produced from then until his death was his completed *Faust*. The *Conversations with Eckermann* are an excellent record of him in his later life. Magnificently versatile and distinguished as he was as a creative writer, Goethe is even more important as a great, representative, widely and deeply influential figure not only of German but of all European literature. He might be said to be his own greatest creation.

GOGOL, NIKOLAY VASILYEVICH: Russian author, born at Sorochintsy in the Ukraine in 1809, died in Moscow 1852. He went to St. Petersburg to work but found life in the civil service frustrating. His first literary success was with his stories of Ukrainian life published in 1831–32, followed by *Mirgorod* and *Arabeski* in 1835 and his comedy *The Government Inspector* in the following year. He visited Rome and during his stay wrote most of the novel *Dead Souls* (1842); in 1848 he visited Palestine, but finally settled in Moscow. He suffered from hypochondria and became partially insane at the end of his life. His genius created a kind of romantic-grotesque-satirical comic writing that belongs to him alone, and his *Dead Souls* is an inimitable masterpiece.

GOLDONI, CARLO: Italian dramatist, poet, prose writer and librettist, born in 1707 at Venice and died in 1793 at Paris. He practised law in Venice and Pisa and was Genoese consul from 1740–44. He wrote some 250 plays in Italian, Venetian dialect and French. After writing for a company of actors in Venice he became a professional dramatist there from 1748 to 1762. In 1762 he left Venice for France, where he directed the Comédie Italienne (1762–64) and later became Italian master to the royal princesses. The French Revolution impoverished him, and his last years were not happy. Goldoni is one of the best eighteenth-century dramatists, a master of ingenious and entertaining theatrical invention, and his best comedies still hold the stage.

GOLDSMITH, OLIVER: Irish poet, playwright, novelist and essayist, born at Ardnagow (Co. Roscommon) in 1728, died in London 1774. Educated in Dublin, he studied medicine at Edinburgh and Leiden and finally settled in London. He became a member of Johnson's Literary Club, founded in 1763, and his reputation as a man of letters dates from about this time. His novel, the *Vicar of Wakefield*, appeared in 1766, and the famous comedy *She Stoops to Conquer* in 1773. His success in several different kinds of literature, during a comparatively short life, he owes to his simple warm humanity, charm and style.

GORKY, MAXIM (pseudonym of Alexey Maximovich Peshkov): Russian writer, born at Nizhni Novgorod in 1868, died in Leningrad 1936. Orphaned at seven, he ran away from his employer when about twelve years old and embarked on a vagrant life. From 1898 onward he enjoyed a remarkable rise to fame in Europe and America as well as in Russia. He founded a publishing house, was active during the 1905 revolution and forced to flee the country, returning in 1913. In 1921 he left Russia once more, then returned to the Soviet Union seven years later as a great cultural figure. He was responsible for the adoption of 'socialist-realism', which was accepted in 1934 throughout the whole of Soviet literature. His works include numerous novels, short stories, plays and autobiographical works. It is probably by these wonderful reminiscences of his early life, and by his portraits of his fellow-authors, that he will be best remembered.

GUTENBERG, JOHANN: German printer, born c. 1398 at Mainz and appears to have died there in 1468. He entered into partnership with Dritzen and Heilmann in 1438 and later with Johann Fust. During the latter period (1450–1455) he is thought to have printed Latin bibles and smaller books, including a Kalendar in 1447 and the *Donatus* in ?1451. But the work was not a commercial success and after he separated from Fust little is known of his activities. He appears to have been printing and to have remained at Mainz, though possibly later moving to Eltville. And if books have meant much to us, then we should think of Gutenberg with gratitude and affection.

HAMSUN, KNUT: Norwegian novelist, playwright and poet, born at Lom in 1859, died at Nørholm in 1952. Of peasant stock, he was brought up at Hamarøy in Nørdland, moving there when three years old. After numerous jobs he spent four years in America during the 1880s and first received literary recognition with the essay *Det Moderne Amerikas Aandsliv* in 1889. The publication in the following year of his novel *Sult*, which attracted a great deal of notice, firmly established his reputation. Numerous works followed, including plays and verse as well as novels, the most famous being his *Markens Grøde* (1917), in which he reacts strongly against current literary ideals. During the Nazi occupation of Norway, he collaborated with the Nazis. A powerful novelist, with remarkable descriptive passages in his work, he had a great international reputation for many years and strongly influenced younger Norwegian writers.

HARDY, THOMAS: English poet and novelist, born at Higher Bockhampton, Dorset, in 1840, died at Max Gate near Dorchester in 1928. Brought up in rather poor circumstances, he was educated first at local schools, then in London, where he studied in the evenings at King's College. From 1856 to 1865 he studied architecture, first with an ecclesiastical architect and then under Sir Arthur Blomfield, becoming a prizeman of the R.I.B.A. and Architectural Association and publishing his first article in *Chambers' Journal* in 1865. His early poetry was not published, but in 1871 his first novel *Desperate Remedies* appeared, followed by many others between then and 1897, including *Tess of the D'Urbervilles* (1891) and *Jude the Obscure* (1896). He then returned to poetry, publishing several collections between 1898 and 1917, while the famous epic-drama in blank verse *The Dynasts* appeared in instalments between 1904 and 1908. It has long been the fashion to prefer Hardy the poet to Hardy the novelist, but in spite of some obvious failings he is a novelist of unusual power and depth.

HAWTHORNE, NATHANIEL: American short-story writer and novelist, born at Salem, Mass., in 1804, died at Plymouth, N.H., in 1864. Educated at Bowdoin College, where he met Longfellow, he spent twelve years at Salem, where he eventually made a name with *Twice-Told Tales* (1837). After working in the Boston Custom House, living briefly at Brook Farm, marrying and living at Concord, he became governor of the port of Salem, where he wrote his famous novel *The Scarlet Letter* (1850), which was followed within two years by *The House of the Seven Gables* and *The Blithedale Romance*. He served as U.S. consul abroad, and in his last novel, *The Marble Faun*, used Rome as its setting. After being under-valued for a considerable time, Hawthorne is now regarded as one of America's representative novelists, and during recent years his work has been the subject of much close and appreciative criticism.

HEINE, HEINRICH: German poet, born in Düsseldorf 1797, died in Paris in 1856. He came of Jewish stock and started life in commerce, later studying law at Bonn and Berlin, where his first poems were published. He devoted himself to writing as a result of the success of the *Reisebilder* (1826); he settled in Paris in 1831, where he did much to further Franco-German understanding. He became paralysed in his last years. His lyrics are exquisite, and his witty and impudent prose, even when he is writing about things now of little or no importance, can still be read with pleasure. He is an original 'little master'.

HOFFMANN, ERNST THEODOR WILHELM (altered to Amadeus): German writer, composer and caricaturist, born in Königsberg in 1776 and died in Berlin 1822. An unhappy home and a gifted but highly-strung nature caused him many difficulties. Working either in government service or in music, he became theatrical composer and designer in Bamberg (1808–13), and was one of Beethoven's earliest supporters. In 1816 his opera *Undine* was performed in Berlin, but being dissatisfied with his ability as a composer he had already turned to writing and was an important literary figure in Germany from 1814 onward. Though the *Tales of Hoffmann* are now better known on the operatic stage than as literature, he is in fact an extremely ingenious and quite original story-teller whose work perhaps deserves more attention that it has received, at least outside Germany, for a long time.

HOFMANNSTHAL, HUGO VON: Austrian poet, playwright and essayist, born in Vienna in 1874 and died at Rodaun in 1929. Of Jewish, Italian and German ancestry, he was established as a poet by the age of sixteen, writing many of his best-known lyrics around this time. His numerous dramatic successes before World War I include *Das gerettete Venedig* (1905) and *Jedermann* (1911), while his co-operation with Richard Strauss produced operatic works such as *Der Rosenkavalier* (1911). His later writings include a number of critical essays. After being under-valued for many years, he has now a growing reputation as one of the representative poets of his period.

HOLBERG, LUDVIG, BARON HOLBERG: Danish playwright, satirist, essayist and historian, born in Bergen 1684, died in Copenhagen in 1754. His father was a Norwegian army officer, but he himself was educated at Copenhagen and settled in Denmark. He travelled in England, France and Italy, and so gained touch with the European thought of the time, particularly French philosophy and literature. By 1730, when he took the Chair of History at Copenhagen, he had already produced several comedies and the poem *Peder Paars* (1719–20) as well as numerous historical writings. He wrote thirty-two comedies for the first Danish theatre, and was created a baron for leaving his fortune to the college at Sorø. Though he never enjoyed a wide international reputation, Holberg is a very important figure in the Scandinavian Theatre and Literature.

HÖLDERLIN, JOHANN CHRISTIAN FRIEDRICH: German poet, born at Lauffen in 1770, died at Tübingen in 1843. Educated at the Tübinger Stift and intended for the Church, he declined orders and became a private tutor. His love-affair at Frankfurt-am-Main (1796–98) was his greatest experience and inspired his poetry. Insanity, which first manifested itself in 1802, returned in 1806, two years after he had been made Librarian at Homburg. For the rest of his life he was looked after by a Tübingen carpenter. *Hyperion* appeared in 1797–99, though fragments had been included in Schiller's *Neue Thalia* earlier in the 1790s; his other works were published by friends after his loss of reason. Gradually he came to be recognised as one of Germany's finest poets, and in our own age his influence on German poetry has been notable.

HUGO, VICTOR-MARIE: French poet, novelist and playwright, born at Besançon in 1802, died in Paris in 1885. The son of a general, he was intended for a military career, but at seventeen he founded a literary review and by the age of twenty had produced his first collection of verse, followed by two more in 1824 and 1826. His first play, *Cromwell*, with its important preface, appeared in 1827 and *Hernani* in 1830. His literary leadership being established, and strengthened by *Notre-Dame de Paris* in 1831, he continued to write plays with varying degrees of success and in 1835 left the Theatre. Between 1829 and 1840 several important books of verse were written. A period of literary inactivity followed, during which time he played an increasingly important political role. After the *coup d'état* of 1851 he was forced to flee the country and finally settled in Guernsey. During his exile he wrote the great epic poems and three novels —*Les Misérables* (1862), *Les Travailleurs de la mer* (1866) and *L'Homme qui rit* (1869). From his return to Paris in 1870 until his death he was honoured as one of the greatest men of his time. Neither his fiction nor his drama is of the first order, but even those French critics who have followed very different fashions in verse cannot deny his enduring greatness as a poet.

IBSEN, HENRIK JOHAN: Norwegian dramatist and poet, born at Skien in 1828, died in Oslo in 1906. Son of a merchant who went bankrupt, he was first apprenticed to an apothecary with a view to reading medicine. An historical drama, his second, was performed in Oslo soon after he moved there in 1850. From 1851 to 1857 he was stage-manager of the new theatre in Bergen, then returned to the capital as director of the Norske Theater. The next six years were disappointing and financially difficult, but after writing *The Pretenders* in 1863 he was awarded a travelling scholarship, and went to Rome, where he wrote *Brand* (1866) and *Peer Gynt* (1867), which finally established his Scandinavian reputation. From then until 1891 he lived mostly in Germany and Italy, writing the plays, from *A Doll's House* to *The Wild Duck* and *Hedda Gabler*, that brought him a great European reputation. After he returned to Norway he continued to write, and the more deeply symbolical plays of this final period include *The Master Builder* and *John Gabriel Borkman*. Ibsen cannot be challenged as the great master of the modern drama of prose realism. His superb stagecraft, probably the result of his years of work actually in the Theatre, introduced many innovations in techniuqe. The skill, force and depth of his finest plays keep them alive still in playhouses all over the world.

JAMES, HENRY: American novelist and critic, born in New York in 1843, died in London in 1916. His family was of Scots and Irish origin and he was educated in New York and Europe; between 1868 and 1875 he spent much time in Paris, Rome and London and at length made his home in England. His first long novel *Roderick Hudson* appeared in 1876 and was followed by many others, including *What Maisie Knew* (1898) and *The Golden Bowl* (1914), a number of short stories, some unsuccessful plays, critical and travel works. During the last twenty-five years his reputation, especially with American and English critics, has been far greater than it was during his lifetime.

JAMES, WILLIAM: American philosopher, born in New York 1842, died at Chocurua, N.H., in 1910. Brother of Henry James, he taught at Harvard, where he organised a psychological laboratory; his famous work *The Principle of Psychology*, published in 1890, was the result of his discoveries and theories in this field. His philosophical writings include the important *Pragmatism* (1907), in which his doctrine is set forth. These works, together with his *Varieties of Religious Experience*, perhaps his masterpiece, made him one of the most influential thinkers of his time.

JONSON, BENJAMIN: English actor, poet, dramatist and critic, born in or near London about 1572, died there in 1637. Leaving Westminster in 1589, where he received a classical education under Camden, he was apprenticed to a bricklayer, and fought in Flanders between about 1591 and 1597. He then acted with a strolling company, was imprisoned twice, the second time for killing a man, and was converted to Roman Catholicism. By 1614 he had become established as a dramatist and man of letters, the tragedy *Sejanus* as well as four comedies, masques, and *Catiline* having being written by that date. A series of disasters, including the burning of his library the onset, of paralysis and the failure of his latest plays, was alleviated in 1631 owing to the aid of Charles I. Although Ben Jonson wrote some enchanting lyrics and some excellent criticism, his name is kept alive by his comedies, especially *Volpone* and *The Alchemist*, written with immense gusto and a good eye for character. It is his misfortune that the more charming, more truly humorous, more poetic comedies of Shakespeare come so close to his and outshine them. But his comedy deservedly still holds the English stage.

JOYCE, JAMES: Irish novelist and poet, born at Rathgar, Dublin, 1882, died in Zürich 1941. Educated by the Jesuits at Sallins, Co. Kildare, and at Dublin, where he read modern languages, took a great interest in music, and wrote several essays before graduating in 1902. He left Ireland in 1904 and spent the rest of his life in voluntary exile, mostly in Trieste, Paris and Zürich, despite poverty, difficulties with publishers and failing sight, writing poetry and prose and a play, *The Exiles* (1918). His famous *Ulysses* appeared in 1922, and *Finnegans Wake* in 1939. He is deservedly recognised as one of the masters of the modern movement, although his actual influence on later fiction has been over-estimated.

KAFKA, FRANZ: German novelist, born in Prague in 1883, died at Kierling near Vienna in 1924. A victim of tuberculosis, he had several spells in sanatoria. A few short stories were published in his lifetime, but all his major works were published posthumously and include the two famous novels *Der Prozess* (1925) and *Das Schloss*. He is a master of strange and deeply symbolic narrative, capable of many different interpretations, and he has had a great influence on modern fiction.

KEATS, JOHN: English poet, born in London 1795, died in Rome 1821. The son of the keeper of a livery stable, he went to school at Enfield, where he had Cowden Clarke as headmaster. He was apprenticed to an apothecary-surgeon and started a medical training, becoming a dresser at Guy's Hospital in 1816. The next year he published his first volume of *Poems* and although it had no success he determined to abandon surgery for literature. *Endymion* (1817) was harshly attacked in the *Quarterly Review* and *Blackwood's Magazine*. Most of his greatest poems were written between 1818 and 1820 and appeared in the great volume *Lamia and Other Poems* published in 1820. He was already ill with consumption, and his condition was probably aggravated by his misplaced passion for the inadequate Fanny Brawne. Sailing to Italy with his friend Severn in the hope of recovering his health, he died, and was buried in the Protestant Cemetery in Rome. Keats was a great poet even during his short life, and had he lived he might have been one of the very greatest. His letters offer more evidence of his force of mind and deep insight.

KIERKEGAARD, SØREN AABYE: Danish philosopher and essayist, born at Copenhagen in 1813, died there in 1855. Brought up in a morbidly religious atmosphere, he studied philosophy and æsthetics at Copenhagen against his father's wishes, but eventually took a degree in theology. His main philosophic books written under pseudonyms between 1843 and 1846 were among his earliest writings, and during this period the first of his *Edifying Discourses* appeared. A feud with the periodical Corsaren in 1846 and the resulting suffering led to a deeper understanding of Christianity and an attack on theologians in a new series of books. The effort he poured into a passionate attack on 'official' Christianity hastened his death. To those who share something of his guilt-ridden temperament, Kierkegaard makes a most powerful appeal, one that has been stronger in this century than it was in his own.

KIPLING, JOSEPH RUDYARD: English poet, novelist and short-story writer, born in Bombay in 1865, died in London 1936. His childhood was spent in India, but he was educated in England, returning to India in 1882 to become a journalist. His early poems and short stories about the English in India, appearing in the late 1880s and earlier 1890s and coinciding with the new imperialism of that period, achieved enormous popularity. After spending some years in America, his wife being an American, he settled in England but spent many winters in South Africa. After the *Jungle Books* and *Kim*, probably his masterpiece, he wrote little about India, which had given him his best work. At his worst, Kipling is a magnificent craftsman, and at his best he has genius, though from middle life onwards the artist in him had fewer and fewer opportunities.

LEOPARDI, GIACOMO, COUNT: Italian poet, born at Recanati in 1798, died in Naples 1837. Son of an erudite nobleman who directed his education, his precocity was soon apparent. As a result of over-work he damaged his eyes and developed spinal trouble. The pessimism which is such a feature of his writing appears to have developed during a period of blindness in 1819. Apart from his famous *Canti* he also produced several prose works, including *Operette Morali* (1827) and *Zibaldone di pensieri*. In spite of his complete pessimism, Leopardi was widely read and admired outside Italy during most of the nineteenth century.

LERMONTOV, MIKHAIL YURYEVICH: Russian poet and novelist, born in Moscow 1814, died at Pyatigorsk in 1841. Son of an army officer, he was brought up in Tarkhany and Moscow by his maternal grandmother. He entered Moscow University in 1830 but transferred to the cadet school in St. Petersburg two years later, after which he became commissioned in a Guards regiment. He was virtually exiled to the Caucasus with a line-regiment as a result of his poem *On the Death of Pushkin*, written in 1837, but was soon allowed to return. During the last four years of his short life he attained great popularity as a poet, and wrote his important works, including the novel *A Hero of Our Time*. A duel with the son of the French Ambassador in 1840 resulted in a further exile in the Caucasus and while there he was killed in another duel. Lermontov was a kind of belated Russian Byron, though more genuinely romantic in feeling than Byron himself. He had remarkable gifts and had he lived to bring them to maturity, he would undoubtedly have been a major writer. *A Hero of Our Time*, embodying a representative Russian type, had considerable influence both on its readers and later Russian writers.

LESAGE, ALAIN RENÉ: French novelist and dramatist, born at Sarzeau (Morbihan) in 1668, died in Boulogne 1747. He came of middle-class parentage and lived uneventfully in Paris, where his large number of plays and novels were produced. Starting with translations from the Spanish, he wrote the satirical comedy *Turcaret, ou Le financier* in 1709. After further productions had been refused by the Comédie Française, he wrote about a hundred farces for the small theatres of the Paris fairs. His first successful novel, *Le Diable Boiteux* (1707) and much of his later work show strong Spanish influence. The famous *Gil Blas de Santillane* was published in 1715. He has not the depth of a great novelist, but *Gil Blas* is a supreme example of the *picaresque* novel and can still be read with pleasure.

LESSING, GOTTHOLD EPHRAIM: Critic and dramatist, born at Kamenz in 1729, died in 1781 at Brunswick. His father was a Protestant pastor, and he went to school at Meissen and to Leipzig University. In 1749 he became a journalist in Berlin, and during the next ten years he attained fame through his plays and critical writings. From 1760 to 1765, while secretary to General Tauentzien in Breslau, he employed his leisure in classical studies, leading to *Laokoön* in 1766. In 1767 he became house critic to the Hamburg Theatre and in 1770 librarian at Wolfenbüttel. He wrote the famous verse drama, *Nathan der Weise* in 1779. His was a noble liberating influence on German literature and Theatre; and he is one of the most attractive figures of his century.

MACHIAVELLI, NICCOLÒ: Political theorist and historian, born at

Florence in 1459, died there in 1527. His political career began in 1498 under the Florentine republic; during the next ten years he was sent on important missions, and was instrumental in raising a militia for the defence of Florence. When the Medici returned to power he was deposed from office, imprisoned, tortured, then placed under house-arrest at San Casciano. Here he wrote *Il Principe* in 1513. From 1519 until they were expelled in 1527, he served the Medici, and wrote the annals of Florence. On the re-establishment of the republic he was considered suspect and, bitterly disappointed, he fell ill and died. Machiavelli's fame and great influence belong to political philosophy rather than to literature proper, but there can be no doubt about their extent, when the adjective coined from his name is still used everywhere.

MALLARMÉ, STEPHANE: French poet, born in Paris in 1842, died at Valvins in 1898. He went to England at the age of twenty, spending nine months in London and returning to France, where he taught English in provincial lycées and eventually in Paris, where he ran a salon in the rue de Rome. His *Poésies* and *Album de Vers et de Prose* were published in 1887. In 1894 he retired to the country. Through Valéry, who married his daughter, and many Symbolist poets in different countries, Mallarmé, with his theory of Symbolism, may be said to have been the greatest single influence in modern poetry.

MANN, THOMAS: German novelist, born in Lübeck in 1875, died in Zürich in 1955. Son of a Lübeck merchant, he published his first novel *Die Buddenbrooks* at the age of twenty-five, which gained him a prominent position in German literary circles. Several shorter novels were written in the twenty-four years before the publication of his famous novel *Der Zauberberg* (1924), which brought him European fame and the award of the Nobel Prize five years later. His later novels include the ambitious *Joseph* series, and *Doktor Faustus*. He is Germany's greatest novelist, and one of the masters of twentieth-century fiction.

MANZONI, ALESSANDRO: Italian poet and novelist, born in Milan in 1785 and died there in 1873. His mother separated from his father, and in 1805 he went to live with her in Paris. Here his friendship with Claude Fauriel brought him under the influence of the Romantic Movement. In 1810 he was re-converted to Roman Catholicism; thereafter over a period of some twenty-five years his sensist philosophic doctrines changed gradually to Rosminianism. His great historical novel, *The Betrothed*, first written in 1827, was published in its final Florentine version in 1840. It has held its place as Italy's masterpiece in fiction, beloved and frequently quoted by every Italian. It contains some faults of construction and manner, but it is a novel of great breadth and rich, warm humanity, all the better because Manzoni, unlike other contemporary historical novelists, takes his central characters from the peasantry and describes seventeenth-century life in Italy from their point of view.

MARIVAUX, PIERRE CARLET DE CHAMBLAIN DE: French playwright and novelist, born in Paris 1688, died there in 1763. Son of a wealthy banker, he started writing as a hobby; on losing his money in 1722 and having to earn a living he produced a number of successful comedies between then and 1739, notable amongst them being *La Jeu de l'amour et du hasard* (1730). He wrote two novels, *La Vie de Marianne* (1731–41) and *Le Paysan parvenu* (1735–36) and became an Academician in 1743. Neither his drama nor his fiction is in the highest class, but both are very personal, with an odd charm and touches of subtlety unusual in his time.

MAUPASSANT, HENRI RENÉ ALBERT GUY DE: French novelist and short-story writer, born at Tourville-sur-Arques in 1850, died in Paris 1893. At the age of eleven his parents separated; through his mother he met Flaubert, who supervised his early writings. He entered the civil service and worked as a clerk from 1872 until 1880, when the success of *Boule de Suif* enabled him to earn a living by writing. Apart from his short stories and novels, including the famous *Pierre et Jean* (1888), he wrote three plays as well as some verse and was one of the most popular and highly-paid writers of his time. His reputation has declined considerably, along with the taste for the particular type of short story he wrote. But his best work still has a large and grateful public, at home and abroad.

MELVILLE, HERMAN: American novelist, poet and short-story writer, born in New York in 1819, died there in 1891. His association with the navy and his travels including a voyage to Liverpool at the age of nineteen and others to the South Seas, provided the themes for several novels, five being written before he was thirty-two which earned him some initial recognition. His famous symbolic novel *Moby Dick*, published in 1851, was not well received and this loss of popularity resulted in poverty for him and his family. His later works include Civil War poems, *Clarel* (1876), inspired by his journey to Palestine in 1856–57, and the novel *Billy Budd*, published posthumously. Undervalued far too long, Melville is now in danger of being over-valued, but of its own kind *Moby Dick* is undoubtedly a masterpiece.

MEREDITH, GEORGE: English novelist and poet, born at Portsmouth in 1828, died at Boxhill in 1909. Partly Welsh by birth, he was educated in Moravia and then articled to a solicitor but soon turned to literature. His early writings were unsuccessful and he was obliged to work as a journalist and a publishers' reader, but towards the end of his life he attained great fame. His first poems appeared in 1851, *Modern Love* in 1862 and a final volume in 1909. Of his many novels, his masterpiece, *The Egoist*, was published in 1879. Meredith's fiction has long been out of fashion, though it may be enjoyed again one day. But the astonishing modernity in the feeling and manner of his *Modern Love* has been recognised and praised by many critics of poetry.

MOLIÈRE, assumed name of Jean-Baptiste Poquelin: French dramatist, born in Paris 1622, died there in 1673. Educated at Paris and probably Orléans, he joined the newly formed Illustre Théâtre, becoming its leader in 1652. After playing in the provinces since 1645 the company returned to Paris in 1658 under the patronage of the Duke of Orléans; by 1661 it was established in the Palais Royal and four years later came under the King's direct patronage. His first personal success was with the satire *Les Précieuses Ridicules*, produced in 1659. Many other comedies, farces and Court entertainments were produced between then and his death, notably *L'École des Femmes* (1662), *Le Tartuffe*, *Don Juan* (1665), *Le Misanthrope* (1666), *L'Avare* (1668), *Le Bourgeois gentilhomme* (1670), *Les Femmes savantes* (1672), *Le Malade imaginaire* (1673). Molière cannot be challenged as one of the masters of world drama, a great comic dramatist who at times, as in *Don Juan* and *Le Misanthrope*, reveals underlying serious depths.

MONTAIGNE, MICHEL DE: French essayist, born at the Château de Montaigne, Dordogne. in 1533 and died there in 1592. He was educated at the Collège de Guyenne, Bordeaux, and then studied law. He was greatly influenced by La Boétie and felt his death deeply. In 1571, after inheriting his father's estate, he retired to Montaigne to study and meditate. After publishing his first two books of *Essais* in 1580 he returned to active life and travelled in Germany, Switzerland and Italy. His political experiences as Mayor of Bordeaux (1581–85) and as a disinterested intermediary between Catholic and Protestant factions in France are reflected in Book III of the *Essais* (1588). On many different counts Montaigne adds up to the total claim of being one of the great original masters and innovators and influences beyond estimation of Western literature. Scores of major writers, in many different forms, derive something important from him.

MUSSET, LOUIS-CHARLES-ALFRED DE: French poet and dramatist, born in Paris 1810, died there in 1857. The son of cultivated parents, he early became a favourite in Charles Nodier's group of young Romantics. He published his first poems in 1830. In the same year his play, *La Nuit vénitienne* was a failure, and from then until when they were produced at the Comédie française from 1847 onwards he only wrote plays for publication in the *Revue des Deux Mondes*. His association with George Sand (1834–35) was followed by the appearance of the romantic poems *Les Nuits* (1835–37) and his *Confession d'un enfant du siècle* (1836). Musset was the last disillusioned child of the Romantic Movement in France, where, after his death, his plays, highly original and full of charm, wit, poetic feeling, captured the Theatre.

NIETZSCHE, FRIEDRICH WILHELM: German philosopher and poet, born at Röcken in 1844, died in Weimar 1900. Son of a Lutheran pastor who died when he was five, he was brought up by devout female relatives, educated at Bonn and Leipzig, and became professor of Greek at Basle University in 1869. He served as a non-combatant in the Franco-German War. During this period he was much influenced by Schopenhauer and was an enthusiastic admirer of Wagner; his work includes *The Birth of Tragedy*. A subsequent revulsion against his former idols is reflected in his later work, headed by the famous *Zarathustra*, published in four parts (1883–92). A nervous breakdown in 1889 led to long periods of mental illness bordering on insanity, and he was never able to finish his final work on the Will to Power. In spite of the fact that translation rarely suggests the brilliance and force of his original German text, Nietzsche's work has been widely studied throughout the Western world, and his influence, not always good, was particularly strong on other writers between 1890 and 1910. Though his values and judgments are often unsound, his fearless questioning of the age and his intuitive feeling that it was hurrying towards catastrophe are still impressive.

O'NEILL, EUGENE GLADSTONE: American playwright, born in New York in 1888, died at Boston (Mass.) in 1953. Son of an actor, he accompanied his father on theatrical tours, and completed his formal education with a year at Princeton. He went to Honduras prospecting for gold, worked in factory offices, became a seaman and voyaged to Argentina, South Africa and England. During a six-month stay in a sanatorium he started to write. After experience at Harvard in the '47 Workshop he joined the Provincetown Players, who produced his plays. In 1920 he was acclaimed America's leading dramatist with *Beyond the Horizon*, and from then on wrote a large number of plays, including the famous *Mourning Becomes Electra* (1931) and *The Iceman Cometh* (1946), being awarded the Nobel Prize in 1936. Though not without certain obvious limitations, he must be considered the best all-round dramatist America has produced so far.

PASCAL, BLAISE: French writer, born at Clermont-Ferrand in 1623, died in Paris 1662. Son of a magistrate, he was educated in Paris and excelled in mathematics, geometry and physics. He was the inventor of a calculating machine. In 1646 with the rest of his family he became influenced by the Jansenists and in 1654, after a few years of worldly living in aristocratic society he experienced a sudden conversion and attached himself to Port-Royal. In *Les Provinciales* (1656–57) he defends the Jansenists and attacks the Jesuits. *Les Pensées*, which was planned by 1658, remained unfinished at his death. A great mathematician, Pascal is also a writer of extraordinary power, profoundly influencing many later writers not repelled by his guilt-ridden, self-tormenting attitude of mind towards religion.

PIRANDELLO, LUIGI: Italian playwright, short-story writer and novelist, born at Agrigento in 1867, died in Rome in 1936. Educated at Palermo, Rome and Bonn, he first achieved success with the novel *Il fu Mattia Pascal* in 1904. Later, when already middle-aged, he rose to greater fame through his numerous plays, which include *Così è—se vi pare* (1918) and *Sei personaggi in cerca d'un autore* (1921). His other writings include a number of short stories and essays. He is Italy's best modern dramatist, whose highly original plays, subjective and sceptical, capture the spirit of the present age.

POE, EDGAR ALLAN: American poet, short-story writer and critic, born in Boston in 1809, died in Baltimore in 1849. His parents, travelling actors, died while he was still a child and he was befriended and educated by John Allan. They parted over the young man's gambling debts, and from then onward Poe's life was a struggle with hack-work, poverty and alcoholism. He wrote some seventy stories and many poems between 1829 and his death, the *Raven and Other Poems* appearing in 1845. With the *Gold Bug* and *The Murders in the Rue Morgue* he may be recognised as one of the originators of the detective story. But his greatest contribution to literature was an indirect one, for through the fascination his poetry had for Baudelaire and Mallarmé his was the strongest original influence on the French Symbolists. Opinion is still sharply divided about the value of his own work.

POPE, ALEXANDER: English poet, born in the City of London 1688, died at Twickenham in 1744. Brought up in the country, where he studied intensively, he was handicapped by physical deformity and suffered poor health all his life. His first work, *An Essay on Criticism*, appeared in 1711, followed by the *Rape of the Lock* in 1712 and a volume of poetry in 1717. After spending many years translating Homer (*Iliad* 1720, *Odyssey* 1726) and bringing out an edition of Shakespeare, he went to Twickenham and there, during the latter part of his life, produced his finest original poetry. Within the strict limits of the contemporary manner, style, range of feeling, Pope is a master.

PROUST, MARCEL: French novelist, born at Auteuil in 1871, died in Paris in 1922. Son of a physician and a wealthy Jewess, he managed by charm and ambition to gain an entrée into Parisian society during his twenties. From the turn of the century onward misfortune, illness and disillusionment caused him to become more and more of a recluse, living in a cork-lined room at 102 Boulevard Haussman from 1907, where he worked by night and slept by day. Between 1907 and 1914 he visited Cabourg each summer. His great novel *À la recherche du temps perdu*, first drafted between 1909 and 1912, was revised and enlarged up to his death. Little attention was paid to the first part, published in 1913, but the second in 1919 won the Prix Goncourt and gained him world-wide recognition. He is unquestionably the greatest French novelist of this century, and one of the masters of modern literature.

PUSHKIN, ALEXANDER SERGEYEVICH: Russian poet, born in Moscow 1799, died in St. Petersburg in 1837. Of noble birth (though with an Abyssinian ancestry on his mother's side) he had a French education at the Tsarskoe Selo Lycée, where he began to write poetry. He then settled in St. Petersburg, nominally as a civil servant. *Ruslan and Ludmila* was acclaimed in 1820, but by the time of its publication some barbed epigrams had already led to his exile in South Russia, where he wrote the *Prisoner of the Caucasus* (1820–21). After further banishment, he was abruptly pardoned by Nicholas I, and thereafter circumstances forced him to be closely tied to the Court. *Boris Godunov* appeared in the year of his pardon (1826) and he was writing *Eugene Onegin* between 1823 and 1831. He made an ill-judged marriage in 1831, and the intrigues and follies of his wife were finally responsible for his being killed in a duel with the French legitimist, Baron Heckeren-d'Anthès. Both in poetry and prose, Pushkin was a major writer, of immense importance to Russian literature. Because of the difficulty of translating him adequately, his originality and power and genuine greatness have not been widely appreciated, even today, outside Russia.

RABELAIS, FRANÇOIS: French writer, born near Chinon (Touraine) c. 1490, died in Paris 1553 or 1554. Son of a prosperous lawyer, he became a Franciscan monk, but later, as a secular priest, took up medicine. While working in Lyons hospital he published *Pantagruel* (1532) and *Gargantua* (1534), which were both condemned by the Sorbonne. In 1537 he took his doctorate at Montpellier. With his patrons, Jean and Guillaume du Bellay, he visited Italy several times between 1534 and 1549. After his *Tiers Livre* was condemned in 1546 he fled to Metz to escape persecution. He later settled near Paris, probably at an abbey of which he was a canon. Rabelais is one of the vast originals of European Literature: a fantastic humorist of genius, a great humanist, as deeply wise as

473

he is wittily exuberant; he is the fountain from which streams of later literature flow; one of France's most magnificent gifts to our world.

RACINE, JEAN: French dramatist and poet, born at La Ferté-Milon in 1639, died in Paris 1699. As an orphan he was brought up by his grandmother, a deeply religious woman, and was educated at Beauvais and by the Jansenists of Port-Royal. He was intended for the Church but after his successful odes (1660–63) he began writing for the Theatre and had his first play produced by Molière in 1664. He then left Molière and had all his other plays produced by the company of the Hôtel de Bourgogne. After an extremely successful career in the Theatre, he left it in 1677 to accept the post of Historiographer Royal, but later, in 1689 and 1691, he wrote two religious plays for Mme. de Maintenon's girls' school at St. Cyr. Although widely admired as a dramatist he had little personal popularity and was on several occasions accused of very doubtful behaviour. But he has long been accepted as the supreme master of French neo-classical tragedy.

RICHARDSON, SAMUEL: English novelist, born in Derbyshire in 1689 and died in London in 1761. He was a successful printer, and after retirement he was asked to prepare "a little volume of letters in common style for the use of country readers". This gave him the idea of writing fiction in the form of letters, a wildly unrealistic method but enabling him to allow his characters to describe at length their thoughts and feelings. *Pamela, or Virtue Rewarded* was followed, in 1748, by his masterpiece, *Clarissa*, and the immense but less successful *History of Sir Charles Grandison*, in 1754. Richardson's success, both at home and abroad, is one of the most startling in literary history. His sentimentality and smug piety, the curious hot-house atmosphere of his fiction, his unconscious suggestion of sexual sadism and masochism, proved to be exactly to the taste of the time, which accepted him as its greatest novelist. This opinion of him did not last, but his influence on fiction lasted for almost a hundred years.

RILKE, RAINER MARIA: German poet, born at Prague in 1875, died at Val-Mont near Montreux in 1926. From his early twenties onward he travelled about Europe, wandering chiefly between Munich, Berlin, Paris, Rome and ultimately Switzerland. His first poems, in the German folksong tradition, were published in 1894 and were followed by others in the same vein, until his Roman Catholic beliefs were replaced by mysticism, giving rise to poems such as *Geschichten vom Lieben Gott* (1900–04) and the *Buch der Bilder* (1902). Some of his best work was written between 1903 and 1912, when he was influenced by contemporary French life and art, producing the two volumes of *Neue Gedichte* (1907–08) as well as several prose works. His later poems include *Duineser*

Elegien (1911–22) and *Sonette an Orpheus* (1922). He is one of the major European poets of this century, and his curious personality has been the subject of many studies.

RIMBAUD, JEAN ARTHUR: French poet, born at Charleville in 1854, died in Marseilles 1891. Son of an army captain who abandoned his wife and child, he rebelled against his upbringing and finally escaped to Paris in 1871, making friends with Verlaine and travelling with him to Belgium and London. In Brussels he was wounded by Verlaine in a quarrel; three months later *Une Saison en Enfer* was published (1873) and he then abandoned literature. After roaming about, doing odd jobs, for some years, he finally settled in Abyssinia, where he became involved in gun-running and slave traffic as well as the coffee business. He died at thirty-seven as a result of an amputation. At once a prodigy and a strange demonic figure, Rimbaud anticipated by fifty years much of what is characteristic of modern literature.

ROLLAND, ROMAIN: French writer, born at Clamecy in 1866, died at Vézelay in 1944. Of bourgeois parentage, he became Professor of Art History at the Sorbonne. His huge novel, *Jean Christophe*, which was serialised in Peguy's *Cahiers de la Quinzaine* between 1904 and 1912, remains his best-known work. At the outbreak of World War I he was living in Switzerland, where he produced a series of pacifist manifestoes. In 1915 he was awarded the Nobel Prize, and after the war became recognised as a revolutionary and independent humanist. He was a man of ideas and ideals rather than an essentially creative writer, though the earlier volumes of *Jean Christophe* contain some very fine passages.

RONSARD, PIERRE DE: French poet, born at the Manoir de la Poissonnière near Vendôme c. 1524, died at Saint-Cosme in 1585. He was intended for a military and diplomatic career and became page to the Dauphin at ten. An illness at eighteen caused partial deafness and he turned to literature. His study of the classics and the Italian poets, such as Petrarch, influenced his work, the *Odes* appearing in 1550 and 1552 and the *Amours* in 1552–53. By 1560, as leader of the 'Pléiade' he was established as an important literary figure. His poems after this date include *Les Discours* (1560–70) and the *Sonnets pour Hélène* (1578). He was almost forgotten during the latter part of the seventeenth and during the eighteenth century, but the Romantics rediscovered him, and now he is acknowledged to be one of the great lyric poets of France.

ROUSSEAU, JEAN-JACQUES: French writer and philosopher, born in Geneva in 1712, died near Paris in 1778. Son of a watchmaker of French

Calvinist stock, his mother died at his birth and the difficulties of his early years increased his instability of character. After years of wanderings and struggles he won the Académie de Dijon essay prize in 1750, which immediately made him famous. His important works date from this time. Two books appearing in 1762 were condemned and caused him to flee to Switzerland; here he started on the *Confessions*. He went to England in 1765 but soon returned to Paris, having already developed the persecution mania that darkened his last years. For good or evil Rousseau's influence, both on literature and political philosophy, was such that it is almost impossible to over-estimate it. The whole Romantic Movement comes out of him.

RUSKIN, JOHN: English writer, born in 1819, died at Brantwood, Coniston, in 1900. Son of a wealthy wine merchant, he was educated at home and at Oxford and travelled abroad. After writing verse at Oxford he anonymously brought out the first volume of *Modern Painters* in 1843. Throughout his life he lectured and wrote on art and art criticism, bringing out the final volume of *Modern Painters* in 1860 and in the same year being made Slade Professor in Fine Art at Oxford. Later his interests broadened to include political economy and social philosophy, and it is as a social philosopher, not as an art critic, that he has had the widest audience and influence during the last seventy-five years. His remarkable style, with its long and elaborate sentences, fascinated Marcel Proust, who imitated it.

SCHILLER, JOHANN CHRISTOPH FRIEDRICH: German dramatist, born at Marbach in 1759, died at Weimar 1805. Instead of entering the Church as intended, he was forced to join the Duke of Württemberg's military academy (1773–80). *Die Räuber* appeared in 1781, when he was regimental doctor in Stuttgart; it displeased the Duke, and the following year he fled to Mannheim. He spent a winter at Bauerbach writing *Kabale und Liebe* and returned to Mannheim as a salaried dramatist in 1783. In 1785 he went to Leipzig, *Don Carlos* being finished in 1787, and then to Weimar, taking a Chair of History at Jena University in 1789. Upon receiving a grant as the result of illness in 1791 he studied Kant's philosophy and produced a number of philosophical writings. His friendship with Goethe began in 1794 and his important historical poetic dramas were written after that date. If not quite a master of world drama, Schiller, a noble and enthusiastic character, is a dramatic poet of stature and enduring fame.

SCOTT, WALTER: Scottish novelist, poet and historian, born in Edinburgh in 1771, died at Abbotsford in 1832. He was educated at Edinburgh, called to the Bar in 1792, and appointed Sheriff of Selkirkshire in 1799. A collector of old Border ballads, he began writing spirited narrative verse himself, but after the great success of his first novel, *Waverley* (1814), published anonymously, he chiefly devoted himself to historical fiction. In 1820 he was created a baronet. After the financial collapse in 1826 of the publishing business in which he was a partner, he made an heroic effort to clear its debts. This meant that he wrote too much, too hastily, and his later novels are not always soundly constructed and well written. Though he is now largely out of fashion, Scott is still the greatest of all purely historical novelists, vigorous, manly, with a fine sense of history and character. His popularity during his lifetime and for many years later was enormous, throughout the whole Western world, and his influence on this particular form of fiction has been everywhere acknowledged.

SHAKESPEARE, WILLIAM: English dramatist and poet, born at Stratford-upon-Avon in 1564, died there in 1616. Little is known about his early life, though it is likely that he was connected in some way with the Theatre while still quite young. He was an actor, though never of major roles, and later, when his fame as a dramatist grew, he became 'a sharer', that is, one of the management. His earliest plays were being produced in 1592–93, and in the latter year *Venus and Adonis* was registered with the Stationers' Company, with *Lucrece* a year later. This same year, 1594, he joined the Lord Chamberlain's company. In 1597 he bought New Place, Stratford, but continued to live in London, where the Globe was built in 1599, and his company acquired the Blackfriars Theatre ten years later. The *Sonnets* were published in 1609, not long before he retired altogether to Stratford. Any comment on the astonishing genius and world-wide enduring fame of Shakespeare is superfluous. But in view of the innumerable books denying his authorship of the plays, it is worth pointing out that all the real evidence (as distinct from fantastic codes and anagrams) in the plays themselves suggests, first, that they are the work of one man, and, secondly, that that man is far more likely to have been someone with Shakespeare's known background than some great Elizabethan nobleman, who would never have known the wide variety of social experience obviously familiar to the author of these plays. And the contemporary references to him, though slight, are entirely convincing. Then the plays' masterly stagecraft suggests an author with an intimate knowledge of the Theatre, which Shakespeare had and none of the other substitute authors can claim at all. Finally, there is nothing strange about a modestly educated middle-class man becoming a great master; it is precisely this class, and not the aristocracy, that has given us most of our masters of literature.

SHAW, GEORGE BERNARD: Irish dramatist, novelist and propagandist, born in Dublin in 1856, died at Ayot Saint Lawrence (Herts) in 1950. Wesley

College, Dublin, was his school and after some instruction in music and painting at home, he emigrated to London in 1876. After nine years of hack writing and unsuccessful novels, he gained a reputation as a critic of music and drama, a book-reviewer and propagandist for socialism, founding the Fabian Society in 1884. His many plays began to be acted regularly from 1910 in England, Germany, America, and within a few more years were acted everywhere. He was awarded the Nobel Prize for literature in 1925 and bequeathed his fortune to research concerning a new alphabetical system. He is already losing some of his stature as a philosophical world figure, but he remains the supreme comic dramatist of the age.

SHELLEY, PERCY BYSSHE: English poet, born near Horsham, Sussex, in 1792, drowned in the Gulf of Spezia in 1822. After schooling at Eton he went on to Oxford but was sent down in 1811 for publishing *The Necessity of Atheism*. He eloped with Harriet Westbrook in the same year. *Queen Mab* appeared in 1813 and the next year he left England with William Godwin's daughter, Mary, whom he married in 1816. He spent most of the rest of his life in Italy. *Prometheus Unbound* was published in 1820, and in the same year he settled in Pisa, where many of his best-known lyrics were to be written. He was drowned when returning from Leghorn in a small sailing-boat; his body was washed up at Viareggio and cremated on the shore in the presence of Leigh Hunt and Byron. His ashes were buried in the Protestant Cemetery in Rome, close beside the grave of Keats, the admired friend whom he had commemorated in *Adonais*. Shelley is one of the representative great poets of rebellious ultra-romantic youth. His poetry is unequal, and is often too mawkish, melting, gaseous, but at its lyrical height it has a strange beauty, unlike that of any other poetry.

SHERIDAN, RICHARD BRINSLEY: Irish dramatist and orator, born in Dublin in 1751, died in London 1816. He was educated at Dublin and Harrow and studied law. His early life was spent in Bath; he moved to London in 1774 at the time of his marriage. The following year he successfully produced *The Rivals*, became a shareholder in Drury Lane Theatre in 1776 and its manager from 1776 to 1809. *The School for Scandal* was produced in 1777. In 1780 he became M.P. for Stafford, Under-Secretary of State in 1782, Privy Councillor and Treasurer of the Navy in 1799. Apart from the famous comedies he was known for his speeches on Irish affairs and on the impeachment of Warren Hastings. Sheridan's comedies, though not on the highest level of the art, have kept their liveliness, wit, and charm, and are still successfully played.

STENDHAL (pseudonym of Marie-Henri Beyle): French novelist, born at

Grenoble in 1783, died in Paris 1842. In 1799 he went to Paris with the intention of entering the Polytechnique, but joined the army, serving as a non-combatant in Napoleon's second Italian campaign. After resigning his commission, he rejoined as a non-combatant officer during the Russian campaign. From 1814 to 1821 he lived in Italy until the Austrian police expelled him for associating with Italian patriots. From 1830 until his death he was French consul at Civita-vecchia. His first novel, *Armance*, appeared in 1827; *Le Rouge et le Noir* in 1830; *La Chartreuse de Parme* in 1839. Almost unknown in his lifetime, Stendhal is now, if anything, over-esteemed, chiefly because his economy and cool dry analysis of character and motive make him seem modern in manner and feeling. Though in fact his fiction is not without some dubious romantic elements, he does anticipate much modern fiction, and at the least must be allowed to be a highly original novelist.

STERNE, LAURENCE: English novelist, born at Clonmel (Co. Tipperary) in 1713, died in London 1768. His father was an officer in the English Army, and he was educated at Halifax (Yorks.) and at Cambridge. Between 1760–67, while a parson in Sutton and Coxwold, he wrote the nine parts of *Tristram Shandy*. A journey to France in 1762 suggested the *Sentimental Journey*, written in 1768; several volumes of sermons were also published. Sterne is important not only because *Tristram Shandy* and the *Sentimental Journey* are enduring masterpieces, but also because his highly subjective, direct and economic method, entirely original, had a very considerable influence upon later novelists, down to our own time.

STRINDBERG, JOHAN AUGUST: Swedish dramatist, novelist, poet, born in Stockholm in 1849, died there in 1912. He studied at Uppsala, was engaged in tutoring and journalism, and in 1874 became assistant in the royal library in Stockholm. His first marriage (there were two others) took place in 1877, and the catastrophic failure of his relations with his first wife helps to explain the almost pathological suspicion and bitterness we find in his later treatment of sexual relationships. After some success in drama and fiction, he left Sweden in 1883, returning briefly the following year to be prosecuted for blasphemy, but being acquitted. After being married and divorced a second time, he lived in Paris and there had a mental breakdown, from which he emerged with a deeper interest in religious themes, compelling him to use much symbolism in his later drama. He returned to Sweden in 1896, wrote numerous plays and some fiction, and founded his own intimate theatre. He lived in isolation during his last years. Though wildly eccentric and unstable in his private life, Strindberg is a master of drama, both in the realistic manner of *The Father* and in his later experimental manner, as in the *Dream Play* and *Spook Sonata*, which influenced much expressionist playwriting. His best plays are masterly in their technique and have extraordinary force.

SVEVO, ITALO: Italian novelist, born in Trieste in 1861, died at Motta di Livenza in 1928. His early works, which include *Una Vita* (1893) and *Senilità* (1898), gained little notice; his eventual recognition as a writer was largely due to the influence of his friend, James Joyce (from whom he learned English), with the French critics some years later. His novels are set in Trieste and the later ones include *La Coscienza di Zeno* (1923). His deeply subjective and very ironical, sceptical humour is even now not as widely known as it ought to be.

SWIFT, JONATHAN: Satirist, poet, pamphleteer. Born in Dublin, though of English parentage, in 1667, died there in 1745. After a childhood of extreme poverty, he went to Trinity College, Dublin, then in 1689 became secretary to Sir William Temple. After some years he returned to Ireland, went into the Church and was given a parish near Belfast. There he wrote his first satires, *A Tale of a Tub* and *The Battle of the Books*. Later he paid frequent visits to London, where he enjoyed the friendship of the chief Whig writers, but in 1710 he attached himself to the Tories and became their most effective pamphleteer, especially in his famous *Conduct of the Allies*. In 1713, to his bitter disappointment, he was not offered a bishopric but only made Dean of St. Patrick's, and retired altogether to Ireland in disgust. His last years were very unhappy. His *Journal to Stella* is addressed to Esther Johnson, whom he loved and may have married, although they never lived together. His masterpiece, *Gulliver's Travels*, appeared in 1726. It is one of the ironies of literary history that the first two parts of this ferocious satire on the whole human race, a monument of misanthropy, have long been favourites with children. Swift had one of the most powerful intellects of his time, and a prose style that is easy, lucid, forceful. Apart from the last part, which is almost insane in its ferocity, *Gulliver's Travels* is a wonderful and enduring satire.

SYNGE, JOHN MILLINGTON: Irish dramatist and poet, born at Rathfarnham, Co. Dublin, in 1871, died in Dublin in 1909. He was of Anglo-Irish stock from Wicklow, and graduated from Trinity College, Dublin, in 1892. He travelled in Germany and France, studying French literature in Paris, where he became secretary to de Joubainville and met W. B. Yeats. Returning to Ireland he spent time in Aran and it was there, as well as in Wicklow and Kerry, that much of his material was gathered. His first play, *In the Shadow of the Glen* was produced at the Abbey Theatre in 1903 and was followed from then until 1910 by others including *Riders to the Sea* (1904) and *Deirdre of the Sorrows* written in the year of his death; he was considered Ireland's leading dramatist. His finest play, the rich and ironic comedy, *The Playboy of the Western World*, is one of the dramatic masterpieces of this century.

TASSO, TORQUATO: Italian poet, born at Sorrento in 1544, died at Rome in 1595. Educated at Naples by the Jesuits, then at Padua, where he published his first epic in 1562. He entered the service of the Estes in 1565 and later became Court poet to Alphonso II. To this period until 1577, when insanity began to manifest itself, his best work belongs. During his incarceration at the Hospital of St. Anne, later at Mantua and finally, after restless wanderings, at Rome enjoying Papal protection, his literary activity was unflagging though genius waned as his madness increased. He is the subject of a poetic drama by Goethe. Though hampered by a gloomy supernaturalism and a thick fantastic-romantic atmosphere, when reasonably free of them Tasso is a poet of great feeling and fine creative energy, and was for a long time the most widely admired of all Italian poets later than Dante.

TENNYSON, ALFRED, 1st Lord: English poet, born at Somersby, Lincs., in 1809, died at Aldworth, Haslemere, in 1892. Son of a clergyman, he was educated at Louth Grammar School and at Cambridge. Two volumes of poems in 1827 and 1830 attracted little attention, but a third in 1832 had more success, though it was attacked by reviewers. His *Poems* published in 1842, which included among others *Ulysses*, and *Morte d'Arthur*, assured his literary reputation. In 1850 he became Poet Laureate and in this year published the famous *In Memoriam* on the death of Arthur Hallam. In addition to the many poems written after this time, including the monodrama *Maud* (1855), he also wrote three plays. Tennyson may not be the very great poet the Victorians imagined him to be; but, a master of both sharp imagery and haunting cadences, he is a much better poet than most post-Victorian criticism allowed him to be.

THACKERAY, WILLIAM MAKEPEACE: English novelist, born in Calcutta in 1811, died in London in 1863. On the death of his father, an important figure in the East India Company, he was sent home to England. After schooling at Chiswick and at Charterhouse, he spent one year at Cambridge, where he was a friend of Tennyson, Fitzgerald and Monckton Milnes. After a brief attempt to read law, he lost money heavily in journalistic ventures, speculation and gambling. He studied art for a time, and while in Paris married an Irish girl who became insane only four years later and never recovered. Returning to England in 1837, he wrote for *Fraser's Magazine* and *Punch* and had already established a reputation when he published his first important novel *Vanity Fair* (1847–48). In 1851 he won a new distinction as a lecturer, the talks comprised in *The English Humourists* and *The Four Georges* having been delivered in England

and America. The *Cornhill Magazine* was launched under his editorship in 1860, and he made many contributions to it before his sudden death. Thackeray no longer has the reputation he had during his lifetime and for some years afterwards, chiefly because his novels now seem too loosely constructed and discursive. He had a keen insight into sexual relationships but, writing for Victorian family reading, could not be reasonably frank about them. But his graceful, easy style, his sense of a wide social scene, his character drawing, still make him a highly rewarding novelist for readers not in a hurry.

THOREAU, HENRY DAVID: American poet and essayist, born at Concord (Mass.) in 1817, died there in 1862. Graduated from Harvard in 1837 and tried teaching, without success; he became a friend of Emerson, joined the Transcendental Club and wrote for *The Dial*. His famous *Walden; or, Life in the Woods*, inspired by his two-year stay in a cabin, was published in 1854, but already in 1849 he had published *A Week on the Concord and Merrimack Rivers*, while his essay *On the Duty of Civil Disobedience* in the same year was one of many contributions he made to the anti-slavery campaign. The secret of Thoreau is his highly individual and very fine prose style, which many later American and English writers have studied with advantage.

TOLSTOY, LEV NIKOLAYEVICH: Russian novelist, dramatist, religious and social philosopher, born at Yasnaya Polyana in 1828, died at Astapovo in 1910. A member of the landed aristocracy, he left the university to serve with the army, then travelled abroad before marrying and settling down on his family estate. He began his literary career in 1852; his great *War and Peace* appeared between 1862 and 1869, followed by his other masterpiece, *Anna Karenina*, 1875–77. He then experienced the 'conversion' described in *Confession*, ceased to believe in creative writing for its own sake, and gradually built up the ascetic and anarchic form of Christianity that came to be known as Tolstoyanism. But, to illustrate and teach his beliefs, he wrote some novels and many tales. Finally, wishing to live his creed, he fled from his wife and home, and collapsed in a little railway station in Central Russia. Tolstoy's gigantic prestige, as a world figure, has suffered little during the half-century since his death. He remains one of the great masters—and many people would say the greatest master—of European fiction. *War and Peace* and *Anna Karenina* are equally remarkable for their breadth and depth, their strength and their subtlety. His was a natural genius, and when it was unhampered by his religious and social convictions, it worked wonders.

TURGENEV, IVAN SERGEYEVICH: Russian author, born at Orël in 1818, died at Bougival near Paris in 1883. Of upper-class parentage, he studied in

Moscow and Berlin, where his liberal tendencies were strengthened. Having launched his literary career with a narrative poem (*Parasha*, 1843) he soon turned to prose and in 1847 published his first story in Sovremennik. This story together with others was published in book form and appears to have inspired Alexander II's determination to abolish serfdom. His first novel, *Rudin*, appeared in 1855. His one famous play, *A Month in the Country*, was belatedly produced in 1872. For the greater part of his working life his reputation abroad was greater than that of any other Russian writer. Turgenev endured a frustrated passion for the singer Mme. Viardot-Garcia, and died while following her on one of her European tours. Though more limited and less powerful than Tolstoy and Dostoyevsky, Turgenev must be considered a great novelist, and with his objectivity, his subtle presentation of character and scene, his poetic appreciation of an atmosphere, he is perhaps the greatest single influence on modern fiction.

TWAIN, MARK (pseudonym of Samuel Langhorne Clemens): American writer of novels, travel sketches and stories, born in Florida, Mo., in 1835, died at Redding, Conn., in 1910. Brought up in Hannibal, Missouri, he left school early and worked as a printer's apprentice, a steamboat pilot on the Mississippi and a frontier journalist. His humorous sketches, published in 1867, earned him initial popularity but his literary reputation was established after a journey to the Mediterranean and Holy Land, resulting in *The Innocents Abroad* (1869). Among his numerous later works are his two masterpieces of the old life on the great river, *Huckleberry Finn* and *Life on the Mississippi*. Though much of his humour and fiction is sadly 'dated', and he is no longer regarded as the representative American writer he once seemed to be, these two magnificent books will keep his name and fame alive.

UNAMUNO Y JUGO, MIGUEL DE: Spanish thinker, born at Bilbao in 1864, died at Salamanca in 1936. An important and powerful figure in Spain for over forty years, he was exiled by Primo de Rivera from 1924 to 1930, joined the republican constituent Cortes and sided with Franco at the beginning of the Civil War though later changed his views. An extensive reader in several languages, he became Professor of Greek at Salamanca where he also held the post of Rector. His works include *Del Sentimiento trágico de la vida* (1912), several novels, of which *Niebla* (1914) is a notable example, and poems, including his famous 'El Cristo de Velazquez' (1920). But it is as the philosopher of the 'tragic sense of life' that he has had the widest and strongest influence.

VALÉRY, PAUL: French poet, essayist and critic, born at Cette 1871, died in Paris 1945. Going to Paris at the age of twenty, he became influenced by

Mallarmé, but gained literary recognition initially with two prose works, *Introduction à la méthode de Léonard de Vinci* in 1895 and *Monsieur Teste* in 1906. After several unproductive years he became famous with his poem 'La jeune parque' in 1917, which was followed by a collection of poems entitled *Charmes* (1922). His subsequent writings were chiefly in prose and include *Eupalinos* (1923) and five volumes of critical essays. He is a magnificent poet, and his influence, not always good, has been important both inside and outside France.

VEGA CARPIO, LOPE FÉLIX DE: Spanish dramatist, poet and novelist, born in Madrid in 1562, died there 1635. After working for the Bishop of Avila he served as a volunteer at Terceira and later in the Armada. He became secretary to the Duke of Alba and in 1595 returned to Madrid, from which he had been banished for libel some years before. In 1605 he met the Duke of Sessa, who became his patron, and two years later entered his service. During this time he was criticised for his new dramatic form. He became a priest in 1614. In addition to the numerous plays he was a prolific writer of prose and poetry, one of his best known works being the novel *La Dorotea* (1632). Lope de Vega, whose originating genius and influence upon the Spanish Theatre are beyond doubt, has been overshadowed outside Spain, where he has never been frequently played, by the greater fame of Calderón.

VERLAINE, PAUL: French poet, born at Metz in 1844, died in Paris 1896. Of middle-class parentage, he became a municipal clerk in Paris. He started writing in 1866, bringing out *Poèmes Saturniens* in that year and *Fêtes Galantes* in 1869. He accompanied Rimbaud to Belgium and England, but was imprisoned between 1873 and 1875 as a result of wounding him in a quarrel. The famous *Romances sans Paroles* appeared in 1874. He worked as a schoolmaster in England and France, but finally succumbed to alcohol and debauchery, becoming destitute and spending his last years in hospital, though continuing to write poetry until the end. He had a natural vein of pure lyricism, very rare in French poetry, and his work strongly influenced English and other poets outside France, especially during the 1890s.

VOLTAIRE (pseudonym of François-Marie Arouet): French writer, born in Paris 1694, died there in 1778. Son of a notary, he was educated by the Jesuits and studied law. His first successful tragedy, *Oedipe*, was produced in 1718 following imprisonment in the Bastille. A second incarceration was followed by several years spent in England (1726–29), which influenced him greatly. Returning to France he wrote *Charles XII* (1731), *Lettres sur les Anglais* (1733–34) and several plays. Through the influence of Mme. de Pompadour he became Historiographer Royal and a Gentleman of the Bedchamber in 1745. He was elected an Academician in 1746. He spent from 1751 to 1753 in Berlin at the invitation of Frederick II of Prussia, then settled near Geneva, writing *Candide* in 1759. His latter years were spent attacking oppression and injustice; he was acclaimed as a hero when in 1778 he took his last play *Irene* to Paris for production. Not quite in the first rank in his various capacities as a poet, dramatist, story-teller, historian, thinker, Voltaire yet remains a tremendous figure, dominating eighteenth-century Western Europe, and immensely valuable as a great liberating influence.

WELLS, HERBERT GEORGE: English novelist and social philosopher, born at Bromley in 1866, died in London 1946. As a boy he was apprenticed to a draper, read widely, then turned to teaching, took a degree in science and soon made a name as a writer with the publication in 1895 of his scientific romance *The Time Machine*. This was followed in 1898 by *The War of the Worlds* and others in the same vein, which subsequently developed into the prophetic books dealing with social philosophy such as *A Modern Utopia* (1905). He wrote a number of novels between 1896 and 1927, of which *Kipps, Mr. Polly* and *Tono Bungay* are particularly memorable; other works include *The Outline of History* (1920) and *Experiment in Autobiography* (1934). His training and outlook were scientific; his temperament and natural genius were literary; and this difference led to a certain strain and confusion in him; but he is certainly one of the world figures of his time.

WHITMAN, WALT[ER]: American poet and journalist, born at West Hills, L.I., N.Y., in 1819, died in Camden, N.J., in 1892. Brought up in Brooklyn, he left school early and worked as office boy and printer's devil, then taught for a time in country schools, finally taking up journalism in New York. His first literary work of importance, a pamphlet of twelve poems, entitled *Leaves of Grass*, appeared in 1855 and was subsequently revised several times and more poems added to each new edition. During the Civil War, when tending the wounded in Washington, he wrote the famous elegy on the death of Lincoln. He entered government service but in 1873 became paralysed and retired to Camden. With all his faults—and he has many—Whitman is a great poet, an original and essentially American master.

WOLFE, THOMAS CLAYTON: American novelist, born at Asheville, N.C., in 1900, died at Baltimore, Md., in 1938. Educated at the University of North Carolina and at Harvard, where he wrote plays, he travelled abroad and then taught English at New York University. His novels—*Look Homeward, Angel*; *Of Time and the River*; *The Web and the Rock*; *You Can't Go Home Again*—contain a great deal of thinly disguised autobiography, have many faults of construction and manner, but their best scenes have exceptional vitality, force, depth.

WOOLF, VIRGINIA (*née* Stephen): English novelist and essayist, born in London 1882, committed suicide in the River Ouse in 1941. She was one of the most important members of the highly influential Bloomsbury Group, writing reviews and two novels before manifesting her peculiarly individual art as a novelist. Her works also included several volumes of essays and two biographies. Her finest novels are exquisite examples of the deeply subjective, interior-monologue method in fiction.

WORDSWORTH, WILLIAM: English poet, born at Cockermouth in 1770, died at Grasmere in 1850. The son of an attorney, he enjoyed a country boyhood in the Lake District, and was educated at Hawkshead grammar school and Cambridge. A visit to France in 1791 made him an enthusiastic republican, but the later excesses of the Revolution caused an extreme revulsion of feeling. After living briefly in Dorset with his sister Dorothy (who was to be his lifelong companion) they moved to Alfoxden, Somerset, where they were neighbours of Coleridge. Coleridge confirmed Wordsworth in his determination to become a poet, and together they wrote *Lyrical Ballads* (first edition 1798, second with the famous *Preface* 1800). Having already started *The Prelude*, which was not to be published until after his death, he and Dorothy returned to the Lake District to live in 1799. He married his cousin Mary Hutchinson some three years later. All his subsequent work was written while they lived very modestly at Dove Cottage, Grasmere, and then rather more spaciously at near-by Rydal Mount. He was made Poet Laureate in 1843. Wordsworth wrote a great deal of conscientious but totally uninspired verse, but in a comparatively small number of whole poems, together with some heightened passages in others, a strong and entirely original poetic genius is clearly evident.

YEATS, WILLIAM BUTLER: Irish poet and dramatist, born in Dublin 1865, died at Roquebrune in 1939. His father, a Dublin painter, encouraged his talent for poetry, and he was brought up in Sligo, and educated in London and Dublin, where he studied art. He spent some time in London, where he founded the Rhymers Club with Ernest Rhys. His first important collection of poems, *The Wanderings of Oisin*, appeared in 1889 and established him as an important influence in Irish literature. On returning to Ireland he became one of the leaders of the Irish Literary Movement, and he founded the Abbey Theatre with Lady Gregory, directing it and writing many plays for it. He was awarded the Nobel Prize in 1923 and was an Irish Free State senator from 1922 to 1928. He is one of the few poets whose work gains in power and depth with age; and he is not only Ireland's greatest poet but certainly the greatest poet, writing in English, of the whole modern period.

ZOLA, ÉMILE ÉDOUARD CHARLES ANTOINE: French novelist, born in Paris 1840 and died there in 1902. Son of an engineer, he was brought up at Aix-en-Provence and was a friend of Cézanne. He returned to Paris in 1858, where, having concluded his studies, he worked with the booksellers Hachette, became a journalist and art critic, strongly supporting Manet and the Impressionists. His first literary success, *Contes à Ninon* (1864), was followed by a great number of novels, short stories and critical writings, in particular the group of twenty novels entitled *Les Rougon-Macquart* and two other groups, *Les Trois Villes* (1894–98) and *Les Quatres Evangiles* (1899–1902). As a result of his active defence of Dreyfus and the publication of *J'accuse* in 1898 he was exiled and lived in England for some time. As the acknowledged leader of what we might call 'documentary' naturalism in fiction, Zola enjoyed enormous prestige in his lifetime and was a world-wide influence. Since then he has been either neglected or under-valued by criticism. His work is unequal and he can be very bad, but his best novels are powerful and memorable works.

Index

A Christmas Carol, 255
A Doll's House, 288
A Farewell to Arms, 373, 435
A Hero of our Time, 177
A Lear of the Steppes, 245
A Lost Lady, 428
A Midsummer Night's Dream, 30, 38
A Month in the Country, 245, 293
A New Way to Pay Old Debts, 34
A Nobleman's Nest, 245
A Passage to India, 355, 356
À Rebours, 258
A Sentimental Journey, 93, 95
A Shropshire Lad, 322
A Vision, 403
A Voice from the Chorus, 399
Aakjær, Jeppe, 336
Abbey of Thélème, 21
Abbey Theatre, 380, 381
Abingdon, 30
Académie Française, 59
Adams, Henry Brooks, 357, 358
Addison, Joseph, 55, 75, 96
Ade, George, 357
Adler, Alfred, 315
Adolphe, 162
AE, 403
Æsthetic Movement, 193, 197, 214, 402
Africa, 42
Agnosticism, 20
Ahab, Captain, 238
Aksakov, 242
Alarcón, Pedro Antonio de, 267

Alberti, Leon Battista, 11
Albertine, 411
Alceste, 71
Alchemy, 401
Alemán, Mateo, 44
Alembert, Jean le Rond d', 99, 107
Alexander VI, 4
All Quiet on the Western Front, 373, 374
Allegory, 7, 12
Alleyn, Edward, 32
Altruism, 16
Alvarez Quintero (brothers), Serafin and Joaquín, 379
Amelia, 91
America, xi, 42, 155, 156, 211-4, 234-42, 356-62
America, 418
American Revolution, 98
Aminta, 14
An American Tragedy, 358
An Apologie of Raymond Sebond, 24
Anarchism, 21
Anatol Playlets, 379
And Quiet Flows the Don, 423
Andersen, Hans Christian, 184
Anderson, Maxwell, 373, 388
Anderson, Sherwood, 431, 432, 433
Andreas, 393
Andrey, 253
Andreyev, Leonid Nikolaevich, 363
Ann Vickers, 430
Anna Karenina, 251, 254, 262
Anna Karenina, 251, 253, 254, 255, 256

Anne, Queen, 57, 96, 226
Annensky, 397
Anouilh, Jean, 388
Anti-Clericalism, 20
Anti-Goeze, 80
'Antilha', 8
Antiochus, 67
Antoine, André, 281, 282
Antonelli, Luigi, 386
Antony, 170
Antony and Cleopatra, 39
Anzengruber, Ludwig, 267
Apollinaire, Guillaume, 371
Arcadia, 9
Arden, Forest of, 278
Aretino, Pietro, 13, 14
Ariel, 151
Ariosto, Lodovico, 13, 15
Aristotle, 64, 79
Armada, Spanish, 26, 27, 42, 50
Arms and the Man, 351
Arnim, Ludwig Joachim von, 126, 127
Arnold, Matthew, 134, 188, 210
Arquebus, 13
Arthur, 6, 7
Artsybashev, Mikhail Petrovich, 364
As You Desire Me, 387
Ascham, Roger, 27
Ashenden, 372
Asia, xi
Aspects of the Novel, 356
Athalie, 66
Atheism, 6
Atheists, 27
Athenäum, 126
Atlantic, 8
Aubigné, Jean Henri Merle d', 19
Auden, Wystan Hugh, 388, 404, 408, 409
Auerbach, Erich, 189, 190, 267
Augier, Emile, 279, 280
Aupick, General, 216
Austen, Jane, 143, 154
Australia, 390, 424
Autobiography, 268

Autos Sacramentales, 43, 44
Axel, 258
Azores, 8
Aztecs, 42

Babbitt, 430
Babbitt, Professor Irving, 150
Babel, Isaac, 423
Bacon, Francis, 28, 34, 54
Bahr, Hermann, 378
Balmont, Konstantin Dmitrievich, 397
Baltimore, 212, 429, 431
Balzac, Honoré de, 87, 163, 165, 167–9, 222, 224, 225, 249, 260
Bancroft, Sir Squire, 277, 278
Banville, Théodore de, 216
'Barbarians', 15
Barbey d'Aurévilly, Jules, 258
Barbusse, Henri, 371
Barker, George, 404
Baroja, Pío, 367
Barrès, Maurice, 337
Barrett, Elizabeth, 209
Barrie, Sir James Matthew, 380
Basques, 310
Bastille, 99, 100, 101, 109
Bataille, Félix Henry, 337
Battle of Books, 58
Baudelaire, Charles Pierre, 156, 157, 171, 188–90, 193, 207, 214–7, 219, 228
Bawdy, 12, 21, 22
Bayle, Pierre, 59
Bazarov, 243
Beaumarchais, Pierre Augustin Caron de, 73, 74
Beaumont, Francis, 34
Becque, Henry François, 281
Beer-Hofmann, Richard, 379
Beethoven, Ludwig van, 125, 340
Before Dawn, 282
Bel Ami, 258
Belinsky, Vissarion Grigorievich, 175, 178, 326
Bellay, Joachim du, 18, 19

Belloc, Hilaire, 344, 345
Bembo, Pietro, 13
Benavente, Jacinto, 379
Benda, Julien, 307
Benelli, Sem, 386
Benevolence, 16
Bennett, Enoch Arnold, 353–5, 425
Béranger, Pierre Jean de, 165
Bérénice, 67
Bergman, Hjalmar, 384
Bergson, Henri, 301, 306, 347
Berlin, 79, 282
Berlioz, Louis Hector, 161, 334
Berlitz School, 367
Bernard, Jean Jacques, 385, 386
Bernhardt, Sarah, 274
Bernstein, Henry Léon Gustave Charles, 337, 436
Betti, Ugo, 386
Between the Acts, 426
Beyond Good and Evil, 189, 204
Beyond Human Power, 285
Bible, 3, 246
Bierce, Ambrose, 273
Bildungsroman, 134, 135, 420, 421, 427
Billy Budd, 237
Biographia Literaria, 149
Bishop Blougram's Apology, 209, 210
Bizet, Georges, 257
Bjørnson, Bjørnstjerne, 267, 285, 342
Blake, William, 135, 140, 141, 152, 404
Bleak House, 232
Blois, 18
Blok, Aleksandri Aleksandrovich, 220, 397–400, 402
Bloom, 417
Blunden, Edmund, 372
Boccaccio, Giovanni, 12, 13, 80
Bodmer, Johann Jakob, 79
Böhme, Jakob, 140
Boileau-Despréaux, Nicolas, 59, 66, 79
Bolkonsky, Prince, 253
Bontempelli, Massimo, 386
Book of Genesis, 194

Book of Job, 53
Books, xii, 3, 4, 7
Booth, Edwin, 274
Border Ballads, 144
Borgia, Cesare, 15
Bossuet, Jacques Bénigne, 59
Boston, Mass., 188, 211, 212, 236, 272
Boswell, James, 96, 143
Boucher, François, 99, 108
Boule de Suif, 258
Bourget, Paul, 258
Bouvard et Pécuchet, 259, 261
Bowen, Elizabeth, 427
Bowra, Sir Cecil Maurice, 399
Brahms, Johannes, 125
Brand, 287
'Brazil', 8, 9
Brecht, Bertolt, 382, 383
Brentano, Clemens, 126, 127
Breton, André, 324
Bridges, Robert, 404
Bridie, James, 388
Brieux, Eugène, 282, 337
Brobdingnag, 58
Brontë Sisters, 188, 225, 226
Brook Farm, 234
Brooke, Rupert, 372
Brookfield, Mrs., 226
Brooklyn, 212
Brooks, Van Wyck, 240, 356
Brown, Charles Brockden, 155
Browne, Sir Thomas, 153
Browning, Robert, 188, 209, 210
Brunswick, Duke of, 80
Brussels, 45, 188
Bryusov, Valeri Yakovlevich, 397
Buddenbrooks, 362, 420
Buddhism, 197
Buffon, Georges Louis Leclerc de, 99
Bulgakov, 384
Bullock, William A., 187, 188, 192
Bunin, Ivan Alekseevich, 363
Bunyan, John, 83
Burbage, James, 32

Burgundy, 6
Burney, Fanny, 154
Burns, Robert, 139
Butler, Samuel, 270, 347
Byely, Andrei, 397
Byron, George Gordon, 91, 93, 117, 143, 145–8, 152, 171, 176, 177, 178, 206, 209, 442

CABOT, JOHN, 8
Caesar, C. Julius, 32, 38, 349
Cagliostro, Alessandro di, 114
Cahiers de la Quinzaine, 371
Caillavet, Madame de, 339
Calas, Jean, 106
Calderón de la Barca, Pedro, 43, 44
California, 383
Calvin, Jean, 19
Camoëns, Luiz Vaz de, 42
Canada, 390
Candide, 105, 106
Cannibals, 8
Cape of Good Hope, 8
Čapek, Karel, 388
Capitalism, 28
Captain Brassbound's Conversion, 349
Captain Maxim Maximych, 178
Captain Singleton, 86
Carducci, Giosué, 342
Carlyle, Thomas, 4, 108, 126, 188, 190, 198, 199, 201
Carmen, 170
Carnap, Rudolf, 314
Caron, Pierre Augustin, 73
Case of Sergeant Grischa, 374
Castiglione, Baldassare, 13
Castilian, 43
Cathedrals, 45
Cather, Willa, 428, 429
Catherine of Russia, 100
Catholics, 27, 40
Cato, 75
Catskill Mountains, 155
Caucasus, 177, 178

Cavalry, 13
Cave paintings, xii
Caxton, William, 3
Celestina, 44
Célimène, 71
Céline, Louis-Ferdinand, 414, 415
Celtic, 6
Censorship, 4, 173
Cervantes Saavedra, Miguel de, 22, 43–6, 48–50, 54, 83, 84, 93, 129, 255, 330, 446
Chambers, Ephraim, 106
Chamisso, Adelbert von, 127
Chaplin, Charles Spencer, 332, 374
Chapman, George, 33
Charlemagne, 6
Charles II, 74
Charles V, 13
Charlus, 413
Charmes, 331
Chateaubriand, François René de, 117, 161, 162, 163
Châtelet, Gabrielle Émilie, Mme du, 101
Chatterton, 165
Chehov, Anton Pavlovich, 245, 278, 288, 293–7, 364, 365, 378, 379, 382, 384
Chesterton, Gilbert Keith, 344, 345, 348
Chiarelli, Luigi, 386
Chile, 389
China, 3
Chinon, 18, 25
Chivalry, 6, 44, 46
Choiseul, Étienne François de, 114
Chopin, Frédéric François, 161, 169
Christabel, 150
Christendom, 5
Church, 49
Church, Catholic, 14, 43, 69
Churchill, John, Duke of Marlborough, 117
Cinq-Mars, 165
City-states, 16
Civilisation, 9, 21

Clarissa; or the History of a Young Lady, 87–90
Claudine, 341
Clayhanger, 353
Cléante, 71
Clemens, Samuel Langhorne, 239
Cleopatra, 28, 39
Cobbett, William, 154
Cocteau, Jean, 378
Code of Conduct, 16
Coleridge, Samuel Taylor, 22, 88, 91, 126, 143, 147–50, 152
Colette, Sidonie-Gabrielle, 341, 342
Collins, Wilkie, 268
Colloquia, 12
Cologne, 3
Colonel Jack, 86
Colum, Mary, 418
Columbine, 72
Columbus, Christopher, 8
Comédie Française, 72, 73
Comédie Italienne, 72
Commedia dell' Arte, 72
Common sense, 48
Commonwealth, 74
Commynes, 6
Compagnie des Quinze, 388
Comte, Auguste, 200, 201
Conchubar, 402
Concord, Mass., 197, 198, 211
Confessions of an English Opium-Eater, 153
Congreve, William, 70, 75, 76
Conquest of Happiness, 312
Conrad, Joseph, 351, 352
Constant, Benjamin, 162, 412
Conversations with Eckermann, 134
Cook, Captain, 86
Cooper, Fenimore, 155, 156
Copenhagen, 78, 182
Coppée, François 216
Corbière, Edouard Joachim, 217
Cordelia, 39
Corelli, Marie, 438
Corneille, Pierre, 44, 65, 66, 68, 79

Counter-Reformation, 10, 14, 19
Courteline, Georges, 337
Cozzens, James Gould, 433
Craft, 16
Crainquebille, 339
Crane, Hart, 405
Crane, Stephen, 273, 357
Crébillon, Prosper Jolyot, Sieur de Crais-Billon, 68
Crébillon, Claude Prosper Jolyot de, 84
Creeds, 6
Creevey, Thomas, 154
Crime and Punishment, 188, 248, 249
Criticism, xiii, 19
Critics, xii, xiii, 19, 20
Croce, Benedetto, 308, 309, 310
Crommelynck, Fernand, 385
Cruelty, 16
Cuchulain, 402
Culture, xi, xiii, 20
Cummings, Edward Estlin, 373
Curel, François de, 282, 337
Cyclopaedia, or an Universal Dictionary of Arts and Sciences, 106
Cynicism, 21
Cyrano de Bergerac, 284

DADA, 323, 324
Dalin, Olof von, 78
Dance of Death, 399
Dance of Death, 6
D'Annunzio, Gabriele, 367
Dante Alighieri, 13, 22, 40, 134, 338
Darwin, Charles Robert, 194, 196, 205
Daudet, Alphonse, 256, 257
David Copperfield, 189, 232
Day of the Locust, 434
Day with Conrad Green, 431
Days of the Turbins, 384
De Quincey, Thomas, 153
Dead Souls, 178, 179
Death, 49
Death in Venice, 362, 420
Decameron, 12

Deceit, 16

Decline and Fall, 427

Decline and Fall of the Roman Empire, 104, 143

Decline of the West, 310

Dee, John, 28

Degas, Hilaire Germain Edgar, 260

Dehumanization of Art, 331

Deirdre, 381

Defoe, Daniel, 86, 87

Dekker, Eduard Douwes, 267

Dekker, Thomas, 33

Delacroix, Ferdinand Victor Eugène, 161

Del Sentimiento Trágico de la Vida, 310

Denis Duval, 228

Denmark, 78

Departmental Ditties, 342

Der Grüne Heinrich, 267

Der Rosenkavalier, 394

Derby, Earl of, 34

Des Grieux, 85

Descartes, René, 54, 60, 392

Desire Under the Elms, 387, 388

Dewey, John, 307

Diaghilev, Sergei Pavlovich, 317

Dias, Bartolomeo, 8

Dickens, Charles, 35, 95, 179, 180, 188, 190, 201, 212, 222, 224, 225, 226, 228–34, 246, 249, 255, 260, 267, 268, 269, 303, 332, 367

Dickinson, Emily, 212

Dictatorships, 17

Diderot, Denis, 73, 87, 89, 90, 96, 98–100, 106–10, 116

Die Heimat, 283

Disenchantment, 372

Disraeli, Benjamin, 201

Dodsworth, 430

Don Carlos, 132

Don Juan, 44

Don Juan, 147

Don Quixote, 45–50, 83, 84, 137, 261, 330

Donne, John, 29

Dordogne, 18, 25

Dos Passos, John Roderigo, 433

Dostoyevsky, Fëdor Mikhailovich, 180, 188, 230, 244, 246–51, 261, 268

Dover Beach, 210

Dr. Faustus, 420

Dr. Jekyll and Mr. Hyde, 272

Dr. Zhivago, 397

Dreigroschenoper, 383

Dreiser, Theodore Herman Albert, 273, 358, 359

Dreyfus affair, 265, 339

Drottningholm, 63

Dryden, John, 75, 79

Du Bartas, Guillaume, 19

Dublin, 323, 333, 349

Dubliners, 417

Duhamel, Georges, 371

Dulcinea, 48

Dumas, Alexandre *père*, 165, 169, 215, 283

Dumas, Alexandre *fils*, 169, 279, 280

Du Ryer, 65

Duse, Eleonora, 74, 376

Dutch, 3

Ecclesiastical Sonnets, 149

Echegaray, José, 342, 379

Eckermann, Johann Peter, 135, 136

Edgeworth, Maria, 154

Edward IV, 7

Egmont, 134

Eichendorff, Joseph von, 127

El Mágico Prodigioso, 44

Elegies, 396

Elektra, 394

Eliot, Thomas Stearns, 133, 134, 331, 333, 388, 405–9

Eliot, George, 201, 223, 269, 270

Elyot, Sir Thomas, 27

Elizabeth I, 12, 26, 27, 28, 34

Elizabethan Age, 26, 27, 29–34, 135

Elizabethan Theatre, 74

Ellis, Havelock, 263

Elmer Gantry, 430

Emerson, Ralph Waldo, 188, 197, 198, 211, 235

Emilia Galotti, 80

Encyclopaedists, 96, 99, 106, 108, 109, 113

Endymion, 152

Engels, Friedrich, 107, 201, 202

England, 3, 12, 15, 26, 101

Enlightenment, The, 98–110

Erasmus, Desiderius, 12, 14, 20, 102

Erewhon, 270, 347

Eros, 12, 21, 215, 236

Esmond, 226, 227, 228

Esther Waters, 353

Etherege, George, 75

Ethics, 16

Eucken, Rudolf Christoph, 362

Eugene Onegin, 176

Eugénie Grandet, 169

Euripides, 87

Europe, xi, 3, 5, 12, 15, 18, 42

Evolution, 16, 194, 196

Ewald, Johannes, 78

Exemplary Novels, 45

Exhibition of 1851, 208

Experiment in Autobiography, 346

Expressionism, 381, 382, 383

Failures, 385

Falstaff, 39, 69

Family Reunion, 388

Fanaticism, 19, 20

Fantasio, 172

Far From the Madding Crowd, 272

Farquhar, George, 75, 76

Fathers and Sons, 243, 245

Faulkner, William, 323, 373, 431, 433, 436–8

Faust, 134, 135, 137

Fénelon, François de Salignac de La Mothe-, 59

Ferdinand of Aragon, 17

Ferney, 101

Ferrier, Susan, 154

Feudalism, 28

Feudalistic wars, 5

Feuillet, Octave, 258

Fichte, Johann Gottlieb, 126

Fiction, 7

Fielding, Henry, 87, 90–5

Films, 377, 378

Finance, 49

Finnegans Wake, 416, 417, 418

First Love, 244

Fitzgerald, Francis Scott Key, 373, 431, 433, 434, 439

Fitzgerald, Robert David, 390

Flaubert, Gustave, 188, 190, 223, 225, 256, 257, 259–62

Fletcher, Phineas, 34

Florence, 10, 11, 13, 14, 15, 17, 50

Florio, 24

Folklore, 7, 127

Fontainas, André, 220

Fontenelle, Bernard Le Bovier de, 59

Fonvizin, Denis Ivanovich, 78

Ford, John, 34, 237

Ford, Ford Madox, 371

Forsyte Saga, 354

Forster, Edward Morgan, 355, 356

Forster, John, 229

Fort, Paul, 220

Fouqué, Friedrich Heinrich Karl La Motte-, 127

Fournier, Alain, 371

Fragonard, Jean Honoré, 108

France, Anatole, 102, 161, 223, 259, 329, 336–40

France, 3, 6, 12, 18, 19, 22, 25, 54, 72, 78

Francis I, 12, 18

Frankenstein, 151, 202

Frederick the Great, 100, 101

Frederick the Great, 188

Freedom and Organisation, 312

Freie Bühne, 282

French, 3, 18

French Revolution, 98, 102, 143, 159, 199

French Revolution, 199

Fréron, Élie Catherine, 109
Freud, Sigmund, 246, 288, 315, 323
Freytag, Gustav, 267
From Morn to Midnight, 382
Frost, Robert, 405

GALATEA, 44
Galileo Galilei, 54
Galsworthy, John, 354, 355, 380
Gargantua, 21
Garine, 415
Gaul, 22
Gautier, Théophile, 161, 165, 170, 171, 193, 216
Gawaine and the Green Knight, 7
Gay, John, 76
Genius, 20, 21
Genoa, 8, 14
Geoffrin, Marie Thérèse, 98, 100
George, Stefan, 126, 220, 393-5, 400
Germans, 3, 4, 14
Germany, 3
Germinal, 263, 264, 265
Germinie Lacerteux, 257
Gerusalemme Liberata, 14
Ghosts, 288
Gibbon, Edward, 91, 104, 143
Gide, André Paul Guillaume, 164, 263, 393, 413, 414
Gil Blas, 50, 73, 83, 84, 95
Gilkin, Iwan, 220
Giono, Jean, 414
Giraud, Albert, 220
Giraudoux, Jean, 385
Gjellerup, Karl, 366
Glasgow, Ellen, 357
Goa, 8
God, 5
Godwin, Mary, 151
Godwin, William, 150, 151
Goebbels, Joseph, 16, 204
Goethe, Johann Wolfgang von, 80, 83, 102, 108, 122-38, 146, 155, 172, 227, 318, 340, 442

Goeze, Johann Melchior, 80
Gogarty, Oliver St. John, 403
Gogol, Nikolay Vasilyevich, 173, 175, 178-80, 242
Gold, 8, 9
'Golden Age', 43
Goldoni, Carlo, 74
Goldsmith, Oliver, 76, 95, 96
Goncharov, Ivan Aleksandrovich, 242
Goncourt, Edmond and Jules de, 192, 243, 256
Gonne, Maud, 402, 403
Good faith, 16, 17
Göring, Hermann, 204
Gorky, Maxim, 252, 362-7, 423
Gothic (design), 4, 5, 6,
Goths, 14
Gotthelf, Jeremias, 266, 267
Gottsched, Johann Christoph, 79
Götz von Berlichingen, 124, 134
Goya y Lucientes, Francisco José de, 199, 413
Granville-Barker, Harley, 380
Grapes of Wrath, 433
Graves, Robert, 372
Gregory, Lady Augusta, 380
Greek, 4, 7, 40
Greene, Graham, 427
Greene, Maurice, 29
Grein, Jacob Thomas, 282
Greuze, Jean Baptiste, 107
Greville, Charles Cavendish Fulke, 154
Griboyedov, Aleksandr Sergeevich, 175
Grillparzer, Franz, 135
Grieg, Nordahl, 384
Grimm, Friedrich Melchior von, 107, 108
Grock, 368
Growth of the Soil, 367
Grub Street, 95, 96
Guard of Honour, 433
Gulliver's Travels, 57, 58, 86
Gurdjieff, 368
Gutenberg, Johann, 3

Guzmán de Alfarache, 44–5
Gyllenborg, Carl, 78

Hail and Farewell, 353
Halévy, Ludovic, 279
Hamann, Johann Georg, 122
Hamburg National Theatre, 79
Hamlet, 28, 36–9, 89, 122, 137, 275, 276, 330
Hamsun, Knut, 366, 367
Hannele, 283
Harding, President W. G., 429
Hardy, Thomas, 223, 270–2
Harlequinade, 72, 73
Harris, Frank, 351
Harte, Bret, 273
Hašek, Jaroslav, 374
Hasenclever, Walter, 382
Hauff, Wilhelm, 127
Hauptmann, Gerhart, 282, 283, 362
Hawthorne, Nathaniel, 188, 225, 234–9
Haydon, Benjamin Robert, 155
Hazlitt, William, 142, 143, 147, 153
He who Gets Slapped, 363
Heart of Darkness, 352
Heathcliff, 225
Hebrew, 4
Hedda Gabler, 286
Hegel, Georg Wilhelm Friedrich, 126, 305, 311
Heiberg, Gunnar, 384
Heine, Heinrich, 114, 127, 130, 172, 207
Hellman, Lillian, 388
Héloïse and Abélard, 353
Helvétius, Claude Adrien, 98
Hemingway, Ernest, 323, 373, 429, 432, 433, 435, 436
Henley, William Ernest, 170
Henriette, 72
Henry IV, 387
Henry V, 39
Henry VIII, 27
Henry, O., 357
Heptameron, 12

Herder, Johann Gottfried von, 122, 123
Heresy, 20
Heritage of Symbolism, 399
Hermann and Dorothea, 134
Hernani, 159, 164, 165, 167
Hervieu, Paul Ernest, 282, 337
Hesse, Hermann, 126, 331, 420
Heyse, Paul von, 267, 362
Heywood, Thomas, 34
Himmler, Heinrich, 204
Hinduism, 197
Hippius (Zinaida Nikolaevna Merezhkovskaya), 397
Historians, 16, 20
History, xii, 17
History of Charles XII, 103
History of the Life of the late Mr. Jonathan Wild the Great, 91
Hitler, Adolf, 16, 204, 388
Hobbes, Thomas, 54
Hoffmann, Ernst Theodor Wilhelm, 127, 128
Hofmannsthal, Hugo von, 379, 393, 394
Hogarth, Catherine, 230
Hogarth, Mary, 230
Hogarth, William, 88
Holbach, Baron Paul Henri Dietrich d', 96, 98–100
Holberg, Ludvig, 78
Hölderlin, Johann Christian Friedrich, 126, 135, 137
Holmes, Oliver Wendell, 211
Homer, 87, 91, 134, 144, 255, 338
Hopkins, Gerard Manley, 404
Hôtel de Bourgogne, 63
Housman, Alfred Edward, 322
Houyhnhnms, 58
Howard, Sidney, 387
Howard's End, 355, 356
Howells, William Dean, 188, 272, 363
Hugo, Victor-Marie, 22, 159, 160, 161, 164–7, 172, 206, 215, 227, 255, 283
Huguenots, 19
Human Comedy, The, 168

Humanism, 15, 20
Hume, David, 103, 104, 123
Humorist, 20
Humour, 20, 21
Humphry Clinker, 95
Hungary, 385
Hunt, Leigh, 142, 153
Huxley, Aldous, 427
Huysmans, Joris Karl, 258, 259
Hyperion, 137
Hypocrisy, 16

I Promessi Sposi, 181
Iago, 40
Ibsen, Henrik Johan, 50, 77, 190, 278, 282, 284–91, 294, 295, 342, 347, 378, 379, 384
Iceland, 389
Idealism, 12, 44
Idols, 9
Idyll, 44
Ilf, Ilya Arnoldovich, 423
Imaginary Conversations, 154
Imperial Palace, 353
In Praise of Idleness, 312
Incas, 42
Independent Theatre, 282
India, 42
Indies, 8
Individualism, 6
Industrial Revolution, 115, 141, 199
Insect Play, 388
Intimations of Immortality, 148
Iphigenia, 134
Irving, Henry, 274
Irving, Washington, 155
Isherwood, Christopher, 388
It Can't Happen Here, 430
Italians, 3, 10, 14, 72, 73, 180, 181, 386
Italy, 3, 5, 7, 10, 12, 13, 15, 18, 19, 26
Ivanov, Vyacheslav Ivanovich, 397
Ivory, 8

JACOBEAN AGE, 15, 33, 56, 237

Jammes, Francis, 337
Jaurès, Jean Léon, 339
Jacobsen, Jens Peter, 267
Jacques the Fatalist, 108
James, Henry, 223, 228, 239, 241, 273, 307, 357–62
James, William, 307, 308
James I, 26, 34
Jane Eyre, 225
Jane Shore, 75
Japanese Puppet Theatre, 291
Jean Christophe, 340
Jenny, 366
Jeffers, Robinson, 405
Jesuits, 19, 60, 99, 107
Jewett, Sarah Orne, 428
Jews, 43
Johnson, Dr. Samuel, 58, 79, 96, 123
Jonson, Benjamin, 33, 56, 75
Joseph Andrews, 90, 91
Jourdain, 72
Journal of the Plague Year, 86
Journalism, 13
Journey to the End of Night, 415
Journey's End, 373
Jowitt, Benjamin, 307
Joyce, James, 50, 323, 324, 333, 352, 367, 377, 415–8
Julius II, 13
Jung, Carl Gustav, 140, 288, 292, 315, 323, 324, 431
Juno and the Paycock, 381
Jutland, 336

KAFKA, FRANZ, 331, 333, 337, 352, 377, 419–21
Kaiser, Georg, 382
Karl August, Duke of Saxe-Weimar, 125
Kangaroo, 424
Kant, Immanuel, 99, 117, 126
Karamazov, Alyosha, 247
Karamazov, Ivan, 247
Karatayev, 253
Karenin, 254

Katayev, Valentin Petrovich, 384, 423
Kean, 170
Keats, John, 151–3, 208, 209
Keller, Gottfried, 234, 267
Kepler, Johannes, 54
Kerner, Andreas Justinus, 127
Keynes, John Maynard, 312
Kierkegaard, Søren Aabye, 182, 183
Kim, 343, 344
Kinck, Hans, 384
Kingsley, Charles, 201
Kipling, Rudyard, 194, 220, 272, 317, 319,
    342–4
Kipps, 345
Kitty, 254
Kleist, Heinrich von, 127, 128
Klinger, Friedrich von, 123, 136
Knowledge, 20
Königsberg, 122
Kornfeld, Paul, 382
Kristin Lavransdatter, 366
Krog, Helge, 384
Kubla Khan, 150
Kuprin, Aleksandr Ivanovich, 363
Kutuzov, 253

L'Arlésienne, 257
L'Assommoir, 264
La Bruyère, Jean de, 60, 133
La Chapelle, Jean de, 68
La Chaussée, Nivelle de, 73
La Coscienza di Zeno, 367
La Cousine Bette, 169
La Curée, 265
La Dame aux Camélias, 169, 279
La Débâcle, 264
La Fayette, Madame de, 83
La Fontaine, Jean de, 59
La Fosse, Antoine de, 68
La Grange-Chancel, Joseph de, 68
L'Île des Pingouins, 337, 339
Le Légataire Universel, 73
La Légende de Saint Julien l'Hospitalier, 259
La Locandiera, 74

La Mancha, 48
La Mettrie, Julien Offroy de, 100
La Parisienne, 281
La Princesse de Clèves, 83
La Révolte des Anges, 337, 340
La Rochefoucauld, Duc François de, 60,
    83, 133
La Tentation de Saint Antoine, 259
La Trahison des Clercs, 307
La Vida es Sueño, 44
Labiche, Eugène, 279
Labrador, 8
Laforgue, Jules, 217, 218
Lagerkvist, Par, 384
Lagerlöf, Selma, 366
Lamarck, Jean Baptiste Pierre Antoine de
    Monet, 348
Lamartine, Alphonse Marie Louis de, 161,
    164
Lamb, Charles, 142, 153
Lancaster, 6
Landor, Walter Savage, 153
Landsknechte, 13
Lanier, Sidney, 211
Laokoön, 79
L'Après-midi d'un Faune, 188
Laputa, 58
Larbaud, Valéry, 367
Lardner, Ring, 431, 432
Lascaux, xii
Latin, 3
Latin Quarter, 165
Laughter, 307
Lavedan, Henri Léon Émile, 337
Lawrence, David Herbert, 292, 424, 425
Laxness, Halldór, 389
Lazarillo de Tormes, 44
Le Bon, Gustave, 304
Le Cid, 44, 65
Le Cousin Pons, 169
Le Diable Boiteux, 83, 84
L'Éducation sentimentale, 188, 259, 260
Le Feu, 371
Le Grand Meaulnes, 371

Leibniz, Gottfried Wilhelm von, 54, 99, 105
Le Malade Imaginaire, 69
Le Mangeur de Rêves, 385
Le Menteur, 66
Lenz, Jakob Michael Reinhold, 123, 136
Le Paradoxe sur le Comédien, 108
Le Père Goriot, 169
Le Voyage de Monsieur Perrichon, 279
Lear, 38, 39, 89
Learning, 4
Leaves of Grass, 188, 189, 207, 212, 238
Lecouvreur, Adrienne, 63
Légende des Siècles, 166
Leigh, Augusta, 147
Leipzig, 79
Lenin, 175, 324, 325
Lenormand, Henri René, 385
Leo X, 13
Leonov, Leonid, 423
Leopardi, Giacomo, Count, 180, 197
Lepanto, 44
Lerberghe, 220
Lermontov, Mikhail Yuryevich, 173, 175, 177, 178
Les Chimères, 171
Les Corbeaux, 281
Les Dieux ont Soif, 337, 340
Les Faux-Monnayeurs, 414
Les Filles du Feu, 171
Les Fleurs du mal, 189, 207
Les Misérables, 255
Les Précieuses Ridicules, 69
Les Ratés, 385
Lesage, Alain René, 73, 83, 84
Lespinasse, Julie de, 98, 100
Lessing, Gotthold Ephraim, 79–81, 103, 108
Lettres de mon Moulin, 257
Lettres sur les Anglais, 58
Lever, Charles, 228
Levin, 254
Lewes, George Henry, 269
Lewis, Cecil Day, 404

Lewis, Matthew Gregory ('Monk'), 154
Lewis, Sinclair, 405, 429–32
Lewis, Wyndham, 317
L'Homme-machine, 100
Library, 4
Life of Nelson, 148
Life of Reason, 308
Life on the Mississippi, 240
Light in August, 437
Lilliput, 58
Lillo, George, 75
Lincoln, Abraham, 212
Lisbon, 105
Lisle, Leconte de, 216
Liszt, Franz, 161
Literature, xi, xii, xiii, 4, 5, 6, 19
Little Dorrit, 232, 233
Locke, John, 54, 101
Logical Positivism, 314
Logos, 12, 215, 236, 341
Loire, 18, 25
London, 27, 28, 30, 31, 45
London, Jack, 363
Longfellow, Henry Wadsworth, 206, 211
Look Back in Anger, 444
Lorca, Federico Garcia, 388
Lorenzaccio, 172
Loti, Pierre, 272
Louis XIV, 54, 55, 59, 67, 69, 78, 83, 103, 117
Louis XV, 99, 114
Louis-Philippe, 190
Love for Love, 75
Lovelace, 88, 89, 90
Low Countries, 3
Lowell, James Russell, 211
Lower Depths, 365
Lucia, 182
Lucky Jim, 444
Lutheranism, 14
Lying, 16
Lyly, John, 29
Lyrical Ballads, 147
Lyrics, 18, 19

MACAO, 8
Macartney, Frederick, 390
Macaulay, Lord, 194, 233, 348
Macbeth, 32, 36, 37, 38, 39
Machiavelli, Niccolò, 14–17, 50
Machiavellian, 15, 16, 17
Mackenzie, Compton, 372
MacNeice, Louis, 404
Macpherson, James, 122, 123
Madame Bovary, 225, 256, 259–62
Madariaga y Rojo, Salvador de, 49
Mademoiselle de Maupin, 171
Madness, 14, 48, 58, 119, 120, 121, 204, 205
Madrid, 45
Maeterlinck, Maurice, 220, 283, 337, 393
Magda, 283
Magic, 15
Main Street, 430
Maintenon, Françoise de, 66, 83
Mainz, 3
Mairet, Jean, 64
Mallarmé, Stephane, 156, 188, 189, 217–9, 337, 390, 391, 396, 399, 402
Malebranche, Nicolas de, 59
Malherbe, François de, 59
Malory, Sir Thomas, 7
Malraux, André, 415, 427
Maly Theatre, 293
Man, xii, 10, 13
Mandragola, La, 14
Manet, Édouard, 260
Manila, 8
Mann, Thomas, 50, 331, 336, 362, 377, 420–3
Manon Lescaut, 85
Manzoni, Alessandro, 180–2, 318
Marcel, Gabriel Honoré, 385
March to the Gallows, 334
Märchen, 127–30
Mardi, 237
Margaret of Navarre, 12
Marguerite de Valois, 169–70
Marianne, 84, 85

Marinetti, Filippo Tommaso, 317
Mario and the Magician, 420
Marivaudage, 73, 84
Marivaux, Pierre Carlet de Chamblain de, 73, 84, 85
Marlowe, Christopher, 33, 34
Marmontel, Jean François, 100, 107
Marot, Clément, 19
Marquand, John P., 433
Marquis of Posa, 132
Marston, John, 33
Martin Arrowsmith, 430
Martin Chuzzlewit, 212
Marx, Karl, 107, 117, 201, 202, 203, 286, 301, 347, 348
Mary Stuart, 132
Mary Stuart, Queen of Scots, 12, 132
Massinger, Philip, 34
Masters, Lee, 405
Matriarchal, 21
Matteo Falcone, 170
Maturin, Charles Robert, 154
Maud, 207, 208
Maugham, Somerset, 372
Maupassant, Guy de, 257, 258
Mauriac, François, 414, 427
Max Havelaar, 267
Mayakovsky, Vladimir, 325, 398
Mazarin, Cardinal, 3
Medici family, 14, 15
Medici, Lorenzo de, 10
Medieval literature, xi
Mediterranean, 7
Meilhac, Henri, 279
Melville, Herman, 188, 211, 225, 226, 237–9, 272
Mémoires d'Outre-Tombe, 162
Memoirs of a Cavalier, 86
Ménard, Louis, 216
Mencken, Henry Louis, 284, 286, 429
Mephistopheles, 16, 109, 137, 347
Mercenaries, 14
Merchants, 6, 7, 8
Meredith, George, 210, 223, 270, 271

Merezhovsky, Dmitri Sergeevich, 363, 364
Mérimée, Prosper, 161, 165, 170
Metternich, Prince Klemens, 135
Mexico City, 8
Meyer, Conrad Ferdinand, 267
Michelangelo, 10, 14
Micromegas, 105
Middle Age, 4, 5, 8, 10
Middlemarch, 269
Middleton, Thomas, 34
Milan, 13, 14
Mill, John Stuart, 196, 203, 313
Milton, John, 56, 79
Mimesis, 189
Mind at the End of its Tether, 346
Minna von Barnhelm, 80
Mirbeau, Octave, 282
Le Misanthrope, 71
Mirsky, Dmitry Svyatopolk, 177
Miss Julie, 289, 292
Miss Sara Sampson, 80
Mississippi, 156
Missouri, 240
Mistral, Frédéric, 337, 340, 342
Mistral, Gabriela, 389
Moby Dick, 189, 190, 211, 226, 237, 238, 430
Mockel, Albert Henri Louis, 220
Modern Love, 210
Molière, 63, 69–73, 78, 117, 255, 275, 349, 377
Moll Flanders, 86
Molnár, Ferenc, 385
Mommsen, Theodor, 342, 362
Monet, Claude, 260
Monks, 4
Mont-Saint-Michel and Chartres, 357
Montague, Charles Edward, 372
Montaigne, Michel de, 9, 18, 19, 22–5, 38, 50, 54, 60, 61, 93, 446
Montesquieu, Charles de Secondat, 99, 104, 105
Montherlant, Henry de, 414

Moore, George, 353, 403
Moore, George Edward, 311, 312
Moore, Marianne, 405
Moore, Thomas, 154, 206
Moors, 43, 44
Moral Tales, 107
Morley, John, 109
Morris, William, 210
Mortimer, 132
Moscow, 174
Moscow Art Theatre, 293, 382
Motion pictures, 7
Mourning Becomes Electra, 388
Mozart, Wolfgang Amadeus, 220
Mr. Pickwick, 50
Mr. Polly, 345
Mr. Rochester, 225
Mr. Squeers, 303
Mrs. Bloom, 416
Mrs. Dalloway, 331, 426
Movable types, xi, 3, 4, 5, 7
Muir, Edwin, 393
Müller, Friedrich (Mahler), 123
Murger, Henri, 165
Musset, Alfred de, 87, 161, 165, 169, 171, 172
Mussolini, Benito, 349
Myers, Leo Hamilton, 427
Myshkin, Prince, 247
Myth, 7, 45

Nana, 265
Nantucket, 238
Napoleon, 117, 138, 143, 159, 162, 252, 253
Natasha, 251, 253
Nathan the Wise, 80
Nationalism, 27
Nature, 53, 119, 149, 385
Nazis, 203, 244, 334, 367, 395, 415, 420
Neruda, Pablo, 389
Nerval, Gérard de, 161, 165, 171
Neuber, Caroline, 79
New Bedford, 238

New World, 8
New York, 188
Newgate, 77
Newton, Isaac, 53, 101
Nicholas I, 173
Nicholas Nickleby, 35, 225
Nichols, Robert, 372
Nietzsche, Friedrich Wilhelm, 188, 189, 202–5, 250, 286, 301, 302, 306, 340, 347
Nightmare Abbey, 154
Nobel Prizes, 337, 338, 340, 341, 342, 354, 362, 363, 366, 367, 379, 386, 388, 389, 428, 429, 436
Noble Savage, 9
Nodier, Charles, 165
Norris, Frank, 273, 357
Norsemen, 8
Norway, 78, 188
Notebooks, 234, 236
Notes from Underground, 249
Notre-Dame de Paris, 166
Novalis, 126
Novels, 45, 50, 82–97
Nušić, Branislav, 336

Obermann, 161
Obey, André, 388
Oblomov, 242
O'Casey, Sean, 381
Odense, 184
Odéon, 159
Odets, Clifford, 388
Odyssey, 416
Œdipus Rex, 64
Of Time and the River, 439
Offenbach, Jacques, 279
Oldfield, Anne, 63
O'Leary, 402
Oliveira, Alberto de, 336
Omoo, 237
O'Neill, Eugene Gladstone, 387, 388
On the Eve, 245
One of Ours, 428
Ophelia, 39

Origin of Species, 205
Orlando Furioso, 13
Orpheus myth, 396
Ortega y Gasset, 304, 331
Ossian, 122, 123
Ostrovsky, Aleksandr Nikolaevich, 276, 293
Othello, 165, 276
Othello, 39
Otway, Thomas, 75
Our Mutual Friend, 188, 190, 232, 233
Our Town, 388
Outline of History, 345
Owen, Wilfrid, 372
Oxford, Earl of, 34

PAGANINI, NICCOLÒ, 161
Pagnol, Marcel, 385
Palissot de Montenoy, Charles, 109
Pamela; or Virtue Rewarded, 87, 88, 90
Pantagruel, 21
Pantaloon, 72
Papacy, 10, 13
Paris, 18, 19, 45, 59, 65, 69, 72, 96, 99, 101, 103, 107, 159, 160, 162, 188, 189
Parnassians, 216
Parnell, Charles Stewart, 402
Parson Adams, 90
Party, 49
Pascal, Blaise, 60, 61, 182
Pasternak, Boris, 397, 398
Pastoral life, 44
Patagonia, 389
Pater, Walter, 215, 224
Patriarchal, 21
Peacock, Thomas Love, 154
Pechorin, 178
Peer Gynt, 188, 287
Péguy, Charles, 341, 371
Peirce, Charles Sanders, 307
Pembroke, Countess of, 34
Pendennis, 228
Percy, Thomas, 114
Pereda, José María de, 267

Peregrine Pickle, 95
Peretz, Yitzchok Leibush, 336
Pérez Galdós, 267, 367
Périgord, 23
Perrault, Charles, 59
Persian Letters, 104
Persuasion, 16
Peshkov, A. M., 362
Peter the Great, 254
Petrarch, Francesco, 13
Petrov, Evgeny Petrovich, 423
Phèdre, 67, 68
Philadelphia, 187
Philinte, 71
Philip II, 42, 132
Philosophers, 99, 100, 103, 110
Picaresque writing, 44, 84, 95
Pickwick Papers, 35, 225
Pico della Mirandola, 10, 11, 13, 14, 17, 50
Pierre, 253
Pierre, 237
Pierre et Jean, 258
Pierrot, 172
Pikemen, 13
Pilgrim's Progress, 83
Pillars of Society, 288
Pincon, 8
Pirandello, Luigi, 50, 367, 386, 387
Pissarro, Camille, 260
Plain Tales from the Hills, 342
Platonism, 10, 12
Plays, xii
Pléiade, 19
Plutarch, 36
Poe, Edgar Allan, 156, 157, 211, 217, 219, 437
Poems and Ballads, 210
Poet Laureate, 208, 209
Poets, 9
Point Counter Point, 427
Politicians, 16
Politics, 16, 17, 19
Poliziano, Angelo, 10
Pommeraye, Mme de, 108

Pompadour, Mme de, 99
Pontoppidan, Henrik, 366
Pope, Alexander, 53, 110, 117
Pornography, 20
Porto-Riche, Georges, de, 337
Portrait of the Artist, 417
Portugal, 8, 42
Portuguese, 8
Potsdam, 101
Pound, Ezra, 317, 405–7, 409
Power, 4, 17
Power of Darkness, 293
Powys, John Cowper, 403, 427
Prejudices, 429
Press, 49
Prévost, Abbé, 85
Principia Ethica, 312
Principles of Literary Criticism, 309
Printing, xi, 3, 4
Progoff, Ira, 316
Prometheus, 151
Prophecy, 11
Prose, 19
Prospero, 40, 150
Protestant, 20
Proudhon, Pierre Joseph, 301
Proust, Marcel, 23, 50, 200, 306, 320, 331, 333, 336, 352, 376, 377, 395, 410–15
Prudhomme, Sully de, 216, 337
Psyche, human, xi
Psychology, 116, 137, 288, 307, 315, 316, 323, 353, 444
Psychology of the Unconscious, 323
Publicity, 13
Pudd'nhead Wilson, 240
Pulci, Luigi, 10
Punch, 438
Purchas's Pilgrimage, 150
Puritans, 27, 34
Pushkin, Alexander Sergeyevich, 173, 175, 176, 179, 245, 255

Quarterly Review, 152, 222
Quijano, Alonso, 48, 49

Quo Vadis?, 366

R.U.R., 388
Raabe, Wilhelm, 267
Rabelais, François, 18–22, 25, 38, 50, 54, 58, 93, 94, 446
Rachel, 274
Racine, Jean, 55, 59, 63, 66–8
Radcliffe, Mrs., 154
Rahmenerzählung, 267
Raleigh, Walter, 34
Ralph, Philip Lee, 187, 189
Rameau's Nephew, 108, 109, 110
Rationalism, 20
Raynal, Paul, 385
Read, Herbert, 372
Reade, Charles, 6, 268
Realism, 6, 7
Recessional, 344
Red Cavalry, 423
Reformation, 10, 19
Regnard, Jean François, 73, 78
Reimarus, Hermann Samuel, 80
Religion, 5, 17, 19, 129, 444, 445
Reliques of Ancient English Poetry, 114
Remarque, Erich Maria, 373, 374
Renaissance, 5, 6, 7, 12–22, 23, 26, 40, 41, 195
Renée Mauperin, 257
Renoir, Pierre Auguste, 260
Renzo, 182
Responsibilities, 401
Restoration Theatre, 75
Resurrection, 256
Reuter, Gabriele, 267
Revolt of the Masses, 304
Revolutions, 17
Reymont, Wladislaw Stanislaw, 366
Rice, Elmer, 387
Riceyman Steps, 353
Richards, Ivor Armstrong, 309
Richardson, Samuel, 73, 85–95, 108
Richelieu, Duc de, 59
Richter, Jean Paul, 126

Right You Are, 387
Rilke, Rainer Maria, 126, 220, 333, 393, 395–7, 400, 402
Rimbaud, Jean Arthur, 188, 217, 218
Rip Van Winkle, 155
Rise of Silas Lapham, 272
Robertson, Thomas William, 276
Robinson Crusoe, 86
Robinson, Henry Crabb, 155
Roderick Hudson, 273
Roderick Random, 95
Rodin, François Auguste René, 396
Rohan-Chabot, Chevalier de, 101
Rolland, Romain, 116, 340, 341
Romains, Jules, 371, 385
Roman Comique, 83
Roman design, 4
Roman Empire, 7
Romances, 6, 7
Rome, 4, 13, 14, 22
Romantics, 19, 113, 117, 139, 142, 178
Romeo and Juliet, 27
Ronsard, Pierre de, 12, 18, 19
Rosegger, Peter, 267
Rosicrucianism, 401
Rosmersholm, 287
Rossetti, Christina, 210
Rossetti, Dante Gabriel, 210
Rosso di San Secondo, 386
Rostand, Edmond, 283, 284, 337
Rostov family, 253
Rotrou, Jean de, 65
Rouen, 65, 256, 262
Rougon-Macquart, 262
Rousseau, Jean-Jacques, 99, 101, 106, 113–22, 124, 140, 143, 145–8, 150, 159, 161, 162, 181, 199
Rowe, Nicholas, 75
Roxana, 86
Rudin, 244, 245
Rural Rides, 154
Ruskin, John, 188, 199, 200
Russell, Bertrand, 16, 311–3
Russell, George William, 403

Russia, xi, 78, 173–80, 190, 191, 242–56, 293–7, 324, 383, 384
Rutland, Earl of, 34
Ruy Blas, 167
Rydberg, Abraham Viktor, 267

Sт. Cyr, 66
Saint Joan, 328
St. Petersburg, 174, 178, 242, 243, 244
Sainte-Beuve, Charles Augustin, 165, 201
Saint-Évremond, Seigneur de, 59
Saint-Simon, Comte de, 59, 200
Salammbô, 259
Salon of 1824, 161
Sam Weller, 50
Sancho Panza, 45, 47, 48, 49, 83
Sanctuary, 437
Sand, George (Aurore Dupin), 87, 161, 169, 171, 269
Sandburg, Carl, 405
Sanin, 364
Santayana, George, 228, 233, 308
Sardou, Victorien, 280, 281
Sassoon, Siegfried, 372
Satan, 215, 216
Satire, 20, 46
Saurat, Denis, 281
Scarron, Paul, 83
Sceptics, 27
Schelling, Friedrich Wilhelm Joseph von, 126, 149
Schiller, Johann Christoph Friedrich von, 80, 108, 123–6, 130–3, 155
Schizophrenia, 7
Schlegel, August Wilhelm von, 64, 71, 126
Schlegel, Friedrich von, 126, 129
Schlick, Moritz, 314
Schmitz, Ettore, 367, 368
Schnitzler, Arthur, 379
Scholarship, xii, 5, 8
Schopenhauer, Arthur, 196–8, 271, 305, 306
Schubert, Franz, 125

Schumann, Robert, 125
Science(s), 15, 16
Scott, Sir Walter, 91, 143–5, 154, 181, 318, 442
Scribe, Augustin Eugéne, 165, 170, 280
Scudéry, Madelène de, 83
Sea and Jungle, 373
Sea-captains, 8
Seeger, Alan, 373
Segur, Nicolas, 338
Self-deception, 17
Selkirk, Alexander, 86
Sémiramis, 63
Sénancour, Étienne Pivert de, 161
Seneca, 30
Senilità, 367
'Serapion Brothers', 325
Serfs, 242
Seven that were Hanged, 363
Sévigné, Marie de, 59
Sex, 12, 39
Shadwell, Thomas, 75
Shakespeare, William, 5, 21, 22, 24, 28–41, 44, 45, 50, 54, 55, 65, 67–70, 79, 122, 134, 135, 144, 152, 159, 255, 274–6, 278, 330, 338, 377, 441, 446
Shaw, George Bernard, 77, 100, 102, 243, 280, 284, 293, 306, 317, 319, 328, 336, 342, 344–53, 380
She Stoops to Conquer, 76
Shelley, Percy Bysshe, 44, 143, 149–52, 154, 213
Sheridan, Richard Brinsley, 76, 87
Sherriff, Robert Cedric, 373
Sherwood, Robert, 387
Shirley, 225
Sholokhov, Mikhail, 423
Shoulder Arms, 374
Siberia, 173, 174, 246, 248
Sidney, Sir Philip, 27
Sienkiewicz, Henryk, 342, 366
Sierra, Martinez, 379
Sister Carrie, 358
Six Characters in Search of an Author, 387

Slaves, 8
Smith, Albert, 228
Smith, The Rev. Sydney, 154
Smoke, 188, 244
Smollett, Tobias, 95, 96
Snow, Charles Percy, 417
Social Contract, 121
'Socialist Realism', 107, 325, 364, 423
Soldiers Three, 342
Soliloquies in England, 308
Sologub, Fëdor, 364, 397
Songs before Sunrise, 188
Songs of Innocence, 140
Sons and Lovers, 425
Sophocles, 64, 65, 68
Sorcery, 16
Sorel, Georges, 301–4, 306
Sorge, Reinhard Johannes, 382
Southey, Robert, 148, 149
Soviet Russia, 175
Spain, 3, 8, 27, 42, 43, 50, 83, 84, 310, 367
Spaniards, 14
Spencer, Herbert, 196, 269
Spender, Stephen, 404
Spengler, Oswald, 310
Spenser, Edmund, 27, 29, 56
Spielhagen, Friedrich, 267
Spinoza, Baruch, 54
Sportsman's Notebook, 243, 245
Squaring the Circle, 384
Squire, 45, 46, 47
Staël, Anne Louise Germaine de, 134, 159, 162
Stalin, Joseph, 100, 348, 423
Stallings, Laurence, 373
Stanislavsky (Konstantin Sergeevich Alekseev), 293, 382
State, 49
States, 17
Steele, Richard, 96
Stein, Gertrude, 431, 434
Steinbeck, John, 433
Stendhal (Marie-Henri Beyle), 160, 162–4, 169, 224

Stephani, de, 386
Stephen Dedalus, 417
Steppenwolf, 331
Sterne, Laurence, 87, 91–6, 108, 126
Sternheim, Karl, 382
Stevens, Wallace, 405
Stevenson, Robert Louis, 170, 272
Stockholm, 63, 78
Storm, 267
Stowe, Harriet Beecher, 234
Strachey, Lytton, 113, 312
Strassburg, 122
Stratford upon Avon, 35, 37
Strauss, Richard, 393
Street Scene, 387
Strindberg, Johan August, 278, 282, 289–93, 295, 378, 381, 384
Sturm und Drang, 123, 442
Sudermann, Hermann, 282
Sue, Eugène, 170
Sumarokov, Aleksandr Petrovich, 78
Superstition, 15
Surface, Charles, 76
Surface, Joseph, 76
Surgères, Hélène de, 12
Surrey, 26
Surtees, Robert Smith, 228
Svevo, Italo, 367, 368
Swann, 411
Sweden, 78
Swedenborg, 140
Swift, Jonathan, 57–9, 77, 86, 91, 105
Swinburne, Algernon Charles, 188, 210
Swiss, 79
Switzerland, 101, 266, 267, 340, 395
Sylvie, 171
Symbolist Movement, 171, 216–20, 248, 258, 259, 264, 317, 331, 353, 377, 389, 390, 392, 394, 396, 397, 399–402
Synge, John Millington, 380, 387

TAINE, HIPPOLYTE ADOLPHE, 201
Tarkington, Booth, 357
Tartarin, 257

Tartuffe, 71
Tasso, Torquato, 14, 15
Tasso, 134
Taste, 55, 56, 59
Taylor, Jeremy, 153
Télémaque, 59
Television, 7
Tender is the Night, 373, 434, 435
Tennyson, Alfred, Lord, 188–90, 192, 206–9
Ternan, Ellen, 230
Tess of the D'Urbervilles, 272
Thackeray, William Makepeace, 94, 188, 225–8, 233, 268, 269
Thaïs, 340
The Adventures of Huckleberry Finn, 190, 240, 430, 435
The Adventures of Tom Sawyer, 240
The Alchemist, 33
The Ancient Mariner, 150
The Angel, 177
The Barber of Seville, 74
The Beaux' Stratagem, 76
The Beggar's Opera, 77, 383
The Betrothal, 283
The Birth of Tragedy, 204
The Blessed Damozel, 210
The Blithedale Romance, 234, 236
The Blue Bird, 283
The Bostonians, 361
The Bronze Horseman, 176
The Brook Kerith, 353
The Brothers Karamazov, 248, 249
The Captain of Köpenick, 382
The Captain's Daughter, 176
The Castle, 331, 419, 420
The Cenci, 151
The Changeling, 34
The Chartreuse of Parma, 163
The Cherry Orchard, 293, 295, 296
The Chimes, 255
The City of the Yellow Devil, 363
The Cloister and the Hearth, 6, 268
The Concert, 378

The Confessions of a Fool, 289
The Confidence Man, 237
The Conquerors, 415
The Count of Monte-Cristo, 170
The Counterfeiters, 414
The Crowd, 304
The Dance of Death, 290, 291
The Dark Forest, 372
The Death of Ivan Ilyich, 256
The Death of Tintagiles, 283
The Demon, 177
The Doctor's Dilemma, 351
The Dream Doctor, 385
The Dream Play, 290, 292
The Drunkard, 264
The Duchess of Malfi, 34
The Duel, 363
The Education of Henry Adams, 357, 358
The Education of the Human Race, 81
The Egoist, 270
The Elective Affinities, 134
The Enormous Room, 373
The Eternal Husband, 248
The Excursion, 147
The Faerie Queene, 29
The Fair Penitent, 75
The Fatal Curiosity, 75
The Father, 289, 290, 291, 292
The Fruits of Enlightenment, 293
The Gambler, 248
The Genealogy of Morals, 204
The 'Genius', 359
The Gentleman from San Francisco, 363
The Good Soldier Schweik, 374
The Good-Natur'd Man, 76
The Government Inspector, 178, 179
The Great Gatsby, 433
The Greatcoat, 178
The History of Sir Charles Grandison, 87, 88
The House of the Dead, 246, 247
The Idiot, 188, 248
The Idylls of the King, 189, 192
The Importance of Being Earnest, 351
The Indian Summer of a Forsyte, 354

The Inferno, 289
The Innocents Abroad, 188, 241
The Just and the Unjust, 433
The King's Italian Players, 72
The Kreutzer Sonata, 256
The Lake Poets, 148
The Last Puritan, 308
The Last Ride Together, 209
The Last Tycoon, 434
The Letter of Lord Chandos, 393
The Life and Death of Mr. Badman, 83
The Little Demon, 364
The London Merchant, 75
The Long Christmas Dinner, 388
The Lotus Eaters, 208
The Lusiad (Os Lusíadas), 42
The Magic Mountain, 331, 362, 420–2, 427
The Maid of Orleans, 132
The Man of Property, 354
The Man that Corrupted Hadleyburg, 240
The Man who Knew Coolidge, 430
The Marriage of Figaro, 74
The Marriage of Heaven and Hell, 141
The Master Builder, 286, 288
The Mayor of Zalamea, 44
The Minor, 78
The Moonstone, 268
The Mourning Bride, 75
The New Machiavelli, 345
The Newcomes, 228
The Nice Old Man and the Pretty Girl, 368
The Nose, 178
The Nun, 108
The Old Wives' Tale, 353
The Ordeal of Mark Twain, 241
The Oxford Book of Modern Verse, 404
The Path to Rome, 344
The Peasants, 366
The Pit, 363
The Playboy of the Western World, 380, 381
The Portrait of a Lady, 361
The Possessed, 248
The Prelude, 147

The Prince, 15, 16, 17
The Princess, 206
The Princess Casamassima, 361
The Procurator of Judea, 340
The Professor, 225
The Professor's House, 428
The Prospects of Industrial Civilisation, 312
The Queen of Spades, 176
The Recruiting Officer, 76
The Red and the Black, 163
The Red Badge of Courage, 273
The Return of the Native, 272
The Ring and the Book, 188
The Rivals, 76, 87
The Road to Damascus, 290
The Robbers, 123
The Root and the Flower, 427
The Scarlet Letter, 234, 235
The School for Scandal, 76
The Scythians, 399
The Seagull, 295, 296
The Silver Box, 354
The Spectator, 96
The Spook Sonata, 290, 292
The Storm, 293
The Story of Our Civilisation, 187
The Sunken Bell, 283
The Talisman, 144
The Tatler, 96
The Tempest, 40
The Three Sisters, 293, 295
The Three-Cornered Hat, 267
The Time Machine, 345
The Titan, 359
The Torrents of Spring, 244
The Trial, 419, 420
The Twelve, 398, 399
The Varieties of Religious Experience, 307
The Vicar of Wakefield, 95
The Way of All Flesh, 270
The Way of the World, 75
The Weavers, 282
The White Devil, 34
The Wide, Wide World, 234

The Wild Duck, 286–8
The Woman in White, 268
The Woodlanders, 272
The World as Will and Idea, 196
The Wound and the Bow, 229
Theatre, xii
Thérèse Raquin, 188
Thomas, Dylan, 409, 410
Thomas, Edward, 372
Thoreau, Henry David, 188, 197, 198, 211, 373
Three Musketeers, 169
Thus Spake Zarathustra, 204
Tidemarks, 373
Tieck, 126–9
Time is a Dream, 385
Tirso de Molina, 44
Titus, 67
To the Lighthouse, 426
Tolerance, 19, 21
Toller, Ernst, 382
Tolstoy, Aleksei Nikolaevich, 423
Tolstoy, Lev Nikolaevich, 102, 116, 188–90, 223, 224, 244, 250–6, 260, 268, 282, 362, 365
Tom Jones, 50, 91, 92
Tomlinson, Henry Major, 373
Tono Bungay, 346
Tories, 57, 143, 149
Tostes, 262
Touraine, 21
Tourneur, 237
Travel Pictures, 130
Treachery, 16
Treasure Island, 272
Treatise on Toleration, 106
Trieste, 333, 367, 418
Tristram Shandy, 93, 94
Trois Contes, 261
Trollope, Anthony, 227, 233, 268, 270
Troy, 402
Truth, 16
Tudors, 26
Turcaret, 73

Turgenev, Ivan Sergeyevich, 188, 242–7, 249, 251, 256, 293
Turks, 7
Turner, Joseph Mallord William, 200
Turner, Walter James, 372
Twain, Mark, 144, 156, 239–42, 272, 273, 363
Twenty-six Men and a Girl, 365
Typee, 237
Tzara, Tristan, 323, 324

UHLAND, JOHANN LUDWIG, 127
Ulalume, 157
Ulyanov, Vladimir Ilyich, 324
Ulysses, 323, 331, 416–9
Un Chapeau de Paille d'Italie, 279
Unamuno y Jugo, Miguel de, 50, 310, 311, 367, 379
Uncle Tom's Cabin, 234, 255
Uncle Vanya, 295
Undertones of War, 372
Undset, Sigrid, 366
United States of America, 78, 98, 190
Unities, 59, 64, 65
Universe, 5
Urbino, 13
Unruh, Fritz von, 382

VADIUS, 72
Valéry, Paul, 156, 331, 337, 390, 391, 392, 397–400, 402, 410, 422
Valois, 18
Vanbrugh, Sir John, 75
Vanity Fair, 226, 227, 228
Vasco da Gama, 42
Vauvenargues, 133
Vega Carpio, Lope Félix de, 43, 44
Vendôme, 18
Venice, 13, 14, 74, 188
Venice Preserved, 75
Verga, 267, 367
Verhaeren, Émile, 220
Verlaine, Paul, 188, 218, 219, 337
Verrocchio, Andrea del, 11

Versailles, 59, 65, 67, 101
Versatility, 11, 13
Vespucci, Amerigo, 8
Viardot, 243
Victoria, Queen, 187, 208
Vie des Martyrs, 371
Vienna, 135
Vigny, Alfred de, 164, 165
Vildrac, Charles, 385
Vile Bodies, 427
Villainy, 16
Villette, 225
Villiers de L'Isle-Adam, 258, 259
Villon, François, 219
Vincennes, 116
Vinci, Leonardo da, 11, 14, 390
'Vineland', 8
Virgil, 208
Virtues, 17
Vizetelly, 263
Voland, Sophie, 109
Volpone, 33
Voltaire, 58, 63, 68, 70, 75, 79, 98–106,
     109, 113, 162, 176, 338, 339, 340
Vronsky, 254
Vulgate Bible, 3

WAGNER, Heinrich Leopold, 123, 136
Wagner, Richard, 217, 340
Walden, 198
Wallenstein, 132
Walpole, Hugh, 372
Walpole, Horace, 103
War and Peace, 188, 251–6
Waring, 209
Warner, Susan Bogert, 234
Warren, Samuel, 228
Wars, 5
Wars of the Roses, 6
Wassermann, Jakob, 420
Waste Land, 331
Waugh, Evelyn, 427
Webster, John, 15, 34
Wedekind, Franz, 379

Weimar, 135, 136
Weir of Hermiston, 272
Wellesley, Arthur, Duke of Wellington,
     117
Wells, Herbert George, 317, 319, 342,
     344–8, 352, 355, 425
Werner, Zacharias, 126
Werther, 124, 133, 134, 135
West, Nathanael, 434
Western Man, xi, xii, xiii, 4, 5, 17, 37, 41,
     42, 44
Westminster, 3
Westminster Review, 269
Wetherell, Elizabeth, 234
Wharton, Edith, 357
What I Believe, 252
What is Art?, 255
What Price Glory, 373
What to Do, 189
Where Angels Fear to Tread, 355
Whitehead, Alfred North, 305
Whitman, Walt[er], 188, 189, 207, 211–4,
     220, 238, 239, 432
Whittier, John Greenleaf, 211
Wieland, or The Transformation, 155
Wilde, Oscar, 77, 193, 351, 353
Wilder, Thornton, 388
Wilhelm Meister, 50, 126, 134, 135, 137,
     427
William Tell, 132
Williams, William Carlos, 405
'Willy', 341
Wilson, Angus, 263
Wilson, Edmund, 229
Winckelmann, Johann Joachim, 136
Winterset, 388
Wit, 20
With the Night Mail, 343
Wittgenstein, Ludwig Adolf Peter, 314
Woe from Wit, 175
Wolf, Hugo, 125
Wolfe, Thomas Clayton, 433, 438–40
Woman, 11, 12, 21, 119, 146, 254, 291
Women in Love, 425

Woolf, Virginia, 331, 425–7
Words, 20
Wordsworth, Dorothy, 149
Wordsworth, William, 143, 147–9, 152
Work of Art, 430
World of Yesterday, 333
Württemberg, Duke of, 125, 130
Wuthering Heights, 225
Wyatt, Thomas, 26
Wycherley, William, 75, 76

YAHOOS, 58
Yankees, 211, 241
Yeats, William Butler, 220, 347, 374, 380, 392, 398–403, 407–9, 435

You Can't Go Home Again, 439
You Never Can Tell, 351
Yorick, 96
York, 6

Zadig, 105
Zionism, 374
'Znanie', 363
Zola, Émile, 188, 189, 192, 193, 223, 256, 260, 262–5, 268, 273, 281, 282, 430
Zoshchenko, 423
Zuckmayer, Carl, 382
Zürich, 79, 267, 323, 324, 333, 418
Zweig, Arnold, 374
Zweig, Stefan, 333, 336

71 72 73 74 75 10 9 8 7 6 5

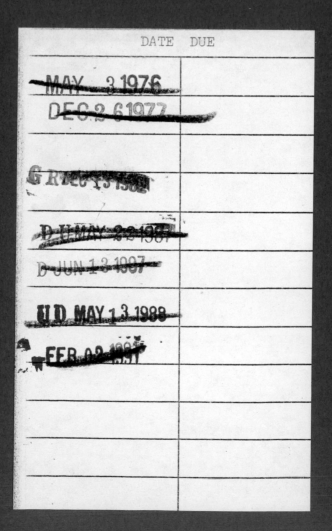